Early Medieval Europe 300–1000

HISTORY OF EUROPE

PUBLISHED

Early Medieval Europe 300–1000 (2nd edn)
Roger Collins

Sixteenth Century Europe
Richard Mackenney

Seventeenth Century Europe 1598–1700
Thomas Munck

Eighteenth Century Europe (2nd edn)
Jeremy Black

History of Europe
Series Standing Order
ISBN 0–333–71699–X hardcover
ISBN 0–333–69381–7 paperback
(*outside North America only*)

You can receive future titles in this series as they are published by placing a standing order. Please contact your bookseller or, in the case of difficulty, write to us at the address below with your name and address, the title of the series and the ISBN quoted above.

Customer Services Department, Macmillan Distribution Ltd
Houndmills, Basingstoke, Hampshire RG21 6XS, England

Early Medieval Europe 300–1000

Roger Collins
Fellow of the Institute for Advanced Studies
University of Edinburgh

Second Edition

First edition 1991
Second edition 1999

Published by
PALGRAVE
Houndmills, Basingstoke, Hampshire RG21 6XS and
175 Fifth Avenue, New York, N. Y. 10010
Companies and representatives throughout the world

PALGRAVE is the new global academic imprint of
St. Martin's Press LLC Scholarly and Reference Division and
Palgrave Publishers Ltd (formerly Macmillan Press Ltd).

ISBN 0–333–65807–8 hardback
ISBN 0–333–65808–6 paperback

This book is printed on paper suitable for recycling and made from fully managed and sustained forest sources.

A catalogue record for this book is available from the British Library.

Cataloging-in-Publication data is available from the Library of Congress

ISBN 0–312–21885–0 cloth
ISBN 0–312–21886–9 paperback

10   9
08   07   06   05   04

Printed in China

Contents

Chronology of main events, 238–1000

British Isles	Western Europe	Eastern Europe	North Africa	Near East
	238 murder of Maximin I			241–72 reign of Shapur I
		244 Gordian III deposed by Philip	248 Cyprian bishop of Carthage	
	253–60 reign of Valerian			260 Shapur I captures Valerian
	253–68 reign of Gallienus		258 martyrdom of Cyprian of Carthage	
	260–73 'Gallic Empire'			
286–93 reign of Carausius	285 Diocletian ruling West	282–3 reign of Carus		283 Carus' invasion of Persia
293–6 reign of Allectus	293 appointment of Caesars	284–305 reign of Diocletian		293–303 reign of Narseh
		303 beginning of 'Great Persecution'		296–7 war with Rome
306 Constantine proclaimed at York	305–6 reign of Constantius I in West	305–11 reign of Galerius	311 reign of Alexander	309–79 reign of Shapur II
	306–37 rule of Constantine in West	313 war between Maximin and Licinius	312 beginning of Donatist schism	
	312 Battle of Milvian Bridge; conversion of Constantine	314 war with Licinius (308–24)		
		324–37 Constantine ruling East		
		324 founding of Constantinople		

Britain	West	East	Africa	Persia
		325 Council of Nicaea		
		330 dedication of Constantinople		
337–50 reign of Constans		337–61 reign of Constantius II		
343 visit of Constans			354 birth of Augustine	
350–3 Britain supports Magnentius		350–3 Gallus Caesar at Antioch		
357–9 Julian's campaigns in Gaul				360 war between Rome and Persia
360 Julian's revolt		361–3 reign of Julian; 'pagan revival'		363 Julian's invasion of Persia
364–75 reign of Valentinian I		364–78 reign of Valens		364 Jovian's treaty
367 raids by Picts, Irish and Saxons; Hadrian's Wall repaired		376 Visigoths admitted into Balkans		
		378 Battle of Adrianople		
383–8 reign of Magnus Maximus		379–95 reign of Theodosius I		
392–4 reign of Eugenius; 'pagan revival'		391 closing of pagan temples	395–430 Augustine bishop of Hippo	
395–423 reign of Honorius		395–408 reign of Arcadius	397 Augustine writes 'Confessions'	
395–408 ascendancy of Stilicho			397 revolt of Gildo	
406 Vandals, Alans, Sueves cross Rhine			413–27 Augustine writing 'City of God'	
406 reigns of Marcus and Gratian			418 Council of Carthage	
407–11 reign of Constantine III				
408 Alaric's Visigoths enter Italy				
410 sack of Rome				
410 revolt of Britain				
c. 411–21 ascendancy of Constantius				

Chronology of main events, 238–1000 (continued)

British Isles	Western Europe	Eastern Europe	North Africa	Near East
Nynia in Galloway and southern Pictland	425–55 reign of Valentinian III		429 Vandal invasion	
431 Palladius sent to Ireland	430–53 ascendancy of Aetius		439 Vandals take Carthage	
	440–61 Leo I bishop of Rome	440s Hun raids on Balkans	442 Vandal treaty	
c. 446–53 appeal to Aetius Saxon treaty				
	451 Hun invasion of Gaul	451 Council of Chalcedon		459–84 reign of Peroz Persian wars with the Hephthalites
		453 death of Attila		
		454 battle on the Nedao		
	455–7 reign of Avitus		455 Vandal sack of Rome	
			468 attack by eastern fleet fails	
Patrick in Ireland	476/480 formal end of western Empire	474–91 reign of Zeno	476–84 reign of Huneric; 'persecution' of Catholics	
				488–97, 499–531 reign of Kavad I; Mazdakite movement
	c. 481–c. 511 reign of Clovis in Gaul			
490s Battle of Badon	493 Ostrogothic kingdom established in Italy			
	507 Battle of Vouillé			
	c. 511 division of Frankish kingdom	527–65 reign of Justinian	523–30 reign of Hilderic	c. 525 Dhu Nuwas in the Yemen
		529 Nika Riots	533 imperial conquest of Africa	531–79 reign of Khusro I

c. 540 Gildas writing 'De Excidio'	535–53 wars in Italy, leading to imperial conquest	527–33 'Corpus Iuris Civilis'	536 Council of Carthage 543 Berber revolt 548 revolt suppressed	540 Persian sack of Antioch
c. 560–c. 590 career of Ceawlin 563/5 foundation of Iona	558–61 Francia united under Chlotar I (c. 511–61) 568 Lombard invasion of Italy under Alboin 569–86 reign of Leovigild in Spain 574–84 'interregnum' in Lombard kingdom 589 Third Council of Toledo 590–616 reign of Agilulf in Italy 590–604 Gregory the Great, bishop of Rome	550s beginning of Slav penetration of Balkans	563 new Berber revolt	570? birth of Muhammad 579–90 reign of Hormizd IV
597 arrival of Augustine in Kent and death of Columba	594 death of Gregory of Tours	590s campaigns against Slavs 602 overthrow of Maurice		591 Maurice installs Khusro II in Iran
604 death of Augustine	613 unification of Francia under Chlotar II 620s Isidore writing 'History' and 'Chronicle'	610 fall of Phocas	610 revolt of Heraclius	610 Muhammad's revelations begin 614 Persian capture of Jerusalem 622 the Hijra 628 murder of Khusro II

Chronology of main events, 238–1000 (continued)

British Isles	Western Europe	Eastern Europe	North Africa	Near East
629–32 Roman mission in Northumbria				630 Muhammad conquers Mecca
	623–38 rule of Dagobert I in Francia	626 Avar siege of Constantinople		632 succession of Abu Bakr
632 death of Edwin	636 death of Isidore of Seville			634 succession of 'Umar
633–42 reign of Oswald in Northumbria	636–52 reign of Rothari in Italy	636 Battle of Yarmuk		636 Arab conquest of Jerusalem
c. 632–55 reign of Penda in Mercia	639 Thuringian revolt	641 death of Heraclius I		640 conquest of Egypt
				642 collapse of Persia before Arabs
642–70 reign of Oswy in Northumbria	649–72 reign of Reccesuinth	649 Arab conquest of Cyprus	646 revolt of exarch Gregory	651 death of last shah, Yazdgard III
655–8 Northumbrian rule over Mercia	654 issue of 'Forum Iudicum'		647 first Arab raid – death of Gregory	656–61 caliphate of 'Ali
				661–80 Mu'awiya first Umayyad Caliph
663/4 Synod of Whitby	657–664/5 regency of Balthildis			
	c. 660–73, 675–80, Ebroin Mayor of Palace in Neustria	668 murder of Constans at Syracuse	669 Arab invasion under 'Uqba	
	673 war between Wamba and Paul	674–7 Arab siege of Constantinople	670 foundation of Kairouan	
		681 Bulgars established in Balkans	683 death of 'Uqba ibn Nafi	680–4 civil wars
685 Battle of Dunnichen				

British Isles	Western Europe	Byzantium	Arab world
	687 Battle of Tertry		**698** Arab capture of Carthage
			700–12 governorship of Musa ibn Nusayr
705 death of Adamnan			
709 death of Aldhelm			
	711 Arab invasion of Spain	**711** overthrow of Justinian II	
	712–14 reign of Liutprand in Italy		
	714–19 Charles Martel gains control of Austrasia and most of Neustria	**717** Arab siege of Constantinople and accession of Leo III	
716–57 reign of Æthelbald of Mercia			
	720s Charles restores control east of Rhine	**726** Leo III's first Iconoclast measures	**724–43** caliphate of Hisham
731/2 Bede finishes his 'History'	**733** Battle of Poitiers		
735 death of Bede	**735** Charles occupies Aquitaine		
	737 and **739** campaigns in Provence		
	741–7 joint rule of Pippin III and Carloman	**741–75** reign of Constantine V; most intense period of Iconoclasm	**744–55** rule of Ibn Habib
			743–50 conflicts in Syria
	749–56 reign of Aistulf in Italy		**749** 'Abbasid revolt
	751 coronation of Pippin III		**750** Umayyads replaced as Caliphs by the 'Abbasids

Chronology of main events, 238–1000 (continued)

British Isles	Western Europe	Eastern Europe	North Africa	Near East
754 death of Boniface	756 Umayyad Amirate founded in Spain			762 foundation of Baghdad
757–96 reign of Offa of Mercia			761 restoration of 'Abbasid rule	
766 death of archbishop Egbert of York – Alcuin's teacher	768–814 reign of Charlemagne		777 Rustamid kingdom in W. Algeria	786–809 reign of Harun ar-Rashid
	772–804 Saxon wars			
	774 Frankish conquest of Lombard kingdom	775–80 reign of Leo IV the Khazar	789 Idrisid kingdom in Morocco	
		787 Second Council of Nicaea		
	790s Frankish Avar wars	796 blinding of Constantine VI		
793 Viking raid on Lindisfarne	800 imperial coronation of Charlemagne		800 Aghlabid kingdom in Tunisia	
802–39 reign of Egbert of Wessex		802 deposition of empress Irene		
804 death of Alcuin	808–10 Frankish conflict with Godefred	811 defeat of Nicephorus by Bulgars		
	814–40 reign of Louis the Pious	813 Iconoclasm revived by Leo V (813–20)		813–19 civil war in Caliphate
	817 'Ordinatio Imperii'	814 death of khan Krum of Bulgars		
829 compiling of 'Historia Brittonum'	822 Louis's penance at Attigny	815 Byzantine–Bulgar peace treaty		
835 beginning of Viking raids on Wessex	830–4 civil wars in Francia		827–78 Aghlabid conquest of Sicily	

Britain	Western Europe / Francia	Byzantium	Mediterranean	Islamic World
	835 beginning of Danish raids on Francia	**830, 837** Byzantine victories over Arabs		**836** Samarra becomes 'Abbasid capital
	840–3 civil wars in Francia			
	843 Treaty of Verdun	**847** end of Iconoclasm		
850/1 first Viking wintering in Britain	**858** Louis the German invades West Francia	**860** Rhos attack Constantinople		**861** murder of caliph Al-Mutawakkil: ascendancy of Turks in the 'Abbasid Caliphate until 945
		864 conversion of the Bulgars		
867 Danish conquest of York	**866–910** reign of Alfonso the Great in Asturias	**867** Macedonian dynasty in Byzantium lasts until 1056	**868** Aghlabids take Malta	
869/70 conquest of East Anglia				
871–99 reign of Alfred of Wessex	**871** Byzantine recapture Bari	**870s** Byzantine campaigns in Asia Minor under Basil I (867–86)		
871 Battle of Ashdown	**872** Louis II forced to leave south Italy			
874 Danes expel Burgred from Mercia	**875** Charles the Bald crowned emperor			
878 Danes winter attack on Alfred; Battle of Edington	**877** death of Charles the Bald			

Chronology of main events, 238–1000 (*continued*)

	British Isles	Western Europe	Eastern Europe	North Africa	Near East
879–92		resumed Viking raids in N. Francia			
881		imperial coronation of Charles the Fat			
882		death of Hincmar of Reims			
885–6		Viking siege of Paris			
886	Alfred captures London				
886–912			reign of Leo the Wise		
887		deposition of Charles the Fat			
889			abdication of Boris		
892	new Danish invasion under Haesten				Baghdad restored as 'Abbasid capital
893			Symeon becomes ruler of the Bulgars		
894	dispersal of the invaders				
909	Wessex armies harry Viking kingdom of York			Aghlabids overthrown by Fatimids	
911		Charles the Simple's treaty with Rollo; Carolingian dynasty in E. Francia extinct			
912–59			reign of Constantine VII Porphyrogenitos		
912–61		rule of Abd ar-Rahman III in Spain			
917–24			Bulgar attacks on Byzantium		
918	death of Æthelflæd; Wessex annexes western Mercia				
920	Wessex conquest of East Mercia				

British Isles

- **924–39** reign of Athelstan
- **937** Battle of Brunanburh
- **944** Edmund of Wessex conquers Northumbria
- **948** Eadred of Wessex harries Northumbria
- **942–9/50** Hywel Dda 'King of all Wales'
- **961–88** Dunstan archbishop of Canterbury
- **973** coronation of Edgar at Bath
- **975–8** reign of Edward the Martyr
- **978–1016** reign of Æthelred the Unready
- **987** end of Carolingian rule in France; Hugh Capet crowned

Western Europe

- **923** deposition of Charles the Simple
- **936** restoration of Carolingian rule in France with Louis IV (d. 954)
- **939** battle of Simancas
- **955** Battle on the Lech
- **960** Hugh Capet 'Duke of the Franks'
- **962** imperial coronation of Otto I
- **972** Otto (II) marries Byzantine princess
- **973–83** reign of Otto II
- **982** Otto II defeated in southern Italy

Byzantium and Eastern Europe

- **920–44** Romanos Lecapenos co-emperor
- **927** death of tsar Symeon of the Bulgars; peace made with Byzantium
- **957** visit of Olga to Constantinople
- **c. 962–71** rule of Svyatoslav in Kiev
- **963–9** reign of Nicephorus Phocas; Byzantium regains Crete and Antioch
- **969–76** reign of John Zimiskes
- **970** defeat of 'Rhos' invasion of Thrace
- **976–1025** rule of Basil the Bulgarslayer
- **978** Vladimir becomes ruler of Kiev
- **c. 987** conversion of Vladimir

Islamic world

- **945** Buyids take Baghdad; 'Abbasid Caliphs under Buyid control until 1055
- **969** Fatimids take Cairo
- **972** Zirid kingdom in Tunisia

Chronology of main events, 238–1000 (*continued*)

British Isles	Western Europe	Eastern Europe	North Africa	Near East
980 Viking raids on southern England				
991 Battle of Maldon	**994** Otto III attains his majority	**995–1000** Olaf Tryggvason king of Norway		
990s mounting Viking attacks	**1000** Conversion of Iceland			
	1002 death of Otto III			

Preface to the first edition

At an early stage in thinking about the question of its contents it became clear that this was doomed to be a book that nobody could like, or at least that if some of its readers were pleased with some of it, none of them would possibly enjoy all of it. There are too many variables in the topics, themes, events and personalities that have to be considered for inclusion in a work of this (relative!) brevity that has to concern itself with so extended a chronological period. It became increasingly obvious that the real decisions to be made were those concerning what was to be omitted, and for an author temperamentally inclined to squeezing limited and fragmentary evidence as far as it will permit, if not beyond, this has been a particularly hard task.

Wholesale omissions and the reduction of complicated and nuanced arguments to bald assertions are bound to dissatisfy the discerning reader (as much as the author). In consequence, what is attempted here has to be a personal approach that may at times seem wrong headed in its concentration on some subjects to the exclusion of others or its occasional descent into detailed argument that seems out of proportion to the scale of the rest of the book. In that sense I can only fall back on the defence of a great, if idiosyncratic, ninth century bishop, that was recently echoed by a much revered Master: *Scripsi quod sensi.*

It may seem strange to those unfamiliar with these centuries that such an apology is necessary, and that a period of such apparent remoteness and obscurity should not manage to encompass itself totally in a book of even half the length of this one. Only brief acquaintance, however, will reveal how substantial is the corpus of evidence relating to this time, and how numerous and varied the problems involved in interpreting it. Moreover, the proper understanding of this period involves the historian in moving his gaze on occasion from the western fringes of Iran to Iceland and from Ethiopia and the edge of the Sahara to the steppes of Central Asia. Such breadth of geographical and chronological vision seems to be less necessary – or less demanded – in later periods.

In trying to present, even in outline, this series of interrelated developments, it was clearly necessary to push the chronological limits of this book back to an earlier period than those of the beginning of the sixth century, which was where it had first been intended to place them. So much of what was to make up the framework of ideas and institutions which shaped subsequent centuries originated in the fourth century that it would have been perverse to start any later than *c.* 300, and, indeed, a lack of Late Roman background has often led to mistaken and misleading interpretations of Early Medieval History. In turn, the decision to start with the fourth century prompted at least some preliminary investigation of the third.

Doubtless such a process could be indefinitely prolonged, recessing ever further back in time, but there is a certain rightness about commencing such a study as this in the mid-third century, when so many of the principal ideas and institutions of Antiquity were undergoing transformation. This period, however little studied and poorly documented, represents the first formative stage of the major changes that were to follow, and it is here that this enquiry begins.

Where to end was to some extent predetermined by the structure of the series in which this volume is to appear, but the disintegration of the Frankish successor empire in the late ninth and early tenth centuries again makes for something of a natural break, at least in some aspects of the history of medieval Europe. Extending the survey slightly further than I might have liked, the symbolic date of the year 1000 makes an aesthetically pleasing, if intellectually not entirely satisfying terminal point. To a certain extent, then, this book could have been given such a subtitle as 'From Constantine the Great to Charles the Simple'! In practice, treatment of the tenth century offered here is less full than for some earlier periods, largely because a number of the major themes that have their origin in this, still relatively little studied, time are best considered in the wider context of their development in the eleventh and twelfth centuries.

Other topics that might have merited inclusion have been omitted partly due to personal style and inclination on the part of the author and partly due to the fact that the lack of other general surveys of this period necessitated the provision of a substantial narrative outline of events, taken together with analysis of and comment on the major sources of evidence. In consequence there may be less economic history to be found in this book than some readers might like. This is conditioned on the author's part by a dislike for generalisation based on an insufficiency of evidence, and this is one of several areas for which the Early Middle Ages are poorly equipped in terms of the survival of source material. It is relatively easy to create general models on the basis of limited evidence, but these tend all too often in such circumstances to rest on *a priori* assumptions as to how societies and their economies should work. Such determinism should be resisted. It is also preferable to ask questions of evidence that its particular nature fits it to answer rather than ones that the historian feels he *ought* to pose.

The first victims of this book – paradoxically, even before it was ever commissioned – were the successive first-year history students in the University of Liverpool, to whom between the years 1974 and 1980 elements of it were expounded in the form of lectures on this period. The most recent guinea pigs to have suffered in its genesis are those former students at the Royal School, Bath, to whom the first edition is dedicated. I am very grateful to them for their enthusiasm in the discussion of a range of issues and topics that are considered in the chapters below. My especial thanks must go to Ian Wood, who read all of the first draft of this book, and whose comments and suggestions on it enabled me to avoid many errors. The greatest debt of all, though, is that to my wife Judith McClure, with whom so much of it has been shared in all of the phases just mentioned and whose role in it is truly omnipresent.

Bath   ROGER COLLINS
September 1990

Preface to the second edition

Thanks to that miracle of modern publishing, the text of a book on computer disk, it has been both possible and relatively easy to make changes and corrections throughout. Not only has this meant that errors detected since the first publication of this book, including the most delightful of all, the entirely spurious Anskar's *Life of Rimbert*, which eluded detection by both author and first readers alike, have been purged, but it has also been possible to make stylistic improvements throughout. In addition, an entirely new chapter on Spain after the Arab Conquest has been included, while the one dealing with the Ottonian Empire has been significantly expanded.

The early medieval centuries have enjoyed a period of remarkable prosperity and growth in terms of the research that has been carried out and the books and articles published on a wide range of subjects relating to them in the course of the 1990s. This flourishing of scholarship has been taken account of as much as has been possible in the preparation of this second edition, and has influenced changes to the text throughout. It will also be seen to be reflected in alterations and additions to both the notes to each chapter and to the general bibliography. In some cases it may be too early to see what constitutes genuine advances in our understanding of this complex period and what may prove to be false starts or misleading trails. Only time will tell.

As in the original edition, the selection of subjects for inclusion and the interpretations offered have ultimately to be matters of personal choice and conviction. While trying to take account of the great wealth of current and past scholarship relating to this period, seven hundred years of the history of Europe, North Africa and parts of the Middle East are not easily to be covered, and fashions in historiography can change rapidly. However, in making revisions I have generally tried to be less judgmental, leaving the reader even greater scope to make her and his decisions as to the merits of the cases argued here.

Edinburgh　　　　　　　　　　　　　　　　　　ROGER COLLINS
March 1998

Introduction

When Gibbon surveyed the centuries of 'decline' in the history of the Roman empire and its Byzantine successor he allowed himself to start with a little mild Utopianism. Of the Antonine period he commented that 'If a man were called upon to fix the period in the history of the world during which the condition of the human race was most happy and prosperous, he would, without hesitation, name that which elapsed from the death of Domitian to the accession of Commodus' (that is AD 96–181). Few might nowadays ask themselves such a question, let alone come up with a response that equates 'the world' exclusively with the Mediterranean and 'the human race' with a small economic and social elite. However, for all of his enthusiasm for second century Rome, some of which was intended as implicit criticism of aspects of his own society of which he disapproved, it was not about this period that Gibbon intended to write.

Periods of tranquillity, social harmony and economic stability do not make very exciting history – even if we now would detect more conflict and change in the second century than was apparent to Gibbon. The turbulent centuries that were to follow pose more interesting historiographical problems, not least because they encompassed the most important developments that would take place in the history of the Near East, the Mediterranean and Western Europe, between the formation of the Roman Empire in the first century BC and the discovery of the New World in the late fifteenth AD. Even then much of the way that the society and economy of the Americas were to be developed and exploited was directly conditioned by a body of ideas and through the means of institutions that had come into being in the period of the Late Roman Empire.

In general, the centuries covered by this book constitute a period of the greatest significance for the future development, not only of Europe, but also in the longer term of much else of the world. They saw, not least, the establishment of Christianity as the majority religion of the Roman Empire, and with it an indissoluble fusing of Judaeo-Christian and Romano-Greek thought. Apart from the first brief period of the founding of the religion in the time of the Early Roman Empire, there was to be no time in the whole subsequent history of the Christian Church so fertile in the development of its distinctive ideas and practices as the 'Patristic Age', lasting from roughly the mid-fourth century to the early sixth.

The writings of such men as Athanasius, Basil, Gregory of Nazianzus, Gregory of Nyssa, Ambrose, Jerome, Augustine and their immediate successors provided the intellectual framework of Christian thinking not only throughout the rest of the Middle Ages, but also for the Reformation and more recent centuries. The distinctive Christian emphasis on Virginity and the extraordinary ideological and institutional structures of monasticism were likewise the products of these centuries. They also saw the challenge to and modification of the Romano-Christian tradition with the rise to dominance of Islam over the whole of the Near East and the southern Mediterranean. The direct relevance of this formative period of Islamic thought and institutions to the modern society of these regions and to various contemporary political and economic issues hardly needs underlining.

In the West the Roman Empire dissolved itself as a unitary political entity in the fifth century, but its intellectual and material cultural legacy continued to direct the fragmentary successor states that came into being in its ruin. Especially true was this of that extraordinary institution the papacy, whose own distinctive view of its nature and purpose was formed in this time, together with many of the institutional features that would enable it to play so dominant a role in Western Europe for centuries to come. As a corollary to this, the most substantial, and still unhealed, rift in Christendom, that between the Latin and Greek Churches, came into being at the very end of this period.

This itself was not uninfluenced by political changes in the West, with the emergence of the short-lived Frankish empire of the Carolingians, which in its territorial expansion both northwards and eastwards further extended the areas of influence of the intellectual culture and some of the material civilisation of Late Antiquity. These would be taken even further to the east in the succeeding centuries, when the German realm that was brought into being under the Ottonian kings and emperors, established itself as the dominant force in central Europe. At the same time a resurgent Byzantine Empire was once more extending its own influence both westwards and northwards, not least into the region that would become Russia, thus creating a long-lasting divide in the cultural traditions of Europe.

To turn once more to the perspective of the historian, it was perhaps easier for Gibbon in an age of relative tranquillity to take a broad, if hardly dispassionate, view of this sequence of events. His approach to it, though, was conditioned by a desire to criticise certain elements in the society of his own day that he found reprehensible, notably its penchant for apparently pointless wars of conquest and the continuing strength of elements of unreason, above all in religion. At the same time, a much more radical critique, symbolised by the French Revolution, was to lead directly to the subversion of much of the social order of Europe and, perhaps paradoxically, to the proliferation of aggressive warfare on an almost unprecedented scale, together with the emergence of ideologies far more menacing to Liberal individualism and reason than the placid religiosity of the eighteenth century. Flamboyant despots of the succeeding period, from Napoleon to Hitler, also turned to the Roman imperial past and its attempted revival under Charlemagne for some of the imagery and the framework of ideas needed to shape and manifest their regimes.

The revival of scholarly interest in the periods of Late Antiquity and the Early Middle Ages can, as much as the historiography of any period, partake of the quality of mere antiquarianism. However, the nature of its subject matter, the scale and significance of so many of its events, and the intellectual force of the thought of so many of its greatest writers should militate against this. History should not necessarily be expected to teach lessons, and certainly is not cyclical, but the study of these apparently remote centuries is as conducive as any to the questioning of received value systems, the evaluation of dogma and the formulation of principles to guide the conduct of states and individuals in complex times.

For Judith

1 Problem-solving emperors

A dynamic age: the Roman Empire, 235–285

In the third century the Roman Empire finally came of age. Problems that had been developing for decades or had even been inherent within its structures from the beginning manifested themselves so strongly that they had at last to be confronted and resolved. The solutions may not have proved permanent ones, but at least the process of looking for them was cathartic. Although the Roman world is often portrayed as only emerging from the period of political and economic problems that marked so much of the century in the reign of Diocletian (284–305), it is worth noting how some of the solutions he was to advance had been prefigured in the reigns of a number of his predecessors.

When the former praetorian prefect Philip seized power from the still adolescent emperor Gordian III in 244, many of the elements that would go to make up what is often called 'the crisis of the third century' were clearly present.[1] In the East the newly emerged but antiquarian-minded power of Sassanian Persia was seeking not only to regain territories lost to Rome earlier in the century by its Parthian predecessor, but was also making a claim to recover all the lands once owned by the Achaemenid Persian Empire, which had been overthrown by Alexander the Great (c. 330 BC) but whose heir it claimed to be. On the Danube and Rhine frontiers pressure was mounting from various Germanic peoples, themselves subject to forces largely beyond the ken of the few Roman authors of this period whose historical works have survived. Similar movements of un-Romanised populations were eroding the Empire's hold on parts of its territory in North Africa.

Within the frontiers problems no less threatening were mounting. For reasons that are still largely opaque the economy of the Empire was over-heating, prices were rising fast and the only remedy adopted by the central government, that of reducing the purity of the silver in the coinage, only added to the inflationary spiral. The impact of this on the army, towards whose needs what passed for economic policy in the Roman world was always directed, added to the political pressures on already overburdened emperors.

The surreptitious foundation of the imperial system by the constitutional fiction of the first of its rulers, Augustus (27 BC–AD 14), taking on a life tenure of a wide range of magistracies and religious and military offices, had effectively concentrated power

1

and central decision-making throughout the Empire in the hands of one individual. The weakness of such a system was that it was only as efficient as the man in whose control it lay. The personal incompetence of many of the first emperors was masked by the limited nature of the problems they had to face. As these mounted the latitude that could be allowed for the eccentricities, lack of ability, or sheer youth of emperors who inherited their power and the burdens of office merely by virtue of family relationship became increasingly slight.[2] However, dynastic succession and even quite a measure of mediocrity could be put up with in periods in which the emperors did not have to establish their credibility as military leaders.

From an emperor having to be able to prove himself as a commander in the field, it was but a short step to a successful commander in the field becoming thereby a contender for the imperial office. Dynastic sentiment could carry some weight. The achievements and popularity with their soldiers of Septimius Severus (193–211) and his son Caracalla (211–17) paved the way for the acceptance by the troops of their distinctly less than competent relatives Elagabalus (218–22) and his cousin Severus Alexander (222–35). The former was able to give himself up to a life of total hedonism in Rome and the latter to endure a long subjection to the dominance of his grandmother and mother without too much strain being put on the imperial office by their lack of ability. However, when after several peaceful years a Germanic threat manifested itself on the Rhine frontier, Severus Alexander was quickly eliminated by his own soldiers and the first of a series of professional military emperors emerged in the person of Maximin I.

This proved unpalatable to the aristocracy. It is not that they were unused to power being transferred by decision of the army. This had happened in 68–9, in 193–7 and in 217–18. What had changed was the kind of man who commanded the armies, and therefore the kind of person who would be chosen by the troops as their emperor. By traditions stretching back into the time of the Roman Republic the holding of major military commands had been a senatorial prerogative. Effective as many of them had proved individually, such amateurism became less tolerable as the threats to the integrity of the Roman frontiers grew in intensity, and the Empire became increasingly defensive in its stance. The time when office and positions of power had been monopolised by a senatorial aristocracy of exclusively urban Roman origin was long past, and emperors and senators were taken from the upper classes of a number of major provinces, notably Spain and Africa, but in Maximin I a man of much lower social origin, from a much more backward province, had been selected by the army.

Indeed, he is portrayed by the contemporary Greek historian Herodian as coming 'from one of the semi-barbarous tribes of the interior of Thrace'.[3] This became embroidered in the peculiar fourth century Latin compilation known as the *Scriptores Historiae Augustae*, a set of imperial biographies supposedly written by a variety of authors at the beginning of the century, but most probably the work of a single writer working towards the end of it. For this author Maximin had been a complete outsider, the product of the marriage of a Goth and an Alan, coming from lands beyond the Empire, adjacent to and not part of Thrace.[4]

Although some historians have, unaccountably, preferred to believe the more picaresque fourth century account of his origins, even the version of Herodian is hardly free from prejudice. Maximin may have lacked the sophistication or the cultural attainments of some of his predecessors, and his pursuit of the revenues needed to pay his armies may have deepened the antipathy between emperor and Senate, but he was an effective military commander. This, however, made him vulnerable when the threat on the frontiers temporarily lessened. An unsuccessful revolt in Africa in 238 provided the inspiration for a more serious rebellion instigated by the Senate, and the emperor was murdered by his own men when bogged down in a protracted siege of Aquileia in northern Italy.[5]

The choice of and also the fate of the next rulers highlights another problem that had dogged the imperial system from at least the murder of Caligula in AD 41. This was the power of the Praetorian Guard, the elite force, generally stationed in Rome, that provided the imperial bodyguard. Control of this body of troops, normally dangerously close to the emperor's person, was vested in one or two Praetorian Prefects, who, when the emperor was personally weak or incapable, were able to exercise a controlling influence on the regime.[6]

The reign of the child emperor Gordian III (238–44) proves the point. He had been selected by the Senate for largely symbolic reasons in that he was the grandson of the elderly proconsul whose short-lived revolt in Africa had initiated the senatorial resistance that brought about the fall of Maximin. Two imperial co-regents who had been appointed effectively to keep the throne warm for the boy were murdered within months by the Praetorian Guard, whose Prefect then became the power behind the regime. In that he made the young emperor his son-in-law he had no need to contemplate dynastic change. However, after his death his successor preferred to take an early opportunity to eliminate Gordian and replace him as emperor.

The events of 238 and 244 demonstrated the fragility of the imperial office. They also coincided with the beginnings of the serious military threats from the Persians and on the Danube frontier. It was in the middle of a campaign against the Sassanians that Philip removed Gordian III. In his own five-year reign, which also saw the millenary celebration of the foundation of the city of Rome, the German pressure on the Danube frontier led to some successful campaigning in the region on the emperor's part in 246. However, in 248/9 a major incursion into the eastern Balkans on the part of the Goths, Vandals, Carpi and others led to chaos. The revolt of the legions in the area was suppressed, but only to have the victorious general responsible proclaimed emperor by his own troops. When he led them into Italy they overwhelmed the army loyal to Philip at Verona.[7]

The death in battle, or more probably at the hands of their own soldiers, of Philip I and his son and co-ruler Philip II left the throne vacant for the rebel Decius. He, however, was faced with the problems that had ultimately led to his predecessor's downfall. The spiralling inflation and the intensified level of military activity had led the state into having to raise more and more money to pay the troops. The massive costs incurred in the celebration of the millennium of Rome had added a further short-term element. Substantial increases in taxation in the later part of Philip's reign proved counterproductive, in that they led to revolts. Additionally, the immediate military threat resulting from the Gothic presence in the Balkan provinces required action, which was to prove fatal to the new imperial regime. In 251, after some initial success, Decius and his eldest son were killed in a disastrous battle with the Goths.[8]

The following two decades represent the heart of the period of crisis. They commenced with a time of political instability resulting from the upheavals of 249–51. Trebonianus Gallus, the general who extricated the remnants of the Roman army from the Balkans after the death of Decius, was able to make himself emperor, but as his regime was the product of defeat and compromise it remained vulnerable. A far from conclusive victory over the Goths in 253 by one of his generals, called Aemilian, led to the latter being proclaimed emperor by his army. When Aemilian invaded Italy, Gallus's men would not fight and instead killed him and his co-ruler Volusian. However, the carefully timed arrival in Italy of the Gallic armies, supposed to be coming to aid the now defunct Gallus, led in turn to Aemilian being killed by his own troops after a reign of less than four months. The commander of the Gallic forces, Valerian, was accepted as emperor, and with his son Gallienus as co-ruler, he was able to enjoy a seven-year respite from similar threats. For him disaster was to take another form.[9]

The Persian threat, put in abeyance by the treaty made by Philip I in 244, reasserted itself. In 260 the Roman emperor Valerian (253–60), while campaigning in the East, was trapped by a Sassanian army and taken into captivity, in which he died.[10] In the aftermath power in Syria, Mesopotamia and eventually Egypt passed into the hands of the indigenous rulers of Palmyra. In the Balkans, following the disaster of 251, no effective campaigning was undertaken to expel the Goths and their allies from the regions they had occupied for the next twenty years.

Military problems on the Rhine frontier also reasserted themselves in this period, after a time of relative tranquillity. In 260 Franks and other western Germanic groups breached the frontier and ravaged their way across Gaul and into Spain unopposed. In the immediate aftermath one of the military commanders in Gaul, Cassius Latinius Postumus, was proclaimed emperor by his troops. He killed the son of the then co-emperor Gallienus (253–68) in Cologne and made himself master of Gaul, Britain and parts of Spain. His rule lasted until he was murdered by some of his own men in 269. He had two successors, who kept this so-called 'Gallic empire' in being until 273.[11]

In this same period the debasement of the coinage finally reached the point at which the precious metal content of the supposedly silver coins known as *antoniniani* was no higher than 5 per cent. The coins themselves were effectively made of bronze, and they had to be dipped in a bath of silver to give them a thin coating before they were issued. No one seems to have been fooled, and the enormous size of some of the hoards of coins of this period testifies not only to the instability that led to their being hidden – and never recovered – but also to the massive production of the coins necessitated by the dwindling of their commercial value.[12]

While cumulatively all of these problems, to which could be added references to plague and famine, seem to add up to a picture of political, economic and to some extent social chaos of 'the Years of Anarchy', as they have been called, the impression is partly deceptive. Many of the areas of the Empire were in practice little affected by these difficulties. For example, between the conclusion of Septimius Severus's campaign against the Caledonians in 210/11 and the revolt of Carausius in 286 Britain seems to have been perfectly tranquil. Similarly, only a few parts of Spain were touched by Frankish and also some Berber raids in the middle of the century. This appears as a period of considerable prosperity for the cities of Roman Africa, which show few of the symptoms of urban decline that can be detected in many other regions of the Empire.[13] Egypt suffered no external threats, nor did most parts of Asia Minor.

In provincial and local terms, moreover, the creation of 'break-away' regimes such as that of the Gallic emperors Postumus, Victorinus and Tetricus, was an essentially healthy sign. When the administration of the legitimate emperor was incapable, for what-ever reasons, of defending a province or a group of them the creation of a locally based imperial regime ensured both better protection and also the exclusive direction of resources to the needs of the region. In these respects, when the western half of the Empire disintegrated in the fifth century it would have benefited from the kind of responses to crisis that can be seen in the third.

Certainly, what is very marked is the rapidity of the recovery from the period of military disaster and defeat. Despite ruling during the very epicentre of the period of crisis the emperor Gallienus was able to survive for fifteen years, the longest reign between those of Severus Alexander (222–38) and Diocletian (284–305). Although this is still controversial, it has been argued that the cavalry army that he instituted in the 260s in northern Italy was the precedent for the mobile field armies that were to become the standard form of imperial defence from the early fourth century onwards.[14] Unfortunately, the early death of one of his sons and the killing of the other by Postumus led to there being no clear answer to the question of imperial succession. This may have contributed to the conspiracy of a group of his leading generals, who arranged his murder.

What followed was a period of the rule of a succession of soldiers of great competence but of relatively low social origins. They were very similar in these respects to Maximin I, but whereas he had stood out as an unusual type of emperor in the first half of the century, Claudius II (268–70), Aurelian (270–5), Tacitus (275–6), Probus (276–82) and Carus (282–3) represent an unbroken line of such provincial career soldiers.[15] Unlike Philip I, Decius, Gallus and Valerian, they were not senators and did not belong to the cultivated upper class world of the city of Rome. They were, on the other hand, very successful in most of the tasks to which they turned their hands.

In a brief reign, terminated by illness, Claudius II disposed of the Gothic menace in the Balkans, expelling them from imperial territory. Aurelian put an end to the independent Gallic empire in 273, even allowing its last incumbent to retire to his estates in Italy, and followed this up by re-establishing Roman control in the East. This was facilitated by the recent demise of the highly successful Sassanian shah Shapur I (241–72) and an ensuing period of internal disorder in Persia. By the time of Carus (282–3) it was possible for the Romans to take the offensive, and this emperor launched an invasion that reached as far as the Persian capital of Ctesiphon, before he himself was, apparently, killed by lightning.[16]

Aurelian was able to increase the silver content in the coinage, and at the same time gave up the pretence of overvaluing it, by abolishing the residual bronze coin denominations that had existed alongside it. Further economic recovery was gradual, and it must be admitted that the actual causes of it were probably as opaque to the rulers of the Empire at this time as they are to modern historians.

The one area in which these emperors did not effect radical change in relation to pre-existing problems was that of internal political stability and the vulnerability of the holders of the imperial office. By succumbing to disease Claudius II was one of only two emperors in the course of the entire century to die of natural causes. The tendency in the army to favour hereditary succession, if only for reasons of self-interest, manifested itself both on his death and on that of Tacitus in 276. On both occasions units of the army proclaimed the late emperor's brother. Neither, however, was able to call on enough support to face the challenge of the candidate chosen by other units of the army. In 270 Quintillus, proclaimed in northern Italy, lasted only seventeen days. In 276 Florian, the brother of Tacitus, was set up by the army in Asia Minor, but was opposed by Probus, the choice of the army in Egypt. Rather than face a war, his own men killed him at Tarsus after a reign of three months.[17]

As well as disputed successions, the period was still marked by occasional military revolts. Probus (276–82) was faced by two: one in Gaul and the other in Syria in 281. It is probable also that his successor Carus, Praetorian Prefect and commander of the army in the Balkans, was in revolt against him in 282, when he was killed by his own men near Sirmium. Although it is recorded that the troops did this because he had transferred them to the digging of drainage ditches, it is perhaps more probable that the murder of Probus represents something of a replay of the events of 276 and that he was killed because his own men were unwilling to support him against Carus.[18]

The basic problem remained the need for the emperor to be in more than one place at the same time, at least in periods of military crisis. He had to command his forces in person, but if more than one frontier was threatened or if a mixture of internal and external threats needed to be countered, control over a significant body of troops had to be delegated to a subordinate general. Success on the part of this man, or even just the prospect of the cash payment traditionally given out on the occasion of a change in the holder of the imperial office, could lead his army to proclaim him emperor. Admittedly, this seems only to have been done if there was a good chance that wider backing for the rebel would be found amongst other military commands. If this was not forthcoming, and the rebel forces looked as if they were not getting a broader basis of support for their candidate, they tended to murder him and revert to their previous allegiance. Even with this relative 'safety mechanism', such revolts and contested successions were frequent in the period 268–85.

The emperor who first tried to put an end to this instability himself achieved power in the same way. Carus was the only one of the military emperors of this period to attempt both to pre-empt the problem of his own succession and to resolve the difficulty of needing an imperial presence in more than one location simultaneously. On his accession he nominated his two sons to the rank of Caesar, or junior emperor. When he undertook his Persian campaign in 283 he promoted the elder of them, Carinus, to the superior rank of Augustus or full emperor, leaving him in charge of the West. The younger son, the Caesar Numerian, accompanied him. On Carus's death in Persia his army then elevated Numerian to the rank of Augustus. In the course of the army's withdrawal across Asia Minor in the winter of 284 the new emperor was secretly murdered. One of the generals, Diocletian, blamed the Praetorian Prefect, killed him and had himself proclaimed emperor by the troops. In the ensuing civil war against Carinus, Diocletian suffered an initial defeat, but the western emperor was murdered by some of his own officers. Diocletian was accepted as sole ruler without further opposition.[19]

The reign of Diocletian, 285–305

Diocletian's appreciation of the scale of the problems facing the holder of the imperial office and the need for the emperor to be able to deal personally with any large scale difficulty that required a military solution was both acute and remarkable. None of his immediate predecessors, apart from Carus, had even faced up to the issue let alone attempted to solve it. The kind of dynastic solution adopted by Carus, following earlier precedents, was only as strong as the emperor's children were competent and popular. Diocletian's answer was both more daring and potentially more risky, but it proved to be both immediate and effective. This was to select one of his generals and promote him to the rank of imperial colleague, with special responsibility for a particular part of the Empire.

In 285 he nominated Maximian as his co-ruler, at first in the junior rank of Caesar. In April 286 Maximian was further advanced to the senior rank of Augustus, making him an equal colleague of Diocletian, who entrusted him with the oversight of the West while he returned to the East.[20] This could have led to civil war, if Maximian had wished to try to make himself sole ruler, but he seems to have had no such ambitions, and was kept busy with a series of military problems in the West, ranging from Frankish and Saxon seaborne raiding in the Channel to a major Berber incursion into the Roman provinces of North Africa. Although probably not originally envisaged in 286, Diocletian's political solution was taken a stage further in 293. In that year, with the consent of Maximian, he nominated two Caesars, Galerius and Constantius, one for the East and one for the West. These two operated under the authority of the senior emperor in their half of the Empire, and with particular oversight of a group of provinces. To further cement the loyalty of the imperial quartet each of the Caesars married the daughter of the senior emperor of his half of the Empire.[21] In 305 the two senior emperors abdicated in favour of their Caesars and new junior emperors were appointed to bring the imperial college up to the number of four once more.

The new Tetrarchic (that is 'four ruler') system did not eliminate the possibility of military revolt, but it certainly limited the extent to which a rebel general in a particular province could threaten the stability of the imperial regime. In 286 Carausius, the commander of the Channel fleet, rebelled. He was proclaimed emperor by the army in Britain, but although his regime lasted for seven years he did not extend his power beyond the island, apart from holding Boulogne and some other locations on the north Gallic coast. He himself was murdered by his finance minister Allectus in 293, and the latter was killed when the Caesar Constantius invaded Britain in 296.[22] It was principally the difficulty of shipping an army across the Channel that allowed this rebel regime to last so long. A prior attempt at invasion in 289 had been abandoned when the imperial fleet was destroyed in a storm. On the other hand a revolt in Egypt in 296 under Domitius Domitianus was suppressed within eight months.[23]

The intention of the fully developed Tetrarchic system was to present the four emperors as working together in the closest harmony and concord. Although there was a distinction in status between the two senior Augusti and their junior partners, otherwise their functions and authorities were equal and interchangeable.

The ideology was represented in art, above all by the elimination of elements of individuality in the portraiture of the rulers. Thus in the coins of these emperors only the inscriptions indicate which of the rulers is being portrayed. The styles vary from mint to mint but the individual rulers are given identical features.[24] The quintessential imperial image of this period may be found in the three-dimensional porphyry sculptures of the four emperors, now embedded in the wall of the Church of San Marco in Venice. Grouped in pairs, with the senior emperor in each case holding his arm around the shoulder of his junior, the men are identical both in their military costume and in their physiognomy.[25] They form a team, an indivisible unit, and are not four separable individuals.

In the official literary depictions of the imperial regime the same imagery may also be found. In 291 in the panegyric or speech in praise of the emperor Maximian on his birthday the Gallic orator Mamertinus imagines the crowd exclaiming as they saw the two emperors together in Milan: 'Do you see Diocletian? Do you see Maximian? There they both are! They are together! How they sit in unity! How they talk together in concord!'[26] This dates from the period before the extension of the numbers in the 'college of emperors' from two to four; something that may have resulted from the incapacity of Maximian, at least to deal adequately with all of the problems besetting the West in the later 280s.[27]

As well as this fundamental change in the imperial office, Diocletian sought to restructure the administration of the Empire. A reorganisation of provincial boundaries increased the number and reduced the size of such units. At the same time civil and military authority within the provinces was generally divided and parallel hierarchies created within both divisions. The smaller provinces were themselves then grouped into larger units, called dioceses, and these were placed under the direction of a new class of official called *Vicarii*, or Deputy Praetorian Prefects. This process was continued under Diocletian's eventual successor Constantine I (306–37), who by disbanding the Praetorian cohorts in 312 finally turned the Praetorian Prefecture into an essentially civilian and administrative office. Later in his reign he increased the number of Prefects from two to four and tied them to regional prefectures rather than being linked to the persons of the emperors.[28]

In the reorganisation of the army as well as the restructuring of the administration it is equally or more difficult to separate the reforms of Diocletian from those of Constantine. Certainly, by the latter's death in 337 an entirely new organisation had been introduced, whereby the army was divided into two types of unit. On the one hand there were the *Limitanei*, garrison groups stationed on the frontiers and intended to provide the first line of defence against incursions, and on the other there were the *Comitatenses,* or units of the mobile field armies that were deployed well behind the frontiers and which moved rapidly to counter specific threats that were beyond the capacity of the *Limitanei* to contain.

The garrison forces were less well armed, equipped and trained and were expected to have only limited mobility. The field armies, on the other hand, contained much larger proportions of cavalry than had existed under the early Empire, when this arm had been considered inferior and its units had been composed exclusively of the second class Auxiliaries. The army reforms of Diocletian and Constantine marked a change in imperial strategy in favour of what is known as 'Defence in Depth'. The frontiers became more intensively defended by the location of garrisons and the construction of more numerous and more complex fortifications, but once this outer shell had been penetrated the protection of the provinces depended on the capacity of the field armies to concentrate and move to meet the threat. This system had certain disadvantages, and the re-deployment of field armies to partici-pate in the numerous civil wars within the Empire in the fourth century could leave the frontier provinces open to sustained penetration and destruction when the *Limitanei* failed to prevent hostile incursions. However, the roots of the change, as with many of the features of the reign of Diocletian, can be traced back to earlier stages in the third century; in this case to the reign of Gallienus (253–68), whose cavalry army in northern Italy is often seen as the precursor of the *Comitatenses.*[29]

A reform that can certainly be ascribed to Diocletian is the measure he took to curb the inflationary price spiral within the Empire. However, economic theory was as underdeveloped in the Ancient World as was technology, and the emperor's sole concern was the cost of supplies for his army. His approach to the problem was direct but ultimately ineffectual. It took the form of an edict on prices, issued in the year 301. This stipulated the maximum price that could be charged for a long list of specified items, most of which, not surprisingly, were of direct importance to the army. The penalty for charging more than the decreed prices was execution. In practice this seems to have had limited effect, in that it ignored the basic mechanisms of supply and demand. Hoarding and 'black market' trading became preferable alternatives to selling on the open market at government-set price levels. The edict had to be repealed.[30] More effective were a series of reforms of the coinage in 296 that reintroduced a bronze denomination and set new ratios of value between bronze, silver and gold. This took up and extended the revaluation tentatively begun under Aurelian.

In general it could be said that the whole thrust of the changes introduced around the turn of the century by Diocletian and by Constantine was aimed at the production of a more regimented and rigid society. Laws that required sons to follow in the professions of their fathers, laws that fixed prices, laws that established exact hierarchies in the civil and military administration, and laws that forbade an increasing range of opinions and practices all cohere in terms of the kind of social ideals that underlie them.[31] This was not just a question of the will of an individual ruler or even of a college of emperors. Many of the elements can be detected earlier in the third century in less developed and coherent form, and the transformation that was wrought within the Empire at the end of it must reflect the growth of the public acceptability of so many of the rules that were then introduced or systematised.

In this sense the culmination of occasional persecution of the Christians in the course of the third century in the so-called Great Persecution initiated by Diocletian in 303 is hardly surprising. This was both more thorough, logical and systematic than anything that had gone before it, and at the same time developed tendencies within Roman society that had been manifesting themselves for a century or more. Leaving aside the rather nebulous Neronian persecution, confined to the city of Rome, and linked to the need to find scapegoats for the great fire in the city in AD 64, serious state-initiated action against the growing Christian communities within the Empire was principally a third century phenomenon.[32]

It began with the brief reign of Trajan Decius (249–51), who in 250 issued an edict requiring his provincial governors, urban magistrates and local Commissioners for Sacrifices to obtain certificates from the citizens to establish that they had taken part in the obligatory public sacrifices to the gods and to the Genius (or guiding spirit) of the Emperor on certain specified days. At least one witness was required to sign the statement. It is thought, though, that many Christians got around these regulations by bribery or influence, and the whole process had no sooner begun than it was terminated by Decius's death in 251.[33]

More sustained and systematic were the measures taken in the middle of his reign by the emperor Valerian, who issued two laws against the Christians. The first ordered them not to assemble in their own places of worship or to use their own cemeteries, and required them to take part in the public sacrifices. The second confiscated the property of still practising Christians, deprived individuals of their existing legal status, and threatened death to those who persisted in their faith.[34] These laws were repealed in 261 by Valerian's son Gallienus, who also restored their property to Christian individuals and communities. No further state action was taken against them until the time of Diocletian.

The sources of evidence for all of the persecutions are generally later in date than the events themselves, and are written from a Christian point of view. Only the chance survival of an odd document, such as the witnessed certificate of attendance at sacrifices sent to the Commissioners for Sacrifices 'in the Village of Alexander's Island' in Egypt by one Aurelius Diogenes 'son of Satabus ... aged 72; scar on right eyebrow', gives any contemporary and non-Christian perspective on events.[35] Thus it is not easy to assess the real causes for the state-initiated persecutions. From the Christian side no attempt was made to explain or understand the causes of the actions being taken against them. The pagan Roman world was expected to be antagonistic and that this occasionally erupted in the form of officially sponsored violence was a matter of no surprise.

It is, perhaps, easier for us to understand something of the motives of the imperial government, when the logic of the Christian position is expounded. Firstly, it needs to be stressed that there was little inherently wrong from a Roman point of view in the proliferation of different forms of religious belief and practice. Nor was secrecy in the performance of ritual necessarily disapproved of, though it could arouse suspicion. A number of 'mystery cults' existed, and attracted high and occasionally imperial favour. That the founding figure of Christianity had been put to death by the imperial judicial system and the strong early links of the new religion to the Jews, who had twice rebelled against the Empire, were probably less causes for concern in the third century than in the previous two. However, the refusal of the Christians to participate in the public sacrifices to the Genius of the Emperor and the principal gods of the Empire was a far more serious worry.

The religious exclusivity of the Christian message meant that no adherent of the faith could participate in any other act of worship. For the Christians the gods venerated by their fellow Romans were not divinities at all, but evil demonic forces, whose hold over the minds of their adherents prevented them from recognising the truth of the Christian revelation. Thus for a Christian to participate in a pagan sacrifice, even in a passive way, was a positive act of apostasy, a renunciation of belief. This was unfortunate when the making of such sacrifices was the principal way in which acts of public loyalty to the emperor were expressed.

In many ways such a sacrifice was a political act in a religious form, but for the Christians the implicit recognition of a divinity other than the one true God made participation an act of spiritual suicide. In consequence, of course, the Christians could seem to be politically subversive. The successive crises affecting the material well-being of the Empire in the mid-third century and the growth in the number of Christians made the taking of repressive measures against such apparent dissidents increasingly likely.[36]

In general the growth of Christianity, particularly amongst the most influential sectors of society, was disturbing to imperial regimes of a conservative cast. The second rescript of Valerian envisaged the possibilities of Christians being found amongst the ranks of the Senate, and the second level of nobility, that of the *Equites*. Similarly, there were thought to be many Christians amongst the members of the imperial household both at this time and later in that of Diocletian. The emperor Decius, who initiated the series of imperial laws requiring Christian participation in the public sacrifices, was particularly anxious to reinforce the imperial cult, not least in the aftermath of his own overthrow of Philip and the spate of revolts in 249. He also issued a series of coins commemorating previous emperors, from Augustus to Severus Alexander, who had been deified or been declared to be gods.[37] That the issue of Christian non-participation in such rites should come to a head at this time is thus little of a surprise. Imperial attitudes and policy are, however, only half of the story.[38]

Although attention normally focuses on the formal measures taken by the state against the Christians in this mid-third century period, and the later accounts of the martyrdoms of those who refused to abandon their faith provide in most cases vivid images of confrontations with the civil authorities, it is notable that the persecutions can also be seen to derive from conflicts and hostilities in local urban contexts. The Christian accounts written in the early fourth century, particularly the *Ecclesiastical History* of bishop Eusebius of Caesarea (d. 339/40), make mention of these. In a letter sent by bishop Dionysius of Alexandria to his colleague Fabius in Antioch, which is quoted by Eusebius, active persecution had broken out in his city a year before the promulgation of Decius's edict. This he blamed on 'the nameless prophet and worker of mischief' who incited the populace of Alexandria against the Christian community, several of whom were lynched.[39]

In the great cities of the eastern half of the Empire, above all in Antioch and Alexandria, the numerical rise of the Christian communities, whose religious practices prevented them from participating in the public festivals of their pagan neighbours, was bound to be a cause of mounting tension in periods of economic hardship and political crisis. It seems very probable that Valerian, who had favoured the Christians to a degree they themselves found surprising at the beginning of his reign, was turned against them after he came east and took up residence in Antioch in 256. Bishop Dionysius in another of his letters put the blame on one of the emperor's civil servant advisers – later to be an unsuccessful emperor-maker – by the name of Macrianus.[40]

A similar personal influence, but again one rooted in the intense inter-communal hostilities of the eastern cities, is thought to have lain behind the initiation of the Great Persecution under Diocletian. It is surprising that he waited until so late a stage in his reign to begin legislating against the Christians if he personally had a deep dislike of them. There is thus a plausibility to the suggestion that the initiative really lay with the Caesar Galerius, whose dominance was increasing in the final years of Diocletian's reign and who was to succeed him within two years.[41] However, it is worth noting that it was Galerius who in 311 repealed the edict of persecution; in other words a year before the conversion of Constantine.

Whatever the motives and the parts played by the individual actors, the strength of anti-Christian feeling and the degree to which persecution was actively pursued in the years 303 to 312 depended largely upon local conditions. In the West, where, apart from Africa, Christian communities were neither numerous nor large, the application of Diocletian's legal measures, which were effectively the re-imposition of those of Valerian, barely outlasted his reign. Constantius I (305–6) seems to have allowed the penalties against practising Christians to lapse and Maxentius (306–12) began the process of restoring their property. In the East, however, the Caesar and later Augustus Maximin II (305–13), who controlled Egypt and Syria, applied the laws in full, not least because of popular anti-Christian agitation within his territories.[42] This is probably what prevented him from following Galerius in ending the persecution in 311.

It is perhaps paradoxical that Diocletian should be responsible for at least the inauguration of the last imperially sponsored attempt to extirpate Christianity. His eventual successor Constantine, who was the heir to so many of his policies, and whose work extended and completed so much of that of Diocletian, took a quite opposite approach and became the first Christian emperor. In many ways this was the more logical step. In the more regulated and authoritarian state that had been created in the third century the hierarchic structures and the Mediterranean-wide organisation of the Church had much to offer the secular rulers of the Empire.

2 The age of Constantine

Imperial rivals, 305–312

The abdication of Diocletian and Maximian in 305, whether envisaged as a fundamental feature of the Tetrarchic system or the product of the senior emperor's recent ill health, opened the way to the emergence of a second Tetrarchy, in which the dominant figure should have been Galerius.[1] His succession to Diocletian as the Augustus in the East was matched by the parallel elevation of Constantius in the West. The two Caesars appointed to assist them, Severus in the West and Maximin II in the East, are presented in the, admittedly hostile, Christian sources, which provide so much of the political narrative for this period, as both being creatures of Galerius.[2] Severus was one of his subordinate officers, and Maximin the new senior emperor's nephew. This latter appointment marks the only concession made to family relationships in the constitution of the new Tetrarchy. Neither the son of Maximian nor the son of Constantius was promoted, and this must represent a deliberate attempt to prevent dynastic succession from coming to play a part in the new imperial system.

If so, this proved to be a fatal flaw. The death in 306 of Constantius I at York, where he had gone to campaign against the Picts, led not to Galerius being able to nominate a new senior colleague, most probably intended to be an old comrade in arms called Licinius, but to the army in Britain proclaiming the dead emperor's son Constantine as his successor.[3] In the same year, with the connivance of the retired emperor Maximian, the army in Rome proclaimed the latter's son Maxentius emperor, in rebellion against the Caesar Severus. Galerius attempted to shore up the disintegrating Tetrarchy by recognising Constantine, but only as a Caesar, whilst nominating the beleaguered Severus as the new Augustus for the West. Maxentius and his father were to be left out on a limb.

Galerius's lack of flexibility was soon to prove fatal to the entire system. Severus's new title proved empty in that he lost the support of his army in Italy and was persuaded, after an abortive siege of Rome, to surrender himself into the hands of Maxentius, who soon had him put to death. An imperial 'conference' held at Carnuntum on the Danube in 308, between Galerius and the retired emperors Diocletian and Maximian (who had just been expelled from Italy by his son) led to another ill-conceived attempt to force the imperial structure back into its required shape.

Licinius was proclaimed Augustus, in succession to the unlamented Severus, Maximian was required to return to his retirement, and Maxentius was proclaimed to be a usurper.[4]

Most of this was foolish. Whatever the constitutional niceties Maxentius was the *de facto* ruler of Italy and Africa, and was consolidating his position in Rome by a major programme of public works. Furthermore, neither Constantine nor Maximin, who had been Caesars for the past two years, was prepared to tolerate the elevation of Licinius over his head. An attempt to placate them with the meaningless title of *Filius Augusti* or 'Son of the Senior Emperor' proved abortive, and in 309 they both had to be recognised as *Augustus* in their own right.[5] As a system the Tetrarchy was dead, replaced by the co-existence of five emperors, four of whom were mutually recognised and one of whom was theoretically still a usurper. In practice it was only going to be a matter of time before all of the rival rulers fell to fighting amongst themselves for larger shares of territory and power.

Galerius's failure to impose a solution of his own devising or to prove himself Diocletian's equal was completed by his invasion of Italy in 310. Although able to bottle up Maxentius in Rome he was unable to take the city, and his army disintegrated under the twin pressures of military failure and the distribution of bribes by the besieged usurper. Galerius was forced to make a hasty and ignominious retreat from Italy, back to his imperial residence at Salonica, where he died the following year. Although just prior to his death he repealed his anti-Christian legislation, his painful terminal illness was reported with relish and much intimate detail in the work *On the Deaths of the Persecutors* of the African Christian rhetor Lactantius.[6]

Whether the continued survival of Galerius would have long delayed the ensuing conflict between the remaining emperors is open to question. The first round was fought in 312, within a year of his death. Constantine invaded Italy, and whereas Maxentius had successfully sat out two previous such threats safe within the walls of Rome, this time he came out to meet him. In the ensuing battle of the Milvian Bridge, just north of the city, Constantine was victorious, and Maxentius drowned trying to flee across the Tiber.[7] By this victory Italy and Africa were joined to Constantine's other provinces of Britain, Gaul and Spain.

The emperor and his new religion

This episode was significant not just because it effected a change in the fluid boundaries of the spheres of authority of rival emperors, but also and more so because it is associated directly with the conversion of Constantine to Christianity. For an event of such importance, at least in the long term, the evidence relating to it is extraordinarily sparse and contradictory. It comes principally in the form of the accounts of the emperor's vision and subsequent conversion on the eve of the battle given in the *De Mortibus Persecutorum* (*Deaths of the Persecutors*) of Lactantius (*c*. 317) and in the Greek *Life of Constantine* and *Ecclesiastical History* of Bishop Eusebius of Caesarea.[8]

Although attempts have been made to suggest that Constantine was being cynically self-interested in his conversion to the faith of those who had been subjected to state persecution since 303, such views are not convincing.[9] The greater number of Christians were to be found in the eastern half of the Empire rather than the west, and it was by no means clear that they would have been prepared to co-operate with the secular aims of the state, even under a Christian emperor. To a considerable extent Eusebius in the 320s was to write for a Christian readership who needed to be taught how to view the advent of such a ruler. It could not be thought that in 312 the conversion would guarantee Constantine a body of military support or a 'fifth column' within the territory of his rivals.

Attempts to understand the conversion ultimately come up against the impossibility of penetrating into a level of individual motivation that is beyond the merely logical. Moreover, in this case, although Eusebius at least could present his report of Constantine's vision on the eve of the battle as being the emperor's personal account of it, given on oath, it has to be appreciated that in the intervening years the latter's own perception of what had motivated him and what it signified had changed dramatically. All in all Constantine was a very different sort of Christian in the 330s from what he had been in 312.[10]

In so far as any interpretation of the groundwork of the conversion is possible, it is significant to note both the devotion to the worship of the Sun manifested by Constantine's father, and the way in which the imagery of the solar divinity Sol/Oriens had been appropriated as a means of depicting Christ in the art of the late third century, as is well manifested in the damaged mosaic found under the basilica of St Peter's in Rome. This was put up on the ceiling of a tomb close to the site of the small shrine erected by Christians in the later second century marking the supposed location of the burial of St Peter. That the mosaic pre-dated the age of Constantine is proved by its position in the buildings that were deliberately buried in the creation of the platform on which Constantine was to erect his great basilica dedicated to St Peter. The iconography of the mosaic, damaged when the excavators, unsuspectingly, smashed their way through the roof of the buried room is significant in that it combines the traditional imagery of the sun god in his two-horse chariot with elements of Christian symbolism, such as the vine.[11]

Constantine preserved on the coins issued by his government for several years after his conversion the reverse legend of *Soli Invicto Comiti* – 'To the Unconquered Sun, Companion (of the Emperor)'. The last of these was struck in 323.[12] Although often assumed to represent a state of compromise between the emperor's new-found faith and the pagan traditions of virtually all of the main sectors of society in the western empire, this continued use of solar imagery by the new Christian may represent a more personal statement. It is significant that Constantine's views of his new religion became more complex and, it might be said, more orthodox after his conquest of the East, the half of the Empire in which Christianity had a firmer and more substantial hold, and where such sophisticated ecclesiastical advisers as Eusebius were awaiting him. In the West only Africa could match any part of the East in terms of the size and strength of Christian communities or learning. There Constantine did not go.

It would be wrong to assume that the senatorial aristocracy of Rome, the self-appointed guardians of the conservative traditions of the city and the empire that it had created, viewed their new emperor's plebeian faith with surprise or hostility. Their lack of enthusiasm for Maxentius may have been less than Constantine's panegyrists wished their audiences to believe, but in the matter of religion there was little initially very startling about the prospect of an emperor who believed himself to be specially favoured by and to have a personal relationship to a or the divinity. Heliogabalus and Aurelian had done the same, and the notion of the emperor's divine *comes* or companion had become a standard one in the imperial ideology of the Tetrarchy.[13]

Constantine's Christianity only seemed peculiar and markedly different from the Sun worship of his father and of Aurelian when allied to the exclusivity of his fellow devotees. Whereas most of the other cults and faiths that co-existed in the Mediterranean world in the late Roman period did so on the basis of mutual toleration and syncretism, the Christians, like the Jews, saw themselves as the exclusive possessors of religious truth and the adherents of the only true divinity, who could in no sense be thought to manifest himself under the guise of some other object of veneration. The Constantinian confusion between Christ and Sol was not long allowed to last.

Similarly, the refusal of the Christians to see their religion as one amongst many or as a faith that could co-exist with a myriad of others by means either of some highbrow philosophising or by the cruder syncretistic equating of one divinity with another, as had been customary in the Empire since its inception, meant that for the first time a specific body of the population was directly and exclusively affected by an imperial decision on a matter of personal religious preference. Because the nature of the Christian perspectives on supernatural truth and on the ends of human life were what they were, the nuances of a change in religious ideology of a new imperial regime assumed a significance hitherto totally lacking in the political life of the Roman Empire. As a devotee of Jupiter Diocletian did not have a defined constituency of supporters, nor was he obliged to consider how to further such a hypothetical body's aims at the expense of, say, those who were peculiarly attached to the cult of Mars. Constantine in 312, however, found himself very differently placed.

It soon became apparent that the co-religionists of the emperor, and this for once meant a minority of his subjects, were going to be especially favoured by the new regime. Amongst the earliest beneficiaries was the Christian community in Rome, or rather its leadership. During his stay in the city after the victory over Maxentius at the Milvian bridge Constantine began the construction of the first overt and explicitly Christian buildings. Previously Christians had gathered discretely in a number of private houses, in which particular rooms were given over to worship and the performance of other rites, such as baptism. There was no distinctive Christian architecture, and no purpose-built structures intended exclusively for their religious requirements. This Constantine altered, not least by the construction of the great basilica of St Peter's, erected on the supposed site of the burial of the martyr.[14]

The basic plan of the new form of building was borrowed from that of the secular basilica, a rectangular structure with an apse at one or both ends, normally serving as a law court and to be found in most of the towns and cities of the Empire. Such a basilica, on a monumental scale, and containing space for half a dozen or more courts had been begun by Maxentius in the Roman forum, and was to be completed by Constantine after 312.[15] The basilican plan had also proved adaptable for the design of imperial throne halls, in which the increasingly formal state ceremonial of the Late Empire could be performed. In such buildings as Constantine's throne room in Trier the rectangular body of the hall provided direction and space for the lesser participants, with the single semicircular apse serving as the location for the imperial throne and the focus of all attention.[16] With courtiers and attendants filling the body of the hall and the emperor enthroned behind curtains in the apse, envoys and others to be received could be led in by the *Silentiarii*, the overseers of court protocol, and brought through the hall. At an appropriate point the curtain concealing the emperor was drawn back and all present made obeisance to the ruler.[17]

It was this adaptation that probably provides the key to understanding why the basilica was adopted as the basic, and subsequently little modified, form of architecture for the Christian places of public worship. The rectangular hall provided the necessary space for the congregation, whilst the need for a focus for the liturgy around the altar was immediately catered for by the apsidal extension towards which all attention could be directed. This was perhaps the first, but certainly not the only way in which the emperor's adoption of Christianity in the early fourth century led to the mingling of imperial and Christian imagery, institutions, and structures.

As well as the extraordinarily rapid creation not only of a distinctive if derivative style of Christian architecture and its practical manifestation in a number of buildings of lavish and substantial construction, Constantine's benefactions to the church in Rome also transformed the economic position and social standing of its leaders. Endowment with income was matched by the grant to the bishops of the city of the Lateran palace, a former imperial residence.[18] The provision of a palatial dwelling and centre of administration, together with the income needed to support it and the transformed lifestyle of the bishop and clergy, added to the sumptuousness of the new Christian places of worship, altered the standing of the leaders of their community within the city. In the late second century one of the bishops of Rome had been a freed slave, and the general social level of the Christians in the city was hardly high, but Constantine's gifts put the bishops on a par in terms of conspicuous wealth and ostentation with the leaders of secular society, the still almost exclusively pagan aristocracy of the Senate.[19]

It became clear that a shared religious affiliation was the best route to imperial favour from Constantine, but although the Senate of Rome marked his victory over Maxentius, whom they may not have disliked, by the erection of a still extant triumphal arch, its members were economically little in need of the ruler's patronage, and the general tendency of emperors in the second half of the third century to exclude senators from government and military office actually allowed them to be less dependent on imperial goodwill than would otherwise have been the case.[20] However, there were some who for reasons of conviction or convenience found it beneficial to share the ruler's religion and thus his munificence.

More widely, and more equitably, Constantine instructed his provincial governors to restore to the Christian communities the property that had been taken from them during the period of persecution. There are indications, however, that this process had already begun in Africa and Italy in the time of Maxentius.[21] Whilst Constantine was unable to legislate for his co-religionists outside the provinces under his direct control in 312, his position as the sole ruler of the western half of the Empire made him the most powerful of the emperors and the person whose alliance both of the two rivals in the east, Licinius and Maximin II, would desire. Maximin was the less well-placed of the two in that he seems to have made some prior commitments to the unfortunate Maxentius, and, as various documents preserved in the *Ecclesiastical History* of Eusebius show, popular opposition to the Christians seems to have been much stronger at a local level in his dominions, particularly Egypt, than in those of Licinius, and he was thus less able and probably less willing to pay the ideological price that Constantine sought.[22]

At a simpler level, Licinius was also closer to Constantine geographically, and it is thus little surprising to find the two emperors meeting in Milan, when their newly forged amity was cemented by the issue of an edict in March 313 ending the persecution of Christians throughout the Empire.[23] Even Maximin found it advisable to give force to this decree. To some extent active persecution, which had been at its height in the first two or three years after 303, had then become little more than a formality, and even Galerius, possibly the most ideologically motivated of the tetrarchs in this respect, had issued an edict of toleration for the Christians just before his death in 311. From 312 onwards, though, whenever official persecution of Christians re-emerged it was more a political stance reflecting the persecuting ruler's attitude towards the increasingly dominant Constantine. Thus Licinius joined Constantine in granting toleration to the Christians in 313, but himself reintroduced persecution in the course of his two unsuccessful civil wars with the western emperor.[24] Likewise, Maximin initially accepted toleration when trying to pacify Constantine and Licinius, but allowed a further burst of persecution when the attempts failed and all-out war with Licinius seemed unavoidable.

It could not be said that the emergence of Christianity as a major force with a growing and socially rising membership was in itself the cause of the increasing divisiveness in Roman society from the later third century onwards, in that the phenomenon can be detected in areas in which religion had no part to play. However, the exclusivity of Christian religious belief, and the concomitant intolerance of other forms of faith, made the intellectual *modus vivendi* of the multitude of different groups, sects, and religions of the Roman world no longer tenable, and exacerbated the divisiveness of other fissures in the society.[25] Although it is hard to blame the victim for the suffering he endures, the initiation of active and legally instigated persecution of the Christian communities by the state at various points in the second half of the third century is a reflection of both the growing hold of Christianity over increasingly prominent sectors of Roman society and the uncompromising nature of its ideology.

For Constantine, despite what he had done for the position of the Christian community within Rome, the city was inevitably a stronghold of opposition to his beliefs. This was because of the conservatism of the Senate, whose tacit opposition to the emperor's religious aims grew stronger the more overt the latter became, and it has been suggested that his decision to move the centre of his government to the east reflected this hostility. However, it has to be borne in mind that, apart from under the regime of Maxentius, Rome had ceased to be the normal place of imperial residence after the death of Gallienus in 268. Diocletian's precedent would suggest an eastern capital, and the greater numbers of Christians resident in that part of the empire might have been only a secondary consideration.

First of all came the acquisition of control over the whole Empire, a final undoing of the political structures that Diocletian and his colleagues had created and sought to maintain with increasing difficulty. Despite initial attempts at compromise, the conflict between Licinius and Maximin II for ascendancy in the East could not long be delayed after Constantine's uniting of the West in 312. Early in the spring of 313, while Licinius was still in Italy, Maximin struck and invaded his rival's territory. However, despite the haste of his return from the West, Licinius routed his opponent in a battle in Thrace on 30 April and drove him back into Asia. Maximin, in flight, died of illness at Tarsus, while Licinius was still busy conquering Asia Minor.[26]

With Licinius as dominant in the East as Constantine in the West, the need for the alliance between them was less obvious once the restoration of single dynastic rule over the whole Empire became their aim. The first clash occurred in 314. Licinius lost two battles against the western armies in the Balkans and was forced to cede some territory as the price of peace. However, the war had been effectively indecisive, and there followed an uneasy decade of co-existence before the outbreak of the final war in 323. Again Licinius was defeated in their two encounters, at Adrianople and Chrysopolis, but this time the victories were clearer and having been besieged in Byzantium Licinius was forced to submit. His life, and that of his son, was spared at the intervention of his wife, Constantine's sister, but neither was allowed to live for long.[27]

Interestingly, in both of the wars Licinius had at crucial moments proclaimed co-emperors, a certain Valerius Valens in 314 and Marcus Martianus in 324. It seems that these were his proposed candidates for western emperor when and if Constantine was disposed of. Both were executed by the man they were supposed to replace.[28] It thus appears that Licinius was still thinking in tetrarchic terms of a possible college of emperors, created by appointment, rather than in the nakedly dynastic aspirations of his rival. Sentiment played little part in Licinius's makeup. He is said to have had the wives and children of both Galerius and Maximin II put to death after they fell into his hands in 313, but in ruthlessness as in political calculation he was far outstripped by Constantine.[29]

It has not been possible for subsequent generations to idealise the first Christian emperor. His treatment of defeated enemies, such as the family of Licinius, was perhaps not untypical of his age, but he was as lethal to his own family as to his foes. His father-in-law, the former emperor Maximian, he had had strangled in 310.[30] His eldest son Crispus was executed in the process of some family and court intrigue in 326, and his own wife Fausta, daughter of Maximian, was put to death in rather obscure circumstances soon after.[31] Constantine displayed a single mindedness, and a sense of purpose that were matched by few emperors, but his ruthlessness was all the more awesome for being veiled in a religious and civilian guise.

After 312 he deliberately played down the starkly militaristic images of the imperial office and its incumbents favoured by the Tetrarchy. Instead a revived classicism manifested itself in the officially sponsored imperial images, to be seen in coin portraits and marble busts. At the same time the special relationship between the secular ruler and his divine mentor was highlighted by those representations which depict him with his eyes turned upwards towards heaven. The styles selected and adapted by his regime set the pattern for the rest of the century as far as imperial portraiture and the visual propaganda of the imperial government were concerned.[32]

In few ways does the massively self-confident and unbridled autocracy of Constantine manifest itself so clearly as in his creation of his new capital of Constantinople, begun in 325 and formally consecrated in 330. The political and, in terms of location, military disadvantages of Rome as the centre of imperial government had long been known to the emperors, and under the Tetrarchy four new imperial residences and centres of administration had been selected for each of the four rulers: Nicomedia, Milan, Thessalonica and Trier. Although some of these cities had come to be particularly associated with and adorned by one or another of these emperors, the idea of a total re-foundation and renaming of a city, in this case the former port of Byzantium, was an innovation of Constantine's.

Although it is often thought that the emperor's experiences in Rome, particularly in his relations with the predominantly pagan Senate, led him to want to create a new and totally Christian capital, with no pagan places of worship, it also needs to be remembered that no emperor had followed the example of the Hellenistic Kings and named his capital with his own name.[33] Nero and Commodus are both accused of having wished to do so in the case of Rome, but even they had not done so in practice, and their examples were hardly savoury ones.[34] However, Constantine's decision, taken within months of the overthrow of Licinius, was implemented and the new 'City of Constantine' became his residence for the rest of his reign and that of his successors in the eastern half of the Empire until 1453.

Constantine's heirs, 324–350

The war between Constantine and Maxentius in 312 and the subsequent conflicts between Licinius and Maximin II in 313 and between Constantine and Licinius in 314 and 323–4 mark a change in the way such conflicts over succession or the aspirations of rival emperors came to be settled in the Roman world. In the third century, although usurpations and revolts were frequent, in no case were the results conditioned by the outcome of direct conflict between the armed forces of the opposing sides. In such episodes as Decius's revolt against Philip I in 249, Aemilian's revolt against Trebonianus Gallus and Volusian in 251, Valerian's opposition to Aemilian in the same year, Probus's challenge to Florian in 276 and possibly Carus's presumed revolt against Probus in 282, although both sides in each conflict had the support of different units of the army and a resolution in war seemed inevitable, in every case the loser fell victim to the swords of his own men before the issue came to be tested in battle.

In each of these cases, and probably others in which emperors fell to assassination and were smoothly replaced by other members of the army high command, as happened to Gallienus in 268, it looks almost as if the Roman army or officer corps as a whole acted as a body, weighed up the merits of rival candidates and then acted to prevent any further unnecessary bloodshed within the ranks of the forces. There was none of the long and bloody fighting between different legionary armies supporting rival candidates for the imperial office that was so marked in the years 69 and 193–7. Some elements of this kind of divisive conflict within the army reappeared in the difficult years following Valerian's capture by the Persians in 260, but this was as much a response to as the cause of a breakdown in central authority within the Empire.

On the other hand, in the fourth century very bloody and protracted fighting between units of the Roman army supporting the claims of rival emperors took place on a number of occasions. The imperial civil wars of the time of Constantine may not in themselves have caused much long-term loss, and the rise of Constantine himself to an unchallenged supremacy in the Roman world is so often assumed to be 'inevitable' or so intrinsically significant that no thought is given to the consequences of the means employed. However, these conflicts were to be the first of a sequence that ultimately proved fatal to the continued existence of the Roman Empire, or at least the western half of it.

One clear message of the political problems of the third century and of Diocletian's attempted solutions of them was that the Empire required the presence of more than one emperor if simultaneous military threats were presented to more than one frontier. The possibility of a successful general being turned by his soldiers into an imperial contender had been demonstrated as a practical reality on numerous occasions between 249 and 282. The alternative 'college of emperors' envisaged by Diocletian had in large measure foundered on the failure to appreciate the rather paradoxical popularity of dynastic succession with the army. Even children or candidates of no proven ability could gain the imperial throne with military backing solely on the basis of family relationship to a venerated predecessor. This occurred in 218 and 222 with the last Severans, in 238 in the case of the infant Gordian III, and in 251 with the child co-emperor Hostilian. Equally notable had been the army support for Constantine and Maxentius in 306, which enabled both of them to take and hold imperial titles.

For Constantine the problem was simpler, in that he had an abundance of sons. The conclusion of the first of his wars with Licinius had been marked by the elevation of two of his sons and his opponent's only legitimate one to the rank of Caesar.[35] All of them were still too young to wield any practical authority, but this marked the abandonment of the tetrarchic system of adoption and made a clear declaration of future dynastic succession. In practice Licinius's line was to prove short-lived, and the Caesar Licinius II

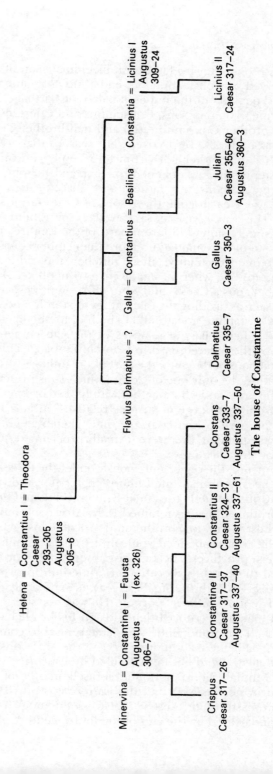

The house of Constantine

Helena = Constantius I = Theodora
             Caesar
             293–305
             Augustus
             305–6

Minervina = Constantine I = Fausta
          Augustus   (ex. 326)
          306–7

Crispus
Caesar 317–26

Constantine II
Caesar 317–37
Augustus 337–40

Constantius II
Caesar 324–37
Augustus 337–61

Constans
Caesar 333–7
Augustus 337–50

Flavius Dalmatius = ?

Dalmatius
Caesar 335–7

Galla = Constantius = Basilina

Gallus
Caesar 350–3

Julian
Caesar 355–60
Augustus 360–3

Constantia = Licinius I
            Augustus
            309–24

Licinius II
Caesar 317–24

was executed soon after his father. An illegitimate son of Licinius I was preserved by Constantine, but ended up as an attendant in the womens' quarters of the imperial palace at Carthage.[36]

Constantine's younger sons, Constantius and Constans, joined their elder brother Constantine (II) and half-brother Crispus as Caesars in 324 and 333 respectively. For reasons that are still far from clear Crispus either fell victim to a family conspiracy, for which his stepmother was blamed, or engaged in some ill-conceived intrigue against his father, and was executed in 326, leaving the way clear for the three sons of Constantine's second marriage. The three Caesars received responsibility for the immediate supervision of different parts of the Empire, although they appear to have remained no more than ciphers during their father's lifetime. Peculiarly, their number was added to by Constantine in 335, when he made his two nephews Dalmatius and Hannibalianus a Caesar and King of Armenia respectively.[37]

This was seen as dividing the cake rather too thinly, and immediately after Constantine's death in 337 both of these, together with most of the other collateral relatives of the late emperor, were massacred by the palace guard in Constantinople.[38] This apparently spontaneous outburst on the part of the military was blamed on Constantius, the only one of Constantine's sons present in the capital at the time, and who together with his two brothers greatly benefited from this purge of surplus relatives. After a hiatus of three months, perhaps caused by the time taken in negotiation of the ensuing settlement, they were formally proclaimed Augusti or emperors by their armies.

In consequence, the regions previously under the three brothers as Caesars became transformed into their territorial divisions as emperors. Constantine II thus held Britain, Gaul, and Spain; his youngest brother Constans retained Italy, Africa and most of the Balkans; whilst the middle brother and probable instigator of the purge of the palace obtained control of Constantinople and all of the eastern provinces. Such a division was pragmatic in that it represented the existing allocation of armies and provinces, but left the eldest son with the smallest, least economically desirable and militarily most difficult portion. He was not slow to object, and began making territorial demands on his brother Constans to the south. The latter's understandable refusal to compromise led to war in 340, but in attempting to cross the Alps Constantine's army was defeated and he himself killed in a surprise attack.[39]

By this windfall Constans found himself master of his late brother's provinces as well, and the Empire was thus effectively divided into eastern and western halves, something that was to become standardised by the end of the fourth century. Although

Constantius's own propaganda suggests that he graciously consented to his younger brother thus acquiring the lion's share of the Empire, something which he must have thought that he had achieved himself in 337, there seems no reason to believe that he was anything other than faced by a *fait accompli*.[40] The generally acknowledged superiority of the western armies, and the fate of the unfortunate Constantine II, would have made further bickering over boundaries rather dangerous. Moreover, Persian threats to the eastern frontier were growing.

In 298, after an initially poor start, the Roman armies commanded by the Caesar Galerius had achieved a major victory over the Persians and had forced the shaky regime of the recently created shah Nerseh (293–302) to make substantial territorial concessions in Mesopotamia as the price of peace. This humiliation Nerseh's grandson Shapur II (309–79) was anxious to avenge, but was initially too weak to undertake.[41] However, by the last year of Constantine I's life a war with Persia was imminent. The first Persian attempt to regain the frontier fortress town of Nisibis was launched in 338, and was repeated in 346 and 350.[42] A general state of equilibrium was maintained between the two great empires, at least as long as a Roman ruler was able to devote his constant attention and military resources to the security of his eastern provinces. When in the 350s Constantius II was forced to look westward the tide in the east turned in favour of the Persians.

The lack of substantial literary historical texts makes it very difficult to assess the politics and personalities of this period. The Tetrarchy can at least be viewed from the admittedly hostile standpoint of the Christian authors, and the years from 353 to 378 are described in considerable detail, often from an eyewitness's perspective, in the surviving books of the history of Ammianus Marcellinus, often described as being the last of the classical historians and a self-appointed continuator of the work of Tacitus. However, the final years of the reign of Constantine and most of those of his sons remain obscure, being described in the briefest of fashions in the diminutive works of some late fourth century historical epitomators.[43]

Despite a general tendency to disparage Constantius II, largely due to an uncritical acceptance of the attitudes and judgements of the historian Ammianus by his modern counterparts, the success of this emperor in maintaining his eastern frontiers against a renascent Persia should not be minimised. In the West his brother was apparently equally active in trying to combat growing pressure being exerted on the Rhine frontier by both the Franks and the Alamans. Constans was the last of the Roman emperors to visit Britain, which he did in 343, in response to some military problems of which we know little. Some reorganisation of the defences of the island took place in consequence, and it has been suggested that the coastal fort erected at Pevensey in Sussex was built on this emperor's orders.[44]

Whatever his other virtues, Constans failed to retain the loyalty of his army, and in 350 he was overthrown in a conspiracy hatched by his finance minister or *Comes Rei Privatae* Marcellinus and a general of possibly mixed British and Frankish origin called Magnentius, commander of units of the field army, who was hailed as emperor by the armies in Gaul. Constans was captured in flight and executed. It has been proposed that the rather enigmatic but substantial mausoleum at Centcelles near Tarragona, whose mosaics seem to date to this period became his final resting place.[45]

The lack of detailed narrative makes it impossible to understand the underlying causes of Constans's fall, which ran counter to the strong sentiment of dynastic loyalty to the house of Constantine which had manifested itself amongst the western armies from the beginning of the century. Equally so, the grounds for the alternative popularity of Magnentius remain unclear, though some prior military success may be assumed. This is particularly regrettable in that the consequences of the coup of 350 were in some respects extraordinarily far reaching, in that they were to have a permanent and detrimental effect upon the military security of the western half of the Empire for the rest of its existence.

3 Frontier wars and civil wars, 350–395

Imperial defence, 350–361

It is particularly regrettable that the sections of the historical work of Ammianus Marcellinus that have survived deal only with the events of 353 onwards. There are a number of tantalising references later on in the extant books of the work to various persons and incidents of the period of the civil war between the eastern and western halves of the Empire in the years 350–3, but the main narrative, which may have been extensive, has been lost. Thus the pattern of events can only be known in outline.[1]

The unexpected overthrow of Constans in 350, and with him of the Constantinian dynasty in the West, seems temporarily to have shaken the political fabric in that half of the Empire. When Magnentius was busy seizing power in Gaul, a relative by marriage of the house of Constantine by the name of Nepotian made a bid to take control of Rome. A few coins struck in his name have survived, and it looks as if, like Maxentius in 306, he was playing on the urban patriotism and the sense of dissatisfaction at being excluded from real political power of the Roman Senate. However, as soon as Magnentius had consolidated his hold in the north he was able to crush the ephemeral regime of Nepotian.[2]

More significant was the proclamation as emperor of another pretender, an elderly general called Vetranio. He had long commanded the imperial field armies in the Balkans, and thus had the backing of a major military following. Although he initially negotiated with both of his rivals, Constantius II in the East and Magnentius in the West, his heart does not seem to have been in it, and he was rapidly persuaded to abdicate in favour of Constantius.[3] Thus his real importance lies in the fact that his brief bid for power prevented Magnentius from gaining control of the western Balkans and the substantial military forces stationed in the region.

Of the ensuing three years of war between Magnentius and Constantius little of the detail is known other than the outcome: which was that after some extremely hard fought and bloody battles in the Balkans and Gaul the western ruler was decisively defeated, and finally committed suicide in August of 353. This made possible the reunification of the Empire under the rule of Constantius II, the sole surviving son of Constantine.[4]

However, the longer term consequences of the war also included the significant weakening of the imperial defences along the Rhine. As the fighting in the civil war grew in intensity, it seems that units of *Limitanei* or frontier troops were transferred to the western field army to assist Magnentius in his increasingly desperate resistance. Certainly, the evidence of Ammianus indicates that in the year 356 virtually all of the Roman frontier fortresses north of Mainz had been abandoned, and doubtless in consequence a substantial, if economically not very productive, piece of imperial territory west of the Rhine and north of the Meuse had passed into the control of various groups of Franks.[5]

More threatening at the time would have seemed the penetration across the Rhine and into the Gallic provinces further south of large numbers of another Germanic people, the Alamans. They even defeated a Roman army under Magnentius's brother, the Caesar Decentius.[6] Although lacking the siegecraft needed to take walled towns, they were able to make themselves masters of increasing stretches of the countryside from the middle Rhine as far westward as Troyes, Autun and Sens. This process of the Alamannic penetration of eastern Gaul began in the period of the civil war of 350–3, and was doubtless made possible by it. It continued unabated until effectively challenged and curtailed in 356 and 357.

The elimination, at least temporarily, of this threat from the Alamans was the work of the Caesar Julian. He and a half-brother called Gallus were the only members of the collateral branches of the house of Constantine to survive the purge of 337, probably thanks to their youth. When Constantius had to turn his attention to the West to conduct the campaigns against Magnentius, he made Gallus a Caesar, and established him with a court at Antioch, to provide an imperial presence and oversee the frontier with Persia. However, in 353, after the conclusion of the civil war, he summoned Gallus to come to him at Milan. The Caesar was arrested on his way across the Balkans, and then executed on the emperor's orders.[7]

Although Gallus, by Ammianus's account, had acted as Caesar in a high-handed and tactless way, thus making himself a number of powerful enemies in the East and in Constantius's entourage, there must remain the suspicion that with the civil war over his services were no longer required. With his elimination the surviving male members of the dynasty of Constantine were reduced to two: Constantius II and Gallus's half-brother Julian. As the emperor had no children the ranks of the imperial family were becoming decidedly thin.

The precedent of Gallus's fate can hardly have been forgotten when a rather similar situation developed in 355. In the East the threat of a Persian offensive was growing again and pressures were mounting on the Danube. At the same time Britain had only recently been recovered and leading adherents of the late Magnentius in the island purged. In Gaul the Alamannic threat had not been countered, and the general appointed to meet it had instead been proclaimed emperor by his troops at Cologne. This new usurper, Silvanus, was of Frankish origin and the son of a distinguished general of the time of Constantine I. He seems to have been driven into revolt by the fear of a court intrigue being directed against him, and this testifies to the fragility of imperial favour and the rapid fluctuations in the fortunes of the leading figures of Constantius's court. Like Vetranio in 350, Silvanus was a very half-hearted emperor, and immediately opened negotiations with Constantius. The latter's envoys, who included the historian Ammianus Marcellinus, then serving as a staff officer, arranged to have Silvanus assassinated, and the revolt collapsed.[8]

Whether because this dangerously weakened the city's garrison or because the murder of Silvanus required avenging by his own people, Cologne was then seized and sacked by the Franks from across the Meuse and left abandoned.[9] By this time the deteriorating conditions in Gaul, together with the existence of equally acute problems elsewhere in the Empire, had determined Constantius II to appoint a new Caesar. This was Julian, whom he had recently sent for from his studies in Athens, and who seems to have had no previous military experience. Proclaimed in Rome in November 355, Julian was dispatched into Gaul, while Constantius prepared to deal with problems on the Danube frontier and ultimately in the East.[10]

Julian's campaigning in Gaul in the years 356–9, described in some detail by Ammianus, is particularly revealing both of the Roman methods of warfare and of the nature of the barbarian threat they were being directed against. Julian set out from Rome for Vienne in the Rhône valley and spent the rest of the winter there. At some point in the spring a force of Alamans attacked the city of Autun, whose walls were apparently in a state of ill-repair. Julian left Vienne to relieve Autun, which he did without any fighting being recorded, and he then proceeded northwards to Troyes. Here, Ammianus records significantly, the inhabitants were almost too frightened to let him in; in other words they could not easily recognise the difference between a Roman army and an Alamannic force. He continued his march to Reims, where the Roman field forces still active in northern Gaul were concentrating. It is reported that Julian's troops were constantly harassed by Alamannic attack throughout this march from the south and that they were particularly vulnerable at road and river crossings. At the same time the Alamans were reported to be raiding in force in the areas around the Roman towns and forts on the middle Rhine, from Mainz as far south as Strasbourg.[11]

However, Julian's priority was the restoration of Cologne, and the whole campaigning season of 356 was devoted to this, and to the making of treaties with the Frankish kings north of the Meuse.[12] It looks as if his intention was to stabilise his rear in preparation for a major assault on the Alamans in 357, and at the same time to regroup and restore the morale of the Roman field forces in Gaul, some of whom had doubtless supported Magnentius and Silvanus or had suffered defeats from the Alamans.

The continuing threat from the latter manifested itself later that year, when after leaving Cologne, Julian dispersed his troops to different winter quarters and he himself took up residence in Sens. There he was besieged for a month by Alamannic forces, who had been informed that he had only part of his army with him. They eventually gave up, appreciating that they lacked the

Julian in Gaul, 355–60

ability to take defended towns.[13] However, the fact that the senior Roman commander in the West could thus be bottled up by a barbarian force for a significant period shows how dependent the Romans were on holding fortified towns, and also how deeply the Alamans had been able to penetrate the Gallic countryside.

The imperial fortunes changed the following year when a no doubt long planned Roman offensive was launched against the Alamans. This involved a two-pronged pincer attack on their principal concentration in the area of the middle Rhine. Julian and the Gallic field armies, which again concentrated at Reims, marched south-east to reach the Rhine in the region of Strasbourg, while a second and possibly larger army of 25 000 men under a general of Germanic origin called Barbatio marched northwards from Italy to the upper Rhine.

The Alamans seem to have been well enough informed about the nature of the threat, and concentrated a large army, said to be 35 000 strong, under two supreme war leaders, Chnodomar and Serapio, and five other kings and ten 'princes'. They also took the classic step of striking before the two Roman armies could combine, in the vicinity of Strasbourg. They intercepted the army commanded by Barbatio and drove it back to the fortress town of Augusta Raurica (near Basel in Switzerland), and having checked that, they turned on the second, and probably smaller, Roman army under Julian. Superior as their strategy had been, their tactics proved deficient, and in the ensuing battle at Strasbourg the Alamannic army was defeated with the loss of some 6000 men and the capture of its commander, Chnodomar.[14]

This single battle really turned the tide as far as the Alamannic penetration of Gaul was concerned. It broke the Alamannic confederacy of tribes, that had largely been built up and held together on the military credibility of Chnodomar, and for the first time enabled the Romans to take the initiative. In the aftermath of the battle Julian marched to Mainz, and despite some reluctance on the part of his troops, crossed the Rhine. Threatened with a Roman invasion of their own territory, the Alamans sought a truce.[15]

With the Alamannic threat countered, Julian was able to seek a more effective settlement with the Franks, who had been raiding Roman territory in the vicinity of recently restored Cologne. He blockaded their strongholds on the Meuse, some of which may well have been abandoned Roman forts, until they were prepared to come to terms.[16] It is notable that Julian made no attempt to penetrate the marshy lands north of the Meuse which the Franks had occupied, and their occupation of this area was not challenged by the Romans. From this small beginning the subsequent Frankish occupation of all of Gaul was to develop.

This, it might be said, was 'the birth of France'. In 357/8, however, what seems to have been achieved was a treaty of federation: Frankish occupation of Roman territory was accepted in return for their participation in the defence of the region. In itself this was a good bargain, and the Franks remained faithful to the terms of the treaty until the eventual collapse of imperial authority in the area in the fifth century.

In 359 Julian was able to restore seven of the principal Roman fortresses on the lower Rhine, to add to those he had previously rebuilt in the region of Strasbourg and across the Rhine near Mainz.[17] For the first time for nearly a decade the Roman frontier along the Rhine had been re-established. Alamannic raiding across the middle part of the river had been halted, and although not expelled, Frankish occupation of the west bank of the lower Rhine had been regularised. Thus much of what had been lost in 350–3 had been regained by the end of 359.

Reactionary rebel: the emperor Julian, 361–363

Julian was now in a position very similar to that of his half-brother Gallus in 353. He had been made Caesar for a particular purpose, and that he had now achieved. His immediate usefulness to Constantius was at an end, and as in 353, he was being subjected to increasing vilification at the emperor's court. Although Ammianus Marcellinus was clearly strongly prejudiced against Constantius II, not least because the historian was in many ways a partisan of Julian, the information he provides does indicate that constant suspicion existed of those who did well, particularly militarily, or who might in any way seem to present a threat to the emperor's security. A recent victim had been the general (*Magister Peditum*) Barbatio, who had masterminded the plot against and execution of the Caesar Gallus and who had commanded the army that was supposed to co-operate with that of Julian on the Rhine in 357. He was executed because of a secret letter written by his wife about an omen that seemed to suggest he might be the next emperor. They were informed on by a maid.[18]

Whether Julian really stood in anything like the same danger as Gallus in 353 is hard to determine. He was now the only other male representative of the line of Constantine, and it is not clear how willing Constantius was to commit dynastic suicide. However, the events of 360 could have given him serious doubts as to his safety. In the East the war with the Persians had started again in 359, and was hardly going well for Rome. The important frontier fortress of Amida fell to Shapur II and the Persians launched a full scale invasion of Roman Mesopotamia in 360.[19] In the circumstances Constantius's need of reinforcements was real, and the now pacified state of the West would have indicated that this was the area in which to find them. On the other hand, if Julian were going to be eliminated he would have to be separated from his troops, who had become devoted to him as the result of his highly successful campaigns. The ruse of summoning the Caesar to consult with the emperor might hardly have been expected to work again, and so the dispersal of Julian's armies would be the necessary first step to his elimination.

Whatever the motivation, which may well have been mixed, the order from Constantius to Julian, sent early in 360, to dispatch a number of his units to the East gave rise to a revolt. Julian, who had deliberately placed himself on the line of march of the soldiers setting out from Gaul, was proclaimed emperor by his armies at Paris, after going through the necessary ritual of refusing the proffered power.[20] This meant yet another civil war, in less than ten years after the last one, as it was made quickly clear that Constantius II had no intention of accepting Julian as an equal colleague. However, its practical as opposed to theoretical outbreak was delayed by Julian's need to secure his position in the West, and quell further trouble with the Alamans, and for Constantius to be able to detach himself from the war with Persia. When he was eventually able to make his way back towards Constantinople, he was taken ill and died unexpectedly near Tarsus on 5 October 361.[21]

Although much maligned by Ammianus and those modern historians who have a Romantic fondness for Julian, Constantius II had proved himself a capable and conscientious emperor, very much in the model of his father, whose ruthlessness and tenacity he had in large measure shared. His tendency to support the theologians of the Arian party also meant that much Christian opinion, following the lead of Bishop Athanasius of Alexandria, whom he twice exiled, was in his own day and thereafter hostile to him. He may have allowed court politics and the power of the secret agents of the state, such as the notorious Spaniard, Paul 'the Chain', to get out of hand, and reach such a pitch that generals might be driven to revolt rather than face disgrace or even death through factional intrigue, but it was the emperor's favour that they sought, not control over him.[22] He did, however, seem to be willing to see his dynasty rendered extinct rather than share power with any of his dwindling band of male relatives.

Julian, on the other hand, in his brief reign (361–3) showed himself to be an emperor of a very different kind. The unforeseen death of his cousin Constantius left him undisputed master of the

Empire, and even those units of the army that were making their way west to fight him promptly accepted his imperial authority. He was thus able to turn what had commenced as a military campaign into a triumphal progress to Constantinople.

Julian's approach to his new office and the policies he tried to develop through it were in many respects reactionary; in the sense that he sought to undo much of the religious, cultural and political transformation to which the Empire had been subjected in the reigns of his predecessors, since the time of Constantine I. This nostalgic and antiquarian tendency in his thinking may well have been a product of his secluded and scholarly upbringing, which had kept him away from public attention, and had certainly not been intended to equip him for future imperial office. Once in Constantinople he purged the court of a number of the most prominent of the supporters of Constantius, and had several of his more notorious officials, such as Paul 'the Chain', put on trial. More controversial, however, was the style of imperial court that Julian tried to create. He dismissed the eunuchs, who had previously been the personal servants of the emperor and his family, and tried to revive the image of the imperial office as no more than the greatest of the civil magistracies. Thus, although he continued to use a throne, he rose from it when senators were presented and came forward to greet them personally, rather than allowing them to perform the by now standard acts of obeisance.[23]

In character with this attempt to return imperial protocol and the political ideas that underlay it to something closer to the standards and practices of the earlier Empire, was Julian's public revelation of his hitherto private paganism. He had been initiated into the Eleusinian Mysteries in the course of his literary studies in Athens, and while maintaining the appearance of being a Christian prince of the House of Constantine he had personally rebelled against the dynastic religion. His accession to power had enabled him to drop the mask, and his reign marked a period of what is normally called pagan reaction.[24] In practice all Julian did was to remove the privileges that had been afforded the bishops and clergy under the previous regime, and at the same time redirect the state funding that had heretofore been channelled into the Church into the resuscitation of classical urban paganism. This meant the directing of state funding into the rebuilding of derelict or neglected temples and the payment of stipends for town priesthoods rather than into the erection and endowment of churches and subsidising of the Christian clergy. Ultimately Julian took the quite logical step of forbidding Christians from holding the state-subsidised professorships of rhetoric and grammar that were to be found in most of the major cities of the Empire. This was based on the argument that it was hardly appropriate for them to teach the literary classics of Antiquity when their writings showed that they were totally at variance with the ideology and religious principles that had prompted and underpinned that literature.[25]

For the Christians all of this constituted persecution, but then for those who have enjoyed privileges their removal is an act of positive disadvantage rather than a merely neutral restoration of equilibrium. Christian hostility to Julian might have become more overtly manifest had he reigned longer, but the brevity of his rule made his reforms a passing fear and for a while thereafter a troubled memory. The hold of Christianity on ever increasing numbers and more and more influential sectors of the population as the fourth century progressed might have been restrained by the change in imperial favour, but was unlikely to have been reversed. The reason for asserting this is less the innate strength of the Christian position, though this should not be under-estimated, than the moribund nature of much of the classical paganism of the Mediterranean world by this time.

The reason that so many temples were derelict and so many town councils had stopped paying the salaries of the priesthoods who should have serviced the temples was more a reflection of the lack of public interest than the result of any overt pressure from the imperial regime of the House of Constantine. Indeed, it is notable that the redoubtable persecutor Maximin II had tried to do what Julian sought and to put new life into flagging pagan religiosity at a time when the Christians in his sections of the Empire were a persecuted and harassed minority. The converse of the rise of Christianity during the third and early fourth centuries was actually the collapse of the public credibility of the long-established religious cults of the towns of the Roman Empire. The upper classes and intellectuals had long preferred either devotion to the increasingly popular mystery cults or, by no means mutually exclusively, the increasingly philosophical reformulation of traditional religious ideas that was associated with Neoplato-nism.[26] However, once it is said that a set of beliefs and associated myths is not actually true, but merely represents a way of express-ing deeper and more complex realities, the popular and intel-lectual levels of religiosity become divorced.

What Julian, who had studied under some of the principal Neoplatonic philosophers of his day in Athens as well as becoming an enthusiast for the performance of the rituals of the old religion, sought to do was to restore the traditional forms of paganism by refurbishing temples, paying for priesthoods, and encouraging the revival of public rites, such as animal sacrifice, and at the same

time to give new intellectual impetus to the religion by dissemi-
nating, not least in his own writings, the philosophical interpretations of it he had learnt from his university masters.[27] Thus he
sought single-handedly to pull together the two increasingly diver-
gent elements in paganism. The result was that he could be
criticised on both sides. The general non-Christian populations
of the towns of the eastern Mediterranean seem to have lost much
of their taste for traditional observances, certainly if it meant
paying for them, and they also found the philosophical under-
pinning that Julian was trying to put back into the religion beyond
their capacity to understand. The intellectual elite found it ludi-
crous that one who had been trained to understand the higher
truths that lay behind the old practices should concern himself
with the popular level of religion.

What is perhaps most notable about Julian's attempts to revive
old ways, in political life, in religion and in local urban patriotism,
is their lack of success, and the degree of indifference, shading
into opposition, with which he was faced. Even his partisans, such
as Ammianus, who valued his military virtues, thought his expulsion of the court eunuchs unjustly harsh.[28] His Republican
approach to the imperial office and its ceremonial was condemned
as being merely undignified, and his sporting of the philosopher's
beard, which he grew after his coming to power, was made into
a matter of ridicule by the local populace during his stay in
Antioch in 363.

This city, to which he transferred his court, both to conduct
operations on the eastern frontier and to get away from the totally
Christian environment of Constantinople, was still home to a
large pagan population, and had long been a major intellectual,
as well as commercial, centre in the Greek East. Even here, though,
Julian could gain little sympathy for his religious and cultural
aspirations. He failed to interest the city council in the restoration
of public buildings and civic religion, and the lampooning of his
personal appearance by the populace led him to write one of his
most powerful works, the *Misopogon* or *Beard-Hater*, in which he
struck back at what he considered to be the Antiochenes' frivolity
and lack of purpose. Had he returned from his Persian expedition
in 363, he would have moved his seat of government from Antioch
to Tarsus.[29]

Significant as were the reactions of the urban councils and the
ordinary populations of the cities of the eastern provinces, perhaps even more telling was the attitude of some of those to whom
Julian appealed directly, and who might have been expected to
share many of his aspirations. These were the pagan philosophers
and teachers, whose cultural and intellectual interests the new

emperor shared, and who in some cases had been his own teachers and fellow students. Although one or two, notably the Neoplatonist philosopher Maximus, came to join his court, many others found excuses to stay away, and wait to see what transpired.[30]

In this they were wise, since Julian's regime proved far more short-lived than might have been expected. The Persians had gained considerable advantage in their war with Constantius II in 359 and 360, and by the capture of some strategic towns had effectively redrawn the frontiers in their favour. In 363 Julian, whose innate if untutored military ability had been demonstrated in his Gallic campaigns, determined on launching an invasion of Persia. For this he gathered from Antioch an unusually large army, 65 000 strong, and marched down the Euphrates towards the Persian capital of Ctesiphon.

How far Julian imagined that he could recreate the military achievements of Alexander the Great, whose image and memory he sometimes drew upon in his propaganda, cannot be judged. Certainly, as recent criticism has indicated, his strategic judgement was faulty in both the conception and the execution of this campaign.[31] The Roman army succeeded in making its way down the Euphrates, but lacked the mobility to force the Persians to give battle or the technical skills to take the city of Ctesiphon. Thus Julian was unable to achieve his military and diplomatic objectives by his mighty display of force, and instead had to undertake the demoralising task of withdrawing his troops from an untenable position, and with an enemy still in full strength and enjoying superior mobility. Unable to take the boats that had brought them down back up the Euphrates, Julian was obliged to burn his flotilla and take his forces overland towards the Tigris in a triangular march back towards Roman territory. The retreat across Mesopotamia was accompanied by frequent attacks from companies of Persian horse archers. In hastening to repel one of these sudden strikes at the army's flanks Julian rushed out from his camp without armour and was mortally wounded in the fray. He died in his tent on 26 June 363, aged only thirty-two.[32]

The argument as to whether or not Julian and his 'pagan revival' really constituted a threat to the growing hold of Christianity in the Roman Empire is essentially academic in the light of the brevity of his reign. Certainly one pagan orator later raised the possibility that he had not been struck down by a Persian arrow but had instead been stabbed in the back in the midst of the fray by a Christian member of his own guard.[33] But it is questionable whether a longer reign would have availed Julian much, in the light of the kinds of responses he did evoke from those who might have been expected to have been his principal supporters.

He was also unmarried and had no designated successor, who might have carried on some of his policies, or at least protected his memory.

Internal conflicts, 363–395

Julian's immediate successor as emperor, Jovian, the commander of the corps of imperial guards called the *Domestici*, was selected by the army in the camp following Julian's death, and was faced with the task of extricating the even more demoralised Roman forces from their intolerable position in the middle of Mesopotamia. This he did by immediately making a treaty with Shapur II, effectively giving back to the Persians all that the Empire had gained in the campaigns of the 290s. After this inauspicious start to his reign he led the army back via Antioch towards Constantinople, only to die of rather mysterious, albeit possibly natural, causes while on the march on 23 February 364.[34]

Once again the army command was in the position of choosing a new emperor, and after some discussion selected a general called Valentinian. He rapidly decided to associate his brother Valens with him in the imperial office and to divide their respective spheres of activity. He installed Valens in Constantinople and himself set off for the West. The need for two emperors, for the first time since 350, was made clear by the renewed threats to the Rhine and Danube frontiers on the part of the Alamans and others, who thus took advantage of the emperors' over-involvement in the East. And in 368 Shapur II abrogated the treaty of 363 on the grounds that he had made it with Jovian and was thus not bound by it to the new imperial regime.[35]

Of the two new emperors, Valentinian I has always enjoyed a good press, from the time of Ammianus Marcellinus onwards, and this is not undeserved. Most of his eleven year reign (364–75) was devoted to constant and effective campaigning on the western frontiers. His brother Valens (364–78), on the other hand, has normally been seen as inadequate to the tasks he was faced with.[36] This is unfair in some respects, and is largely conditioned by the knowledge from hindsight of his eventual unfortunate fate. Also, his continuing support, like that of Constantius II, for the Arian faction in the great theological dispute that divided the Church for much of the century, led to his vilification by the adherents of the ultimately triumphant orthodox party.[37]

Valens proved competent enough to survive the revolt and seizure of Constantinople by the usurper Procopius (365–6), a former general and relative of the emperor Julian, whom he claimed had promised him the imperial succession.[38] In 367 and

369 Valens led armies across the Danube against the Visigoths, who had provided military assistance for Procopius, and in the latter year defeated their principal leader Athanaric, forcing them to sue for peace. Such campaigning outside the frontiers of the Empire was normally considered very risky, and only a small and select number of late Roman emperors ever undertook it. Although Ammianus, who had left the army early in Valens's reign, makes all too brief mention of it, this was no mean military achievement.[39]

As well as the purging of the army of the supporters of Julian, another reason for Ammianus Marcellinus's hostility to Valens may have lain in the personal danger he came into in his native Antioch in 371, when accusations of treason were being bandied about and imperial agents were conducting a series of investigations and trials of prominent citizens suspected of being disaffected towards the regime.[40] Similar inquiries were also carried out in Rome by appointees of Valentinian, and a number of Senators were tried and convicted of using magical practices in 372.[41] Several were executed. In the Roman world secret consultations of oracles and other forms of soothsaying were always looked at askance, as they were often assumed to have political intentions.

With the relative brevity of imperial reigns and the lack of dynastic continuity, the seeking of supernatural information as to how long an emperor would live and what might be the name of his successor was a sign of political dissidence, and the possible first step to conspiracy. As in parts of the third century, friction between the highly cultured civilian aristocracy of the Senate and the middle class provincials who made up the officer class led to hostility and ultimately violent measures on the part of the emperors. This became particularly marked in the reigns of Valentinian I and Valens, who employed officers of similar background to themselves and from their home province of Pannonia in the Balkans in many positions, not least in the city of Rome, which required more tactful exercising than they were willing or able to provide.

The personal need for dynastic continuity, and the way that the sentiments of the army could be manipulated in this matter, become clear in the various succession arrangements of the House of Valentinian. He himself selected his elder son Gratian, then aged only eight, to be titular co-emperor of the West with him in 367. In 375 after a highly successful series of campaigns around the lower Rhine, Valentinian transferred his attention again to the Danube, to counter the depredations of a people called the Quadi. However, late in the year, being it seems of a naturally choleric disposition, he died of a stroke brought on by a fit of rage in an imperial audience at what he considered the insolence of the excuses offered to him by envoys of the Quadi.[42]

This should have left the way open clearly for Gratian, who had been left at Trier, but the generals commanding the army on the Danube found it convenient to proclaim as emperor the four-year-old child Valentinian II, son of Valentinian I by a second wife. The reason given was that the Gallic contingents could not be trusted not to take the opportunity of setting up a new emperor of their own choosing.[43] When it is remembered that each election of an emperor was accompanied by the distribution of a cash donation to the troops, the creation of a new, albeit token, emperor made much political sense in the circumstances.

Whatever the truth of the elevation of Valentinian II, in practice effective authority in the West was exercised by Gratian or his advisers, with the infant Valentinian established together with his mother in a court at Milan. Gratian, who was initially much influenced by his former tutor Ausonius, a professor of rhetoric from Bordeaux and a poet of some skill, proved himself capable of at least serving as the figurehead for successful military operations against renewed Alamannic pressure on the upper Rhine.[44] In 378 he and his armies defeated a major incursion by one of these tribes, called the Lentienses, killing 35 000 of them, and then crossed into their own territory between the headwaters of the Rhine and Danube to force them to submit.[45]

However, Gratian's popularity with his own military waned. As with so many of these imperial dynasties, the lack of competence of the second generation eroded the initial sense of army loyalty to a line founded by a popular commander and emperor. In 383, when a general of Spanish origin called Magnus Maximus was proclaimed emperor by the armies in Britain, the troops in Gaul, after an initial defeat by the rebel, rapidly deserted Gratian, who had lost their support through his affection for his barbarian bodyguards and his occasional adoption of the latter's national dress. He tried to flee to the East, but was captured and executed.[46] Amongst those who joined Maximus was Merobaudes, a leading general under both Valentinian and Gratian, of German origin.[47]

The regime of Valentinian II in Italy, dominated by his mother Justina, was thus left to look to its defences, but with little by way of military backing being available to it. However, the first concern of Magnus Maximus, now master of Britain, Gaul and Spain, was to secure his recognition as a colleague by the emperor in the East, Theodosius I (379–95). This and some astute, if possibly mendacious, diplomacy on the part of Bishop Ambrose of Milan prevented Maximus from crossing the undefended Alps to make himself master of Italy as well.[48] In the outcome Theodosius proved willing to tolerate Maximus's rule in the West as long as Valentinian II and his court were left in control of Italy and Africa. Only when Maximus felt strong enough to face an outright breach with Theodosius, in 387, did he finally cross the Alps and thus make himself master of all the West without any opposition.[49]

This the eastern emperor was not prepared to tolerate, and there commenced yet another civil war between the two halves of the Empire, which if short was, as usual, bloody. Theodosius invaded the West in 388, and in a hard fought battle in the Julian Alps defeated Maximus, who was captured and executed at Aquileia.[50] Valentinian II was sent to set up his court at Vienne in Gaul, and Theodosius spent a few months in Milan before returning East. Although he was thus able to reinstate Valentinian II, who had been an exile in his court since the previous year, as ruler of the West, he made sure the latter remained as much a puppet as he had been throughout his previous reign, by installing one of his own generals, a Frank called Arbogast, as the commander of the western field armies.

Whatever the short-term benefits of this arrangement, it was to provoke yet another civil war within four years. In 392 the unfortunate Valentinian II, who enjoyed perhaps the most consistently depressing imperial career of any wearer of the Purple, became so incensed by his powerlessness in the hands of Arbogast that when he failed in an attempt to dismiss the over-powerful general he committed suicide.[51] This was hardly in Arbogast's interests, although he has been accused of murdering Valentinian, and he had to find an alternative emperor to fill the vacancy. He selected a former teacher and civil servant called Eugenius. This was a strange choice but his own Germanic origins made him unacceptable himself, and he could hardly elevate another military man without losing his own pre-eminence in the army.

Needless to say, Theodosius I was not pleased and began to plan yet another invasion of the West. This materialised in 394, just six years after the last one. In the meantime the regime of Eugenius and Arbogast, which had based itself in Gaul, had sought to appeal to all possible interest groups, not least the still largely pagan senatorial aristocracy in Rome. Measures restricting pagan worship were abolished, and some evidence of the restoration of cult sites has survived from this brief period. Perhaps in consequence, some of the most noted senators, led by Virius Nicomachus Flavianus, who became Praetorian Prefect, the principal civilian administrator in Italy, threw themselves into active support of Eugenius's government.[52]

It was of little avail. In 394 Theodosius invaded Italy, and in another and even bloodier battle in the Alps in September on the river Frigidus, the western army, after some initial success, was totally defeated. Eugenius was captured and killed. Arbogast and Nicomachus Flavianus committed suicide.[53] Theodosius I, however, did not long survive. After the battle he established himself in Milan once more, but died there unexpectedly in January 395, leaving the Empire to his two young sons.[54]

It is not always easy to understand why the emperors of the second half of the fourth century were so unwilling to tolerate the existence of imperial colleagues in other sections of the Empire whom they had not selected themselves. Constantius II could have come to an understanding with Magnentius as the latter wished, despite the loss of his brother: family sentiment was not strong in the House of Constantine. He could also have tolerated Julian, his only living male relative, as a colleague in the West, when he himself was so committed on the Persian frontier. Theodosius, likewise, could have come to terms with sharing the Empire with Magnus Maximus or with Eugenius. However, in each case the issue had to be tested in war, with consequent bloodshed and damage to the armies.

In the latter respect, whether or not there was a shortage of manpower in the late Roman Empire matters less than the fact that these perennial conflicts destroyed the quality of the army, because the losses of highly trained Roman veterans in the ranks of the elite field armies could only be compensated for by the recruitment of either untried civilians or militarily competent but culturally ambivalent barbarians from across the frontier. The principal element in Theodosius I's victory over Eugenius on the Frigidus, apart from some luck with the weather, was his large contingent of Visigothic troops. How they came to be there requires a look at other aspects of this turbulent second half of the fourth century.

4   The battle of Adrianople and the sack of Rome

The coming of the Huns

Much of eastern and central Europe had been the scene of almost continuous movement and jostling of peoples, settling, migrating, fighting, forming and reforming ethnic identities from long before the inception of the Roman Empire. This period of instability could be said to have begun by the middle of the first millennium BC and was to continue until at least the very end of the first millennium AD. In this context Rome's wars against its 'barbarian' neighbours form only a part of a longer and more complex whole. Mutually interactive as they were, the chronologies of the great civilisations of the Mediterranean basin and of this 'Age of Migrations' further to the north are by no means synchronous.

In terms of written evidence, at least until the fifth century AD, the only perspective available to the modern scholar on the events taking place beyond their frontiers comes from the writings of those Roman historians who were prepared to include brief accounts of the doings of the 'barbarians' in their treatments of contemporary events. Even when the frontier wars required some attention to be paid to those against whom these struggles were waged, it is unwise to place too much reliance on the detail of the accounts given of non-Roman societies and their customs. For one thing there was the attitude of mind of the Romans that divided all of the inhabitants of the world into two groups: the citizens of the Empire, who alone enjoyed the benefits of civilisation, and the rest, the 'barbarians' who did not.[1] The Romans were even less ethnographically minded than the Greeks, and were, moreover, far more prone to mere antiquarianism.

There was little to be gained from describing the habits of those who were considered savages, and this included even such, to a modern perspective, advanced societies as that of the Persians. No civilised reader would be expected to take a serious interest in such matters. At the same time, though, a Roman author would be expected to display his erudition and his knowledge of the work of past historians and geographers by referring to the inhabitants of particular regions in his own day in the way his predecessors had. Thus for fourth and fifth century writers the Huns, who dominated the northern bank of the Danube for much of that time, had to be called Scythians as Herodotus had called the inhabitants of that region in his time. In subsequent centuries, long after the collapse of the Hun hegemony in the mid-450s, the members of subsequent cultures who rose to prominence in the same region, such as the Avars, continued to be called Huns by eastern Roman authors.

Even had a classically trained Roman historian developed a real ethnographic interest in the barbarians living beyond the imperial frontiers, the acquisition of detailed and reliable information would not have been easy. Only one of the known historical writers of the fourth and fifth century seems to have had really first-hand experience of a barbarian society, and this is Priscus, who was an imperial ambassador to the Huns in the 440s. Unfortunately only fragments of his work survive as extracts in later texts, above all in the *Biblioteca* or 'Library' of Photios, Patriarch of Constantinople (858–67, 877–86).[2]

Thus it is fair to say that much of the information that would be needed to explain the inner workings of the societies living beyond the imperial frontiers and to explain their actions from their own perspective is entirely lacking. Archaeology is of little help here, in that it can hardly be expected to shed much light on mental processes, and moreover the association of particular material cultures with named societies known from the historical record is by no means as easy as might be assumed. Several populations that are known from the literary record to have been socially and politically distinct shared a common material culture, and thus can not be distinguished archaeologically. A good case in point is that of the Goths, who in the first three centuries AD probably formed just one component of what the archaeologists label the Wielbark culture, which gradually extended itself from the southern shores of the Baltic to the Carpathians. A far from reliable literary account of their history in this period can be found in the *Getica* or 'Gothic History' written in 551 by Jordanes, but there is no way that archaeological research can confirm or deny its claims.[3] There is thus no archaeological evidence *stricto sensu* for the existence of the Goths in this period.

Therefore, it is not surprising, if regrettable, that the causes of the most significant upheaval in the order and distribution of the peoples to the north of Rome in the imperial period remain largely unknown and unknowable. This is the phenomenon often called conveniently if too simply as 'the Coming of the Huns'. In its traditional form this is presented as a manifestation in Antiquity of the modern military-political concept of 'the Domino Effect'. Thus, the sudden eruption out of the steppes of Central Asia of the hitherto unknown nomadic people called the Huns caused the collapse of the previously stable Gothic kingdom of the Greuthungi centred to the north-west of the Black Sea.[4] This, and the consequent westward flight of defeated Greuthungi, led in turn to the fall of the adjacent confederacy of the Theruingi. The latter, too, were driven westwards and southwards, and arrived in increasing numbers as refugees along the north bank of the river Danube, and thus on the frontier of the Roman Empire. The pressure was relieved by the decision of the emperor Valens to admit the refugees into imperial territory in the Balkans, but with ultimately disastrous consequences for the Empire.[5]

Even put as simply as that, the flaws in such an account are obvious. It is rather like the argument from 'the First Mover': if the Huns pushed the Goths and the Goths pushed the Romans, then who pushed the Huns? Normally, this question is not asked, because there is a tendency to assume that nomads are almost instinctively led to prey upon their settled neighbours. In fact nomadic society is far more fragile than that of agriculturalists, and if anything even more conservative.[6] Thus long established patterns of movement, and fixed areas of winter and summer grazing for the flocks are preserved by such societies, unless dramatic changes in external conditions force them to alter their time-honoured procedures. Therefore the unprecedented appearance of the Huns in an area that stretched ultimately from the west of the river Don to the banks of the Danube, is itself in need of explanation.

Likewise, the nature of the impact of the Huns on the Goths also requires closer analysis. By the middle of the fifth century the Huns had organised themselves into a large and formidable confederacy, with many subject peoples under them, and for the first time had a single leader over them.[7] However, such unitary kingship is nowhere recorded of them in the last quarter of the fourth century, when they first came to the attention of the Romans. This kingship was something that grew out of the Huns' success in establishing their hegemony, and was not the cause of it. In the later fourth and early fifth century Roman sources the Huns are described in terms of the activities of several quite separate groups. So it is necessary to avoid thinking of their successes against the Goths in this period as being due to the leadership of some anonymous Hun equivalent of Genghis Khan. If, though, as can be demonstrated, the Huns lacked a unified social and political organisation, but operated in relatively small bands and were not particularly numerous, how were they able to subvert what is normally seen as the powerful kingdom of the Greuthungi?

The latter have long been taken as being if not identical with then immediately ancestral to the later Gothic confederacy known as the Ostrogoths, which came to dominate Italy for most of the first half of the sixth century. This in itself is a dubious assumption. Even more so is the belief that there were no more than two major groupings amongst the Goths at this time: a larger and more powerful Greuthungic kingdom and a somewhat lesser Theruingian one.[8] The Roman sources for the period extending from *c.* 370 to around 408 reveal the presence of more numerous and smaller Gothic confederacies, several of whom remained permanently outside of Roman territory. One of these consisted of a group of Goths, elements of whose language and culture survived in the Crimea until at least the seventeenth century.[9] The Goths as a whole were thus little more unified than the Huns.

Their role in the south-Russian steppe from the mid to late third century until the 370s would seem essentially to have been that of a dominant military aristocracy, ruling over a mixed subject population of very different ethnic and cultural composition. Their own material culture was almost certainly that named by modern archaeologists after two of its most significant sites: Cernjachov and Sîntana de Mures.[10] Allowing that this Cernjachov/Sîntana de Mures culture, which has several striking similarities with the preceding and slightly overlapping Wielbark culture, was that of the Goths, it can also be demonstrated archaeologically that their subject peoples would have included groups of Slavs, nomadic Sarmatians, some of the Hellenised population of the region of Pontus, as well as other Germans. How this Gothic hegemony was achieved is quite unknown, but chronologically it must be related to the period of upheaval and of pressure on the Roman imperial frontiers that took place in the second half of the third century.[11] It was thus of relatively recent creation, and probably by no means stable.

The intrusion of the Goths into this region between the Danube and the Don is particularly remarkable in that it seems to represent the first case of a primarily agrarian, Germanic speaking confederacy, coming from the North-West, establishing dominance in this area. Before the mid-third and from the late fourth century onwards, hegemonial power was normally exercised by a steppe nomad confederacy; previously the Scythians and the Sarmatians, and subsequently the Huns, the Avars, the Bulgars and the Magyars. All of these came from the east. Viewed in a long-term perspective, the establishment of the Goths in this region was an aberration, and one that was likely to be rectified once a new nomad confederacy formed itself east of the Don. Related to this may be the indications of climatic deterioration in northern and eastern Europe in the second half of the fourth century.[12] The implications of the hypothesis outlined here would be that the phenomenon to be investigated is not so much an unexpected and unprovoked invasion of Gothic lands by the nomadic Huns, as the rapid re-nomadisation of the Don–Dniester–Danube after a brief interval of domination by a more sedentary agrarian society. To turn, though, from the causes of the rise of Hun power to its consequences for the Roman Empire is to enter a much better documented area. The events of the years 376–8 form the final section of the historical writing of Ammianus Marcellinus, and the defeat of the emperor Valens at the Battle of Adrianople was to be the climax of the work.[13]

The Goths and the Empire, 376–395

In 376, as the result of the extraordinary changes taking place to the north of the Black Sea, large numbers of Theruingi and some of the Greuthungi arrived as refugees on the north bank of the Danube, and petitioned the emperor Valens to admit them into the Roman Empire and give them land in return for military service. This he agreed to.[14] In itself there was perhaps nothing reprehensible in such a scheme, and it had its equivalent in the treaties Julian seems to have made with the Franks in north-east Gaul. It would have provided military manpower, and reduced the burden of provincial taxation in the areas in which the Gothic detachments were settled. However, it was vitiated by the greed and corruption of the Roman military commanders responsible for controlling and settling the Goths in the eastern Balkans, who are reported to have made them pay for supplies that the emperor had intended them to receive free.[15]

Their growing discontent at this treatment led the Roman commanders to move the Gothic contingents, under leaders called Fritigern and Alavivus, away from the Danube, and south to the city of Marcianople near the Black Sea, which was then the headquarters of the military command in Thrace. There the incident took place which sparked off the incipient Gothic revolt. Some of the Goths tried to force their way into the city to obtain food while the Roman general Lupicinus was entertaining their leaders to a banquet. He panicked and tried to take his guests as hostages, killing their bodyguards. In the confusion Fritigern at least was able to escape and take command of the various groups of Goths around the city. When Lupicinus marched out against them his army was routed and he was forced to flee for refuge back into Marcianople. Other Gothic detachments further south joined the revolt when the Roman authorities tried to hustle them on across the Dardanelles into Asia Minor.[16]

Despite some initial successes in restraining the Goths and pinning them down in the Dobrudja, the region between the lower Danube, the Black Sea and the Balkan Mountains, the Roman generals proved alternately overcautious and overconfident, and so by the late summer of 378 a large-scale operation had to be mounted against them by the emperor Valens in person, with an army of some 40 000 men. The Theruingi, together with a significant detachment of Greuthungi cavalry, concentrated their forces just to the north of Adrianople. In the ensuing battle on 9 August the Roman forces were heavily defeated. Two-thirds of the army was destroyed and the emperor was killed.[17]

In itself the battle of Adrianople struck a severe, if short-lived, blow at Roman military morale and revived memories of the destruction of the emperor Decius by the Goths in 251. However, its significance in itself was probably much less than is sometimes claimed. It was the eastern Roman army that suffered the defeat, and yet that half of the Empire was to survive for more than another thousand years. Its own immediate impact, despite the apparently shattering nature of the defeat, was also limited, in that within four years the Goths had been brought to heel by a new emperor, Theodosius I, and were settled by treaty on imperial territory. They then served as vital components in the armies Theodosius used to invade the western half of the empire in 388 and again in 394.[18]

The reason for the apparent tractability of the Goths in the aftermath of what should have been a major military achievement was their dilemma in respect of food. They entered the Empire as refugees, and although promised supplies and locations for settlement, these did not materialise. Within months of crossing the Danube they were at war with the Empire. There was no question that they could in such circumstances grow their own food. They had to take whatever they could find. As they proved, not least to themselves, that they lacked the necessary military skills and technology to capture towns, and with them the state granaries, they had to obtain what they needed from the countryside. This first of all limited their ability to acquire food to certain seasons. There was no point taking harvests that were not ready for consumption. Also the crops produced in any one district would only be capable of feeding a relatively small number of people. Thus, even more significantly, it meant that they could only keep together as a body for military purposes for very restricted periods of time. The commissariat problems of trying to feed a total body of population estimated to be in the region of 200 000 men, women and children, were insurmountable in these circumstances. Thus to feed themselves they had to break up into smaller groups and scatter widely across the countryside. In military terms this was suicidal, if their enemy, the Roman army, was able to mount effective mobile operations against them, and cut off the roaming bands of Goths one at a time.[19]

Although Fritigern proved an able commander of his people in these very difficult circumstances, and at one stage came close to capturing Theodosius, soon after his appointment as emperor by Gratian, all of the advantages really lay with the Romans.[20] Thus it was that the Theruingi came to terms in 382, and the detachments of the Greuthungi, their allies in the battle of Adrianople, even earlier, in 380.[21] The problems that the Gothic leaders faced in the years 378–82 were to be perennial ones for hostile forces operating within the imperial frontiers during the course of the next century or more, and the military and political triumphs that the Empire secured were almost always the result of skilful exploitation of this weakness. On the other hand, direct confrontation with massed barbarian armies, as at the battle of Adrianople, generally favoured the latter and threw away the Romans' primary advantage. Slow but steady wearing down of their opponents by limiting their freedom of movement and access to the necessary quantities of food paid far better dividends than risking all in the chances of a single military encounter. This had proved a crucial tactic in turning disaster into victory in the Second Punic War in the Republican period, and was often well understood by the more intelligent, if therefore less flamboyant, emperors and generals of the late imperial age.

On the other hand, the establishment by the treaty of 382 of a large Gothic presence in the eastern Balkans added an element to all military and political calculations for three decades to come.[22] Theodosius I found his new source of manpower so valuable that he cashiered one of his generals who went too far in trying to control them, and when in 392 a large band of them under the leadership of Alaric broke away from their establishments on the Danube and started looting civilian areas in Thrace he prevented his field commander Stilicho from completing his initial victory and eliminating them.[23] It was this predominantly Gothic confederacy, drawn from a variety of different Theruingian and Greuthungic groups which formed around Alaric in the early 390s, that became the group normally known as the Visigoths. (They may well have just called themselves the Goths, but to avoid confusion with the other grouping of Goths that developed in the Balkans in the mid to later fifth century they will be known here as the Visigoths.)

Whether or not in conscious imitation of the example of his former imperial master, when after the death of Theodosius I Stilicho became regent in the western half of the Empire, he failed on three further occasions to take advantage of available opportunities to destroy the newly formed Visigothic confederacy. In part this may have been on both Theodosius and Stilicho's part an understanding of the lesson learnt at Adrianople that open battle was too risky and that the enemy was at his most dangerous when he stood to lose all. On the other hand both emperor and general hoped to gain military and political advantages from winning the active co-operation of the Goths in the struggles between the eastern and western halves of the Empire.

Although blame is often apportioned, even to otherwise traditionally 'good' emperors like Theodosius I, for failing to produce a final solution to the barbarian problem, the greater fault may lie in their continuing tendency to conduct or be willing to conduct civil wars within the Empire. Such a conflict could have occurred in 397 and another was imminent in 407/8.[24] Stilicho's career as regent and virtual military dictator of the West falls between these two dates.

Stilicho or Honorius? The conflict of two strategies, 395–410

Stilicho had exercised the chief military command under Theodosius I in the West after the fall of Eugenius, and continued to do so after the emperor's premature death.[25] By his own account he claimed that Theodosius on his death-bed had entrusted him with guardianship of both his sons, the emperors Arcadius (395–408) and Honorius (395–423). This the former, ruling in Constantinople, and backed by a succession of alternative mentors, was unwilling to countenance. Much of Stilicho's interest was thereafter directed either at turning this aspiration on his part into reality or at least, if he were to be confined only to a western sphere of activity, to securing the return to the West of the diocese of Illyricum, which the emperor Gratian had ceded to Theodosius I when he proclaimed him his co-ruler in January 379.[26] In this second, more limited but more practical ambition Stilicho had to take account of the Visigoths, who now constituted the most powerful military force in the Balkans.

Whether or not their leader Alaric belonged to an ancient royal clan, a problem long disputed by historians, matters less than the fact that he was the first man to emerge with authority over all of the Visigoths in the Balkans since Fritigern, and in the circumstances of the time he was able to play off the rivalries of the two halves of the Empire to the advantage of his followers.[27]

The exact nature of the Gothic establishment in the Balkans after 382 is not easy to determine. It is often implied that they became some kind of farmer-soldiers, being given land on which to settle in return for providing detachments for the imperial army. However, recent studies of similar agreements to provide 'hospitality', made between imperial governments and barbarian forces in the fifth century, have shown that, despite the apparent terminology of the treaties, what was at issue was not redistribution of land, but the reallocation of tax revenue.[28] If these arguments are allowed to hold force for this slightly later period, then they must also be true of the 380s and 390s. There was no legal basis by which the imperial government could appropriate its subjects' property at will and redistribute it to barbarian 'guests'. Nor is there any evidence to prove that it did. In fact, had Alaric and his Visigoths possessed a secure landed base in the Balkans they would not have been subject to the pressures which they were under.

For although from one point of view Alaric and his Visigothic confederacy, established as garrisons throughout Thrace and Illyricum, were in an ideal situation to exploit the rivalries of Stilicho and his eastern opponents, they had their own particular difficulties to face. Not having their own land meant that they continued to be dependent upon at least one of the imperial regimes to provide them with food supplies. Furthermore, whatever the roots of Alaric's claim to status amongst his own people in the hoary antiquity of the vanished Gothic past, his actual survival depended not on their sense of history but on satisfying their immediate practical needs. Thus for Alaric his standing amongst his followers would be enhanced by his ability to combine the traditional role of the Germanic war leader with demonstrable status in the new order of the Roman Empire in which the Visigoths now moved. In other words what he wanted were regular subsidies from the imperial government and a title for himself.

Thus, throughout the period from 395 to 410 Alaric's persistent demands were for regular supplies of food, annual payments of cash and the office of Master of the Soldiers. This latter, which would have given him the rank, status, and salary of commander of one of the imperial field armies, was necessary not only for the material benefits it conveyed and the way it would locate him and his followers in the imperial order, but also to make concrete Alaric's hold over his own following. Even if Alaric was a relative of the great Theruingian 'judge' Athanaric, who died in Constantinople in 381, it should be appreciated that there appears to have been no form of permanent central authority amongst the Theruingi prior to their entry into the Empire in 376, and that kingship amongst them was at best the temporary war leadership of a section of the people.[29] The structures of power within those groups of Goths who had established themselves in Roman territory in 376 were thus transformed during the last quarter of the fourth century by the emergence of Alaric as the permanent leader of all or the greater part of them.[30]

While Alaric could hope to play off the rivalries of East and West as far as the Empire was concerned, his own political and above all material requirements were too finely balanced for him to have much room for manoeuvre. The imperial governments could try to control him and the Visigoths by playing on their constant need for supplies. Thus on occasion Alaric tried to put pressure on one or other half of the Empire by direct action, raiding and looting civil settlements and the countryside of the western Balkans. In 402 for the first time he led a raid in force into Italy but was defeated by Stilicho in a battle at Pollentia.[31] Each time Stilicho took steps to contain the Visigoths, but no campaign was decisive. Some damage was inflicted on Alaric's forces, but on each occasion, in 392, 395, 397 and 402, he and his men were allowed to escape from apparent encirclement by imperial forces.

Stilicho's favoured mouthpiece, the Egyptian poet Claudian, did his best in a series of long panegyrics, or formal poems of praise, to make his patron seem merciful, and to enhance the significance of the victories that were won, but the speed with which the Visigothic threat reasserted itself must have underlined the hollowness of his claims.[32] In the first case the responsibility lay with Theodosius I, and in 395 and 397 Stilicho had much to gain from turning Alaric to his side in thus securing western control over Illyricum, but the invasion of Italy in 402 was surely an indication of just how uncontrollable his prospective ally might be. In 407 Stilicho actually came to an agreement with Alaric to obtain for him the regular supplies, subsidies and the title that he so long had sought, in return for a change of allegiance on the part of the Goths.[33] The eastern half of the Empire closed its ports to westerners, Stilicho was declared a public enemy and civil war seemed imminent.

In the East the apparently barbarophile sentiments of the court of Theodosius I were replaced in the year 400 by outright hostility to the domination of the state by Germanic generals and their soldiers. The population of Constantinople rose against the city garrison controlled by a Gothic general called Gainas, who was seeking to make himself into the eastern equivalent of Stilicho. In the aftermath an essentially civilian regime, which included prominent literary and cultural figures, came to power. Although the actual political groupings did not remain stable, a consistent feature of the attitudes of the eastern court thereafter throughout the first half of the fifth century was fixed hostility to military domination of the state, and with it, because the two were almost synonymous, to the Germanic soldiers and their commanders.[34]

A similar attitude seems to have developed in the West in the first decade of the century. Legislation was introduced forbidding the wearing of such barbarian garments as trousers or the sporting of long hair.[35] The Senatorial aristocracy of Rome, who in their own eyes at least were paying the costs of Stilicho's policies, which seemed to be edging them closer to war with the East, nearly refused to provide the funding for the implementation of his agreement with Alaric, around which his ambitions had come to settle. Whether this stand was instigated by the imperial court, which in 402 had moved from Milan to the greater security of Ravenna, or was taken advantage of by the emperor and his entourage, it marked the end for Stilicho. Having lost imperial support he fled to sanctuary in a church, but was persuaded out and then executed on the orders of his son-in-law, the emperor Honorius. His son and a number of senators who owed their offices to him were similarly put to death. Barbarian soldiers under his command were massacred by regular Roman troops, though many escaped from Italy to join up with Alaric.[36]

Whether he was deliberately mischievous and self-seeking in his dealings with Alaric, or merely militarily timid or incompetent cannot be assessed with certainty on the basis of the evidence, but the consequences of Stilicho's policies were highly damaging to the Empire and to the city of Rome. The Senate repudiated the recent, much hated, agreement to pay the Visigothic leader 4000 pounds weight of gold. In consequence of that and of the attack on the Gothic and other Germanic troops in Italy, Alaric led his men in the autumn of 408 into the peninsula to put direct pressure on the imperial government to honour the treaty. He marched on Rome.[37]

The sequence of events in Italy over the next two years, which culminated in the Visigothic sack of Rome in August 410, is by no means easy to untangle or to recount in outline. The principal players in the drama were to be found in a variety of locations. Firstly, and most importantly, there was the imperial court, securely located behind the almost impenetrable marshes that guarded Ravenna. The emperor Honorius and his advisers are often criticised for passivity in these crucial years, but the very immobility of their stance was itself a positive decision of policy, and one that, despite the calumniations of historians both ancient and modern, actually paid off. Freed from the over-mighty dominance of Stilicho, Honorius had no wish to subject himself or the western half of the Empire to the control of another Germanic military dictator. Safe in his capital the emperor was ideally situated to outface the Visigothic leader and to ignore his demands.[38]

Unable to exercise any direct leverage on Honorius or threaten his personal security, Alaric was once again, although militarily unchallenged in Italy, in an increasingly difficult position. He had failed to secure the rewards for himself and his people that the agreement with Stilicho had promised. He had then taken the dramatic step of once again invading Italy to obtain enough of what had been promised to provide for their requirements and to maintain his own credibility. Thus, weak as Honorius's position might seem to be, the pressure was really on Alaric to achieve at least some of the objectives that he had publicly set himself.

To bring this about he did enjoy the coerced co-operation of the third set of actors in this drama, the Senate of Rome. Alaric's first move on entering Italy in the autumn of 408 had been to blockade Rome, and by the end of the year the Senate had agreed to pay him 5000 pounds of gold, 30 000 pounds of silver and a large quantity of silk, skins and spices to lift the siege.[39] They also promised to intercede with the emperor to try to persuade him to make the treaty the Goths wanted. Honorius continued to stand firm, even though some of his advisers supported the Visigoths' demands.

After nearly a year of fruitless negotiation Alaric marched on Rome again and after a further blockade obtained entry, and had the Senate proclaim a new emperor for him in the person of Priscus Attalus, then the Prefect of the City, or principal magistrate and civil administrator of Rome.[40] Although Attalus was delighted to be able to invest Alaric with the office of Master of the Soldiers, the position was essentially farcical so long as the legitimate emperor remained inviolate in Ravenna. Moreover, the usurper in Rome depended entirely upon the protection afforded him by his Gothic master.

Thus, in 410, when Alaric decided that the best solution for the Goths was to have them shipped from southern Italy across to Africa, long regarded as the granary of the western empire, to obtain the regular supplies of food and the security that they sought, Attalus was forced to thwart his master's intentions, as otherwise he would have been left defenceless to face the vengeance of Honorius. Thus even a puppet emperor was no solution to the problems that Alaric faced, and so he forced Attalus to abdicate in the summer of 410 and tried to renew negotiations with Honorius, perhaps feeling the latter would be grateful to him for pulling down the usurper he himself had set up.[41] All was to no avail, and Alaric was even attacked by other Goths, who had reverted to the imperial allegiance; as well they might in view of the consistent failure of Alaric to achieve any of the objectives he had set himself. By now his position was desperate, above all in relation to his own supporters, and he turned to Rome for a third time. After a further siege of the city his men broke through the wall on 24 August, and gave over the city to a three-day sack.[42]

Appalling as doubtless was the suffering endured by the inhabitants during those few days, and demoralising as was the blow to an imperial patriotism that still associated itself with the city that had given the Empire its name, the infamous Sack of Rome by the Visigoths has to be seen as the last desperate measure of a leader whose every policy had failed and whose every ambition had been thwarted. In part it may have been an insensate act of revenge, though this was hard on the inhabitants of Rome who had done their best as far as honour and their material resources were concerned to comply with Alaric's demands, but it is probably best seen as a move to stave off the insistent demands of his followers and to provide them with at least short-term satisfaction.

After leaving devastated Rome with their loot and their hostages the Visigoths turned south, probably again to try for Africa. However, before the year was out and before they came to the coast Alaric was dead. He was succeeded as leader of the Visigothic confederation by his wife's brother Ataulf.[43] Under his direction they finally gave up all hopes of establishing a position for themselves in Italy or of using it as a base for a crossing into the greater security of Africa. Early in 412 Ataulf led the Visigoths over the Alps and out of Italy. Honorius's policy had worked, and Italy was not to be subjected to domination by a Germanic people until after the end of imperial rule in the West.

The lack of evidence relating to both imperial and Visigothic actions and intentions in Italy in the year 411 is regrettable, as it would be interesting to know if the emperor wished or expected Ataulf and his followers to become participants in the complicated affairs of Gaul rather than see them return east into the Balkans. In Gaul the years from 406 to 411 had seen considerable upheaval. In 406 the army in Britain, which had thrown up Magnus Maximus in 383, rebelled again and created and murdered two emperors, Marcus and Gratian, in quick succession.[44] A third choice, in the person of a certain Constantine, selected because of the fortunate associations of his name, lasted longer. This he may have achieved by giving his troops something else to think about by leading them across the Channel to make him master of Gaul.

Here he was needed. On the last day of 406 a group of three peoples, the Vandals, the Sueves and the Alans, crossed the Rhine while it was frozen and were thus able to penetrate the Roman defences.[45] Here the Franks were able, at least initially, to show the worth of the agreements they had made with Julian. They took on one branch of the Vandal forces and defeated them, but were then themselves pushed aside by the Alans.[46] Over the course of the next three years this group of confederated peoples made their way across Gaul and in September 409 crossed the Pyrenees into Spain.[47] In their wake they clearly left devastation, in that they had to loot and forage for their own maintenance.

The effects of their penetration of the frontiers also created a power vacuum in Gaul, which was swiftly filled by the rebel emperor Constantine III from Britain. Landing at Boulogne, his forces restored some semblance of order in the rear of the barbarian's passage, and he made himself master of Gaul and also of Spain. From his base at Arles, Constantine III was poised to intervene in events in Italy, and at least one of Honorius's ministers in Ravenna was in treasonable correspondence with him. He tried to secure the legitimate emperor's recognition of him as an imperial colleague, and descended with an army into northern Italy in 410.[48]

However, Constantine's power base was weak and his regime correspondingly ephemeral. One of his generals, a Briton called Gerontius, led a revolt against him in Spain, defeated and executed his son and recently appointed co-emperor Constans, and bottled up the would-be master of the West in Arles. Only the arrival of imperial forces from Italy commanded by a new Master of the Soldiers called Constantius saved Constantine III from death at the hands of his own rebel general. Instead this gave Honorius the pleasure of ordering his execution when Arles capitulated to the imperial army.[49]

Thus in less than a year after the Sack of Rome, Honorius's forces sent from Italy were restoring imperial control in at least the southern parts of Gaul. Eastern and northern sections remained still to be resuscitated, and Britain, which had also rebelled against the luckless Constantine III in 410, had to be left in practice to go its own way, though it would be wrong to assume that Honorius regarded it as subsequently detached from the Empire.[50] Whatever the psychological reverberations of the Visigothic looting of the Eternal City the imperial regime in Italy displayed remarkable resilience and activity once the threat of a barbarian domination of the state had been lifted. This would seem to have been the positive outcome of Honorius's policy of passivity in the face of Alaric's threats.

5 A divided city: the Christian Church, 300–460

Christianity and the Empire

The Sack of Rome in 410 may have caused a sense of profound shock in many of the intellectual circles of the Latin-speaking half of the Empire, but it seems to have aroused little recorded comment in the predominantly Greek East. Equally uncertain was the attitude towards the disaster and its implications of the leaders of Christian thought. From Bethlehem in a letter written in 412, the priest and ascetic teacher Jerome (331–419), a westerner and formerly an *habitué* of some of the most exalted Christian aristocratic circles in Rome, showed how the twin literary heritage of Classical and Christian learning could be combined in lamenting this disaster, by quoting from the Psalms: 'O, God, the heathen have come into thine inheritance; thy holy temple have they defiled; they have made Jerusalem [that is Rome] an orchard' and then following it by a passage from Book Two of the Aeneid: 'The ancient city that for many a hundred years ruled the world comes down in ruins.'[1]

Even so, his feelings for the city of Rome, manifested not least in other sections of this very same letter, could be ambiguous. In this work, which is principally an account of the spiritual career of the lady Marcella, in whose house in the city his particular group of disciples had frequently met in the early 380s, he also called Rome a 'slander-loving place', in which 'it was the triumph of vice to disparage virtue and to defile all that is pure and clean'.[2] Jerome had had long and close associations with Rome and with many of the leading members of its society, and was someone for whom classical Latin literature, much of which was centred on the city, never lost its appeal. Other Christians had less personal involvement with either the city or the literary culture that had grown up around it. For them, as perhaps for Constantine when he left it for Constantinople, the pagan traditions of Rome's past and of so many of the aristocratic families who still dominated it were unpalatable. In 392–4 the 'pagan revival' under the emperor Eugenius had largely been orchestrated by the great Roman families of the Nichomachi and the Symmachi, and even as recently as 408, when the city was threatened by Alaric, it is possible that pagan sacrifices had been held.[3]

Yet despite the intense conservatism which really underlay the continuing devotion to paganism of the aristocracy and which made Rome as a whole less amenable to Christianity than any other of the great cities of the Empire, for the Christian intellectuals the sack of 410 was an acute embarrassment. Whatever their personal feelings, Rome was, as Jerome called it, 'the city that had taken the world', and which itself had never fallen to invasion in the course of a history that traditionally spanned over 1100 years. Now, within years of the final triumph of the new Christian dispensation in the Empire of Theodosius I, it had been captured and sacked. The pagan intelligentsia, subjected to increasingly intolerant restrictions under the Christian emperors of the late fourth century, were now able to make some riposte by claiming that this disaster was due to the desertion of the old gods, who had for so long preserved and made prosperous the Roman state.[4]

Whatever literary form these pagan arguments took cannot now be shown, as none have survived, and they may have been fewer in number and less strident than the Christian replies might seem to suggest. To some extent it is permissible to wonder if the Christian apologists who sprang into action in the aftermath of the sack were really writing to ease the minds of their own co-religionists, to whom these very obvious questions would have been far more unsettling than to the chivvied and repressed minority of pagan intellectuals.

The first substantial Christian work of justification was written by a Spanish priest called Orosius, and appeared in 418.[5] He entitled it *Seven Books of History against the Pagans*, and it took the form of a synoptic, but by no means brief, survey of the history of Rome and its empire. The principal argument of Orosius's work was that, however unfortunate contemporary events in the period of Christian rule over the Empire might be, far worse things had happened in the past in the time of pagan domination. In particular he stressed how the Goths under Alaric, who had been converted to Christianity, admittedly of the unorthodox Arian form, in the late fourth century, were especially merciful to the inhabitants of Rome in 410 because of the tenets of their new religion. The principal purpose of his *History* was to highlight the bloodiness and misery of past events, while playing down such elements in recent ones. This was neither intellectually very satisfying nor frankly very credible history, and even fellow Christians, including Augustine, Bishop of Hippo (354–430), to whom the work was dedicated, were not convinced by its tendentious arguments.[6] However, Orosius's *Seven Books* remained very popular throughout the Middle Ages and survived in many manuscripts, largely thanks to the substantial quantity of historical information that it contained.[7]

It was to be Augustine himself who produced the most substantial, in terms both of bulk and of the quality and sophistication of argument, analysis of the meaning of these events and of how they should lead contemporary Christians to view their association with the secular state. This took the form of his magisterial *On the City of God*, written in twenty-two books over the course of twelve (413–25) years. In it he undermined the necessary identification of the Roman imperial state with the Christian Church and the need to regard the former as the eternal or divinely chosen vehicle for bringing about the aims, by achievement of the universal acceptance of its tenets, of the latter.[8] Such a view was in no sense a condemnation of the Roman state, and only implicitly a recognition of its current weakened political and military condition. It was basically an explanation of the irrelevance of secular human institutions in the achievement of individual salvation, and thus incidentally a vital stage on the way towards the fuller elaboration of his ideas on divine grace and predestination that absorbed much of Augustine's last years.[9]

Although not presented in an explicitly controversial context, these arguments also challenged a dominant strand of Christian political thinking in the eastern half of the Empire. Ever since Constantine had established himself in the East, where both traditions of absolute monarchy and of state repression of Christianity were far stronger than in the West, a series of Christian thinkers had sought to intensify and make indissoluble the links between Church and state. The identification had been first articulated by Constantine's adviser and biographer Bishop Eusebius of Caesarea, and the emperor's own personal involvement in internal Church affairs, notably in presiding over the Council of Nicaea and in using the powers of the state to try and solve theological disputes, established precedents that his successors did not relinquish.

In the East the emperor's role in the Church was marked by his powers of appointing bishops, of applying secular punishments to them if they displeased him, of giving force to theological statements by his approval of them, and of his enjoying such priestly privileges as having a seat in the sanctuary in church, a location otherwise exclusive to the clergy.[10] In general all of this took place within an intellectual context in which the eternity of the Empire and its role as God's chosen vehicle for the achievement of human salvation was not called into question. Despite various vicissitudes, such attitudes and such imperial authority survived in the East with little modification up until the final extinction of the Empire in 1453.

This was perhaps all the more surprising in that the emperors had shown themselves capable of backing the wrong theological horse as early as the mid-fourth century, and on a number of occasions the strength of popular religious opinion outweighed the personal theological preferences of individual rulers. The Arian controversy, which broke out in the Church of Alexandria during the reign of Constantine, indicated something of the problems of imperial involvement in doctrinal arguments. The Alexandrian priest Arius's trinitarian formulation in which the Son and the Holy Spirit are both neither co-eternal with nor equal to the Father was strongly resisted by Alexander, the bishop of the city (313–26), and by his successor Athanasius (326–73).

The condemnation of Arius by a local Egyptian council in 321 proved insufficient and the controversy gave the emperor his first opportunity to hold a council of all of the Church in the Empire. Thus he called the first Ecumenical council, that held at Nicaea in 325, in which in theory if not in practice the whole Christian body was represented. The bishops under the presidency of the emperor condemned Arius's teaching, and Constantine exiled him to Illyria. The Council also promulgated the first formal statement of orthodox faith, which from its origin became known as the Nicene Creed. However, Constantine was subsequently persuaded, not least by his sister and by various ecclesiastical advisers, that Arius had been misrepresented and so he ordered his restoration in 331.[11]

Although in its extreme form this theology never won many adherents, subsequent provincial councils increasingly modified orthodox teaching so as to effect some kind of compromise with Arianism, which was in many ways more immediately appealing and simpler to understand than the rarified abstractness of the orthodox doctrines on the Trinity. By the end of his reign Constantine had himself come to accept a modified Arian position, one that his son Constantius II, at the cost of his later reputation, was therefore anxious to maintain. Those bishops, such as Athanasius of Alexandria, who refused any compromise, fell under imperial displeasure and could be punished accordingly. They could in the process also become pawns in imperial power politics.

Athanasius was exiled to Trier in Gaul by Constantine I in 336, sent back to Alexandria by Constantine II in 338, and was exiled again by Constantius II in 340. Constans forced his brother to accept Athanasius back again in 346, but Constantius II was able to send him off once more in 356, after he had made himself ruler of the whole Empire. The bishop remained in exile until after the death of Constantius in 361, and was then allowed back to Alexandria by the pagan emperor Julian, who was happy to intensify the divisions within the Christian ranks. Athanasius was very nearly exiled again under Valens, the last of the emperors sympathetic to a form of Arianism, and in whose reign Christianity was preached to the Goths.[12] The accession of the westerner Theodosius I as ruler of the East ended the line of emperors whose theological views were Arian-leaning, and under his direction the First Council of Constantinople in 381 finally condemned all forms of Arianism. As with Constantine in 325, so in 381 it was imperial preference that dominated ecclesiastical decision making.

During all this period, although a number of individual bishops, such as Potamius of Lisbon, adopted quasi-Arian theological views, the Church in the West as a whole remained staunchly orthodox.[13] Western rulers such as Constantine II, Constans and Valentinian I may not have shared their eastern colleagues' beliefs, or perhaps more pertinently proved themselves to be less interested in abstract theological niceties. Indeed the attitudes of the two halves of the Empire, the Latin-speaking West and the Greek-speaking East, were fundamentally different. In part because Christianity was less well established in the West at the time of the conversion of Constantine and in part because most of the earliest Christian writing had been in Greek and so its learned tradition was accessible only to readers of Greek, the western Church was less interested in and also less able to understand the divisive theological controversies that aroused so much passion in the East.

Only towards the end of the fourth century did a series of great Latin writers appear, who catered for the needs of the growing western Church by translating works originally written in Greek or who adapted techniques and ways of thought that had been developed in the East.[14] Amongst the most prominent of these was the priest Jerome, who undertook a new and much improved Latin translation of the Bible and the writing of a series of large-scale commentaries on many of its books.[15] This exegetical work was greatly influenced by that of the third century Alexandrian writer Origen (d. 254), a number of whose own works were translated into Latin by Jerome's erstwhile friend Rufinus of Aquileia. Jerome and Rufinus fell out when, because of certain speculations in some of his writings, Origen was posthumously condemned by various church councils around the year 400.[16]

Amongst the principal western beneficiaries and transmitters of eastern theology was Ambrose, Bishop of Milan (374–97), who in his life more than in his writings articulated an alternative view of Church–state relations in the Empire.[17] The son of Constantine II's Praetorian Prefect, Ambrose was himself on the middle rungs of the ladder of an official career when he was elected bishop by the populace and clergy of Milan. In that by this stage the bishop had become not just the spiritual head of a town's Christian community, but also its economic, social and political leader, episcopal elections were peculiarly significant. If a town could obtain the services of a wealthy or politically influential man as its bishop then his value to the community could be considerable. Particularly useful candidates could almost be forced into taking the office, and their previous ecclesiastical credentials could be slight or even non-existent.[18] Ambrose was not even a member of the clergy, but was actually the civil governor of the province when chosen by the people of Milan.

As the principal city of northern Italy Milan was undoubtedly a place worth being the bishop of, but as the platform for a spectacular career in politics its role was dramatically transformed by the death of Valentinian I in 375. The creation of a separate imperial sphere of authority for the infant Valentinian II made Milan the seat of an imperial court, for the first time since 305. Ambrose was able to influence and increasingly to dominate the court, not just by strength of personality but by a series of carefully stage-managed confrontations.

Although this was relatively rare in the West, Valentinian II's mother Justina was, for personal or political reasons, an Arian sympathiser, and her attempts to require Ambrose to surrender one of the major basilicas in the city to serve as a church for the German Arian soldiers of the imperial guard gave him the chance to mobilise public support by barricading himself and other clergy inside the building. Only by violence and ultimately a massacre could the empress have secured her ends, and at this prospect she lost her nerve.[19] The discovery, apparently as the result of a divine revelation, of the relics of Saints Gervasius and Protasius then made Ambrose's position within the city impregnable.[20] For all its secular importance Milan had no specifically local patron saints, whose special celestial protection could be invoked and whose relics would serve as the focus for Milanese patriotic devotion. This position was rectified by Ambrose's very public search for and uncovering of the bodies of these two previously unheard of martyrs, whose histories the bishop also conveniently revealed.

So strong did Ambrose's influence on the court become that he was able to intervene on the wider stage in matters concerning the Church. Thus when in 384 Quintus Aurelius Symmachus, the Prefect of the City of Rome, petitioned the emperor Valentinian II to allow the restoration to the Senate House of the Statue of Victory, which the emperor Gratian had had removed as a pagan abomination, Ambrose was able to veto the appeal without more ado. This he could do by the simple expedient of threatening the thirteen-year-old emperor with excommunication: 'you will come to the church – and your bishop will not be there'.[21] This threat he was actually able to put into practice in a confrontation with Theodosius I, who established his court in Milan during his stays in the West in 388–91 and 394–5.

In 388 the Christian community in Callinicum, urged on by its bishop, destroyed both the meeting house of a deviant Christian group and the principal local synagogue. The emperor ordered the latter to be rebuilt at the bishop's expense and also the perpetrators of the outrage, many of whom were monks, to be punished. Ambrose intervened to secure the rescinding of these instructions. When a letter he sent to Theodosius failed to achieve his ends, he staged a confrontation with the emperor in church. Having preached on the subject, he came down from the pulpit to face Theodosius directly, and he made it clear that he would not go to the altar to perform the rites of communion if the emperor did not promise to withdraw his orders.[22]

A similar episode was taken a stage further in 390. When a riot broke out in Thessalonica over the detention of a popular charioteer arrested as a male prostitute, the garrison commander and other soldiers were killed. Theodosius I ordered an attack on the racing fans in the city as a reprisal. This got out of hand and a massacre ensued. Ambrose, when he heard of it, wrote to the emperor making it clear that he would not celebrate communion in Theodosius's presence until such time as the latter had purged himself of the guilt by a period of penance. This apparently took the form of the ruler attending church divested of his imperial robes and abstaining from communion until Christmas. He seems in fact thus to have followed some or all of the normal requirements of those entering a canonical state of penance.[23]

Whatever the rights and wrongs of the occasions for these confrontations, they expressed a very different view of the relations between the emperor and the Church to that which, for example, Theodosius I would have encountered in the East. Implicitly Ambrose was requiring the emperor to accept the role of being yet another individual who, whatever his secular status, was subject to ecclesiastical discipline and who in matters pertaining to the Church and to Christian moral conduct had to accept the superior authority of his bishop. In practice Ambrose could only force the emperor into these acts and concessions by public humiliations. These depended on the physical presence of the ruler in Milan and the fact that emperor and bishop shared the same system of values. The weakness of Ambrose's position was revealed by his inability to oppose the pagan revival conducted by the emperor Eugenius in 392–4.[24] Because Eugenius was not present in Milan, never entered Ambrose's church and probably would not have cared whether the latter celebrated communion or not, the bishop was powerless to oppose him. Influential as Ambrose's example might be, it would take the growth of an institution to turn an individual's view of Church-state relations into a reality.

The primacy of Peter

Constantine's gifts in the aftermath of his conversion had transformed the economic and social standing of the bishops of Rome. Moreover the special status of the city gave the leader of its Christian community an immediate importance beyond the confines of Rome. However, Africa outstripped any other region of western Christendom in terms of the number of believers and of the attainments of its principal churchmen. The intellectual leaders of the Latin Church of the third century had been the Africans Tertullian (d. 240) and Bishop Cyprian of Carthage (executed 258), and Rome had produced no figures of comparable significance.[25] Even in the late fourth century the holders of the see of Rome were outshone not only in learning but also in political influence and sheer stage-holding magnetism by Ambrose of Milan. It was Ambrose, not Pope Damasus (366–84), who ensured that the Altar of Victory was not returned to the Senate House. In this period the leaders of lay society in Rome, the members of the great senatorial families, were still predominantly pagan, and the bishops seem to have gone out of their way to avoid any conflict with them or with those aspects of the life of the city with which they were intimately involved.[26] Thus, not until the late fifth century would the popes challenge the continuance in Rome of such quasi-pagan festivals as the Lupercalia.

On the other hand, the clergy of Rome were busy forging an institution that would claim and in large measure attain an unrivalled power over the Church in the West, and which would not be dependent on the strengths and weaknesses of the individuals who became the head of it. In this respect the Roman Church was probably fortunate that the city was very rarely an imperial residence, in that they were not tempted into relying on the vagaries of personal influence over the secular rulers, but could instead try to evolve a system that was capable of standing independent of external political ties.

The first requirement was a self-justifying ideology. The Roman Church was unusually fortunate in that it alone of the major Christian centres of the West could claim to have been founded by an Apostle, St Peter, who came to be regarded as the first bishop of the city. According to Christian tradition Peter was also executed and buried in Rome, as was St Paul. From the late second century onwards the supposed site of Peter's burial was being venerated, and on this and the comparable grave of Paul two great basilicas were erected by Constantine I and by Pope Damasus respectively. No other western Church, and few of the eastern ones, had founding figures of such significance, and this gave Rome a particular prestige. Nor was this all: Peter was the acknowledged leader of the Apostles, and moreover in the Gospel of Matthew Christ addresses him, when changing his name from Simon to Peter, with the words 'You are Peter and on this rock I will build my Church' (Matthew 16.18).

In itself this phrase is not self-explanatory, and it is not easy to see what it meant to the author of this particular Gospel. Certainly from the perspective of his own day and cultural outlook he could never have entertained the notion that it instituted the headship of a hierarchical clerical elite. This statement, however, from the later fourth century was made the theoretical basis for claims to special authority on the part of the bishops of Rome. What they insisted belonged to them were the rights of final jurisdiction in all ecclesiastical disputes and the right to be informed of and to confirm all episcopal appointments in the western provinces of the Empire.[27]

While the other independent churches might be prepared to accord that of Rome a primacy of prestige on the basis of its apostolic foundation, they had no immediate inclination to accept these more practical demands. However, the fact that these claims were consistently reiterated by successive bishops had the paradoxical effect of making them increasingly acceptable. Furthermore, they did actually offer things that more and more of their fellow bishops in the West came to want. Thus in a period in which the political and economic importance of bishops in the urban communities was rapidly increasing, disputed elections and subsequent attempts to eject incumbent bishops became ever more common. In the local context the stakes involved in an episcopal election could be very high.

Therefore the role of a third party demanding to be able to confirm all elections and also to act as final court of appeal in all local disputes, to whom disappointed candidates or deposed occupants of sees could address their claim, became increasingly important. Thus it became increasingly customary for bishops to seek papal confirmation of their election as a security against subsequent attempts to replace them. In the same way, Rome's claims offered an opportunity for one party in a doctrinal dispute to secure a more than localised victory. For example, the African Church was particularly firm in resisting Roman pretensions as far as interference in local affairs was concerned. However, when in 417/18 Augustine and the African bishops wanted to secure the condemnation in the West of the teachings of Pelagius on divine grace and free will, they assiduously courted the bishops of Rome and thus implicitly came thereby to accept the papal claim to right of final jurisdiction in disputes and in matters of doctrine.[28]

What is particularly striking is the consistency and tenacity of the Roman bishops' claims. In large part this was due to their being not just the ideas and statements of the individual holders of the see, but being policies developed and perpetuated by a large and sophisticated ecclesiastical corporation. The late fourth century also saw the growth of the institutional complexity of the Roman Church. In particular this took the form of the establishment of a series of interconnected regional *tituli*, centred on sectional churches within the city, each with its own clergy, the senior members of which formed an advisory and administrative body or *curia* around the bishop.[29] Rome also had the advantage, unlike its principal eastern rivals of Antioch and Alexandria, of not being internally divided and wracked by theological disputes, as in the various stages of the Arian controversy. The East was also liable to disputes between its great churches, which included the *parvenu* but politically important Constantinople and the prestigious but less significant see of Jerusalem.

The early fifth century saw the power of the Church in the city of Rome greatly enhanced. The fall of Eugenius's regime in 394, continuing imperial encouragement, and insidious family pressures all combined to hasten the extinction of paganism amongst the senatorial houses. The sack of the city in 410 also led to the dispersal of some of the families and in general their wealth was adversely affected by many of the events of the fifth century.[30] By the middle of it the secular aristocracy of Rome had been financially outstripped by the Church, which came increasingly to take over the functions formerly filled by the senators as the principal patrons of the city. The Roman Church took over the charitable work and much of the political patronage of the senatorial families, many of the members of whom were either entering its ranks or committing themselves to ascetic lifestyles that placed them under ecclesiastical discipline. As well as material benefits, the Church was also providing new spiritual patronage for the city as a whole and for each of its component regions.

The growth of the cult of the martyrs who had been executed during the persecutions of Decius and Diocletian's reigns provided new focuses for local loyalty. Each urban region had come to acquire its own special saint or saints, whose relics, which could be either whole bodies or various limbs, were translated into specially built churches from the cemeteries outside the city.[31] Thus each section of Rome had its special saints and particular churches, while overall loomed the great patronal figures of Peter and Paul. At the same time an increasingly elaborate liturgy was being evolved to honour all of these saints, and in the form of long and colourful processions from church to church, culminating in the pontifical basilicas of St Peter's or St John Lateran, tying them all together into one interrelated whole, and to emphasise the special role of the bishop. At the same time these processions and the liturgy of the great feast days provided alternatives to the public festivities of the pagan holidays that the Church was trying to suppress. A number of these, which their supporters saw as being non-Christian but not actively pagan, a distinction that did not appeal to the clerical mind, survived into the sixth century.[32]

The ideological framework on which claims for the special status and authority of the Roman Church were based received a further and more complex elaboration during the pontificate of Leo I (440–61). Like his predecessors he took as his starting point the so-called Petrine text of the Gospel of Matthew, but he interpreted it in the light of concepts borrowed from Roman law, according to which an heir inherited all of the rights and also all of the obligations of a testator. In other words, in a legal sense he became that person. Thus Leo argued that Peter had been the bishop of Rome and had passed on his authority to his successor Clement. (This idea actually derived from the forged text known as the Pseudo-Clementine Epistle.) Clement in turn passed on what he had received from Peter to his own successor and so on through a supposedly unbroken episcopal succession. Therefore the subsequent bishops of Rome, according to Leo, received what Christ had given to Peter, in other words the powers of 'binding and loosing'. But, more than that, by application of the legal principles mentioned above, they *were* Peter; an identification that Leo made quite explicit in a number of his surviving sermons and letters.[33]

What did this doctrine mean in practice? Leo claimed that as Peter's heir, indeed as Peter himself, he alone had the right and the duty of making final and binding decisions on matters of doctrine. This was particularly significant at this time in that the East was once again wracked by violent theological divisions, and it was to be as the self-proclaimed unique source of authority in matters doctrinal that Leo involved himself in these complex and acrimonious disputes, the theology of which he did not always understand in the same way as the eastern bishops.

With the questions of the relationships between the Three Persons of the Trinity more or less settled with the termination of the conflicts over Arianism at the Council of Constantinople in 381, it was not long before a fresh controversy was generated over the attempt to condemn the total corpus of the writings of Origen (d. 254). This was but one aspect of a wider tendency in the Church at this time to make the definitions of orthodox belief more rigid and to exclude many previously acceptable theological ideas and speculations, and also those who had believed in them. This assault on Origen's teaching caused much conflict in the East, especially in Egypt around the turn of the fourth century. Its immediate causes and consequences, however, may have lain more in the field of ecclesiastical politics than of abstract theological argument. In particular this affair enabled Bishop Theophilus of Alexandria (385–412) to pose as the champion of orthodoxy and to establish himself as an apparently sound ally of the see of Rome in their common hatred of the bishops of Constantinople.[34] It also enabled the Alexandrian Church to score a moral victory over its other rival, the see of Antioch, whose intellectual tradition owed much to Origen's methods of biblical exegesis.[35]

The rise of the see of Constantinople to prominence as the result of the city's role as imperial capital aroused the jealousy and hostility of the leaders of the other great eastern patriarchal sees, especially Alexandria. Any political or ideological weakness on the part of the incumbent of the see of Constantinople was eagerly seized on by his peers. Thus the great orator and moralist St John Chrysostom, Bishop of Constantinople (398–404), who as a former cleric of the rival see of Antioch was thus doubly hated by the Alexandrian Church, was successfully undermined by his ecclesiastical opponents when he lost the favour of the imperial family.[36] Rome was not entirely easy about this affair, not least as it involved the exile of a bishop by the secular power;

something that was rare in the West and also quite at variance with Rome's claim to be the final court of appeal in matters ecclesiastical.

However, the next victim of Alexandrian aggression was much more acceptable, and his elimination strengthened rather than strained the Rome–Alexandria axis. This was the deposition of Patriarch Nestorius of Constantinople (428–31). Like John Chrysostom, he was an Antiochene, and he underlined the link by instituting a festival in the Church of Constantinople to commemorate Chrysostom. Unlike his great predecessor, Nestorius's error was not one of tact but of teaching. On the subject of the combining of divine and human elements in Christ he took a sharply discriminatory line, and argued for the existence of two natures and two persons. In consequence he was able to present Mary as the mother of only the human Jesus and to deny her the title of *Theotokos* or 'God-bearer', which she had attracted in popular devotion.[37]

This inevitably lost Nestorius much support and ultimately laid his theology open to condemnation by a council of the eastern church held at Ephesus in 431. The whole episode was brilliantly orchestrated by Bishop Cyril of Alexandria (412–44), the ablest ecclesiastical politician of an age of able ecclesiastical politicians. Nestorius himself was permitted to retire into a monastery, but his theology did attract a following amongst some of the Syriac-speaking Christians. Nestorians, as they became called, also came to form the dominant element amongst Christians under Persian rule and spread their distinctive theology to various communities in Central Asia and the borders of China.[38]

In opposing Nestorius, Cyril had put forward a strongly contradictory theology. For Two Natures in Two Persons he effectively substituted the doctrine of One Nature in One Person: the human and divine in Christ were indistinguishable and inseparable. At the Council of Ephesus in 431 Cyril and Nestorius and their respective backers had excommunicated each other. The emperor Theodosius II had been prepared to see both deposed, and although Nestorius voluntarily resigned, Cyril was forced to modify his explicit theological stand in order to gain restoration to his see. In the later 440s the supporters of the extreme One Nature, or Monophysite, theology attempted to overturn this reverse and have the full version of the teaching accepted as orthodoxy. In this they had the useful support of the powerful imperial chamberlain Chrysaphius. At a second council of Ephesus in 449 Bishop Dioscorus of Alexandria (444–51) was able to win an extraordinary victory, which included the deposition and exile of his rival, Bishop Flavian of Constantinople

(446–9), and the acceptance of the One Nature theology as orthodox.[39]

In their hour of triumph, however, the Alexandrians over-reached themselves, and in formulating doctrinal statements to confound Nestorius they had gone too far in the opposite direction. In due course Constantinople was able to strike back, and even Rome felt that its former ally was misguided. A change of emperor heralded a reversal of the Monophysite triumph. Marcian (450–7), who had had Chrysaphius executed, was per-suaded by Bishop Anatolius of Constantinople (449–58) to hold a general council of the whole Church to lay down authorita-tive teaching on this matter of the Natures and Persons of Christ. This gathering met at Chalcedon in 451, condemned the Mono-physite theology of Bishop Dioscorus of Alexandria, and pro-duced the orthodox formulation of 'Two Natures in One Person'.[40]

This procedure was not entirely what Rome had envisaged. While Leo was convinced that the Monophysite doctrine required to be condemned, for a council to do so was a funda-mental rebuff for the Roman view that only the holder of Peter's chair – Peter himself – could make authoritative pronounce-ments on doctrine. Leo produced a theological statement, known as the Tome, which he sent with his envoys to the Council of Chalcedon.[41] In his view this should be read out there and, Peter having spoken, no further discussion should be allowed or required. In practice the document was received, and its orthodoxy acclaimed. The eastern bishops, who were willing to concede to Rome a primacy in prestige but not in authority, accepted the Tome as orthodox because it cohered to the doc-trinal statements of earlier ecumenical councils. For Rome, though, it was the authoritative statement of orthodox belief solely because Leo–Peter had issued it. A fundamental and ultimately irreconcilable divide over the sources of authority in the Church had come into existence.

Leo was also highly displeased because in the authoritative canons that it promulgated by way of stating the conclusions that had been reached, the Council of Chalcedon had accorded special prestige to the see of Constantinople. In Canon 28 it gave Constantinople precedence over both Alexandria and Antioch, and also augmented the territory under the ecclesiastical control of the imperial see. Although Rome was hardly affected by this, Leo accused Anatolius of 'self-seeking' and of 'depraved cupidity'.[42] This was to be but the start of a series of acrimonious exchanges between the two sees, which were intensified when the title of 'Ecumenical Patriarch' was adopted by the bishop of

Constantinople, possibly as early as the patriarchate of Acacius (472–89).[43]

The Monophysite controversy was far from settled by the decisions at Chalcedon. This merely prevented one side from obtaining outright dominance. Although the power of the secular arm was applied and various eastern bishops who supported the Monophysite theology were exiled from their sees, this teaching gained and preserved a majority following amongst the Christian populations of Syria and Egypt, and at the slightest weakening by the government the expelled prelates were restored on a wave of popular backing. Violence was frequent and many bishops were killed by the partisans of the other side in this bitter theological controversy, which was still raging when the eastern provinces passed into Arab rule in the seventh century.[44]

The rise of monasticism

Not the least violent of the participants in all of the eastern theological disputes were the monks. The rise of the monastic movement is yet another area in which eastern ideas influenced the West, but came to be transformed and given a very different institutional character. The origins of monasticism are to be sought in Egypt in the second half of the third century. Traditionally the founding figure is St Anthony, but he is probably best seen as a representative of the earliest stages of the movement. Information about him comes from a substantial *Life of Anthony* written by Bishop Athanasius of Alexandria around the year 355, and translated into Latin during his fourth exile in the West.[45]

According to the *Life* Anthony (*c.* 250–*c.* 355), aged eighteen and following the death of his parents, heard the Gospel text in which Christ states that those who would be perfect should sell all they possess, give it to the poor, and then come and follow him. This command Anthony felt obliged to follow literally. An initial qualm about what provision to make for his sister was stilled by a subsequent hearing of the text 'Take no thought for the morrow'. He retired firstly to a tomb on the fringes of the desert and then to an abandoned fort, where he lived a life of renunciation and mortification for twenty years. After the ending of the persecution under Maximin II in 313, in which he had gone down to Alexandria to try to achieve martyrdom, he retired deeper into the desert, to what he called his 'inner mountain', where he remained until he died, leaving only a cloak, two tunics and a hair shirt.

He had not been alone, and it was the pressure of the attention that he aroused that caused him to move in stages into remoter and ever harsher terrain. At the time of his death he was accompanied by two disciples. The rigours of his self-mortification attracted growing numbers of visitors and would-be followers to him, impelled by the belief that special power and holiness were vested in those who so gained mastery over their bodies and the lusts of the flesh. This veneration for ascetics and belief in their special powers may have had its roots in earlier and pre-Christian traditions in Egyptian society.

What Anthony and his emulators were doing was undertaking firstly a geographical flight, away from their homes and families in the villages and small towns of the Nile valley into the uncultivatable semi-desert, where they lived in caves and amongst wild animals. In other words they sought out the very conditions most at variance with their former modes of life. They renounced their possessions and all former human ties, living on the minimum possible amounts of food gathered from the land or obtained by such manual labour as basket weaving, the products of which were sold in the villages. The purpose of all of this was the salvation of the soul of the individual, by taking Christ's teaching on renunciation at face value and by the deliberate seeking of conflict with the passions of the mind and body, which were externalised as demons. These were fought against and vanquished by showing that they had no hold over the individual holy man, who aimed to bring his body into total subjection to his will.[46]

Not everyone who shared such ideals could undertake the mortification and the conflicts with the 'demonic' forces in solitude, at least not initially. Thus, many aspirants to such an ascetic life looked first to subject themselves to the guidance of an already established holy man of proven prowess. Some, like Anthony, felt such involvement to be a snare, and escaped further and further away from society. Others, however, were prepared to help their fellows on the spiritual path. Pachomius (*c*. 295–350), having himself become a noted hermit, gathered large numbers of disciples and began to organise them into communities.[47] In these monasteries, or effectively monastic villages, each monk had his own hut and supported himself out of his own manual labour, but they all came together for the liturgy and were all under the direction and supervision of their spiritual father (*abba* – hence abbot).

These communities could be very large indeed and contain 300 or more members, but there was no sense that the communal life was in itself beneficial.[48] Each man was there only to secure his own spiritual salvation and the relationship with the abbot was personal. The communal or *coenobitic* life was seen only as the first stage, a kind of spiritual primary school, to be followed if possible by the monk going out to lead the solitary life in a remote location, far removed from any other society. In practice many of the monks never aspired to or failed to be able to advance to this next step and remained in the coenobia. Communities of female ascetics also came into being in this period, although there were fewer of them than of men, and in general the women were never expected to move on to the full solitary life. They remained under the direction of male abbots.[49] Those women who did attempt to lead an individual ascetic life could face misunderstanding, abuse and even violence.

The movement began to attract interest outside Egypt and similar forms developed in Palestine, where the monastic communities were known as *Lavra*, and in Syria.[50] In Syria, where the sharp distinction between desert and cultivated land that was characteristic of Egypt was somewhat blurred, a novel form of escape was created with the appearance of the Stylites. These were solitaries who escaped not horizontally but vertically, by establishing themselves on the tops of pillars.

Traditionally, the first of these was St Simeon Stylites (388–460), who began his ascetic career as an ordinary hermit, on the Egyptian model. From 413 to 423 he lived in an enclosed cell near Antioch, but in 423 he began to build himself a pillar, gradually extending it upwards until by 430 it was 60 feet high. The top was said to be only 3 feet in diameter. There he remained, with a manacle around his neck, until his death, engaged in meditation and conflict with demons. He attracted many visitors who came to him for spiritual and also secular advice, and was consulted on various political matters by the emperors Theodosius II, Marcian and Leo I. Questioners ascended to him by a ladder, up which also his disciples brought occasional supplies of food.[51]

Mortification, but also conspicuous display of it, was taken to its extreme by Simeon and other Syrian pillar saints, such as Daniel the Stylite (died *c.* 490), who inherited Simeon's pillar and lived on it for 33 years. His legs were said to be completely putrefied by the time of his death. Unlike Anthony or even Pachomius, such men as Daniel could exercise considerable influence in secular affairs because of their reputation for outstanding sanctity and their relative accessibility. The opposition to his religious views on the part of Daniel helped bring about the rapid fall of the usurper Basiliscus (475–6).[52] As the division between the Orthodox and the Monophysites grew in intensity and also the number of such

Stylite saints increased, so it became more common to encounter pillar saints on adjacent columns shouting theological abuse at each other across the Syrian landscape.[53]

In the West, whither Athanasius brought the news of the new movement during his enforced exiles, monasticism took on a rather different character. For one thing it was initially much more of an urban than a rural phenomenon, and the idea of the superiority of the solitary rapidly gave way to priority being given to the corporate quest of the community. Aristocrats created house-monasteries in their own properties, in which, with selected friends and companions, they lived a life of modified asceticism, following a set of rules of their own devising. Rome was a particular centre for such establishments, and a number of individual spiritual guides became highly fashionable. Jerome was one such popular mentor until he left in 385 for Bethlehem, where with two of his Roman lady disciples he established male and female monastic communities.[54] Other westerners, lured also by the growing cult of pilgrimage to the Holy Places, moved to the East, particularly after the sack of Rome and the flight of some of the leading aristocratic families from the city.[55]

On the other hand the theological controversies in the East in the same period led to a migration westwards of a number of monastic teachers. The most influential of these was John Cassian, who left Egypt in the course of the conflict over the teachings of Origen, became a follower of John Chrysostom in Constantinople, and came west to try to gain papal support for the Patriarch in 405. After John's death he moved to Marseille in Gaul, where he set up male and female monastic communities. Around 420, at the request of the local bishop he wrote a work called the *Institutes*, a collection of monastic rules and regulations, much influenced by the Greek rules and advice of Bishop Basil of Caesarea (370–9). He followed this with his books of *Conferences*, recounting the oral spiritual teaching of a series of Egyptian holy men and monastic founders.[56] Both of these works of Cassian remained highly influential in the West and became classics of Latin monastic literature.

In both East and West the individualism of the monks and their leaders and their lack of answerability to the established ecclesiastical hierarchy made them difficult to control. The theological divisions and the sheer number of the monks in Egypt made them dangerous partisans in the faction fights within the cities. Monks were responsible for the murder of the pagan philosopher Hypatia (410), for the sacking of the last great temples, and for the lynching of a number of bishops with whose theological views they were at variance.[57] In the West the more limited and more aristocratic nature of the phenomenon prevented any such developments, but individual monastic teachers could threaten the growing consensus on the nature of orthodox belief being developed by such bishops as Augustine. In trying in 418 to suppress one of these teachers, Pelagius, formerly a fashionable leader of the aristocratic monastic life in Rome, Augustine was happy to obtain the secular aid of the state. For all the arguments of *The City of God*, the Empire still had a role to play in coercing its citizens into right belief.[58] However, Augustine had been right: he died in 430 while Hippo was under siege by the Vandals, and the rule of Rome in Africa did not long survive him.[59]

6   The disappearance of an army

Shrinking the western Empire, 410–454

One of the most striking features of the period between the years
395 and 476 is the lack of reference to specifically Roman armies
in the literary sources relating to both the eastern and the western
halves of the Empire. Certainly there is a great deal of military
activity recorded in these decades, much of it conducted by
generals acting for and in the name of a succession of emperors.
But in very few cases are the troops under their command found
to be other than federates or mercenaries. This contrasts strongly
with the situation in previous centuries, in which the formation,
deployment and movement of unequivocally Roman armies can
be documented in considerable detail. It is thus not surprising to
find that many modern historians of the Roman army discreetly
terminate their studies around the year 400.[1]

It is possible to be quite precise as to when the presence of
Roman field armies was last recorded in many of the provinces
of the western half of the empire. In 407 the usurper Constantine
III withdrew the mobile forces from Britain.[2] None were ever sent
back to the island. After this emperor's fall in 411 and the
elimination of the rebel regime of Maximus and Gerontius based
in Barcelona, the field army was withdrawn from Spain.[3] Some
form of garrisoning was retained in the north-eastern province
of Tarraconensis throughout most of the fifth century, but the
other Spanish provinces were left without a Roman military presence. Africa, where most of the Spanish field army units were
directed in 413, was equally denuded of its troops in 432 when
the general Boniface shipped his army to Italy to engage in a civil
war with his rival, Aetius.[4] They were not returned, and by 439
Carthage and all of the North African provinces were in the hands
of the Vandals, whose rule was recognised by the imperial government in a treaty made in 442.

The situation in Gaul is less clear cut, in that what occurred
there was a gradual contraction of the Roman military presence over the course of several decades, with at the same time
an increased dependence on mercenary or federate troops to preserve an ever dwindling enclave of direct imperial rule. The settlement of the Visigoths in Aquitaine in 418 marked the beginning
of the process.[5] The last time a Roman general, in the person of
Aetius, then Master of the Soldiers in Gaul, appeared in the region
of the lower Rhine, once a principal area of imperial campaigning,

was the year 428.[6] Direct control of the area north of the Loire and west of the Seine seems to have been preserved at least until the murder of the emperor Majorian in 461. The Auvergne was retained under imperial rule until 475, hut its defence depended exclusively on local resources from the 450s onwards.

At the same time, the employment of non-Roman forces in imperial defence in Gaul grew dramatically. The Visigoths were used against the Burgundians and the usurping emperors Jovinus and Sebastian in the Rhineland in 413.[7] They were subsequently sent into Spain against the Vandals and Alans from 416 to 418, and were then established by treaty as federates in the province of Aquitania Secunda in south-west Gaul. When the kingdom they created around Toulouse after the treaty with the Romans in 418/19 began to expand into areas that the Empire wished to retain under its direct rule they themselves were subjected to attacks by armies of Hun mercenaries in imperial service. Aetius's deputy in Gaul, Litorius, was even able to threaten Toulouse with a Hun army in 439, but he proved overconfident and was defeated.[8] Hun units had previously been used by Litorius between 435 and 437 in suppressing Bagaudic banditry north of the Loire, and were also turned on the small Burgundian kingdom in the middle Rhineland in 437.[9] In 442 Aetius settled the remnants of the Burgundians in the region of Savoy to garrison the western Alpine approaches into Italy.[10]

Unlike the fourth century, for much of which the large-scale contemporary narrative history of Ammianus Marcellinus is available, the fifth century is not well served in terms of surviving literary historical records. Our principal sources of information come in the form of short chronicles, the most important of which was completed around the year 455 and was the work of an Aquitanian layman with strong theological interests, called Prosper. He wrote the final versions of his chronicle in Rome. Another chronicle, written by a Bishop Hydatius of Chaves (*Iria Flavia*) in Galicia about 469, gives a north-western Spanish perspective on events and is our principal source for the history of the peninsula in the fifth century.[11] Such works do give an outline of leading events, at least from their authors' points of view, but they tend to offer no interpretation of them, nor any assessment of motive or of personality. Thus most of the leading actors in these events remain two-dimensional, and their policies and actions can only be interpreted on the basis of what can be assumed to be their results.

What emerges from the records of Roman military activity, and equally significantly the lack of it in certain areas, is the diminishing capacity of the imperial government in the West, still centred in Ravenna, to provide direct administrative control over and military defence of its provinces. The exercise of central government authority was gradually but consistently reduced from the crisis period of 406–11 onwards. Up to that time there are no indications that the emperors would contemplate ignoring the defensive needs of any of the component parts of the western Empire or of delegating their direct rule over the provinces to other authorities. Once the process started, in Britain in 410, in Spain in 411 and in Gaul in 418, it accelerated rapidly. Politics at the imperial court seems largely to have taken the form of deciding between options as to which areas of the western Empire were regarded as dispensable and which had to be retained under direct imperial rule at all costs.

Simply put, the decision made and maintained between the 420s and the mid 450s was that Gaul was the only area other than Italy that deserved such special attention. The responsibility for making and implementing this policy rests largely with one man, the general Flavius Aetius. For some historians Aetius is 'the last of the Romans', the indefatigable defender of a declining empire. More recently and more pertinently it has been suggested that 'if Aetius was the last of the Romans, it was because he left nothing to his successors'.[12] The record of his activities and their outcome would seem to give greater weight to the latter view.

His father, although originating in the province of Moesia, made a successful military career for himself in Africa and subsequently in Gaul, where he became Commander of the Cavalry (*Magister Equitum*) during the ascendancy of Constantius in the years 411–21.[13] Probably in consequence of his father's military prominence Aetius was sent as a Roman hostage first to the Visigoths and then to the Huns. The contacts he made with the latter led to his being despatched to recruit an army of Hun mercenaries to fight for the Emperor John (423–5), who had been elevated by the western army after the death of Honorius.

Whether deliberately or otherwise, his return to Italy with a Hun army proved to be too late to save John, who was overthrown by the forces of the eastern emperor Theodosius II in 425, in the last of the succession of civil wars between the two halves of the Empire.[14] Aetius was able to secure a military command for himself under the new western regime of Valentinian III and his mother Galla Placidia, the sister of Honorius, in return for removing his Hun forces from Italy. He received the post of Master of the Soldiers, or Commander in Chief, in Gaul and initiated the series of campaigns that he was to fight there by relieving Arles from a Visigothic siege.

In 429 Aetius returned to Italy to take up the post of junior of the two Masters of the Soldiers 'in the Presence' (that is of the emperor), in other words becoming the second senior general in the West. In 430 he arranged for the murder of Felix, his immediate superior, and took over his post.[15] In 432, however, he was challenged by Boniface, the military commander in Africa, whose influence at court he had undermined in 427. Boniface was invited to Italy with his army and given the Mastership of the Soldiers by the Empress Galla Placidia, then acting as regent for her still infant son. Aetius did not give up easily. In the ensuing civil war Boniface was victorious in a battle near Rimini, but died soon after from his wounds.[16] His son-in-law Sebastian was appointed to succeed him as Master of the Soldiers, but lacked the strength to resist Aetius, who forced his own reinstatement in 433.[17] From that year until his murder at the hands of the emperor Valentinian III in 454, Aetius exercised an unchallenged military and political supremacy in the western half of the Empire.

The main lines of his policy have already been outlined. Throughout the 430s and early 440s he used increasing numbers of Hun mercenaries to maintain imperial control in Gaul. At the same time no resources were diverted to assist in the defence of other western provinces. An appeal for military assistance against the raids of the Picts and Scots was sent from Britain to Aetius between 446 and 454, but seems to have received no reply.[18] A similar request from the towns of Galicia in 431 had been answered only by the despatch of a single officer, sent by Aetius to negotiate with the Sueves, whose kingdom was rapidly engulfing the province.[19] More serious still was the failure of Aetius to take any action to stem the Vandal seizure of Africa.

In this latter case it may be suspected that the predominance from 425 to 432 in the North African provinces of his rival Boniface predisposed Aetius against making strenuous efforts to retain them. On the other hand, the years of the Vandal conquest did coincide exactly with those of the greatest conflict in Gaul between Aetius's forces and the Visigoths, and it is possible that the resources did not exist to enable war to be waged by the Empire on two fronts simultaneously. Whatever the cause, Aetius clearly allowed no other claim on his attention to distract him from his ultimately unsuccessful attempt to eliminate the Visigothic kingdom in Gaul, and in consequence he was prepared to concede practical control of Africa, supposedly the 'granary of the western Empire', to the Vandals. The treaty made in 442 that formalised this recognition included the betrothal of the Emperor Valentinian III's daughter to Huneric, the eldest surviving son of the Vandal King Gaiseric.[20]

Despite the defeat and subsequent execution of Litorius at the hands of the Visigoths in 439, Aetius did manage to limit their expansion beyond the areas with which they had been entrusted in 418. He had in that sense faced a genuine problem, in that the Visigothic kingdom based on Toulouse had become openly aggressive and expansionary after the death of its King Wallia (415–18) and the accession of Theoderic I (418–51). Moreover, Aetius, who had forced himself on the western court in 425, in 430, and again in 433, clearly lacked the support of, and indeed seems to have aroused the enmity of, the empress Galla Placidia and her son Valentinian III.[21]

In consequence he had to build up a network of powerful allies in other directions. His principal backing appears to have come from his Hun armies, some members of whom had ties of personal loyalty to him. With such military support he could also look for political backing from elements in the senatorial aristocracy, particularly those with interests to preserve in Gaul.[22] Also the occasional hostility that had manifested itself in the fourth century, and more acutely from 408 onwards between senators in Rome and the imperial court in Milan and then Ravenna, meant that a commander out of favour with the latter could expect some support from the former. However, it should be noted that wealthy as they still were, the senatorial aristocracy could not themselves provide Aetius with the military backing upon which his survival depended. That came from the Huns.

The 430s, however, saw a profound change come over the political structuring of Hun society in the plains north of the Danube, which then seems to have been the centre of their area of settlement and control. The Huns, who had contributed to the collapse of Gothic power north of the Black Sea in the 370s, do not appear then to have recognised any form of central political authority. There was no one 'king of the Huns' at this time. The subjection of a variety of subject peoples, and the eventual restoration of stability in the north Danubian regions under Hun hegemony, seem to have given rise to, rather than to have been created by, the emergence of a unitary ruling dynasty amongst the Huns. A certain Rua appears by the early 430s to have been wielding authority over all the people, or at least this is the perspective of contemporary Roman accounts. He was succeeded between 433 and 435 by his nephews Bleda and Attila, and the latter secured complete domination by the murder of his brother around the years 444/5.[23]

The emergence of an apparently effective single authority amongst the Huns meant that by the mid 440s the continued supply of Hun mercenaries for the armies of the western Empire depended on the continuing goodwill of their king or khan. For most of the 430s and 440s the Huns were exploiting their proximity to the

Roman Empire in two ways. They were providing more and more of the military manpower used by the western government to maintain its authority in Gaul and to repress the Visigoths, Burgundians and Bagaudae, and thus at the same time to keep Aetius in power. They were also using the threat and occasionally the reality of raids in force across the Danube into the Balkans to extort annual payments of tribute from the eastern half of the Empire, then under the rule of Theodosius II (402–50).[24]

The death of this emperor in 450 led to a dramatic change of policy in Constantinople. The new ruler Marcian (450–7), who married his predecessor's sister, purged the leading figures of Theodosius II's regime, and refused to continue the agreed annual payments to the Huns. For reasons that have never been effectively explained, this did not lead to a Hun invasion of the Balkans, as had occurred in 441 and 447. Instead, in 451 Attila took his armies westward into Gaul, thus using against western Roman interests the very forces that had previously defended them for most of the preceding two decades.

Although there are some indications that the intended victims of the Hun assault were to be the Visigoths, the contemporary references locate the Hun army in the Rhineland and around the city of Metz, which was sacked.[25] A later saint's life also has the Huns undertaking an unsuccessful siege of Orléans in the Loire valley.[26] Aetius was forced to make a rapid reversal in his policy. Having, since his first campaign in 425, sought to confine or even eliminate the Visigothic kingdom, he was forced in the new circumstances of the Hun incursion to make an alliance with Theoderic I against this common threat. In the ensuing battle 'of the Catalaunian plains', in the vicinity of Troyes, the main role was played by the Visigoths. Aetius may not have been present in person, and the limited nature of the Roman response again seems to highlight the reduced size of the imperial military establishment at this time.[27] The Visigothic King Theoderic was killed, but the Huns were defeated, and in consequence were forced to withdraw from Gaul.

It has been suggested that Aetius dissuaded the new Visigothic king, Thorismund (451–3), from following up the victory with an effective pursuit of the retreating Huns.[28] Such a view depends upon the rather over elaborate account of the whole episode that is to be found in the mid-sixth century *Getica* or *Gothic History* of Jordanes, but it may make sense in the light of the previous pattern of Aetius's policy. For him the principal enemy remained the Visigoths, and it is possible that he hoped to continue to do business with the Huns, in the matter of the providing of mercenaries for the defence of Roman interests in Gaul.

If so, he was rapidly to be disillusioned. In 452 Attila and his Hun army once again invaded imperial territory, but this time their target was Italy. The Huns crossed the Danube and broke through the eastern Alpine passes unopposed. What is particularly striking about this campaign is the total absence of any Roman military response. The Huns sacked Aquileia and advanced into the Po valley without any resistance being offered. The only reply made was the despatch from Rome of an embassy, consisting of two leading senators and Pope Leo I. According to the contemporary chronicle of Prosper, himself the pope's secretary, it was their pleas that led Attila to withdraw and retire beyond the Danube once more, but it is at least feasible to suspect that other factors, such as an epidemic amongst the Huns, may have helped persuade them to leave the apparently defenceless Italian provinces.[29]

What might have happened in the following year can only be a matter of speculation, in that Attila died in 453, and his empire collapsed under the competing claims of his sons and the revolt of most of the subject peoples. A confederacy of the latter defeated the Hun army in the battle of the Nedao in 454 and in the aftermath the Hun dominion disintegrated even more rapidly than it had first been formed.[30] It is hardly coincidental that these events were paralleled by the elimination of Aetius. His principal allies had turned against him in 451. He had failed to defend Italy in 452, and the future prospect of using Hun mercenary armies ceased to be viable in the collapse of their power in 453/4. Aetius had outlived his usefulness, and those who had long hated and feared him were able to treat him as he had treated some of his own earlier rivals. Aetius was killed in the palace in Ravenna in 454, possibly by the emperor's own hand, and with him died the Praetorian Prefect Boethius, one of his foremost senatorial allies.[31]

Unfortunately for Valentinian III, his elimination of Aetius led directly to his own murder. Although his principal military following had been lost with the reversal of support on the part of the Huns, Aetius still retained the loyalty of a number of officers who had served under him and of a force of bodyguards of barbarian origin, who by the traditions of their own society were bound to seek revenge for a betrayed leader. Two of these men were easily suborned by the former Consul and Praetorian Prefect Petronius Maximus to murder the emperor in the course of a military parade in Rome on 16 March 455, a mere six months after the death of Aetius.[32]

For the sixth century chronicler the Count Marcellinus, writing in Constantinople, the western Empire was lost in 454 with the murder of Aetius. Some modern historians have agreed, and have echoed sixth century Byzantine views that would see Aetius as 'the last of the Romans'.[33] In fact the elimination of Valentinian meant the end of the imperial dynasty that had through its branches ruled the West since 364, and the initiation of a period in which the imperial office ceased to carry much weight in the western half of the Empire. It might also be argued that had Aetius been murdered a good few years earlier the western Empire would have had a better chance of survival.

An age of military dictators, 455–480

The career of Aetius has been followed in some detail, not only because it is crucial to the understanding of the making of Roman imperial policy over a vital three decades that effectively decided the fate of the western Empire, but also because it typifies a wider phenomenon, that of the role of the 'military dictator' in the fifth century. In the West an almost unbroken succession of generals can be found exercising the real power in the state in all matters relating to the army, military strategy, the making of major political appointments, and the deployment of financial and other resources from the time of Stilicho, if not earlier, right up to the ending of the line of separate western emperors in 476–80.

They can be listed as follows – all of them held the office of *Magister Militum praesentalis* or Master of the Soldiers in the (imperial) presence:

Arbogast	388–94
Stilicho	395–408
Constantius	411–21
Castinus	423–5
Felix	425–30
Aetius	430–2
Boniface	432 (Sebastian 432–3)
Aetius	433–54
Ricimer	457–72
Gundobad	472–3
Orestes	475–6
Odovacer	476– (became 'King of Italy', 476–93)

Some proved short-lived or unsuccessful, as in the cases of Boniface and of Castinus, who provided the military backing for the failed regime of the emperor John. Certain periods of particular turmoil, such as the years 408–11 or 454–7, could also see a number of competitors struggling to gain the kind of ascendancy that men like Stilicho, Aetius and Ricimer were able to exercise over long periods, but failing to attain it. This was not, however, an exclusively western phenomenon. A similar list of such men can be drawn up for the East:

Gainas	399–400
Fravitta	400–1
Aspar	431–71
Zeno	473–4 (became emperor in 474)
Theoderic Strabo	474–5, 475/6, 478–9
Theoderic 'the Amal'	476, 477–8
Vitalian	518–20

However, as the list makes clear, the situation in the East throughout the fifth century is not so clear cut, largely because the military needs of that half of the Empire were less consistent, and it was often possible to prevent the commanders of the armies from exercising the kind of general control of political life and dominance of the imperial court that was so typical of their counterparts in the West. Thus Gainas, one of a number of officers of Gothic origin who rose to prominence in the reign of Theodosius I, tried to establish a control over the eastern court similar to that being exercised by Stilicho over the western one, but was driven out of Constantinople in an anti-German riot and was subsequently defeated by another of the Gothic generals, called Fravitta. The latter succeeded to Gainas's post, but within a year had been killed in a coup organised by one of the court factions.[34]

In general the eastern court was able to maintain a more consistently civilian image and to prevent its leading generals from acquiring a monopoly of power even in military matters. Aspar, who held the office of Master of the Soldiers for at least forty years, was never able to exercise the dominance over policy making and appointments long held by his western contemporary Aetius. Under Theodosius II his influence was limited, and even the succession of Marcian in 450, who had been one of his staff officers, seems neither to have been his work nor to have specially benefited him. Only with the death of Marcian in 457 did Aspar achieve a real supremacy in the eastern court, when he engineered the succession of Leo I (457–74), another of his military subordinates.[35]

Even so, his supremacy was not secure. By the late 460s Leo was creating a counterweight to the forces controlled by Aspar by recruiting Isaurians, mountain dwellers from central Asia Minor. He married his daughter to one of their leaders called Tarasis the son of Codissa, who then changed his name to Zeno, probably in honour of an earlier Isaurian general. By 471 Leo was strong enough to seize and execute Aspar and his eldest son, who had been Master of the Soldiers in the Eastern Provinces.[36] The limitations on Aspar's power and his ultimate failure contrast markedly with the hold over a succession of emperors that was exercised by the principal military commander in the West in the 460s, a general called Ricimer. His rise to power was the product of the period of confusion that followed the killings of Aetius and then of Valentinian III, and was marked by dramatic changes in several areas of western policy. These were initiated by the events of 455.

Having arranged the death of Valentinian III, Petronius Maximus was able to secure his own proclamation as emperor on the following day, and he linked his family to that of his predecessor by himself marrying the latter's widow and uniting his son Palladius with the former emperor's daughter. This, however, broke one of the terms of the treaty made in 442 between Valentinian III and the Vandal King Gaiseric, which had included the betrothal of the former's daughter Eudocia to the latter's son Huneric. Thus in 455 Gaiseric was not only able to claim that the new imperial regime had violated this treaty, but could also present himself as the avenger of his son's would-be father-in-law. A Vandal fleet sailed from Africa, and descended upon an undefended Rome, giving the city a second sack, and perhaps a more thorough one than that of 410. As the Vandals arrived the wretched Petronius Maximus, who had based himself in the city, tried to flee. An enraged citizen threw a well-aimed brick at him, thus bringing his brief reign to an appropriate end.[37]

The sack of Rome of 455 had the immediate effect of making the potential Vandal threat to Italy seem of far greater moment than the more distant menace of Visigothic ambitions in Gaul. Although the Vandals returned to Africa with their loot, the whole episode brought home in a way that was previously not appreciated how vulnerable Italy, and Rome in particular, was to seaborne raiding, and how easy it was for a hostile power in North Africa, in control of the mercantile fleets of the coastal towns of the African provinces, to conduct such warfare. The Vandal menace and the ambition of regaining direct control of Africa became the mainspring of imperial policy throughout the last years left to the western half of the Empire.

The lack of functioning Roman armies in the heartland of the western Empire, which was apparent from the absence of resistance both to Attila in 452 and to the Vandal sack of Rome in 455, meant that Gaul had to be looked to as the source of military manpower for the defence of Italy. Petronius Maximus had probably already realised this, as he appointed as his Master of the

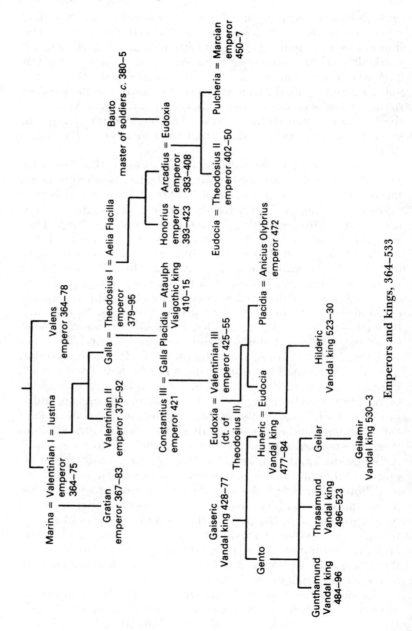

Emperors and kings, 364–533

Soldiers in the Presence a Gallic aristocrat called Eparchius Avitus, who had served under Aetius and who also had close personal ties to the Visigothic royal house. This Avitus is reported to have persuaded Theoderic I to ally with Aetius against the Hun threat in 451. In 455 he was sent by Maximus to the Visigoths, this time it may be assumed for aid against the Vandals. While Avitus was still at the Gothic court in Toulouse the news of Maximus's death arrived, and with the support of the new Visigothic king Theoderic II (453–6) he was proclaimed emperor by the army and an assembly of Gallic aristocrats at Arles.[38]

The Senate in Rome and the army commanders in Italy accepted this Gallic seizure of the initiative because of their pressing need for assistance, but clearly resented the necessity. Although Avitus came with a largely Visigothic army to Rome, his interests and those of his principal backers lay in Gaul. His close ties to the Visigoths also meant that the threats the latter posed to Roman interests in Gaul were greatly reduced. It is hardly coincidental that in 456 the Visigothic king Theoderic II led an army into Spain against the Suevic ruler Rechiarius, whose expansionary activities were threatening the last imperial enclave in the peninsula, the north-eastern province of Tarraconensis.[39] Thus, as under Wallia, the Visigoths came once more to play the role of Roman federate troops, acting in the imperial interests, but at the same time were able to expand their own control over areas that were of secondary concern to Avitus and his Gallic aristocratic supporters. It is possible that this move into Spain was also presented to the Italian senators, now obsessively concerned with the Vandal threat, as the necessary preliminary to an invasion of Africa.

If so, the lack of immediate action against the Vandals and the ignominy of accepting provincial emperor-making made Avitus's regime increasingly unpopular in Rome, although it had been recognised by the eastern emperor Marcian. In 456 a general of mixed Visigothic and Suevic origin called Ricimer won a battle at sea against a Vandal force. In itself it may not have been militarily significant, but it seems to have enabled the Italian high command to feel it could dispense with Avitus. Another of Aetius's former officers, but one who had fallen out with him, called Majorian, with the backing of Ricimer renounced his allegiance to the Gallic emperor, who then tried to escape from Rome back to safety in his home province. However, Avitus was intercepted and his forces defeated by Majorian and Ricimer at Piacenza (*Pollentia*) in October 456. After the battle the emperor was promptly ordained as Bishop of Piacenza, a manoeuvre to formalise his deposition. His death followed, perhaps suspiciously, soon after.[40]

The belated determination to regain Africa dominated western imperial policy for the next fifteen years in the same way that the not always real Visigothic menace had obsessed it in the time of Aetius. In 457, after an interval probably spent in securing eastern recognition, Majorian was proclaimed emperor.[41] His first steps were to impose himself on the remaining imperially controlled regions of Gaul, where the deposition of Avitus had been badly received, but this was only the preliminary to the invasion of Africa, towards which the making of an agreement with the Visigothic King Theoderic II was the second step. With these barriers removed, in 460 Majorian was the last of the Roman emperors to appear in the Iberian peninsula. He made a formal *adventus*, the ceremony to mark an imperial arrival in a city, into Zaragoza, and then proceeded to the south-eastern coast, where a fleet was being assembled to transfer his army to Africa.[42] Here, however, in the same year, disaster struck. Being forewarned, the Vandals made a pre-emptive strike on the imperial fleet, destroying or capturing the bulk of it. The campaign had to be called off.

Worse was to follow, in that Majorian then agreed to the Vandal King Gaiseric's request for a treaty. As far as it is now known, this seems to have been an acceptance of the terms of the previous treaty of 442, conceding Vandal control of Africa in return for peace. On his return to Gaul in 461 Majorian disbanded his army, mainly composed of Germanic federates, and in the autumn he headed for Rome, only to be intercepted by the forces of Ricimer, deposed and executed.[43] Although it is normally attributed to a power struggle between the two men, the unfortunate end of Majorian may relate to his ignominious failure in the abortive African venture.

Decisive as Ricimer's move had been it only served to further fragment the dwindling territories controlled directly by the western emperor. When in November 461, two months after the death of Majorian, he set up as emperor of his own choosing a senator called Libius Severus, the former ruler's Master of the Soldiers in Gaul, a general called Aegidius, refused to accept him.[44] Thus Roman territory north of the Loire ceased to be ruled from Italy. Ricimer incited his Visigothic allies to attack Aegidius in return for being given control of Narbonne. Aegidius in turn opened up communication with the Vandals for joint action against the regime of Ricimer and Severus. The latter was further hampered by the refusal of the eastern emperor Leo to recognise his would-be western colleague.

The situation was ameliorated in 465 by the deaths of both Aegidius and the Emperor Severus. Poison and Ricimer were suspected in both cases.[45] This does not seem to have led to the return of northern Gaul to imperial rule, but it did make possible a rapprochement between East and West. This reached fruition in 467, when the Roman Senate, or more exactly Ricimer, accepted an eastern nominee for the western throne in the person of Anthemius, in return for the eastern Empire funding and launching an invasion of Africa to dispose of the Vandals. Leo I hereby benefited from the removal to the West of the dangerously well-connected Anthemius, who was not only a distant descendant of the Emperor Julian, but also a son-in-law of the former Emperor Marcian and a contender for the imperial office in the East in 457.[46]

In that sense Leo got the better of the bargain. The eastern expedition to Africa in 468, which was commanded by his brother-in-law, proved to be a disaster. The fleet was subjected to a surprise attack by fire ships off the African coast, and the invasion was abandoned.[47] In the West conflicts of authority between Anthemius and Ricimer reached such a point that civil war broke out. Anthemius, whose eastern origins were used against him, not least through giving him the derisive nickname 'the little Greek', seems to have had limited popular support. His opponents may also have accused him of being a pagan, a charge for which no evidence can be found. Ricimer's forces took Rome, and Anthemius was dragged from sanctuary in a church and executed in July 472.[48]

By this time it must have been clear that effective military action against the Vandals was beyond the capacities of either half of the Empire, and so Ricimer in the last stage of his career himself came to an agreement with Gaiseric. This was represented in his choosing as the new western emperor the senator Anicius Olybrius.[49] This man was the husband of the former emperor Valentinian III's second daughter. Her elder sister, pledged to Gaiseric's son by the treaty of 442 and then forcibly married to the son of Petronius Maximus, had been taken off to Africa and married to Huneric by the Vandals in 455. Thus the selection of this brother-in-law of the Vandal king's heir marked a final and in practice irrelevant rapprochement between the western Empire and the Vandal kingdom.

In the event neither Ricimer nor the emperor Olybrius lived out the year, both dying of natural causes before the end of 472. By this time the Empire in the West had for all practical purposes become reduced to the bounds of Italy, the Auvergne and eastern Provence. The Visigoths were the masters of everything south of the Loire and west of the Rhône, and were to add the Auvergne to their territories in 475. The Burgundian kingdom encompassed Savoy and a large section of the middle Rhône valley. Imperial rule over the Ebro valley and related Catalan coast was terminated by the Visigothic king Euric (466–84) in the early 470s.[50] So little did Italy matter that Ricimer's successor and nephew Gundobad preferred in 473 not to remain to support the regime of the puppet emperor Glycerius, whom he had created, but to go instead to compete for control of the Burgundian kingdom in Gaul.[51]

Thus abandoned, Glycerius had no military resources available to resist an eastern imperial nominee, Julius Nepos, the Master of the Soldiers in Dalmatia.[52] Glycerius was deposed and sent as bishop to Salona in Dalmatia. However, like Anthemius, Nepos had little real support in Italy, and after a reign of just over a year he was expelled from Italy back to Dalmatia. His supplanter was his newly appointed Master of the Soldiers, Orestes, who made his own son Romulus emperor in October 475. In August 476 Orestes himself was overthrown and killed by another and more experienced general of mixed Germanic origin called Odovacer. The young Romulus was permitted to retire into private life on an estate in south Italy, where he may still have been living around the year 510.[53]

Formally the deposition of Romulus, and the taking of power in Italy by Odovacer under the title of king in 476 did not mark the end of the western Roman Empire. The ejected Julius Nepos still lived and controlled Dalmatia, preventing an eastern recognition of the *status quo* in Italy. The murder of Nepos in 480, possibly engineered by Bishop Glycerius, the man he himself had deposed in 474, removed this obstacle, and also may technically be said to mark the end of the Roman Empire in the West.[54] In that sense it died not with a bang or with a whimper, neither in Rome nor in Ravenna, but at the end of an assassin's knife in a villa in Salona in Dalmatia.

What is genuinely striking about the process of the 'Fall of the Roman Empire', to which it is necessary rapidly to add 'in the West', as its eastern half was to survive for another 1000 years, is the haphazard, almost accidental nature of the process. From 410 onwards successive western imperial regimes just gave away or lost control of more and more of the territory of the former Empire. At the same time, it must be appreciated, no emperor or Master of the Soldiers would have thought they were actually abandoning or putting outside the Empire the various provinces that they thus surrendered. In terms of constitutional theory practical authority in areas of administration and defence were being delegated to imperial appointees in the persons of the Germanic kings. These remained in theory subordinate to the higher authority of the emperors, even though the latter ceased to obtain material benefit from or to exercise direct control over the provinces.

In this way the western Empire delegated itself out of existence. It was perfectly logical for Odovacer to set himself up as King of Italy and to declare that there no longer needed to be two separate divisions within the Empire.[55] The events of 476 or 480 meant in theory, and this was how both Odovacer and the Emperor Zeno saw it, that instead of the Empire being divided and there being eastern and western sections there was now just one indivisible Empire again, and the rights and authority of the western ruler over his subordinates, the Germanic kings, merely passed to the thenceforth sole emperor ruling in Constantinople.

Obviously in practice this was not much more than a constitutional fiction, albeit an ideologically powerful one. Direct imperial rule over most of the West had been lost in the course of the fifth century, and was in most areas either not to be or only briefly restored. However much continuity can be detected, and there is an impressive quantity of it, in terms of administrative, fiscal, legal and institutional survivals at the provincial level, the actual disintegration of direct imperial rule is a process that it is clearly important to understand.

In that the ability of the emperors or their officials in the imperial capital, which fluctuated between Ravenna and Rome throughout the century, to exercise personal authority in practice over the provinces depended as always on their ability to enforce their will, the problem is a military one. If a self-consciously Roman army, commanded by officers established in a hierarchy that culminated in the emperor and his senior military advisers in Italy continued to exist, then so too did direct imperial rule over the provinces throughout which that army was stationed When the army was not present, so too disappeared the central government's ability to coerce and to enforce its decisions.

The mysterious disappearance of the Roman army is one of the most extraordinary phenomena of the fifth century. Generals abound and so do barbarian soldiers. The old Roman units do not, even though such archaising texts as the *Notitia Dignitatum* of *c*. 425, appear to prolong their lives. Only the supposed existence of traditional units in Britain and Spain at a time when other evidence shows they were not there reveals the unreliability of this as a statement of the actual as opposed to theoretical deployment of the Roman army at the end of the first quarter of the fifth century.[56]

Inevitably, as the areas under direct imperial control diminished in size, so too were traditional recruiting grounds lost to the Roman army. From the later fourth century onwards pressure from the troops themselves had reduced the quantity of armour worn and other long established features of Roman military practice and equipment.[57] By 425 the surviving units of the Roman army would have been in appearance, including dress and weaponry, little different from the various enemies they were required to fight, most of whom had themselves become increasingly Romanised in terms of material culture over the course of the previous decades. The loss of training and expertise, the expense of maintaining a standing army, and the political difficulties that could result from having one, all combined to make it seem easier, cheaper and safer to use barbarian federates to fight in the emperor's name. In consequence those who directed them were able to demand more and were being given more by way of control over the government and revenues of the provinces in which they were situated.

At the centre, the only perspective was one of the protection of Italy and of any other interests that were close to the hearts of those exercising political control there. Thus Africa could be dispensed with in order to concentrate on the preservation of parts of Gaul in the time of Aetius. Under Ricimer there was a change to almost exactly the opposite order of priorities. In consequence neither Africa nor Gaul was preserved and the Empire itself became in practice no larger than Italy. Odovacer was right to put an end to the fiction and to make of Italy only one among the several kingdoms into which the West had become divided.

The fall of Rome?

The analysis offered here may seem strangely limited as an answer to the perennial question of why did the Roman Empire fall. What has been suggested is that in large measure it gave itself away: the central administration of the western half of the empire relinquished day to day control over more and more of its provinces as its capacity to defend and police them, and therefore to administer them directly, declined in the face of a mounting series of military problems. This, it should be stressed, was seen at the time by the emperors and their advisers as no more than a temporary expedient, and in no sense did they feel that they were alienating their intrinsic authority over the western provinces. In practice, however, as can be seen with hindsight, direct imperial rule was never to be reimposed on most of these territories, and the central administration of the western Empire succumbed to the process it itself had instigated.

On the other hand, as will be seen in subsequent chapters dealing with the events in the West in the aftermath of the elimination of the last western emperors in 476–80, the intellectual, governmental and material cultural traditions of the Later Roman Empire continued to enjoy vitality in the West long after the disappearance of the unitary political structure that had previously sustained them, but which in practice had proved not to be integral to their survival. 'The Fall of the Roman Empire in the West' was not the immediate disappearance of a civilisation: it was merely the breaking down of a governmental apparatus that could no longer be sustained in the light of current economic and political realities. Ultimately, of course it may be argued that the removal of the institutional prop facilitated the withering of certain aspects of the social organisation and cultural traditions that had rested upon it, but this was to be a gradual process, extending far beyond the period in which discussions of 'the Fall' normally confine themselves. Many features of the Late imperial Romano-Christian intellectual tradition survive to the present, and have helped shape all of the societies that have been formed in the Mediterranean and northern Europe from the fifth century onwards.

In previous decades arguments concerning the 'Fall of the Roman Empire' have tended to be formulated rather differently, largely due to the way in which the significance of the process has been viewed. If the disappearance of the overall political structures of the western Empire be taken as corresponding exactly with the undermining of the intellectual and material culture of Rome, then a far more complex and cataclysmic process would have to be thought to have occurred. Consequentially, the explanations advanced to make sense of it would have to look to very different kinds of causes. In part the previous tendency to treat the process as one of the 'fall' of a civilisation resulted from overemphasis of the supposedly Germanic nature of the successor states that came into being in the West in the aftermath of the disappearance of the Empire, and from seeing the interaction of Rome and the so-called Barbarians simply in terms of confrontation.

Viewed in terms of the conflict of opposed, albeit unequal, cultures, it is not surprising that the issue was taken as being a moral one: how could the beneficiaries of a 'higher' civilisation fail to triumph over the representatives of a 'lower' one? The answer would have to lie, according to the intellectual predilections or ideological presuppositions of the questioner, in a range of moral or structural possibilities. The simplest level of answer was that which manifested itself in a correspondence in *The Times* a few years ago, in which the merits or otherwise of the 'lead pipe' theory were debated. According to this the prevalence of lead piping in the Roman urban water distributory systems – aqueducts, underground channels and so forth – led over the course of time to the toxic effects of this metal being transmitted genetically. In other words, the mental capacities of the Romans gradually deteriorated, as the brains of successive generations were atrophied by the lead. Thus, while they were still capable of dealing with a complex series of threats to their society in the third century, by the fifth they had lost the necessary mental ability.

While ingenious, this theory has not much recommended itself to professional practitioners of the historical art. Their arguments have tended to be more complex, if not necessarily always more credible. However, it has generally been recognised that while the western half of the Roman Empire disappeared in the fifth century, the eastern half survived, despite various modifications, for another thousand years. Thus, any explanation that may hope to be considered viable has to take account of the very different fates of the two components of the Empire. This effectively undermined the arguments eloquently advanced by Edward Gibbon, who placed the blame squarely on the effects of the adoption of Christianity, which he saw as including a rise in 'other worldliness', manpower shortages from the growth of popularity of monasticism and Christian teachings on virginity, and an ambivalent attitude to warfare.[58] All of these features, however, even without assessing their inherent validity, would have to have been as true of the eastern half of the Empire as of the western.

More recent commentators have therefore taken account of the need to produce arguments that stress differences between the two parts of the Late Empire. Most of these tend to revolve around supposed differences in the social structure and economic organisation of the Roman world in the fourth and fifth centuries. In so doing they tend rapidly to depart from the hard reality of the available evidence. The first, most basic, if unpalatable truth about the economy of the Late Roman Empire is that insufficient evidence survives to sustain *any* generalisations about its nature and functioning. It is certainly possible for historians to propose what are in the main ideologically pre-determined models of how that economy in their view *ought* to have worked, but these may only convince those who share their beliefs.

Thus, to take only a moderate and mild interpretation, influenced by ideals of an English liberal kind, it was argued by A. H. M. Jones in his monumental *Later Roman Empire* that western senators were wealthier than eastern ones, and that there 'were probably more medium landowners in the East, and fairly certainly more peasant proprietors'.[59] While allowing credit for the qualifying adverbs, it must be pointed out that no valid statistical information exists to support or deny such an assertion, and that underlying it are the assumptions that free peasant proprietors are economically productive and intrinsically patriotic. Jones's arguments are actually a little more complex, in that for him this productivity and patriotism have to be seen in the context of the ability of the society to support 'idle mouths'. These latter, amongst whom were included monks and aristocrats, he regarded with the deepest moral indignation as the cause of the imperial ruin, and he assumed his readers would share this particular perspective. On the other hand, the great Russian historian Rostovtzeff, who was driven into exile by the 1917 Revolution, saw the undermining of the upper class culture of the Mediterranean cities by peasant soldiers as the true cause of Rome's fall.[60] In other words, this is one of those topics that can tell the reader more about a historian's personal prejudices than about the historical reality that he seeks to describe.

7   The new kingdoms

War lords and kings

There is a danger when trying to visualise those whom the Romans of the fourth and fifth centuries would have called 'the Barbarians' of using images from other and generally earlier ages. Without due caution and letting the pejorative nature of the name speak by itself it would be easy to imagine them as being little better than savages, naked, hairy and doubtless garishly painted. In practice, however, the various German peoples were, in terms of material culture, little different from the Roman provincials. Their items of personal adornment and practical necessities such as brooches, belt buckles and other fastenings were in most cases either of Roman manufacture or were modelled on Roman originals.[1] A major source of inspiration were the buckles, fastenings and other items of jewellery used in the uniforms of the Roman army, in whose ranks substantial numbers of the Germans, individually and collectively, had served. Trade and the acquisition of loot added to the stock of such items amongst the Germans, and in general these Roman styles of jewellery and practical metalwork became the accepted norm in their societies. It is thus possible to find identical objects, dated to the fifth and sixth centuries, amongst the Anglo-Saxons, Franks and Visigoths, and scattered over an area extending from southern Britain to the centre of Spain.[2]

In terms of clothing the debt may have run as much in the opposite direction. In the early imperial period such items of dress as trousers, worn by both the Germans and the Persians, were regarded by the Romans as being quintessentially barbaric, yet they had become the norm except in the highest levels of society by the end of the fourth century. In 397 the emperor Honorius issued a law forbidding the wearing of trousers and also of a type of Germanic footwear called *tzangae* within the city of Rome. That his law had to be reissued in 399 and again in 416, although the stipulated penalty was exile and confiscation of property, suggests that even within the limits of Rome it proved hard to enforce such a decree.[3] In the law of 416 the wearing of long hair, another supposedly barbarian trait, was added to the list of offences.

It is possible, however, that it was not so much the barbarian associations of these items and styles that gave offence as their military connotations. In the *Theodosian Code*, the compilation of

Roman imperial law issued in 438 and in which the text of these three edicts was preserved, they accompany an earlier law of 382 forbidding senators from wearing military dress within the city.[4] By the beginning of the fifth century so interdependent had the two become that in such aspects as dress and adornment Roman soldiers and Germanic warriors would not easily have been told apart, as can be seen for example from the representations of the imperial bodyguard on such contemporary works of art as the silver *missorium* of Theodosius (388) or the carved obelisk base erected by the same emperor in the Hippodrome in Constantinople (*c.* 390).[5]

Individual Germanic soldiers of Frankish, Vandal and other origin were able to rise through military service within the Empire to high commands in the army and admission to the Senate, where apart from their names they seem to have been indistinguishable from their Roman civilian counterparts. This process dates back at least to the reign of Constantine I, under whom the Frank Bonitus commanded the Seventh Legion. His son Silvanus was commander of the infantry in Gaul between 352 and 355, and was driven by political intrigue at the court of Constantius II into proclaiming himself emperor at Cologne in the latter year. Only a passing reference in Ammianus Marcellinus reveals his Frankish origin and thus that of his father, as in their case they had perfectly acceptable Roman names.[6]

Such officers of Germanic origin were not just to be found exercising commands in areas close to their own homelands. A Frankish general called Richomer became Master of the Soldiers in the East in 383, with his headquarters in Antioch. In the following year he was Consul and from 388 until his death in 393 was the commander in chief of the eastern armies under the emperor Theodosius I.[7] In fact he was the first of a dynasty of military office-holders. His nephew Arbogast was the Master of the Soldiers in the West in the same period and the man responsible for the murder or suicide of Valentinian II and for the elevation of Eugenius.[8] One of his descendants, also called Arbogast, is to be found holding the post of Count of Trier around the year 477.[9]

How consciously Frankish such men were and what kind of contacts they maintained with their people is impossible to judge. When Silvanus was murdered by agents of Constantius II in 355, the Franks sacked Cologne. Was this revenge or just a good opportunity for loot? Certainly such prominent soldiers of barbarian descent were normally more than just illiterate boors. Richomer became a friend of the sophist and orator Libanius in Antioch, and the younger Arbogast was praised by the Gallic author and bishop Sidonius Apollinaris (died *c.* 486) for his literary skill and knowledge of the classics.[10] Roman attitudes of contempt for barbarians certainly did not lead to the isolation of such highly placed officers of Germanic origin in the upper ranks of society. The daughter of the Frankish Master of the Soldiers and consul (385) Bauto married the emperor Arcadius (383–408) and became the mother of his successor Theodosius II (402–50).[11]

It would be interesting to know to what extent the rise of such men as these was influenced by any prior social status they held in their own societies, but in most cases nothing is known about their earlier lives. However, there are indications that some of them at least were in this sense 'self-made'. Arbitio, who was Master of the Cavalry under Constantius II in the years 351(?) to 361 and Consul in 355 started his career as an ordinary soldier in the ranks.[12] On the other hand a certain Mallobaudes, who held the Roman military rank of *Comes Domesticorum* or commander of a unit of the imperial bodyguard, was also described at the same time as being a Frankish king.[13] His Roman appointment may have come from his having a ready made military following, but he was certainly holding a junior staff appointment over twenty years earlier.

These examples – and many more could be produced – indicate something of the way in which the Roman Empire had been absorbing increasing numbers of Germans from the beginning of the fourth century, if not earlier, into the army and through it, in the cases of some of them, into the upper echelons of society and into positions of real wealth and political power. In itself this is not to be seen as a simple contributory cause of 'the Fall of the Roman Empire', not least as this process was as marked in the East as in the West, and Germanic officers and men continued to play important parts in the armed forces of that half of the Empire well on into the sixth century. As has been shown, many of the leading Germans became highly Romanised, as in material cultural terms did the societies from which they had sprung.

Indeed the very absence of a clear-cut sense of 'us' and 'them' may have contributed to the disintegration of the western half of the Empire in the course of the fifth century. No consistent policy was followed as to who was the enemy. At the same time the virtual disappearance of self-consciously Roman units in the western army meant that the imperial regimes had to be on good terms with one or more of the competing Germanic groups if they were to obtain the military force necessary to control others who seemed to be threatening the interests they held vital. The lack of consistency in determining whom to do business with and whom to try and destroy led to a fatal vacillation.

Several of the leaders of barbarian confederacies came to take on roles in relation to the Empire analogous to, or in some cases identical with, those exercised by imperial Masters of Soldiers, many of whom were themselves of Germanic origin. This is particularly true of a period of extraordinary entrepreneurial enterprise that followed the disintegration of the Hun domination north of the Danube in 453/4. In the aftermath several groups and individuals who had been subject to the Huns made their way into the Empire, where some of them were to prosper exceedingly, Although the history of this period is normally presented in simple terms of the movements of whole peoples, in practice many of the groups and also of the individuals who rose to prominence in the second half of the fifth century were decidedly mixed in their ethnic origins and were busy forming new cultural and political entities rather than continuing old ones. A good example of all of these phenomena can be seen in the cases of Odovacer and his brother Onulph.

Their father, Edeco, is thought to have been a Hun, and their mother was a member of the probably Germanic people called the Sciri. Edeco features in one of the fragmentary but contemporary Greek histories of the period as a bodyguard of Attila and one of his leading advisers.[14] In the 460s Edeco and Onulph were in the Balkans, leading the Sciri in a war with the Ostrogoths, both independently and in alliance with the Sueves.[15] In the very same decade Odovacer is first recorded, leading an army of Saxons in Gaul. He and his men made themselves masters of Angers, but in 469 lost it to the Frankish king Childeric and a Roman count called Paul.[16] By 471 he had moved to Italy and supported Ricimer in his civil war with the Emperor Anthemius. In the years after the death of Ricimer he gained a considerable ascendancy over the imperial forces in Italy, which were by now drawn almost exclusively from the ranks of some of the minor German tribes, and when they fell out with their commander Orestes in 476 it was under Odovacer's lead. After the execution of Orestes and his brother he was made king of Italy by the army.[17]

Less distinguished in its final outcome, the career of his brother Onulph was equally varied. After fighting on behalf of his mother's people against the Ostrogoths in the 460s, he appears in the service of the eastern Empire, holding the officer of Master of the Soldiers in Illyricum from 477 to 479. This in part was the reward for murdering his patron and predecessor at the instigation of the emperor Zeno. In the 480s Onulph moved to Italy, where in 488 he commanded his brother's armies in a victorious campaign against the Rugi around the upper Danube. He was later dragged from sanctuary and killed immediately after Odovacer's murder in 493.[18]

At the very least two such careers indicate the geographical range and the variety of opportunity open at this time to those with the necessary military talent. A pre-established position in a social hierarchy was not the prerequisite for success, though this was something that could be exploited in certain circumstances. Thus, just as Odovacer and his brother rose to positions of power in societies to which they were in origin outsiders, it was equally possible for those inheriting authority within an established social group to use it to extend their personal power and that of those who followed them. The best examples of this phenomenon in the later fifth and early sixth centuries come in the cases of the Ostrogothic leader Theoderic and the Frankish king Clovis.

It might be thought, though, that a comparison on the one hand of such entrepreneurial adventurers as Odovacer, lacking a power base within an established Germanic 'barbarian' society, and on the other hereditary rulers of such societies, as Theoderic and Clovis are normally considered to be, is matching chalk with cheese. This is far from being the case. The achievements of Theoderic and Clovis only make sense when seen in the context of the conditions that also threw up Ricimer, Aspar, Count Arbogast of Trier, and Odovacer.

It is dangerously simple to think of the Germanic societies that in the late fifth and sixth centuries were taking control of more and more of the former territories of the western Roman Empire as ethnic constants. This is the kind of conception that underlies those all too frequently to be encountered maps of the *Volkerwanderungzeit* or 'Age of Migrations', with long spaghetti-like lines sprawling across the continent.[19] Each arrowed line has its own colour and each marks the movement of a 'people', starting in their supposed first home, usually located in Scandinavia, and having squiggled its way through centuries and several thousands of miles it terminates in their final home. For the Franks this is France, for the Ostrogoths Italy, the Visigoths Spain and the Vandals Africa.

At the lowest level such thinking – and such maps – leaves little room for the various elements of the 'tribes' that got left behind on the way. The Sueves *ought to* be in north-west Spain, where they had arrived soon after 409, but what are Suevic kings and their followers doing fighting in the Balkans against the Ostrogoths in the 460s? How can Heruli be both making seaborne raids on the northern coast of Spain in 455 and 459 and also be established in southern Moravia after the fall of the Hun empire?[20] The answer to this and many other similar questions is that individuals, families, groups and whole sections of these large-scale ethnic entities either became detached or had detached themselves from the main body. They remained aware of their particular origin and this could on occasion colour their actions. Thus it has been suggested that Aspar deliberately sabotaged eastern imperial ventures directed against the Vandals in Africa, because the main body of his own people, the Alans, had become a component part of the Vandal confederacy.[21]

Many of the older discussions of the history of this period take tribal continuity for granted. However long and tortuous their wanderings, however varied their political fortunes and however powerful the alien cultural influences to which they were subjected, the existence of the people as a whole remains constant. Yet, how can this be? To take the example of the Visigoths: between the middle of the fourth century and the second half of the fifth they had as a group changed their name, moved from the area north-east of the Danube to the south-west of France, via the Balkans, the south of Italy and Spain, converted to Christianity and accepted the unitary rule of a single dynasty of kings for the first time in their history. In other words their society had undergone an extraordinary range of internal changes. Although their case provides one of the best examples of such a series of transformations, it is far from being unique.

Theoderic and the Ostrogothic kingdom in Italy

The Ostrogoths, like the Visigoths, offer us a history that is more notable for its discontinuities than its continuities. Not least of these may well be a hiatus in the ruling line of kings across the period in which the Ostrogoths, who were then anyway known as the *Greuthungi*, were a subject people of the Huns; that is from the 370s to the 450s.[22] Depending upon the brief *History of the Goths* or *Getica* written in Constantinople by Jordanes around 551, many historians have accepted the claim of Theoderic and his family to be descendants of an earlier line of Gothic kings, known by the dynastic name of the Amals. This continuity in the ruling house has been seen by some as the principal explanation for the long-term survival of the people. However, it has also been suggested that Theoderic's claim to Amal descent was spurious, and was made to give *de iure* legitimacy to his rule. Perhaps even more convincing are recent arguments to the effect that what was propagandistic and invented was the whole notion of the antiquity of the Amals. Theoderic's family was thus genuinely part of an Amal clan, but this kin-group had no special claim to status amongst the Goths nor had it ever previously exercised royal authority over them.

The problem of sorting fact from fiction in the history of the Ostrogoths is essentially, and unsurprisingly, one of evaluating written sources, in particular the *Getica* or *Gothic History* of

Jordanes, mentioned above. Little is known of this author. It can be said that he was at least partly of Gothic descent, and that he was almost certainly writing around the year 551. By his own statement he intended to produce an abbreviated version of the *Gothic History* in twelve books of his contemporary, the great Roman civil servant Cassiodorus, but as this latter is entirely lost his claim cannot be tested. Arguments have been presented for and against it.[23]

Jordanes's own Gothic descent, despite the highly Romanised cultural context within which he lived and worked, has led historians to believe that his short work must contain genuine Gothic traditions about their own past. Much weight has also been given to the phrase used in an official letter congratulating Cassiodorus on his *Gothic History*, the model for that of Jordanes, that he 'made the Origin of the Goths into Roman History'. In other words that he took the Goths' own oral legends and turned them into written history. However, the sentence in question continues: 'gathering as if into one crown the flowering shoots that were previously dispersed throughout the fields of books'.[24] In other words, it states in the florid rhetoric much loved by the late imperial government and its successors that he had been using literary, which is to say Roman, sources.

In fact most of the texts that underlie Jordanes's account and by implication that of Cassiodorus can be identified. Apart from one royal genealogy there is no element of Gothic origin to be found in the work.[25] Studies of the nature, composition and historical reliability of such genealogies in other early medieval societies must dampen any hope of placing much reliance on the details of this one. All too often such things represent political manifestos of the period in which they were composed, that is to say that of the most recently dated figure to be found in them, with the limits of their historical trustworthiness extending back no more than four or five generations.[26] Interest in establishing continuity in a royal line was far more the product of Roman presuppositions about the working of Germanic societies than it was a reality in those societies. In the first half of the sixth century the Ostrogothic regime ruling in Italy needed a history and a constitutional role for itself that fitted in with the intellectual expectations of the Roman upper classes upon whose good will and co-operation it depended, and who also liked to imagine great family continuities between themselves and the aristocracies of the Republic and Early Empire.

The reality of Ostrogothic history in the second half of the fifth century was rather different, and more impressive. In the aftermath of the collapse of the Hun supremacy north of the Danube, that resulted from the death of Attila and the defeat of his sons by their subject peoples in the battle on the river Nedao in 454, a number of Germanic groups were admitted into the Empire. Amongst them were the followers of a certain Valamer, who were settled in Pannonia in the western Balkans by agreement with the emperor Marcian (450–7). Valamer was killed soon afterwards and his position was taken by Theodemer, who is described as his brother; though this may be yet another piece of subsequent genealogical falsification.

In the same period another group comprised primarily but not exclusively of Goths appears in the eastern Balkans under the leadership of a certain Theoderic Strabo (or 'the Squinter'). This Theoderic was a relative of the wife of the Alan general and Master of the Soldiers Aspar, much of whose military power may have derived from this connection.[27] Yet other prominent Goths had been in imperial service for considerably longer and from before the fall of the Hun empire: Arnegisclus and his son Anagastes held the office of Master of the Soldiers in Thrace in 447 and 469–70 respectively and had personal followings similar to those of Theodemir and Theoderic Strabo.[28]

Anagastes failed to maintain any political influence after his abortive revolt in 470, but the history of the Balkans in the 470s and early 480s may safely be said to consist of the struggle for supremacy between on the one hand Theoderic Strabo and his son Recitach and on the other Theodemer and the latter's son, another Theoderic. The ultimate prize, though, was not an anachronistic and unobtainable unification of all of these Balkan Goths under a single dynasty but the succession to the power of Aspar as Master of the Soldiers in the imperial presence and dominant figure in the eastern court. However, the existence of two rival groups of barbarian soldiery enabled successive emperors to play off their rivalry, until the death of Strabo in 481 and the murder of Recitach in 484 left Theoderic the son of Theodemer in a position to unite both groups.[29] Even then, although given the coveted title of Master of the Soldiers, the imperial government was able to deny him real power by cutting off the supplies of food needed to keep his army together. The strength of the defences of Constantinople meant that the capital could resist a siege in 487, as it had previously in 481 when threatened by Strabo, and in 488 a final solution was reached when Theoderic, abandoning his ambitions in the East, agreed to invade Italy on behalf of the emperor Zeno.[30]

The war between Odovacer and Theoderic, initiated by the latter's invasion of Italy in 489, lasted for some four years, but much of it consisted of a protracted siege of Ravenna. Theoderic made himself master of Italy fairly rapidly but Odovacer held out in the former imperial capital until 493, when a power-sharing agreement was reached between the two. However, once admitted into Ravenna Theoderic promptly murdered Odovacer.[31] Several of the leading Roman supporters of the fallen regime, such as the finance minister Cassiodorus, had already transferred their allegiance to Theoderic. At least one of them, the senator Liberius, refused to take office under the new ruler while their old master still lived.[32] This may merely have hastened the demise of Odovacer, and Liberius certainly felt no qualms about accepting the office of Praetorian Prefect of Italy in 493 from the hands of his murderer. With such adjustments made and Odovacer's military following replaced as the army of Italy by Theoderic's Goths, a new Germanic kingdom came into being.

Ostrogothic Italy is normally viewed as a forcing ground for and a highly successful experiment in Romano-Germanic co-operation and mutual appreciation. To some extent this is true, but it is necessary to appreciate that what is at issue is not the relationship between two equal, autonomous partners. Although subject to the political authority of the Ostrogothic ruler in Ravenna, the upper classes of Roman society, who provided the personnel and expertise for the maintenance of the administration and who set the cultural goals for the new regime, were supremely confident of the values of their society and their standing within it. On the other hand, the Ostrogothic element, probably concentrated in the area to the north of the river Po, was still relatively unformed and malleable.

Their real past extended back no further than the cultural melting pot of the period of the collapse of the Hun empire. The ancestors of those who in Italy in the first half of the sixth century would have thought of themselves as (Ostro)goths may have called themselves Sciri, Rugi, Gepids, and much else besides. It was also in this period that the conversion of many of them to Christianity occurred. Out of the confused conditions that had existed in the Balkans in the 450s, with the combination of Germanic soldiers who had served under Aspar, John the Vandal, Arnegisclus and others with newer groups of Goths admitted to the Empire after the battle on the Nedao, a fusion had only been achieved in the 480s.[33] The Italian conquest of 489–93 further welded together the disparate parts in a common enterprise, and the resulting kingdom gave them the chance to develop a more distinct sense of a common ethnic identity and a common purpose.

The prime movers in these processes, however, were the Romans. From their perspective the followers of Theoderic were ready-made to fill the role in Italy and regions adjacent to it that had been exercised by Odovacer's forces and previously by the various other Germanic units who had constituted the army of the last century of the western Empire. At the same time, though, they recognised that their new military defenders were ethnically distinct from themselves and that their leader was a *rex* or king, that is to say the ruler of a *gens* or people. He could not be a new western emperor in name, even if he could be taught to fill most though not all of the functions of one.

The *gens* itself had to be given a sense of its past, but a past that fitted Roman expectations. Cassiodorus, son of the former finance minister and himself to be Master of the Offices (head of the civil service) and Praetorian Prefect of Italy, set about providing this in his *Gothic History*.[34] As evidenced in its possible abridgement by Jordanes, this was drawn almost entirely from Greek and Roman literary sources and made to cohere to the Roman understanding of the past. For the Romans barbarians had kings: had not Tacitus told them this was the case in his *Germania* of AD 98?[35] So, as well as the people, its ruling dynasty was given a history, not least in a genealogy whose lack of coherence in the pattern of names raises immediate suspicions.

Theoderic himself, though, was no untutored barbarian. He had spent about ten years as a hostage in Constantinople (*c.* 461–71), and had twice succeeded in extorting the title of Master of the Soldiers out of the emperors (476/7–8 and 483–7).[36] He knew about imperial courts, had received a Roman education, and was well aware of the political power of the commanders of armies. He was thus willing and able to co-operate with his Roman officials both in fitting his Gothic following into its appointed niche in Italian society, and in his own person and government fulfilling Roman expectations of continuity.

Odovacer had undertaken some restoration of public buildings, evidenced not least by the provision of a new set of named seats for members of the Senate in the Coliseum, the principal amphitheatre in Rome.[37] Theoderic's programme of new buildings and the restoration of existing ones was far more extensive, and included the erection or repair of aqueducts, public baths, city walls and palaces – these last being centres of administration and not just private residences – in a variety of major Italian cities, including Rome, Ravenna, Verona and Pavia.[38]

Other traditional and politically valuable aspects of late Roman imperial government were revived with the re-establishment of the distribution of free supplies of corn to the poor in the City of Rome, and the holding of very expensive but popular circus games. Probably the most magnificent of these will have been the games held in Rome in 500 to mark Theoderic's visit to the city.[39] So 'bread and circuses' came back, albeit briefly, after an intermission caused by the economic weakness of the last imperial regimes in the West and the Vandal seizure of Africa, the traditional source of grain for the dole.

In his visit to Rome in 500 Theoderic also enjoyed the last western *Adventus*, the formal and elaborate late Roman ceremonial used when an emperor entered a city. A special medal was also issued to commemorate the event.[40] Many of the trappings of the old imperial rule continued in use, and western senators nominated by Theoderic continued to be able to enjoy the honour of the consulship in conjunction with colleagues appointed by the emperor in Constantinople. After the hard times of the years 455–76 the regime of Theoderic – and perhaps that of Odovacer had tried to do the same – offered the upper classes of Roman society a sense of security and continuity with a much valued past.

The material security of Italy was not just imaginary. Odovacer had defended northern Italy with a forward policy beyond the Alps. The defence of the southern part of the province of Norricum had been reorganised and the Rugi, who had been threatening the area, were effectively destroyed in 488.[41] Theoderic went further, by seizing control in 504/5 of the province of Pannonia, although nominally under direct imperial rule, which thus secured the access into Italy from the East. He established a similar *cordon sanitaire* in the West by annexing Provence in 508 after the collapse of the Visigothic kingdom in Gaul.[42] Alliances, cemented by marriages of one of Theoderic's sisters and of one of his daughters to the Thuringian and Burgundian kings respectively, preserved the security of the areas north of the Alps, and a similar link with the Vandal ruler Thrasamund (496–523) helped to ensure good relations with Africa.[43] The annexation of the Visigothic kingdom in Spain in 511 thus seemed to turn the western Mediterranean into 'an Ostrogothic lake'.

The image that is normally presented of Italy under the rule of Theoderic contrasts strongly with that of the Frankish kingdom in Gaul that was being created by his contemporary, the Merovingian king Clovis (481?–511?). The latter appears as a violent, rather unsophisticated but militarily very successful ruler, under whose reign a small kingdom centred on Tournai in modern Belgium was transformed into a realm extending from the Channel to the Pyrenees and the Rhône Valley. Stories of Clovis burying his axe in the head of one of his soldiers who had once thwarted him over the distribution of some loot seem to reinforce the presentation of the Frankish king as a 'barbarous' war lord, far removed from the Roman-imitating ruler of Ravenna.[44]

Yet what we have here is more a conflict in the types of evidence than in their contents. Apart from the near-contemporary *Gothic*

History of Jordanes, itself probably an abridgement of a work written around the year 519, most of the sources for the reign of Theoderic come in the form of contemporary documents: above all the letter collections of Bishop Ennodius of Pavia (d. 521) and of Cassiodorus.[45] The latter is particularly important in that it contains many of the items of official correspondence that he composed for the Ostrogothic kings while holding the offices of Quaestor (a kind of state secretary) in 507–11 and Master of the Offices in 523–7. The collection of letters was issued in 537. Thus, much of the material is both contemporary and official in character (even allowing for the fact that Cassiodorus took careful and self-interested account of the changed political realities of the later 530s in making his selection of which letters to include).

Clovis

In contrast to the quantity and variety of contemporary literary evidence relating to the Ostrogothic kingdom, the principal source that has to be used for the reign of Clovis (481?–511?) in Gaul is the second of the *Ten Books of History* of Bishop Gregory of Tours (d. 594), a work completed a short while before his death.[46] It thus dates from around 100 years after the heyday of Clovis. It is clear that Gregory's information relating to that period is both slight in quantity and was handled by him in a selective and ideologically motivated way.[47] His Clovis, in other words, had a part to play in the didactic purposes for which the great work was written. Scholars have long doubted the truth of the dating he provides for the baptism of Clovis (497), preferring later ones around 503 or 507/8, and other aspects of the reign may be equally unreliable in their chronology.[48] More significant still is the suspicion that Gregory's Clovis is in many respects a model figure, fitting an ideologically preconceived image of the Catholic warrior king.

In this respect there is a strong probability that Gregory deliberately placed the baptism of Clovis prior to his final conflict with the Arian and thus heretical Visigoths, and also passed over indications that the Frankish king had been under some considerable Arian influence himself prior to his finally opting for the Catholic form of Christianity. In fact, there exist some indications, based on contemporary texts, and contradicting Gregory of Tours's version of events, that would make Clovis, as well as one of his sisters, a practising Arian Christian rather than a pagan prior to his conversion to Catholicism.[49] With such flaws at the heart of it, the greatest reservation must be used in approaching any aspect of Gregory's account of Clovis.

Unlike the case of Theoderic, there is very little contemporary material extant that relates to the reign of Clovis. What there is consists of a small number of letters from Bishops Remigius of Reims and Avitus of Vienne and one issued in Clovis's own name.[50] Remigius's letter to Clovis makes it virtually certain that Clovis was a Christian by around the year 486. In fact, once it is appreciated that Gregory's view of Clovis as converting from paganism is untrustworthy then there exist no grounds for believing that he was *ever* a pagan. Nor does his father Childeric I (d. 481) have to be other than a Christian. The fact that he was buried with treasure and in a funeral mound, discovered and excavated in the seventeenth century, is no proof that he was a pagan, when it is recorded that the assuredly Christian Visigothic king Alaric I received such a burial.[51]

In fact, the letters written to, by and about Clovis put him in a typical late Roman context. Remigius refers to him as having taken over the administration of the province of Belgica Secunda, and advises him to listen to the advice that he may be given by the bishops under his rule; an injunction that would hardly make sense if not addressed to a Christian.[52] The letter sent in his name to the bishops of southern Gaul in 507/8 is couched in the formal rhetoric and uses the administrative terminology of late Roman government. There is little to distinguish this text from the kind of administrative document currently being produced in Theoderic's Italy. Its oddity resides in its being unique. It is thus wise to envisage Clovis operating in the area of civil administration within the traditions of late Roman government, and employing in it the northern Gallic equivalents of those Romans who worked for the Ostrogothic king in Ravenna. They were provincials rather than metropolitan senators and their administration was less complex for being that of a province rather than the vestiges of the imperial central government, but when it is appreciated that a fifth century Gallic aristocrat such as Sidonius Apollinaris could produce a letter collection as mannered as that of his Italian counterparts and could also become Prefect of the city of Rome (in 469) the distinction should not be pushed too far.[53]

In military matters Clovis should be seen in the light of the activities of his father Childeric, whose tomb was found near Tournai. Qualitatively, although the ruler of one of the groups of the Salian division of the Franks, Childeric was little different in his career from such late imperial commanders as the Master of the Soldiers Aegidius or Count Paul.[54] He could equally be compared to Odovacer, when the latter was campaigning in the Loire valley with a Saxon army, or to a certain Riotamus, whose services were retained in 469 by the Emperor Anthemius and who commanded an army said to be 12 000 strong, composed of emigrants from Britain recently established in the region around Orléans in the Loire valley.[55]

When to this mix is added the Visigothic kingdom south of the Loire and the Burgundians in the Rhône valley, some of whom were ruled by Gundobad, the former Master of the Soldiers in Italy, it must be appreciated that in the period 461–86 there existed a large number of rivals competing for power in northern Gaul. Moreover, no real qualitative distinction can be made between competitors whose military backing was largely mono-ethnic, that is to say those who would normally be classed as barbarian or Germanic kings, and those who commanded mixed forces of multi-ethnic origin. Indeed, it would be unwise to envisage individuals and groups behaving as if ethnic allegiance was the principal constraint on their actions. Thus, some of those whom by their material culture we would classify as Frisians and Franks appear alongside Jutes and Saxons as settlers in south-eastern Britain at this time.[56] Also, at some point those Franks who followed Childeric transferred their allegiance to Aegidius, forcing their king to take refuge with the Thuringians, probably until the Roman general's death in 464.[57] In other words not all Franks felt it necessary to be attached to Frankish kings, whilst the latter could have in their service those who were not Frankish in origin.

Nor is it necessary to think of the power of the leaders of these competing armies as being exclusively territorial or as being aimed just at the physical expansion of a wholly contiguous area of territory. The centre of Childeric's domain was probably Tournai, where he was buried in 481. But in 469 he is found fighting around Angers and between 476 and 481 he was in negotiation with Odovacer, by then ruler of Italy, over a campaign against the Alamans around the upper Rhine.[58] Neither of these areas was adjacent to his own territories, which were all to the east of the Seine and north of the Aisne.

It was from this base that his son Clovis was to launch a career that put an end to this period of rival 'war lords' in northern Gaul and transformed the political geography of an even larger area. When an alternative based on contemporary sources is lacking it is necessary to fall back, with some reservations, on the chronological structure provided by Gregory of Tours's account, and from this it appears that in 486 Clovis, in his early twenties, launched a successful attack on Soissons, then the administrative centre of an area – the province of Belgica Secunda referred to by Bishop Remigius of Reims – ruled by Syagrius the son of Aegidius.[59] In 491 he made himself master of his mother's people the Thuringians (at least temporarily), and he won a victory over the Alamans, dated by Gregory to 496/7, but possibly identical to one recorded in contemporary sources from Ostrogothic Italy as occurring in 506.[60] The details of the Frankish–Alaman wars of this period are highly obscure. Some fighting certainly took place at this time between the Alamans and another group of Franks, those settled in the Rhineland and known as the Ripuarians, who had kings of their own ruling from Cologne.[61] They achieved a victory over the Alamans at the battle of Tolbiac.[62] What role, if any, Clovis played in this is unknown, but the battle in 506, at which he probably was present, led to the absorption of some of the Alamans into his confederacy, while others put themselves under the protection of Theoderic, who used them to defend the northern approaches to Italy against the threat of Frankish aggression. An intervention around the year 500 in a conflict between the Burgundian kings Gundobad and Godegisel proved less productive, and ultimately led only to the strengthening of the former, who was able to eliminate his brother, despite the latter's Frankish backing.[63]

In 507, a rather better documented conflict arose with another of the main participants in the earlier wars, the Visigothic kingdom. This still had its centre in Toulouse but by this time also controlled much of Spain, and in the north extended up to the Loire valley, where it threatened the expansionary interests of Clovis.[64] The latter also enjoyed the support in this war of the Burgundians, who confronted the Visigothic kingdom across the middle Rhône. In practice, though, this amounted to no more than a jackal-like bid to scavenge Visigothic towns in the lower Rhône valley once the issue had been decided. A battle between Clovis and the Visigoths at Vouillé near Poitiers settled the matter.[65] The Visigothic King Alaric II (484–507) was killed and the Aquitanian provinces of the Visigothic kingdom passed into Clovis's hands in the course of 507 and 508. More might have been gained but for Theoderic's intervention in 508 to secure control of Provence, and in 511 to annexe the whole Visigothic kingdom, then ruled from Narbonne and Barcelona.

Although no dates are given, the final stage of Clovis's career was devoted to the elimination of some of the other small Frankish kingdoms, based on Cologne, Cambrai, Thérouanne (?) and Le Mans (?), most of which were ruled by his own relatives.[66] Gregory of Tours implies that Clovis himself died in 511, though a reference in the *Liber Pontificalis,* the official set of papal biographies, to a gift that he sent to Rome would suggest that he was still alive *c.* 513.[67]

Although seen, above all from the perspective imposed on these events by Gregory of Tours, as being the Frankish conquest of

Gaul, just as Theoderic's triumph over Odovacer may be presented as the Ostrogothic capture of Italy, this is in large measure to muddle consequences with causes. Both Clovis and Theoderic emerged from a range of rival rulers of their respective peoples. Theoderic eliminated his fellow contestants at the beginning of his career: Clovis was able to wait until nearly the end of his. Had Theoderic remained in the Balkans he might have inherited Aspar's role within the imperial government, but an autonomous Ostrogothic kingdom would not have emerged.

In the case of Clovis the issue was not so much emancipation from the attraction exercised by and domination of the Roman state, as a contest between rival claimants – different types of Frank, Saxons, Burgundians, descendants of Roman generals and others – to vacant political authority in Gaul. Clovis's aspirations and achievements were conditioned by pre-existing Roman administrative and military structures in very much the same way as Theoderic's were. In his case, though, the distant imperial government in Constantinople could afford to recognise his authority, by the grant of an honorary consulship in 508, while it remained suspicious of the greater power of the Ostrogothic dominion in Italy. This difference in imperial attitudes helped condition the subsequent history of the Frankish and Ostrogothic kingdoms in the sixth century.

8 The twilight of the West, 518–568?

Prelude: Constantinople and Rome

Imperial attitudes to Clovis's kingdom in Gaul and to Theoderic's in Italy were markedly different. Although Gregory of Tours preserves only a rather enigmatic account of it, Clovis's victory over the Goths in 507 resulted in some form of imperial recognition in the following year. According to Gregory this was the granting of an honorary consulship.[1] Clovis's baptism, and thus his formal renunciation of Arianism, may have also taken place at this time. Although the emperor's grant of some kind of honorific is often associated with the greater acceptability of Clovis once he had become a Catholic, this itself was perhaps little more than a symbol of his determination to break once and for all with the Arian Goths, hitherto the dominant powers in the West. It is hardly accidental that Clovis's breach with the Visigoths followed the first period of overt hostilities between the Empire and the Ostrogoths, or that it should have led to the establishment of diplomatic ties between Constantinople and the Frankish kingdom.

The then emperor, Anastasius I (491–518), could not easily pose as an upholder of religious orthodoxy in that he was himself a Monophysite, and he faced considerable opposition in Constantinople later in his reign, culminating in a riot which nearly overthrew him in 511.[2] However, this was either not known or not understood in the West, where the presence of the Arian Germans loomed much larger than the slightly abstruse Christological controversies of the eastern Church.[3]

Disappointingly little evidence survives relating to the relatively long reign of Anastasius I, but as in his religious affiliation so in many other areas did he reverse the policies of his predecessor Zeno. The latter had largely risen to power thanks to the military backing he could command from his fellow Isaurians, members of a mountain-dwelling people in central Anatolia, whom Leo I had used to break the dominance in Constantinople of the German troops of Aspar.[4] In turn Anastasius, selected in 491 by his predecessor's widow, the daughter of Leo I, had to face the hostility of Zeno's Isaurians. Their insurrection in 492, led by Zeno's brother, took five years to crush.[5]

How far Zeno had been content with the terms of his agreement of 488 made with Theoderic cannot be judged, as he died before the Ostrogothic conquest of Italy was even complete. Anastasius probably renegotiated it around the year 498, though it is not clear exactly what in eastern eyes Theoderic's constitutional position in the West really was. The ambiguity that is palpable in the evidence relating to this question may have been a deliberate feature of the treaty of 498. In that the inhabitants of the eastern Empire continued to call themselves 'Romans' (*Romaioi*), and indeed were to do so right up until 1453, the control of the city of Rome by a barbarian ruler, whatever his formal constitutional ties to the emperor, was bound to seem dishonourable and irksome. The material and political problems of raising and maintaining armies limited the emperor's ability to intervene in the West, as did the Isaurian war of 492–7 and then the renewed war with Persia in Mesopotamia, which lasted from 502 to 505.[6]

Although possibly willing to accept Theoderic as a subordinate ruler in Italy in 498, Anastasius was clearly disturbed by the re-extension of Ostrogothic power into the Balkans in 504, when Sirmium was taken from the Gepids and in 505, when an army of Bulgars, who may have been imperial allies, was defeated on the river Morava. Although he was not able to take direct military action, this led to an imperial naval raid on the coasts of Italy in 508 and, as has been seen, the diplomatic rapprochement with the emergent power of Clovis's Franks.[7] However, Ostrogothic military strength, the death of Clovis and division of his kingdom, and the emperor's own internal problems prevented more overt conflict.

The seizure of power after the death of Anastasius in 518 by Justin, the Commander of the Imperial Guard, led to a further deterioration in relations between the Empire and the Ostrogothic monarchy, though initially this was not obvious.[8] In 519 Justin was willing to share the consulship with Theoderic's son-in-law Eutharic.[9] However, the new emperor, who came from the Balkans and was a native Latin speaker, was far more interested in re-establishing imperial ties with the Roman aristocracy and Church. Thus 519 also marked the restoration of formal relations between the Papacy in Rome and the Patriarchate of Constantinople. Unlike Anastasius, Justin was impeccably orthodox, and at his direction a council in Constantinople condemned the former Patriarch of the city, Acacius, whose theological formulation, known as the *Henoticon* (482) had been an attempt to compromise with the Monophysites, but had served only to infuriate the Roman Church. This long-sought-for condemnation opened the way to the formal reconciliation of the two churches, which had broken off communion in 484.[10]

In turn this development may have led to more frequent and closer dealings with Constantinople on the part of a few of the leading Roman senatorial families, many of whom had eastern branches. A particular case is that of Quintus Aurelius Memmius Symmachus, a descendant of the pagan orator of the late fourth century and himself the author of a lost *Roman History*.[11] Like many of his fellows he had held high office under Odovacer, as Prefect of the City and Consul (485), but had found no difficulty in making an accommodation with the new Ostrogothic regime, from which he acquired the honorific title of Patrician. Two of his daughters were leaders of the aristocratic ascetic movement in Rome in the early sixth century, and another married the senator Anicius Manlius Severinus Boethius, himself the son of another of the great office holders of the age of Odovacer.[12]

Boethius, like Symmachus, enjoyed the highest social status under the rule of Theoderic, gaining the title of Patrician and holding the consulship in 510.[13] In 522 he and his family were particularly honoured by his two sons being nominated joint consuls. This initiative must have come from the Emperor Justin or have been approved by him, but as Boethius himself took over the duties of Master of the Offices, effectively the head of Theoderic's civil service, in the same year his acceptability to the Ostrogothic government could hardly have been in question. However, in 523 he was accused of treason, tried, and executed. The same fate befell his father-in-law Symmachus in 525.

Much debate has been generated by this affair, probably out of all proportion to its real importance.[14] In large part this is due to Boethius's intellectual interests. He had a fine command of Greek, by that time an increasingly unusual attainment in the West, and he had translated a number of the works of Plato and Aristotle into Latin and was engaged upon writing a series of commentaries on them at the time of his death.[15] He also wrote some short theological treatises. While in prison awaiting a painful and lingering form of execution, Boethius composed his most famous and influential work, *On the Consolation of Philosophy*. This used, wrongly, to be interpreted as evidence that he lapsed into paganism in his final days, but is rather to be seen as demonstrating something of the powerful hold that classical literary and philosophical culture could still exercise over the Christian intelligentsia in Rome at this time. The work itself and the circumstances under which it was created combined to immortalise its author and to cast a lasting shadow over the reputation of the government at whose hands he died. Interestingly though, immediately contemporary comment centred more upon the unfairness of the fate of his father-in-law Symmachus, who may only have been guilty by association.[16]

The misleading importance of the Boethius–Symmachus affair lies in the fact that it is held to mark a sudden and unreversed deterioration in the relations between Theoderic and the Senate, and thus more widely in the previously harmonious co-existence of Romans and Goths. There is in fact not a shred of evidence to support such an allegation. It is worth noting, for example, that in 523, when Boethius was arrested, Cassiodorus, who claimed family connection with him, promptly succeeded him as Master of the Offices and held the post until 527.[17]

It is important to appreciate that the accusation of treason levelled against Boethius was made by a fellow senator called Cyprianus, son of Odovacer's finance minister and himself a high official in Theoderic's government. Three other senators testified against Boethius and the trial was conducted by the Prefect of the City of Rome.[18] In his *On the Consolation of Philosophy* Boethius claimed that his accusers had either been bribed or had joined in the attack on him to obtain pardon for offences of which they themselves stood suspected.[19] This may or may not be true. Senators were always in danger of prejudiced charges being made against them by political rivals. What is important, though, is to appreciate that the procedures used were Roman, as were the accusers and judge. The only participation by Theoderic was the carrying out of the sentence.

It is often forgotten how potentially dangerous a senator's life could be, and that the price of office and influence was envy and political malice. For example, the senators Basilius and Praetextatus were accused in 510/11 of engaging in magical practices, a capital crime. Both were tried before the then Prefect of the city and condemned. Although Basilius managed to escape disguised as a monk, he was hunted down, brought back to Rome and burnt alive.[20] No one has bemoaned his fate or seen any deeper political implication in it. Equally unremarked is the fact that Boethius's own grandfather was put to death by the emperor Valentinian III without the benefit of any judicial processes whatsoever.[21]

Related to the execution of Boethius, and equally seen as symptomatic of a violent deterioration in Roman–Gothic relations was the fate of Pope John I (523–6). A member of Boethius's social and intellectual circle, and dedicatee of three of his theological tractates, John was one of the Roman clergy particularly pleased by the re-establishment of religious orthodoxy in Constantinople in 519, and he may have been much less willing to compromise with the Arianism of the Ostrogoths than his immediate papal predecessors.[22] When by 525 Justin I, possibly here advised by his nephew Justinian, began to enforce legal measures against non-orthodox Christians in the empire, be they Monophysites,

Nestorians or Arians, John was sent by Theoderic as his envoy to try to obtain greater toleration for the last group, most of whom were of Gothic origin.

Although the emperor proved surprisingly willing to compromise on most matters, he could not allow those Germans in Constantinople who had recently been forcibly rebaptised as Catholics to lapse back into Arianism, as this implicitly denigrated their Catholic baptism. Theoderic is said in consequence to have regarded the embassy, which returned in 526, as a failure and to have blamed this unfairly on the pope, who had been greatly feted in Constantinople. John was in consequence detained, though not imprisoned, in Ravenna. Unfortunately for Theoderic's later reputation, John died there.[23] However, this did not lead to any breach with the Catholic establishment in Italy or with the Church in Rome, whose choice of a successor to John I was the more diplomatic Felix IV (526–30).[24] As with the execution of Boethius, the demise of John I in these circumstances seems to have left no immediate mark on relations between the Romans and their Ostrogothic rulers. The consequences of the accession of Justin's successor Justinian (527–65) were of far greater significance for the history of Italy.

Justinian I and Africa, 527–533

There has been a tendency amongst historians of the period to treat the reign of Justin I as being no more than the first phase of that of Justinian, but this is to take the propagandistic self-presentation of the latter at face value.[25] Justinian's apologists presented him as the obvious and unchallenged heir to his uncle in the same way that writers of the age of Justin II (565–78) would make him out to be the natural successor to Justinian.[26] In neither case should these political myths be fully believed. In both 527 and 565 other members of the reigning emperor's family stood equally close to the throne.

Until officially selected as co-emperor by Justin I in April 527, Justinian had been one of two competing nephews of the old emperor. The other and ultimately unsuccessful one, Germanus, held the important post of Master of the Soldiers in Thrace throughout Justin's reign, and won a major victory over a Slav confederacy in the course of it.[27] Both nephews were involved in the negotiations to end the Acacian schism and restore links with Rome in 519, and only subsequently did Justinian gain the advantage over his cousin with his appointment as Master of the Soldiers in the Presence in 520.[28] This gave him a commanding position in the palace and capital. When he died in 565 Justinian himself had not even indicated which of his three nephews he favoured. One of them was Justin, the son of Germanus, and currently Master of the Soldiers in Illyricum. However, as in 527, a position in Constantinople proved to be a greater asset, and it was another Justin, holding an office in the imperial palace, who was able to seize power on the death of Justinian.[29]

The changed nature of the imperial role that kept the emperors essentially static in the capital city and not expected to lead their armies in person – a state of affairs that lasted from the reign of Arcadius (395–408) to that of Phocas (602–10) – made them especially vulnerable to currents of unrest in Constantinople. Anastasius was nearly overthrown by an urban riot in 511, as was Justinian in 532. The geography of the city, and the special significance of the Hippodrome, gave the inhabitants of Constantinople a potential hold over the emperor denied to any other group of his subjects.

In the late imperial period every major city of the Roman Empire had a hippodrome, in which chariot and horse races were held. These had become the principal forms of public entertainment for all social classes, and had eclipsed the more bloodthirsty enjoyments of the amphitheatre in the time of the first Christian emperors. Gladiatorial games seem to have ended in the fourth century, and wild beast fights were abolished, in theory at least, in 499.[30] However, such buildings were not just sources of amusement: the hippodrome, as with the amphitheatre before it, was the place in which governors and governed came face to face. Emperors, provincial governors and urban magistrates all attended the principal public performances in their cities, and their formal entrance into the special boxes reserved for them was greeted with well-orchestrated public acclaim. Such acclamations could express both praise and disapproval, and represented the way in which local public opinion could make itself felt to the rulers. The large numbers involved meant that strong criticism and explicit political demands could be expressed with impunity.[31]

It is not easy on the basis of the evidence available to see precisely how the acclamations were orchestrated. A well-placed claque could get a particular slogan started, which if it represented something that individuals currently felt strongly about, might then be taken up by more and more of the crowd. Certainly, local administrators and ultimately the imperial government ignored such demonstrations of public opinion at their peril. For example the official *relationes* or reports that the Prefect of the City of Rome Quintus Aurelius Symmachus sent to the emperors in the year 384 are full of information about such local feelings and demands. The emperors clearly expected to be told about them,

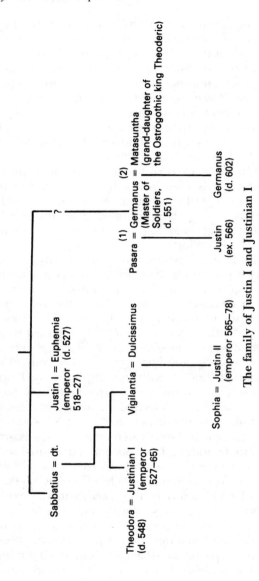

The family of Justin I and Justinian I

and the Prefect's warning that failure to respond could lead to disturbances was amply justified on various occasions in the late fourth century when riots broke out in Rome.[32]

In Constantinople the Hippodrome, which was elaborately adorned by Theodosius I, was immediately adjacent to the imperial palace, and the emperor's box was entered directly from his residence. Thus physically the centre of government and the principal focus for the demonstration of public support for or disapproval of the regime were contiguous. This was formally recognised in the ceremonial of Late Roman imperial ordination. When the new emperor had received the regalia from the hand of the Patriarch in the principal church in Constantinople, he then proceeded to the Hippodrome to be seen by and receive the acclamations of the city populace.[33]

By the sixth century the situation had become complicated by the rise of the circus factions. In the major cities of the eastern Empire racing teams and their supporters had divided into two major groupings or factions, called the Blues and the Greens. Competition and rivalry between the two could on occasion escalate into violence. This provided or articulated an additional element of instability in Late Antique urban life.[34] Normally interfactional rivalry and mutual hostility were so strong that emperors and provincial governors could manipulate them in the interests of preserving local order, but mutual co-operation between the factions could be very threatening to the state.

This is what occurred in the Nika riots of January 532. When some faction members had been condemned to death for crimes about which we are not informed, the Blues and Greens in Constantinople made a truce with each other and instead raided the public jail, freeing their supporters and killing various guards and officials. From this first step into lawlessness, which would inevitably lead to punishment, a more overtly political confrontation with the government was the only escape. The only account of the episode, given in the *History of the Wars* written by Procopius in the 550s, glosses over some of the crucial stages.[35] It seems that rioting and destruction of property in the centre of the city intensified and that Justinian dismissed two of his principal ministers, the Praetorian Prefect John and the Quaestor Tribonian – the latter being the emperor's speech drafter and principal legal adviser – as a sop to the populace.

This move was insufficient to stop the rioting, and the proclamation as emperor of Hypatius, one of the nephews of Anastasius I, by the rioters seems a natural progression in the escalating seriousness of the affair. Hypatius was taken to the Hippodrome for a public proclamation, while only the remonstrances of his wife Theodora prevented Justinian from abandoning the palace and fleeing the city. Some units of the imperial guard appear to have openly supported Hypatius, and others remained neutral. Justinian, however, had the backing of two of his principal generals, Belisarius and Mundus, and a well-timed attack on the rebels in the Hippodrome led to the capture and subsequent execution of Hypatius and his brother, and the massacre of large numbers of the rebellious populace, estimated by Procopius as being in the region of 30 000.

It has been argued that it was these riots that led Justinian into undertaking the campaigns to re-establish direct imperial rule over parts of the former western Roman Empire, that so mark his reign.[36] In such a view, although the emperor had suppressed the actual disturbances, he needed to launch some dramatic undertaking to distract attention in the capital away from the violent suppression of the riots and the underlying tensions that had caused them. For this a military venture, with the prospect of glory and possibly some more tangible economic benefits, would seem to fit the bill.

Tempting as such an idea may be, it should probably be resisted. There are implied chronologies in the narrative of Procopius that show that the expedition against the Vandal kingdom in Africa was in its planning stage prior to the outbreak of the Nika riots. Belisarius, who had been commanding the imperial army in Mesopotamia, was in Constantinople in January of 532 because Justinian had just concluded a war with Persia that had been going on since 527. Furthermore, following Procopius, who was attached to Belisarius's staff during both the Persian war and his subsequent campaigns in the West, Justinian made a treaty with Persia at this point because he wanted to free his hand to launch the expedition against Africa.[37]

It also must be admitted what a risky venture such an expedition could turn out to be; something that Justinian's ministers stressed. In 442, 468, and 470 eastern emperors had, at the behest of western colleagues, launched maritime attacks on the Vandal kingdom in Africa. All had proved to be expensive fiascos, and by the reign of Zeno (474–91) German units of the eastern army were agreeing to serve only on condition that they were not sent to Africa.[38] Although it was possible to send an army by land from Constantinople to Africa – this was to be done in the reverse direction in 602 – any element of surprise would be lost and the problems of communications and logistics would be acute, especially in the final stages across northern Libya. Thus a seaborne operation was the only feasible option for Justinian in 533, as for his predecessors.

This raises the question of the danger of Vandal naval power and so-called Vandal piracy. Much has been made of this, and at one time it was used as a counter to the thesis of the Belgian historian Henri Pirenne, which saw the breaking of the cultural and economic unity of the Mediterranean as being the product of the Arab conquests of the seventh and eight centuries. Other historians, notably N. H. Baynes, argued that this process should be dated earlier, and attributed responsibility for it to Vandal piratical attacks on shipping.[39] Although the actual 'Pirenne Thesis' may now have little to recommend it for other reasons, this at least was an ill-grounded criticism of it. For one thing, it depends on a model of piracy that was essentially that of 'Blackbeard' and the eighteenth century Caribbean.

By their conquest of Roman Africa the Vandal kings became masters of a large amount of shipping: the grain fleet that transported wheat, oil and other commodities to Italy. This could be, and against Rome in 455 was, used to ferry Vandal armies to make descents on selected targets. By this means the Vandals were able to gain control of all of the major islands of the western Mediterranean. Piracy, however, is something else. It is clear, for example, from the wide distribution of the finds of fifth century North African 'red slip ware' pottery in Italy and southern Gaul, that trade continued between these areas at this time and beyond.[40] Cargoes were conveyed from Africa in mercantile vessels, which were 'Vandal' in that the state to which they belonged was the Vandal kingdom centred on Carthage.

With the break up of a single political authority in the western Mediterranean, in other words the Empire, no overall system of law enforcement any longer existed. Thus North African ship owners who cared to, could augment their revenues from trade by making occasional raids on isolated or poorly defended coastal settlements. The kingdom itself on the other hand had been in a state of peace with all its Mediterranean neighbours since 472. The impression that either the Vandal state possessed a specialised war fleet or its vessels were lying in wait to prey on commercial shipping on the high seas needs to be resisted.

What Justinian's expedition had to fear in 533 was not the prospect of a naval battle – none had been fought since Actium in 31 BC – but the threat of the Vandal land forces being able to oppose the disembarkation and thus catch the imperial forces in their most vulnerable position. Here secret diplomacy played a vital part. The Vandal viceroy in Sardinia was persuaded into revolt, and in consequence part of the main Vandal forces had been despatched to regain control of the island at the time when Justinian's army of 15 000 men arrived in Africa in the summer of 533.[41]

The operation, which had been undertaken with considerable trepidation in Constantinople, proved in the outcome to be extraordinarily successful. The landing in the bay of Tunis was unopposed, and the Vandal army was defeated in a battle ten (Roman) miles from Carthage. In the aftermath Belisarius was able to occupy the capital, where the imperial forces were received with great delight by the Roman inhabitants. When the hastily recalled Vandal force that had been sent to Sardinia returned and was reunited with the remnants of the main body, a second battle took place in the vicinity of Carthage in December 533, with the same result as before. The Vandal King Geilamir (530–3) fled inland, and was besieged in a stronghold in Numidia and starved into surrender. He and the remainder of his followers were transported to Constantinople. Geilamir himself was given an estate to which he retired, but the remaining Vandals were absorbed into the ranks of the miscellaneous Germanic federate soldiers in imperial service, and rapidly lost their distinctive ethnic identity. They are not heard of again.[42]

The Vandal war raises obvious questions: why was it undertaken, and how did the outcome prove to be so decisive so rapidly? The argument based on the Nika riots has already been considered and found wanting. Procopius, who was writing later in the reign and thus probably still expressing much of the official view of these events, claimed that Justinian was personally responsible for initiating the plan, although opposed by all of his advisers. However, a bishop from the eastern provinces told the emperor that he had been instructed by God in a vision to reprimand him for having undertaken to liberate the inhabitants of Africa from Arian heretical rule and then losing his nerve.[43] As the principal opponent of the venture was the Praetorian Prefect John the Cappadocian, his removal from office in 532 during the Nika riots may not be entirely coincidental.

Procopius's account of the episode of the vision and his narrative of the events leading up to the war emphasise two interrelated imperial motives for undertaking it, which may well have been those that the government wished to present to the citizens of Constantinople and to the army in 533. The first of these was Justinian's sense of his obligation as emperor to free the orthodox Christians of Africa from subjection to the hostile rule of heretics, and the second was his acute awareness of his imperial responsibility to preserve the correct legal order within all of the territories that had once formed part of the Roman Empire. While these motives fit closely to what else is known of Justinian's high sense of the imperial office, the military realities of the campaign enabled him to draw long-term material reward from its outcome.

The reasons for the rapidity and completeness of the conquest depend largely upon conditions in Africa prior to 533. Of all the Germanic kingdoms that were established in the lands of the western Roman Empire, that of the Vandals was the least stable. Relations between the indigenous inhabitants and the conquerors were almost consistently poor. In the reign of Gaiseric (428–77) many of the principal Roman landowners of Africa either fled or were expelled, though some families were subsequently permitted to return.[44] A persistent attempt was made to break the entrenched power of the Catholic bishops and priests as the ideological and economic leaders of the African communities, and to replace them with a largely Vandal Arian clergy. This was to be achieved by exiling Catholic bishops to other parts of the kingdom, not least to Sardinia, where their local links would be broken. The process could on occasions be violent, though few lives were actually lost.[45]

The considerable intellectual strength of the African Church was hardly weakened by such treatment, and its leading luminary in the century after the death of Augustine, Bishop Fulgentius of Ruspe (d. 527 or 532) spent most of his pontificate in exile, not least in producing a series of masterly anti-Arian writings.[46] One of his contemporaries, Bishop Victor of Vita, wrote around the year 500 an intentionally lurid and propagandistic account of the treatment of the African Catholic clergy and Church at the hands of the Vandals, which was almost certainly intended to be circulated in the East.[47] Imperial awareness of the self-proclaimed sufferings of the Catholics in Africa was strong, and particularly appealing to Justinian, who had intense if idiosyncratic theological interests. However, the position of the Catholic hierarchy in Africa in the sixth century was nothing like as bad as it had been in the fifth. Under Thrasamund (496–523) Arian–Catholic debates had been held, and the exile of bishops had been ended and most of the restrictions on Catholics had been lifted by his successor Hilderic (523–30).[48]

The Vandal monarchy employed an unusual system of royal succession, whereby authority passed through all the surviving members of one generation before moving on to the next. Thus, although Hilderic was the son of Gaiseric's successor Huneric (477–84), the latter had had an elder brother Gento, who died before his father.[49] On the early death of Huneric, who was a particularly active persecutor of the Catholic establishment, the throne passed to his nephews, the sons of Gento, Gunthamund (484–96) and Thrasamund (496–523). Hilderic thus had to wait for 40 years before he could succeed to his father's throne. He also enjoyed the unusual distinction of being the last heir of the former imperial dynasty of Theodosius I, in that his mother was one of the daughters of Valentinian III.[50] Whether it was this heritage or an acute sense of changing political realities that caused it, from his accession Hilderic aligned himself increasingly with the Empire. He also imprisoned his predecessor's widow, the sister of Theoderic the Ostrogoth.[51] The ensuing closening of ties between Carthage and Constantinople led Theoderic in 526 into constructing a fleet to defend Italy against what he saw as the very real threat of an invasion from Africa. In practice this never materialised, and in 530 Hilderic was overthrown by his cousin and intended heir Geilamir.[52] He remained a prisoner and was murdered by Geilamir when the news arrived of the landing of the imperial forces in Africa in 533.[53]

Hilderic's deposition prompted the sending of the imperial letters quoted by Procopius in which Justinian demanded the restoration of the rightful king.[54] The emperor presented himself as the upholder of the will of Gaiseric. Thus, at the diplomatic level at least, the war was initiated by the emperor in order to preserve the rules of succession to the Vandal throne laid down by the founder of their African realm. As Justinian put it in a letter quoted by Procopius he was acting 'to avenge Gaiseric'. He may have hoped to win backing from those in the Vandal kingdom who had supported Hilderic, though in the outcome this does not seem to have been forthcoming. Indeed, the murder of Hilderic by Geilamir was more beneficial to the emperor than to its perpetrator. In the light of the military success the opportunity of eliminating the Vandal kingdom entirely proved irresistible, and with Hilderic dead the emperor was relieved from the obligation of replacing him on the throne, which had been the stated purpose for starting the war.

The speed and completeness of the military success of the expedition commanded by Belisarius is not hard to explain. Popular resentment against Vandal rule was obviously strong, and there were no reservations in the support given to the invaders by the indigenous population, especially in Carthage. More significant still are the implicit indications to be gained from Procopius's narrative that the Vandal presence in Africa was still little more than a military occupation. Although individual Vandals owned estates, the bulk of the people still seem to have lived as garrisoning forces, particularly in Carthage and some of the coastal towns of the Sahel region.

Indicative of this was the speed with which Vandal units were mobilised to meet the unexpected threat and the fact that the Vandal soldiers were accompanied by their wives and families.[55]

They were, thus, not deeply entrenched in local society and after the military defeats of 533/4 could be rounded up and shipped off *en masse* without being able to conduct any effective guerrilla resistance. The impression of a lack of a local Vandal presence is also confirmed by the evidence of a series of land documents written on wood in Numidia during the Vandal period, now known as the Albertini tablets.[56]

The Italian wars, 535–553

Rather different conditions from those encountered in Africa were to be faced by the imperial forces and their commanders in their next undertaking, the invasion of Italy in 535. On the other hand, the ostensible reasons given for the intervention were very similar to those proffered in 533. After the death of Theoderic in 526 the throne had passed to his grandson Athalaric, who was still a child. Effective tutelage and with it control of the government were vested in his mother Amalasuntha, Theoderic's daughter. In practice the administration continued as before. The indefatigable Cassiodorus carried on as Master of the Offices and subsequently became Praetorian Prefect (533–7). Other senators proved equally committed to the existing regime, and one of them, Flavius Maximus, a descendant of the Emperor Petronius Maximus, married an Ostrogothic princess in 535.[57]

The death of Athalaric in 534, however, created a crisis for the Ostrogoths. They had never been ruled by a woman: this would create a gulf of credibility in a kingship that was still articulated primarily as military leadership. Thus Amalasuntha could not take power in her own right. In consequence the throne passed to an elderly nephew of Theoderic called Theodehad (534–6). According to Procopius, Amalasuntha sent for Theodehad to take the throne, but persuaded him first of all to take a secret oath that, while he enjoyed the title, she could continue to exercise the real power in the state.[58]

Frankly this is incredible, although generations of historians have been happy to believe it. Secret oaths are the stuff of rumour, not of accurate reporting. Besides which, Amalasuntha was in a position of considerable weakness. There was no way in which she could have had the royal title herself, and Theodehad was the senior male representative of the dynasty. At best this story is a rationalisation of the conflict that obviously did develop between the principal beneficiary of the former regime and the new king.

The propagandistic *Gothic History* of Jordanes, which aimed at a Romano-Gothic reconciliation, provides a briefer but essentially similar account.[59] According to Jordanes, who does not mention any oath, Amalasuntha selected Theodehad and called him from retirement to take the throne. This made her subsequent imprisonment and murder on his orders acts of peculiar ill-gratitude. Procopius, however, makes it clear that she was killed by some Gothic nobles as an act of vengeance for those of their relatives she had had executed during the reign of her son. These were probably the three military commanders she had had killed around 527.[60] In general both Procopius and Jordanes might well be suspected here of providing us with the official Byzantine version of events. Justinian could only be presented as acting to avenge Amalasuntha, whose killing in any case had not been carried out on the orders of Theodehad, if the latter's own intrinsic rights to the throne were concealed.

In 535, after the death of Amalasuntha, Justinian had by the threat of military intervention nearly intimidated Theodehad into abdicating voluntarily in the emperor's favour.[61] The Gothic king was a committed Romanophile and a scholar, and in 533/4 had contemplated retiring to Constantinople if he could obtain a title and a pension from the emperor. However, while negotiations were still under way the Goths made a pre-emptive strike into Dalmatia and in a battle near Salona killed Mundus, the Master of the Soldiers in Illyricum, and one of the two defenders of Justinian in the Nika riots.[62] Thus war became inevitable.

Unlike the conquest of Vandal Africa, the fighting in Italy was protracted, divisive and highly destructive. Procopius provides a lengthy narrative of the wars, which lasted from 535 to 553, though the final phases had to be covered in the work of his continuator Agathias.[63] The conflict falls into two chronological parts: the first from 535 to 540 and the second from 540 to 553. With recently recovered Africa as a base, the imperial invasion of Italy could be launched, using some of the units that Belisarius had commanded in 533. However, whereas 15 000 men had been sent to Africa, only 7500 were sent into Italy, and this was probably many too few.[64] Moreover, hardly had the invasion been launched when Belisarius had to return to Africa to quell a mutiny amongst the imperial forces, whose pay was, as often happened, grievously in arrears.

The opening stages were almost a 'phoney war'. Despite the trouble in Africa, Belisarius was able to occupy Sicily without resistance and cross to the mainland. Although the Roman inhabitants of Naples refused to admit him and asked him to pass by, he forced his way into the city and then advanced on Rome without meeting any opposition from the Gothic forces.[65] By this time the apparent paralysis of the administration had so incensed the leading Ostrogoths that they rebelled against Theodehad and elected as king one of their own number called Wittigis

(536–40).[66] Theodehad tried to escape to Ravenna, but was over-taken and killed by one of Wittigis's followers who had a grudge against him.

Although the Gothic garrison initially abandoned Rome, Wittigis was subsequently able to besiege Belisarius and the imperial troops in the city for over a year, from the summer of 537. This, however, merely served to tie the Ostrogothic forces down, while a new imperial army some 5000 strong was able to be landed by sea at Naples and eventually to cut Wittigis's line of communication with Ravenna by taking Rimini.[67] The dispirited Goths had to abandon the siege, and the whole war moved northwards. By 539 the position had been entirely reversed, with Belisarius preparing to besiege Wittigis in Ravenna. The blockade of the city, which was almost impregnable, began in 540.

At the same time negotiations were opened for a political settlement with the now thoroughly despondent Gothic regime. Amongst the diplomatic proposals discussed at this time was the restoration of Italy south of the Po to direct imperial rule, while the main area of Ostrogothic settlement north of the river should form a much reduced kingdom under Wittigis.[68] This would have created a valuable military buffer in the north (and would have constituted the best possible outcome for both sides). In the event, though, a rather different solution emerged. Procopius's account is ambiguous, but it appears that Belisarius refused to agree to an Ostrogothic surrender on the terms just mentioned, which had been agreed with the emperor's envoys, but entered instead into secret negotiations of his own. The Gothic leaders, including Wittigis, agreed to surrender Ravenna to him if he would proclaim himself the new emperor of the West. He refused to take such a step until the city was in his hands, and so they surrendered it, thinking he would not fail then to proclaim himself emperor.[69]

This was indeed typical of the kind of risk to be faced from a military commander achieving success in a distant field of action, and may have been behind Justinian's deliberate limiting of the resources of manpower and money that he put into the western campaigns. It is not clear whether Belisarius used this possibility of a revolt on his part just to trick the Ostrogoths into surrender, as in the outcome he did not proclaim himself as emperor, or whether he had intended to do so, but then found that he lacked the support needed amongst his own officers and men, many of whom were highly suspicious of him. In any event the war appeared to have been concluded, with the capture of the Ostrogothic king, the royal treasure and the capital. However, this was nothing like the decisive victory that had been won in Africa in 533/4.

Indeed, although the main royal army had been defeated in the war of 535–40, it was far from a complete conquest. Ostrogothic garrisons and commanders still held most of the principal towns of northern Italy and other tribal units in Ostrogothic service, such as elements of the Rugi and Gepids, were still active.[70] After the cessation of fighting in 540 something of an impasse followed, while a permanent political settlement was evolved. However, Justinian was now faced by new problems on the eastern frontiers; paradoxically these were the result of the Italian war. In 539/40, facing military defeat, Wittigis had appealed to the Persian Shah Khusro I for help: in other words for the opening of a second front in Mesopotamia.[71] This indeed is what then happened, very possibly because the Persians feared that a Roman Empire rejuvenated by the military and economic resources obtained from the western reconquests would soon turn its aggression eastwards.

Thus in the summer of 540 Khusro broke the 'Endless Peace' signed in 532 and invaded Mesopotamia, marching unopposed by an imperial army as far as Antioch, which he took and sacked. He then carried off the surviving inhabitants back into Persia. In consequence, and in dire need of trained military manpower, Justinian ordered Belisarius to return from Italy and to bring Wittigis and the Ostrogoths captured in Ravenna with him, doubtless to reinforce the imperial armies, who in this period were made up almost exclusively of Germanic and other 'barbarian' units. Any idea of a more firmly based political settlement in Italy was thus abandoned. The leaders of the Ostrogoths in northern Italy gathered in Pavia, elected as king one of their number called Ildebad (540–1), and after another failed attempt to persuade the departing Belisarius to proclaim himself emperor of the West, renewed the war.[72]

The ensuing struggle, largely fought under the direction of Ildebad's nephew Baduila (541–52) was protracted and bloody, and required ever increasing numbers of imperial soldiers to be sent into Italy. Belisarius returned to resume command, but failed to achieve the successes of the 530s. He was eventually superseded by a eunuch and former imperial treasurer called Narses, under whose direction the war was concluded. In 552 Baduila (called Totila in Procopius) died after a major defeat at the battle of *Busta Gallorum*, and his successor Teias met the same fate later in the same year in a final confrontation near Mt Vesuvius.[73]

By this stage the operations in Italy were involving other Germanic peoples from north of the Alps, notably the Franks and Lombards, who were drawn into the conflict, which they exploited in their own interests. The Franks, who first intervened under their King Theudebert I (533–48), looted Milan in 539 and established a hold over Venetia and other regions of northern Italy, from which they were only dislodged in the reign of his son Theudebald (548–55).[74] In 568 the Lombards, who had been admitted into Pannonia by Justinian during the Gothic wars, invaded Italy and established a kingdom of their own in the north, based on Pavia, which was to last until 774. Other Lombard detachments soon after established semi-independent duchies centred on Spoleto and Benevento in the centre and south of Italy.[75]

The Empire retained control of Rome and Ravenna and a network of other towns and fortresses, but much of what had taken twenty years of warfare to win was lost to the Lombards in less than five. At the same time the cost and military effort involved in the Italian wars prevented any further expansion of direct imperial rule in the West. An intervention in a civil war in Spain secured for Justinian only a small strip of coast in the south-east of the peninsula, and no further efforts were made to expand this imperial enclave.[76] At best this created a further defence for the reconquered regions of Africa, and it may be that by 551 the emperor's ambitions extended no further.

For Italy the costs of the war were incalculable. It is clear enough from various anecdotes in Procopius that many of the Roman aristocracy were less than enthusiastic about their imperial 'liberators'. A number of prominent senators, including Flavius Maximus and Pope Silverius, were expelled from Rome by Belisarius prior to the Ostrogothic siege.[77] On the other hand, the Goths became equally suspicious of them as collaborators with the invaders. Wittigis executed all of the senators whom he was holding in Ravenna in 537.[78]

By 552 attitudes had become so extreme that Teias massacred 300 Roman senatorial children he was keeping as hostages, and many Roman adults, again including Flavius Maximus, whose life illustrates so many of the changing aspects of mid-sixth century Italian history, were killed out of hand by the Goths at this time.[79] Although both quantitatively and qualitatively the evidence is less good from this point onwards, the great families of Rome disappear from the historical record – as do the Ostrogoths – with the conclusion of these wars. Archaeological evidence also supports a view of widespread destruction and dislocation of the great villa economy in this period.[80]

The balance sheet on Justinian's western ventures is hard to draw up, even from a purely Constantinopolitan viewpoint. The cost and returns of the African war were very different from those of the Italian. The turning point was undoubtedly the year 540.

Had the terms offered to Wittigis and the Ostrogoths by the emperor at that time been implemented, a relatively rapid war with limited involvement of men and money would have produced good material results in terms of re-established imperial control of most of Italy and its tax revenues, while the problems of defence against peoples beyond the Alps would have been solved by the presence of the truncated Gothic kingdom in the north. However, for whatever reasons, Belisarius prevented that from occurring, and then failed to take the western imperial title himself, which might have been the next best thing. The great Persian raid of the same year entirely altered Justinian's sense of priorities, and the Italian situation was left without any sensible solution. Thirteen more years of bitter fighting merely served to leave an enfeebled Italy liable to have its taxes drained away to Constantinople in return for a military defence that was too weak to stop the Lombards from taking most of what the Empire had spent two decades fighting for.

9 Constantinople, Persia and the Arabs

The Roman Empire and Iran

The violent swings of fortune, from the Roman point of view, on their eastern frontiers in the late third and fourth centuries gave way to a period of greater stability in the fifth. After Julian's disastrous invasion of Persia and Jovian's ignominious retreat and treaty, periods of conflict between the two empires became less frequent and the scale of operations more restricted. In general, apart from the opening and the closing phases of the Sassanian Empire, in the mid-third and early seventh centuries, Persian ambitions were confined to far more limited goals than the recreation of the old Achaemenid domination of the eastern Mediterranean. In that hardly any literary source material survives from the Sassanian period, it is necessary to recreate their aims and objectives from the evidence of what they tried to achieve and what a small number of authors writing within the Roman Empire said about them.[1]

Simply put, it could be said that Persian concerns were directed almost exclusively towards the achieving of minor adjustments on the common frontiers with Rome, and occasionally using the threat of war and sometimes its practice to extort regular payments from their neighbour as the price of peace. The principal area of contact between the two empires was in Mesopotamia, and the control of certain key fortress towns in this region became the basic cause and focus of conflict. More complex were the problems to the north in the mountainous areas of eastern Anatolia. Here the kingdom of Armenia existed as a buffer state between the two rival powers. The conversion of the Armenians to Christianity at the very beginning of the fourth century – prior indeed to the conversion of Constantine – brought the kingdom more firmly into the Roman cultural zone. This in turn resulted in the Persians trying to exercise a tighter control over it, and at various times trying to impose their own Zoroastrian religion on the inhabitants. Armenian revolts in defence of their indigenous Christianity could not fail to attract Roman support, and this became a complicating factor in the 'superpower' diplomacy of the two empires.[2]

Except when provoked beyond a certain level, as in 282–3, 297–8 and 363, Roman responses to Persian aggression tended to be low-key and limited to reinforcing the defence of threatened frontiers. Pitched battles between Roman and Persian armies were exceedingly rare, and none were in any sense decisive. In general Persian ability to maintain a state of active but restricted aggression was greater than Roman interest in combating it militarily. As the economic and political problems of keeping large armies in the field grew, so it became cheaper and easier for the Roman Empire to buy peace from the Persian.

The Sassanians recognised Rome as a fellow, if lesser, civilised power, and in diplomatic exchanges could compare the two empires to the Sun (Persia) and the Moon (Rome); both eternal and stable, if of two different orders of brightness and importance.[3] Roman attitudes were culturally less accommodating, and the Persians were to them as barbarous as the Germans, but even so the power of Persia induced in practice a grudging respect, and the presence of the Persian empire on the eastern frontiers was felt to be preferable to that of other less tractable neighbours.[4] Thus when the Persian Shah Peroz (457–84) was taken prisoner by the Hephthalite nomads it was the emperor Zeno (474–91) who paid the ransom for his release.[5]

In the fifth century both empires shared common problems and a common threat. This was the pressure exerted on their northern frontiers by large-scale nomad confederacies. The difficulties the Romans had with the Huns were matched by those the Persians faced from the Hephthalites.[6] In neither case were the nomads interested in acquiring territory, but they did intend to extort tribute, and in the process were able to exercise a measure of political constraint on their victims. The regime of Theodosius II proved generally pliant to Hun demands, and the western half of the Roman empire became militarily dependent on them, to its own great detriment. In Persia the Shah Peroz made two unsuccessful attempts to break the power of the Hephthalites in war, in the second one of which he was killed. The Hephthalites were subsequently able to impose his son Kavad I (488–97, 499–531), who had been a hostage with them, as their candidate for the throne in 488, and restored him in 499 after he had been deposed by his brother.[7]

According to the Syrian chronicler Zachariah of Mitylene, writing in 569, the Persians blamed the Hephthalite menace and the disaster that befell Peroz on the Romans, and this led to renewed war in 502.[8] However, the contemporary *Chronicle of Joshua the Stylite* of 507 makes it clear that the Persians, both under Valkas (484–8) and Kavad I, were trying to extort money from Rome in order to pay the tribute owed to the Hephthalites.[9] In practice the need to organise an effective military response to the Hephthalites, finally achieved in the reign of Kavad's son Khusro I, and to ensure Persian control of vulnerable frontiers, led to increasing conflict between the two empires in the sixth century.

Minor adjustments in control of the principal fortresses in Mesopotamia continued to occur, but more intensive fighting took place in Armenia under the Shah Khusro I (531–75), as the Persians tried to draw this region more firmly into their cultural orbit. Further north still the small region of Lazica, south-west of the Caucasus mountains, saw the most protracted warfare of all, that continued even when truces had been agreed in other zones of conflict.[10] The reason for this would seem to be the potential strategic significance of this otherwise unimportant area. The Persians feared that if the Romans controlled it they could allow nomads from the north of the mountains to come through the passes and raid the vital agricultural areas south of the Caspian. On the other hand, control of Lazica would give the Persians access to the Black Sea, and thus opportunities for naval raids on the north coast of Asia Minor and even down the Bosphorus to Constantinople.

Although the survival of the evidence is poor, and reliance has to be placed on generally unsympathetic Roman reports of developments inside Persia, there are indications that a series of major ideological and economic changes was taking place within the Sassanian Empire in the course of the sixth century. The reign of Kavad I coincided with the rise of the Mazdakite movement, whose Manichaean-inspired doctrines also included the forcible imposition of a communal ownership of property. Mazdak and his followers were encouraged by the shah, not least as a means of breaking the power of the great aristocracy, many of whom claimed descent from former independent regional kings, and a number of outrages were perpetrated against them with the ruler's support. The Mazdakites were eventually suppressed late in the reign. Whatever their role in helping achieve it, it is notable that a decisive change in the balance of power between the shahs and the great families was brought about under Kavad I and Khusro I.[11]

This was also manifested in the greater prominence of a lesser, more locally based rank of nobles called the *dihqans*. These were more directly linked to and subservient to the central government, which at the same time became increasingly bureaucratised and effective.[12] A new taxation system, modelled on that of the Roman Empire, was introduced under Khusro I. A substantial programme of urban construction was inaugurated in Mesopotamia. These new towns became centres of royal administration and were free of the control of the old aristocratic families. They also required the presence of specialised population, as the lifestyle and economic activities of towns require particular skills. In part this could be provided by the wholesale transportation of town dwellers captured in the wars with Rome. Thus the population of Antioch carried off by Khusro in 540 was resettled by him in a new foundation grandly called 'The Better Antioch of Khusro'.[13]

The problems the Persians faced with the Hephthalites beyond the river Oxus and with other nomads north of the Caucasus, as in the case of Rome's dealings with the Huns, were complex and affected the Sassanian regime in a variety of ways. On the one hand the threat of the Hephthalites and their backing for his rule was valuable for Kavad I in his confrontations with dynastic rivals and with the nobility. They also provided him, again very much like the Huns in the West, with manpower to use in his war against Rome, itself intended to extort the money needed to pay the Hephthalites. On the other hand such allies were neither reliable nor easy to control, and the humiliations suffered under the Shah Peroz continued to rankle. The shifts of nomad populations in Central Asia and the inability of the Sassanian Empire to confront the Hephthalites militarily led to greater Persian diplomatic involvement with other confederations. Ultimately they were able to use the Turks to destroy the power of the Hephthalites.[14] In the same way the Emperor Justinian manipulated the rivalries between a number of confederacies north of the Black Sea to try to prevent a dominant nomad power emerging on the frontiers of the Roman Empire.[15]

Such Great Power involvements in the fragile balances between the various nomad groups to the north of their respective empires bred mutual suspicion. At the same time the Sassanians were trying to make additional profits out of the Romans by closing their direct access to eastern trade and forcing them to purchase such luxuries as silk and spices from state controlled Persian intermediaries. One unanticipated by-product of this was to be the creation of an imperial silk industry in Syria, when in 552 the emperor Justinian agreed to the proposal of some monks that they smuggle some silkworms out of the oases of Sogdia in Central Asia. Hitherto the Chinese had preserved a monopoly in the manufacture of silk by preventing the export of these essential creatures from their territories and dominions.[16]

Even if in this area the Persian economic blockade, which may in part have been dictated by fear of the growth of Roman economic and political influence on the peoples of Central Asia, was by-passed, the attempts of the two empires to spread their spheres of cultural domination and exclude each other reached into further and further regions. In the year 525 Dhu Nuwas, the ruler of the Yemen, converted to Judaism, and in consequence began to persecute the minority Christian population in his kingdom. This in due course led the leading Christian power in the southern Red Sea area, the Axumite kingdom of Ethiopia, to intervene, over-throw Dhu Nuwas and establish a protectorate over the Yemen.[17] This was done with the connivance and support of the greatest of all the Christian rulers, the emperor in Constantinople.

Even when the Ethiopian governor Abraha broke away from his allegiance to Axum and created an independent kingdom of his own in the Yemen he continued to enjoy Roman support. The Yemen was in fact a vital economic entrepôt, receiving a variety of goods by sea and then sending them on by camel caravan up the Red Sea littoral. Amongst the items of trade that were of particular interest to the Romans was incense, produced in the south-east corner of the Arabian peninsula, and used daily in all the churches of Christendom. Spices, precious stones and other luxuries were also traded across the Indian Ocean and up the coast of East Africa. All in all, the Christian kingdom of the Yemen under Abraha (*c.* 535–70) was a vital cultural and economic outpost of the Roman Empire.[18] This made the Sassanians more determined to block this Roman egress onto the Indian Ocean, and in 575 a Persian expedition conquered the kingdom and annexed it.

At the same time as this struggle for cultural dominance was being played out in the south of Arabia, more active Roman and Persian interference was taking place with the tribes of northern Arabia. For several centuries the two empires had maintained close links with the Arab tribes established in the southern fringes of Mesopotamia. The regular payments of subsidies to the rulers of these tribes made them into defenders of the vulnerable desert frontiers of the empires and the irregular troops who fought for their masters against the rival empire. The two great Arab con-federacies of the Lakhmids and the Ghassanids benefited in parti-cular from this situation and became the principal desert allies of the Persians and the Romans respectively. Neither, however, was entirely reliable as far as their masters were concerned. Some of the Lakhmids were Nestorian Christians and in the mid-sixth century were receiving subsidies from the Emperor Justinian. The Romans' formal allies, the Ghassanids, were largely Christian, but of the heretical Monophysite kind.[19]

The intensification of conflict between the two empires and their respective doubts about their Arab allies led around the turn of the century to ill-judged attempts to force the latter into closer affiliation with their masters. The Persians attempted to impose Zoroastrianism on the Lakhmids and the persecution of

Monophysites in the Empire under the Emperors Maurice (582–602) and Heraclius (610–41) led to the detention in Constantinople of successive Ghassanid leaders.[20] In practice the effect was merely to alienate the two groups from their traditional paymasters and in consequence leave the Mesopotamian frontiers of the two empires vulnerable to an unlooked-for threat from the desert.

Before this actually manifested itself the military conflict in the Near East attained to proportions quite unprecedented since the third century. In 590 Hormizd IV, the son of Khusro I, was overthrown by a noble coup and replaced by Vahram VI, the first non-Sassanian ruler, whose prestige had been created by a victory over a Turkish invasion. Hormizd IV's heir Khusro fled to the emperor Maurice, who was able to intervene in 591, expel Vahram, and restore Sassanian rule in the person of Khusro II (591–628).[21] The price for this was a considerable readjustment of the frontiers in Armenia and Mesopotamia in Rome's favour.

Although this brought the endemic warfare between the two empires that had continued throughout the 570s and 580s to a satisfactory conclusion from the Roman point of view, and led to an eleven-year period of peace, the territorial settlement was a considerable embarrassment to the regime of the new shah. The overthrow of the Emperor Maurice in 602 by a military insurrection in the army in the Balkans gave Khusro the chance to renew war, as well as to pose as the avenger of his benefactor.[22] The resumed hostilities took the usual form during the reign of the emperor Phocas (602–10), with neither side making significant advances. However, the overthrow of Phocas by an expedition launched by the governor of Africa and his replacement as emperor by the latter's son Heraclius (610–41) was followed by a most extraordinary military collapse and political disintegration on the part of the Roman state.

Modern historians of the eastern Roman or Byzantine Empire have tended to take the propagandistic self-image of the Heraclian regime at face value, but it is notable that it was under his rule that the Roman defences suddenly crumbled, on two fronts simultaneously. In 610 a Persian army was able to reoccupy Armenia, all of which had been ceded to Rome in 591. The Persians were then able to march across Asia Minor to Chalcedon on the opposite shore of the Sea of Marmora from Constantinople. In 611 Caesarea in Cappadocia, the principal city in the centre of Asia Minor, fell to them as well. On the Mesopotamian frontier even greater Sassanian successes were to be recorded. In 611 they captured Antioch and in 614 took Jerusalem. There exists a short but vivid contemporary account of the siege of Jerusalem, written by Antiochos Strategos, which reports that many Christians were massacred by the Persians, abetted by the local Jewish community, and numerous churches were looted and destroyed. In 616 Egypt was invaded and occupied without significant resistance, and in the same year a Persian army reappeared at Chalcedon, divided from the Roman capital only by the waters of the Sea of Marmora and the Bosphorus. The eastern provinces of the Empire were lost and all of Asia Minor open to Persian penetration at will.[23]

What caused this dramatic or, as it was viewed by some, apocalyptic collapse of the Roman Empire's eastern defences is hard to tell. Blame has been placed upon internal disorder within the main cities of the Empire, in every one of which factional violence centred upon the rivalry of 'the Greens and the Blues', the two great divisions into which chariot-racing teams and their supporters had separated themselves. Arguments exist as to the degree to which, if at all, these divisions also mirror other political and religious cleavages in the society.[24] Certainly the emperors from Justinian I onwards found it useful to lend their support to one or other of the two factions, and in turn receive some more personal degree of loyalty from their adherents. Phocas had been given strong backing by the Blues, and in consequence the Greens turned out for Heraclius in the coup of 610.[25]

However, attempts to link the factions to the rivalry between Orthodox and Monophysite Christians are less convincing, and the root causes of these divisions within the major cities, which polarised all classes and sectors of society, have never been satisfactorily analysed. Indeed the search for a unitary solution seems to be something of a Chimera, in that the causes supported by and the issues dividing the two factions appear to vary from city to city, although the factional labels under which the divisions articulated themselves remained constant across the Empire.

Although not capable of being correlated with the circus factions and the violence that these spawned, the religious divide in East Roman or Byzantine society at this time was another cause of instability and political disaffection. No statistical information exists, but it seems reasonably clear that the majority of the indigenous populations of the eastern provinces of the Roman Empire adhered to the various branches of the Monophysite church. Under Justinian I, whose wife Theodora was a Monophysite, a large measure of official toleration was extended towards them, but Maurice resumed what were regarded as persecuting practices.[26] These amounted mainly to the deposition and exile of bishops who propounded Monophysite doctrines, but as they enjoyed a large degree of popular support in their dioceses this could alienate their adherents from the central government. As the majority populations in the eastern provinces also spoke Syriac (Syria and Palestine) or Coptic (Egypt) rather than the Greek of the government and its officials, a further dimension of cultural alienation was introduced. However, it is important not to take this too far and see in these deeply felt theological distinctions a covering for anachronistic incipient nationalism.[27]

Whatever the contributory causes of the collapse, the military state of the eastern Roman Empire looked extraordinarily parlous for most of the first quarter of the seventh century. The eastern provinces and much of inland Asia Minor had been lost to the Persians. At the same time the Slavs, who coming from across the Danube had penetrated deep into the Balkans in the 540s and 550s, were thus gaining an ever increasing grip on the countryside of the only remaining large area of territory in imperial hands.[28] Behind them the nomad confederacy of the Avars, which had come to dominate the area north of the Danube in the late sixth century, became increasingly menacing. In 626 both the major military threats to the Empire were nearly able to combine, quite possibly as the product of Sassanian diplomacy. A large Avar force, with Slav contingents, besieged Constantinople, while a Persian army once again made its way across Asia Minor to the shores of the Bosphorus with the intention of carrying out joint action against the imperial capital. In the event, the Roman navy was able to prevent the Persians from crossing and, lacking the technology that the Sassanian forces could provide, the Avars failed to make any impression on the defences of the city and eventually had to lift the siege.[29]

It is particularly frustrating that when so much of the warfare and diplomacy of the sixth century is so well recorded in the works of Procopius and his two continuators, Agathias and Menander Protector, and in the *History* of Theophylact Simocatta (which covers the years 582 to 603), the far more dramatic campaigning of the early seventh century is almost totally hidden from sight. For not only was the original collapse of the Roman position in the East both rapid and far-reaching, but the imperial recovery was even more extraordinary. Yet of the details of it we know frustratingly little, and have to rely on just a few hints in the panegyric poems on the Emperor Heraclius composed by George of Pisidia, and some of the final sections of the comparatively brief *Paschal Chronicle*.[30]

It seems that in the 620s Heraclius effectively left his capital to fend for itself, largely under the direction of its bishop, Sergius. The emperor himself from 622 was campaigning in Asia Minor and Armenia, and may have at this time introduced a series of *ad hoc* reforms in the raising and maintaining of troops that developed into the classic but highly controversial system of military 'Themes' of the middle period of the Byzantine Empire (eighth to twelfth centuries). Whatever the truth of this, his campaigning in eastern Asia Minor enabled him in 628 to pass behind the main Persian armies operating further west and make an unchecked descent on the Persian capital of Ctesiphon in Mesopotamia. At the approach of the imperial forces to the vulnerable city a palace coup occurred. Khusro II was deposed and murdered by one of his sons, who promptly made a treaty of peace with Heraclius.[31] Thus, although the Persian armies were not confronted directly, the Roman emperor had gained the strategic advantage that was crucial and enabled him to win a victory that would have been almost impossible if the war had been conducted as an attempt to regain the lost territories by frontal assault.

The treaty involved the restoration of the frontiers of the Empire to the positions in which they had been prior to the outbreak of the war. Not surprisingly, the still undefeated Persian armies were in little mood to tolerate the regime that had accepted this humiliation. The new Shah Kavad II was himself murdered the same year and a period of intense political instability followed in the heart of the Persian empire. At least eight different shahs ruled in the years 628 to 632.[32] All met violent ends and the Sassanian dynasty came to an end. One of these ephemeral rulers, previously one of the principal Persian generals in the conquered Roman provinces, completed the terms of the treaty with Heraclius and returned the relic of the 'True Cross', discovered originally by Helena, the mother of Constantine the Great, and carried off to Ctesiphon after the capture of Jerusalem in 614. It was restored to Jerusalem by Heraclius with great ceremony in 630.[33] Within fifteen years it was gone for ever.

Islam and the Arab conquests

In the Great Power rivalry of Rome and Persia in the sixth and early seventh centuries to some extent trade may have 'followed the flag', but so to an even greater degree had religion. To a hitherto unprecedented degree religious affiliation was made concomitant with political allegiance. Deviation and pockets of unorthodoxy were looked upon askance. Christian missionary activity was actively promoted by the emperors to spread Roman cultural influence both northwards into the steppes and southwards down the Nile into Nubia. At the same time the Persians made repeated efforts to impose Zoroastrianism on Armenia.[34] Subtly, too, it looks as if Khusro II made attempts to portray himself as being sympathetic to the Monophysite Christians at a

The Near East in the sixth century

time when they were being oppressed by their own government in Constantinople.[35]

Thus this period saw something of a religious ferment. Nor were Christianity in its various forms and Zoroastrianism alone in competing for more adherents. As has been mentioned, the Arab King Dhu Nuwas converted to Judaism. Other references indicate the existence of whole tribes practising Judaism in Arabia in the course of the sixth century and the first appearance of the Jewish Falashas in Ethiopia should probably be dated to this period. As with the later conversion of the Khazars in Central Asia these pieces of evidence relate to active proselytising and conversion to Judaism on the part of individuals and groups who

were not Jews by descent.[36] Although this is a process that the subsequent history of Judaism and the implications of some modern
political arguments require to be denied and the phenomenon
explained by reference to 'lost tribes' and other historically untenable claims, the evidence of a considerable expansion in the
numbers of adherents of Judaism in Arabia and the horn of Africa
at this time cannot be ignored.

This is the background to probably the most dramatic and
far-ranging set of changes that were to affect the Near East, the
whole Mediterranean basin and much of western Europe in the
period between the break up of the Roman Empire in the fifth
century and the discovery of the 'New World' in the fifteenth.
This was the emergence of Islam and the creation of the Arab
Empire that resulted from it.

For a complex process of such significance, whose opening
stages extended over a not inconsiderable period of time, the
evidential basis upon which it may be studied is truly appalling.
It falls into two distinct and by no means mutually compatible
halves. On the one hand there are those texts in Arabic relating
to the life and teaching of the Prophet Muhammad, which represent the foundations upon which the orthodox Muslim presentation of these events rests. On the other, there exists a variety
of works that are non-Islamic in origin and which, having little
to say about the incubatory period of the new religion and being
far from sympathetic to its teaching, relate principally to various
aspects of the military conquests carried out by the Prophet's
followers in the period after his death.[37]

The traditional and long accepted account of the outline of
Muhammad's life and the genesis of his revelation comes from a
genre of biographies of the Prophet that became popular from the
eighth century onwards. The most substantial and authoritative of
these is the work of Ibn Ishaq (d. 768), which only survives in the
expanded version of it prepared by Ibn Hisham (d. 833).[38] It has
been argued that this material, dating from 150 years after the
death of the Prophet, is contaminated by later pious traditions and
the distortions of eighth century orthodoxy. In other words, the
reader should no more expect to find objective biographical reporting in this and comparable works than he would in the Gospels.

For the authoritative teaching of Muhammad the primary source
has to be the compilation of the revelations he received from the
Archangel, known as the *Qu'ran*. This, however, is traditionally said
to have been given its canonical form in the reign of the Caliph, or
Successor to the Prophet, 'Uthman (644–56).[39] The earliest independent testimony to its existence comes from the end of the
seventh century. According to the traditional version of its genesis,

it was put together from a variety of scraps of writing, enscribed on animal bones and other forms of record. In its present form the *Qu'ran* consists of a series of individual revelations, grouped together according to their size, with the shortest coming last. The contents are thus not organised on a chronological basis and they are exclusively theological and legal in character. The individual sections or *Suras* contain a mixture of different types of material within a single revelation.

Thus to take as an example the *Sura* called 'The Table', it begins with a series of commandments relating to food, listing what is forbidden. There follows a section relating to the ritual procedures necessary before prayer. Then come some lengthy passages that recast biblical texts in order to present the Jewish and Christian messages as partial revelations awaiting their fulfilment in that of Muhammad. This section also contains injunctions as to the treatment of Jews and Christians. The *Sura* then returns to laying down legal rules, forbidding Muslims from drinking wine and from 'arrow-shuffling' – a form of divination – and it concludes with another long section on the role of Muhammad as the Messenger of God, intertwined with depictions of Jesus as a similar if lesser Messenger. The whole is cast in a diction that could fairly be called poetic, despite the injunctive nature of some of the contents. Modern scholarship, working on clues in the text, has assigned the composition of this *Sura* to the final period of Muhammad's life.[40] Some scholars would, however, as with the biographical texts, warn of the danger of interpolation and the danger of rewriting to validate teachings and practices that postdated the time of the Prophet.

The alternative interpretations of the life and message of Muhammad, that have been advanced largely on the basis of trying to put the Arab sources to one side and to effect a reconstruction on the strength of the other body of evidence that is non-Islamic in origin, have generally failed to convince. Partly this must be due to the equally flawed nature of much of that corpus of evidence. Few of the limited number of extant texts from the Byzantine Empire and the eastern Mediterranean that relate to this period are genuinely contemporary, or have not themselves undergone textual transmissions as extensive and suspect as those of the Arab works. Thus the Chronicle written in Greek and/or Coptic around 690 by the Egyptian Bishop John of Nikiu only survives in two seventeenth and eighteenth century manuscripts of an Amharic translation made in 1602 of a lost Arabic translation of the equally lost original.[41]

At best, then, it is as necessary to be as cautious about the Arabic traditions as about the non-Arabic and vice versa. But in such a state of critical impasse it must suffice for now to give the 'ortho-dox' account of the Prophet's life and teaching, while drawing attention to the very serious evidential problems with which it is surrounded.[42] Thus the birth of Muhammad is placed around the year 570. He was a minor member of the Quraysh, the dominant tribe in and around the town of Mecca in the Hijaz, the coastal plain of western Arabia. Mecca was basically a cult site, in which a number of divinities were venerated, especially a sun god in the form of a large meteorite, whose shrine was the rectangular struct-ure known as the *Kaaba*.

Muhammad's early career was as the manager of the camel caravans of a wealthy widow called Khadija, whom he was in due course to marry. Around the year 610 he experienced his first vision or revelation, in which the Archangel Gabriel appeared to him. Despite his initial reservations he continued to have these experiences and from them developed a coherent body of doctrine and religious practice, with which he began to attract followers. The basic theological tenet was the Oneness of God, the affirma-tion of which became the first and most important of the five 'Pillars of Islam', and to which was tied the acceptance of Muhammad's role as the prophet or Messenger of God. The others were concerned with religious observance and included the requirement to pray five times daily at stipulated times, to fast annually during daylight in the month of Ramadan, to give a fixed proportion of income in alms for the poor and, a late addition, to attempt to make the pilgrimage to Mecca at least once in a lifetime.[43]

This final element was doubtless a sop to the Meccans, probably to be dated to the period after Muhammad's conquest of the town, traditionally said to be in the year 630. Initially, however, his new religious message, while attracting a growing body of adherents, was viewed with considerable alarm by the leaders of the Meccan community, who regarded it as a threat to the continued well-being of the town and its dominant tribe. Mecca's position as a cult centre was linked to its economic role as a market and as the centre of the caravan trade that ran up the Red Sea littoral from the Yemen to southern Palestine and ultimately Syria. Because of its religious sig-nificance Mecca enjoyed a special role as a neutral point in which, during an annual month of truce, members of tribes in a state of mutual war and feud could meet without a threat of violence. The tribe of Quraysh thus had considerable influence over other neigh-bouring tribes as middle men in the resolution of feuds and also through the wealth they were prepared to distribute to ensure the safe passage of their caravans. Much of this seemed threatened by Muhammad's religious message that looked likely to undermine the special status of the town and thus of the Quraysh.[44]

In consequence a plot was hatched in 622 to murder him. As he was himself of the Quraysh no individual member of the tribe could be responsible for his death, as the others by the strict obligations of bloodfeud would have to avenge it. Thus it is said that a cumbersome scheme had to be hatched in which many of the leading men of the tribe would be involved in a simultaneous attack on him. Muhammad was soon aware of this, and having recently received an invitation to establish himself there, was able to remove himself and his followers to the town of Medina before the Meccans could prevent it. This emigration to Medina in the northern Hijaz is known as the *Hijra* or 'Flight', and from it is dated the first year of the Muslim calendar.[45]

Medina itself had no dominant tribe, but was effectively divided between two rival confederacies, and it was to act as arbitrator in their quarrels that Muhammad was invited to the town. He agreed but was able to require acceptance of his religious reforms as the price of his services. Increasingly those, including a number of Jewish tribes, who were not willing to do so were evicted from the town. At the same time the strategic location of Medina enabled Muhammad to exercise a growing economic stranglehold on Mecca, cutting the caravan routes to the north. Attempts by the Meccans to dislodge him by force were defeated in 624 and 627, and by the end of the decade, gaining control of the town of Taif to the south-east, Muhammad was effectively blockading Mecca. In 630 the Meccans capitulated, putting the town in his hands and accepting his religious reforms.[46]

Within two years the Prophet had died, but in the meantime much of Arabia is said to have submitted to his authority and to his religious teaching. This included the Persian-ruled Yemen, whose governor is supposed to have embraced Islam in 630.[47] Both the speedy establishment and the wide geographical extent of the Prophet's grip on much of Arabia, secured in no more than the two-year period from 630 to 632 must raise some doubts, though no evidence exists to provide an alternative to the traditional version. It may be that a wider time-scale and more complex processes were involved. The interpretative context that emphasises the role of trade and economic forces both in establishing Muhammad's grip on Mecca and on drawing the Arabian tribes into his allegiance, is the fruit of modern scholarship, though it has recently come under challenge.[48] In itself it can only be a partial reconstruction, and whether it be accepted or not there still remains a very large number of questions that need to be asked about the career of Muhammad and its immediate impact on Arabia. Unfortunately, what is lacking are the answers that might be given.

To turn to the period following the death of the Prophet is to move into a slightly better documented age, at least as far as the impact of the Arabs on their neighbours is concerned. Traditionally the death of Muhammad was followed by what is called the *Riddah* or 'Apostasy', when many of the tribes that had so recently accepted his authority and his religion reverted to their previous faiths and broke their political ties to Mecca. A crisis amongst the inner circle of Muhammad's followers as to how the community was to be led in the absence of the Prophet was resolved with the nomination of the elderly Abu Bakr, traditionally the first to receive his message, as Caliph or Successor. The claims to authority of Muhammad's cousin and son-in-law 'Ali on the basis of ties of blood were rejected.[49] Under the rule of Abu Bakr (632–4) the tribes that had defected were forced back into allegiance, and a series of large-scale attacks on the Arabs' northern neighbours, the great powers of Persia and Byzantium, was launched.

In 634, just prior to the death of Abu Bakr and his replacement by 'Umar, another of the inner circle, the Byzantine forces in Syria were defeated by an Arab tribal army at the battle of Al Ajnadan. The Persians suffered a major defeat in the same year. In 635 Damascus surrendered to an Arab expedition, and faced by this growing threat to the recently recaptured eastern provinces the Emperor Heraclius prepared to intervene in person. In 636 the imperial army was defeated at the battle of Yarmuk, and Heraclius's brother was killed.[50] The emperor evacuated his forces from Syria, and Jerusalem surrendered to the Arabs. The Caliph 'Umar (634–44) made a triumphal entry into the city riding on a donkey.[51] Thus six years after its recovery from the Persians the Holy City was lost to the Roman Empire for ever, and the relic of the 'True Cross' fell into Arab hands and was probably destroyed.

For the Persians, though, the year 637 was even more fateful. In May or June their army was routed at the battle of al-Qadisiyah and its commander killed. In the aftermath the Persian capital of Ctesiphon was captured without further resistance. Most of Persian Mesopotamia passed under Arab rule. The last of the shahs, Yazdgard III (632–51), tried to organise resistance in the western regions of Iran but was forced to flee east after the disastrous battle of Nihavand in 642. He was unable to resist further Arab advances across the Iranian plateau, and in 651 was murdered by some of his own men near Merv.[52]

After the defeat at Yarmuk in 636 only negligible attempts were made by Heraclius's government to hold on to its eastern provinces. Reinforcements were sent to Alexandria, which held out until 642, but the rest of Egypt was conquered by the Arab commander Amr in 640–1.[53] In the latter year the Emperor

Heraclius died. In his last years he suffered from an obscure phobia that made it impossible for him to view the sea. Whether this inhibited his military capacities cannot be said, but the victor over the Persians proved no match for the Arabs. A succession crisis developed after his death and both of his sons came to violent ends within the year. Authority if not power passed to his young grandson Constans II (641–68).[54]

Arab access to the ports of the Syrian coast provided them with a new military arm, and in 649 their fleet took Cyprus. An attempt in 655 by the Emperor Constans II to check the growth of Arab naval power was ended by his disastrous defeat in a battle in the Aegean. Imperial control of the sea was lost. By 674 Constantinople itself was being blockaded by the Arab fleet, while an Arab army was encamped across the Sea of Marmora at Chalcedon. As in 626 the continued existence of the Empire seemed under threat.[55]

In the same period the Arab expansion westward was continuing. The first incursions into Byzantine controlled North Africa occurred in 647. At the time the governor or Exarch was in revolt against Constantinople and had proclaimed himself emperor. However, he was defeated and killed by the Arab invaders near his fortress town of Sbeitla (*Sufetula*) in southern Tunisia.[56] Actual Arab occupation of parts of Africa was slower to develop, but in 670 the city of Qayrawan (Kairouan), their military and administrative centre, was founded in the Sahel. From this base a more determined attempt to conquer North Africa was launched under a succession of commanders. The indigenous Berber tribes put up more sustained resistance than had been encountered in any other region, but by 698 the Arabs had definitively conquered Carthage.[57] By 711 North Africa was so far subjugated that the Arabs were poised to extend their activities to western Europe by the invasion of the Iberian peninsula.

The success of the Arab armies in conquering a swathe of territory that in the 100 years between the death of Muhammad and the battle of Poitiers had extended itself to stretch from the borders of India to the north of the Pyrenees has often been commented on, but never satisfactorily explained. Some interpretations concentrate particularly on the state, in terms of morale and of morals, of the various victims of the Arab expansion. The Persian and Byzantine empires are seen as being militarily exhausted after their titanic mutual struggles in the years 602–28. Persia was rent by internal social divisions and political disorder among its governing classes. The Monophysite majority populations in Syria, Palestine and Egypt can be argued to have felt distanced from the Greek government in Constantinople that was persecuting their religious leaders. Byzantine rule in Africa can be presented as being no more than the perching of an alien ruling elite on top of an indifferent or hostile mass of the indigenous Berber population.

Even if elements of these arguments are allowed, they can at best be only partial explanations. To them is often added the activities of 'third columns' that actively co-operated with the Arabs. The most prominent of these were the Jews, and some have seen the Copts and Jacobite Monophysites of Syria as being more than just alienated from Byzantium, and as being active collaborators with the invaders. The evidence for such involvement is actually very small. There is no proof at all for any claims that Christians of any type openly sided with the Arabs, and that relating to Jewish involvement is both slight and geographically restricted. Although conditions for the Jews in the eastern Roman Empire were far from good, Muhammad had turned against the Jewish tribes in Arabia when they refused to accept his religious message, and thus an Arab and Islamic take-over of the state was not necessarily to be anticipated by them with pleasure. More to the point was the magnitude of the events that were taking place and the scale of violence and disorder that accompanied them, which led some Jews to expect the Messianic coming.[58] Thus, apocalyptic expectations, not political calculations, determined their actions.

More concrete factors might include the nature of the warfare and the political geography of the territories affected. In the pursuit of strengthening the defences against Persia Justinian had devoted much money and material into the rebuilding of town walls and the erection of forts along the east-west frontier in Mesopotamia. However, the eastern fringes of south Syria and of Palestine that fronted onto the desert received no such treatment, as no major military threat was anticipated from that direction, and the allied Arab tribes in these regions were expected to provide sufficient defence against occasional raids by hostile tribes.[59] However, not only did a threat of unprecedented magnitude develop in the 630s, but the previously tractable Arab tribes had been alienated by the treatment they had received from the Emperors Maurice and Heraclius. Thus there were neither fortresses nor allied troops to defend these areas against the unforeseen invasions from Arabia.

The terms and conditions the Arabs offered to the inhabitants of the towns of Syria, Palestine, Egypt and Mesopotamia were calculated to eliminate any threat these might pose and to maximise the Arab war effort by freeing them from the necessity of installing manpower-wasteful garrisons in the towns. The choice offered was that if a town surrendered without resistance the

inhabitants would retain their lives, liberties, local self-government and religious freedom, in return for the payment of land
and capitation taxes. If, on the other hand, they fought and the
town was taken their property would be forfeit and they would
be enslaved. Lacking the prospect of immediate succour from
imperial armies, few towns decided on the second option. If the
emperor eventually triumphed, as he had over the Persians, then
nothing would be lost, and in the meantime the taxes due to the
Arabs were no greater – and may have been less – than those
owed to the Byzantine government. As the walls of those towns
not restored by Justinian were doubtless in a state of poor repair,
the decision cannot have been difficult to make.[60]

Persia was peculiarly vulnerable, in that its capital Ctesiphon
was situated in Mesopotamia and in the immediate front line of
the Arab attack. Its fall was an early and demoralising blow. For
the Byzantine Empire, however, the location of Constantinople
was a strength. The Arab armies, largely of light cavalry, were not
suited to mountainous terrain, and it is notable that although they
penetrated Asia Minor on numerous occasions no attempts were
made to occupy and hold it. By the time the Arabs were in a position to launch a joint sea and land attack on the city, the Byzantines
were able to deploy a 'secret weapon', in the form of Greek Fire,
a highly volatile unrefined petroleum from the area around Baku,
which ignited on contact with water. Jetted out of hydrants on the
Byzantine ships into the sea around the Arab vessels its effects
were devastating, and its use to terminate the great siege of
Constantinople in 674–7 in practice marked the limit to the
threat the Arabs were able to make against the continued existence of the Empire.[61]

Just as at first the Arabs were disconcerted by the Byzantines'
Greek Fire, so previously had many of their victims been by the
nature and ferocity of Arab tactics. Romans and Persians had long
been used to each other's fighting practices and had adapted their
own procedures accordingly. Thus Roman heavy cavalry mirrored
Persian. None of the armies of the victims of the Arab assaults,
other than the Berbers in North Africa, had the mobility to match
them, and a series of resounding victories over forces used to
set-piece battles was the result. This was to be as true in Spain in
711 as it had been in Mesopotamia in the 630s and 640s.

10 Decadent and do-nothing kings

Visigothic Spain, *c.* 589–711

The unpalatable fact that in any given battle one side or the other tends to win or at least gain the advantage was not fully understood by those who used to wish to characterise the final stages of the Visigothic kingdom in Spain as decadent, and who saw the proof of this in the rapidity of its overthrow. This was a view that was once common amongst historians of Visigothic Spain, and has only relatively recently been finally put to rest. If anything, quite the contrary conclusion can be drawn from the 'battle in the Transductine Promontories' between the Visigothic royal army and the Arab invaders in 711 and the collapse of central authority in the kingdom which resulted from it.[1] It was the extraordinary achievement of the Visigothic kings and their advisers, above all a series of outstanding bishops, that in land as geographically and culturally diverse and presenting such problems of movement and communication as the Iberian peninsula, they had been able not only to impose their own central authority but had created structures and institutions that maintained it for well over a century.[2]

The turning point in the relations between the Visigoths and their Hispano-Roman subject population was the Third Council of Toledo in 589, or more exactly the less well documented personal conversion from Arianism to Catholicism on the part of King Reccared (586–601) in 587 and the acquiescence in this of the Visigothic Arian bishops.[3] By the time the council was held in May 589 most of the practical administrative problems had been settled. The council was able to view the conversion of the king and the people as already established, and the assembled bishops went on to legislate for the first time for a unified church in the Iberian peninsula.

However, the real impetus towards a closer integration of the majority Roman population with the ruling Visigothic elite had been created by the achievements of Reccared's father Leovigild (569–86).[4] Under his immediate predecessors the extensive military occupation of most of the peninsula that had existed since the Visigothic conquests of the 450s and 470s had disintegrated. Individual towns and regions broke away from Visigothic rule. King Agila (549–54) lost control of Córdoba, and was then overthrown in a civil war against one of his own magnates. One of the two parties in this conflict had appealed to the Emperor Justinian for aid, and the resulting Byzantine intervention in 551 led to the establishment of an imperial enclave all along the south-eastern coast of Spain from Cartagena to Medina Sidonia, which survived until the 620s.[5]

Under Leovigild the fortunes of the Visigothic monarchy revived. In a series of campaigns from 570 to 578 he regained control of all northern Spain from the Pyrenees to the borders of the Suevic kingdom in Galicia in the north-west. He also inflicted some defeats on the Byzantine forces of occupation and retook Medina Sidonia. In 572 he reimposed royal control on Córdoba. Like several of his successors he had difficulties with the Basques, who were raiding the upper Ebro valley from the valleys of the western Pyrenees. He undertook a campaign to curb them in 581 and also founded a new town of *Victoriacum* (probably modern Olite in Navarre) to try to force some of them to settle.[6] In 585 the conquest of the Suevic kingdom, where the previous royal house had been overthrown by a usurper, completed Leovigild's highly successful imposition of Visigothic authority over the whole of the northern half of the peninsula.[7]

In the south his work was left incomplete. He failed to eliminate the Byzantines, and in 579 his elder son Hermenigild revolted and established an independent kingdom of his own centred on Seville. This Leovigild seems in practice to have been willing to tolerate until the rebel ruler's growing rapprochement with Byzantium began to look dangerous. This was marked by Hermenigild's conversion from Arianism to Catholicism: an obvious sign of the new political affiliation, which though often dated to the beginning of his revolt probably only occurred in 582.[8] In campaigns in 583 and 584 Leovigild regained control of Mérida and Italica, before finally forcing his son to surrender in Seville. In 585 Hermenigild, initially exiled to Valencia, was killed in Tarragona by a certain Sisbert. Why and on whose orders this occurred cannot be known.

The achievement of a political reunification of most of the peninsula by Leovigild could only be an empty victory while a fundamental divide over religion separated the two principal elements in the population. Leovigild had hoped to win over more of the Catholics, who by now included a number of prominent Goths, by holding a synod in Toledo in 580 which modified Arian doctrine by accepting the equality of Father and Son but not of the Spirit, and by removing the need for converts to be rebaptised. However, this seems to have generated a Catholic apologetic offensive in works by Bishop Leander of Seville and others, and even the military defeat of Hermenigild failed to weaken Catholic intellectual resistance.[9] On the other hand, there are indications that in the last few years of his reign Leovigild was moving closer to Catholicism, and a rumour even spread that he himself was converted prior to his death. That his surviving son and heir took such a decision within a year of his accession is thus unsurprising.

The willingness of the Catholic bishops, who in most cases were as much the political and social leaders of their communities as the spiritual, to co-operate with the Visigothic monarchy, once the problem of the Arian heresy was removed, had no parallel in western Europe. It was largely their involvement, which became increasingly regularised through a series of kingdom-wide councils held in Toledo from the 630s onwards, that knitted the disparate regions of the peninsula together.[10] The lack of military challenge, especially after King Suinthila (621–31) had eliminated the Byzantine enclave in the south-east, led to a diminution in the standing forces of the state. The raising of local levies by Romano-Gothic landowners provided the main way of augmenting the nuclear *comitatus* that followed the person of the king. Thus it was not by coercion and the threat of force that the monarchy maintained its authority over the peninsula. The bishops provided spiritual sanctions against those who plotted against the monarchs or who conspired against the existing political order. By the 670s it was possible for the bishops of Toledo to define legitimacy in terms of having received unction in the 'royal city', which from the time of Leovigild had been the principal residence and administrative centre of the kingdom.[11]

On the other hand, it must be admitted, the bishops were not prepared to apply those spiritual sanctions to rulers, such as Sisenand (631–6) and Chindasuinth (642–53) who were successful in overthrowing their predecessors. The success of their coups or revolts was itself proof of divine favour and selection. It was against those who tried and failed that the Church directed its ire. What was far more important than the bishops' threats of excommunication was the fact that they were willing and able to meet to discuss such political matters and to serve as partisans and propagandists for the monarchy in their sees. For them the existence of a peninsula-wide kingdom, embracing all five of the ecclesiastical provinces of Spain and Septimania, to the north-east of the Pyrenees, was vital to the well-being of the Church. Reform could be imposed in matters such as monastic observance, the conduct of the clergy, and the economic management of dioceses, and also uniformity could be sought and decreed in matters of liturgy and the acceptance of a common body of canon law, much of which was in the process of being created at the sixteen Councils of Toledo that took place between 589 and 702.[12]

Obviously these aims and objectives had to be widely acceptable to those who held positions of authority in the Church under Visigothic rule, but much of the direction and impetus came from the guidance of a succession of bishops distinguished for their erudition and also for their political acumen and firmness of purpose. The most prolific of these men as a writer was Isidore, Bishop of Seville (599/600–36), brother of the Bishop Leander who had been a spiritual mentor to both Hermenigild and Reccared.[13] Isidore's most substantial and best-known work is his *Etymologiae* or *Etymologies*, a vast encyclopaedia in twenty books embracing a wide range of subjects, from grammar (bk I.iii) to God (bk VII.i) and from geometry (bk III.i–iii) to gladiators (bk XVII.vii). The internal organisation of the individual books is generally logical, though after the first five, devoted to Grammar, Rhetoric, Mathematics, Medicine and Law, their ordering is less so. The guiding principle of the elucidation of the subjects discussed is that of the etymology of names: as Isidore saw it 'the investigation of anything is much easier if its etymology is known' (I.xix.2).

As well as providing in this and in a range of other works intended for grammatical and biblical study a corpus of educational texts, Isidore also wrote two brief historical works, a chronicle, giving a synoptic history of the world from its foundation, and a *History of the Goths, Vandals and Sueves*.[14] In these two books he placed the recent history of Spain and above all the creation of the Visigothic kingdom in the peninsula into the contexts, firstly of biblical history and secondly of Roman. If the ideological contents of these works, especially the *History of the Goths*, make them into propaganda for the Visigothic monarchy and the order it had imposed, at least it was willingly written. As well as presiding over a series of synods in his own metropolitan province, Isidore presided over the IVth Council of Toledo of 633, which resumed the task initiated by the IIIrd Council of 589 in making the Church the primary supporter of the kings.

After Isidore's death, Seville was eclipsed by Toledo. A succession of outstanding bishops – Eugenius II (646–57), Ildefonsus (657–67) and Julian (680–90) – produced a body of work in the form of law, theology, history, grammar and above all liturgy, that was quite unparalleled in Western Europe in the seventh century in both the quantity and the quality of its writing. They were also all astute politicians, and amongst other things created for their own see an unchallenged primacy over the church of the Visigothic kingdom. Although technically equal to those of Braga,

Mérida, Narbonne, Seville and Tarragona, the metropolitans of Toledo by the time of Julian were able to ordain bishops in the capital to fill sees in the other ecclesiastical provinces.[15] They were also able to impose Toledan liturgy as the norm for the Spanish Church. What is more surprising still is that they met no recorded opposition from their fellow metropolitans, who appear to have co-operated fully in these processes. By 690, contrary to the rules observed throughout the western Church, a bishop of Seville was translated to the see of Toledo, in itself an eloquent witness to the superior status of the latter.[16]

The principal difficulty to be encountered in understanding the society and politics of Spain in the Visigothic period resides, not surprisingly, in the nature of the available evidence. The problem is not just a simple one of quantity. If the total corpus of the civil and ecclesiastical law produced in the Visigothic kingdom in the seventh century is added to its liturgical and theological output then it far outstrips in size the quantity of written materials produced in any other region of the former Roman Empire in the same period, and indeed might go a long way towards equalling the entire known literary output of the time. However, it is the particular nature of these texts that limits their utility for the modern historian. We know a great deal about what *ought* to have happened in Visigothic Spain, but very little about what actually did.[17] That is to say, the greater part of the evidence is legal and normative, and there is a corresponding absence of historical writing giving details of personalities and events.

No large-scale narrative history was ever written in early medieval Spain. Isidore's two works are very brief, and after them no historical composition was undertaken at all in the Visigothic period apart from Julian of Toledo's *History of Wamba*, which confines itself to the campaign fought in 673 by King Wamba (672–80) against a rebel count Paul, who was based in Narbonne.[18] Thus it is impossible to provide the kind of vivid narrative of events that is possible to offer for sixth century Gaul and seventh century Britain on the strength of the existence of the large-scale historical works of Gregory of Tours (d. 594) and Bede (d. 735). In consequence modern historians of Visigothic Spain have tended to provide broad and often chronologically unspecific discussions of general themes, such as 'the army', 'the economy', 'the Gothic population', 'the Roman population'. The resulting presentations can be, in consequence, rather dull and to a greater or lesser degree divorced from the concrete realities of this society.

The problem is largely one of historians approaching Visigothic Spain with predetermined questions in their minds, rather than looking first at the generic strengths and weaknesses of the available evidence, and deciding on the basis of these exactly what may or may not be asked and which topics the sources are capable of illuminating and which not. What must already be clear is that the evidence relating to the ideals and aspirations of the society, in terms of the civil and ecclesiastical laws and some of the treatises of the leading bishops of the kingdom, is unusually abundant, and that relating to the concrete realities of the interplay of personalities and politics and to the practical application of the legislators' normative injunctions is almost non-existent. Even administrative texts are extraordinarily scarce and are principally represented by five very mutilated fragments of documents written on parchment.[19]

After the relatively detailed narrative accounts that can be given of most periods of the Later Roman Empire and of Frankish Gaul, these evidential problems can make the study of Visigothic Spain seem rather too austere and abstract. However, it is possible to conceive of alternative approaches to the subject that should be both illuminating and sufficiently grounded in the realities of the time to be stimulating as well. New discoveries and recent research have opened up other ways of looking at various aspects of the period.

The archaeology of Visigothic Spain has entered a period of considerable vitality, although the nature of its organisation and funding means that certain geographical areas are better served than others. In particular our knowledge of the church building of the seventh century kingdom has been greatly enhanced by excavations in the region of Mérida, the principal city of the Roman and Visigothic province of Lusitania, and a major investigation of the church of Santa Maria de Melque near Toledo, which had hitherto been dated to the tenth century.[20] Current excavations within the city of Mérida are also providing much new information on the wider context of changes in town life from the early Roman imperial period, through that of the Visigothic kingdom and well on into the centuries of Islamic rule. As well as this important work on new sites, more critical study of the five extant churches in northern Spain and Portugal that have long been assigned to the Visigothic period has modified older certainties.[21] All in all these investigations, taken together with the few saints' lives and the writings of the monastic founder Fructuosus of Braga (650s and 660s), and of the hermit Valerius of Bierzo (690s), help to put a lot more flesh on the bare bones of the ecclesiastical regulations concerned with monastic life in the canons of the councils.[22]

Equally valuable, and able to be given a context in relation to textual sources, are the recent discoveries and studies of a series of rock churches and hermits' caves in the upper Ebro valley. Hitherto knowledge of this aspect of the ecclesiastical life of Visigothic Spain had been restricted to the reading of the *Life of St Aemilian*, a late sixth century hermit and 'holy man', written by Bishop Braulio of Zaragoza (631–51), a pupil of Isidore of Seville. The discovery in Alava and the Rioja of large numbers of these cave churches and associated dwellings shows something of the extensiveness of the eremitical communities in this area; a fact entirely concealed in the *Life*.[23]

Another and very different local society in another area of the peninsula can be extraordinarily well illustrated from the wide range of administrative and other documents that it produced, and which to our good fortune were written down on sheets of slate rather than on perishable parchment. The existence of many of these slate documents, found in relatively large numbers in various sites in the area between Avila and Salamanca, has been known for a relatively long time. However, their first transcriber and editor made a large number of mistakes in his copying of them, and in consequence many of the texts appeared to be meaningless. However, a new study and edition has revealed how comprehensible and valuable many of them are, damaged as most of them may be.[24] The range of subject matter is impressive, and includes land transactions, sales, curses and school exercises. In the course of time it will be possible to present far more precise and detailed accounts of the rural society of this region in the late sixth and first quarter of the seventh centuries.

Post-Roman archaeology has hitherto had to confine itself largely to the study of cemeteries and grave goods. Even towns which on the basis of documentary evidence can be shown to have been occupied in the early medieval period have failed to show traces of themselves archaeologically, though Mérida is here starting to prove itself a particularly important exception. Indications of rural settlements are even rarer, although the number of these that have been found and studied is increasing. A sixth century village has been excavated in north-eastern France, but as its sole *raison d'être* seems to have been the servicing of a nearby royal villa it cannot be taken as typical.[25] Another, in the vicinity of Caen in Normandy, shows evidence of occupation of the site from the Late Bronze Age to the twelfth century AD.[26] A village dating to and continuously occupied throughout the period 450–650 has also been discovered in north-east Yorkshire, but it will be some while before a full report on this excavation appears.[27] Visigothic Spain, too, has its own offering to make to this select band.

On the southern banks of rio Segre about fifteen miles west of Lerida in Catalonia is the site of El Bovalar. That this centred on the foundations of a church, probably to be dated to the sixth century, has long been known, and the building itself was excavated in 1967. A more substantial campaign was launched in 1976, and this has uncovered a second and more extensive area of construction extending around the church, and forming what is believed to be a village. The particular interest of this site lies in the fact that the settlement was clearly abandoned in haste and at a single time. Moreover, this can be dated to the reign of the late Visigothic King Achila (710–13) by the existence of a number of his coins found abandoned in the rooms. The rapid abandonment, associated with a destruction by fire, has meant that a wide range of items of everyday use, together with much information relating to diet and the local economy, has been recovered from the site. The apparent precision in dating and the violent destruction of the location, though not apparently of its inhabitants – no bodies having been found – has led to the plausible suggestion that this should be associated with the Arab conquest of the mid and lower Ebro valley, which occurred in the years 712/13.[28]

This one site, therefore, seems to take us directly to the final phase of the Visigothic kingdom in the peninsula, and helps to confirm the impression gained from the *Chronicle of 754* that the Arab campaign in the Ebro was particularly destructive.[29] This is actually of far greater utility and interest than the fanciful constructs that historians have frequently been led to make of the supposed events and the interplay of personalities and politics in the heart of the kingdom, and which derive almost exclusively from a late sources of dubious historical worth. Stories of the betrayal of King Roderic (710/11–711) by the sons of his predecessor Wittiza (693/4–710), and even of their inviting of the Arabs into the peninsula, lack any foundation in reliable, let alone contemporary, evidence.[30] Conflict between Roderic in the south and north-west of the peninsula and Achila in the north-east at the time of the Arab invasions can, however, be substantiated, and the first discovery at El Bovalar of a coin of Achila that was struck at the mint of Zaragoza proves that he ruled over the principal city of the mid Ebro valley as well as over Narbonne, Gerona and Tarragona.

It is clear enough that Visigothic kings were still expected to be the leaders of their own armies. In practice hereditary succession was the norm, but if a minor or an incompetent succeeded, the challenge of opposition from some of the regionally based aristocracy might unseat them. Count Paul in Narbonne attempted to do this to the new King Wamba in 673 but failed. In 710 Roderic had been selected to replace Wittiza and was facing a similar challenge from the same region, as well possibly as problems with Basque raiding in the upper Ebro, when the Arab attacks occurred.[31] Following the nearly contemporary *Chronicle of 754* rather than the much later and fanciful Arab accounts, it is clear that several such incursions were made and that at least two Arab armies were operating in the peninsula when Roderic was defeated and killed at the battle 'in the Transductine Promontories', probably in 711.

With the king dead and his noble following killed or dispersed, the capital fell rapidly to the Arabs, who with the seizure of Toledo gained control of the central administration and of the one place in which the complicated procedures of kingmaking were expected to occur. The possibilities of further centrally organised resistance evaporated, and individual towns and regions submitted on the kind of terms offered to their counterparts in the east. Those that did not suffered the consequences. Within a decade the tide of conquest passed through the peninsula, which broke up into small localised units now lacking the capacity or the need to resist. By 721 the Arabs were poised for the extension of their conquests beyond the Pyrenees.[32]

Merovingian Gaul *c.* 511–687

If the history of the Visigothic kingdom, subjugated by the Arabs between 711 and 720, is difficult to reconstruct and dependent on the teasing out of clues from complex sources, then the previous history of the next victims of Arab aggression, the Merovingian kingdoms in Gaul, can seem deceptively easy to understand. Or at least that is how much of its sixth-century phase might appear. The problem here is the superabundance of the type of evidence so lamentably lacking in the Spanish case. The *Ten Books of Histories* written by Bishop Gregory of Tours, and completed soon before his presumed death in 594, provide a wealth of detailed information on personalities and events, particularly for the period *c.* 550 to 592 (books IV–X).[33]

Gregory's knowledge of events affecting his own episcopal city of Tours during his pontificate (571–94) was obviously first-hand in most instances. Moreover the importance of the city in the Loire valley, its proximity to other major urban centres such as Poitiers, and the relatively frequent shifts in the political boundaries of the Frankish kingdoms, which could affect its political allegiance, all combined to make Gregory peculiarly well-informed about the wider politics of Merovingian Gaul. Furthermore, his upbringing in Clermont and the network of his family connections provided additional sources of information for him to draw on in depicting not only the Romano-Frankish society of his own day but also something of its past. Nor were his works confined generically to history alone. The *Ten Books of Histories* were matched by *Seven Books of Miracles* and one of saints' lives, which if smaller in size and more limited in their content are also mainly concerned with Gaul and with the fifth and sixth centuries.[34]

The sheer bulk of Gregory's contribution to the study of sixth century Gaul makes his perspective on events not only the most accessible but also dangerously persuasive. The problems of accepting his account of the career of Clovis have already been discussed, and so too the difficulty of finding the wherewithal to create an alternative view to put in its place.[35] It might be argued that Gregory himself was disadvantaged in writing about someone, whatever his importance, who was so far removed in time from his own day, and that the information he provides in so much more detail of periods closer to and including his own lifetime should be expected to be more worthy of trust.

In fact, Gregory is a very dangerous historian. It is easy enough to show on the basis of comparison with other contemporary sources that he deliberately distorted his account of the conflicts taking place in Spain in the late 570s and 580s and that his version of Visigothic history is highly prejudiced.[36] It is also easy enough to prove that much of his information relating to Italy is highly erroneous.[37] Unfortunately, there are few such controls to enable us to monitor his treatment of Frankish history, which looms so much larger in his work. It is easy enough to see from such examples as his very prejudiced account of the Frankish King Chilperic (561–84) how passionate Gregory's animosities could be, and his overweening personal and family vanity is if anything even more apparent in his hagiographical works than in his historical.[38]

If this intense and somewhat baleful personality exercises such a hold over the interpretation of so many aspects of the history of sixth century Gaul, how may he be circumvented? It is not easy, in that the author of the principal seventh century Frankish chronicle, known as that 'of Fredegar' or Pseudo-Fredegar, derived much though not all of his sixth century information from Gregory.[39] The only independent contemporary source is the all-too-brief chronicle written in the 590s by Bishop Marius of Avenches.[40] However, if Gregory's value judgements are viewed with caution and if his ideological and personal *bêtes noires*, such as Arianism and King Chilperic, be identified, his copious materials can at least be evaluated on the basis of the sources that he was either explicitly or probably relying on, and how much weight should be allowed them. A full-scale historical commentary on his work would be much appreciated, though it must be admitted that scholars have yet to advance convincing answers to such fundamental questions as what were Gregory's motives in writing his histories, and whom he may have envisaged his intended audience to be.

It would hardly be possible here to offer a synoptic version of Gregory's account of the history of the Frankish kingdoms from the death of Clovis up to his time of writing in the early 590s. To some extent it would be irrelevant, and the presentation of sixth century Gaul that is little more than a retelling of Gregory's narrative is largely responsible for making this society seem so violent and savage. It is preferable to try to isolate the salient features of the society and the principal developments of the period, using his materials, but also trying to supplement them from other documentary sources and from archaeological materials.

Synoptic studies of the latter, not least in the form of large-scale exhibitions and catalogues, have been much encouraged recently, not least by various schemes for Franco-German co-operation and the notional fifteen hundredth anniversary of the conversion of Clovis. It still looks most probable that Frankish settlement continued to limit itself to northern and especially north-eastern Gaul, despite the enormous extent of the territory that Clovis had brought under his political sway.[41] Although it is easy enough to envisage the distribution of garrisoning forces of Franks drawn from the area between the Seine and the Rhine in other parts of the kingdom, it has to be remembered that the fifth century history of Gaul indicates that there were considerable indigenous resources of military manpower already available to be drawn on, and this was a society far more organised for war than, say, that to be found in Italy in the same period.

At the same time the administrative structures that Clovis had available to him were far less sophisticated and extensive, especially in northern Gaul, than those of metropolitan Italy. To put it simply, he was able to fit into the role of something approaching that of a Late Roman provincial Master of the Soldiers, while for Theoderic in Italy there existed the vacant functions though not the title of western emperor. Moreover, the political and cultural unity of Italy had not been compromised in the fifth century to anything like the degree of that of Gaul. Until the Lombard invasion of 568 political control of Italy always remained in the hands of one central authority and the territory changed hands as a unit between successive political masters. The same was largely true of Spain, other than for the Suevic-ruled north-west, until the mid sixth century, and unitary rule over the whole peninsula was reimposed in the 570s and 580s.

Thus the Frankish kings who succeeded Clovis were the heirs of the Late Roman state to a lesser degree than were the Ostrogothic and Visigothic monarchs. They do not seem to have availed themselves of the powers and resources that this might have offered them, or only attempted to do so selectively and intermittently. An instance of this is their almost certain failure to maintain the complex but highly lucrative system of Late Roman taxation. When the innovative and Romanised king Chilperic (561–84) did try to revive the lapsed procedures and introduce new *descriptiones* or tax registers he was met with considerable opposition, organised not least by the Church, and bishops such as Gregory told him that the ill-health (and subsequent deaths) of his children resulted directly from this, to their mind impious, intention.[42] In Spain, on the other hand, the bishops appear as intimately involved in the raising of tax revenue for the monarchs.[43]

This failure to preserve such apparently crucial features of the organisation of the centralised state may seem to imply that the Frankish kings were unsophisticated or more barbarous than their Gothic counterparts. Such an impression would be highly misleading. The problems of continuity really lie in the fifth century rather than in the sixth. Moreover, such a line of argument ignores the structural realities of Gallic society in Late Antiquity and the Early Middle Ages.

From a modern perspective France looks like the model of the centralised state, and favourable historical judgements on various phases of its past all too often seem conditioned by the degree of political unity and central authority seen to be existing in them. The creation of the unified France is every bit as much product of a 'Whig Interpretation of History' as the development of the British Constitution and Parliamentary Democracy. In other words these were long seen by historians as the natural ends to which these particular societies were 'progressing' and that those who assisted in these processes were to be deemed to be 'good', 'great' and 'wise', and those who failed to forward them – or worse, whose actions were thought to retard them – were held to be 'weak' and 'incompetent'.

Thus Clovis for his military unification of so much of what was to be France has always been historigraphically highly aclaimed, while his successors, especially the so-called *rois fainéants*, or 'do-nothing kings' of the later seventh century have tended to be ignored and belittled.[44] Similarly, Charlemagne's 'achievements' contrast with his successors' 'failures', and the latter are seen as leading to the 'disastrous' tenth century, in which centralised royal authority almost disappeared. In fact, when the history of France from around the year 400 to the end of the tenth century is surveyed the periods of powerful and effective central authority are few in number and were all essentially fleeting.[45]

In large part this was due to the strength of regional differences and of local communities and their leaders. The Romans had imposed their form of political unity on a large number of disparate Celtic tribes, but even they did not achieve a single administrative structure for Gaul. Equally instructive is the political settlement that followed the death of Clovis around the year 511. According to Gregory the king's four sons divided the kingdom 'in equal measure between them'. The reality must have been very different, in that of the three younger sons, the product of Clovis's marriage to the Burgundian Clothildis, perhaps only Chlodomer (*c.* 511–24), the eldest, would have reached the legal age of majority by this time. Their half-brother Theuderic was considerably older and had already been campaigning with their father. Whoever did the dividing it was not all of the sons. Nor, contrary to what is often asserted, are there any intrinsic reasons why any division of the kingdom between all potential heirs should have taken place at all.[46] An opportunity to create a single unified Frankish kingdom of Gaul then existed and was deliberately rejected in favour of a division. Why?

The nature of this division is not described by any source, but has to be pieced together from subsequent references to the territories controlled by the four monarchs. What emerges is that the component parts of any one of these king's lands were generally not contiguous. That is to say that between any two regions of the kingdom of one of them was likely to be a piece of the kingdom of another. One explanation for this is that each of the new kings had been allotted a section of the original territory controlled by their father Clovis before 486 and added to this were portions of all of the other regions that he conquered. Whether or not this is the rationale for such an extraordinary division, unparalleled in the other great kingdoms of the West, it certainly inhibited the growth of efficient and centralised royal administration.[47]

This crucial process, which provided the precedent for a similar division among the sons of Chlotar I in 561, is extremely murky. That it even took place immediately after Clovis's death is uncertain, as there is an almost complete blank in Frankish history between *c.* 511 and 522, but its long-term effects were considerable. The conquest and elimination of the Burgundian kingdom in 534 and the cession of Provence by the Ostrogothic King Wittigis in 536 completed the Frankish expansion within Gaul, other than for Visigothic controlled Septimania.[48] This meant that further territorial aggrandisement had either to be made at the expense of neighbouring kingdoms or to take the form of civil war between the Frankish realms within Gaul.

In practice in the time of the first generation after Clovis sufficient such opportunities existed for the kings to co-exist reasonably harmoniously. The first attempt to conquer the Burgundian kingdom cost the life of Chlodomer in 524, but his kingdom was then able to be divided between his two full brothers Childebert I (*c*. 511–58) and Chlotar I (*c*. 511–61), who murdered his infant sons to achieve it.[49] Ten years later the Burgundian kingdom was dismembered by Childebert, Chlotar and Theudebert I (533–48), who had just succeeded his father Theuderic.

Theudebert was undoubtedly the greatest of the Frankish kings of the sixth century.[50] He and his father before him benefited from controlling much of the Rhineland and the eastern frontiers of the Frankish lands. This gave them the potential for territorial aggrandisement on a very large scale. By the time of Theudebert's death, the Frisians, the Saxons, the Thuringians and a number of lesser peoples east of the Rhine acknowledged his authority, and his kingdom had extended itself over the Alps into parts of northern Italy. In the latter stages of the war between the Empire and Justinian, Theudebert may have been presenting himself to the Romans in Italy as a possible new protector. The emperor was also taking seriously the alliance of peoples Theudebert was putting together north-east of the Alps and the threat of a Frankish invasion of the Balkans.[51]

Theudebert's style was deliberately intended to be imperial: he presided in the Hippodrome of Arles, and was the first to break the imperial monopoly in the minting of gold coins. He issued a series that faithfully copied the designs, weight and fineness of the eastern Roman gold *solidus*, but with his own name and royal title substituted for that of the emperor.[52] Within Gaul, or Francia as it may now be called, he appeared to have worked to consolidate a block of territory stretching from the frontiers of Visigothic Septimania and the Mediterranean to the Rhine and beyond.

This domain disintegrated after his death in 548 and that of his son in 555, and successful Saxon and Thuringian revolts put an end to this first Frankish extension east of the Rhine.[53] By the time of the death in 561 of Chlotar I, the last of the sons of Clovis, who had for the final three years of his life ruled over all of the kingdoms, the possibilities for further Frankish territorial aggrandisement had come to an end. A division between Chlotar's four sons exacerbated the problems of territorial competitiveness in that the kingdom of one of them, Chilperic (561–84), was entirely surrounded by lands belonging to his brothers. By 569 war had broken out between them, which lasted with few interruptions until the murder of Sigibert, the most powerful of them, in 575.[54] Subsequent conflicts or the threats of war continued until 613, when, as in 558–61, all of the kingdoms were again united under one ruler, Chlotar II (584–629), the son of Chilperic.[55]

The history of Merovingian Gaul in the seventh century has been long neglected, in comparison with the attention devoted to the periods that precede and follow it. The reason is largely, as is often the case, an evidential one. After the vivid large-scale narratives of Gregory of Tours, the sources available for the 150 years following his death in 594 seem very meagre indeed. They consist of the final book of the *Chronicle of Fredegar*, which is much briefer in its treatment than Gregory and also ends its basic narrative in the year 642. One or two references in the text indicate that its author was writing no earlier than 658/9, but he did not complete his work up to this point.[56]

For the second half of the seventh century the only narrative sources are very thin indeed. They consist of a continuation of the Fredegar Chronicle and the short work known as the *Liber Historiae Francorum*. Both of these were written in the eighth century, and were much influenced by later perspectives.[57] Certain historical references can be found in a small number of hagiographic texts composed in the seventh century, but even these can be contaminated by attitudes that were clearly the product of the political conflicts of the final decades of the century, and are not necessarily reliable reflections of the realities of earlier ones. A case in point is that of the *Vita Arnulfi*, a life of Bishop Arnulf of Metz (614–27/8), who was one of the ancestors of the Pippinid family, which dominated Austrasia, the East Frankish kingdom, for much of the century. A marked characteristic of this work, as of most other Pippinid-influenced hagiography and historiography, was its hostility to the Merovingian Dagobert I (623–38), probably the most powerful and effective of the Frankish kings in this century.[58]

Equally tainted with a deliberately distorted historiographical perspective, though beginning its account with a later period, is the chronicle known as the *Annales Mettenses Priores*, or 'Earlier Metz Annals'. While previously dismissed as the product of a much later period, in that the work extends its coverage up to the year 831, it has recently been argued that the first section of it, concerning the years 687/9, should be regarded as a more or less contemporary product.[59] Even so, the account of these events, which describe the means whereby the Pippinids gained power in Neustria (West Francia), is highly tendentious and represents no more than dynastic propaganda, interesting as that is in its own right.[60]

In view of the limited quantity of and the interpretative problems raised by the historical narratives, other forms of evidence become even more significant. For seventh century Francia this means charters. Of these a substantial corpus survives, though relatively few of the individual charters are originals.[61] Most of these pertain to the abbey of Saint-Denis, just north of Paris, which was especially patronised by Dagobert I, under whom the expansion of the abbey church probably took place, and who was buried there.[62] With all Early Medieval charters problems of forgery and interpolation of new material into genuine early texts have to be faced.[63] Even when such questions of the reliability or otherwise of the documents have been answered, it has to be admitted that the nature of the information that such texts can give us is severely circumscribed. As evidence for the landholdings of an institution they are, once authenticated, invaluable, but as testimony to the political and social processes that lie behind the various gifts, sales and exchanges, they are highly ambiguous.

Into the evidential vacuum modern historians of this period have sometimes attempted to coax all sorts of other bits and pieces of information or new methodological approaches to try to flesh out the very bare bones of what the seventh century in Francia has left of itself. Some of the procedures adopted are of limited helpfulness. The occasional reliance on texts written in later centuries in the hope that they may contain orally transmitted information of ultimately seventh century origin is one of the more unsatisfactory of these approaches. Less uncertain are the arguments of some prosopographers, who on the basis of identity of names (often in sources of widely different date and reliability) seek to tease out the genealogical links of possible aristocratic kinships.[64] At best these can be suggestive, but the evidential base for proper genealogical research only really becomes strong from the eighth century onwards.

All of these evidential difficulties are particularly frustrating in the light of the obvious significance of the period. In the course of the years *c*. 638–*c*. 714 the hitherto dominant Merovingian dynasty lost its grip on practical power, and although this was to be delayed until 751, the process leading to its replacement by that of the Pippinids, or Carolingians as they came to be known, had been initiated. Traditionally, this loss of power was attributed to a variety of factors of a personal kind: the dynasty was considered to be physiologically and mentally decadent. This was seen as involving a mixture of inherited genetic weaknesses and the effects of a congenital enjoyment of unhealthy living. These features were supposed to manifest themselves in the early deaths of the kings, a supposed decline in their mental powers, and a consequential sequence of long minorities, in the course of which the aristocracy obtained a firm grip on royal resources and on the processes of policy making.[65]

Admittedly, three of the Merovingian kings – Theudebert II (596–612), Charibert II (629–32) and Clovis II (638–57) – are described as being 'simple-minded' or 'mentally affected', but this can be as much if not more of an authorial comment on their political decisions than any real judgement on their sanity.[66] In other words it is probably no more than a reflection of prejudice or propaganda, and no real evidence exists for mental instability in the Merovingian family. The other general charges levelled against them tend to evaporate or become attenuated on closer inspection. The number and length of minorities are in practice far fewer than has often been allowed. Only four reigns began with minorities: those of Sigebert III (634–56), Clovis II (638–57), Chlotar III (657–73), and Childeric II (662–75). As, technically, such minorities ended at the age of twelve the years which they covered would only have been 634–42, 638–45, 657–65 and 662–c. 666 respectively. Admittedly, a twelve year old might not be expected to have exercised a very firm grip on events, so some extension would be needed to the periods in which the kings were not exercising effective personal rule.

It also needs to be appreciated that, unlike the period 567–613, much of the seventh century was not a time of warfare between the Frankish monarchs. The existence of rival and competitive Merovingian kingdoms was actually much rarer at this time, and after the death of Dagobert II of Austrasia in 678/9 an unbroken unitary kingship over all the component parts of Francia was preserved until 714.[67] All the kings between these dates exercised their authority from Neustria. (This actually allowed the Mayors of the Palace in Austrasia, where there was normally no resident royal court, to gain an even greater grip on the resources and patronage of the monarchy in this region.) In this same period, it should be noticed, there were no minorities and two of the kings achieved, at least by Merovingian standards, ripe old ages: Theuderic III (673, 675–690/1) was approximately thirty-five at the time of his death, as was his son Childebert III (695–711).

However, for all of that, the sources do not speak, as they had of Chlotar II and of Dagobert I, of the kings taking the lead in events or initiating policies in this period. From the narrative sources it is clear that in both the Neustrian and Austrasian courts from 638 onwards the prime movers were those officials holding the office of Mayor of the Palace. These men ran the royal administration and exercised patronage over royal lands and appointments, including those to bishoprics, in the kings' names. Under them were a variety of other officers, including the Count of the Palace, who controlled the royal household.

Initially the Mayors were chosen by the kings, but in the minorities that were occasioned in Neustria by the deaths of Dagobert I in 638 and of Clovis II in 657, it was the Frankish nobility that appointed the wives of the former kings (Nantechildis and Baldechildis) to act as regents for their sons and named the new Mayors of the Palace (Aega and Ebroin).[68] Nantechildis and Aega co-operated closely in the years 638–42, as initially did Baldechildis and Ebroin, though it is possible that the latter forced the queen to retire into the monastery of Chelles in 664/5 when her son Chlotar III attained his technical majority.[69] From this point onwards few of the kings are found exercising personal authority. Some tried to, such as Childeric II after he became king in Neustria in 673, but he was murdered by an aristocratic faction in 675.[70]

Although the older arguments concerning the personal failings and psychological weaknesses of the Merovingian line may not have much to commend them, it does seem to be the case that the period from 638 to the 660s saw a crucial transformation in the exercise of central authority within Francia. In both Neustria and Austrasia the periods of royal minority in these decades enabled powerful factions to form amongst the aristocracy, leaders of which were put into place primarily through control of the office of Mayor of the Palace. Some of these men, notably the Neustrian Ebroin, proved effective manipulators of factional politics.[71] On occasion internal conflicts within the ruling class could erupt into violence, as when Ebroin and his newly appointed Merovingian king Theuderic III were temporarily overthrown in 673.[72] A similar factional conflict in Neustria in 687 led to one party calling on the Austrasian Mayor of the Palace, Pippin II, for assistance. This led to the battle of Tertry between Pippin and his Neustrian allies on the one hand and the Neustrian Mayor Berchar and the King Theuderic III on the other. From this, as will be examined in chapter 15, emerged an Austrasian ascendancy over Neustria.

It might be thought that the relative powerlessness of the kings was a symptom of the lack of functioning on the part of central authority and administration in Francia. Paradoxically, the contrary is probably true. At a formal level the central governmental apparatus of the Frankish kingdom, as inherited from the Late Roman Empire and modified in the earlier Merovingian period, appears surprisingly well maintained in the seventh century. Frankish royal charters, unlike, for example, those of the Lombard monarchy in Italy, still took the form of mandates from the king to the local count – addressed, in late imperial style, as *magnitudo seu utilitas vestra*.[73] These were royal commands to the count to invest the person or institution named in the document with the property or rights that were delineated, and not just records of a title granted verbally. Such a form of text was predicated upon the continuance of ties between central authority and its local representatives.

The kings, or those who controlled their policy, had available to them their powers of appointment to the principal offices that conveyed local authority, those of *dux* and *comes* – 'duke' and 'count'. The titles derived from the Late Roman military administration, and the functions of the office-holders did not differ much from those of their imperial prototypes. Identical functionaries could be found in Visigothic Spain at the same period. Simply put, the dukes commanded regional armies, and the counts were the principal royal officials in the *civitates* (the main towns and their related territories) of the Frankish kingdoms, with responsibility for any garrison troops, and for the maintenance of local order, and possibly with oversight of the collection of royal revenues from estates and customs duties (*telonea*). Subsections of the *civitates*, called *pagi*, were under the supervision of the count's deputies, known as *Vicarii*.[74]

As well as through his written mandates, other procedures existed that served to keep the ruler in touch with his leading representatives and the most powerful elements in the local society of his kingdom. Perhaps most significant in this respect was the annual assembly of the principal men in the kingdom, held in theory on the Kalends of March (1 March) at a site stipulated by the king. This gathering was of crucial significance, as it was here that discussion of current problems, grievances and military strategy took place. Legal deliberations were also held between the king and 'the elders and Frankish nobility', and these led to the issue of a number of decrees that recorded the decisions reached. A small number of these have survived.[75]

The earliest known Frankish law code, the *Lex Salica*, does not present itself as the product of royal will and, contrary to general belief, the evidence for its being promulgated by Clovis is slight. The earliest manuscript dates to 770, and the earliest reference to the existence of such a corpus of law comes in an edict issued by King Chilperic (561–84), dated to about 574.[76] However, the legal principle referred to in the edict does not feature in the known text of *Lex Salica*. Not before the issue at Cologne of a systematised form of the text by Childebert II on 1 March 596 does any evidence emerge for the existence of the written text of *Lex Salica*.[77] No mention of Clovis may be found in the code, other than for an ambiguous statement in a preface written in the mid-eighth century that the first sixty-five sections were the work of 'the first king of the Franks'.[78] This could apply as much to Childeric I as to Clovis, if not to one of their predecessors, and it actually serves no more than as an assertion of the antiquity of this section of the text.

While it remains perfectly possible that the earliest form of *Lex Salica* was a systematised collection of the edicts of Clovis (possibly including similar decrees and decisions of his father), there is no proof that it was actually put together in his reign. That it did indeed derive from or consisted of some form of compilation of royal edicts is a reasonable deduction, and it can be shown from internal references that some of these can have dated from no earlier than 507/8. On the other hand, what probably should be avoided is the notion that this code was therefore no more than a propagandistic manifesto, designed to enhance the status of a Frankish monarch, who might thereby be made to look more Romanised or even quasi-imperial. Whatever else may be said about it, it should be seen as being intended to have practical as well as symbolic significance, and it did not derive from any hoary pre-Merovingian past of the Frankish people.

The survival of procedures of centralised administration and law-making gave the Merovingian monarchy a particular inherent strength, irrespective of the capacity or otherwise of those nominally supposed to wield authority. It thus became far more attractive for those who wished to advance themselves, their kin and their followers to try to co-operate in gaining control of the apparatus of central government rather than to try to ignore it and look to the building up of purely regional and localised power bases. Hence the rise of aristocratic factions competing to secure their dominance over Neustria or Austrasia, and ultimately over both together.[79] The final stages and consequences of this process after the battle of Tertry in 687 will need to be examined in a subsequent chapter.

11   The re-creating of Britain

Entrepreneurial rulers, 410–597

Britain is often treated as being very different to other regions of the former western Empire in respect of its history in the centuries following the end of Roman rule. In part this is a reflection of the insularity of the English historiographical tradition, but it is also a reaction to genuine dissimilarities in the development of Britain and other parts of Western Europe. However, these may be fewer and less significant than is usually believed. It is only when British conditions are seen in comparison with those of the rest of Western Europe in the fifth and sixth centuries that a proper perspective on British history at this time can be achieved.

The principal problem, as always, is one of evidence. The sources for the history of Britain in the fifth century are exceedingly scanty, even if, paradoxically, more substantial than for some of the earlier periods when Britain was generally a sleepy if contented part of the Roman Empire.[1] Where the trouble lies is in the interpretation of the evidence, and more particularly in the assessment of the relevance or otherwise of individual items of it. The problems are largely methodological ones, and depend principally upon the degree of willingness or otherwise on the part of individual historians to take account of materials that are considerably later in date than the period under consideration, and whose acceptability as sources depends upon belief either in 'missing links' in the transmission or in oral tradition.[2]

The best example of this difficulty comes in a text known from its manuscript title as the *Historia Brittonum* or 'History of the Britons', and which also has been known as 'Nennius', after its supposed compiler. This Nennius, whose name does not appear in all of the manuscripts, was a disciple of a certain Elvodug, who has been argued to be the same as Elfoddw (d. 809) 'archbishop of Venedotia' (probably the see of Bangor in Gwynedd).[3] This is a far from certain identification, as is Nennius's responsibility for the work of compilation, but the evidence of the earliest manuscript seems to place the date of completion of the work in the year 829/30. No two of the manuscripts of it are identical in their contents, and the 'core text' formed by the original compiler has to be reconstructed by deduction.[4]

The *Historia Brittonum*, as it is probably safest to call it, contains a variety of items relating to the history of the island, not least a section that contains the first reference to 'Arthur' in a list of twelve battles that he is supposed to have fought against the Saxons as war leader of the Britons.[5] This has particularly aroused the enthusiasm of those who wish to see an historical Arthur behind the figure of medieval legend, but it represents only one facet of the Nennius problem.[6] The dearth of contemporary evidence has led to many of the elements in this compilation being used in the interpretation of the fifth and sixth centuries in Britain. Only recently has such an approach been challenged, but the swing away from general acceptance of the testimony of the *Historia Brittonum* is now marked.[7]

The only issue that might remain contentious about this text concerns one of the sections, which unlike any other of the various components, is dated by reference to consulships.[8] This form of dating for historical texts was abandoned by the last quarter of the sixth century throughout Europe, not least due to the abolition of the consular office by the Emperor Justinian in 551. This would imply that this section of the text, which is very brief and contains only a few chronicle-like entries relating to the fifth century, may be of genuinely early date. However, the ultra-cautious amongst the modern historians of this period in Britain are inclined to suspect that later elements have been interpolated into the original chronological framework, and that it is in consequence impossible to rely on any of its information. This principally means that the date it gives for the arrival of the Anglo-Saxons in Britain, in the fourth year of the reign of Valentinian III (428/9), cannot be trusted.

Other texts that once were allowed some significance in elucidating the history of this period, but which are now distrusted or entirely ruled out of court, include the collection of apparently interrelated poems known as the *Canu Aneirin* ('Song of Aneirin') or also as the *Gododdin*.[9] These represent a series of bardic laments over a group of British warriors, who at the behest of the King of Gododdin, a British kingdom centred on Dun Eddin (Edinburgh), fought against the Saxons at Catraeth (Catterick in Co. Durham), around the year 600. The text has proved extraordinarily difficult to understand; so much so that one of its first editors revised and translated it as if it were concerned with a battle fought in 1098 in North Wales between the Norman Earl of Shrewsbury and King Magnus III of Norway![10] If more recent scholarship has rescued the work from that fate, and shown it to concern a 'Dark Age' battle instead, it has not been able to prove either the reality of the war described or the proximity of the date of composition of the poems to the events they purport to describe. Similar problems attend the rest of the small corpus of early Welsh (in language) poetry relating to historical episodes in this period.[11]

If, as seems necessary, all of the *Historia Brittonum* materials and the Welsh heroic poems have to be put to one side as representing no more than later elaborations or legendary accretions, then the amount of evidence that is genuinely pertinent to the study of Britain in the period *c*. 410–*c*. 597 is very small. Its largest component is the work of the monk Gildas, entitled *De Excidio Brittonum* or 'The Ruin of the Britons'. Whilst, again, there existed a tendency amongst earlier generations of historians to take Gildas's work as if it were an historical composition, and to try to stretch its scanty references to fifth century events as far as they would go, there is now a great readiness to see it for what it really is, a work of moral exhortation, that makes some use of historical material in a deliberately tendentious way. It is thus very like the early fifth century Gallic work, *De Gubernatione Dei* or 'On the Governance of God' of the priest Salvian. This too tended to be rummaged in by historians looking for information about the economic and moral well-being (or rather lack thereof) of the western Roman Empire.

Problems still exist as to the date at which Gildas wrote (probably *c*. 540, but possibly as early as *c*. 520), the region in which he was working, and other aspects of his life.[12] Later Celtic *Lives* of Gildas seem to offer no reliable information, and little trust should be placed in the idea that he spent his later years in Brittany.[13] A brief penitential for monks is also ascribed to this author. From the details of the penances it imposed – referring to British cheese and Roman units of liquid measurement – it is certainly a British work, but how far the manuscript ascription of it to Gildas should be believed is highly debatable.[14]

Possibly the most important thing to appreciate about Gildas's *De Excidio* is that the opening historical survey, which is intended to provide the material for his denunciation of British vices, is not chronologically sequential. Thus it appears that the problems the Britons faced in the late fourth and fifth centuries with the Picts and the Irish precede all their conflicts with the Saxons; whereas Gildas has actually arranged his materials so as to discuss the wars with the Irish and the Picts before those against the Saxons.[15] Non-recognition of this important truth has led, not surprisingly, to some chronological problems for historians of the period.

Without going in detail into the arguments, it is possible to suggest on the basis of this all too limited body of evidence the following clear features. Firstly, from soon after the withdrawal of the units of the Roman field army from Britain by Constantine III in 407, parts of the island were subjected to raids, and in limited areas some colonisation on the part of the Picts and the Irish took place. Secondly, from some point in the first half of the fifth century onwards, Saxons, who themselves had been conducting seaborne raids on the south coast, were taken on by the rulers of parts of southern Britain as federates to provide defence against the Irish and the Picts. Thus they came into the island, very much in the way that the Franks and the Visigoths established themselves in northern Francia and Spain, to take on the role and fill the niche in society that had once been occupied by the Roman army. Increasing numbers of these Saxons appear to have been established at various points in eastern and northern Britain in consequence of such agreements. It is possible that the imperial government, then controlled by Aetius, was involved in the making of such a treaty of federation around the year 442, but the primary responsibility may rest with the various local potentates and oligarchies that gained control of parts of the island after the ending of direct Roman rule.[16]

Now it is normally thought that the most significant feature of the period between 410 and the time when Gildas was writing his *De Excidio* (*c.* 520/40) was the revolt of the Saxons against the Britons and their consequent conquest of much of the eastern half of Britain. This used also to be allied to a view which saw the Saxons as effectively 'pushing' the Britons westwards into the regions of Wales, Cumbria and the south-west. In fact, the perspective to be gained from reading Gildas's work is that the problems with the Saxons had been settled after some heavy fighting some forty years prior to the time of his writing, in other words in the 480s or around 500. For him the Saxon menace was actually a thing of the past.[17]

Taking the period *c.* 410–*c.* 540 as a whole, what was probably far more significant than the occasional difficulties with the Saxons, was the disappearance in Britain of centralised government. In 410 a unitary authority had existed in the island – other than in the regions north of Hadrian's Wall – which by the mid-sixth century had totally disappeared, to be replaced by a series of small-scale and mutually antagonistic kingdoms. Gildas refers to the rulers of a number of these: Constantine of Dumnonia, Aurelius Caninus, Vortipor of the Demetae, Cuneglasus and Maglocunus.[18] Dumnonia is easily located (in the area of Devon) because of the implied relationship with the Celtic tribe of the Dumnonii, and Maglocunus is almost certainly to be identified with a king of Gwynedd known in later vernacular sources as Maelgw(y)n.[19] Attempts have been made to locate the other kingdoms, but these can be at best approximate, and because of the subsequent fame of Gildas's work little reliance should be placed on the apparent appearance of some of these names in later Welsh royal genealogies.[20]

Even so, the phenomenon they represent is well attested, not only in the west, but also in the north and beyond Hadrian's Wall, where tribal kingdoms had long existed. Moreover, such kingdoms were also coming into existence in the centre and east of the island in the course of the sixth century. That the populations subject to the rulers of these kingdoms were in some cases exclusively Celtic-speaking, and in others Celtic- and Germanic-speaking, is of rather less importance than is often assumed. That the Saxons extirpated or expelled the British inhabitants of the lowland parts of the island is no longer believed, and even in areas that were, politically speaking, under Saxon rule there is now no question that substantial elements of the former Romano-British population continued to exist.[21] In such regions intermarriage and mutual cultural assimilation seem rapidly to have produced quite homogeneous societies, in which, for example, Anglo-Saxon-speaking kings could have Celtic names.[22]

Difficulties of understanding have largely been created by imposing the perspectives of later centuries onto the realities of the later fifth and sixth. By the middle of the seventh century relatively large kingdoms had come into being in Britain, which had not existed 100 years earlier. Subsequently, in at least one of these, the dominant southern kingdom of Wessex, a historiographical tradition had been developed that sought to give its monarchy a past in a period in which it had in reality not been present. Thus the compilers of the late ninth century original version of the *Anglo-Saxon Chronicle* looked for, and thought they had found, the antecedents of their kingdom in a period, the sixth century, in which no such entity had existed.[23]

The second half of the sixth century in Britain was an entrepreneurial age in which a series of individuals and families of mixed Anglian or Saxon and Romano-British origin struggled to create local bases of power for themselves. The scale of operation of such 'war lords' was generally quite small and geographically restricted, but in comparative terms some did very well for themselves indeed. A case in point would be that of Ceawlin (fl. 556–93), one of those presented by the *Anglo-Saxon Chronicle* as being a king of Wessex, although the area of his activities, in the upper Thames and the Cotswolds, was far removed from the heartlands of the later kingdom, as it was also from the areas in the south of modern Hampshire in which the same source locates his supposed relatives and predecessors.[24]

In that the dates for Ceawlin's career come exclusively from the *Anglo-Saxon Chronicle*, the chronological exactitude of which is particularly suspect for any period up to the late ninth century, some latitude must be given in trying to provide an exact account of his activities. Taking the *Chronicle* references as at best approximations (and at worst as guesses), it is under the year 556 that Ceawlin first appears, fighting together with a certain Cynric against the Britons at *Beranburh*. However, as this same Cynric, the son of Cerdic, is recorded in the *Chronicle* as arriving in Britain in 495, it is somewhat incredible, to say the least, to find him apparently still going strong over 60 years later.

There is in fact an unbridgeable chronological gulf between the supposed founding period of the notional kingdom of Wessex in the late fifth century and the next period in which supposed members of its ruling house are to be found, which is to say in the second half of the sixth. In practice much of the information relating to the early phase is of a distinctly 'folklorique' character: Cerdic and Cynric land at a place called *Cerdicesora*; they kill a 'Welsh' king called Natanleod, and henceforth that district is called *Natanleod* (Netley near Southampton), and so forth.[25] The suspicion must exist that the place names preceded the persons referred to, rather than the other way around, and that the history of the latter was to some extent concocted to explain the existence of the former.

Genealogical information is equally suspect. Ceawlin's relationship to Cerdic and Cynric is never specified in the body of the *Chronicle* though he is said under the year 560 to have succeeded to the kingdom of Wessex that they created.[26] For 568 it is reported that Ceawlin and a certain Cutha fought against Æthelberht of Kent. In 577 he appears fighting alongside a certain Cuthwine against the Britons in the battle of Dyrham (probably the manor of that name close to Bath). To make matters worse an otherwise unattested Cuthwulf is reported to have fought the Britons at *Bedcanford* in 571. The continuators of the original version of the *Chronicle* were as confused as are modern historians by all of this, and one of them, the scribe of the 'E' or Parker version, added to the text concerning the year 571 the statement 'That Cutha was the brother of Ceawlin.' In that this is not common to all of the versions of the *Chronicle* it cannot belong to the core text, and can only be a later insertion. Unfortunately, modern scholars clutching for evidential straws have often wanted to believe it.[27]

The battle reported to have taken place at Dyrham in 577 in which Ceawlin and Cuthwine fought against and killed the kings of Bath, Cirencester and Gloucester, is peculiarly intriguing. It implies for one thing the continued occupation of these Roman towns and the existence of various otherwise unattested small kingdoms in the Cotswolds and valley of the Severn. Unfortunately, archaeology cannot yet confirm any occupation of Bath between the fourth and seventh centuries; though it is possible that this should be sought for in the context of a reoccupied hill-fort rather than in the former Roman settlement. In the case of Cirencester, however, fairly extensive excavation has revealed that the former Roman amphitheatre, outside the city walls, was converted for occupation in the fifth century.[28] This is something that certainly happened in a number of towns in the south of France in the seventh and eighth centuries, but so far in the case of Cirencester no evidence of occupation into the sixth century has yet been detected.

If a battle was fought at Dyrham – possibly around the hill-fort there – in the late sixth century, and if, as the *Chronicle* records, this led to the conquest of the three small kingdoms by Ceawlin and his allies, this certainly should not be seen in the context of an 'Anglo-Saxon' advance at the expense of the 'Britons', as the later Wessex sources would like to portray it. For one thing the archaeological evidence from the Severn valley does not confirm a Saxon presence in cultural terms at this time.[29]

As has been stressed above, it is important to separate the 'Anglianisation' of the culture and language of lowland Britain from the political history of the various kingdoms of mixed Saxon and Celtic origin that were being created – and in many cases also destroyed – in this formative period of the sixth and first half of the seventh century. Perhaps the nearest the *Anglo-Saxon Chronicle* gets to capturing the reality of this time is in its entry for 597, when it records that Ceolwulf, whom it presents as King of Wessex, 'ever fought and made war either against the Angles, or against the Welsh, or against the Picts, or against the Scots'. Quite how he got his hands on any Picts is not clear, and the only people whom the *Chronicle* actually record him as fighting against were the South Saxons, but as a piece of literary invention this brief entry captures the spirit of this entrepreneurial age.[30]

Christian kingdoms, 598–685

By the very end of the sixth century larger, more coherent, kingdoms had emerged in Kent under Æthelberht (565?–616) and in Northumbria under Æthelfrith (*c.* 593–617). The latter was created from the uniting of the two smaller kingdoms of Bernicia and Deira, divided by the valley of the Tees, which both had Celtic names, testifying again to the fusion of Anglo-Saxon and Romano-British elements in the formation of so many of the societies that developed in the eastern and central parts of Britain in the sixth century.[31]

An obvious question in relation to cultural survivals from the earlier Roman domination of the island is that concerning continuity in the practice of Christianity. Evidence relating to the establishment of Christianity in Britain in the fourth century is extremely hard to find, but there are few grounds to doubt its presence by the time imperial rule had come to an end in 410.[32] What is particularly notable is the strength of Christianity in those areas of Britain which under the Empire were least Romanised or where the imperial presence had been primarily military: in the mountains of Wales and along and beyond the northern frontiers.

The penetration of Christianity into these regions may well have been in part the product of a cultural osmosis between the British kingdoms north of Hadrian's Wall and the Empire to the south. Although it is often suggested that the north of Roman Britain was essentially a military zone, with little civilian settlement and limited Romanisation, the evidence of the impact of Roman material culture north of the Wall might give grounds for doubt. Conflict and resistance in military terms should not be equated with indifference or hostility in cultural ones.

It is possible, though, that the disintegration of the fixed frontier between the Empire and the British tribes to the north of the Wall, that came about in the late fourth century, accelerated the process of communication and exchange, in which the import of Christianity from the south was a major component. By the middle of the fifth century a Christian community certainly existed in Galloway, as recorded both in inscriptions from Whithorn and Kirkmadrine, and in the brief account of the career of the missionary Bishop Nynia that was put by the Anglian monk Bede into his *Historia Ecclesiastica Gentis Anglorum* of 731/2.[33] The inscriptions record the existence of various named bishops and clerics in this region *c.* 450, and also the possible dedication of a church.[34] Nynia, who cannot be easily dated on the basis of Bede, may have lived up to half a century earlier or later. What is particularly significant about him, though, is the claim that he was engaged in expanding the hold of Christianity further north still to the kingdom(s) of the Picts.

The Picts have sometimes been seen, like the Basques, as being one of the oldest and longest established of the peoples of Western Europe, with an origin in the period before the Indo-European migrations into Western Europe in the early Iron Age. Such a view depended primarily upon the linguistic analysis of a handful of inscriptions dating from the seventh to ninth centuries, some elements of which were thought to be non Indo-European. However, this has recently been challenged, and all of the scanty linguistic evidence relating to Pictish can be interpreted in the light of its being a Celtic language of the 'P', as opposed to 'Q', family (Welsh, Cornish and Breton as opposed to Irish and Scots Gaelic). Despite some origin legends of probably Irish origin, recorded by Bede, that would make the Picts post-Roman immigrants into Scotland, archaeological evidence supports the continuity of their presence on the Scottish mainland and in the northern isles from at least the Iron Age onwards. Although the best known Pictish monuments dating to the period after the ending of Roman rule are a series of finely carved free-standing symbol stones, the exact purpose and meaning of which continue to be a source of debate, there are good grounds for believing that this society also produced written records, hardly any traces of which have survived.[35] This literacy was almost certainly confined to the clergy, but was a reflection of the success of outside influences in bringing about the spread of Christianity in the Pictish lands in a period extending from the fifth to early eighth centuries.

Conflicting traditions as to the routes and timing of the penetration of Christianity, and with it some of the intellectual culture of the Mediterranean Roman world, into their society have led to the belief that at least two separate groups of Picts have to be envisaged. On the one hand Bede has Nynia converting the 'southern Picts' in the fifth century, while the Irish Abbot Columba (d. 597), the founder of Iona, is made responsible for converting those Picts subject to a King Bruide.[36] It has therefore been assumed that Nynia's mission from Galloway was to a southern Pictish kingdom, whilst that of Columba was to a northern one perhaps centred around Inverness, with a dividing line between the two lying somewhere in the region of the Mounth.[37] However, serious reservations have been expressed as to the validity of both of these accounts of missionary activity. The special roles claimed for both Nynia and of Columba may be a reflection of the importance that came to be attached to them in the traditions of Whithorn and of Iona respectively, and not constitute reliable evidence of their actual personal involvement in such missionary labours. As in the parallel case of Patrick in Ireland (see chapter 13) it is possibly unwise to place too much emphasis on the activities of single individuals, and preferable to look to gradual dissemination through prolonged cultural contact and exchange.

Survival of Christianity in the lowland regions of central and southern Britain, which came under the domination of rulers of Anglo-Saxon origin, and where the bulk of the waves of new immigrants had settled, is an even more contentious issue than that of its northwards extension beyond Hadrian's Wall. The simple view, derived from the great *Ecclesiastical History* of Bede (d. 735), is that the Anglo-Saxon kingdoms and all their inhabitants were pagan until the arrival of the mission sent to Kent by Pope Gregory the Great in 597. Yet even Bede's own account, deriving from information he received from Canterbury, reveals certain anomalous features.

The King of Kent, Æthelberht, to whom the mission led by the monk Augustine had been sent, had married the daughter of the Frankish King Charibert (561–7). In so doing he had had to agree that she should be permitted to continue the practice of her own religion, and she had been accompanied to Kent by the Frankish Bishop Liudhard, who is usually described as her chaplain.[38] However, when it is appreciated that in this period bishops are never to be found without an episcopal see and were never sent or consecrated other than to existing Christian communities, the fact that a Frankish bishop was exercising his ministry in Kent in the second half of the sixth century indicates the pre-existence there of a body of fellow believers.[39] For them to need a bishop means that more than a kind of Frankish *corps diplomatique* was involved, and that several clergy of lesser rank would have already been functioning. However imprecise an indicator, the previous presence in Canterbury of Liudhard might prove the existence of a Christian community in Kent prior to Augustine's arrival in 597.

Even so, the advent of the group of monks sent from Rome by the pope was unquestionably crucial in that it led to the baptism of the king and of substantial numbers of his followers.[40] A new ecclesiastical organisation was able to develop, despite a brief setback caused by the initial apostasy of Æthelberht's son Eadbald (616–40). He subsequently came to accept the advantages offered by conversion, and his son and successor Eorcenberht (640–64) became a still more thoroughgoing Christian, even imposing the observance of Lent on his subjects.[41]

The Roman mission to Kent in 597 had extended its sphere of influence northwards in 625 when a sister of Eadbald had married King Edwin of Northumbria, who agreed to accept Christianity as well as a wife. One of the Roman missionaries, Paulinus, had accompanied the queen to Northumbria and begun the conversion of the king's followers. However, Edwin's death in 632 in battle against King Cadwallon of Gwynedd and Penda the King of the Mercians led to the collapse of his mission. Paulinus, recently appointed as the first Archbishop of York, fled south, and was subsequently assigned the see of Rochester in Kent.[42]

In practice the most significant consequence of these events was that power in Northumbria passed back into the hands of a rival branch of the royal dynasty, whose leader, Oswald, defeated and killed the invading Cadwallon in 633. Oswald (633–42) the son of Æthelfrith had been converted to Christianity by Irish monks while in exile after Edwin had overthrown his father. (The contentious issues of the establishment and nature of Christianity in Ireland will be discussed in chapter 13 below.) Thus, once secure on the throne of Northumbria he turned to the Irish monks of Iona to take the place of Paulinus and his southern followers, who had been so closely associated with the rival regime of Edwin.[43]

The nature of ecclesiastical organisation that had developed in the Mediterranean in the time of the Late Roman Empire depended upon the existence of towns for its primary structure. The intimate relationship between town and countryside that characterised Late Antiquity provided this ready made. Towns were the centres of local administration and fiscal organisation, and the principal local landowners would in most cases also have urban residences. Towns were also the principal market places for the surplus goods of the countryside and the centres in which skilled trades, such as pottery making, could be established, depending upon a network of exchange relationships with rural as well as urban consumers. Thus just as civil magistrates, many of whose responsibilities they came to share, administered justice from the towns, so too could the bishops oversee the ecclesiastical organisation and discipline of their dioceses from an urban centre. Similarly, in pre-Christian times the towns had been the cult centres for the surrounding region, and this was something that the new religion had been able to capitalise on, installing the Christian martyrs as the spiritual patrons of the towns and their hinterlands.

This was the kind of pattern that Christian organisation depended upon, and which Gregory the Great had obviously envisaged as being established in the Anglo-Saxon kingdoms as conversion spread. He had already devised a blueprint for new episcopal sees and their locations, in which archiepiscopal sees would be established in London and York, with each having twelve suffragan dioceses under its jurisdiction.[44] In practice the realities of the situation were rather different from those envisaged in Rome. Thus London, the principal administrative centre of Late Roman Britain, and probably the largest town in the British provinces, was by the late sixth century in the territory of the relatively minor kingdom of the East Saxons, and not a suitable headquarters for a church primarily dependent on the patronage of the kings of Kent. Instead Canterbury, described by Bede as the *metropolis* of all of Æthelberht's domain, became the see of Augustine and his successors.[45] In the north, while York did become the seat, albeit intermittently, of an archbishop, it long remained the only episcopal see in the kingdom of Deira. While its only suffragans were to be three bishoprics based on monasteries in Bernicia and a fourth briefly established at Abercorn near Edinburgh during the period of Northumbrian expansion northwards in the mid-seventh century.

It is thus quite vital to understand something of the state of towns in Anglo-Saxon England in this period if the nature and organisation of the Church are to be understood. The tendency in the past, partly based on misleading views of a thorough 'Germanisation' of lowland Britain, and partly on the negative results of excavations, was to deny post-Roman urban survival in the island. Yet, as previously mentioned, more recent excavation, using more sensitive techniques and, perhaps more importantly, actually looking for such traces, has uncovered some evidence of continuing occupation of much-reduced town sites in a number of cases, including Cirencester, Wroxeter and, most recently, Carlisle. More such discoveries may follow.

Relatively slight as these traces are, they do confirm the impression given by the written sources that some Roman towns still functioned as centres of administration, even if their economic roles as markets and centres of population had declined. Canterbury is obviously a case in point, and in Northumbria it seems likely that York remained an important if occasional royal centre, where the king's palace may have been located within the former Roman military headquarters complex. In some cases, strategic or other considerations had led to the relocation of the new centre to a site close to, but no longer within the confines of the previous Roman settlement. This was the case with Cirencester and also *Verulamium*/St Albans. Other 'towns' that feature in the albeit problematic literary sources include Bath, Gloucester, Lincoln, Rochester, Dorchester (Oxon.), Edinburgh and Dumbarton.[46]

The number of such survivals was small and in none of these cases, any more than with York or Canterbury, should large-scale occupation be imagined. As previously mentioned, the need for towns as specialised centres of production and as market places for rural produce had declined greatly, not only in Britain but throughout most of the former western Roman Empire from the fifth century onwards. Where towns continued it was more as ceremonial and government centres. Because of the previous pattern of ecclesiastical organisation and the pre-existing links between urban cult sites and rural votaries, the stone-built church complexes – involving several church buildings, baptisteries and episcopal palaces – continued to be occupied and to serve the periodic liturgical needs of an increasingly ruralised congregation. Thus it is possible to imagine that the major festivals of the Church's year and local patronal festivals would attract country-dwelling worshippers to the urban cult sites, doubtless with opportunities for regional market exchange taking place at the same time. Similarly the rulers, or in larger kingdoms their local representatives, would periodically conduct business in such settings: holding courts and conducting consultations with the leading men of the area or of the kingdom.

It is important also to note the role of rural royal residences and administrative sites, such as that excavated at Yeavering in the Northumbrian kingdom of Bernicia.[47] These would be especially prominent in such kingdoms as Bernicia or East Anglia, which for historical reasons lacked the major Roman urban centres of some of the other realms, but it is important also to bear in mind that the Merovingian kings likewise appear to have spent most of their time in rural palaces and only occasionally held assemblies and winter courts in towns such as Soissons.

Overall, the nature of the ecclesiastical organisation that developed in lowland Britain in the sixth century was conditioned by such factors as the pre-existence and survival of towns. In a few cases, such as that of Canterbury, where towns were still used as major royal centres, episcopal monasteries of the type that were common in continental Europe (see chapter 13) could develop. Thus, the monks who accompanied Augustine to Kent in 597 were established in the monastery of St Peter, later known as St Augustine's, which became the burial place for the first archbishops, and for several of the Kentish kings. In other areas, notably in Northumbria, rural monasteries were the norm.

Very similar monastic establishments to those then to be found in Ireland and on Iona were created under Irish inspiration in Northumbria in the mid-seventh century, notably at Lindisfarne and in the joint monastery of St Paul at Jarrow and St Peter at Wearmouth, in which Bede lived and worked.[48] These latter were, however, subject to other than exclusively Irish influence, in that after the Synod of Whitby in 664, a debate on the respective merits of Irish and Roman customs relating to the calculation of the date of Easter and the form of the monastic tonsure, that was held in the presence of the Northumbrian King Oswy (642–70), continental ties grew in strength.[49]

Because of the papal inspiration behind the Augustinian mission and the role that Gregory the Great and his successors played in instructing and advising both Augustine, who was consecrated as Archbishop of Canterbury in 599, and the kings of Kent and Northumbria, very close ties were formed between the Roman Church and that in the Anglo-Saxon kingdoms. It became customary for the archbishops of Canterbury from Augustine onwards to receive from the popes after their consecration a *pallium*, a thin stole worn around the neck in the performance of the liturgy, as a sign of the special and subordinate relationship of the one to the other. The first account of the life of Gregory the Great was written early in the eight century in the Northumbrian monastery of Whitby.[50] Thus, despite the largely Irish origins of Christianity in the Anglo-Saxon kingdom of Northumbria, by the later seventh century kings such as Oswy and aristocratic monastic founders such as Benedict Biscop were looking to Rome for instruction – as were the Irish themselves.

Biscop, the founder of Wearmouth (674) and Jarrow (681), made a number of journeys to Rome to buy books, to obtain the service of specialist craftsmen in such arts as glass making and to obtain direction on Roman liturgical procedures. For the latter Pope Agatho (678–81) sent the papal arch-cantor John to Wearmouth and Jarrow with Biscop to provide instruction on the spot – and also to carry out an investigation into the orthodoxy of the teaching of the English Church.[51] By the early eighth century the monastery of Jarrow was able to produce such a masterwork of Mediterranean-style calligraphic and book-painting art as the *Codex Amiatinus* (pre-716), which was to be sent as a present to Rome, that it was long difficult for modern palaeographers to accept it as a manuscript of English provenance.[52]

The fusion of Irish and Mediterranean traditions in northern Britain has also left tangible results of itself that can be seen in the artistic products of Northumbria in the later seventh and eight centuries, particularly in the fields of manuscript illumination and of sculpture. In both areas what is most notable is the juxtaposition or co-existence of elements that are either clearly Celtic or Roman in inspiration In such well known manuscripts as the Lindisfarne Gospels, written a little before the year 698 by Eadfrith, Bishop of Lindisfarne (698–721), the text is decorated in a purely Celtic fashion, while the full page portraits of the four evangelists are clearly dependent on Late Antique models from the Mediterranean.[53] Similarly, the earliest works of monumental sculpture produced in the northern Anglo-Saxon kingdoms, principally a series of large free-standing crosses, can display a combination of sophisticated and well understood use of Mediterranean models for figurative art with decorative features that are purely Celtic in inspiration – or they can adhere exclusively to one style or the other.[54]

The Mercian hegemony, 633–874

By the time that this artistic and intellectual revival was taking place in the north the kingdom of Kent had become, politically speaking, something of a backwater, and had long been overtaken in terms of size and respective strength by the more recently developed kingdoms of Wessex and Mercia. The latter, which derived from the amalgamation and conquest of a large number of very small kingdoms (often seen, rather deceptively, as separate 'tribes' or peoples), only really emerges into historiographical view under its King Penda (626?–55).[55] He was a pagan until his death, although initially the ally or possibly the subordinate of the Christian King Cadwallon of Gwynedd (north-west Wales), and this, together with his conflicts with neighbouring kingdoms, has inevitably coloured his presentation in the major narrative sources pertinent to the period: the Northumbrian (and partly Kentish) *Ecclesiastical History* of Bede and the West Saxon *Anglo-Saxon Chronicle*.

In practice, though, Penda may have been the first of the kings of the central part of Britain who, through conquest and diplomacy, was able to put together a powerful confederacy uniting a number of hitherto disparate small kingdoms. Some of those elements may still be represented in an eighth century document, possibly a tribute list of the Mercian kings of that period, known as the *Tribal Hideage*.[56] It would be unwise to see the various 'peoples' represented in this as being separate ethnic entities or survivals of earlier Germanic tribal divisions. These are merely traces of the small kingdoms in the central parts of the island that had come into existence in the fifth and sixth centuries, but which were finally swallowed up by the most successful of their number, the Mercian kingdom of Penda, in the first half of the seventh. The most substantial of these conquests at this time was probably another large-scale kingdom, though one in what may be called larval or embryo form, that was known as the kingdom of the Middle Angles. Although artificially preserved as an appanage until 656, this then disappeared as a political entity.[57]

For all his success in subjecting these smaller components of what was to become the kingdom of Mercia, together with the elimination of the rival Middle Anglian kingdom, Penda was not in the 630s able to compete with the longer-established, large-scale kingdoms that surrounded his. Hence, when threatened by Northumbrian ambitions, he found it expedient to ally with the dominant British kingdom of the west, that of Gwynedd. This pagan–Christian/Saxon–Celt (distinctions which clearly mattered little in the 630s) confederacy was the product of the threat posed to both by the expanding power of the Northumbrian King Edwin (617–32), who was defeated and killed by the allies at the battle of Hatfield Chase.[58] As seen through the eyes of Bede, the Northumbrians take the centre of the stage in the complex pattern of events of the middle of the seventh century, but in practice these could be reinterpreted as the successful resistance of the Mercians to this threat of domination from the north and their consequent rise to effective overlordship over all the various kingdoms of southern and central Britain.

The problems of small-scale Early Medieval warfare are well illustrated by the outcome of the overthrow of Edwin in 632. The two component kingdoms of Northumbria split, each taking a new king from the rival branches of the royal line, but both of these monarchs were killed by Cadwallon in 633. Oswald, the brother of one of them, Eanfrith of Bernicia, was able, however, to defeat and kill the British king in yet another battle in 633 at *Deniseburn*.[59] The small size of the armies and the difficulties of a king, whose centre of power was in North Wales, in imposing his authority over the region of modern Yorkshire made Cadwallon's attempt to hold on to Northumbria extremely vulnerable. Oswald was in consequence of his victory able to resume his predecessor Edwin's ambitions, which included dominance over the kingdoms of central Britain. It was not until 642 that Penda was able to mount a renewed resistance to Northumbrian hegemony, defeating and killing Oswald at the battle of *Maserfelth* (probably Oswestry) – possibly, to judge by the location, with British assistance.[60]

This battle was crucial in that in practice it marked the end of Northumbrian attempts to expand south-westwards. From 642 to 655 Penda and his new Mercian kingdom represented the greatest power amongst the kingdoms of Britain. One of the sons of the next Northumbrian king, Oswy (642–70), was kept a hostage at the Mercian court. Cenwalh the King of Wessex was briefly expelled from his kingdom by Penda (645/6?) and the East Anglian King Anna was killed by him in 654.[61] It is notable how many kings died in battle in this period, and it is likely that the fate of the commander was crucial in determining the outcome of these inter-kingdom conflicts. Penda himself was killed in an invasion of Northumbria in 655 in a battle fought on the river *Winwaed*, probably near Leeds.

Although these events might suggest rapid and dramatic fluctuation, it is clear that Penda's achievements, little as we may now know of them, were permanent ones. In Northumbrian tradition Oswy emerged as having authority over the kings of the south, but in practice this was short-lived. After the overthrow of Penda he had set up the latter's son Peada as king of the southern part of Mercia, keeping the northern territories for himself. But in 658 Peada was murdered by the Mercian nobility, who set up his brother Wulfhere (658–74) as king, and re-established freedom from Northumbrian hegemony.[62] Bede again conceals this process, but it is clear that Wulfhere re-established his father's ascendancy over the East Saxon kingdom – and very probably over that of the

East Angles as well. He also regained control of the northern parts of Mercia, including former dependent territories such as the kingdom of Lindsey (Lincolnshire).[63] His heir Æthelred (674–704) also visited destruction on the kingdom of Kent in 676. The latter also reimposed Mercian rule on Lindsey after this region briefly passed back into Northumbrian control *c.* 674.[64]

Although under Oswy's son Ecgfrith (670–85) the Northumbrian kingdom kept up its hopes of regaining influence in the south and also substantially extended itself northwards, seeing off any remaining British kingdoms between Hadrian's Wall and the Firth of Forth, this expansion was terminated and then rapidly reversed in consequence of the king's defeat and death at the hands of the Picts at the battle of Dunnichen or 'Nechtan's Dun'.[65] Thereafter a truncated and confined Northumbria entered a period of considerable internal instability and stagnation.

On the other hand, the Mercian kingdom was able to exploit the achievements of Penda and Wulfhere and turn its hegemony over the other realms of southern, eastern and central Britain into the norm. There has existed a tendency to talk of this period of Mercian ascendancy as being a product of the eighth century, but it is important to see how much of it had already been achieved from the 640s onwards, and the degree to which the eighth century kings were preserving a state of political affairs that they inherited from their predecessors.[66]

Christianity was introduced into Mercia, firstly through Irish and Northumbrian influence in the 650s. A single bishopric for the kingdom, including Lindsey, was established around 653 and held by a succession of Irish or Irish-trained bishops.[67] Under Bishop Chad (669–71) an episcopal centre was established at Lichfield, which became established as the principal seat of the Mercian bishops. A second diocese was established in the eastern region of the kingdom *c.* 674.[68]

The particular links between the papacy and the Anglo-Saxon kingdoms were emphasised by the growth of traditions of kings renouncing their thrones to retire into monastic life either in Britain or in Rome.[69] The Mercian King Æthelred had retired to the monastery of Bardney in Lindsey in 704. His nephew and successor Ceonred (704–9), withdrew to Rome; a step so unusual that it was recorded in the official collection of papal biographies known as the *Liber Pontificalis*, as well as in the approving pages of Bede.[70] In this he had, however, been preceded by King Caedwalla of Wessex, who had gone to Rome specially to be baptised by the pope in 688. He had, however, died there nine days later, so it is not clear whether or not he had proposed to make his stay a permanent one in the way Ceonred did.[71]

The successors of both of these kings, Ine of Wessex (688–728) and Ceolred of Mercia (709–16) are reported to have fought at Alton Priors in Wiltshire in 715.[72] The outcome is unknown, but the location would argue that this was an act of Mercian aggression, very much in line with the style of kingship followed from the time of Penda onwards. Ceolred's successor Æthelbald (716–57) appears as a monarch of the same stamp, anxious to impose the pre-eminence of his kingdom, and to obtain material benefits from it.

Evidential shortage is peculiarly frustrating in the case of the eighth century in Britain, especially in contrast with the relative profusion of the source materials relating to the seventh. Bede, who was writing in the 730s, has much less to say about the early decades of the eighth century, but does at least confirm that in 731 'all of these kingdoms [Wessex, Essex, Sussex, East Anglia, Kent, and the kingdom of the Hwicce] and the other southern kingdoms which reach right up to the Humber, together with their various kings, are subject to Æthelbald, king of Mercia'.[73] The details of how this was achieved and precisely how it expressed itself are not revealed. The whole nature of 'overlordship' is peculiarly difficult and has been bedevilled by comparisons with artificial Irish legal categorisations of the rights of superior kings over their subordinates, and by the supposed existence of the title of *Bretwalda*.

The blame for the latter really rests with Bede, although he never used the term himself. In book two of his *Ecclesiastical History* he listed seven kings who ruled over all the territories of the *gens Anglorum* south of the river Humber.[74] In the ninth century West Saxon vernacular translation of his work this was formalised as the title of *Bretwalda*, despite Bede not having suggested anything so precise. Bede's seven were Ælle of the South Saxons, Ceawlin, Æthelberht of Kent, Raedwald of the East Angles, and three successive Northumbrians: Edwin, Oswald and Oswy.

It has long been recognised that there are some historical impossibilities here. The evidence relating to Ælle (470s/490s) is slight and highly dubious; that concerning Ceawlin has been examined above and found equally wanting. What is clear is that neither of these exercised much authority over anybody beyond the area of their immediate activities, which were East Sussex and the upper Thames valley respectively. The case of Æthelberht of Kent is far from conclusive, and Raedwald (d. *c.* 625/7) is almost unknown, despite his being the favoured candidate for the man buried in the greatest and first excavated of the mounds in the supposedly royal cemetery at Sutton Hoo (near Woodbridge, Suffolk). Only with the three Northumbrians does a stronger case for some form of hegemony over other kingdoms emerge, and in that of Oswy it can have lasted no more than three years (655–8). Yet, on the other hand, Bede is very specific about Æthelbald of Mercia exercising a supremacy over all of the kingdoms south of the Humber in his reference in book five, even though he does not include him in his list of such rulers in book two! A slightly less reverential approach to the text of Bede might have convinced historians long since that he was not attempting to enshrine a fundamental truth about 'the Olde English Constitution' in this clearly partisan Northumbrian reading of history.[75]

More significant than this problem is the practical one of what precisely such overlordship consisted of. It is surely probable that it depended above all on the continuing ability of the 'overlord' to be able to back up his demands for tribute or acts of submission with a credible threat of force. Any wavering in this would change the relationship. Thus, it is believed that Æthelbald's successor Offa (757–96) lost control of Kent during the period 775–85, and that an indigenous dynasty then re-established its independence in that kingdom, as would happen again in 796.[76]

While the claim to authority could be backed by force, it consisted in all probability of the annual receipt of a fixed tribute from the subordinate kings. It may also have manifested itself in the dominant ruler's ability to travel at will through other kingdoms and hold assemblies in them, in which his superior status would ritually have been made manifest. Thus, for example, Bede records Oswald of Northumbria as being present in Wessex at the time of the consecration of Birinus as the first Bishop of Dorchester (Oxon.). Bede states that both kings gave him the *civitas* as the place to establish his episcopal see.[77] As Dorchester was in the Thames valley, on the frontiers between the West Saxon and Mercian kingdoms, and far from Northumbria, it is usually taken that Oswald, as the superior king, confirmed the grant made by King Cynegisl (611?–42?) of Wessex. Certainly by the time of Offa a number of the charters or documents recording gifts made by some of the lesser kings of southern England also contain the Mercian ruler's signature, indicating either his presence at the time of the making of the donation or the recipient's subsequent wish to obtain his confirmation of the local ruler's deed.[78] The absence of such confirmatory signatures from Kentish charters in the years 775–85 is one of the major pieces of evidence used to substantiate the independence of this kingdom from Mercian overlordship during the decade.[79]

It must be noted, however, that the number of such charters that have survived in total – virtually all in later cartulary copies – from this period is very small, and that, statistically, it is unwise to make too many subtle deductions from so small a sample. Of Offa himself only forty-three charters are known for his thirty-nine years of rule, and of these seventeen have been judged to be spurious or interpolated by some or all of the scholars who have commented on them.[80]

In general the reign of Offa has long vexed historians, who have recognised this king's importance but have been faced with an extremely limited body of evidence with which to interpret it. Thus, for example, Offa's most famous legacy, in modern eyes, must be the great dyke that bears his name, and which runs from the river Dee near Chester in the north down to the mouth of the Wye at Chepstow in the south. Not a single item of contemporary evidence actually connects this impressive piece of engineering and state-directed public works to the king. It is only on the basis of a statement in the late ninth century Welsh Bishop Asser's *Life of Alfred* that the association rests, though few would now deny it.[81] The nature of the work, be it boundary marker or defensive system between Offa's kingdom and those of the Welsh kings to the west, remains contentious and open to alternative interpretations based on archaeology largely because no documentary record remains of its creation.[82]

Offa was one of the few Anglo-Saxon kings whom we know to have had close diplomatic dealings with continental rulers, in his case the Frankish monarch Charles the Great (768–814), with whom letters were exchanged dealing with questions relating to English merchants and pilgrims in Francia. These were accompanied by various diplomatic presents. There were also periods of strained relations, as when Offa sought a marriage for his son with one of Charles's daughters (*c.* 790). The diplomatic row that this engendered seems to have led to Frankish ports being closed for a while to traders from Britain. This was finally resolved through the intermediacy of the abbot of Saint-Wandrille in the Seine valley. Letters from Charles's adviser, the Northumbrian Deacon Alcuin, to Offa also hint at the Mercian king's efforts to develop schools for the training of the clergy in his kingdom.[83] This was in line with the kind of programme that the Frankish ruler was trying to foster in his own realm at this same time.

Archaeologically, little is known of the centres of Offa's government. Some traces have been found of what may have been his palace at Tamworth, but little more. From his few charters and the records of assemblies of bishops held in his presence, for example at the fortified enclosure at Gumley in Leicestershire in 772 and 779, some idea can be gained of the peripatetic movements of his court and armed following. Under him the Mercian bishopric of Lichfield may have been substantially patronised, and after the probable difficulties with Kent in 775–85, Offa persuaded the pope (with Frankish support?) to elevate the see to archiepiscopal rank in 786.[84] This would have made the ecclesiastical order correspond with the political, but the promotion was reversed early in the ninth century. The legatine synod of 786, held under the direction of envoys from Rome and attended also by representatives from Francia, was another testimony to both the papal and Frankish ties and the programme of reform within the English church that Offa was interested in promoting.

To use hindsight it would be possible to argue, somewhat anachronistically, that the period of Mercian domination was to be a cultural 'dead-end'. The Viking conquests of the ninth century and the wars of the tenth apparently so effectively destroyed the material and intellectual records of the Mercian kingdom that all that now survive for us are a handful of charters, a small number of manuscripts (notably the Book of Cerne), some fragmentary stone carvings in the church of Breedon on the Hill and the great frontier dyke that Offa (almost certainly) built between his realm and those of the Welsh kings.[85] Of the Mercian laws, which did exist, and of the kingdom's historiography, which may have done so, few elements survive.[86]

The conflicts of the ninth and tenth centuries were in most respects to prove equally destructive in Northumbria, whose political stability had never been very secure, and in Wessex. However, both of these kingdoms have left more traces of themselves, not least through what they had managed to export, which therefore was not available to be destroyed in the wars with the Vikings and in the long and very destructive conquest of the Anglo-Norse kingdom of York by Wessex in the course of the tenth century. This is not just a matter of the survival of a certain number of manuscripts, but represents the evidence for a very significant and distinctive contribution to the cultural and artistic development of Western Europe in the seventh and eight centuries.

After the relative splendour of the period of Mercian supremacy under Offa in the late eighth century, the ninth century in Britain can seem rather more sombre. As often the case, this is largely a reflection of the character of the evidence. Under the West Saxon King Alfred (871–99) a chronicle was compiled, using various earlier annals, which has become known as *The Anglo-Saxon Chronicle*. Its name is misleading, in that, especially in its ninth century and earlier sections, it is a predominantly West Saxon work. The indigenous historiography of the two other large kingdoms, of Mercia and of Northumbria, is only represented by brief entries in two much later compilations, those ascribed to 'Florence of Worcester' and 'Symeon of Durham', that are held in part to derive from otherwise lost annals composed in these regions. These are neither numerous nor detailed enough to compensate for the predominantly West Saxon view of the history of ninth century England, which also contaminated all of the later accounts of the period, including those written in areas that at the time had been hostile to Wessex. The same could also be said, with even greater truth, for the history of England in the tenth century.

It is necessary, also, to note that most of the minor kingdoms that had existed in the later seventh century still were to be found in the ninth, although they have left us hardly any record of themselves.[87] After the death of Offa an independent kingdom re-emerged in Kent under a certain Eadbert Praen (796–8?). It may have been rapidly stifled by a still powerful Mercia, but two further indigenous monarchs were recorded soon after: Cuthred (d. 807) and Baldred, who was expelled in 825.[88] In the latter year the kingdom was conquered by the West Saxons, and for several decades it became an appanage, to be held by the eldest son of the West Saxon ruler.

Independent kings continued to exist in East Anglia, until its definitive conquest by the Vikings in 870. The names of most of these monarchs remain unknown. Initially still menaced by Mercia, the East Anglians were able to resist its attempts to reimpose over-lordship and two Mercian kings, Beornwulf (823–5) and Ludeca (825–7) were killed in battle by them.[89] Even more shadowy in this period is the kingdom of the East Saxons, but by 839 at the latest it, like Kent, had become a subordinate monarchy to be held by the eldest son or heir of the ruler of Wessex.

Northumbria, which had been highly unstable in the eighth century, may have been generally less so in the ninth – at least until the crucial decade of the 860s. Of its kings all too little may be known beyond their names and probable chronology. One of them, Eanred, held his throne for 33 years (*c*. 808–41). His son Æthelred was killed *c*. 850, and power was taken by a king Osbryht, possibly the descendant of an earlier king Osbald (796). In about 863 Osbrhyt was challenged by a certain Ælla, and expelled from York. They were still in conflict when the Danish army invaded Northumbria in 866.[90]

Mercia retained some of the pre-eminence it had achieved in the eighth century under Cœnwulf (796–821), a representative from another branch of the ruling house, who took power after the sudden death of Offa's son Ecgfrith (796). He retained over-lordship over Kent and East Anglia for some of his reign, but his death was followed by a period of weakness. Defeats by the West Saxons (825) and the East Angles (825 and 827) were followed by a brief conquest of the kingdom by Egbert of Wessex in 829–30.[91] Although the Mercian king Wiglaf (827–41) was able to regain his throne this decade of the 820s had weakened the kingdom.

The principal beneficiary of, and in part the architect of, Mercia's decline was Egbert of Wessex (802–39), who may well have been of Kentish origin and the son of a short-lived ruler of that kingdom called Eahlmund (*c.* 784/5).[92] Despite the legitimist claims of later Wessex genealogies, it is possible that the line of kings that traced itself back to Cerdic came to an end with the death of Cynewulf in a civil war in 786, and that the next king Beorhtric (786–802) was a Mercian candidate.[93] On the latter's death in 802 the Kentish adventurer Egbert was able to take power. In the 820s he expelled the Mercian candidate Baldred from Kent (825) and conquered the kingdom and that of Essex permanently, and Mercia temporarily (829/30). He also forced some of the Welsh to submit to him, and made an agreement with the Northumbrian ruler Eanred.[94] In West Saxon propaganda Egbert was later presented as a new *Bretwalda*, the first since the Northumbrian Oswy. This was a notion taken directly from Bede and deliberately revived in the interests of promoting the status of the founding figure of the new West Saxon dynasty. It is not surprising that this West Saxon historiography did not bother with a retrospective endowment of this title on the powerful Mercian kings of the late seventh and eighth centuries.

In practice Egbert's predominance over the Anglo-Saxon kings south of the Humber proved short-lived, though his gains in Kent were not lost. He was subjected to a series of Viking attacks in the south in the 830s as well as war with the British in Cornwall. His successor Æthelwulf (839–55) faced similar, if less frequent, attacks in the 840s.[95] All of this may have made possible a restoration of the Mercian ascendancy. By 851 it is clear that Mercia had regained control of the lands north of the Thames, probably including Essex, and although West Saxon historiography presents it as a plea for help, in 853 contingents were sent from Wessex to serve under King Burghred of Mercia (852–74) in his subjection of the Welsh princes.[96] However, the traditional pattern of the Anglo-Saxon kingdoms and the normal preeminence amongst them of Mercia was finally and irrevocably disrupted by the Viking wars and conquests of the period 865–79, which will be considered in chapter 19.

12 The Lombard achievement, c. 540–712

The acquisition of Italy, 540–572

The people who were to make themselves masters of much of Italy in the course of the late sixth and early seventh centuries were one of the few protagonists of the events of this period who, by name at least, might have been familiar to readers of classical authors. The Lombards were given a brief mention in the *Germania* of Tacitus (AD 98), and were there noted for the smallness of their numbers and their hardiness as fighters.[1] They appear to have been located at this time along the southern banks of the Elbe.[2]

Despite such apparent antiquity as an ethnic group, absolute discontinuity exists in evidential terms between the 'Longobardi' of Tacitus, and those referred to in the writings of Procopius and his continuators in the mid- to late sixth century. The occasional notices afforded them in these works were concerned primarily with their participation in contemporary events, and it may be thought preferable to look instead for a Lombard view of their own history. For such a literary text that provides an account of the people's past it is necessary to turn to the *History of the Lombards*, written in the monastery of Monte Cassino by Paul the Deacon in the 790s, and probably intended for presentation to the Beneventan Duke Grimoald III (787–806).[3]

This is a work that is full of problems for the historian.[4] Composed in the aftermath of the Frankish conquest of the Lombard kingdom (see chapter 15 below), by an author who had himself spent some years in Francia in the service of the conquerors, it depends for its information on a variety of sources, not all identifiable, and of uneven worth. Amongst these is a brief text known as the *Origo Gentis Langobardorum* or 'Origin of the Lombard People'. From its own internal references it would seem to belong to the period of the second reign of King Perctarit (672–88), prior to his association of his son Cunincpert as co-ruler in 679.

To the *Origo* and to Paul's *History* can be added another very short anonymous work, found in only one manuscript, providing a synoptic account of Lombard history. This was written between the years 806 and 810, but appears to be largely independent of the two earlier works. None of these texts should, however, be treated as objective accounts of the pre-Italian phases of Lombard history. Nor should some of the more naïve-seeming narratives in them be treated, as has tended to happen, as survivals of ancient legends of the people.

In all three works the length of time envisaged as passing between the first formation of the Lombard people and their entry into Italy in 568 is no more than eleven generations. Some more precise chronological pointers can be found. Thus, for example, the second of the kings of the Lombards, who belongs in the fourth of these generations, a certain 'Lamissio' or 'Laiamicho', is recorded under the entry equivalent to AD 423 in an interpolated version of the *Chronicle of Prosper* as ruling at that time and for a period of three years.[5] In general, the history of the Lombards as represented in these three works of the seventh to ninth centuries extends back in real chronological terms no earlier than the late fourth.[6]

In practice all three works, with the interesting variants that exist between them, represent the views of the Lombard past that were formulated in Italy from the seventh century on under the influence of Roman ideas of Germanic ethnic formation, and were also affected by similarly Romanised accounts of the history of their predecessors in Italy, the Ostrogoths.[7] Thus, as in Jordanes's account of the Goths, the Lombards are represented as a single, homogeneous people moving, partly of their own volition and partly in consequence of a series of accidents and adventures, from an original homeland in Scandinavia to a new homeland in Italy. Such narratives are the *Genesis* and *Exodus* of the peoples concerned, and their historical reality should be regarded with the same degree of scholarly scepticism as would those of the first two books of the Bible.

In the light of such difficulties with the Lombard historiographical tradition it is infinitely safer to fall back on the, albeit often hostile but more clearly contemporary, Byzantine sources and on the evidence of archaeology, to try to establish the nature and causes of the Lombard involvement in Italy in the late sixth century. As will be seen, the information to be found in Procopius in particular can be made to present a rather different, and also, once assembled, a more complex and more credible version of the history of the Lombards in the preceding eighty years than that offered by Paul and the *Origo*.

Although not expressed in such terms, it is clear from Procopius's account that the events of the 480s led to major changes in the location and roles of the principal Germanic ethnic groups in the regions just north of the Danube. Odovacer's elimination of the Rugi in 488 and the removal in the following year into Italy of Theoderic and all his following left a power vacuum in the northern Balkans and the upper Danube. Into this the confederacy of the Heruls may have been the first to move, but they failed to hold their own against other competitors, notably the Gepids and the Lombards, although briefly dominating the latter.[8] If Procopius is to be believed the Lombards were Christians before the accession of Anastasius I in 491, testifying to an already high degree of Roman influence on them.

Although the details of the process are unclear, it seems that in the 540s Justinian relied on all three of these rival groups to secure the Danube frontier in the western Balkans, in the regions between the river and the Illyrian mountains to the south. The Gepids were given control of Sirmium once it was regained from the Ostrogoths, and the Lombards were persuaded to move south of the Danube to establish themselves in south-western Norricum and western Pannonia. The Heruls, who provided significant contingents for the armies fighting in Italy, were by this time located further east, in the area around Singidunum (Belgrade). Their establishment in and control over contiguous regions secured the Danube frontier and provided some defence for the more valued southern regions of the Balkans. However, the degree of imperial control over any of the three confederacies was clearly limited, although individuals and groups were recruited from amongst them to serve in the imperial forces.[9] As with the rival forces supporting the two Theoderics in the 470s, imperial political influence was maintained by preventing any one confederacy from establishing a clear domination. Throughout the reign of Justinian this seems to have meant providing greater support for the Lombards against the more powerful Gepids.[10]

This policy was completely reversed by Justin II (565–78), who seems almost to have made a principle of turning his predecessor's diplomatic objectives on their heads. From the chronicle of Theophylact Simocatta and the fragments of Menander's continuation of Procopius and Agathias, it would seem that the new emperor was prepared to give his support to the Gepids against the Lombards, and in consequence the latter appealed for help to the leaders of the nomad confederacy of the Avars, who were currently developing into the dominant power to the north of the Danube.[11] They were already hostile to Justin II because of his refusal to continue the payment of annual subsidies to them that had been initiated by Justinian, and may have had their own reasons to wish to put an end to continuing Gepid occupation of the Carpathian basin.[12]

The outcome was disastrous as far as the retention of imperial control not only over the western Balkans but also over Italy was concerned. In 567 the Avars and Lombards combined to destroy the Gepid kingdom centred on Sirmium. Although in later

Lombard tradition their role was made to be central, there can be little doubt from the contemporary Byzantine sources that the primary participant in these events was the Avar confederacy.[13] The emperor intervened to secure control of Sirmium and gave refuge to the fugitive Gepid King Usdibad, but the rest of the lands occupied by the Gepids passed under Avar control, and the remnants of the people would appear to have been absorbed into their confederacy or that of the Lombards. Although Justin II and then Tiberius II (578–82) were able to retain Sirmium, it was lost to the Avars by early in the reign of Maurice (582–602).[14]

Although their own role in these events may not have been as heroic as they were later to make out, the Lombards were deeply affected by them. The relatively limited threat of the Gepids had been replaced by the expansionary power of the Avar confederacy, and it was probably in consequence of this change in the Carpathian basin that in the following year the Lombards abandoned their own fortresses in western Norricum and crossed the passes in the Julian Alps into Italy.[15] According to the Lombard historiographical tradition they voluntarily gave up their lands to the Avars, on condition that if they ever needed them again they would be returned![16] However, the contemporary chronicler Bishop Marius of Avenches indicates that they deliberately devastated their former homeland, thus creating a *cordon sanitaire* between themselves and the Avars.[17]

Interestingly, and evidence of the continuing existence of a Mediterranean-wide network of contacts, a story is to be found in Isidore of Seville, writing in Spain in the 620s, and in the Burgundian *Chronicle of Fredegar* (later seventh century) as well as in Paul the Deacon's *History* to the effect that the Lombards were invited into Italy by the Patrician Narses in revenge for his having been dismissed from office by the Emperor Justin II.[18] Considerable doubt has been expressed as to the worth of this tradition, not least as Narses apparently retired to the imperially controlled city of Naples and did not die until the mid 570s, thus being easily accessible to imperial vengeance.

The question may turn upon the point at which Narses was replaced as the commander of the imperial armies in Italy. Fighting against surviving groups of Ostrogoths in northern Italy had continued until 562, when Verona, their last stronghold, fell. In 567, as has been seen, a major upheaval occurred on the Danube, leading to war between the Empire and the Avars over the control of Sirmium and Justin II's refusal to hand over the fugitive Gepid king. It is possible in these circumstances that Narses, who had previously employed Lombard contingents in his campaign against the Ostrogoths, entered into some negotiations with them with a view to securing the defence of northern Italy.[19] Such an arrangement, if it existed, might well have been repudiated by Justin II when Narses was replaced.

The details of the conquest are to be found in Paul the Deacon. Two of the sources for this part of his *History* have been identified. In addition to sections of the historical work of the not very well informed Gregory of Tours, he had access to an otherwise lost *Historiola* or 'Small History' of Bishop Secundus of Trento (d. 612). The latter, devoted to the history of the Lombards and the earliest phases of their rule in Italy, was doubtless extremely valuable, though probably primarily concerned with events affecting Trento.[20] However, it has not proved easy to determine in full which parts of Paul's text derive from this near-contemporary source.

It would appear that in the period 568–72 much of northern Italy was occupied by the Lombards. Milan admitted them with little or no resistance, whereas Pavia required a three-year-long blockade to force it into submission. A number of towns and their related territories did continue to hold out, of which the most important by far were Ravenna, the headquarters of the recently re-established imperial administration of Italy, and Rome, which as well as being the papal residence was also the administrative centre of an imperial duchy. Although much of the land in between these two cities passed into Lombard control, the continued imperial retention of Perugia enabled contact to be maintained between them. A number of other enclaves of imperial rule, such as Padua and Mantua and various coastal towns, survived in the north and more extensive territories were preserved in the south.[21]

Alboin established himself at Verona; a significant choice in that it had been the last stronghold of Ostrogothic resistance, only falling to the Empire in 562.[22] His successors, though, were to establish first Milan (until at least 616) and then Pavia as their preferred centre of government. It was at Verona that Alboin was murdered in 572, apparently at the instigation of his wife Rosamund, who thereby avenged the killing of her own father, the Gepid King Cunimund. An elaborate account of this episode and its Romantic ramifications is given by Paul, but in that most of the episodes were so private that no source could be relied on to have given him an accurate version of events, it is highly unwise to take much of it at face value. The simple affirmation of the *Chronicle of Fredegar* that Alboin was poisoned by his wife, whose father he had killed, might thus be preferred.[23]

Moreover, one source that is very close in time to these events suggests other motives, the barest echo of which may be found in Paul. In the early 580s Bishop Marius of Avenches concluded his brief chronicle. Because of his location in the western Alps he was well informed on events in northern Italy, and his work, despite its brevity, must be allowed considerable authority. He confirms that Alboin's wife was involved in the murder and that she subsequently married the other leading conspirator, a certain Hilmagis, whom Paul describes as the dead king's foster brother. But whereas Paul has the guilty couple fleeing to Ravenna almost alone, Marius reports that they were accompanied by 'part of the army'. In other words this episode seems to represent a real divide in the Lombard ranks between those anxious to preserve the independent kingdom that Alboin had created and those who wished to submit to imperial authority, and quite possibly, like the Ostrogoths before them, be relocated within or beyond Italy as part of the emperor's army.[24] Hilmagis and his supporters also took with them to Ravenna the Lombard royal treasure, a vital economic and symbolic resource of the monarchy.

Whatever the nature of previous contacts, imperial reactions to the Lombard presence in Italy were hostile and generally remained so throughout the ensuing period of their kingdom. This has tended to colour both Byzantine and papal sources relating to the Lombards, and until recently much modern historiography.[25] They have been presented as being peculiarly 'barbarous', and their presence in Italy a disaster. It was in this respect their misfortune that attitudes had clearly been so affected by the horrors of the protracted thirty-year war between the Empire and the Ostrogoths. The replacement of the Ostrogothic presence by a Lombard one offered little attraction to those for whom the achievements of the age of Theoderic were at best a dim memory, overlaid by the years of mutual atrocity and savagery that had intervened.

Dukes and kings, 572–584

It is clear that the regime of Justin II had no wish to see the Lombards established as a federate people in Italy, filling the role of the Ostrogoths. As well as the fact that enormous effort had been expended in the regaining of Italy for direct imperial rule, the Lombards were not necessarily safe allies. Not least significant in this respect were their links with the Franks. In the 540s the Frankish King Theudebert I (533–48) had tried to put together an alliance against the Empire with the Lombards and the Gepids, and may even have envisaged a joint invasion of the Balkans and a march on Constantinople. This came to nothing, but in the 550s or 560s a definite Lombard–Frankish alliance was symbolised by the marriage of Alboin to Chlotsuintha, one of the daughters of Chlotar I (d. 561).[26]

It is possible that the relationship involved a certain subordination on the part of the Lombards, in that sections of other peoples known to be under Frankish hegemony, such as the Saxons, were involved in the Lombard entry into Italy in 568.[27] Moreover the foremost modern Italian historian of the Lombards has suggested very plausibly that the recorded Lombard invasion of Provence and the lower Rhône valley in 574 was undertaken at the behest of the eastern Frankish King Sigibert I (561–75) as part of his war against his brothers Chilperic and Guntramn.[28] Subsequently, in 582 when Sigibert's successor Childebert II (575–96) received imperial subsidies to undertake a campaign against the Lombards, the latter were obliged to buy his withdrawal from Italy, and the tributary status of their kingdom was reaffirmed in treaties made with the Frankish monarch in 590/1.[29] Only the emergence of a reinvigorated Lombard monarchy under Agilulf (590–616) seems to have led to a more active and effective resistance to Frankish military and diplomatic bullying.[30]

Despite the constantly abusive language used about them in such texts as the imperial letters to the Frankish king, the Lombards were by no means the barbarians that they have often been depicted as being. As has been noted, they were reported to be Christians by the late fifth century, and their common adhesion to the Catholic faith, as opposed to the Arianism of the Gepids, was used as a diplomatic counter in their relations with the Empire in the time of Justinian.[31] Admittedly, this cannot be true of all of the people, as in the generation after their invasion of Italy many of them are reported still to have been pagans.[32] Furthermore, by the time of Alboin (c. 560–72) some of the Christian Lombards seem to have become Arians, possibly in consequence of Gepid influence in the period c. 548–67.[33]

In material culture they show themselves no different from the Ostrogoths, Visigoths or Franks.[34] Their dress and weapons were, like those of these other peoples, strongly influenced by Roman traditions and above all by the styles favoured by the late imperial army. The period of the conquest itself was doubtless violent and disruptive, as all such phases in the history of early medieval societies tended to be. Perhaps, though, the most striking feature of the early period of the Lombard occupation of northern Italy was the speed with which they were able to establish a new military and administrative order on these regions; one, moreover, that was markedly Roman in its character. In particular their creation of a system of duchies has most aroused modern historians' interest.

That Paul the Deacon was most probably using the near-contemporary work of Bishop Secundus of Trento and that aspects of his account are confirmed by independent Frankish sources gives credence to at least the outline of his description of the creation of the Lombard duchies. According to Paul no sooner had Alboin crossed the Alps than he appointed his nephew Gisulf to be the first *dux* or duke of the region of Friuli. By 573/4, so the historian claimed, there were thirty-five such officials to be found in the kingdom, each based on a city. It is possible that numerically this is an exaggeration as far as this period is concerned, but several if not all of the later duchies did come into existence at this time.[35]

Something of the nature of the office can be deduced from clauses in the law code that was produced by the Lombard King Rothari (636–52).[36] It is clear from these references that the dukes, who were based in the principal cities and towns of Lombard Italy, were responsible for the military and judicial administration of the regions under their authority. Another class of official, the *gastald* (possibly also called *comes* or 'count') acted as something of a counterweight to the duke, being responsible for the overseeing of royal estates and their revenues in the duchy and for ensuring that the duke did administer impartial justice. In certain areas, particularly those not incorporated within the territories of duchies, *gastalds* could exercise the equivalent of ducal functions and were directly responsible to the king.[37]

Rather different conditions existed in the south of Italy, where, for example in the seventh century, the *gastalds* appear to have been responsible to the dukes rather than to the distant monarchs in Pavia. This resulted not only from the greater distances between the southern duchies and the Po valley, but possibly also from the circumstances of their formation. Whereas the north of the country was divided up into a large number of territorially quite small duchies, the centre and south of Italy contained only two: those of Spoleto and of Benevento. It has been suggested that these were the products not of Lombard encroachments under royal aegis, but, quite contrarily, were set up by the imperial government to resist the Lombard kingdom.[38]

This is not as paradoxical as it may seem, in that, as previously mentioned, detachments of Lombards had been used by the Empire in the late stages of the war with the Ostrogoths. Political cohesion amongst the Lombards was far from strong, and numerous other ethnic groups, including Gepids, Sueves, Saxons and Utigur and Kutrigur Bulgars, were involved in the movement into Italy in 568. Paul the Deacon provides examples of Lombard dukes in Italy who were prepared to ally with the emperor and his representative in Ravenna, the exarch, against the Lombard kings.

A certain Duke Droctulf, of Suevic origin, is particularly singled out as a collaborator with the Empire, and his obituary inscription in Ravenna was recorded by Paul.[39] Also, as has been seen, a major division of opinion may have existed amongst the Lombards over the question of co-operation with or resistance to the Empire.

Intriguing and even plausible as this theory is, it has no positive evidence to support it. Indeed the first appearance of a Duke of Spoleto in Paul's *History* is in the context of an attack on the exarchate of Ravenna. Faroald is reported to have taken and looted Classis, the port of Ravenna, probably around the year 579.[40] Whether the duchy of Spoleto was itself in existence by this time is far from certain, and it is possible that the entrepreneurial Faroald went on to carve out a dominion for himself on the strength of such exploits as his seizure of Classis. The origins of Benevento are equally obscure. What does seem clear is that both duchies existed by the time of King Authari (584–90) and that he was able, perhaps briefly, to impose royal authority over both of them.[41] This could not always be effectively maintained by his successors.

A location of the formation of the great duchies of Spoleto and Benevento in the early 580s makes particular sense in the light of the conditions then existing. Following Alboin's murder, which brought to an end his dynasty, which itself had only endured for two generations, one of his dukes by the name of Cleph was chosen by the Lombard army to succeed him.[42] He lasted for little more than a year before being murdered by 'his boy'; a rather enigmatic fate that neither Paul the Deacon nor Marius of Avenches further illuminates.[43] There followed a ten-year inter-regnum in which no king was chosen, and regional authority was exercised by the dukes alone.[44]

This has been frequently held against the Lombards, as proof of their lack of sophistication. More recent interpretations have, rightly, been far less critical.[45] Even so, some have tended to assume that such a phenomenon must represent an aberration, explicable only as a manifestation of hostile and external influences working on Lombard society. Byzantine gold has been deduced as the particular motive for and instrument of the 'crime'.[46] However, other historians have argued that Paul the Deacon was indicating that what occurred was effectively a ten-year-long regency for Cleph's son Authari, and that his investiture as king was merely delayed until he was of suitable age.[47] If less appealingly machiavellian, the latter solution has the virtue of simplicity. However, a further modification will be suggested below.

The period of the interregnum and of the succeeding reign of Authari (584–90) also mark the point at which what had so far been little more than a military occupation of certain Italian towns and cities began to be transformed into a more permanent Lombard settlement. As with the Visigothic kingdoms in southern Gaul and Spain and the Ostrogothic one in Italy, the first step towards this had to be a fiscal one: the establishment of a mechanism whereby the Lombard soldiery could receive regular pay and supplies, and thus not have to rely on the profits of war or random extortions. As in the case of the other and earlier established post-Roman societies in the West this meant the application of a system of *hospitalitas.*

Although attempts are still being made to shore up older views that see such a process exclusively in terms of the requisitioning and redistribution of ownership of land, these are generally unconvincing.[48] What is at issue is unquestionably a fiscal arrangement. However, it is perplexing to find even the progenitor of the new understanding of the ways in which the needs of Germanic soldiery came to be integrated into the financial organisation of the late and post-imperial states abashed at the prospect of extending the logic of this perception to the Lombard Kingdom.[49] In part this is due to too much weight being given to the negative image of the Lombard presence in Italy, itself almost totally the product of prejudice, ancient and modern.[50]

Two passages in Paul's *History* are of especial relevance. After recording the arrangements made following the murder of Cleph he reports that: 'In these days many of the noble Romans were killed from love of gain, and the remainder were divided among their "guests" and made tributaries, that they should pay the third part of their products to the Lombards.'[51] For some this has meant that after a fairly thorough-going slaughter of the surviving Roman upper classes, the remainder of the subject population were divided up, effectively as serfs for the conquerors, bound to the land and obliged to render up a fixed proportion of the produce of their labours to their Lombard overlords.[52] Once again, this is no more than a reflection of a strange predisposition to expect the worst of the Lombards, and implicitly, to accept the verdict on them of their enemies.

It is not unreasonable, instead, to translate the word *tributarii* in this passage as in its more natural meaning of 'taxpayer'.[53] Moreover, it is clear enough from the construction of the phrase that the 'remainder' referred to represents the Roman upper classes and not the whole non-Lombard population. The passage, if anything, is proof of the survival rather than of the elimination of elements of the Roman landowning class in the territories under Lombard rule. This is also what might be expected from the strong imprint of Roman ideas and institutions on Lombard government and administration.[54]

The second pertinent passage in Paul's *History* is to be found as part of his account of the elevation of Cleph's son Authari to the kingship (584).[55] In this single sentence certain ambiguous words hold the key to the meaning, and these are likely to be interpreted in the light of how the previous passage has been understood, and more generally in accordance with *a priori* expectations of Lombard society and its behaviour.[56] In Foulke's classic translation of Paul the sentence is rendered: 'The oppressed people, however, were parcelled out among their Langobard guests.' It is quite possible, though, to translate this passage as meaning that there took place in 584 a redistribution of 'those under a fiscal obligation'.[57]

In earlier instances of the application of *hospitalitas*, the receipts due from taxpayers under obligation to provide fixed proportions of their produce (be it in cash or in kind) were assigned directly and personally to the intended recipients, the Germanic soldiery, thus eliminating the role of the state in collecting and redistributing this revenue.[58] Prejudice apart, and allowing for the continued existence of Romans capable of advising on such matters, there are no good grounds for doubting that such a system could have been reapplied for the benefit of the Lombards in 573 and 584.

The second of these was caused by the process, referred to in the same chapter of Paul's *History*, whereby the dukes surrendered half of their *substantiae* to the king in order to provide him, his court and his officials with a sound financial basis on which to maintain themselves. In that the royal administration had been in abeyance since 573, and that the allocation of taxpayers to recipients had occurred during that time, it was inevitable that the re-establishment of a royal household and government apparatus would involve an adjustment in the allocation of taxpayers. In 573 those obliged to pay had been assigned to the dukes and their followers, in that there was no king and court to take a share. Thus the *substantiae* referred to, already understood to mean 'productive resources from which public revenues flowed', need to be seen also to include rights to a proportion of the taxes due from Roman landowners.[59]

If this is accepted, it throws a slightly different light on the period of the interregnum. It is surely significant that the first major effort to set up a new administrative and fiscal system took place immediately after the monarchy had effectively been suspended, whether under pretext of a long regency or not. Not Byzantine gold but the opportunity for the dukes to acquire the potential resources of the monarchy may have been behind the decision not to replace Cleph. The previous loss of the royal treasure in 572 also meant that the monarchy would have required considerable financial underwriting if its economic position was to be restored and this may not have been felt to be worthwhile at this time. The dukes were thus able in 573 to take control of those resources that would otherwise have been by right those of the king, and to establish fiscal arrangements that directly benefited themselves and their own followers, whose needs were catered for without the necessity of recourse to royal patronage, as was the case in Francia.

By 584 the mounting belligerence of the Frankish King Childebert II and the increasingly threatening moves of the Empire against the Lombard kingdom made a return to a central authority inevitable, and a new king was installed. As has been mentioned, in consequence the dukes were forced to relinquish some of the resources they had made their own in the course of the previous decade. But what is perhaps more striking is that they were able to retain half. This in practice gave them an independence *vis-à-vis* the king that was unmatched on the part of the greater nobility in both Visigothic Spain and the Frankish kingdoms. It is thus not surprising that the duchies became hereditary offices, and that the kings often had great difficulty in imposing their will on the dukes. All too often this could only be done by direct military confrontation.

It is also permissible to suspect that the rather unusual nature of the office of *Gastald* sprang from these circumstances. In each duchy certain revenue-producing estates and also rights to proportions of taxation were conceded to the crown in 584. It was clearly necessary for a class of royal official, in theory independent of the local duke, to be instituted in each duchy to oversee the management of the royal lands and the collection of dues owed to the crown. Hence the Lombard administrative pattern, which otherwise has many generic resemblances to those found in the other Germanic kingdoms in the West, developed its distinctive characteristics. Whereas in Francia and Spain both the urban magistrates and governors, the counts, and the military commanders, the dukes, were royal appointees working together, at least in theory, in a unified administrative structure, the peculiar conditions and events of the early period of the Lombard settlement in Italy led to the creation of more powerful, often autonomous duchies, which frequently inhibited the exercise of royal power over the whole of the kingdom.[60]

The kingdom of the Lombards, 584–712

From the arrangements made in 584 there emerged a much revitalised monarchy. Not least was this due to the personality of the new king, Authari, who seems to have enjoyed the approval of

Paul the Deacon and thus most probably that of his principal source, Bishop Secundus of Trento. Militarily Authari's short reign was vital to the survival of the Lombard kingdom. He won a major victory over Byzantine forces in 586, though defeated by them in renewed conflict the following year.[61]

More significant still were relations with the Franks. Having received hefty Byzantine subsidies the previous year, Childebert II dispatched an expedition into Italy in 585, but this may have been more to impress the Emperor Maurice than to achieve long-term objectives. In 588, to end the threat of further invasion Authari tried to negotiate a treaty with Childebert II of Austrasia, doubtless involving some form of tribute paying, which was also to be symbolised by his marriage to the Frankish king's sister. This fell through, as Childebert preferred to betroth her to the newly converted Visigothic King Reccared (586–601), and instead decided to honour the undertakings made to and paid for by the Emperor Maurice, by launching another invasion of Italy. This proved to be a disaster.[62]

In 590, however, a very large-scale Frankish invasion occurred. The Lombards survived by holding the principal cities, notably Pavia and Milan, against Frankish blockade until the latter were forced to withdraw due to the rising incidence of disease. Various fortresses were taken, and it seems probable that the primary purpose of the invasion was to force the Lombards into accepting some form of Frankish suzerainty and the regular payment of tribute. After the withdrawal of the Frankish forces, said to have been commanded by twenty dukes, Authari opened negotiations with Childebert II, also trying to secure the good offices of the latter's uncle, Guntramn, the Frankish King of Burgundy. Negotiations were still in train when the news came of Authari's death.[63]

Prior to his death he had engaged in a marriage that was to be of considerable importance for the future of the Lombard monarchy. Deprived of the proposed marriage to Childebert's sister (her betrothal to Reccared proved equally short-lived) he turned instead to the Bavarian ducal house of the Agilolfings. He married Theodelinda, daughter of Duke Garibald (d. 592). The particular significance of this was that her mother, Garibald's wife, was the daughter of an earlier Lombard King, Waco (d. *c.* 540), whose dynasty, at least according to later tradition, had ruled over the people for the previous seven generations.[64] His line in the male descent had died out soon after, and the kingship passed to the short-lived dynasties of Audoin and of Cleph.

In that a Frankish marriage had seemed more desirable in 588, it is unlikely that Authari made this match out of a high sense of the need for dynastic legitimation. The Bavarians, a people whose origins – be they partly Roman or all Germanic – have been a matter of much debate, were potentially valuable allies for the Lombards in view of their location immediately to the north of Italy.[65] However, on the premature death of Authari in 590, Theodelinda came to represent the best way in which a new king could be grafted onto the stock of the former royal line. That she was given a free choice between all of the dukes, as Paul would have us believe, is not entirely easy to credit.[66] Hard political bargaining or even naked force must have underlain the ritual acts.

Dynastic continuity and legitimacy became increasingly important for the Lombards, and although Theodelinda's own male descent died out with her son Adaloald (616–26), marriage to her daughter Gundiperga legitimised two further kings, and when even these lines failed the descendants of Theodelinda's brother Gundoald (d. 616) provided most of the Lombard monarchs up to the year 712. The only alternative royal dynasty, that of Audoin and Alboin, was able to impose a representative in the person of Grimoald (662–71), a descendant of Alboin's nephew Duke Gisulf of Friuli, but even he found it expedient to marry into the 'Bavarian' royal line (see genealogical table). Although the Lombards have been criticised for the number of coups and conspiracies that convulsed their monarchy in the seventh century, what is most striking is their fidelity to dynastic continuity and, paradoxical as it may seem, this can represent another instance of strong Roman influence on their political expectations and institutions.

The new king, symbolically 'chosen' by Theodelinda, was Agilulf, of partly Thuringian origin and previously Duke of Turin. His reign (590–616) marked the achievement of a much greater degree of stability and security on the part of the kingdom. He brought the negotiations for peace with the Franks, initiated by Authari, to a successful conclusion. The removal of the threat of Frankish intervention, whatever it may have cost in tribute, freed the king's hands to take a more active role in Italy. It also enabled him to impose much greater royal control over the dukes, at least in the north of Italy. A number of them are recorded by Paul the Deacon as having conspired against the king, who had originally been one of their own number, and several of these he had executed. In some cases he used the royal army to break their power.[67] He replaced them with men expected to be more faithful to himself, but did not or could not change the basic administrative structures.

The increasing military problems of the Empire, firstly with the Slavs and Avars in the Balkans and then with the Persians and the Arabs on the eastern frontiers, meant that fewer and fewer resources could be spared for the defence of imperial interests in Italy, let alone the initiation of major campaigns against the Lombards.

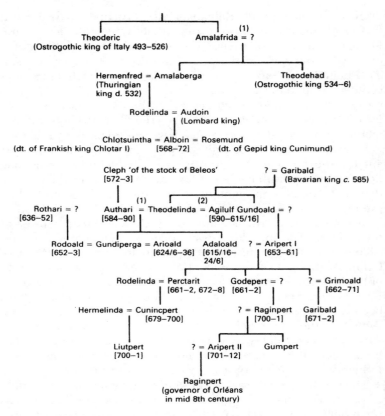

A simplified genealogy of the Lombard royal dynasties *c.* **568–712**
(regnal dates of the Lombard kings are enclosed in square brackets)

Agilulf on occasion made use of an alliance with the Avars in his campaigns against the Byzantine forces in Italy, and was even able, late in his reign, to use them as a threat against the Franks.[68]

In such circumstances Agilulf was able to renew the expansion of the kingdom. He may also have been spurred on in this by the need to curb the growing territorial power of the two great dukes of Spoleto and of Benevento. The first major Lombard attempt to take Rome was that of the Duke Faroald of Spoleto in 579, and his successor Duke Ariulf (591–601) made another attempt in 592. He was also able briefly to make himself master of the key fortress town of Perugia. Agilulf's own, more protracted, siege of the city in 593 may well have been a response to the fear of Rome falling into the hands of these overly independent dukes.[69] In all cases Rome held out, but it was Agilulf who had become master of Perugia by the end of these campaigns.

It must be wondered, if Agilulf had been able to take Rome, whether the position of the Lombards in Italy would not have been immeasurably strengthened, and whether a genuinely united Italian kingdom, on the lines of that which had existed under the Ostrogoths, would have emerged. It is impossible to say if the papacy, which remained implacably hostile to the idea of Lombard political control of Rome throughout the whole existence of the kingdom, might not have proved more pliable if this had actually been imposed, and if it had become necessary to work out a *modus vivendi* with the conquerors. But while the city and territories of the duchy of Rome remained an imperial enclave the popes had at least a political obligation to remain opposed to the Lombards. This was initially accentuated by religious divisions.

Despite the deliberately heightened language with which they were described in Byzantine and papal documents, in which their supposed 'frightfulness', 'abominableness' and 'savagery' are constantly referred to, there was little about the Lombards that should have made them any less acceptable to the civilian population of Italy than their Ostrogothic predecessors.[70] Like the latter, they were, in the early stages of their settlement south of the Alps, Arian Christians, but in that the popes had collaborated easily enough with Theoderic and his successors this should have been no insuperable bar to good relations with the Church of Rome.

In fact, the religious history of the Lombards is far from easy to understand.[71] Alboin appears to have been an Arian in the 560s, if the letter of Nicetius of Trier to his Frankish wife is to be believed, despite the Lombards having portrayed themselves to the emperor Justinian as fellow Catholics only a decade and a half earlier. Authari also seems to have been an Arian, and at Easter 590 he is said to have forbidden Lombards to receive Catholic baptism.[72] Agilulf's position is not known for sure, though Theodelinda was certainly a Catholic, as was their son Adaloald (616–26). The next two kings, Arioald (626–36) and Rothari (636–52), were Arians. Only with Aripert I (653–61) did these fluctuations in theological allegiance cease, although some historians have seen Grimoald (662–71) as the last Arian king.

This is quite unlike anything to be found in any of the other Germanic kingdoms in which the kings and the people passed through an Arian phase before becoming irrevocably Catholic. In the cases of the Burgundians and the Visigoths (and possibly the Franks) periods of conflict and debate preceded the decision of the king to convert, but once this was made the issue ceased to be a live one. In Spain in the brief period between the announcement of Reccared's conversion in 587 and the formalising of the conversion of the kingdom through the holding of the Third Council of Toledo in

May 589 virtually all of the contentious issues of the dismantling of the institutions of the Arian church and the redeployment of its personnel had been resolved.[73] After 590 Arianism was a dead issue in the Visigothic kingdom; there were no more Arians.

The constant shifts in religious affiliation on the part of the Lombard monarchy thus require explanation. For some historians this is no more than proof that religion, uniquely in Early Medieval Europe, was not a matter of real concern at anything above the individual level in the Lombard kingdom. Others would like to see these fluctuations as representing the shifting ascendancies of rival groups: one forward looking and willing to compromise with Roman cultural norms, the other conservative and wedded to the ancestral Germanic traditions of the people.[74] Neither of these approaches is satisfying.

What must be clear, from comparison with the Spanish case, is that whatever the fluctuations in the religious affiliations of the monarchy this did not directly affect the existence and functioning of an Arian Church within the kingdom. Very little is known of this institution, but certain casual references prove its existence. Arian Lombard bishops certainly functioned, and a number of churches consecrated by earlier generations of Arians in Italy still existed in the 580s, even in Rome.[75] Slight as the information is, it seems to suggest that initially the Arian bishops and clergy were attached to the Lombard garrisons, rather than having a fixed urban base. The Arian bishop referred to in Gregory the Great's *Dialogues* comes into Spoleto to try to obtain a church for Arian use, but does not, as was the case in Spain prior to 589, appear to be Arian Bishop *of* Spoleto, that is to say part of a parallel and rival hierarchy. His miraculous discomfiture is said to have dismayed the Lombards garrisoning the region. On the other hand, if Paul the Deacon is to be believed, such parallel Arian and Catholic hierarchies had definitely come into existence in a number of cities, including Pavia, by the time of Rothari (636–52).[76]

In general it would seem reasonable to suggest that support for and maintenance of an Arian clergy and church depended on the religious affiliation of the local *de facto* rulers, which in the Lombard state meant that an Arian duke could set up or preserve an Arian establishment in his duchy, even when the king was a Catholic. The kings lacked the strength to impose religious uniformity on the duchies, particularly those in the south. This also meant, in the light of the way that the monarchy passed through the hands of a number of ducal families in the period 572–672, that it was quite possible for a duke, chosen for whatever political reasons, or who managed to take the crown, to be an Arian or a Catholic king, according to his previous religious affiliation.

This was doubtless facilitated by the existence of a division within the Catholic Church in Italy, which was only finally healed in 612, known as the Istrian Schism. A number of the north Italian bishops had felt that the papacy had failed to make an adequate condemnation of the Emperor Justinian's attempt to modify orthodox doctrine in the interests of affecting some kind of reconciliation with the Monophysites. His formal denunciation of the teaching of three earlier and strongly pro-Chalcedonian theologians had generated what came to be called 'The Three Chapters Controversy'. The opposition to this on the part of Pope Vigilius had led to his arrest and considerable ill-treatment in Constantinople. His successor Pelagius I (556–61) had therefore been somewhat less passionate in his disagreement with the emperor, and in consequence had fallen foul of the north Italian bishops. Their continuing alienation from Rome may have meant that the Catholic Church in Italy took a much less unified stand on the matter of Lombard Arianism.[77]

Nor, apart from Authari's attempt to prevent Lombards receiving Catholic baptism, does the division between Arians and Catholics in the kingdom look to have been very contentious.[78] There are no accounts of theological debates or of confrontations over the ownership of churches. Although some bishoprics remained vacant, there is an equal lack of evidence to suggest that the Catholic establishment was downtrodden or incapable of maintaining itself.[79] Probably Arian rulers such as Agilulf proved willing to patronise Catholic shrines and even Catholic monks. He donated a votive crown to his wife's foundation of the Basilica of St John the Baptist at Monza, and the earliest extant Lombard royal charter is the king's grant of 613 to the newly established monastery of Bobbio, founded with Agilulf's support by the Irish Abbot Columbanus after his expulsion from Burgundy.[80] Last, and not least, Agilulf was prepared to have his son and heir baptised as a Catholic, doubtless at the behest of his wife Theodelinda (*c.* 604). In such general circumstances it is perhaps less surprising that Lombard Arianism should expire gradually and without notice, rather than for the issue to require a single authoritative but contentious resolution.

With the death of Bishop Secundus of Trent in 612 Paul the Deacon's primary source of information came to an end. His account of the rest of the seventh century is in consequence extremely brief, and whole reigns can receive but the barest mention. Thus of Arioald (626–36), who replaced the young Adaloald when the latter apparently went mad, Paul can only say 'Concerning the acts of this king hardly anything has come to our knowledge.'[81] His successor Rothari (636–52) has left more trace of himself, not just in Paul's report of his conquest of various imperial fortresses on the Ligurian coast, but most substantially in the law code that he promulgated in the eighth year of his reign (643/4).[82]

Paul the Deacon's statement on the nature of the law contained in Rothari's code, or Edict, as it should more properly be known, has generally been taken at face value. According to Paul the king 'collected in a series of writings the laws of the Lombards which they were keeping in memory only and custom'. This appears to be a reflection of the statement on the procedures followed in collecting the laws, which is to be found in the Edict itself.[83] It is important to appreciate, however, how marked is the impression of Roman ideas on the formation and character of the code.

In his preface the king declared: 'The collection which follows makes evident how great was and is our care and solicitude for the welfare of our subjects …' as '… we have perceived it necessary to improve and to reaffirm the present law, amending all earlier laws by adding that which is lacking and eliminating that which is superfluous.' Such a statement corresponds remarkably closely to the declarations of purpose that preface such Roman legal collections as Justinian's Code and Institutes and the earlier Theodosian Code. Likewise, the title given to the code is a direct reflection of the interpretative and emendatory Edict that the Late Roman Praetorian Prefect was empowered to issue, in order to modify or make pertinent the application of imperial law. It was also the title given to the similar but briefer compilation of Rothari's Italian predecessor, the Ostrogothic king Theoderic.[84]

Certain items in the Edict can in no sense represent ancestral custom. Thus, a law punishing the forging of charters by the loss of a hand is thoroughly Roman, both in the importance implicitly ascribed to written titles to property, and in the jurisprudential principles underlying the penalty to be inflicted.[85] Similarly, all tariffs of compensation for injuries – and this is what most of the Edict is concerned with – are calculated in the Roman unit of value, the *solidus*. Perhaps most significant of all is the fact that the laws of the Edict, whatever their supposed traditional origins, were intended to be applied to all subjects of the monarch, whether they were Lombards or not. This is stated explicitly both in a concluding section of the Edict and in one of the laws that states that all foreigners entering the kingdom shall be subject to these rules of law unless the king agrees otherwise.[86] This was, in other words, intended to be a fully territorial code, that is, applicable to all living within the geographical regions subject to the authority of the king of the Lombards.

Some of the laws have been ridiculed as representing quaint survivals of primitive Germanic superstition and savagery. For the great English historian of Early Medieval Italy, Thomas Hodgkin, writing in the late nineteenth century, 'the Code of Rothari, promulgated on the sacred soil of Italy, ... is like the black tent of the Bedouin pitched amid the colonnades of some stately Syrian temple, whose ruined glories touch no responsive chord in the soul of the swart barbarian'.[87] Such laws as those forbidding the killing of someone else's female slave on the suspicion that she is a vampire would be used to support such a contention.[88] However, other texts, such as the *Dialogues* of Gregory the Great, provide proof, if it be needed, that such 'irrational' beliefs were to be encountered widely in Italy, as indeed elsewhere and at all periods of Antiquity and the Middle Ages, and were in no sense a Lombard contribution to the society of the peninsula. Nor should the concentration in the Edict on rural contexts and the legal problems that were to be encountered in them blind the historian to the importance of urban survival in Lombard Italy, and their particular contributions to it.

What is so impressive about the Lombards is that they took over, not without difficulty, a society in which towns were still the administrative and economic centres of their regions, even if the size of their populations and the state of their former public buildings were in serious decline. To this situation the Lombards adapted expeditiously and effectively. Indeed, as has been seen, this is what saved the kingdom during the great Frankish invasion of 590, when the Lombards held the cities against them. Their royal and ducal centres of government were town based.[89] What is more, certain types of public works continued to be carried out in the towns under Lombard rule. These included repair to fortifications, and in one case at least this may have been paid for by the royal or ducal administration.[90] Urban church building and monastic foundation on the part of several of the seventh century kings and dukes is well recorded in Paul the Deacon.[91] This continued to be a marked feature of the Lombard kingdom in the eighth century, as is testified to by such surviving monuments as the monastic church of San Salvatore in Brescia.

Certain aspects of Late Roman ceremonial and protocol were also preserved in the Lombard kingdom. In 604 Agilulf held a great ceremony in the amphitheatre in Milan, in the presence of envoys of the Frankish King Theodebert II, in which his infant son Adaloald was associated with him as king. Similarly, in the 670s King Perctarit (661–2, 672–88) had a special ceremonial gate built in the palace at Pavia.[92] Indeed, war and victory remained central both to the formal role and to the practical functioning of the Lombard monarchy. The continuing pressures from both beyond the Alps and the surviving imperial enclaves in Italy placed a premium on military competence, and despite such moves as that of Agilulf in 604 and a similar association of his son Cunincpert by Perctarit in 679, proven ability in war remained the primary quality required for the survival of a Lombard king.

Thus when Godepert and Perctarit, the sons of Aripert I (653–61), began fighting amongst themselves in 661/2 they were quickly overthrown by the experienced Duke of Benevento Grimoald (662–71), at the behest of at least one of his northern ducal colleagues. His reign, coincidentally, was to see the most serious military threats posed to the continued existence of the kingdom since the 580s. He faced a Frankish invasion from Provence and a major Avar incursion into Friuli, while the most serious threat of all developed in the south, directed against his duchy of Benevento, which he had delegated to his son Romuald (duke 662–87). The Byzantine Emperor Constans II (641–68) transferred his capital to Syracuse in Sicily in 663, and initiated a campaign of conquest against the Lombard holdings in the south of Italy. All three of these invasions were met and ultimately defeated, and the murder of Constans II in 668 led to the return of the imperial government to Constantinople.[93]

If external threats decreased after the reign of Grimoald, the problem of the entrenched power of the dukes remained as a permanent challenge to royal authority.[94] The death of Grimoald in 671, leaving a minor as heir to the kingdom in the person of Garipald (671–2), led to the rapid restoration of Perctarit, who had passed an adventurous exile amongst the Avars and Franks, before crossing to England. A trace of this may be found in the fact that his son Cunincpert (679–700) married an Anglo-Saxon.[95] Both of these kings faced serious threats to their authority from Alahis, Duke of Trento and additionally of Brescia, who early in the sole reign of Cunincpert was able to expel the latter from Pavia and briefly seize the crown.[96]

The 'Bavarian' dynasty was to be irrevocably displaced by a similar coup in 712, although its own internal divisions may have played a part in this. When the inevitable crisis of credibility was created by the succession of a minor, Cunincpert's son Liutpert (700–1), power was seized violently by a rival branch of the family, represented by Raginpert (701), Duke of Turin and son of the King Godepert (661–2) who had been killed by Grimoald. The new king died the very same year, but was succeeded by his son Aripert II (701–12). He in turn had to struggle against a rival aspirant in the person of Duke Rothari of Bergamo, who briefly proclaimed himself king.

Amongst those displaced by the coup of 701 was a certain Ansprand, whose origins are never revealed by Paul but who was obviously a figure of considerable importance in the following of Cunincpert, as he was appointed *tutor* (guardian?) to the latter's heir. It was this Ansprand who in 712 invaded the kingdom with an army provided by Theotpert, the Duke of the Bavarians. Paul's account of the outcome is highly obscure, in that he states that Aripert II defeated the invading army, but then felt he ought to flee to Francia, only to be drowned swimming across the river Ticino.[97] His brother Gumpert did manage to escape to the Frankish kingdoms, and his descendants were still living there and holding offices of some significance at the time that Paul the Deacon resided at the court of Charlemagne.

Although the crown thus fell into the hands of Ansprand in 712 he died the same year, and was succeeded by his son Liutprand (712–44). Under this monarch a revival of both royal power and the territorial expansion of the Lombard state was to take place. At the same time, though, changing conditions in the Empire, in Francia and in Rome would lead to a combination of circumstances that would ultimately prove fatal to the continuing existence of the independent Lombard kingdom.[98] But in looking back over the period of the ascendancy of the 'Bavarian' dynasty (590–712), it is hard not to be impressed by the Lombard achievements, especially in the light of unremitting hostility on the part of so many of their neighbours and the political difficulties caused by their resulting inability to recreate a single unified Italian kingdom. It is depressing to see how much of the prejudice of the non-Lombard sources, revitalised in the great nineteenth century narrative histories of early medieval Italy, still lives on into the present, to condition and distort the interpretation of a significant and interesting society.

13 The sundering of East and West

Survivals of cultural unity

The Arab conquest of North Africa in the late seventh century completed the demolition of the intellectual power house of Latin Christianity. Ever since the third century the African Church had produced the majority of the outstanding thinkers of the western tradition. Even after the death of Augustine in 430 and the Vandal conquest, Africa had continued to produce writers of high intellectual stature. Nor had they been of purely local significance: from exile in Sardinia Bishop Fulgentius of Ruspe (d. 527 or 532) had exercised considerable influence on ecclesiastical circles in both southern Gaul and in Rome through his letters and treatises.[1]

The restoration of direct imperial rule over Africa in 533 by Justinian had proved a mixed blessing as far as the Church was concerned. Militarily the imperial armies took over the struggle against the raids of the Berber tribes in the south which the Vandals had been losing for the last three or four decades of their rule in Africa, and after some hard fighting re-established stable if reduced southern and western frontiers.[2] However, the theological interests of Justinian proved as unwelcome to the African bishops as had the Arianism of their former rulers. The emperor's condemnation of the work of three respected fifth century theologians was resisted in various parts of the Empire and beyond, and generated a fresh, if not very long lasting, division in the Church known as the dispute over the 'Three Chapters'.[3]

Some of the Africans, who anyway disputed the emperor's right to determine theological orthodoxy by imperial will, led the resistance and wrote a series of works in defence of the threatened authors and challenging Justinian. They suffered exile for their pains, and attempts to impose the imperial views by force led to a migration of African clerics and monks into Spain. They and the books they brought with them made a vital contribution to an intellectual renaissance of the Spanish Church in the last quarter of the sixth century. Subsequent Spanish manuscript transmission thereby saved a number of African writings that would otherwise have been entirely lost.[4]

Other Africans moved, willingly or as exiles, to Constantinople in the course of the sixth century, and it is from the extant writings of the grammarian Priscian, the poet Corippus and the historian

Bishop Victor of Tunnunna (Tunis) that we can appreciate the continuing vitality of Africa in so many areas of learning. Another later indicator may be the influence exerted in Britain of the African Abbot Hadrian, who was appointed in 668 by Pope Vitalian to accompany the new Archbishop of Canterbury, Theodore of Tarsus, and who soon became abbot of St Peter's monastery (better known as St Augustine's) in the city. Amongst his pupils was the poet and grammarian Aldhelm, later Bishop of Sherborne (705/6–9), who as poet and letter-writer became the leading intellectual figure in the Church in southern Britain in his day.

That an African-born monk could end his life as an abbot in south-eastern Britain, and quite possibly also be a correspondent of a bishop of Toledo (Julian), gives some qualitative impression of the continuing network of contacts and the scope for travel and movement still existing within the former territories of the Roman Empire, even in the middle of the seventh century.[5] A Spanish cleric from the north-west of the peninsula in the same period, Bishop Fructuosus of Braga (*c.* 655–75), planned, though he was prevented from carrying out, a visit to the eastern Mediterranean, and his contemporary Bishop Eugenius II of Toledo (646–57) wrote a now lost work on the Trinity to send to Africa and the East as a contribution to the then raging dispute over the One or Two Wills (or Energies) of Christ, known as the Monothelete Controversy.[6] Even more striking may be the indication in the work of the Irish abbot of Iona Adamnan (679–704) entitled *On the Holy Places* that his informant, a Frankish bishop called Arculf, had travelled to Arab-ruled Jerusalem, probably in the 680s, and had spent nine months there.[7]

The controversy that Bishop Eugenius II of Toledo had wished to embroil himself in had resulted from yet another ill-judged attempt to settle the dispute within the eastern Church between the Orthodox and the Monophysites. This was launched by the Emperor Heraclius in 639 in a document called the *Ekthesis*. The imperially sponsored theological formula, which allowed that Christ had two Natures and two Persons but only a single Will or 'Energy', which it was hoped would bring about a reconciliation, failed to attract most of the Monophysites and was subsequently strongly condemned in Africa and Rome. An imperial edict of the emperor Constans II in 648, known as the *Type* or 'Rule' forbade any further discussion of the issue, but instead only served to exacerbate opposition, which even punitive measures against Pope Martin I (649–53) and others failed to stem.[8]

Much more acceptable in the West and expressive of the sense of a continuing cultural community within the former Roman imperial lands were the canonical decisions of the Third Council of Constantinople of 680–1, finally condemning the Monothelete theology. In advance of the main Council a synod was held in Rome in 680 under Pope Agatho (678–81) to co-ordinate western theological views and condemnations of the Monothelete teaching. Various provincial gatherings were also held under papal inspiration, of which the council of the Church in the Anglo-Saxon kingdoms held at Hatfield under the direction of Archbishop Theodore of Canterbury (669–90) is the best recorded.[9] Subsequently the Fourteenth Council of Toledo was specially called in November 684 to accept the pronouncements of the meeting in Constantinople.[10] Thus, the tradition of Ecumenical Councils, of which III Constantinople had been the sixth, representing all the orthodox components of Christendom, was still a living one in practice and not just in theory in the late seventh century.

Trade is the subject concerning which the greatest attention has been paid to the problems of continuities and discontinuities in patterns of contact and communication within the Mediterranean and beyond. The evidence on which any hypothesis has to be based is slight, but that is true for almost any facet of the economic life of Antiquity and the Early Middle Ages. Much weight has been placed on an episode in the seventh century *Life* of the Patriarch of Alexandria called John the Almsgiver (610–19). In this a ship, whose trading mission was funded by the Alexandrian Church, returned from Britain with a cargo of tin. That the tin was found on arrival to have transmuted itself miraculously into silver would suggest that a certain care is needed in treating this story as an objective account of contemporary realities.[11] At the very least, though, it shows that the author of the *Life*, Leontius of Byzantium, both knew of Britain and was correct in referring to tin, a relatively rare metal, as a product of the island. Rather more significant for arguments concerning seventh century contacts are the continuing finds of Mediterranean products, notably various kinds of pottery, in a wide number and location of trading and residential sites around Britain. In the same way other such 'harder' pieces of evidence, as that for the continued use of papyrus imported from Egypt in documents produced in Ravenna, Gaul and Spain, confirm the impression of continuing economic activity throughout the Mediterranean in this period, even if no quantitative assessments can be made.[12]

On the other hand, all these exchanges of personnel and of ideas and of goods need to be seen against a background of growing linguistic incomprehension. St Augustine did not learn Greek at school and only seems to have made himself master it later in life. After his death in 430 few of the leading figures of the western Church could be said with any certainty to have done the same. The layman Boethius, who translated works of both Plato and Aristotle, was certainly fluent in the language, but he was exceptional. Neither Isidore of Seville nor Pope Gregory the Great (590–604), the principal Latin authors of the early seventh century, seem to have been able to read much if any Greek at all, or to have felt that this was a lack on their part. This, in Gregory's case, was despite a five-year stay in Constantinople as papal representative at the imperial court.[13]

In Constantinople Latin came increasingly to be associated with the 'barbarians' who were the political masters of most parts of the former western Empire, and its use declined accordingly. It had been the language of the law in both parts of the Empire, and when in 528 Justinian set up a commission to codify the imperial edicts, systematise and excerpt the writings of the jurists, and produce a new introductory textbook for legal studies, all of these were issued in Latin.[14] The textbook, known as the *Institutes*, which was published in 533 and was to be used by students in the two principal legal schools of the Empire, those of Beirut and of Constantinople, presupposed the continuing use of Latin in the learning and the practice of law in the East. Yet before the end of the reign all new imperial legislation was being issued exclusively in Greek.

On the other hand, it is important not to become too apocalyptic about this phenomenon. Some scholars have measured the level of learning in the West primarily on the basis of individual authors' knowledge of, or more often lack of knowledge of, Greek.[15] But as the yardstick for the measuring of cultural attainments this is limited. The ignorance of Latin in the East is not regarded as equally reprehensible. Besides which, even when the two halves of the Mediterranean appear to have become uncompromisingly monolingual, numerous exceptions can be found. The African Latin poet Flavius Cresconius Corippus expected to be understood when he wrote a verse panegyric in Latin in Constantinople to celebrate the accession of the Emperor Justin II in 565. Nor did the Latin-speaking Gregory have problems in engaging in a public debate with the patriarch Eutychius in 582, during his stay in Constantinople.[16] Equally striking is the fact that a number of his seventh century successors as pope were native Greek speakers from Sicily, and that it was possible for two native Syrians, Theodore (642–9) and John V (685–6), to become bishops of Rome in the same period.

The first serious divide within the fabric of the Mediterranean world was between north and south, and was occasioned by the Arab conquests. However, reactions to the unforeseen rise of Islam and the extraordinary military success of the Arabs helped to fracture the cultural cohesion of the Christian-ruled northern shores of the Mediterranean as well. As will be seen, the succession of demoralising military defeats and the theological challenge that Islam seemed to present caused a series of dramatic reassessments within the eastern Roman Empire, not only of both strategy and administration, but also of the nature of the relationship between God and Man. The effects of this, together with the diminution in the Empire's ability to play a significant military role in the defence of the West against a still expansionary Arab Empire, led to strain and severance in the ties binding together the component parts of the Christian world. Within the former Christian-ruled territories to the south of the Mediterranean and in Spain the changes in political control produced equally profound intellectual change.

Christian communities survived and Latin remained in use in some coastal parts of eastern North Africa until at least the eleventh century, but it was by then no more than the second language of a rapidly dwindling minority of the population.[17] Unlike Egypt, however, where sizeable numbers of Christians continued to dominate the villages of the Nile valley, the tribal organisation of the Berbers of North Africa led to more rapid and extensive mass conversions to Islam. In such a society conversion was not a matter of individual choice but the decision of whole communities who elected their own leaders. Muslim holy men, whose tombs or *marabouts* dot the north African landscape, also played an important part in this process, commensurate with that of their earlier Christian counterparts in the evangelisation of the Syrian and also possibly the Spanish countryside.[18]

The Arab conquest of Spain, that was in military terms completed in the decade after 711, enhanced the detachment of the African Church from western Christendom. As in Egypt, the rate of conversion from Christianity to Islam was far from rapid in Arab-ruled Spain, known as *Al-Andalus*, and it is quite possible that the majority of the population in the south of the peninsula were still Christians in the early eleventh century. Despite the changed political circumstances the clergy of Toledo continued to exercise an intellectual leadership throughout the eighth century, but a controversy that broke out in the 780s over Bishop Elipandus of Toledo's use of terminology that implied that Christ's human nature was adoptive led to the increasing isolation of the Christian communities in the south from the rest of the Latin Church.[19]

Other and more extensive theological disputes, allied to a real divide in religious sensibilities, had by this time also brought about a fundamental rift between East and West in the areas that were still ruled by Christian monarchs. In general, the first three-quarters of the eighth century was marked by increasing and ultimately irrevocable fragmentation within the greater cultural community of those areas that had previously been linked by their common inheritances from the Roman Empire and the Christian religion. To understand this process requires some consideration of the political changes in the eastern Mediterranean in the early eighth century.

Iconoclasm: divisions in the East

In the eastern Roman or Byzantine Empire the dynasty of Heraclius had come to an end in 711 with the overthrow of the flamboyant if unstable Justinian II (685–95, 705–11). Although a by no means incompetent ruler during his first reign, his single minded pursuit of revenge on those who had previously opposed him or who had failed to help him during his ten-year exile led to another army revolt.[20] The period of political turmoil that had been initiated by his first deposition in 695 intensified after his second deposition and ensuing murder. Three emperors ruled between 711 and 717, and a fourth seized power in yet another military coup in the latter year.

The new ruler, Leo III (717–41) might statistically have been expected to be as short-ruling as his predecessors, not least as the year of his accession saw another sustained effort by the Arabs to capture Constantinople. However, the 'Greek Fire' proved as effective against the Arab fleet as it had in the siege of 674–7, and the Arab army was prevented from establishing itself on the European shores of the Bosphorus. After a year the last major attempt by the Arabs to take the imperial capital was abandoned, and not until after the accession of the Umayyad Caliph Hisham (724–43) were their land-based attacks on the imperial territories in Asia Minor renewed.[21]

The removal of the immediate military problem gave Leo III an opportunity to establish a more firmly based regime than those of his predecessors, and the dynasty that he founded lasted for eighty-five years. Sources of information relating to it are very sparse, and come principally in the form of the relevant entries in the *Chronicle* attributed to Abbot Theophanes of Megas Agros in north-west Asia Minor (d. 818). Until recently, modern accounts of the reign of Leo and his son Constantine V (741–75) have tended to offer little more than paraphrases of the chronicler's words.[22] However, Theophanes is by no means a friendly witness. Although not distant in time, his annalistic account is fairly brief, and more importantly, he was deeply hostile to the religious policies of Leo and his successors. Thus, for example, he recorded the story of the infant Constantine V defecating into the font in the course of his baptism.[23] This was not vulgar abuse: it was intended as a symbol of the damage that Theophanes and those who thought like him felt that Constantine was to inflict on the Church in his reign.

The cause of this hostility was the imposition of Iconoclasm by Leo III and his son. Simply put, this was the prohibition of the depiction of natural figures in religious art and in consequence the removal of all images of Christ, the Saints and Old Testament scenes from places of worship. The process began in 726, when some form of imperial edict was issued condemning the veneration of icons, and one of the principal sacred pictures in the city of Constantinople, the portrait of Christ that adorned the Chalke or Bronze Gate into the Palace, was destroyed on the emperor's orders.[24] More extensive measures were delayed until 730, but popular hostility to the imperial attack on religious art had already been aroused. An insurrection in Constantinople had been crushed in 727 and a revolt by the imperial armies in the southern Balkans and the Aegean islands was defeated, again largely by use of 'Greek Fire'.[25]

The roots of this imperially sponsored attack on the veneration of holy pictures are not easy to untangle. A strand in Christian thinking had long existed that considered the attempt to depict Christ, in other words the Divinity, in art was a fundamental breach of the second commandment. This had been a view expressed very forcefully by Bishop Epiphanius of Salamis (d. 403) amongst others in the late fourth century. This was the period in which a distinctively Christian art was developed, and the traditional iconography of Christ, Angels, the leading Apostles and the representation of biblical scenes was formed and indeed became fixed. Images that are now long standardised, of Christ with long brown hair and beard and Angels with the wings of classical Victories and wearing the robes of silentiaries of the Roman imperial court, were all developed at this time, and they became permanently established by the middle of the fifth century. However, minority currents of opposition to the whole notion of representing the sacred in human art continued to exist.

Particular impetus may have been given to the re-emergence of Iconoclast, or image-hating, theology by the corresponding intensification of image veneration in the course of the late sixth and seventh centuries, especially in the East. Images of Christ and the Saints became regarded by many worshippers as ways of special access to the objects of their veneration. Such icons were not just pictures but were spiritually linked to their prototypes, that is to say Christ or the Virgin Mary or the saint who was depicted in the image. Some icons were thought to be particularly powerful. The saint worked miraculous power more effectively or more willingly through some images rather than others. Thus one particular icon of the Virgin Mary, known as the Hodegetria, was regarded as a very special and powerful defence for the city of Constantinople, and to its strength was attributed the lifting of the Arab siege of the city in 718. When Theophanes and other Iconodules (image venerators) had to explain such military successes on the part of the hated and heretical regime of Leo III it was by attributing the victories to the continuing veneration of icons throughout the Empire, despite the attempts of the imperial government to destroy them.[26]

Certainly the rising tide of popular veneration of religious images must have stirred up the counter-current of doubt as to the rightness of such devotion and the fear of idolatry, but it is often suggested, not least by Theophanes, that the catalyst for the triumph of Iconoclasm at this time was the decree of the Umayyad Caliph Yazid II (720–4) forbidding the Christian veneration of religious images in the Arab-ruled territories.[27] Much doubt, however, has been cast on the reality of this edict, and it is possible that the whole purpose of the story was to portray the Christian Iconoclasts as being no better than Muslims, whose religion was seen at this time as being nothing more than a particularly aberrant and heretical form of Christianity.

Even so, the frequency with which the Iconodules accused the Iconoclast emperors and their ecclesiastical supporters of being influenced by both Arab, in other words Muslim, and also Jewish arguments and doctrines suggests that the critiques that both of these religions directed against Christian religious art and the framework of ideas that underlay it had some impact at this time. In particular, the series of major territorial losses in both east and west suffered by the Empire since 634 and the succession of military humiliations at the hands of the Arabs could easily have led to a sense that divine chastisement was being inflicted on the Christians because of deviation from right belief or practice. The identification of this as the recent growth in the veneration of images would make sense in a context in which Old Testament and Apocalyptic strands in Christian thinking were again coming to the fore.

For the modern student of this vital period the absence of the evidence that would lead to a better understanding of the conflicting ideas and *mentalités* of the participants is peculiarly frustrating. The Iconoclasts under Leo III and Constantine V destroyed much of the religious art of the greatly diminished Byzantine Empire, and thus such things as the mosaic decorations of the great churches that Justinian I had erected in Constantinople are completely lost to us. In turn the aniconic or imageless art with which they replaced the naturalistic decorative schemes of earlier generations was destroyed after the final restoration of icon veneration and the formal condemnation of Iconoclasm in 843.[28]

Similarly, the theological treatises and conciliar pronouncements of the Iconoclasts were rapidly destroyed after the end of the period in which they dominated the Byzantine Church. Thus it is very difficult to recapture much of their thinking, which is now only represented in some of the attacks made on it by their enemies. These, however, can not be relied on to present an objective picture of the Iconoclast position. Moderation was not the way of the times in such theological conflicts. For Theophanes the enthusiastic Iconoclast Constantine V was 'a totally destructive bloodsucking wild beast ... deceived by wizardry, licentiousness, blood sacrifices of horses, dung and urine'.[29] Thus many problems remain in the interpretation of the issues and their causes, which in the absolute absence of the necessary evidence will probably never be fully understood.

What is clear is that, despite some intense initial opposition in the capital and the remaining western regions of the Empire, the Emperor Leo III enjoyed sufficient support amongst the armies in the eastern provinces in Asia Minor to be able to impose his theological will. Indeed, the situation may have been the other way around, and that the emperor adopted an Iconoclast stance because this was the position already favoured by the most numerous and powerful elements in his regional armies.[30] The lack of good evidence and deliberate suppression on the part of the ultimately victorious Iconodules makes it impossible to delineate how broadly based and popular the attack on the veneration of images actually was. However, it is reasonable to assume that it enjoyed significant support in those sectors of society upon which the emperor relied to keep himself in power, and this means some if not all of his army. In particular the units of the Anatolic and Thrakesian Themes supported Constantine V against the usurper Artavasdos (742–3), when the latter claimed that the restoration of Orthodoxy was the aim of his revolt.[31]

By this period the Empire had been split up into a small number of military commands, called Themes, which geographically were based on previous Roman administrative divisions. The nature of the organisation of the army within these areas is by no means clear. It used to be thought that the Themes emerged in their fully developed form as early as the first quarter of the seventh century, and also that the troops attached to each Theme were remunerated and sustained by being settled on state-owned lands within each region. They were thus farmer-soldiers, whose loyalty and commitment to the defence of their particular Theme were ensured by their being given a physical stake in it in the form of the lands allotted to them.[32]

Such a view would cohere with older interpretations of the nature of the accommodations made with the Germanic peoples in the West by the imperial regimes in the fifth century. Traditionally, the Roman system of *hospitalitas* (hospitality) that was employed in making such arrangements with the Visigoths, Burgundians and others, was seen as involving the state expropriation of one-third or in some cases two-thirds of the estates of the principal Roman landowners (the 'hosts') in the regions in which the Germanic troops were being established, in order to give the lands, together with fixed percentages of the unfree population attached to them, to the occupying forces or 'guests'.

However, this view of the procedures involved has rightly come under renewed scrutiny recently and has been found wanting. It has been more realistically suggested that what was distributed was a fixed proportion of tax assessments.[33] In other words the taxpayers, in the form of the Roman landowners, were linked directly to the beneficiaries, in the form of the soldiers who were due to receive the assigned revenues. This reduced the intermediary role of the state and its cumbersome apparatus for the centralised collection and then redistribution of tax. Although many of the finer points of the arguments still need to be elaborated, such an interpretation is inherently more sensible and convincing than the older view. In the light of this historians of the Byzantine Empire would do well to look again at some of their apparent certainties about the organisation of the Themes in the period before the tenth century.[34]

The origin of the system in the time of Heraclius has also rightly been doubted, and it is more sensible to see the reorganisation of the army as a product of the very changed military and geographical state of the Empire after the rapid period of Arab expansion in the 630s and 640s. The reign of Constans II (641–68) is the earliest in which such changes could be looked for, but so limited is the evidence that all that can be stated with assurance is that by the end of the reign of Constantine IV (668–85) the four principal Themes of Asia Minor – the Anatolic, Armenian, Opsikian and Thrakesian – were in existence, together with another in Thrace. To these Justinian II added Themes in Greece (Hellas) and Sicily, and Leo III created the Kibyrreot Theme in south-west Asia Minor, which was an exclusively naval force.[35]

The greatest concentration of troops was thus in the east, in Asia Minor, where lay the ever-present threat of attack from the

Arab Caliphate. Under Hisham (724–43) this took the form of virtually annual raids into the Byzantine territory in Asia Minor. To the west the Empire, apart from Sicily and the various enclaves in Italy, had been reduced to little more than the area of modern Greece and the plains of Thrace. Former Roman territories to the west and north in the Balkans were in the hands of the Slavs and the Bulgars. The latter, a steppe confederacy, had crossed the Danube around the year 680 and established themselves south of the river under their Khan Asparuch after a decisive victory over the emperor Constantine IV (668–85).[36]

Under Constantine V (741–75) the religious reforms, that may have been prompted by the territorial decline and military defeats of the Empire, were taken considerably further than under his father, and embraced a wholehearted attack on monasticism and on the veneration of relics. As usual our evidence comes only in the form of the deliberately distorted accounts of the ultimately victorious enemies of Iconoclasm, but the references in Theophanes to the emperor forcing monks to shave off their distinctive beards and to marry are specific enough to be credible.[37] This process seems to have started in the year 765 with the execution of a famed monastic teacher and ascetic called Stephen, and is probably a reflection of the role played by monks in leading the opposition to Iconoclasm. The *Life* written of this martyr for the Iconodule cause provides one of the few additional, if highly prejudiced, sources of information for this period of Byzantine history.[38]

Rome between Constantinople and Francia

The effects of the developments in the Empire on the West were considerable. In the late seventh century the emperors were still taking the lead, for better or worse, in the formulation of religious doctrine and practice. Ecumenical councils representing all the orthodox churches of Christendom were still only held in the East and were conducted under the authority of the rulers of Constantinople: In 680–1 the sixth of the series of Ecumenical councils was held in Constantinople by command of the Emperor Constantine IV to condemn the Monothelete theology, which taught that Christ might have Two Natures and Persons but only had one Will or Energy. Under Popes Leo II (682–3), who had its acts translated into Latin, and Benedict II (684–5) the Roman Church actively co-operated in the task of securing the acceptance of this Council throughout the West.

The next such imperial venture in the holding of a general council proved, to the westerners at least, much less successful.

In 692, at the bidding of Justinian II, another such gathering was held in Constantinople, which was intended to supplement the work of the previous Fifth and Sixth Ecumenical Councils of 553 and 680–1. From this it got its name of the 'Quinisext' (or 'Fifth-Sixth') Council. Doctrinally there was nothing that should have caused difficulties in this council's deliberations. However, because it included in its acts certain regulations that for the first time formalised certain differences between the Greek and Latin Churches in terms of ecclesiastical practices it proved to be extremely divisive. The principal problem concerned clerical marriage.[39]

From the fifth century onwards any form of clerical marriage was formally disapproved of in the West, and provincial councils had legislated against it on a number of occasions. However, the eastern position was different. Bishops were not expected to have wives, nor could the members of the lower orders of the clergy marry after their ordination. However, married men were admitted into the priesthood. This distinction had thus existed for some two to three centuries by the time of the holding of the 'Quinisext' Council, but by committing the eastern rules to written form in its acts, which had to be sent to the western churches for their ratification, this gathering, probably quite unintentionally, forced an open debate on this hitherto tacitly accepted difference.

Pope Sergius I (687–701), a member of a Syrian family resident in Sicily, refused to accept the decisions of the Council, although the acts had been signed by his representatives at the meeting. He took his stand not only on the issue of clerical celibacy but also on the renewed precedence given to the see of Constantinople over the older Churches of Jerusalem, Antioch and Alexandria. This was an issue that first emerged in the Council of Chalcedon in 451 and was one of the contributory causes of Pope Leo I's dissatisfaction with that gathering.

Justinian II's resort to coercion in 692 only served to show how limited imperial authority had become in Italy by the late seventh century. In 649 when Pope Martin I had convened a synod in Rome that opposed Constans II over his Monothelete *Type*, the emperor had promptly ordered his arrest. The exarch or imperial governor, in trying to carry out these orders, had found the support in Rome for the pope so strong that he was able to manipulate it for his own purposes, and rebelled against the emperor with papal backing. However by 653 it proved possible for a new exarch to seize Martin and send him to Constantinople for trial. He was sentenced to death and died in captivity.[40] In 692 when Justinian II wanted to use the same tactics against Sergius I, not only was support for the pope's stand overwhelming in Rome but the army in Ravenna mutinied and marched south to defend him. The commander of the emperor's bodyguard who had been sent to Rome to arrest Sergius was thus forced to appeal to the pope for protection against units of the imperial army.[41]

Not only had the position of the popes within the city of Rome become invulnerable as far as the emperor was concerned, but the possibility of effective imperial military intervention in Italy ceased to be a reality with the collapse of the regime of Justinian II in 695 and the ensuing quarter century of military and political instability. However, initially the popes were still willing to see themselves in secular terms as subject to the emperor and to defend his interests. Pope John VI (701–5) protected the Exarch Theophylact from murder at the hands of mutinous militia, and John VII (705–7) was willing to try to compromise with Justinian II over the acts of the 'Quinisext' Council. He did, however, also adorn the church of Santa Maria Antiqua in the Forum in Rome with a set of frescoes in which his predecessor Martin I, who had suffered at the hands of Constans II, was depicted as a saint.[42] Pope Constantine (708–15) was persuaded to visit Constantinople in 711 and was extraordinarily well received by Justinian II.[43]

The papal willingness to co-operate in the political sphere with the emperor was put under considerable but not ultimately fatal strain by the initiation of the Emperor Leo III's Iconoclast measures in 726. In the seventh century imperial involvement in theological arguments had lain behind all the major disputes with Rome, though the popes were normally able to rationalise this by putting the blame on the Patriarchs of Constantinople for misleading their imperial masters. However, the Emperor Philippicus (711–13), who overthrew Justinian II, reintroduced Monotheletism by his own decree and the fiction of imperial innocence could hardly be further sustained.[44] In 726 Pope Gregory II (715–31) strongly condemned not only the Iconoclast doctrine favoured by Leo III but also the whole principle of the emperor having authority in the making of doctrinal pronouncements.[45]

The stand taken by Gregory II was far tougher than those of Martin I in 649 and Sergius I in 692, but the emperor's ability to take punitive measures against him was very limited. Instead, between 726 and 730, he tried unsuccessfully to bring the pope to accept the Iconoclast doctrine. Leo's unenforceable threat to depose the pope only led to revolts in those parts of northern Italy still under imperial control, which had also been alienated from the new dynasty by its attempts to impose massive increases in taxation after 717.[46] The dispatch of an imperial fleet to Italy in 732 proved disastrous, in that much of it was destroyed in a storm, with the loss of men and materials that the Empire could not easily afford, and so no further attempts were made to impose a solution by force.[47]

Despite the strain in relations at this time, what is most striking is the survival of political loyalty towards Constantinople on the part of all the popes of the early eighth century. Neither Gregory II nor his successor Gregory III (731–41), another of the numerous popes of this period who was of Syrian origin, wavered in their allegiance to the Empire. Gregory II dissuaded the rebels in northern Italy from setting up an emperor of their own. The tenacity of the Roman imperial traditions that underpinned the papal world-view was remarkable in a period marked by the popes' consistent resistance to Leo III's religious policies. They were not looking to create an independent 'papal state'.

On the other hand circumstances in Italy had forced them, from the time of Gregory I (590–604) onwards to play an occasionally independent political hand. Thus Gregory I, faced in 593 by a serious threat to the city of Rome from the Lombards and with no prospect of a military intervention on the part of the exarch, who was based in Ravenna, made a separate treaty with King Agilulf. For this he was criticised by both the exarch and the Emperor Maurice, but it was their inability to defend the city that had prompted his action.[48] For the same reason Pope Zacharias (741–52) made a twenty-year truce for Rome with the Lombards in 742.[49]

Increasingly, as the military problems facing the Empire in the East grew in magnitude the defence of Italy came to be neglected or left only to such resources as the exarchs could assemble. In these circumstances the popes came to play a leading role in organising the defence of Rome. For example, a repair of the city walls was carried out by Gregory II.[50] They also came increasingly to represent wider Italian interests, and to act as spokesmen in various confrontations between the provincials and the imperial government, as represented by the exarch. The ecclesiastical importance of the popes gave them an access to the emperor that was denied to other Italians, and enabled them to go over the heads of the exarchs if need be. Thus it was Pope Gregory II who led the resistance to the increased rates of taxation that Leo III sought to impose on imperial territories in Italy.

For such reasons, in the political circumstances of the seventh and early eighth centuries the popes also came to play a vital role as diplomatic intermediaries between the exarchs and the Lombard rulers. The importance of this function intensified as the military situation in northern Italy turned further and further to the disadvantage of the Byzantines. In 743 Pope Zacharias persuaded King Liutprand (712–44) to halt his attack on the almost defenceless exarchate, and he repeated this achievement in negotiations with King Ratchis (744–9) in 749.[51] However, the latter's successor Aistulf (749–56) was less easily persuaded and in 751 he captured Ravenna and thus finally eliminated the Byzantine exarchate.[52] Apart from Sicily, Apulia and Calabria in the far south, only two tiny enclaves in Venetia and Istra remained of the former imperial territories in Italy.

King Liutprand had brought Spoleto and Benevento, the two great and hitherto largely independent Lombard duchies of central and southern Italy, firmly under royal control, and Aistulf had maintained this. He had then gone on to capture Ravenna. The logic of a political reunification of Italy under the aegis of the Lombard kingdom of Pavia was surely irresistible. Apart from the minor Byzantine holdings, the only remaining anomaly was the duchy of Rome, controlled for the emperor by the pope.

However, it is possible that the Lombard rulers were in two minds as to the desirability of adding the city of Rome and its most important inhabitant to their kingdom. The popes had, largely through the imperial inability to defend the central Italian duchy and the city, made themselves into the *de facto* secular rulers of the region, although still acknowledging the suzerainty of the emperor. They had also come to take on a wider role in Italian politics and could, as under Pope Gregory III, ally themselves with the neighbouring Lombard dukes of Spoleto in opposing the expansion of royal authority. There was therefore much to be gained from the king's point of view in annexing the Roman duchy and preventing it from remaining a potential military and political threat.

On the other hand, the popes' influence extended far beyond the confines of the duchy and even of Italy, and as the foremost bishops in the West they could hardly be treated in the same way as, for example, recalcitrant dukes of Spoleto or Benevento. Nor could the Lombard rulers control the election of popes in the way they could, from the time of Liutprand onwards, control the succession to the other duchies. From what they may have known of papal–imperial relations, it is possible also to suspect that the kings of the Lombards would not have relished the kind of relations with the popes that would have resulted from incorporating Rome directly into their kingdom.[53] All in all, it seems likely that in the early 750s the Lombard rulers would have been more anxious to neutralise Rome than to annexe it. This must explain the fact that when in the spring of 752 Aistulf invaded the duchy of Rome he was willing to make a forty-year treaty of peace with the pope rather than press his undoubted military advantage and take the city.[54]

From the point of view of the pope, now Stephen II(III) (752–7), the integration of the Roman duchy into the Lombard kingdom offered no attraction, and within months of making the treaty with Aistulf in June 752 he had appealed to Constantine V for military aid. This was not forthcoming, as the emperor was busy taking advantage of the chaos following the overthrow of the Umayyad Caliphate in 750 to regain Theodosiopolis (Erzurum) and Melitene in eastern Asia Minor.[55] In Italy Aistulf, warned that the pope was already attempting to subvert the treaty made in the summer, prepared to launch a major assault on Rome in the spring of 753. Stephen II(III) turned for immediate aid to the greatest Christian power in the West, the Arnulfing or Carolingian kingdom of Francia, whose ruler already stood in debt to the papacy for support in replacing the previous Merovingian dynasty in 751. The Frankish King Pippin III's subsequent intervention in Italy proved decisive in bringing about the final detachment of the papacy from Byzantine political allegiance and the creation of a new western Empire.

14 Monks and missionaries

The processes that led to the cultural realignments of the seventh and eighth centuries were by no means exclusively negative ones. One of the most striking features of the second half of this period in particular was the way in which the former physical and intellectual boundaries of the Roman world came to be superseded. The frontiers of the Empire had represented the limits of the civilised world as far as its inhabitants were concerned, and those who lived beyond them were of little or no interest, other than so far as they represented a periodic menace to peace and good order. There was no sense in which it was felt necessary to try to export the benefits of Roman civilisation to such 'barbarians'.

Inevitably, elements of Roman material and intellectual culture did seep across the borders, which became in the process increasingly attractive in the literal sense to those who lived beyond them. In due course, as has been seen, this contributed directly to the implosion of the frontiers under external pressure and ultimately the disintegration of the old political order. In the formative centuries that followed what is customarily called 'the Fall of the Roman Empire', the large-scale political structures of Late Antiquity vanished in the West. But equally significantly, the static political and intellectual boundaries of the older order were replaced by an expanding cultural frontier. Geographical areas such as Ireland, Central Europe east of the Rhine, the steppes of southern Russia, Scandinavia and Iceland, that had scarcely or never been touched by Rome, were brought gradually into a cultural continuum as the result of the active export and dissemination of Christianity.

In the East, despite the conscious survival of a Roman identity and attitudes, from the sixth century onwards the imperial government came to realise the value that this export of Christianity through missionary activity could play in bringing potentially hostile peoples beyond the frontiers into the cultural orbit of the Empire and thus into a more tractable frame of mind politically. Both in the final stages of conflict with the Zoroastrian regime of Sassanian Persia and in the confrontation with Islam, religion played a crucial role in the ideology and the politics of confrontation. Similarly, too, in the Balkans the very serious threats presented to the Empire by such peoples as the Slavs and the Bulgars were ultimately contained not so much by military means, which proved only occasionally and temporarily successful, but by bringing about a cultural realignment that turned the Balkan kingdoms and khanates into what has usefully been termed 'the Byzantine Commonwealth'.[1]

In the fourth and fifth centuries a number of large-scale conversions to Christianity had occurred on the part of Germanic peoples entering the Empire. This was almost a 'rite of passage'. To wish to participate in the benefits offered by Rome meant, for the Visigoths, Ostrogoths, Franks and others, accepting its religion. Extraordinarily little information exists concerning the mechanics of this process. This is not just a question of the loss of evidence but a positive absence of it, due to the fact that contemporaries apparently did not think these were matters of sufficient interest or importance to record. On the other hand, an extensive literature of conversion came into being from the late seventh and eighth centuries onwards, which provides considerable, if rarely unambiguous, evidence concerning the processes of conversion of the Anglo-Saxons, of the various Germanic peoples east of the Rhine, and of Scandinavia.

In these processes it is not easy to distinguish the purely religious dimension from its wider cultural context. Conversion was attractive to those proselytised because it brought with it a whole range of other benefits. Thus, to take a simple example, because Christianity was a religion of the book, which depended upon the knowledge of reading and writing for the understanding of the central features of its message and the way in which that message had been interpreted over the course of many centuries, the introduction of these arts always accompanied it in those societies in which they were not yet present. This could also, in the case of the Slavs in the Balkans, lead to the creation of a distinctive script needed to represent the special characteristics of the spoken language.[2]

In the West the principal architect of the movement to expand the frontiers of Christianity has often been seen as being the papacy, and a starting point has sometimes been assigned to the process in the dispatch of the Roman mission to the Anglo-Saxons in 596. There is some, but only a limited, truth in this. As will be seen, papal interest in evangelism was actually a relatively late phenomenon, and was largely the outcome of a particular pope's highly developed sense of his personal pastoral responsibility. This in turn was not so much an aspect of the ideology of the special nature of papal authority, that had been developing in Rome since at least the late fourth century, as a product of the growth of monastic ideas and institutions.[3]

Western monasticism: Augustine to Gregory the Great

When Augustine became Bishop of Hippo in 395 he established a house-monastery in which to live with his immediate episcopal entourage and from which he would carry out the various pastoral and administrative duties of his new office. He may have been one of the first western provincial bishops to do this, but he was adopting a tradition already well established in the East. Noted bishops and theologians such as the three 'Cappadocian Fathers' – Basil, Bishop of Caesarea (370–9), his brother Gregory of Nyssa (372–95), and their friend Gregory of Nazianzus (Bishop of Constantinople 379–81) – had set up 'private' monastic institutions on their own property and had attempted to combine office in the Church with continuing personal commitment to an ascetic life.[4] Under their inspiration a number of laymen created similar monastic households.

From the late fourth century this was also the way in which many monastic institutions developed in the West. Wealthy individuals or families decided, under the inspiration of the ideal of achieving personal salvation through renunciation and the leading of a disciplined and regulated life of prayer, meditation and good works, to turn their houses into monasteries in which they would live with selected companions, following a pattern of such a life of their own devising. The founders of such establishments were almost always wealthy, in that they depended on their own financial resources to create them, though it is possible in some cases that communities were set up on deserted or unclaimed land.

A number of bishops, especially in Gaul, founded and endowed monastic houses, over which they themselves did not preside. Instead they appointed abbots to govern them. Such institutions were intended to be permanent, in a way that aristocratic household monasteries might not be. It would be unwise, however, to draw too many distinctions between such establishments. In some cases founders of 'private' monastic houses were subsequently persuaded into accepting episcopal office, and then turned their private foundations into regular and permanent monasteries. For example, Martin, Bishop of Tours (d. 397) founded Ligugé, south of Poitiers, prior to his episcopal election, and then after his ordination set up another monastery at Marmoutier on the Loire from which to direct his diocese.[5]

A similar case is that of the famous island monastery of Lérins, near Cannes on the Côte d'Azure.[6] This was founded by Honoratus (d. 430), a member of a Gallic aristocratic family. He attracted a growing number of followers willing to join him, and when he was persuaded to become Bishop of Arles in 427 he appointed one of them, Maximus, to succeed him as head of the community. In turn Maximus became Bishop of Riez in 433, and his successor as Abbot of Lérins, Faustus, in due course also took over his episcopal see.[7] By this time Lérins had established itself as probably the most influential monastic house in the Rhône basin and Provence. Others of its products, and not necessarily former abbots, were sought for episcopal appointments throughout the region. One of these, Caesarius, Bishop of Arles (502–42) founded a major monastic house for women in his diocesan city, and wrote a rule for its inmates.[8]

Such monasteries were frequently urban, but a number also came to be set up on rural family estates. Cassiodorus (d. *c.* 580) retired to his country property at Vivarium in the south of Italy after the final elimination of the Ostrogothic kingdom, and set up such a monastery there. For the monks he admitted to it to live under his direction he wrote his *Institutes*, providing advice on what they should read and how they should copy books and check their doctrinal orthodoxy and textual accuracy.[9] Many such monasteries cannot have survived the death of their founders, but from the sixth century onwards it became increasingly common for those who set up such houses to try to ensure their continuance by committing the regulations under which their inmates lived to writing, to guarantee that the rule of life by which they lived would be preserved. In some cases these may have been no more than the Latin translations of some of the Greek monastic rules produced by Basil of Caesarea (d. 379) and others.

Fuller and more comprehensive sets of regulations did, however, start to appear in the West by the sixth century. Amongst the earliest of these is the anonymous work known as *The Rule of the Master*, written around the year 525, possibly somewhere in the vicinity of Rome. Slightly later in date (*c.* 540) and in part dependent on *The Rule of the Master* is the more famous *Rule of Benedict*.[10] This work is the first of the major western Rules whose author is known, at least in so far as the testimony of some of the manuscripts of the work may be believed. Biographical information concerning this Benedict derives from the account of him in Book II of Pope Gregory the Great's *Dialogues*, a series of stories concerning the lives and miracles of recent Italian holy men, written in 593.[11]

It would be unwise to place great reliance on the details of Gregory's stories concerning Benedict, which were intended to be didactic and edifying. Only the barest outline of his life can in fact be drawn. Benedict (*c.* 480–547) is said to have been educated in Rome but to have retired into a spiritual retreat in a cave at Subiaco around the age of twenty. He is reported to have founded some twelve monastic communities in the area over the next few years and to have received the children of a number of senators from Rome for education. He subsequently moved further south and established his most famous monastic community on the site of a former pagan temple on Monte Cassino in the Apennines north-west of Capua around the year 529.[12]

The *Rule* composed by Benedict for the observance of his monks has aroused particular admiration. Even so, it is important to appreciate that in the sixth and seventh centuries it was one amongst a number of such Rules, composed in Italy, Gaul, Spain and Ireland, and that its general dissemination throughout western Europe as the principal blueprint for the monastic life was largely the result of Carolingian attempts in the early ninth century to establish uniform patterns of monastic, canonical and liturgical observance. Although less ferocious in its discipline than the majority of early medieval Irish monastic Rules, the twelve 'degrees of humility' propounded by *The Rule of Benedict* envisage an abbatial authority that is frighteningly strong and very wide ranging.

No totalitarian dictator could hope to control the minds and behaviour of his subjects in quite the way that Benedict's abbot should be able to. The individual monk was required to be obedient to his abbot in all things, to have no will of his own, not to complain about any injuries or ill-treatment to which he might be subjected when under obedience, to 'be content with the meanest and worst of everything', to call himself and think of himself as being the lowest of the low, to take no independent action, not to speak except in reply to a superior, and to avoid laughter.[13]

Benedict's *Rule*, like that of 'the Master', was unusual in its own time for being so all-embracing in terms of the aspects of the monastic life it sought to regulate. The anonymous or pseudonymous rules that were followed in the monasteries of southern Gaul tended to remain closer to eastern originals, in that they were concerned more with the nature of the spiritual instruction to be provided and less with the minutiae of the practicalities of communal life. That the *Rule of Benedict* would emerge as the best known and most widely used of all western monastic rules was probably less a product of its intrinsic merits than the chance combination of the way it came to the attention of one of the most significant and influential of early medieval popes, and its subsequent influence, albeit mixed with indigenous traditions, on the Irish Church. Both of these were also to play a significant role in the development of the missionary ventures of the seventh and eighth centuries.

Of the popes of the early middle ages Gregory I (590–604) – known as 'the Great' – is by far the most outstanding. In part this may be a reflection of the fact that more is known about him than about virtually all of his predecessors and most of his successors before the twelfth century. The survival of approximately 850 of his official letters (albeit only a small proportion of the total that once existed) provides an extraordinary amount of insight into both the practical problems he faced during his pontificate and the working of his mind.[14] To this can be added the substantial corpus of his exegetical writings, composed during his period as papal representative in Constantinople (*c.* 580–5) and in the opening years of his pontificate.[15]

Most, if indeed not all, of these were composed for monastic audiences and readers. For where Gregory was truly novel was in being the first pope who had previously been a monk. He belonged in this respect to the tradition of the founders of aristocratic 'house-monasteries', having turned his family house on the Caelian Hill into a monastery. Like a number of bishops, he also maintained a modified monastic lifestyle during his pontificate.[16] It was from his monastery on the Caelian that he drew the group of monks whom he sent under Augustine to evangelise the Anglo-Saxon kingdom of Kent in 596.

The subsequent history of missionary ventures has often been seen as a symbiosis between Irish monasticism (which will be discussed below) and the Roman traditions deriving from Gregory's venture in sending monks to Kent. The apparent propensity of the Anglo-Saxon Church from the later seventh century onwards for producing missionaries anxious to spread the Gospel to the pagans east of the Rhine (not least their own continental Saxon 'relatives') is seen in this perspective as a consequence of these twin elements in its own genesis. In turn the special ties that linked the Anglo-Saxons to the Papacy became the route through which the Frankish rulers, under whose political aegis the missionaries had to work, renewed their contacts with Rome. From these derived not least the papal support for the replacement of the Merovingian dynasty by the Carolingian in 751 and ultimately the coronation of the second king of this line as the new Roman emperor in the year 800.[17]

This pattern of relationships at least has the virtue of neatness. However, the reality of the past is rarely as tidy as historians' reconstructions of it, and this particular set of events is a case in point. Although both Irish monasticism and the papacy had roles to play in the expansion of Latin Christianity and in the political and cultural realignments of eighth century Francia, it is unwise to highlight these to such an extent that other elements are

obscured or concealed. In this chapter the first parts of these processes, the missionary ventures, will be examined, while the political developments in Francia will be considered in the next two.

The making of the Irish Church

Ireland was the first territory beyond the Roman imperial frontiers that was converted to Christianity by missionary activity, and
in turn the Irish Church was to play a crucial role both in the
promotion of monastic activity elsewhere in Western Europe and
in the further spreading into new areas of the Christian religion,
and with it many aspects of the intellectual culture of Late
Antiquity. Thus, the origins, growth and distinctive characteristics
of Irish Christianity, as well as the society in which it was to be
implanted, should be considered here. However, these are topics
that have formed and continue to provide a scholarly battle-
ground. The problems are, not surprisingly, evidential ones, but
they are intensified by a linguistic dimension, that has provided
the ammunition for some of the most savage exchanges between
students of early Irish history.[18]

A large part of the source material is written in Old Irish
('archaic' and 'classical') and in Middle Irish, and much of it is
sufficiently far removed from the modern language for genuine
difficulties of interpretation to occur.[19] In particular, there have
been problems to be faced in trying to assign dates to many of
the vernacular texts by linguistic criteria. Dating is, of course,
central to the question of how much weight to allow to the testimony of particular sources, especially when, as in the case of many
of the Irish texts, the extant manuscripts are all relatively modern
and thus no guide in themselves.[20]

The dating and status of the law tracts have proved amongst
the most contentious of issues, but those of the various sets of
annals upon whose testimony the chronological framework of
Early Medieval Ireland might be expected to hang have been
scarcely less so.[21] The generally accepted view, though, might be
said to be that contemporary recording of events in the extant
sets of annals cannot have begun earlier than *c.* 730.[22] Some
annals and narrative histories have been shown to be both much
later in date and more heavily larded with literary invention –
that is, fiction – than was once thought.[23] Other quasi-historical
texts, such as saints' lives, which also used to be accorded considerable weight as evidence, have been subjected to increasingly
critical scrutiny. While such works are of considerable intrinsic
interest in their own right, their value as genuine records of the
Early Medieval centuries has in most cases been reduced to nil.[24]

The limited quantity and nature of genuinely pertinent evidence relating to a number of subjects of central interest, and the heavy overlay deriving from later legendary accretions or deliberately distorted versions, makes the study of this period peculiarly difficult. Not the least controversial topic is that of the coming of Christianity into Ireland. Within the indigenous tradition the primary role has always been ascribed to Patrick. However, to say that there is still no firm agreement as to whether to place his activities in the first or second half of the fifth century is merely to allude to the beginning of the problems concerning him.[25] Greater probability, it should be stated, now probably belongs to the late fifth century dating.

To avoid prolonged historiographical discussion, it is fair to say that the only sources concerning Patrick that may be treated as being of direct relevance to the study of his life are the works that he wrote himself. Two subsequent *Lives* (or rather a *Life* and a *Memorandum*) by Muirchú (*c.* 690) and Tírechán (*c.* 670), do not lead back to the realities of the fifth century.[26] Likewise, the substantial *Tripartite Life* of *c.* 895/900 is a marvellous guide to the aspirations of the monastery of Armagh, which claimed Patrician foundation and predominant status and authority in the Irish Church on the strength of it, but is even further distanced from the real Patrick.[27]

His own writings, as opposed to the beguiling but illusory certainties of the later *Lives*, are tantalisingly obscure. They consist of a *Confessio*, which seems to be a defence against various slanders that were being circulated about him, and a letter directed to the soldiers of a certain Coroticus.[28] In the former he referred to various events in his life: how at the age of sixteen he had been taken from Britain to be sold as a slave by an Irish raiding party, and how he had escaped after six years. Then after he had returned to Britain (the chronology at this point becomes extremely vague), he had experienced a vision in which he received letters from Ireland via a certain Victoricus, appealing to him to come back.[29] In consequence he seems then to have devoted the rest of his life to missionary activity in Ireland, becoming a bishop in the course of it. There may have been some doubts at the time as to the validity of his episcopal ordination, which may have been irregularly performed. It has also been proposed recently that his primary interest there was in groups of fellow Britons, who like himself had been carried off in Irish slave raids.[30] This certainly accords well with the norms of Late Roman ecclesiastical practice, but there is no easy way to prove or disprove this hypothesis. If it is correct, the consequences are that we do not and cannot know exactly when, how and by whom the Irish were converted to Christianity.[31]

Although the authors of later *Lives*, who shared with the modern historian the problem of making a coherent account out of Patrick's own elliptical writings, attribute the introduction of Christianity into Ireland and the conversion of the most powerful kingdoms to his missionary labours, this is almost certainly a gross exaggeration. Both from independent sources and even from the logic of Patrick's own words it is clear that Christians were to be found in Ireland before he began his work there.

Although never politically a part of the Roman Empire, and in consequence retaining elements of a pre-Roman Iron Age social order much longer than most other regions of Western Europe, Ireland was inevitably influenced by the culture of its dominant neighbour, from the first century onwards.[32] That this involved the gradual penetration of Christianity, mediated either through Britain or northern Gaul, is proved not least by the reference in the contemporary *Chronicle of Prosper* to Pope Celestine sending 'the Irish believing in Christ' a certain Palladius to be their 'first bishop'.[33] In his *Life of Patrick* Muirchú, who knew Prosper's work, had to kill off Palladius after an abortive visit, so as to ensure Patrick's status as the true founding father of the Irish Church.[34]

In view of the evidential obscurity it is hard to say more than that it is certain that Christianity was establishing itself in Ireland in the course of the fifth century, as it was also doing at this time in Roman Britain and amongst some of the independent Celtic kingdoms north of Hadrian's Wall.[35] It is not certain how soon monastic communities began to appear in either Britain or Ireland, though some certainly existed in the former by the time of Gildas (fl. 520/40). The Irish evidence is even less clear, in that the subsequent centuries saw a proliferation of monasteries anxious to extend their origins backwards into a largely invented past, and to endow their founders with appropriate miraculous powers and deeds. However, it is possible to say that by the end of the sixth century at least a small number of monastic communities did exist in Ireland, and in such areas as western Scotland, into which elements of Irish population had been migrating since the fifth century.

Such establishments should in no sense be visualised as in any way corresponding to the type of constructions familiar from the numerous remains and survivals of later medieval monasteries. Nor were they like the aristocratic 'house monasteries' set up in towns in the south of Gaul, in Rome and in North Africa, and which represented the main form of monastic institution before the spread of the Irish monks. The nearest extant equivalents are probably to be seen in the monastic sites of Ireland that date from before the Anglo-Norman conquest of the twelfth century, as for example at Glendalough, Clonmacnois and Monasterboice. Such monasteries are very reminiscent of the earliest communities of Egypt and Syria, in that within the compound wall each monk had his own individual hut or cell. The only stone buildings were the small and very simple churches, each dedicated to a different saint, which were places of pilgrimage and meditation rather than being intended to accommodate the entire community in corporate liturgical acts.[36]

Those Irish monasteries that are known to have existed by the late sixth century include Bangor (Co. Down), founded by Comgall, probably Ciaran's foundation at Clonmacnois, and certainly the three linked communities of Derry, Durrow and Iona (in the Inner Hebrides) that were created by Columba (d. 597).[37] It is possible that others were equally firmly established by this time, but the nature of the relevant evidence is too unreliable for certainty in most cases. The foundation of Iona either in 563 or 565 represents the first establishment of an Irish monastery outside the island.[38] Even more wide reaching, though, were to be the travels and the monastic foundations on the Continent in this same period of an Irish abbot from Bangor called Columbanus (d. 615).

Before considering the nature and effects of the Irish impact on Europe, it is necessary, briefly, to look for the answers to two questions: why did monastic communities come so rapidly to play such an apparently dynamic role in Irish society; and why did they prove to be such useful vehicles for the transmission of a learned, and only recently received, intellectual culture to other regions outside Ireland? A total absence of towns, at least before the tenth century, and the peculiarities of the political structures of Irish society made the creation of dioceses on the pattern employed in the former lands of the Roman Empire a practical impossibility in the island. However, monasteries that resembled those of Egypt in terms of their size and organisation, provided an alternative. Although the evidence is far from being impressive either in its quantity or its clarity, it is possible that by the seventh century the greater monastic communities had become the principal ecclesiastical landowners in Ireland, and that their abbots were by then the primary founts of authority in its Church. It is often pointed out that monasteries might in consequence contain one or more bishops to perform the liturgical functions that were particular to their office, but they were subordinate to the power of the abbot.[39] It is necessary, however, to be very cautious in the light of the limited evidence. Such a system may have been peculiar to the monastic confederacy created by Columba.[40]

Attempts have been made to explain such developments, which were quite anomalous in terms of the organisation of the Church elsewhere in Europe. Rejecting those that depend on nothing more than a Romantic view of the special *Volkgeist* of the Celts, the most comprehensible answers relate to the lack of large-scale political structure in Ireland at this time. Still allowing for the fact that the principal historical sources, the *Annals*, are far from contemporaneous at this time, the evidence suggests that Ireland was divided into a large number of small and not very stable kingdoms, perhaps between 80 and 100 in number.[41]

It is necessary to reject the kind of rigid categorisation beloved by the creators and later glossators of some of the legal texts, that would present us with a pattern of different types of kingdom, neatly and hierarchically arranged, and with the rights of 'over-kings' in relation to their 'subkings' precisely tabulated.[42] The reality was altogether messier, with dramatic shifts in local and regional power depending upon the competence as war leaders and providers of reward (treasure, cattle and beer) of individual kings. On such a basis a small kingdom could grow into a big one or just as easily be overrun by a neighbour. The king of a *tuath*, the basic small tribal–political unit, might find himself obliged to pay tribute to a more powerful local ruler, but only for as long as the latter seemed to have the material power to enforce it.

In such circumstances monasteries, endowed with lands and herds by local rulers, and in many cases with the royal house also enjoying something of a monopoly in the abbatial succession, proved easier to establish than episcopal dioceses, whose boundaries would rarely have been able to correspond to the more fluctuating realities of political frontiers. The lack of centralised authority in Ireland also meant that there was no secular power to guarantee the protection and functioning of the kind of ecclesiastical organisation to be found elsewhere in Western Europe.[43]

Monks were also better able than secular clergy to fit into the slots in Irish society recently vacated by the pagan learned and priestly classes. Rigorous asceticism and mortification seem to have formed part of the initial training and subsequent lifestyle of the *druid* and the *filid* or 'seers' – who may for convenience be called the magicians and the poets. The latter in particular were of vital importance in pre-literate Irish society, for their memorisation of laws, genealogies, and heroic poems provided the only vehicle for the preservation of the records of the kingdoms, and thus the historical dimension of their separate identities.[44]

With the introduction of writing the monasteries, many of which were established in close proximity to the main royal centres, took over most of these functions. The monks also came to enjoy the legal status and immunities once enjoyed by the pagan learned classes. A number of the monasteries became intellectual centres to which aspiring monks were drawn, as much by the reputation for learning as for the ascetic sanctity of their abbots. These latter exercised a power over their charges and a responsibility for their spiritual welfare that was again very reminiscent of the Egyptian founding fathers of coenobitic monasticism, but which also corresponded to the intensely hierarchical nature of authority in the pre-Christian Irish intelligentsia.

Because Ireland had never formed a part of the Empire, the Latin language and the literary culture of Rome and of Christianity were alien to its society. This is not though, to say that the Irish were unaware of their powerful neighbour, but it meant that the conversion of the Irish involved not just a change in religious allegiance but also a major cultural transformation.[45] Irish clerics became avid to obtain whatever they could of the literary apparatus of their new faith. They were also, because they themselves had had consciously to learn Latin as a foreign language to master the texts that they needed to read, uniquely well qualified to instruct others who were similarly placed, such as the Germanic-speaking Anglo-Saxons.[46]

In a way that is again most reminiscent of the traditions of Egyptian and Syrian monasticism, the Irish monks took very seriously and literally the injunctions concerning self-negation and renunciation. In that the equivalent of desert could hardly be found in Ireland, this often took the form of physical withdrawal to rocks and small islands off the coast, most dramatically illustrated by such a site as Skelig Michael in the south-west. But withdrawal could also be achieved by any form of self-imposed exile away from the local society which guaranteed the individual his freedom and status, and where his strong family and tribal ties would be located. In consequence, there developed the tradition of what became known as the Greater and the Lesser *Peregrinatio* or pilgrimage, in which the aspiring ascetic withdrew from the protection that came from his own family and *tuath*. In the Lesser form he removed himself from the boundaries of his own kingdom, in which his security had been guaranteed by his family and his ruler. In the Greater form he withdrew entirely from Ireland, under a self-imposed vow not to return.[47]

It has often been assumed that this tradition of *Peregrinatio* was what led Irish monks to cross the seas to Britain and to the Continent, and to found or join existing monastic communities there. It would, in this perspective, be the real motivating force behind the impetus given by the Irish to Western European monastic reform and expansion. This, then, is the mainspring of the whole movement of missionary activity. Yet, as with so many of the traditional certainties of the scholarly consensus on early

Irish history, it starts to crumble away in the hand the harder it is examined. The evidence, inevitably, tends to post-date the supposed early stages of the phenomenon, and in the classifications of *Peregrinatio* we may once again be encountering the love of artificial systematising that is typical of so many of the normative texts, both secular and ecclesiastical, produced in early medieval Ireland. It is clear that Columba, who according to the rules should never have returned to Ireland after the foundation of Iona in 563 or 565, is frequently to be found back in his home land thereafter.[48]

Certainly, Irish monks in their self-imposed (if probably reversible) exile took themselves to the Continent, following long-established trade routes, and founded fixed communities in what were intended to be remote locations in Gaul and northern Italy. The best known of the continental Irish monastic founders is Columbanus, whose rule for the ordering of the daily life and discipline of his monks has survived, together with a small collection of his letters. He was also the author of a penitential, which in three sections devoted to monks, the secular clergy and the laity respectively, laid down the penances to be imposed as expiation for a large number of offences.[49] This work shows traces of borrowings from an earlier British or Irish penitential ascribed to a certain Vinnian, who might be identified with a correspondent of Gildas of the same name.[50] All these works were written in a distinctively florid Latin. At some point before *c.* 660 an Italian disciple and monk of Bobbio, called Jonas of Susa, wrote a *Life of Columbanus* which is the principal source for our knowledge of its events.

On the basis of Jonas's work it can be said that Columbanus arrived in Francia around the year 590 and established two monastic communities in the Vosges, at Annegray and at Luxeuil. His relations with the Gallic episcopate were not good, largely because of the liturgical and other differences between Irish practices (not least concerning the dating of Easter) and those more generally followed in the Latin Church.[51] Despite this he enjoyed royal protection, until he offended king Theuderic II (596–613) by refusing to bless his illegitimate children. This led to his expulsion from the Frankish kingdom of Burgundy and his eventual removal into Lombard Italy, where with the backing of King Agilulf he established the last of his foundations, at Bobbio, prior to his death in 615.[52]

Such monasteries on the Continent attracted other Irishmen to them, either to join or to visit on the course of pilgrimages. In consequence they became channels through which more Christian Latin texts were passed to Ireland. For example, a number of the works of Isidore of Seville reached Ireland soon after their author's death in 636, probably by transmission via Bobbio.[53] These Irish monasteries also began to interest the indigenous inhabitants of the regions in which they were established, and many entered them as monks. Thus Columbanus's successors as abbots of Bobbio were not to be of Irish origin.[54] In general, this phenomenon must warn us not to overemphasise the Irishness of these monasteries, particularly after the first generation. If non-Irish speakers were being attracted into them it was because the Irish linguistic element in them was not strong. The language of the liturgy, the works of exegesis and scriptural study, and of the monastic and penitential rules, was Latin. The language used by the monks in general to communicate with each other must have been one that was mutually comprehensible – this could not have been Irish.

As such foundations proliferated they started to attract the attention of members of the local Frankish aristocracy, who in some cases began to be interested in themselves becoming monks or in establishing such settlements of monks on their own estates.[55] Thus the Frank Wandregisel founded the monastery of Fontanelle in the Seine valley in 648, apparently in consequence of a dream in which he saw the life of the monks of Bobbio, an at least implicit indication of debt to Columbanus's work.[56] The neighbouring monastery of Jumièges was founded around 655 by another Frankish aristocrat called Philibert, apparently under some form of Irish influence. It was largely, though not exclusively, through this Irish-inspired movement that such monastic houses began to proliferate in certain parts of Francia.

It is important, though, to recognise firstly that what may be called indigenous Gallic monastic traditions were already long established and, secondly, that some regions of the Frankish kingdoms were more rapidly and more intensely influenced by the Irish than others. The sites for most of the Irish or Irish-inspired monastic foundations in Francia in the seventh century are to be found within the area between the Seine and the lower Meuse, or in parts of central Burgundy between Besançon and Strasbourg. Very few of the new houses were to be encountered outside these regions.[57] Thus, while Irish traditions, such as the *Peregrinatio*, and Irish monks were to have an important part to play in the expansion of the frontiers of Latin Christianity, it is necessary always to be aware of the existence of alternative sources of inspiration. Over 200 new monasteries are known to have been founded in Gaul in the seventh century, and only a limited number of these can be linked to Irish connections or influence. Indeed, in view of the slight nature of the evidence, it is possible to speculate that the growth of Irish monasticism in this same period may have been stimulated by these continental developments.

Although now reduced to more sensible proportions, there used to be a fashion for attributing virtually every development in the intellectual and spiritual life of Western Europe in the later seventh and eighth centuries to Irish influence. Extraordinary claims were once made for the learning of the Irish scholars, which in some cases was supposed to extend to a fluent knowledge of Greek.[58] In practice, though, the number of texts that can be traced to Ireland itself, as opposed to continental monasteries that had some Irish links, is both small and of limited character. By and large such works consisted of biblical exegesis and other aids to scriptural study, computus (necessary for liturgical calculations), and relatively simple grammars.[59]

These were also the kind of texts that were in turn produced by Irish writers. The more enthusiastic Irish scholars came to the Continent not just for pilgrimage and monastic retreat but also to uncover its store of learning. In consequence they did blow the dust off some books that may have ceased to be read, and have awoken some of their Western European contemporaries to the treasures in their midst. Even so, what they were looking for was not a revival of the secular literature of Antiquity, but more and better works of exegesis, grammar and monastic spirituality and Rules. The Irish appreciated the *Rule of Benedict* almost before anyone else, and a number of the monasteries they founded or influenced lived under a mixed Rule, combining Benedict's work with that of Columbanus.[60] This also influenced the hold that the *Rule of Benedict* obtained on the monasteries of Northumbria, though here the special reverence of the Anglo-Saxons for Gregory the Great, who had mentioned the rule in his *Dialogues*, may have also played a part.

The rigorousness of Irish monasticism, the reputation for sanctity of many of its leading ascetics, and the new impetus given to scriptural studies there began to attract visitors from the Continent by the middle of the seventh century. Amongst these was the Frankish aristocrat Agilbert, who was in due course to become Bishop of Wessex (650s) and then of Paris (667/8–*c.* 680).[61] Ireland in these respects began to provide some of the spiritual facilities once offered by the desert monasteries and ascetic teachers of Egypt and Palestine, access to which was now reduced or closed by the upheavals attending upon the Arab conquest. From this milieu of Franco-Irish monastic development was to spring much of the impetus behind the great missionary ventures of the seventh and eighth centuries.

Spreading the word

The roots of the processes that led to the spread of Christianity, and with it elements of the intellectual culture of Late Antiquity, into regions beyond the former frontiers of the Roman Empire are complex, to say the least. The primary vehicle by which it was achieved, however, has long been recognised to be monasticism. Monks were ideally suited for missionary ventures, in that not only were they tightly disciplined and under obedience to their superiors, but the monastic ideal of renunciation, involving physical relocation, and the enduring of bodily privation, made them ready to move into potentially hostile territories and to put up with considerable hardship.

They were also better able to operate in lands, such as Britain had largely become by the seventh century, in which there were few if any functioning towns, around which non-monastic ecclesiastical structures would normally expect to organise themselves. As proved by Augustine of Hippo and others in the fifth century, it was quite possible for bishops to perform their administrative, pastoral and liturgical functions whilst living within a monastic household.[62] Thus, in due course it proved relatively easy for the diocesan administration of territories which had no towns to be centred on monasteries. Additionally, monasteries were also able to serve as schools, a dimension of their activity that was particularly important in societies in which town life, around which the older Roman secular educational system had evolved, was declining or absent.[63]

However much, in retrospect, monasticism seems the obvious instrument for the physical expansion of Christianity in these centuries, it must not be forgotten how many elements intrinsic to it at this time should have militated against such a development. For one thing, and particularly in the West, there was a considerable emphasis placed on stability. Individual monks and ascetics not under the authority of recognised superiors or resident in fixed locations were intensely distrusted. Several regional churches legislated against 'vagrant monks' in the acts of their provincial synods.[64] Moreover, the whole tenor of monastic spirituality was directed towards the inner, contemplative life, rather than the cultivation of active programmes of 'good works'. It was to escape the distractions of the *Saeculum* that monks were to gather together in withdrawn communities and devote themselves to regular observance.

However, especially in Gaul, there had long existed supplementary traditions of monastic participation in, or indeed initiation of, evangelisation. These stretched back to the time of

Martin of Tours (d. 397), the founder of Ligugé and Marmoutier, who, according to the *Life* written by his aristocratic disciple Sulpicius Severus, had devoted much effort during his episcopate to the extirpation of paganism in the rural parts of his diocese.[65] The spread of the cult of Martin after his death is also closely associated with evangelism. In north-west Spain the conversion of the Suevi from Arianism to Catholicism is associated by Gregory of Tours with the arrival of relics of Martin from Tours.[66] Similarly, the church at Whithorn in Galloway that may have been the centre of Nynia's preaching of Christianity to the southern Picts in the fifth century was subsequently dedicated to St Martin, relics of whom must have been deposited in it.[67]

It is important also to appreciate that in general the Frankish Church was by no means unaware of the existence of pagans living on the fringes of the Merovingian kingdoms, or hostile to attempts to convert them. When Pope Gregory was preparing the dispatch of his monks to the kingdom of Kent he wrote to the bishops of the various Frankish dioceses through which they would pass, soliciting their support for the missionaries.[68] Even more significantly, in certain of the Anglo-Saxon kingdoms Frankish ecclesiastics played a crucial role in the early stages of the establishment of Christianity. The second bishop in the kingdom of Wessex (*c.* 650) was the Frank Agilbert, whose nephew Leuthere was later to be Bishop of Winchester (670–6). Similarly the first bishop of the East Angles (*c.* 630) was a Burgundian called Felix, who established his see at *Dummoc* (Dunwich?).[69] However, the degree of Frankish involvement in Britain should not be exaggerated. There is, despite ill-grounded assertions to the contrary, no evidence for a Frankish political hegemony over any of the southern Anglo-Saxon kingdoms. The latter is a good case of an idea that is first advanced as a speculation, but which turns itself into a dogma through constant repetition and the lack of a challenge.[70]

It is notable that Frankish royal support for missionary ventures on the frontiers of their realms pre-dates the beginning of the Roman and Irish inspired Anglo-Saxon missions to the Continent, which got under way in the late seventh century. In particular Dagobert I (623–38) may have inspired and certainly supported the activities of the Frankish evangelist and monastic founder Amandus. As with so many of the leading figures of the Gallic Church in the sixth to ninth centuries, information concerning Amandus comes principally from a *Life*. Unfortunately, many of these hagiographical compositions, whose authors are usually unknown, are either hard to date or have been shown to have been written at periods relatively removed from the lifetime of their subject. There was clearly a more developed tradition of such composition in Francia, probably related to liturgical commemoration of particular founders, patron saints and bishops of special note in their own dioceses.[71] In the ninth century it appears that numerous such *Lives* of the luminaries of the Gallic church were composed or existing ones were rewritten to make them more appropriate for contemporary needs. Thus in the great five-volume edition of Merovingian saints' lives produced in the late nineteenth century by the *Monumenta Germaniae Historica*, very few of the texts there published were held genuinely to belong to that period. The editor, Bruno Krusch, attributed the greater part of them to the Carolingian centuries. This view has been revised somewhat in recent decades, and a few of the works that Krusch distrusted have been allowed to be seen as genuine compositions of the Merovingian period. Also more allowance is now made for the existence of earlier elements being preserved within a Carolingian rewriting.[72]

The *Vita Amandi* is less problematic than some of these texts, but its history is by no means straightforward. In that one of its stories was apparently vouched for by a named monk known to the anonymous author, the work would appear to have been written soon after Amandus's death, which occurred *c*. 675.[73] However, strong grounds exist for placing the actual date of composition somewhere in the middle of the eighth century, and it is clear that the chronological structure of the *Life* is by no means fully reliable.[74] Although this must affect the assessment made of the work and the weight to assign to the individual features of its account, it is at least useful testimony to what the monks of Elnone, amongst whom was probably numbered the author, believed they knew of their founder at that time.

Particularly pertinent is the association made between Amandus's vow of perpetual exile, and also his entry into the clergy, with a visit to the tomb of St Martin at Tours. He was an Aquitanian, and although the cult of Martin was by this time widespread it was particularly powerful in the Loire valley and northern Aquitaine. Amandus's roots would thus appear to be located in the Martinian tradition, and not in Irish monasticism, which had made little impact on Aquitaine.[75] Even the reference to 'exile' is no indicator of Hibernian influence, in that Martin, who came from Pannonia, had undertaken all of his monastic and episcopal activities in regions far from his native land.

The second element that the author of the *Life* wished to underline in Amandus's motivation was Roman. After a period of ascetic preparation in the vicinity of Bourges, lasting apparently for fifteen years, Amandus went to Rome to visit the shrines of the saints. In the basilica of St Peter, where he passed the nights, he experienced a vision of the Apostle, who instructed him to undertake the task of 'preaching' (*praedicatio*). This term was one much used by and endowed with special significance by Gregory the Great. It did not mean 'sermonising', but rather the under-taking of a charge of spiritual responsibility and guidance.[76] It is clear also from the author's words that this charge, although presented in a visionary context, was essentially a papal one. Amandus received the blessing of the pope (unnamed) and was given relics, the prerequisite for the foundation of churches. The pope in question was almost certainly Honorius I (625–38), who was the first since Gregory the Great to maintain a monastic lifestyle during his pontificate, and who had turned his family mansion in Rome into a monastery.[77] He was a conscious emulator of Gregory, and his support for Amandus's missionary plans must be seen as a dimension of this.

Amandus's missionary activities covered a wide geographical range. The first and ultimately most important of the areas affected by him was the region to the east of the river Scheldt, which, although under Frankish rule, was still predominantly pagan. In his missionary activities here Amandus operated with the backing of Bishop Acharius of Noyon (d. 640), and through him that of Dagobert, who was probably the donor of the royal estates on which the monastery of Elnone (later called St Amand) was to be founded.[78] The *Life* speaks generally of Amandus's success in this area, although he encountered difficulties with at least one of its Frankish counts. He is also reported to have travelled and preached 'across the Danube' to the Slavs.[79] This is vague but must indicate another missionary venture further to the south: possibly in the old Roman provinces of Norricum and Pannonia.

Amandus was not just the evangelist and wonder worker that the author of the *Life* is so anxious to depict. He was also a figure of considerable political importance. Certainly in the 640s he was closely allied to the powerful family of the Austrasian Mayor of the Palace, Grimoald (d. 657), and it is possible this was also true of the time of the latter's father Pippin I (d. 640). Moreover, he was chosen by Dagobert I to be the 'co-father' of his son Sigebert. This is significant in that, firstly, the relation of conpaternity – between the father and the godfather of a child – was a very close one; thus Dagobert was anxious to forge such special ties with Amandus.[80]

Secondly, and possibly the reason for Dagobert's choice, Sigebert was illegitimate. Columbanus had refused even to bless the illegitimate sons of Theuderic II, and none of them had managed to maintain themselves in the kingdom of Austrasia after their father's death in 613. Whether this was the precedent that worried Dagobert, or whether problems of the acceptability of illegitimate sons were deeper rooted in the Frankish political tradition is not clear. However, Amandus's influence in Austrasia was obviously significant, and it is possible that his Roman connections were also important. His acceptance of the role of godfather may thus have been crucial to Dagobert's nomination of the infant Sigebert (III) as King of Austrasia in 634.[81] For Amandus this act gained him the immediate support of the most powerful Merovingian king of the seventh century, and the prospect of future backing from his new godson. It is notable that he did not take the kind of stand that Columbanus had, and although it is hard to generalise from one example, it is possible to suggest that the greater rigidity of Irish adherence to the rules of canon law and emphasis on public penance made them less compromising and thus less effective in their dealings with the secular powers on the Continent.

Involvement with the interests of the ruler may also have influenced Amandus's next choice of mission field. This was to be amongst the Basques south of the Garonne, the future Gascony. It is notable that this coincided with Dagobert's acquisition of the kingdom in Aquitaine previously held by his half-brother Charibert II (629–32) and with a large-scale campaign to subjugate the Basques of the western Pyrenees in 635. Although no mention is made of this in the *Life* the timing suggests that Amandus was attempting with royal support to attach the Basques more firmly to Frankish control by conversion, which meant the adopting of the value systems of the conquerors. As in later complaints about the Vikings, the Basques are frequency denounced in the Frankish sources for 'perfidy', that is the breaking of oaths. But if the value systems of the two parties to an agreement are different, what is sacred to one side is no more than expedient to the other. In practice Amandus does not appear to have succeeded in his task, and the division of the kingdom on Dagobert's death, with the legitimate Clovis II acquiring Aquitaine, terminated his efforts in this area and led to his return to Austrasia.[82]

Here, at the behest of Grimoald, the Mayor of the Palace, he became Bishop of Maastricht in 648/9, but was faced with considerable opposition on the part of his clergy to his programme of spiritual regeneration, which led him to resign the see in 650/1.[83] However, the establishment and relative strength of the cult of Martin in the Scheldt valley in the seventh century may be the product of his influence. His continuing links with Rome at this time are demonstrated by the chance survival of the text of the letter sent to him in 650 by Pope Martin I (649–53), dealing with the recent papal condemnation of Monotheletism.[84] He was also particularly involved with the family of the Mayor of the Palace in the creation in 648/9 of the monastery of Nivelles on their estates and the installation of Grimoald's sister Geretrudis (d. 659) as its first abbess. Two other monasteries may have been founded by the Pippinid family with Amandus's aid at this time: those of Fossès (651?) and of Moustier-sur-Sambre (650?).[85]

Paradoxically, the longer term beneficiaries of this burst of monastic foundation were to be Irish monks. When in *c.* 651 the Irish abbot Foílleán and his followers were expelled from Péronne by the Neustrian Mayor of the Palace, Erchinoald, they were given refuge at Fossès, and Nivelles, which had begun as a single monastery for women, was then transformed into a double monastery, a peculiarity of the Irish tradition.[86] Amandus, on the other hand, seems to have lost wider influence after his retirement from Maastricht, possibly affected by the temporary eclipse of the Pippinid family in the period 657–*c.* 675. It is likely that he continued his evangelising ventures from his monastery of Elnone, but apart from an attempt, resisted by the local bishop, to found a monastery in the diocese of Uzès in the south of the kingdom of Burgundy, little is recorded of him until his death in 674/5. Even so, the fact that his southern venture enjoyed the backing of Childeric II and that it coincided with that king's brief extension of his authority from Austrasia into Neustria and Burgundy in the years 673–5 suggests that once again Amandus was playing a role that was as much political as spiritual.[87]

The case of Amandus is particularly important, in that it highlights the contributions being made by indigenous Gallic monastic and missionary traditions, and the links between Amandus, the Frankish rulers and Rome in the mid-seventh century closely parallel the kind of ties that were to develop between the Anglo-Saxon missionaries, the Papacy and the Carolingian dynasty in the middle of the eighth. In the case of Nivelles it is also possible to see that a monastery that has long been thought of as a product of the Irish revival of continental monasticism actually owed its creation to the indigenous tradition.

It is important not to make too much of a dichotomy between the insular (Irish and Anglo-Saxon) and continental traditions. For one thing the Gallic impact on Ireland and on the Irish Church should never be underestimated. Nor was there a clear conflict between the two strands, though there could be between their patrons. The Neustrian Mayor of the Palace, Erchinoald, had founded the monastery of Péronne in the valley of the Somme, burying in it the body of the recently deceased Irish hermit Fursa, who had previously been established in the ruined Roman fort of Burgh Castle in East Anglia. But soon after (*c*. 650/1) Erchinoald expelled his Irish monks from Péronne, who were promptly given refuge by the Pippinids in their foundations in the valley of the Maas.[88] This was indeed a frontier area between the two kingdoms, and it is possible, though not vouched for in the sources, that Erchinoald's unexplained turning against his former Irish protégés was due to their openness to Pippinid blandishments.

The Irish were no less willing than the indigenous monks to become involved in the increasingly turbulent politics of Francia in the middle of the seventh century. When Sigebert III died in 656, Grimoald the Mayor of the Palace had the king's young son Dagobert tonsured and sent off to Ireland, and put on the throne instead of a certain Childebert (656–62?), whom hostile sources claim was actually his own son.[89] The patronage extended to the Irish monks in the Pippinid monasteries of the Maas may well explain the Irish dimension in this conspiracy. It did Grimoald himself little good, in that he fell into the hands of the Neustrian Clovis II later in 656 or in 657 and was executed. His Childebert, however, continued as king in Austrasia until around 662; which may argue that he was, indeed, a genuine Merovingian.

The political turbulence of Francia in the period of the 670s and 680s seems to have limited the ability of the indigenous Frankish monastic founders and missionaries to pursue the example set by Amandus, and it was to be to the Irish-inspired and frequently Irish-trained Anglo-Saxons that the Pippinids were to turn in the very late seventh century, when they sought once again to link the extension of Christianity with that of the secular power of the Frankish kingdom. The region thus targeted was Frisia, the flat marshy land between the Rhine and the North Sea, whose inhabitants were noted for their maritime and trading activities and who had contributed a small but distinctive element to the Germanic settlement of Britain in the post-Roman period, but who had so far resisted both Frankish political overlordship and conversion to Christianity.[90] The extension of missionary activity into this area was a natural development from that of the adjacent regions of the Scheldt and the Maas, which had been undertaken by Amandus and others in the mid-seventh century. In the 690s, however, it also coincided with the efforts of the now dominant Mayor of the Palace, Pippin II, to bring the Frisian kingdom back into subjection to the Frankish monarchy.

The origins of the evangelisation of Frisia can be said to lie in the visit of Bishop Wilfred of York (d. 709) in the winter of 678/9 and his attempt while delayed there on his journey southwards to begin the conversion of the inhabitants and of their King Aldgisl.[91] Wilfred is often represented as the most Roman-minded of the Northumbrian clergy, and he had been the victorious spokesman at the Synod of Whitby of the party in the Church that wanted to introduce the customs of Rome in such matters as the dating of Easter. However, as will be seen, in many ways he enjoyed close ties with Ireland. Notably, in 676 when on his way to Rome Wilfred was asked by leading men in Austrasia to engineer the return of Dagobert from his monastic exile in Ireland. This Wilfred was able to do and Dagobert II (676–8) was duly installed as King of Austrasia.[92] Moreover, it is important to remember that the Easter issue was by this time only affecting the Church in the northern part of Ireland and in the great monastic confederacy founded by Columba. The southern Irish monasteries and clerics had already gone over to the Roman customs.

In 678/9 Wilfred was on his way to Rome again, to appeal for the backing of Pope Agatho against the ultimately successful attempt of Archbishop Theodore of Canterbury to split the enormous diocese of York into four new smaller sees.[93] Although Stephanus, the author of *The Life of Wilfred*, presents his patron's work in Frisia as being highly successful, it is clear that at best only a small beginning had been made. The next effort in this direction was to have come directly from Ireland in the 680s, where a Frisian mission was one of the plans formed but not carried out by a Northumbrian called Egbert, who had gone to study in the monastery of *Rath Melsigi* (probably to be identified with Clonmelsh in County Carlow).[94] He was later to establish himself in Iona, after the Columban confederacy had finally accepted the Roman customs on Easter observance. His frustrated intention of undertaking a mission to the Frisians was subsequently taken up by another Anglo-Saxon called Willibrord, who had come to *Rath Melsigi* to study under Egbert. It is notable that Willibrord had previously been a monk in the monastery of Ripon founded by Wilfred and of which he remained abbot.[95] Although no textual source links Egbert and Wilfred directly, the common theme of the Frisian mission suggests close ties between them, and it may be assumed that Willibrord went to *Rath Melsigi* and thence to Frisia under Wilfred's aegis.

In the 690s Willibrord and a group of companions sailed from Ireland and established themselves in the ruined Roman fort of Utrecht. His efforts at converting the Frisians, now under a King Radbod (d. 719) received the backing of the effective ruler of Francia at this time, the Mayor of the Palace Pippin II, who in the 690s was trying to bring Frisia back under the Frankish control to which had been subject in the sixth and earlier seventh centuries. Fear of Frankish reprisals may have provided the missionaries with the necessary protection, but on the other hand the clear association of Willibrord and Pippin linked conversion to Frankish overlordship, and not surprisingly Radbod refused to accept Christianity. But some success was registered, as the Christian community became sufficiently large to require its own bishop.

Bede, writing in the early 730s, records that when Willibrord was given permission by the Frisian king to preach to his people, he decided first of all to go to Rome to receive papal approval and to try to obtain some relics for the churches he hoped to found in Frisia. His companions in the mission field selected another of their number, a certain Swithberht, to serve as bishop, and he returned to Britain in order to receive his ordination, significantly enough, from the hands of Wilfred.[96] He subsequently went on to preach outside Frisia. By 695 the situation of the Church in Frisia looked sufficiently well established to induce Pippin II to send Willibrord back to Rome with the request that he be consecrated archbishop of the Frisians, giving him supreme ecclesiastical authority in the region.[97] Pope Sergius (687–701) complied, and Willibrord established his archiepiscopal seat in the former Roman fortress of Utrecht (*Traiectum*).

The death of Pippin II in 714 led to a five-year period of political upheaval in Francia and to the Frisians breaking free of Frankish control. In practice this also halted Willibrord's missionary activities in Frisia, and he may have withdrawn to a settlement in Antwerp, founded in the mid seventh century by Amandus. This again is a reminder of the crucial role played by the latter and his followers in these north-eastern frontier regions of the Frankish kingdoms.

Willibrord was able to re-establish the Church in the southwestern parts of Frisia after the death of Radbod in 719, but made little further progress. In the years preceding his death in 739 he may instead have been devoting his attention to the evangelisation of Thuringia from his base in the monastery that he founded at Echternach (in Luxembourg).[98] The Thuringian Duke Hedeno appears to have backed him, and from the evidence of charters it is clear that he as well as the Pippinids endowed Willibrord with land for the foundation and material support of his monasteries.[99]

Willibrord's intended heir in the Frisian mission field was another Anglo-Saxon monk called Wynfrith. Unlike his predecessors, he came from Wessex, which under the leadership of Aldhelm, abbot of a monastic community at Malmesbury and later Bishop of Sherborne (705/6–9), had developed its own intellectual tradition, which like that of Northumbria fused elements obtained from Ireland with ever increasing debts to Rome and to Francia.[100] Wynfrith, whose name was later changed to Boniface, had been educated in monasteries at Exeter and at Nursling (near the later port of Southampton), before undertaking a brief voyage to Frisia in 716. He arrived there to find the mission in a state of collapse, due to the current state of war. His next visit to the Continent came in 718 and this took him directly to Rome, where he told the pope of his commitment to undertake some form of missionary activity and was in consequence, in May 719, commissioned by Gregory II (715–31) to carry out just such work and to report to Rome on its progress.

Boniface first of all spent three years (719–22) with Willibrord, assisting in the revival of the Frisian mission before moving southwards to establish his own field of operations in the region of Hesse. He devoted most of the next thirty years to work in Hesse and Thuringia, though in 753 he was to undertake a missionary journey into the hitherto neglected area of northern Frisia, where on 5 June 754 he and his companions were attacked and murdered by a band of pirates.[101] One of three extant manuscripts that are thought to have been his personal property is marked with cuts that might validate the story in his *Life* that presents him as defending his head with a book in this savage and fatal encounter. However, as none of these impinge upon the text of the manuscript but are all rather neatly and improbably orderly in their placing, it seems more likely that they were added at a later date, to give a greater appearance of authenticity to this treasured relic.[102]

Much of Boniface's missionary career, like that of Willibrord, was passed in regions that had once enjoyed some exposure both to Christianity and to Roman civilisation as mediated through Francia. These elements had diminished or had been eliminated in the period of the political decline of the Frankish kingdoms in the second half of the seventh century. The new rulers of Francia, therefore, had considerable interest in promoting the missionary activities that went hand in hand with their own restoration of political influence and ultimately of control over these regions east of the Rhine. Pippin II's son Charles Martel (d. 741) may have been slightly less helpful than his father, but much of his attention was devoted to the securing of his power in Aquitaine and Burgundy. His sons proved more active allies, especially Carloman (741–7), who had secured the eastern frontier regions in the division of territories in 742. The missionaries, for their part, depended on the Frankish rulers not just for the promise of protection or at least reprisals against the peoples amongst whom they were working, but also as a counterbalance to the distrust and hostility of the bishops of many of the major Rhineland sees, close to whose dioceses they were often working but under whose authority they were not placed. These men, normally members of the great aristocratic families of Austrasia, had little reason to like the missionaries, who were not only aliens and outwith their episcopal authority, but were also noted for their reforming zeal and were in direct contact with the see of Rome.[103]

Unlike the Augustinian mission to Britain in 596/7, the papacy had not initiated the continental ventures of the Anglo-Saxon and Irish monks, but rapidly came to see their value, not just in terms of evangelisation but also in the spread of Roman doctrinal views and liturgical practices. In his mandate to Boniface of 15 May 719, Gregory II had required the new missionary to 'insist upon using the sacramental discipline prescribed by the official ritual formulary of Our Holy Apostolic See'.[104] In its sponsorship of the Anglo-Saxon missionary ventures on the Continent the papacy may have hoped to outflank the entrenched Frankish episcopate, whose resistance to self-reform on the model envisaged by Rome went back to the time of Gregory I if not earlier.

With the support of the Mayors of the Palace of the family of Pippin II, who were not displeased to be able to make their own links to Rome and who had much to gain from fostering alternatives to the independent and powerful Austrasian episcopal families, the popes found themselves able to appoint to bishoprics within the political sphere of Francia. Willibrord as archbishop of the Frisians should have been able to create a network of subordinate episcopal sees, although this was limited by the effective stagnation of this missionary field after 714. Boniface was given an archiepiscopal *pallium* by Gregory III (731–41) in 732, and in 738, deflecting him from an interest in pushing on from Thuringia into the lands of the Saxons, the pope gave him instead some new responsibilities further to the south in Bavaria.[105]

This region had close ties to the Lombard kingdom in Italy and a line of dukes of its own, who were anxious to resist Frankish political domination as far as was practically possible.[106] Boniface, as representative of Rome, may have been more welcome, at least to the ducal house, and under his direction four episcopal dioceses were said to have had their boundaries established, to provide the basic structure of ecclesiastical organisation within the duchy. Boniface returned northwards in 741, and in practice the dominant role in evangelisation in Bavaria was to be played thereafter by the Irish Bishop Virgil of Salzburg, with whom he notoriously failed to get on.[107] Back in Thuringia, Boniface created new dioceses to which he appointed fellow Anglo-Saxons, and in 744 in Hesse he founded, as his own spiritual retreat and as the centre of planned missionary expansion into Saxony, the monastery of Fulda. This, together with his monastery at Fritzlar in Saxony, was placed under direct papal authority, thus exempting it from the jurisdiction of future local bishops.[108]

In a territory that was rapidly taking on an ordered ecclesiastical structure, Boniface found himself in the anomalous position of being an archbishop but lacking a fixed see. In 746 a vacancy in the great Rhineland archbishopric of Mainz, following the deposition of the previous incumbent, was used to give him the needed institutional setting, and this see, once the preserve of Frankish aristocrats, passed after his death to his fellow Anglo-Saxon and missionary disciple Lullus.[109] It is possible, though far from certain, that his last great public act was to serve in 751 as the consecrator of the former mayor of the Palace Pippin III as the first king of the new ruling house of Francia.[110]

For all his undoubted importance, which is in part allied to the survival of a relatively substantial body of evidence, in the form of letters and *Lives* – of both Boniface and some of his associates – it is important not to overlook the work of other bishops and monastic founders working on the eastern frontiers of Francia and its dependencies, both at this time and earlier. In particular the areas to the south-east of the Frankish kingdoms, around the upper Rhine and upper Danube, owed most to the activities of men of very similar background to Amandus, who himself had made at least one missionary foray into this region.

Amongst those who came after him was Emmeram, a fellow Aquitanian from the area around Poitiers, who was inspired to think of a mission to the Avars in the plains around the Danube. Because of war then going on between the Avars and the Bavarians he was persuaded at Regensburg by Duke Theoto (d. 717) to work among his people rather than go on to the his original destination. After an apparently fruitful period of missionary labour in Bavaria in the area of Regensburg he was savagely murdered; the victim of a conflict within the ruling ducal house (*c.* 690).[111] Another outsider persuaded by Duke Theoto around 693 to work amongst the Bavarians was Hrodbert, later known as St Rupert, who established a bishopric in the former Roman settlement of Salzburg, where he also refounded the monastery of St Peter, as well as creating a new house for nuns.[112] In the early eighth century a Frank from Melun, south of Paris, called Corbinian (d. 730), established another monastic bishopric in Bavaria, based on the natural fortress of Freising. His church was dedicated to St Martin, as were several others in the duchy.[113] With both Salzburg and Freising in existence and the cult of a founding saint well established at Regensburg, it has to wondered if the importance and success of Boniface's activities in Bavaria in the years 738–741, mentioned above, have not been exaggerated in the sources generated by his followers. Likewise, his return northwards in 741 may be more due to the well-entrenched opposition that he faced from already firmly established ecclesiastical bodies in Bavaria than to any sense of the fulfilment of his purposes.

In Bavaria, as also in some of the regions east of the Rhine – and as had been the case in England – the missionaries and monastic founders were working in regions that had once been influenced by Christianity, or in which Christian and non-Christian practices co-existed. In part this was the product of the weakening of the Frankish empire after the death of Dagobert I. Territories and peoples once subject to Frankish political and cultural sway (or in the case of Bavaria with Christian traditions stretching back to the Late Roman Empire) lost whatever ecclesiastical 'infrastructure' of church organisation that had once existed. On the other hand, it is necessary not always to accept reformers' views of themselves. Monasticism was still a relatively new departure in the West, especially in its more intense Franco-Irish rural forms, and it is possible that what monastic authors saw as the sweeping away of paganism or of pagan contaminations of Christianity was instead the elimination of older, more easy going Late Roman attitudes to religious belief and practice.

15 Towards a new western Empire, 714–800

Charles 'the Hammer'

The change of dynasty in Francia in 751 inevitably coloured the perspective of all of those historical works that were composed in the period that followed. Moreover, the final century of the rule of the preceding dynasty has left us so few accounts of itself that it is fair to say that the last Merovingians do not speak for themselves. So much that we know about them is through the distorting mirror of the Carolingian historiographical tradition. Even a work that is firmly Merovingian in its original date of composition, such as the so-called *Chronicle of Fredegar*, received continuations that were Carolingian in their inspiration and intent. The core text, that was completed in the later seventh century, was augmented by an equally anonymous author in the middle of the eighth, working, as he notes, on the orders of Count Childebrand and of his son Count Nibelung. Childebrand was the half-brother of Charles Martel, the Mayor of the Palace and father of the first Carolingian king.[1]

A number of minor sets of annals composed in the eighth century do exist, but virtually all of these were composed in the period of Carolingian rule or when their ascendancy in most parts of Francia was already assured. Although there are some earlier materials contained within them, the earliest possible date of composition for the first of these sets of annals would have to be placed in the 730s, and it is notable that a number of them choose the death of the Carolingian Drogo (708), Duke of Champagne, as the starting point for their retrospective record of events.[2]

The only narrative history that may be said to be, at least in part, free of Carolingian political bias is another anonymous work, known as the *Liber Historiae Francorum*, or *Book of the History of the Franks*, composed around the year 727 somewhere north of Paris. Arguments concerning a more precise location have centred on the royal monastery of Saint-Denis and, less probably, on Rouen. A recent study has made a strong, though not decisive, case for Soissons.[3] The Neustrian or West Frankish perspective of the author is undoubted, but he was writing in a time in which the political authority of the Carolingian Mayor of the Palace, Charles Martel, was firmly established. His account is also extremely brief, and its accuracy can in a number of instances be faulted. It is worth noting that various hagiographical texts might reveal aspects of their, usually anonymous, authors' perspectives on contemporary Frankish events, but it is unwise to separate such works too rigidly into 'pro-' or 'anti-Carolingian' categories.

Thus it is not easy to assess the final stages of the Merovingian period in Frankish history. The image of the late seventh century kings as *rois fainéants* or 'do-nothing kings' has already been briefly examined and found in several respects to be wanting. It is in part the product of the Carolingian historiographical perspective. However, it is equally clear that by the first quarter of the eighth century the kings had ceased to exercise any practical authority, and were little better than puppets in the hands of rival aristocratic factions, of which that led by the Arnulfings, later to be known as Carolingians, who were dominant in Austrasia or East Francia, was the most powerful.

The Arnulfings themselves, though, were to pass through a period in which they suffered from some of the same problems as the kings in whose name they wielded power. In 710 or 711 Childebert III died and was succeeded by his young son Dagobert III (710/1–15). Pippin II had made arrangements for succession to his own authority by appointing his surviving legitimate son Grimoald as the Mayor of the Palace in Neustria, but while he himself was ill Grimoald was murdered at Liège, for reasons that are never explained. In consequence Pippin designated the latter's infant son Theudoald as the new Mayor in Neustria.[4] To be able to appoint a child to such a post is a sign of Pippin's power at this time, but it was hardly a compliment to the Neustrians. The only hope for the future of such an arrangement was the continued longevity of Pippin, but on his death in December 714 the vulnerable and flawed structure he had created for his own succession collapsed.

Pippin's widow Plectrudis assumed control in Austrasia, but the Neustrians, waiting for the chance to break free of Arnulfing domination, revolted against the rule of her infant grandson Theudoald, and defeated his supporters in battle. They appointed Raganfred, one of their own number, as Mayor and in 715 invaded Austrasia. On the death of Dagobert III in the same year, they set up another Merovingian of their own choosing in the person of Chilperic II, who had formerly been confined to a monastery. At the same time they made an alliance with the pagan Frisians, whom Pippin II had been trying to conquer during the later years of his ascendancy.[5]

According to both the continuator of 'Fredegar' and the author of the *Liber Historiae Francorum*, who admittedly were writing either under his rule or during the reign of his son, it was only the decisive action of Pippin II's illegitimate son Charles, known from the ninth century on as Charles Martel or 'Hammer', that saved the day for the Arnulfings. It did, however, take him a while to bring this about. He had been imprisoned by Plectrudis during the sensitive period following his father's death, but was able 'by God's help' to get free.[6] As the only male member of his line of fighting age he was better able to rally support than the infant Theudoald.

His first efforts were not impressive. He led his forces against the Frisians, who were invading Austrasia under their King Radbod as the allies of the Neustrians. However, after heavy fighting he was forced to retreat. The Frisians were able to unite with the Neustrian army that had made its way through the Forest of the Ardennes. The allies advanced on Plectrudis's base at Cologne, and she was forced to come to terms with them, surrendering 'much treasure', which may well have included that taken from Neustria by Pippin II in 687. The Neustrian army was ambushed on its way home by Charles at Amblève in April 716, but although the Fredegar continuator speaks of 'heavy losses', this was hardly decisive, in that the fighting continued unabated the following year.[7]

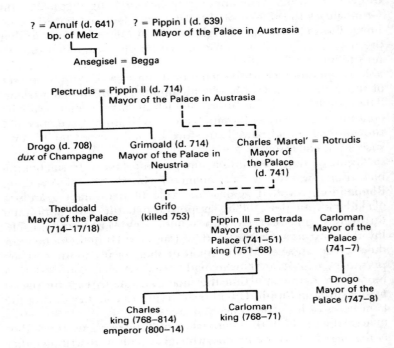

The early Carolingians

Renewed war in the spring of 717 proved crucial. The Neustrians tried to crush Charles, and despite his offer of a peace treaty forced him to battle. In the ensuing conflict at Vinchy on 21 March Charles was victorious and drove King Chilperic and Raganfred back to Paris. He was then able to turn on Plectrudis, defeat her supporters and force her to surrender Cologne and the remainder of the treasure she controlled. Charles then set up a Merovingian called Chlotar IV (d. 719) as King of Austrasia, and in 718 was able to ensure the security of the eastern frontiers of the kingdom by a victory over Radbod and the Frisians.[8]

Although Neustria and Austrasia were once more divided, with separate kings and mayors of the palace, it was clear that this was no more than a temporary solution. Looking around for new allies, the Neustrians had sought aid from the effectively independent Duke Eudo of Aquitaine, who could provide an army of Basque mercenaries. However, when war was resumed Charles and his now united Austrasian forces were able to overrun eastern Neustria.[9] Eudo may have been more concerned about the growing threat to southern Aquitaine posed by the Arabs, who first crossed the Pyrenees in 720. He came to an agreement with Charles, handing over the person of the Neustrian King Chilperic, who then briefly reigned over a nominally reunited kingdom until his death in 721 or 722. Even so, Raganfred and his followers continued to hold out in western Neustria, probably based at Angers, until about 730/1.

In comparison with what may be known of the crucial events of the years 714–721, the rest of the period of Charles's ascendancy is particularly badly documented. The *Liber Historiae Francorum* ends its account with the death of Chilperic, and in the continuations of 'Fredegar' something of a hiatus occurs between 721 and 733.[10] However, it seems clear, if only from what little the chronicles and annals do say, that although Charles had made himself master of most of the region between the Seine and the Rhine and had set up his own tame Merovingian in the person of Theuderic IV (721/2–37), his power at first extended little further. Large areas of Francia, notably Aquitaine, Burgundy and Provence, remained under the rule of independent dynasties of dukes, descendants of office-holders appointed by the seventh century Merovingian kings. Nor is it clear that his hold over Neustria was necessarily secure. Here he shared problems faced by his father before him.

Although it is normally assumed that the battle of Tertry in 687 made Pippin II the undisputed master of both Austrasia and Neustria, this is certainly an oversimplification. In Neustria the previous Mayor Berchar and his supporters had been overthrown in the aftermath of the battle, and they were replaced in the court and other offices by those who had opposed them, several of whom had previously taken refuge with or appealed to Pippin in Austrasia for assistance. These included Bishop Reolus of Reims and Count Audramnus.[11] Thus, in 687 Pippin was able to assist in the installing of a new ruling group in the Neustrian court, composed of his allies such as the new Mayor Norbert and Audramnus, who became Count of the Palace by *c*. 693. Some of the Neustrian nobility also found it expedient to form even closer ties with the powerful Austrasian Mayor: the widow of Berchar was married by her family to Pippin's eldest son Drogo.[12]

All of this had enabled Pippin to turn his attention elsewhere, not least in the 690s to campaigns to regain Austrasian hegemony over Frisia, but it must be recognised that his hold over Neustria was at best vicarious, and depended upon the alliances he had made with prominent Neustrian aristocrats. It is clear, too, that the influence that he and his family was able to exercise over Neustria became increasingly resented, and this manifested itself openly on his death.

Some historians have turned to the charters, and above all the records of the *placita* or legal hearings conducted by some of the late seventh century Merovingians, for indications of rising political tensions of this kind. In particular Childebert III (695–710/1) has been singled out as a ruler able to take an unusually independent line for a late Merovingian king, and one that was, moreover, markedly anti-Pippinid.[13] The evidence offered in support of this view consists of three of these *placita* documents, recording cases heard before the king in which the losing parties were the sons of Pippin.[14]

Unfortunately, this evidence will not easily bear the weight of the interpretation put upon it, in that it is to say the least ambiguous. Even if the legal decisions (which could of course be prompted as much by justice as by politics) did indicate such sentiment, and that the hearings were deliberately intended to inflict pinpricks of humiliation on the Pippinids this would not prove that the king rather than the Neustrian court nobility was orchestrating them. However, it is equally possible that another interpretation altogether should be preferred, which would view such apparently confrontational legal disputes as a formal device by means of which a secure title to property could be obtained, with a documentary record being created to preserve it.[15] Even if this particular approach to the politics of the period is weakened by its ambiguity, at least the principle is sound: Pippin depended for his hold on Neustria on a network of allies within that kingdom, and after 719 his son Charles had to do the same.

By dint of harder and longer fighting in the years 714–19 Charles had probably won a far more decisive military victory over Neustria than his father had in 687, and he was not so beholden to a powerful faction of the Neustrian aristocracy in the way Pippin had been. Even so, as it is clear that he did not wish to tie himself to the royal court, which continued to be principally resident in Neustria, he had to establish a body of allies and supporters in that kingdom to run it for him. The evidence of narrative history being almost entirely absent by this time, and with few royal charters surviving, it is not easy to delineate this group in detail.

One of those who almost certainly must be included in it was Charles's nephew Hugh. By 724, when he became Abbot of Fontanelle (Saint-Wandrille), he already held the archbishopric of Rouen, and the bishoprics of Bayeux and Paris. He also became Abbot of Jumièges, where he was to be buried in 732/3.[16] This gave him control of virtually all the major churches of the lower Seine valley and the area of the future Normandy. Some indication of his personal landholdings may be gained from the brief references to the gifts he made to his abbey of Fontanelle. The estates in question, which he inherited from his parents, were located in the valleys of the Oise and the Somme. In that these may well have been once owned by his grandfather, the Neustrian Mayor of the Palace Waratto (680s), it is possible to see Hugh as a representative both of the dominant Austrasian line of the Pippinids and of the well entrenched greater aristocracy of Neustria.

It has recently been argued, against older views, that Hugh should not be seen as an automatic supporter of Charles, and that he might, indeed, have been opposed to him.[17] This is based on Hugh's being a grandson of Pippin II by his wife Plectrudis, whereas Charles was the product of Pippin's probably unsacramental relationship with Alpaida. That Charles had been able to replace the legitimate and older line in acquiring the office of mayor should thus have left that branch of the family hostile to him. However, Hugh's case is an odd one, and there are signs that another and more crucial division had taken place within the Pippinid line at an earlier point. Hugh's father Drogo had been Pippin II's eldest son and Hugh himself, born *c.* 695, had been both an adult and still a layman at the time of Pippin's death. Yet in the arrangements made by Pippin after the death of his son Grimoald, which were then maintained by Plectrudis, Hugh and at least one other adult brother of his were passed over in favour of appointing Grimoald's infant son Theudoald (d. 741) to the office of Mayor of the Neustrian Palace – with disastrous consequences. That Hugh had been so treated in 714 may well have made him more willing to co-operate with Charles in the control of Neustria after 719.

Another of the probable partisans of Charles in Neustria was Godobald, who was made Abbot of the great monastery and royal pantheon of Saint-Denis by *c.* 726/7. He had been a supporter of Dodo, the probable brother of Charles's mother Alpaida, and at his instigation had been involved in the murder of Bishop Lambert of Maastricht (*c.* 705).[18] According to later Saint-Denis tradition he undertook a penitential pilgrimage to Rome and benefited from a miraculous cure, but it is hard not to suspect that he received the important abbacy as a tried and trusted friend of Charles's family.[19] Few of them as we can now detect, it is with the support of such men that Charles was able to keep Neustria loyal to himself and to free his own hands for ventures east of the Rhine.

There he had to face a problem that was to occupy his successors throughout the century: the gradual movement of the Saxons into areas across the Rhine that the Franks either held or had an interest in controlling. The continental Saxons had previously been established in the low-lying and marshy lands around the rivers Weser and Aller, but by the early eighth century were edging themselves south-westwards onto the high ground south of the river Lippe.[20] It was in this area that many of the Frankish–Saxon wars were to be fought throughout the century, and what was at issue was control of this region. The Frankish chroniclers always speak of the Saxons as being 'in revolt', but this was only a harking back to the first half of the seventh century in which they had paid tribute to the Franks. Charles Martel's first encounter with the Saxons occurred *c.* 720, and another and more serious campaign had to be undertaken in 738.[21]

In 725 Charles launched a major expedition east of the Rhine against the Alamans, Thuringians and Bavarians, all of whom had been subject to the Franks during the heyday of the Merovingian dynasty, but who had long been allowed to go their own way under ducal dynasties of ultimately Frankish origin. They were, as the continuator of Fredegar puts it, 'punished' and 'subjugated'. The wife and daughter of the former Bavarian Duke Grimoald (717–25) were taken off as hostages.[22] In practice Charles was in no position to impose his authority directly over these peoples, but they had been brought firmly back within the sphere of Frankish political influence. Closer integration had to await the time of his grandson in the 770s and 780s.

The next extension of Charles's power was largely the result of a windfall. The duchy of Aquitaine had retained its practical independence throughout the 720s. Charles had begun a series of attacks on it around 730, following his obtaining of control over western Neustria. At the same time the Aquitanian Duke Eudo, menaced since 720/1 by Arab attacks in the south of his territories, had allied himself with the leader of the Berber garrisons that the Arabs established in the western Pyrenees. When the Berbers' revolt was crushed by the forces of the Arab governor of Spain, a punitive campaign was also planned against the Aquitanians. This was launched in 732 or 733. Duke Eudo was defeated by the Arab army on the river Garonne and was forced to appeal to his northern enemy, Charles Martel, for assistance. The Frankish army intercepted the Arab forces under the governor 'Abd al-Rahman ibn Gafiqi as they were moving northwards towards Tours, having sacked Poitiers.[23]

The ensuing battle of Poitiers of October(?) 732 or 733, in which the Arabs were defeated and forced to retreat to Spain, may not have saved Christendom from imminent Islamic conquest, as is sometimes asserted, but it certainly left Aquitaine open to the re-imposition of political control from the north. When Duke Eudo died in 735 Charles returned to Aquitaine, occupied Bordeaux and imposed his own garrisons on the principal fortresses and towns of the duchy.[24] As in the duchies to the east of the Rhine, a formerly more closely integrated component of the Merovingian kingdom had been restored, albeit temporarily, to Frankish control.

In the meantime, in 734, with the duchies east of the Rhine cowed and Aquitaine neutralised, it had proved possible for him also to impose his authority on the former Frankish kingdom of Burgundy. He appointed new officials and according to the continuator of Fredegar, carried out an extensive redistribution of lands in favour of his own followers and supporters. This was clearly resented, and in 736 he had to invade the region again, and take Lyon by force. With Burgundy thus bludgeoned into accepting his authority, the way lay open for penetration further down the Rhône valley into Provence.[25] A campaign in 737 was directed there, initially under his brother Count Childebrand and then under Charles himself. It was prompted by the recent Arab conquest of Avignon, which had effectively cut off the Rhône valley from the Mediterranean, but the chronicler implies that the ultimate target for the Franks was Duke Maurontus of Marseille, whom he calls 'base', 'craven', and 'heretical'.[26]

Maurontus was also explicitly accused of being in alliance with the Arabs. It is just possible that this was true, as they provided the only possible counterweight to the growing power of the Frankish Mayor, but it is worth noting that the continuator of Fredegar also accuses Duke Eudo of Aquitaine of being allied to the Arabs at the very time when the latter were invading his duchy, defeating his army and sacking his cities.[27] In fact the events in Provence in 737 and 739 are almost a doublet of those that occurred in Aquitaine in 733 and 735.

It is possible to wonder, if nothing stronger, whether Charles's campaign of 737 was not launched in response to an appeal for help from Duke Maurontus in countering the rapidly developing Arab conquest of Provence. The Frankish army retook Avignon, but failed to capture Narbonne, which was the principal Arab fortress in south-west France. Charles did, however, sack and burn Nîmes, Agde, Béziers and probably Maguelonne as well.[28] All these towns, it may be salutary to appreciate, had, apart from their Arab or Berber garrisons, entirely Christian populations.

In 739 Charles was back in Provence again. This time his target was explicitly Duke Maurontus. Avignon, which may have been given or returned to Maurontus in 737, was taken again and the duke was forced to flee from Marseille to take refuge on an island off the coast. His eventual fate is unknown.[29] It looks, as in Aquitaine in 735, as if an initial intervention by Charles and his Frankish forces against an Arab threat could lead to a subsequent armed annexation of the region. The inhabitants of Aquitaine or of Provence may have preferred Frankish rule to Arab, but not necessarily to that of their own dukes. From Charles's point of view, however, the Arab attacks on both Aquitaine and Provence were providential, in that they provided the openings for military intervention, to be followed up by the imposition of greater control on these regions that had been able to go their own way during the period of Merovingian political weakness in the mid to late seventh century.

Thus, in a series of campaigns lasting from 732/3 to 739 Charles, from his base in north-east Francia, made himself master of virtually all of the south and of the west. His methods were generally violent and ruthless. His treatment of those who turned to him for help was cynical to say the least. On the other hand, those elements in local society upon whom he relied benefited considerably from his favour. A century later he was castigated by the Church for his treatment of monasteries, particularly in his forcing them to make precarial grants of property to those upon whom he depended for military support. Such grants were in effect leases for life in return for fixed annual renders. In themselves they were not intrinsically harmful to the grantor, in that a regular income was thereby guaranteed. They were only detrimental in periods of escalating prices or land values, in which higher returns could be guaranteed by shorter or more flexible leases. There are no reasons to suspect that the 730s were part of such a period, and it is likely that this particular accusation owes much more to the political and economic circumstances of the 830s than to those of the 730s.[30]

What Charles had tried to do by these and other practices was to build up networks of local supporters, controlling the principal offices and with a powerful landed base, who could transform what were military conquests into a longer-term re-imposition of central-ised authority, exercised still in the name of Merovingian kings by the Pippinid Mayoral dynasty. As well as lay magnates, institutions of the Church gained from the patronage that Charles was able to exercise on an ever increasing scale. In return he looked to those whom he rewarded for political loyalty and other signs of gratitude, spiritual as well as material. Thus the monastery of Saint-Denis to the north of Paris, formerly the pantheon of the Merovingian dynasty, benefited particularly from a grant by Charles of the former royal villa and estate of Clichy, and it was in Saint-Denis that he was to be buried, following his death on 22 October 741.

Pippin 'the Short'

The legacy of Charles Martel, from the point of view of the Arnulfing house and its northern Frankish aristocratic allies, was primarily inherited by his two eldest sons, Pippin III (known as 'the Short') and Carloman. A third son, Grifo, the product of a liaison with the daughter of Duke Grimoald of Bavaria, may have been intended to receive a share of power, and seems to have been established in Thuringia after their father's death, but his half-brothers lured him into a trap at Laon and imprisoned him in a monastery until 747. Another victim of this period was the former Mayor of Neustria, Theudoald, who was killed in 741, possibly because he represented a threat from a rival line of the dynasty. His survival to that date is perhaps evidence of the kind of political compromises and alliances that Charles Martel had had to make, even at the height of his power.[31]

Although Pippin III and, more briefly, Carloman were to be able to consolidate and augment the conquests made by their father in the last years of his life, this was only after facing their almost complete collapse. On the death of Charles Aquitaine regained its independence under Duke Hunald, the son of Eudo; the Alaman Duke Godefred threw off his enforced subservience to the Arnulfing Mayors; and Odilo the Duke of the Bavarians gave his support to Grifo. Needless to say the continuator of Fredegar presents Pippin III and Carloman's reactions to these diverse threats as being decisive and almost instantly successful. Thus in 742 they invaded Aquitaine, and are said by the chronicler to have 'stood as victors around'. The reality of what he describes is rather less impressive: they burnt the suburbs of Bourges, but did not take the city, and otherwise only captured the fortress of Loches, just south of the Loire.[32] In practice Duke Hunald was able to establish himself without serious challenge, and the brothers were obliged to accept the re-emergence of the duchy by a treaty made in 745.[33]

As far as the Alamans were concerned an autumn campaign in 742 produced the submission of some of them, but they were not finally defeated until after further campaigning in 744 and 746.[34] At this point the independent ducal line was terminated. Similarly, the Bavarians under Duke Odilo (737–48) were not quickly forced to accept the authority of the two joint Mayors, despite what the chronicler records as a defeat in the year 743. Only after Odilo's death in January 748, when the Bavarians initially refused to accept the rule of his infant son Tassilo, whose mother was the sister of Pippin III and Carloman, were the Franks able to make a decisive intervention in Bavaria. Grifo, who had escaped from monastic incarceration in 747, briefly seized the duchy by virtue of his part Bavarian descent, but was quickly driven out by Pippin. The latter's nephew Tassilo was imposed as duke, and held the office as a normally loyal subordinate of successive Frankish rulers for the next forty years.[35]

It thus took some eight years for the influence exercised by Charles Martel over the duchies east of the Rhine to be recovered, and it was going to take another twenty years and much hard fighting before the independence of the duchy of Aquitaine was to be extinguished. The process of the restoration of Arnulfing power may have been assisted when in 747 Carloman decided that he wished to enter a monastery and left for Rome.[36] It is possible that he did so in the expectation that his son Drogo would in due course succeed to authority over all of the Frankish lands, as Pippin at this time was probably still unmarried and had no children. In the meantime Drogo succeeded his father as Mayor of the Palace in Austrasia. However, Pippin married a lady called Bertrada and their first son, Charles, was born in 748. Soon after, and perhaps in consequence, Drogo seems to have been deprived of his office by his uncle. Even so, he and his supporters continued to resist Pippin in various regions across the Rhine until as late as 753.[37] So too did the latter's half-brother Grifo, who was finally killed in the Alps during this same year, while on his way to solicit Lombard assistance against Pippin, who by this time had made himself King of the Franks.

The achievements of Charles Martel and Pippin III in re-imposing a greater measure of centralised authority, as exercised by themselves, on the primary components of the Frankish realm and over most of its peripheral duchies raise a number of questions. Notably, these relate to the nature of the problem which they faced and the means by which they overcame it. It is worth considering these briefly here, in that they relate to the structures of the Frankish state that emerged in consequence of their activities, both military and political.

It is, perhaps, easy to imagine the duchies east of the Rhine, the Frisian kingdom, and the great southern and western duchies of Francia – Aquitaine, Burgundy, and Provence – as being naturally prone to breaking away from Frankish overlordship. In many of these cases the inhabitants of the territories were not Frankish in origin and had their own distinct cultural traditions and long independent histories. Even to the west of the Rhine modern historians have seen continuities in Burgundian and Aquitanian ethnic identifies which, taken together with limited Frankish settlement as opposed to military occupation of these regions, should have made them likely to break free of this alien domination whenever the opportunity arose.

However, recent research has also emphasised the Frankish origin of many of the dominant families in all these regions. Moreover, there are indications that even in times of relative political and military weakness in the late seventh century some of these men still found it useful or necessary to travel to Neustria to attend the royal court.[38] Other recent arguments also cast doubt on the reality of some of the claims for the genuine survival of separate Aquitanian and Burgundian identities.[39] This has led to suggestions that it was the rising power of the Pippinids and their attempt to take over the still considerable authority of the kings that drove such regional potentates into trying to build up their own independent local power bases. At the same time, the existence of long-term feuds between the principal aristocratic families within the regions enabled the Pippinids to find useful allies in local society, who would serve their interests both in the military subjugation and in the subsequent government of one of these great duchies. The best documented case of this is probably that of a certain Abbo, member of a long-established and powerful southern Burgundian aristocratic kinship, who seems to have supported Charles Martel against Maurontus, and was rewarded with the office of Patrician (*Patricius*) of Provence after 737.[40]

Whereas there is no evidence of Burgundian, Provençal or Aquitanian revolts against the Merovingians in the seventh century, this is not true of the eastern regions. The Saxons had been able to free themselves from paying regular tribute to the Franks in the time of the otherwise powerful Dagobert I (623–38). This may have been a consequence of the latter's hard-fought war against the Wends, a Slavic people who seem to have been forged into an aggressive confederacy by a Frankish adventurer called Samo. The Alamans are recorded as winning a significant victory over the Wends at the same time as the Franks suffered a humiliating defeat, and this may have enabled them to break free of Merovingian tutelage. The other significant group across the river in the area of the central Rhine, the Thuringians, broke into open rebellion after the death of Dagobert and defeated his heir Sigebert III (634–56) in 639. The *Chronicle of Fredegar* records the revolt as being a direct consequence of a victory they had won over the Wends.[41] If less dramatically, it seems that the Bavarians also broke free of Frankish tutelage in this period under a ducal family of Frankish origin known as the Agilolfings.

Although little is known of the ducal families of the various peoples east of the Rhine, and substantial gaps exist in their genealogies, it does seem true that they were all of ultimately Frankish origin.[42] This is almost certainly also the case with the Aquitanian ducal line that emerges with Eudo, and probably also with the line of the counts of *Vasconia*, the region of Basque settlement between the Garonne and the eastern Pyrenees.[43] As was to happen on a larger scale in the ninth century, such dynasties of Frankish 'viceroys', initially installed by the Merovingians to keep the various tributary and subject peoples under control, came increasingly to identify with the interests of their new territories. It is thus not fanciful to suspect that the processes that had got under way across the Rhine in the mid seventh century were starting to extend themselves west of the river in the early eighth. In other words genuine regional powers were developing in Aquitaine, Burgundy and Provence, which the military and political activities of Charles Martel and Pippin III cut short.

It must be wondered how they were able to do this, when the previous half century or more had favoured the secessionist tendencies of the duchies. The answer lies in the nature of military power in Francia. Control of the eastern duchies had been an important resource for the Merovingians, and the rulers of Austrasia in particular had called upon levies of Saxons, Thuringians and others to assist them in their wars, not least the conflicts between the kingdoms that had been prevalent in the period 567–613. Sigebert I had used such forces against his brother Chilperic in 574, as did Theudebert II in 612.[44] It is possible, therefore, that Charles Martel's greater military strength in the 730s derived from renewed access to such sources of manpower.

This itself can only be a partial answer in that a further explanation is needed as to how Charles, following his father's precedent in Frisia, had been able to gain a military advantage over the various eastern duchies. Here the answer must lie within Francia. For none of the other major kingdoms in the West in the aftermath of the disintegration of the Roman empire was as effectively and continuously organised for warfare as was that of the Franks.

The primary institution, which was also an instrument of political control, was that of the annual assembly or 'Marchfield' (which actually could be held between March and May).[45] To this the leading territorial magnates of the kingdom(s) were summoned, and various issues were discussed there, not least new laws, and the ensuing military campaign was agreed upon and initiated. The nobles came to the assembly attended by those who were dependent on them, and who formed the basis of the fighting forces they then contributed to the royal army. Such assemblies guaranteed both a large measure of consensus behind royal decisions and a ready-made military force to direct against internal or external foes.

With such a system the power of the Merovingian state should hardly have been subject to the prolonged decline it appears to have suffered in the period from the late 630s to the 690s. However, it did depend upon certain variables. Above all it rested upon the credibility of the kings as war leaders. In the generation after Dagobert I a real crisis of credibility may have arisen. Although the Merovingians suffered from fewer and less prolonged minorities than is sometimes assumed, the most protracted of them occurred in the crucial period of the very late 630s and 640s, when the consequences of Frankish defeats at the hands of the Wends were making themselves felt in the break up of their hegemony east of the Rhine. Well may it have been recorded that Sigebert III 'wept unrestrainedly' after his defeat at the hands of the Thuringians; he was after all only ten years old.

In the decades that followed rival aristocratic factions established themselves in control of the two kingdoms of Neustria and Austrasia, with the kings able to play only an occasional part. In the circumstances of factional conflicts within the kingdoms combined with periods of tension between them, it is not surprising that large-scale ventures to re-impose Frankish domination east of the Rhine were not undertaken. Equally so, it is understandable that the elimination of open conflict between Neustria and Austrasia by Pippin's victory at Tertry and the political settlement that he was able to impose opened the way for the resumption of more aggressive warfare on the frontiers and the beginnings of the process of re-establishing Frankish power in the east. This process was threatened again by the internal conflicts of 714–19, but was resumed more fully and effectively in consequence of the more thorough-going resolution of the political problems that was achieved by Charles Martel. Although some ground was lost again in the 740s his sons, and Pippin III in particular, were able to consolidate their father's work.

The establishment of relative tranquillity east of the Rhine, and the temporary acknowledgement that Aquitaine had to be allowed to exist as an independent duchy, freed Pippin's hands to turn to other matters. In 743 he and his brother had set up another Merovingian king, Childeric III, possibly a son of Chilperic II (715–21).[46] This followed a six-year gap in which no king had held office. The fact that they felt they needed a Merovingian to legitimise their regime is perhaps indicative of the relative weakness of their position in 743, but may also suggest that their own relations with each other were such that they could not easily co-operate without some kind of formal structure to condition their actions. By 749 Pippin III felt that he could dispense with the king, whom he had felt to be so necessary in 743.

In 750 he sent Bishop Burchard of Würzburg and the royal chaplain Fulrad, Abbot of Saint-Denis, to Rome. As recorded in the *Annales Regni Francorum*, or *Annals of the Kingdom of the Franks*, which may have begun to be written between the years 787 and 793, they were to ask Pope Zacharias if it were right for the kings of the Franks to rule but without wielding power. The pope's reply was that 'it was better to call king the one who had the royal power'. In consequence, on his 'Apostolic authority' he commanded that Pippin be made king.[47]

The contemporary continuator of the Fredegar chronicle is rather more circumspect. He records that a mission was sent to Rome and that what followed was done with papal consent, but makes the constituting of Pippin as king the product of 'the election by all of the Franks … consecration by the bishops and the acknowledgement of the princes' (that is the dukes).[48] The account in the *Annals of the Kingdom of the Franks* seems to betray the contamination of the ideological preoccupations of a slightly later period, and greater weight should probably be placed on the Fredegar continuator's version of events, even allowing for its author's partiality for the Pippinid or Carolingian house. Papal consent may have been needed primarily to persuade the Frankish bishops of the legitimacy of the deposition of the existing king and the replacement of his dynasty.

In political terms what was really crucial was clearly the agreement of the Franks, probably obtained at one of the annual 'Marchfield' assemblies, and the acknowledgement of the new ruler's status by his former peers, the other leading Frankish nobles, and those of the other areas subject to Frankish overlordship. The liturgical procedure adopted for the ceremony in 751 in which Pippin was made king may have involved anointing with chrism, following the Old Testament parallel of Samuel's pouring oil on the heads of Saul and David.[49] However, this is by no means as certain as is often made out. There is no reference to such a procedure in the contemporary sources, and it first appears in the later *Annals of the Kingdom of the Franks*.

What would seem undeniable is that this ritual was used in 754 when Pippin was re-consecrated, together with his two sons, by Pope Stephen II(III).[50] This probably strengthens the arguments of those who see the introduction of this particular practice into Frankish royal consecration as the product of papal influence. It had never previously been employed in Francia. Although used by the Visigothic kings, at least from 672 onwards, it is unlikely that this was the precedent for its adoption in 754 (or 751). Others have argued that the influence came from Ireland via Iona, but no evidence exists for any actual Irish royal unction or anointing.[51]

The pope had come to Francia in the winter of 753/4 to seek Pippin's aid in restraining the Lombard King Aistulf, whose advances into Roman territory in the summer were bringing him ever closer to Rome. Aistulf obviously felt that no serious threat was to be expected from Francia, as he had made no effort to prevent Stephen from passing through the Lombard kingdom on his way north, and he disregarded Pippin's request that he desist from further attacks on Roman territory.[52]

In this he proved unwise. Pippin's position in Francia may not have been very secure, but the papal request for aid gave him the opportunity of cutting a figure on a wider stage; also the chance of an expedition into Italy, which could and did prove financially lucrative, had obvious attractions as far as welding together some of the supporters of the new Frankish royal regime was concerned. Thus in the spring of 755 Pippin led an army across the Alps. He was able to besiege Aistulf in Pavia and force him to agree to terms. These consisted of a guarantee of inviolability for Roman territory and the giving of hostages and 'rich presents' to Pippin and the Frankish magnates.[53]

The papal source, the *Liber Pontificalis* or Pontifical Book, a series of generally contemporary biographical records of the popes, gives a rather more elaborate and ideologically slanted version of these events, which some historians have taken on trust. In this period, however, the Papacy lost its previously secure sense of its secular alignment to the Empire, and rather frantically and under pressure of events, notably the growing Lombard threat to its independence, began to create a new political role for itself. In so doing history was deliberately distorted and documents falsified. Without further investigation it would be unwise to place too much weight on exclusively papal interpretations of the events of this period.

In the 'Life' of Pope Stephen II(III) Pippin is made out to have been consecrated by the pope only after he had promised to obey his instructions, and an elaborate account is given of the initial reception of Stephen at Ponthion in January 754 at which Pippin prostrated himself before the pope and kissed his stirrup.[54] Contemporary Frankish sources omit such details, as well they might, and there is no real way of assessing which of the versions gets nearer to the truth. By 754 the pope probably had more to gain from Pippin than the other way round. The title of 'Patrician of the Romans' that he gave to Pippin at his anointing was high-sounding but meaningless, and may have been primarily intended to commit the Frankish king to the continuing defence of Rome and the Papacy.

Aistulf certainly did not expect any further Frankish interference after his defeat in 755 and not only failed to carry out the territorial restorations he had promised, but renewed his threats to the independence of the Roman duchy. Pippin led a second expedition into Italy in 756 and, paralleling the events of the previous year, besieged Aistulf in Pavia once more. The treaty was renewed, though it seems that the Lombard king was on the point of breaking it yet again when he died later in the year in consequence of a hunting accident.[55]

After his two successive interventions in Italy, and despite subsequent papal pleas, Pippin then ceased to involve himself in events south of the Alps. The latter part of his reign was principally devoted to checking the Saxons and to trying to conquer Aquitaine. In 758 he defeated some of the Saxons, destroyed various forts they had built on the Lippe, and forced them to pay an annual tribute of 300 horses.[56] In 760 he was free to turn his attention to Aquitaine, now ruled by Duke Waiofar (745–68), son of Duke Hunald (742–5). In a series of annual campaigns between the spring of that year and his death in 768 Pippin plundered and slaughtered his way across Aquitaine.[57] Much destruction is recorded: perhaps far more than was to be inflicted by the Vikings on the region in the ninth century. Although Waiofar had been made a fugitive and then murdered and armed Aquitanian resistance apparently crushed, the conquest was still not complete when Pippin died at Paris on 24 September 768.

Charles 'the Great'

Prior to his death, and with the consent of the Frankish nobles and the bishops attending on him, Pippin had divided up his kingdom between his two sons. To Charles, later known as Charles 'the Great', or Charlemagne, he gave the primary Frankish territories of Austrasia and a rather thinned down Neustria. To his younger son Carloman he entrusted the territories that he and Charles Martel had conquered: Burgundy, Alamannia, Provence and Septimania.

The period of the co-existence of the two kings, which lasted from 768 to 771, could not be described as easy, perhaps no more than could that of the co-rule of their father and uncle between 741 and 747. One cause of conflict may well have been Aquitaine, which the continuator of Fredegar, in his penultimate section, described as being intended to be divided between the two brothers, but which the later *Annals of the Kingdom of the Franks* state was given entirely to Charles.[58] Certainly, when in 769 Charles invaded Aquitaine to suppress continuing local resistance, now led by Hunald II, the son of Duke Waiofar, some form of confrontation or dispute seems to have occurred between the brothers at Moncontour, north of Poitiers. Whatever the cause, Carloman then withdrew from Aquitaine.

It seems that in 770 a series of alliances was devised to encircle Carloman. The diplomacy for this appears to have been conducted principally by his own mother, Pippin's widow Bertrada, and the parties who were brought into alliance against him were his brother Charles, Duke Tassilo III of Bavaria, and the Lombard King Desiderius (756–74). Pope Stephen III(IV) was initially uneasy at the prospect of some of his Frankish protectors allying themselves with his Lombard enemies, but his support was gained by the violent elimination of a group of powerful clerics in Rome, who had close ties to the family of his predecessor and who had hitherto dominated the papal court and policy making. However, the death of Carloman from natural causes in December 771, followed soon after by that of the pope, led to the dissolution of this confederacy.[59] Charles sent his Lombard wife back to her father, to whom also now fled the widow and infant children of Carloman when the principal secular and religious leaders of the latter's kingdom decided to accept the rule of his brother.[60] Thus in 771 Charles acquired control of the whole of the kingdom that his father had once ruled. Without this the succeeding period of military conquest and expansion could never have occurred.

As well as the titles and territories that he had acquired from his two predecessors Charles also inherited various problems. Of these the greatest, certainly in terms of the time and effort involved in solving it, was that of the Saxons. Individual campaigns by Charles Martel and Pippin had checked the Saxon pressure along the Lippe, but had certainly not made Frankish rule a reality in the area, let alone Saxony more generally. In 772 Charles set out to achieve an effective subjugation of the southern group of Saxons. This involved not just a military conquest, but an integration of the victims into the Frankish cultural orbit by their forcible conversion to Christianity.[61] Whether this was part of his intentions from the start is not clear, but it had certainly become so by 775.

The campaign of 772 was directed at the seizure of a Saxon fort on the Lippe at Eresburg and the destruction of the shrine of the sacred object known as the Irminsul. The exact nature of this idol is uncertain, but its location in probably recently acquired territory on the expanding southern frontier of Saxon territory would suggest that it was not just an object of traditional reverence but something directly associated with military victory and conquest. Thus, its destruction was not only lucrative, in terms of the seizure of the treasure kept as offerings in the shrine, but also intended as a blow to Saxon morale.[62]

The Saxons retaliated in 774, when they overran and destroyed Eresburg and tried to take the Frankish fort of Syburg in the valley of the Ruhr. They also penetrated further south to attack the monastery of Fritzlar on the upper Weser, which had been established by Boniface as a centre for evangelising the region. This may have been a direct response to the destruction of their sacred Irminsul in 772. The *Annals of the Kingdom of the Franks* are restrained and imprecise about the Frankish riposte ordered by Charles after his return from Italy later that year. It was certainly left to a major expedition, which he commanded in person in 775, to regain the forts lost in 774. This campaign was one of the most extensive conducted in Saxony, and took the Frankish forces through the disputed lands around the Lippe, the Ruhr and the Diemel, across the Weser, where a Saxon army was defeated, to the river Oker.[63]

On the Oker the Eastphalian Saxons came to terms with the Frankish king, giving hostages and promising their loyalty. Charles received a similar submission from the southernmost Saxon confederacy, that of the Angrarii, while returning west to rejoin the detachment of his forces that he had sent against the Westphalians. The propagandistic distortions of the court chronicle, the *Annals of the Kingdom of the Franks* are tellingly exposed by the account given of the activities of this force, which was recorded as having won a great victory in which many Saxons were killed. The anonymous author of the revised version, probably produced after Charles's death, reveals a quite contrary story, in which the overconfident Franks had their camp penetrated by the Saxons and were taken quite by surprise. It was only when

Charles arrived with the main body of the army that the West-
phalian Saxons were defeated and forced, like the Eastphalians
and Angrarii, to come to terms with the Frankish king.[64]

These humiliating submissions were effective only as long as
Charles and the main Frankish army were thought to be in a position to enforce them. In 776 when he again had to go to Italy the
southern Saxons attacked and destroyed Eresburg and threatened
Syburg. Another large-scale expedition had to be launched by
Charles in the autumn, which recovered the lost territory and led
to the Saxons again submitting to him. This they did at the sources
of the river Lippe, a place of particular significance for them.
They promised to become subjects of the king and of the Franks
and to accept Christianity. A significant number of them appeared
before Charles in 777 at his new settlement of Paderborn, built
significantly close to the sources of the Lippe, to receive Christian
baptism.[65] These enforced agreements, however, proved as fragile
as those made in 775.

In part the problem in subduing the Saxons was the difficulty
of the marshy terrain in or on the edges of which the fighting
had to be conducted. This was a region that had ultimately baffled
the Roman efforts at conquest in the time of Augustus. But
perhaps more significant still was the nature of the Saxons' social
and political organisation. They had no kings or permanent
institutions of central authority. Nor, apart from such forts as
Eresburg, did they have any large settlements. The basic Saxon
social units were the extended families, and these occupied fortified farmsteads, rather like small villages. A good idea of these
types of settlement can be gained from the one excavated at
Warendorf.[66]

Thus the Saxons could not be incapacitated by the defeat of a
single leader, nor could the seizure or destruction of key settlements lead to a rapid conquest. It is only because they did band
together to fight, either offensively or defensively, that they could
be brought to battle as a group. Only in the aftermath of such
large-scale encounters do the annals record the different Saxon
confederacies submitting or making agreements with the Franks.
In comparison with the Franks, the Saxons were relatively few in
numbers and poorly organised for conducting offensive warfare
against their powerful neighbour, and in most respects, it must
be appreciated, this was a most unequal struggle. Though in material culture, not least in terms of weapons, the Saxons and the
Franks were very similar.

The social structure and political organisation of Charles's
other principal victim in the 770s, the Lombard kingdom of Pavia,
were at the opposite extreme from those of the Saxons, and the

difference in the speed and decisiveness of the two conflicts is directly related to this. As was demonstrated in 755 and 756, the Lombard kingdom in northern Italy could be incapacitated by a single military defeat and by a threat to its centre of administration and principal royal residence in Pavia. What the events of those years had also shown was that it was difficult for Frankish rulers to impose on the Lombards a permanent political settlement of outstanding problems if they were going to return to the north of the Alps at the end of the current year's campaigning season. To force the Lombard kings to make treaties under duress was very different from ensuring the subsequent fulfilment of the terms of the agreements.

In 773 Charles received an appeal for help from the new pope, Hadrian I (772–95) against renewed Lombard threats to the independence of Rome. He had his own reasons to be interested in a show of force in Italy at this time, in that the widow and children of his brother Carloman had taken refuge with the Lombard King Desiderius. According to the *Liber Pontificalis* the latter was hoping to use them against Charles.[67] This may have been true – or it may have been a piece of papal disinformation intended to ensure the Frankish king's help for Rome against the Lombards. Whatever the cause, Charles invaded Italy with a large army in 773. One detachment of his forces outflanked the Lombard attempt to hold the Alps, and Desiderius was rapidly besieged in Pavia, like his predecessor Aistulf in the 750s.

Unlike the sieges of 755 and 756, this one was protracted and lasted on into 774. After six months Charles himself, who had been joined outside Pavia by his new wife Hildegard (d. 783) and their son, proceeded to Rome, where he met Pope Hadrian. On his return after Easter 774 the siege of Pavia finally came to an end. Unlike the submissions of 755 and 756, on this occasion the Lombard king was required to surrender himself, his family and the royal treasure.[68] The Lombards were obliged to submit to Frankish rule, and Charles himself took the title of King of the Lombards. By the late summer he had returned to Francia, where fighting with the Saxons had now resumed, leaving a garrison in Pavia.

What or who had prompted Charles to take the extreme measure of annexing the Lombard kingdom is unknown. It was quite unprecedented for a ruler of one ethnic group to style himself as king of another. In the fifth and sixth centuries such a conquest would normally have been followed by the elimination of the defeated people's separate ethnic identity, as happened to the Vandals, Sueves, Ostrogoths and others. Similarly in seventh century Britain, where in a number of cases kings of more powerful peoples defeated and killed the rulers of the smaller neighbouring kingdoms, in no case did this lead to, for example, the ruler of Mercia proclaiming himself to be King of the East Angles.

It is possible that Pope Hadrian played a particular role, during Charles's Easter visit to Rome, in persuading him that a final solution to the Lombard kingdom was required. The limited usefulness of earlier Frankish interventions from the papal point of view was quite obvious, and it is unlikely that Charles had at such an early stage in his reign developed fixed intentions of extending his personal rule beyond the frontiers of Francia. But for the *Rex Francorum* to proclaim himself to be *Rex Langobardorum* by virtue of the defeat of his notional predecessor is far more extraordinary than is generally appreciated. Charles had adopted this title by September 774 and used it consistently, and not just in documents relating exclusively to Italy, even after both his royal titles were supplemented by his imperial one.[69] Despite much conquest and territorial expansion in both the sixth and early seventh centuries such a move was quite alien to the world of Frankish political ideas and practices.

Although the centralised nature of royal government was such that the occupation of Pavia and the exile of Desiderius to a monastery in Francia proved sufficient to establish initial Frankish control over the Lombard kingdom, the great duchies of Spoleto and Benevento had in practice to be left under their indigenous rulers. The newly installed Duke Hildeprand of Spoleto, who was a papal ally, acknowledged Charles's overlordship, in 774 or 775, but Benevento under its Duke Arichis only came to terms with him in 787.[70] Even in the north, the return of the new 'King of the Lombards' to Francia led in 775 to a revolt by Duke Hrodgaud of Friuli, which forced Charles to undertake an expedition into Italy early the following year to eliminate the rebel.[71]

The simple lesson would seem to have been that if the king was in Francia there would be trouble in Italy, and if he were in Italy the Saxons would resume fighting. Faced by such a dilemma it is surprising then to find Charles undertaking a campaign in Spain, as he did in 778. The foundation of Paderborn and the mass conversion of some of the Saxons may have convinced him that the Saxon problem had been dealt with. At the Paderborn assembly in 777 he received envoys from the *de facto* independent Arab rulers of Barcelona and Zaragoza, who were threatened by the rising power of the Umayyad Amir of Córdoba, 'Abd al-Rahman I (756–88), who was had gradually made himself master of most of the south and centre of the Iberian peninsula in the course of the previous twenty years.[72] For Charles a Spanish venture represented yet another way in which, as in Aquitaine, Italy and across the Rhine, he could pursue some of the traditional Frankish aims of his Merovingian and Carolingian predecessors. Since the sixth century Frankish kings had been interested in the possibilities of loot if not of conquest offered by the great Roman towns of the Ebro valley and the area of modern Catalonia, and Charles's father Pippin III had managed to conquer all of the remaining Arab ruled areas in south-western Gaul, culminating in his capture of Narbonne in 759.

Traditional as may have been the motives and unexpected as was the opportunity suddenly offered by the appeal from the Arab regional potentates, the expedition that Charles led into the Ebro valley in 778 was probably ill-conceived, and it turned out to be the nearest that any of his undertakings came to disaster.[73] As in his Italian campaign of 774 he divided his forces into two columns, to cross the Pyrenees in different places: one in the East to approach Zaragoza via Barcelona and the other, led by him in person, to cross the western end of the mountains and descend the Ebro. However, one of his two erstwhile Arab allies had by now murdered the other. The Frankish forces were refused admission into Barcelona and found Zaragoza held against them. As an Umayyad army approached the Ebro from the south Charles was obliged to withdraw his army back up the valley and into Francia, dismantling the fortifications of Pamplona, which he had occupied. In the retreat across the Pyrenees the rearguard of his army was set upon and annihilated by the Basques, and a number of prominent officers of his court were killed.

Even ignoring this humiliation, which the *Annals of the Kingdom of the Franks* omit entirely from the account of this year, the whole expedition had failed to achieve any of its objectives, and in the meantime the Saxons had risen up against the Franks while the king was absent. They penetrated as far as the east bank of the Rhine at Deutz opposite Cologne and also destroyed the new Frankish settlement on the Lippe, which Charles had rather unwisely named after himself. In response, a retaliatory expedition in 779 defeated the Westphalians and induced other Saxons east of the Weser to send hostages for their future good conduct. This was reinforced by a major progress through Saxony as far as the Elbe that Charles conducted in 780, and a large number of Saxons submitted to mass baptism on the river Oker.[74]

Even after these major displays of force the submission of the Saxons was still far from secure, and the Frankish chronicle sources, notably the *Annals of the Kingdom of the Franks*, cannot conceal this fact, despite repeated assurances of great Frankish victories and the slaughter of numerous Saxons. Charles had to go to Italy in 781, not least to obtain papal coronation for two of his young sons: Pippin as King of the Lombards and Louis as

King of the Aquitanians. The substantial campaigns that then had to be launched against the Saxons in 782, 783, 784 and 785 show that not only had their resistance still not been broken, but also that, as in 774 and 778, the king's absence in other parts led to major Saxon revolts.[75]

As had clearly been the case with the continuators of the *Chronicle of Fredegar*, the compiler of the *Annals of the Kingdom of the Franks*, working in or around the royal court in the 790s, was happy to distort the truth in the interests of presenting an unremittingly triumphalist view of the king and of his reign. Thus, although forced to record that two leading Frankish nobles were killed, he presents the 782 campaign against the Saxons, which was not directed by the king in person, as yet another military success. Fortunately, the author of the revised version of these annals was more open and admits that the Frankish forces were severely defeated and two of the king's principal officials and four other counts killed. Charles reacted to this reverse with a massive show of force and the subsequent massacre at Verden of 4500 Saxons who had been surrendered to him.[76]

The protracted campaigns of the first half of the 780s were ultimately to bring the Saxons to heel in 785, when, as the Annalist put it, Charles was able 'to march through all of Saxony, wherever he wanted, on open roads and with no one resisting him'. Widukind, the leader of Saxon resistance since 777 and possibly the scion of a former ducal dynasty, was forced to submit and to receive baptism.[77] In practice this was to be only a temporary pacification, in that Saxon resistance was renewed in the later 790s, but it was at least sufficient at the time for Charles to feel that his grip on Saxony was secure, and therefore that he was able to turn his attentions to Italy once more.

He spent Christmas of 786 at Florence and proceeded south to Rome in the spring. Faced with the first real prospect of royal intervention in the south, Duke Arichis of Benevento seems to have offered some form of token submission, but Pope Hadrian persuaded Charles to invade the duchy, and force him into a more abject surrender. The first manifestation of Frankish power in southern Italy in 781 had encouraged the imperial government in Constantinople to try to make an alliance with Charles, who had then received a proposal from the Empress Irene, then acting as regent, that one of his daughters be betrothed to her son, the Emperor Constantine VI (780–97). The reappearance of the Frankish king in southern Italy in 787 led the Empire to push for the implementation of this agreement.[78]

However the Franks viewed this invitation, it is important to understand that for the Byzantine court such a marriage of a member of the imperial family to someone who was regarded as a 'barbarian' could be a useful diplomatic act. Constantine VI's father Leo IV (775–80) had been the son of a Khazar princess, whom Constantine V had married when it was expedient to look for allies north of the Black Sea.[79] In 787 it was advisable for the imperial government to neutralise any threat that Charles presented to their surviving enclaves of territory in southern Italy, and at the same time the empress may have been looking for wider support at a time when she was alienating some of the units of her own army by reversing her predecessors' religious policies. A first attempt to put an end to imperially sponsored Iconoclasm had foundered in 786 when soldiers had broken up a council in Constantinople. A second attempt to hold such a gathering took place in Nicaea in 787, where Iconoclast theology had been formally condemned.[80]

With both Italy and Saxony more firmly under royal control, it is hardly surprising to find that the next move on Charles's part was the elimination of the principal power in the region in between. Although as a Duke Tassilo III of Bavaria was subject to the Frankish king, to whom he was related, the kind of regional independence such a local ruler could enjoy had been amply demonstrated by the line of the dukes of Aquitaine. Tassilo is accused in the Frankish sources of having conspired with the Saxon leader Widukind in the period before 785 and with the Avars and Slavs in the year 788.[81] However, Frankish chroniclers' accusations of treachery must by now seem to be rather debased coinage, and less than full trust should be placed in this one.

Tassilo failed to attend the assembly held by Charles at Worms in 787 after his return from Italy, and in consequence his duchy was invaded. When obliged to submit by this overwhelming display of force he was reinvested with his office, but the following year at the assembly at Ingelheim, which he was constrained to attend, he was accused of treachery and condemned to death. During his attendance at the assembly, Frankish troops had entered Bavaria and taken his family as hostages. In the circumstances he found it expedient to confess his guilt, and was imprisoned in a monastery. His deposition and that of his dynasty was later confirmed by the council held at Frankfurt in 794.[82]

Mysteriously, the allies with whom the unfortunate Tassilo was said to have been conspiring, the confederacy of the Avars, who controlled the plains of Hungary, twice invaded Bavaria in 788, and met with stiff resistance from the inhabitants.[83] As with the Arab raid into Aquitaine in 733 and their capture of Avignon in 737, it is rather surprising to find those whom the Frankish chronicles describe as allies actually engaged in desperate struggles with each other. There are thus very good grounds for doubting the truth of the charges made against Tassilo III, and for suspecting that his confession, repeated in the Council of Frankfurt in 794, has as much validity to it as those of the victims of Stalin's 'show trials' of the 1930s.

Frankish military expansion in the course of the first two decades of the reign of Charles created its own problems. In all areas the extension of their power seriously worried those living beyond the initial targets of Frankish aggression. The wars in Saxony led to problems with the Slavs and then with the Danes, the Italian conquest alarmed the Byzantine Empire and also led to difficulties with the Slavs in the western Balkans, and the intervention in the duchy of Bavaria contributed directly to a confrontation with the Avars. This latter conflict, which began in 788, continued intermittently throughout the early years of the 790s.

In 788 the Avars had twice invaded Bavaria and also sent an army into the March of Friuli in the north-east of Italy, but in all cases had been repulsed by local forces. Charles himself came into Bavaria later in the year to establish frontier defences against further Avar attacks. In 790 an attempt was made to settle the disagreements over boundaries by negotiations held at Worms, but to no avail. In 791 at an assembly or 'Marchfield' held at Regensburg it was decided that a campaign should be launched against the Avars because of 'the excessive and intolerable outrage committed by the Avars against the Holy Church and the Christian people'. What exactly was implied is not known, but it is clear that the expedition, which was clearly planned long before Charles came to Regensburg, was to be given a strongly religious motive.

The ensuing war is not easy to understand. Our only accounts of it come from the Frankish annals, augmented by such chance survivals as a letter from Charles to his wife Fastrada (d. 794) written at the end of the 791 campaign. What is most perplexing is the nature and causes of the Avar collapse. In 791 a Frankish army sent from Italy under Charles's son Pippin defeated an Avar force, while Charles himself was able to enter their territory and proceed along both banks of the Danube without meeting any significant resistance. The explanation for or possibly the consequence of this Frankish triumphal progress in 791 appears to have been a civil war amongst the Avars and the break-up and rapid disappearance of their confederacy. Frankish armies from Italy were able to march unopposed into Avar territory north of the Danube in both 795 and 796 and loot and ultimately destroy a great ceremonial centre known as the Ring.[84]

By this time Charles was campaigning in person less frequently, and from 794 his court came most often to spend the winter

months in the newly developed palace complex at Aachen.[85] Later
still he would remain at or in the vicinity of Aachen throughout
the Summer months as well. In the same year he also convoked
a general council of the Frankish church, to which some Italian
and British bishops also came, not least to consider the implications of the Byzantine restoration of image-veneration at the
Second Council of Nicaea in 787. One of the king's principal
theological advisers, a Goth called Theodulf, who was later to be
Bishop of Orléans, had been preparing a substantial critique of
what was seen as the heretical views of the Greek bishops. This
work was made to appear to have been Charles's own, and in
consequence it later became known to scholars as the *Libri Carolini*
or *Caroline Books*. Both Theodulf and the bishops attending the
council at Frankfurt in 794 were generally critical of Byzantine
image-veneration, which they suspected of verging on idolatry.[86]
Pope Hadrian I, however, had welcomed the restoration of what
he regarded as sound doctrine in Constantinople with considerable enthusiasm, and the papal espousal of the decisions of
II Nicaea may have resulted in the suppression of the probably
still unfinished *Libri Carolini*, which were not presented to the
bishops assembled at Frankfurt.

Emotional and ideological ties linking the Church of Rome and
its bishop to the Empire were still very strong, despite the practical need the Papacy had come to have for Frankish military
backing. An imperial attack in 788 on the duchy of Benevento,
recently subdued by Charles, may have been intended to break
up the new political alignments in the West before they became
too firmly fixed. However, the Byzantine forces were defeated by
the armies commanded by the appointees of the Frankish king.[87]
It must have been clear in Rome that the Empire was in no
position to re-impose its practical control on Italy and that at least
in the short term the future lay with the Franks.

Indeed, developments in Constantinople in the 790s would
have reinforced such a belief. Constantine VI was able to take
power into his own hands in 790 when a military insurrection
overthrew his mother, the regent Irene. However, he allowed her
to return to Constantinople in 792, where she began to conspire
against him.[88] A scandal over his sudden divorce and remarriage
in 796 sapped his popularity with the Church, and fears seem to
have existed that he was being strongly influenced in favour of
restoring Iconoclasm. In July 797 the empress was able to seize
power in a coup backed by the imperial guard, and the unfortunate emperor was blinded, to render him formally incapable of
holding the imperial office. Whether intentionally or not this was
done so brutally that he died in consequence of it.[89]

Even the chronicler Theophanes, for whom as a committed Iconodule Irene, the restorer of image-veneration, was the 'wise and God-loving' empress, 'who had struggled for the true faith in a martyr's fashion', found this act incapable of justification. On Constantine's deposition and death his mother took the throne in person. However, no woman had ever ruled the Empire in her own right, and for those who opposed her the imperial office was considered to be vacant. Her increasingly unstable regime tottered on until she was deposed in 802 in a coup led by her finance minister. In the meantime she had had to look for allies wherever she might find them, and far from renewing war against the Franks in Italy she had even proposed a marriage between herself and Charles. The theoretical vacancy of the imperial throne also proved opportune in the context of a rapid and unforeseen series of developments in the West.[90]

There another blinding was to have quite different consequences, and led directly to the creating rather than to the killing of an emperor. On Christmas Day of 795 Pope Hadrian I died, to be succeeded by Leo III (795–817). By this period the secular power of the papacy within the City of Rome and the substantial material wealth that it controlled, augmented by territories regained from the Lombards, made the office highly sought after, especially in relation to its role in local politics and the rivalries between various noble factions within the city. In particular, control of the office provided opportunities for the relatives and friends of the incumbent pope to obtain positions of authority and financial benefit for themselves. Senior positions in both the ecclesiastical and secular administrations tended to be given to such supporters, and a change of pope meant inevitable changes amongst such principal officials.[91] The elective nature of the papal office, however, made it difficult for one family or faction to monopolise it, but this did not prevent them from trying. Leo III was elected against an opposition centred on the two nephews of his long-reigned predecessor, who were understandably loath to give up the power and influence they had previously enjoyed. Despite the election they continued to hope to oust Leo.

They had, however, overlooked the new Frankish dimension in Roman affairs. Leo III had taken the precaution of announcing his election to Charles, a procedure normally reserved for the emperor in Constantinople.[92] He was the first pope to do so. On 25 April 799 the conspirators struck, ambushing Leo in the course of a procession. He was seized, blinded and had his tongue cut out, before being incarcerated in a monastery. However, unlike the Byzantines in 797, his enemies made a botched job of it. Leo was able to escape from the monastery and from Rome, and make his way north to Charles, who was then at Paderborn.[93] Even worse for his enemies, the blinding and mutilation had been so ineffectually carried out that the fugitive pope regained use of all his senses and was able to claim a miraculous healing.[94]

Agents of those who had overthrown Leo III came after him to appear before Charles and present their accusations of fornication and perjury against the pope. The Frankish king's position was not an easy one, in that serious accusations had been made against the pope by those associated with his predecessor, whom Charles had long regarded as a friend.[95] On the other hand Leo had been anxious to present himself as Charles's creature from the very start of his pontificate. To complicate matters, a number of the king's ecclesiastical advisers, notably the Northumbrian Deacon Alcuin (d. 804), on the basis of arguments developed during the Laurentian schism in the time of the Ostrogothic King Theoderic, pressed on Charles the need to accept that the Bishop of Rome could neither be judged in a secular tribunal nor, because of the Petrine foundation of his see, could he be answerable to any of his ecclesiastical inferiors, even in a council.[96]

After discussions almost totally concealed from us, Leo was restored to Rome with Frankish backing in the summer of 800, and in November Charles himself arrived in the city, in theory to preside over a council that would enquire into the accusations against the pope. This body, meeting at the beginning of December, shared Alcuin's view and declared itself to be incompetent to carry out such a role, and instead Leo was permitted on 23 December to take a public oath that he was innocent of all the charges levelled against him. Two days later, in the course of the celebration of the Mass of Christmas, he crowned Charles as emperor.[97] What Belisarius had been unable or unwilling to do in 539 was thus achieved, and three and a quarter centuries after the deposition of Romulus in 476 a new emperor was created in the West.

Although often seen as the natural culmination of the military conquests of Charles and his Frankish kingdom, the imperial title and coronation at the hands of the pope were the products of particular and limited circumstances, and were by no means the natural ends towards which the king and his advisors had been working.[98] At best the coronation was brought about by purely Italian or even Roman circumstances, and was the outcome of the particular events of the years 799–800, helped by the peculiar constitutional position of the current ruler in Constantinople. If anything the imperial title was to be more of a hindrance than a help to its recipient, and was to be the most ambiguous of the legacies that he would to pass on to his successors.

16 The new Constantine

The meaning of Empire

It is doubtful if any of the participants in the dramatic imperial coronation in St Peter's on Christmas Day in the year 800 knew for certain what they were doing or precisely where it was intended to lead.[1] This is true even in the literal sense, since there had been no imperial ordination in the West since the fifth century and the liturgical procedures followed were new and neither traditional nor borrowed from the Byzantine Empire. The use of a crown was unprecedented and was not to be a feature of imperial investitures in Constantinople before the tenth century. Thus the Roman Church invented its own rites for the occasion.[2]

According to Einhard, a former member of Charles's court, who wrote a *Vita Karoli* or *Life of Charles* in the mid to late 820s, the king declared that if he had known what was going to happen he would never have entered the church that day.[3] This is probably no more than a reflection of the tradition, current since Antiquity, of the refusal of power. Prospective emperors and also bishops had, either in literary tradition or in formal ritual, to resist attempts to elevate them to their new status. There are indications that the idea of an imperial coronation had been discussed in Charles's presence at least since he arrived in Rome in November of 800.[4] Even so, at the very earliest the whole scheme could not have been developed prior to the unexpected flight of Leo to Paderborn and the king's decision to restore him to Rome.

The rapid expansion of the Frankish kingdom under Charles and the conquest of other peoples had inevitably led to the use of the terminology of *imperium* or empire in the correspondence of members of the court, but this was conventional in such circumstances, and had been used, for example, by Bede in writing about some of the seventh century kings of Northumbria.[5] Such usage did not imply an imperial title or even any aspirations towards one. For one thing, in the Roman imperial tradition, which was the only one known in this period, and which was preserved in the ideology of Byzantium, the Empire was one and indivisible. It was possible for two emperors to co-exist but only as colleagues ruling a single Empire. Frequent civil wars had been fought in the fourth century over the refusal of an emperor to accept a self-proclaimed imperial colleague. In 800 it was only the theoretical vacancy in Constantinople, that had come about with the death of Constantine VI on 15 August 797 and the rule of Irene, which gave the Roman Church its excuse for elevating Charles.

The nearest that the king's advisers in Francia seem to have come to articulating the view that the extent of his power required an enhancement of his status were references in letters of Alcuin (d. 804) to an *Imperium Christianorum* or Empire of the Christians.[6] It is important to grasp that hitherto the whole notion of an Empire had been tied to Rome, not so much the city, though this was the symbol of it, as the civilisation. If a Frankish king could not or did not wish to claim to be a Roman emperor, an entirely new ideological base had to be found for such a change in his status.

How far the kind of ideas that lay behind Alcuin's usage could ever have been developed in practice cannot be said. Certainly the conquest of the Saxons had been turned into an armed evangelisation, the Spanish expedition of 778 was transmuted in retrospect into a bid to succour the Christians under Islamic rule, and the Avar campaign of 791 was seen by the king at the time as an act of Christian vengeance and was accompanied by litanies and fasting on the part of his army.[7] But whether the notion of a kind of Christian citizenship could have provided a new ideological cement for the disparate peoples under Charles's rule or could have overcome the Roman overtones of the imperial office and thereby Frankish suspicions of it is unknowable, in that the still incoherent process was given a new direction and impetus by Pope Leo III and his advisors.

It could be argued that just as the popes of the mid-eighth century had been anxious to tie the rulers of the Franks to Rome and its dependent territories to protect them from the Lombards, so Leo III wanted to make the link even closer to ensure his personal protection from his factional enemies within the city. The events of 799 had shown that without Charles's support his own survival was in jeopardy, and just as Stephen II(III) had tried to institutionalise the relationship between the Frankish ruler and the City of Rome by investing Pippin and his sons with the title of 'Patrician of the Romans', so Leo had to go a step further and make Charles into the *Imperator Romanorum* or Emperor of the Romans.[8]

Even if papal motivation was not as narrowly personal as such a view would imply, it is likely that the impetus for a recreation of a western emperor was largely Italian in origin and direction. In part the problem was one of authority. Since 774 Charles had been *Rex Langobardorum*, but the extent of the former Lombard kingdom within Italy was limited, and the constitutional relationship between the monarchy that had been centred in Pavia and the two great central and southern duchies of Spoleto and Benevento was by no means certain; all the more so since the Beneventan rulers had arrogated to themselves the title of prince in the aftermath of the Frankish conquest.

Leaving the problems of the loosely structured Lombard kingdom to one side, there still remained difficulties to face in respect of virtually every other area of Italy as far as Charles's right to rule, as opposed to his power to do so, was concerned. The area of the former exarchate of Ravenna and its related region of the Pentapolis had been taken from imperial control by the Lombards in 751, but this had never been recognised by Constantinople. The popes had claimed these territories for themselves, most probably by virtue of their continuing role as administrators of the imperial duchy of Rome. Attempts to persuade the Frankish rulers to secure the surrender of Ravenna and the Pentapolis to the papal administration both in the 750s and after 774 had come to nothing, but the status of these territories and the right by which Charles ruled them remained highly ambiguous. This was if anything even truer of the city of Rome and the lands of its duchy. At the beginning of the century the popes had been politically subject to the emperors, even if enjoying much *de facto* freedom of action. This situation had not changed in formal terms, despite the ever growing rapprochement between Rome and the Frankish kings.

Some scholars have argued that the popes and their advisors in this period were gradually and consciously working towards the creation of a fully independent territorial state, a 'Republic of St Peter'. However, there is no clear evidence that this was something that any of them would have aspired to, let alone achieved. There would seem instead to have existed a situation of pragmatic uncertainty about the relationships between Empire, papacy and Frankish kingdom for much of the second half of the eighth century. Leo III's decision to send formal notification of his election to Charles instead of to Constantine VI is the first real sign that this was breaking down, and that one of the parties, the Roman Church, was seeking a clear and unambiguous realignment of its relationship to the other two. In other words, the creation of a new western emperor would resolve the lingering constitutional difficulties faced by the popes in terms of their secular allegiance. At the same time, it would provide a new and more satisfactory framework for the exercise of authority by the Frankish ruler over all parts of Italy (and all and any other parts of the former Roman empire in the West).

This may have suited the interests of the pope and to some extent those of Charles himself, but it was totally unacceptable in Constantinople, the capital of a much diminished state but one which still saw itself to be the one and only Roman Empire. War was unavoidable once the regime of the Empress Irene was swept aside, but under her successor Nicephorus I (802–11) the Empire was too weak to make any impression and merely lost more of its remaining territory in Istria to the Franks. At the same time the growing power in the Balkans of the Bulgars under their Khan Krum (805–14) presented a far more serious threat to Byzantium than the coronation of Charles. In 811 Nicephorus was defeated and killed by the Bulgars, and his skull was turned into a drinking vessel for the khan. In 812 the new Emperor Michael I (811–13) made a treaty recognising the imperial status of the Frankish ruler, though only as *Imperator Francorum* or Emperor of the Franks.[9]

By this time, however, the nature of the title and of Charles's own view of his new office had changed significantly. He had returned to Francia late in 801 and never went to Italy again. He and his advisers devoted themselves to working out what his new status might mean in a Frankish context. By the middle of 801 the imperial title, as used in official documents, had been changed from *Imperator Romanorum* to the rather more abstract *Imperator Imperium Romanum gubernans* or 'Emperor governing the Roman Empire'. This usage had antecedents going back to the time of Justinian I, but may have been particularly attractive in divorcing the imperial office from what to the Franks would appear to be the ethnically delimiting 'of the Romans'.[10] This for the Franks meant the inhabitants of the City of Rome and its territories. The form of the title as used in Rome by Leo III at the coronation, which subsequently appeared in the *Liber Pontificalis*, was thus far too limiting, and also seemed to involve an undesirable tying of the office to the City of Rome and to the papacy.

Einhard in his *Vita Karoli Magni* specifically links the reform of the two codes of law under which the Franks lived and the writing down of the laws of their subject peoples to the aftermath of the imperial coronation.[11] He presents them as tasks that were not only carried out after Charles became emperor but were only possible once he had attained that status. As in the classic 'refusal of power' attributed to Charles in his words about the ceremony at St Peter's, this looks like a reminiscence of Roman constitutional ideas. Only the emperor was permitted to make new legislation, although certain of his subordinates could 'interpret' existing laws in such a way as to give them new application and meaning. Thus Procopius had specifically praised the Ostrogothic King Theoderic for not making law, although in fact a set of regulations, known as the 'Edict of Theoderic' has long been ascribed to him.[12] If this was his work he was in it doing little more than would have been permitted to a Praetorian Prefect in the period of the later Roman Empire.

The existence of a version of the law code used by the main body of the Franks, the *Lex Salica*, that can be attributed to the revision of the year 802/3 referred to by Einhard has been recognised by modern scholarship.[13] Less critical, though, has been the reaction to the second element in Einhard's description of Charles's legal activity: the writing down of the laws of the subject peoples. A number of collections, many of which are very brief, that purport to be the codes of the laws of the Thuringians, the Saxons, the Alamans, the Bavarians, the Chamavian Franks and others, are known and have received modern editions. That the redaction of most of these should be associated with the programme described by Einhard has long and rightly been accepted.[14] What, however, is far too frequently asserted and credited is that these really do represent no more and no less than the written form of the customary laws of the peoples to whom they are ascribed.

Many of them, for example the *Leges Saxonum* (Laws of the Saxons) or *Lex Thuringorum* (Law of the Thuringians), are very brief indeed and represented little more than lists of compensations for injury and homicide, moderated by the legal status of the victim. All of these, however, are assessed in terms of *solidi*, which were in origin the principal denomination of gold coin used in the later Roman Empire but which became theoretical units of valuation in the Frankish and Visigothic kingdoms. Whatever else they were, *solidi* were neither indigenous to nor used in any form by the Saxons and Thuringians. Similarly there exist in these codes regulations concerning the punishment of those who commit murder or other offences in churches or of those who plot against the King of the Franks or his sons. As Christianity was introduced and then imposed on the Saxons only from the mid-eighth century onwards and as they became subject to the Franks only in the 780s there are no grounds for seeing these as representing ancestral custom or traditional law amongst them. In other words these are Frankish rules that the Saxons were required to abide by.[15]

This is by no means an isolated phenomenon. A number of other indications exist that show the Franks of the late eighth century trying to 'tidy up' their neighbours and to impose firm ethnic identities on them and give them distinct customs and laws. They seem to have been, from our perspective, strangely anxious to think of their neighbours and also non-Frankish groups within their own territories as being distinct *gentes* or peoples. It is in looking at the treatment of Aquitaine and Burgundy that this comes out most closely, but the implications of this are highly significant when it comes to weighing up the value of Frankish information relating to those peoples beyond their frontiers whom they subjected to political control in the time of the first Carolingians.

It is thus highly significant that the contemporary sources that refer to the Frankish wars in Aquitaine in the period 733–69 never treat the inhabitants of the region as a distinct ethnic group and refer to their leaders only as dukes or princes of Aquitaine. However, slightly later Frankish sources, such as the *Annals of the Kingdom of the Franks*, always call them dukes of the Aquitanians, and imply a common ethnic identity to all the inhabitants of the duchy. In so doing they are, as can easily be demonstrated, deliberately altering the earlier historical sources upon which they rely for their information relating to this period.[16] In fact, to put it very briefly and simply, there is no evidence whatsoever for the existence of a common Aquitanian 'national' or ethnic identity before the period in which this Frankish annalist was writing, which is to say in the 780s.[17] This is also the decade in which Charles set up his youngest son, then aged only three, as 'King of the Aquitanians' (781). This kingdom was in fact an almost wholly artificial creation that fell apart when first subjected to serious strain in the 830s and 840s.[18]

Similarly, a recent study has shown how equally unreal is the supposed Burgundian identity that is also brought out in the Carolingian historical and legal texts of the later eighth and ninth centuries.[19] Although there had once been a Burgundian people and kingdom, centred on the middle Rhône and western Alps in the period 442–533, total discontinuity exists between it and the notional Burgundians of the Carolingian texts. These people were supposed to be legally distinct from the Franks in that they lived under the norms of the code known as the *Lex Gundobada* or 'Law of Gundobad', named after the Burgundian king (d. 518) who was held to be responsible for the first version of it.[20] However, it may be truer to say that the Carolingian rulers required them to be thus distinct and to use a code of law supposedly encapsulating their 'national' tradition. In the same way the 'Aquitanians' were required to use Roman law, because the Franks regarded them as a distinct people of Roman origin.

Once this is appreciated, the whole notion of the 'personality of the law', whereby an individual would be judged only according to the legal rules of his own ethnic group, becomes far more of a Carolingian Frankish invention and much less of something that should be expected to have applied in earlier periods.[21] Much earlier legislation makes more sense when seen as applying territorially, in other words to all the inhabitants of a state, irrespective of their particular ethnic origin.[22]

What, though, does all this mean in terms of the ends the Carolingian rulers and their advisers were trying to achieve? How conscious this process was is by no means possible to gauge, but it does seem as if under Charles the Franks were trying to define their own identity against those of all surrounding groups, who were forced by their Frankish conquerors or political masters into accepting far more rigid and formal definitions of their customs, history and ethnicity, that were in many respects anachronistic. At the same time the older divisions within the Frankish body politic, notably the division between Neustrian and Austrasian kingdoms, virtually disappear.

All of this in turn has important consequences for the strength and stability of the political structure created by Charles and his immediate predecessors. The Roman Empire had achieved the extraordinary feat of turning a large and disparate number of subject peoples, most of whom had been forcibly submitted to Roman rule, into a single, long-lasting and more or less culturally coherent political entity. For many of the Celtic peoples in the West, Rome had represented an intellectually and materially superior culture that had much to offer, at least to the dominant elements in their societies. In the Greek East the situation was almost reversed, but in both cases the concept of a common Roman citizenship and a shared set of values and cultural ideas provided the ideological cement to hold together the upper classes of the Roman Empire from Hadrian's Wall to the Mesopotamian frontiers with Persia, and from the Danube to the fringes of the Sahara.[23]

In comparison with this, the task facing the Franks was much easier, in that their empire was geographically more limited, and they did have the advantage over some of the ethnic groups submitted to their rule of having definite intellectual and material inducements to offer, largely in the form of things they had themselves inherited from Rome. However, there had to be some overarching sense of community if a viable single political entity were to be created to hold together all the ethnically diverse components of the new Frankish Empire. Here the kind of 'empire of the Christians' idea that Alcuin was rather vaguely articulating around the year 800 might have served the purpose. An ideological unity might have been able to outweigh the linguistic, historical, and material cultural divisions between the different ethnic components of the Empire. This is what to a large extent Islam had done for the Arabs and was in due course to do for many of the large numbers of non-Arabs subject to their rule.[24]

However, it is important to note that in the case of the Arab Empire the ability of the Arab tribes to absorb additional and ethnically different elements of population into themselves by means of the ties of clientage was a vital feature in bringing about the cultural unity of the ruling classes. In other words, within a century, there were a relatively large number of non-Arabs, in terms of their family's actual ethnic origins, who were thinking of themselves and their ancestors as being Arabs. Similarly, the exact identity of the regions of Arab political control and of the practice of the Islamic religion strengthened the mutual identification of the two.

The Franks, on the other hand, were trying at the very period of their greatest expansion of territorial control to be ethnically exclusive and to force the peoples subject to them to recognise that not only were they not Franks but also they were very decisively Saxons, Thuringians, Lombards or whatever else, with very strong cultural traditions of their own. It was also impossible, even if it had been attempted, to present the frontiers of Christendom and of the Frankish Empire as being conterminous.[25] Thus, whatever the Franks had to offer to their subject peoples – and this was by no means negligible – it was not backed by the inducements necessary to create a new ethnic or cultural identity, which in turn would have made possible the survival of their Empire as a single political entity.

The machinery of government

An alternative, though ultimately limited, solution to the problem of the integration of the different peoples of the Empire might have been possible if a governmental machinery had existed that was complex enough and extensive enough to enable the state to function irrespective of the personal competence or otherwise of its titular heads.[26] A professional bureaucracy still functioned in the Byzantine Empire, where anyway the common sense of Roman identity and Christian orthodoxy kept the citizens united throughout a period of grave military crisis.[27] In the West, though, whatever had survived of the apparatus of imperial government into the time of the Ostrogothic kingdom was disrupted by wars of reconquest under Justinian and then the division of Italy following the Lombard invasion. In Gaul the breakdown of central authority in the fifth century had meant that the Frankish kings inherited little of the governmental apparatus of the Roman Empire, and the problems they faced in this respect have already been considered.

What the earlier Merovingians had, but their Carolingian successors seem entirely to have lacked, were instruments of local urban self-government. The survival of such Roman institutions as the municipal archives appears reasonably securely documented into the early seventh century, and a number of major urban centres were clearly still flourishing in Aquitaine, Burgundy and Provence at the beginning of the eighth.[28] These, however, were in many cases smashed by the campaigns of Charles Martel and Pippin III.

Under Charles, as under his immediate predecessors, the governmental apparatus of the state was minimal.[29] Counts still served as the principal royal local officials, but to assist them they had no more than an officially stipulated minimum of one notary to write the documents they needed to produce. Deputies or viscounts they might have, at least from the early ninth century onwards, but in practice they depended upon the goodwill of local landowners for any effective imposition of justice. The ultimate sanction that lay behind them beyond their own immediate followings was that of the military might of the king, as represented by the army that could be assembled annually at the 'Marchfield' and which could as easily be directed against internal dissidents as external foes. This, however, was a fairly clumsy weapon, whose utility was greatly reduced in periods of military crisis or political incompetence at the centre.

The best inducement that a king such as Charles could offer to win and maintain the loyalty of the leading families of Francia and the other regions under his rule was military success and the rewards that came from it.[30] Those who served in his expansionary campaigns could expect to profit from them, as their equivalents had in the time of Clovis and his sons. When, however, expansion stopped, as it did under Charles's son the Emperor Louis the Pious, and campaigning became defensive in nature, the interest of those who turned out to fight was blunted by the lack of expectation of profits and office, and they became increasingly aware that better opportunities might be offered in exploiting internal divisions within Francia or in promoting their own purely local concerns.[31]

Like Clovis, Charles did well for himself by an almost continuous process of expanding the frontiers and rewarding his Frankish following by the loot obtained in war and the offices that needed filling in the governing of conquered territories. On the other hand, both Clovis and even more so Charles left impossible legacies to their successors. No state could support itself on a process of indefinite expansion. New structures and institutions had to be created to provide a proper administration of the conquered territories and to absorb the energies of those who had hitherto depended on the profits of war for their sustenance.

Whatever else his achievements were, Charles made no significant improvements to the governmental apparatus of the greatly expanded kingdom that he himself had created. The actual central administration remained minimal, and consisted of no more than the ruler's immediate entourage. Those documents that were not left to their beneficiaries to produce were written for the king by the clerics of the royal chapel, which thus doubled as the governmental writing office.[32] Policies and military and administrative decisions were still made at the annual assemblies, and the king was able to oversee his local officials, notably the counts, only by means of special emissaries or *missi*, dispatched from the court to carry out enquiries and to report back on the functioning of the local administration. Decisions taken at the annual assemblies were also communicated to the peripheral counties through such *missi*. Such decisions and sets of instructions were not necessarily written, or were recorded only by a series of headings rather than in full.[33]

It would be unfair to suggest that Charles was unaware of these problems – though he would doubtless have expressed them differently – or that he did not have a well developed sense of his royal and subsequently imperial obligations. Indeed what is most impressive about the Carolingian regime at this time is the very high-minded nature of its declarations of principles. The putting of these into practical effect was not so easy, but the frequent failure to do so was not for want of the will to try.[34] The more frequent and more extensive use of *missi* was a sensible expedient in the light of the very real limitations that the restricted nature of existing administration forced on the king.

A bureaucracy could not be called into being by a simple declaration of the royal will. It depended, amongst other things, upon the prior existence of a sufficiently well-educated class of men able to understand the needs of an administrative system dependent upon writing. In Francia in this period such a knowledge of even the basic requirements of reading and writing was to be found only amongst the ranks of the clergy. Even there it seems much ignorance and illiteracy were to be found. According to Einhard, Charles himself only began to learn to write late in his life, and made but limited progress with it.[35]

At the same time, as is well evidenced in some of the capitularies – royal administrative orders to the *missi*, records of councils etc. – and in the light of the motivation given for some of the military campaigns, it is clear that Charles felt a strong sense of responsibility for the good order of the Church in his kingdom and of the interdependence of this and the secular well-being of the state. Thus, for these reasons relating to his conception of his office and the duties it entailed, and for the more practical needs of starting to develop a sufficiently extensive learned class, capable of undertaking the administrative tasks that the growing size and complexity of the Frankish kingdom demanded, the king and his advisers devoted themselves to ecclesiastical reform and a revival of learning.

The ideological programme

From such beginnings grew what is generally called 'the Carolingian Renaissance'. The title is not unfair. Just as in the Late Medieval Renaissance, what the scholars of this period achieved was a sustained attempt to recover and make use of some of the learning and the arts of Antiquity. That this was successful to a significant degree can be seen from the fact that most of the works of classical Latin authors that are known today have only survived thanks to their having been copied and preserved in manuscripts of Carolingian date.[36] However, the primary impetus was Christian and its motivation practical. The pagan content of much of the art and literature of the Roman past could still arouse unease in Charles and many of his advisors in the way that it had in Pope Gregory the Great.[37]

Also it should be recognised that the degree of literacy that Charles and his advisors sought to achieve was perhaps no more than the equivalent of that of the primary level of education in the time of the Roman Empire, and it was aimed principally at elevating the attainments of the clergy rather than at affecting wider sections of lay society.[38] Even so, such aspirations and the degree of their achievement need to be measured not so much in absolute terms as against the base from which they departed.

In particular, Charles was interested first of all in attracting into his entourage a selection of scholars to advise him and to invest his regime with the aura of intellectual sophistication associated with Late Roman and even some of the earlier Merovingian courts.[39] The conquest of the Lombard kingdom gave him access to the resources of learning in northern Italy, and the first major luminary of the court was the Deacon Peter of Pisa, who is reported to have instructed the king in (Latin) grammar.[40] Other notable Italians included Paul the Deacon, who had written a *Roman History* prior to the overthrow of the Lombard kingdom, and who was persuaded to stay for four years in Francia when he came in 782 to seek the release of his brother, who had been taken hostage after the revolt of Duke Hrodgaud of Friuli. During his stay in Francia he composed an account of the lives of the bishops of the see of Metz, including the important Carolingian ancestor St Arnulf, and he later prepared an edition of the *On the Meaning of Words* of Sextus Pompeius Festus, which he dedicated to Charles. His most famous work, the *History of the Lombards* was also written after his return from Francia in 786 and his entry into the monastery of Monte Cassino. It was probably intended for dedication to Duke Grimoald III of Benevento (787–806).[41]

The same period of the early 780s saw the arrival in Charles's entourage of two other foreign scholars: the Visigoth Theodulf, who was to become Bishop of Orléans (798–818) and the Deacon Alcuin from York (d. 804). The precise place of origin of Theodulf is uncertain. It used to be thought that he came from the former Visigothic region of Septimania in south-west Gaul, but it is possible that he arrived in Francia in the aftermath of Charles's failed intervention in the Ebro valley in 778 and was a native of the western Pyrenean region.[42] His most significant intellectual contribution was his almost certain authorship of much of the initial draft of the *Libri Carolini* (794).[43] He was also a skilled poet, with the rare distinction for his time of knowing the work of Ovid. He was implicated, perhaps falsely, in a conspiracy in 818 and died in disgrace in 821.

Alcuin is the best known of the scholars who surrounded the Frankish king.[44] He was a Northumbrian, educated at York, who rose to become head of its archiepiscopal school. It is possible that the survival of so many of his writings has somewhat distorted his significance in the Frankish context, and he may have been less frequently at court than was formerly believed. Although he may have met Charles in Italy in 781, he does not seem to have joined the court before 786 at the earliest. He was back in Northumbria again between 790 and 793, and after 796 he passed most of his time in the monastery of St Martin at Tours, whose abbacy he had just been given. He died there in 804.

A poet and theologian and teacher, Alcuin's influence has been detected in a number of the key texts produced at the Carolingian court, notably some of the most important of the capitularies. Some of his poetic and epistolary writings also illuminate aspects of the life of that court, even in such minor details as the nicknames that Alcuin gave to his colleagues. He most frequently addressed Charles himself in such works as 'David', referring to the Biblical monarch who was the effective founder of the kingdom of Israel and was, as the putative author of the Psalms, also a poet and scholar. The image of a Frankish king as a new David had in fact already been used in the Merovingian period, and was thus not original to Alcuin, but he gave it new and more extensive expression.

The preservation of a large corpus of Alcuin's letters, over three hundred in number, has made available an illuminating source of information on a wide range of aspects of the central period of Charles's reign, in particular from *c.* 789 to 802. He may also have had a role in the compiling of the *Libri Carolini*, and he was the principal spokesman in the dispute with Bishop Elipandus of Toledo over the latter's use of a heterodox terminology in writing of Christ's adoption of his human nature.[45] His Northumbrian origin also made him the natural spokesman for Charles's relations with the principal Anglo-Saxon kings of the period, notably Offa of Mercia (758–96).[46] He also became the principal teacher of the members of the noble families who were attached to the king's immediate following. It has also been suggested that his work *De Orthographia* was intended to initiate or assist in a revision of spelling and of the pronunciation of Latin throughout the Carolingian Empire.[47]

While each of these men offered different skills and provided individual expertise in such matters as the formulation of the king's theological views, the provision of textbooks that might be used to encourage the attainment of set goals of simple literacy amongst the clergy and so forth, overall the aim of the reforms was to impose standardised norms in such matters as grammatical education, liturgy, canon law and, subsequently, monastic observance. The norms were almost always those that could be drawn from Rome. Thus, the current version of the Gregorian Sacramentary, the papal Mass book of the Roman Church, was obtained from pope Hadrian I, as was the collection of ecclesiastical laws known as the 'Dionysio-Hadriana'.[48]

Although it is customary to speak of this group of scholars in the service of Charles as 'a court school', it is hard to understand what in practice might be meant by that term, particularly in the period prior to the establishment in 794 of Aachen as the king's favourite though by no means exclusive residence and centre of government. Much of the king's time was spent on campaign, and normally he and his entourage were peripatetic. However, a fairly extensive winter stay was passed each year at one or other of the royal residences, and it is probable that these were the occasions for Charles's meetings with his court scholars and other ecclesiastical advisers. It is clear, too, that they were a far from homogeneous group and were on occasion given to mutual jealousy and academic 'cattiness'.[49]

The achievements of Charles's advisors are perhaps most impressively displayed in the formulation of the objectives and the ideological basis of his regime. These are most clearly expounded in the royal capitularies, particularly those issued between the years 789 and 806.[50] The authors and inspirers of these various sets of instructions and decrees are nowhere named. Nor, unlike most other sets of early medieval charters, is it possible to build up a picture of Charles's entourage from the signatures appended to royal documents, as in the case of the Frankish series such attestations by witnesses were not recorded. Indeed from the court annals, themselves – significantly entirely anonymous, it is clear that the officially sponsored impression was to be that all major decisions and actions were taken and initiated by the king alone. It is possible to speculate, though, that leading roles were taken in practice by such figures as Archbishop Hildebald of Cologne (785–819), the arch-chaplain, and the Abbots Fardulf of Saint-Denis (792–806) and Angilbert of St Riquier (d. 814), and that, just as in the 790s Alcuin's influence was strong, so in the last years of the reign was that of the emperor's relatives Abbot Adalhard of Corbie and his brother Count Wala.[51]

The capitularies are not an easy body of documents to define, largely because their role as written texts is entirely secondary to the purposes for which their contents were originally formulated.[52] That is to say, they represent written records, full, partial or merely in note form, of administrative decisions and decrees delivered orally, and whose authority lay in their spoken rather than their written form. They could deal with a variety of subjects and could range from records of gatherings that were largely or almost exclusively ecclesiastical in composition, to sets of legal regulations that were promulgated to augment or modify the rules to be found in the various legal codes under which the inhabitants of the Frankish Empire lived. Such capitularies of laws 'added to the codes' concerned themselves exclusively with the two Frankish codes, the Salic and the Ripuarian, and in theory the Frankish ruler did not seek to alter the supposedly traditional laws of his other subjects. Other capitularies represent sets of instructions given to the *missi*, the royal officials sent to oversee and report on the working of the local administration of the Empire.

Because the authority behind the various rules, injunctions and instructions lay in the spoken word of the king, their recording was rather haphazard, and the subsequent preservation of the written versions again depended on individual initiatives. Abbot Ansegisis of Saint-Wandrille made one such collection of capitularies of various sorts in the late 820s in the time of the second Carolingian emperor, Louis the Pious.[53] It is possible that this was carried out at the request of the emperor and his advisers, who certainly made use of it on occasion, as no other mechanism existed whereby oral decrees made under previous rulers could be preserved for the use of future governments.

This lack of an established procedure for the written recording of the administrative and legal pronouncements of the Frankish rulers has nothing to do with Germanic traditions of oral law, but reflects identical problems to be encountered in the Late Roman Empire, in which no mechanisms existed to ensure the preservation and distribution of the imperial legal decisions made in the emperor's court, which thereby had the force of law.[54]

The capitulary known as the *Admonitio Generalis* or *General Encouragement* represents the records of a primarily ecclesiastical assembly held, probably at Aachen, in 789. The document consists of a collection of eighty-two canons drawn from the acts of many of the earlier Ecumenical councils of the Church (fourth to sixth centuries), which were here recast as royal decrees. Probably at the same time and place another set of injunctions were issued relating in large measure to aspects of monastic life.[55] What is so striking about this process is that it involved the secular power using its own procedures to issue what would previously have been regarded as purely ecclesiastical laws. For Charles and his advisers it seems that the need for monasteries to ensure that the right sort of monks were appointed to the office of cellarer was a matter of direct concern to the good working of the entire kingdom.

In their own minds the distinction made here between the secular interests of government and the discipline and order of the church would be incomprehensible. As Charles declared in the preamble to his *Admonitio Generalis*: 'Considering with the salutary judgement of a pious mind, together with our bishops and counsellors, the abundant clemency of Christ the King toward us and our people, and how necessary it is not only to render unceasing thanks to his goodness with all our heart and voice but also to devote ourselves to His praise by the continuous practice of good works, that He who has conferred such great honours on our realm may vouchsafe always to preserve us and it by His protection.'[56] Such a view had many precedents that stretch back to the earliest days of the Christian Roman Empire, but never before had the well-being of the state been so closely related to the proper observance of the minutiae of ecclesiastical regulations and discipline. The moral health of the Church in his territories was seen by Charles to be at the very heart of and indissolubly linked to the material prosperity of his empire.

In 792 the failure of a conspiracy directed against Charles at Regensburg by his illegitimate son Pippin (known as 'the Hunchback') led to a new and significant burst of legislative activity.[57] The conspirators, when accused of treason, apparently claimed that they had not taken any oath of loyalty to Charles, and were therefore not guilty of perfidy in plotting against him. In consequence in 793 Charles sent out panels of *missi*, normally consisting of an abbot or bishop and a count, to require all of the bishops, abbots, counts, principal landholders and other lesser officials both secular and ecclesiastical of his kingdom to take such an oath of loyalty.[58]

Although their not having made such an undertaking did not protect the conspirators of 792 from punishment – 'Some were hanged, some beheaded, some flogged and exiled' (*Chronicle of Moissac*) – it was clearly felt that the lack of direct personal ties between the ruler and his principal subjects could lead to the hatching of such plots, which threatened the stability of the kingdom. It was not just that such actions were politically unsettling, but as the contemporary Lorsch annalist saw it, for a king to achieve power through the murder, as was planned in 792, of his own father and brothers was bound to lead to divine vengeance that could affect the whole realm.[59]

The bishops gathered with Charles at Regensburg also decreed, as recorded in another capitulary of the spring of 793, that they would all say three special masses: one for the king, one for the army and one for help in this 'present tribulation'.[60] They also ordered the holding of a two-day fast on the part of all the clergy and all landowners, together with graduated sums that were to be given in alms by all bishops, abbots, abbesses, counts and royal vassals. A kingdom-wide act of reparation and penance was thus clearly envisaged as being needed to atone for the threat to the divine ordering of their society that was represented by the conspiracy of Pippin the Hunchback and his associates.

The same set of ideas influenced another burst of capitulary-producing activity that followed Charles's return from Italy in late 801 and may give some idea of his reflections on the significance of his new imperial title. In 802, following a great assembly at Aachen, he sent out panels of *missi* with instructions both to investigate and to rectify any cases of injustice and also to require the taking of a new oath, similar to that made to Charles as king in 793, but this time addressed to him as emperor. Unlike that of 793, the text of this oath, in two versions, is preserved in an abbreviated version of the main capitulary, probably drawn up for one of the panels of *missi*. The fuller version of the decrees, because it lays down a whole new ideological framework for the relations between ruler and ruled, has come to be known as the 'Programmatic Capitulary'.[61] The oath of 793 had only to be taken by major office-holders and landowners, but the oath of 802 was to be taken by all men aged twelve and above, though whether this was achieved in practice is not known. A subsequent capitulary, issued at Thionville in 805, forbade the taking of oaths of loyalty to anyone other than the monarch.[62]

The implications of the oath of loyalty were, however, interpreted by Charles and his advisers as being far more extensive than just a promise not to conspire against the ruler's person or against the security of his kingdom, together with an obligation not to conceal any knowledge of proposed infidelity on the part of others. In the capitulary of 802 the *missi* were instructed to expound and explain the wider implications of the oath to all those to whom they administered it. It was to be taken to mean that each individual thereby promised 'to strive to the best of his understanding and ability to maintain himself fully in God's holy service', and that he would refrain from a whole series of acts that were seen to be detrimental to the material welfare of the ruler.[63] Thus, by the stated interpretation of the new oath contained in the 'Programmatic Capitulary', it became an act of disloyalty to move a boundary marker on lands owned by the emperor, to disregard any imperial order, or not to pay any rent owed to him.[64] It also became an act of disloyalty and the breaking of faith not to turn out for the required period of military service.

What might seem like relatively harmless offences thus became acts of high treason, and liable to capital punishment, because they were now seen as being breaches in the compact made between ruler and ruled that was created by the taking of the oath. Even more striking is the way that any malpractice in the administration of justice was similarly taken as an act of infidelity. This could involve trying to argue on behalf of someone known to be guilty or failing to testify to the best of one's ability for someone believed innocent. The responsibilities of judges were strongly and frequently reaffirmed.[65] It is clear that for Charles and his advisers the continuance of divine support for the emperor and his regime was intimately connected to the maintenance of true justice for all of his subjects.

The implications of these lines of thinking were worked out in considerable detail, and their consequences drawn in relation to a number of areas. Thus in a document normally classified as a capitulary but which generically takes the form of a letter, addressed to Abbot Baugulf of Fulda, and probably dating to the later 790s, Charles worries about the effects of monks not being able to express themselves in a grammatically correct fashion – 'those who seek to please God by right living may not neglect to please Him also by right speaking'. More serious consequences still could attend upon such mistakes as the king had found in a large number of letters that he had recently received from monasteries: 'Wherefore it came about that we began to fear lest, as skill in writing was deficient, so also wisdom for understanding the holy scriptures might perchance be less than it ought properly to be.'[66] From this, in turn, could spring doctrinal error – heresy – and that would incur divine displeasure, and the threat of disaster for ruler and kingdom alike.

It was such a belief that made Charles and such ecclesiastical advisers as Alcuin so anxious to act against the perceived threat of heresy in the acceptance by one bishop in the Frankish-ruled eastern Pyrenees of the Adoptionist theology developed by Elipandus of Toledo. There was in practice probably little prospect that Felix of Urgel would win over more adherents in Francia, but the very existence of a single dissentient mind in the episcopate was seen to threaten the required doctrinal uniformity of the Church in Charles's territories. So the bishops assembled for the council held at Frankfurt in 794 'rejected and unanimously denied adoption and decreed that this heresy must be wholly eradicated from the holy church'.[67]

This ideological thoroughness is one of the most striking features of the reign of Charles. In part it may be seen as the nearest that the Carolingian rulers ever came to trying to work out a system of public obligation that would in practice compensate for the inadequacy of the governmental and bureaucratic structures of their Empire. They could not rely on the notions of citizenship and legal obligations that had helped underpin the Roman Empire. Nor did they even try to establish a political consensus around a reformed common cultural identity. Instead they tried to create ties of personal loyalty on the part of subjects towards their ruler, based on the sanctity of oaths, using a set of ideas that can be traced back to Rome and to the Christian writers of the fourth century. In practice, though, this was not going to be sufficient to hold together the heterogeneous group of territories and peoples forced into political unity in consequence of Charles's campaigns of the 770s–790s.

17 Frontier societies: Christian Spain, 711–1037

The Christians of Al-Andalus

The Arab and Berber conquest of the Iberian peninsula that had commenced in 711 had been extremely rapid. By 714 the conquerors had reached the Ebro valley, sacking Zaragoza, its principal city, and in 720 they crossed the Pyrenees, and eliminated a vestigial Visigothic kingdom centred on Narbonne. In part the lack of sustained resistance that they encountered prior to their first attacks on Aquitaine in 721 was a reflection of the previously peaceful and also relatively centralised nature of the Spanish Visigothic kingdom. There had not been the kind of external threats to the integrity of the realm in the seventh century that had been faced in the sixth, and unlike that of Francia, the society of Visigothic Spain had not needed to be one that was primarily organised for war. The Iberian peninsula also benefited from naturally defensible land frontiers, which were far removed from the principal court centre of Toledo.

In such circumstances difficulties had been experienced by some of the Visigothic kings in trying to mobilise forces even for small-scale campaigning, primarily in response to Basque raids and in the course of disputed royal successions.[1] There were thus only limited and slowly mobilised military resources available to deploy against the invaders or to be used in protracted resistance to the conquest. At the same time, the special status of the *urbs regia* of Toledo, the only site in which the rituals of royal inauguration could be carried out for a legitimate king, made the rapid fall of the city to the invaders a fatal blow to any hope of raising a centrally organised opposition.[2]

The Arab accounts of the conquest are all to be found in sources of much later date, and although some of these make use of the work of earlier writers, whose accounts may otherwise be lost, none of the latter are earlier than the later ninth century in date. Nor, in the light of what is known of the general development of historiography amongst the Arabs, could we expect this to be otherwise.[3] There are real problems, some hardly yet recognised, in the tradition and transmission of some of these texts, and problems of interpolation and deliberate distortion and invention for ideologically inspired reasons have been detected in some sources, including the earliest.[4] While these difficulties decline, though are far from eliminated, as the gap narrows between the periods being written about and those in which the first extant Arab historians were working, this still leaves the eighth and most of the ninth centuries as evidential minefields as far as Spain is concerned.

There is one contemporary Latin account that can provide a way into understanding some of the history of the peninsula in the first half of the eighth century. This is the text known as the *Mozarabic Chronicle* or *Chronicle of 754*, which was probably composed in Toledo by an anonymous cleric some time close to the year 754, which is that of the last event that the work records. From this text it has been possible to deduce something of the pattern of events and the major developments in Arab rule in the four decades following the conquest.[5]

The rule of the governors that lasted from the conquest up to the Umayyad *coup d'état* in 756, which established an independent Arab monarchy in Al-Andalus, falls into distinct periods. The earliest of these saw almost continuous fighting, with the conquest being extended to and then across the Pyrenees. At this time predominantly Berber garrisons were established in a small number of major cities in Spain, but most areas were permitted to retain autonomy under local leadership in return for political submission and the payment of regular tribute. The latter was fixed by the terms of the more or less standardised treaty of capitulation made between the conquerors and local officials.[6]

Within ten years governors, who were still appointed by the Umayyad caliphs in Damascus and were subordinate to the *wali* or governor of North Africa (*Ifriqiya*), had begun to extend their own authority over conquerors and conquered alike and impose centralised administrative and judicial processes. In 731/2 the first Berber revolt broke out, amongst garrisons in the eastern Pyrenees, fuelled by accounts of conflicts that were intensifying in North Africa. The outbreak of a major revolt amongst the Berbers in Africa in 739/40 led to a parallel rising in Spain. This was crushed after some hard fighting thanks to the arrival of a relief force sent from Syria. The members of the latter then remained in Al-Andalus, and friction was generated between them and the longer-established Arabs, exacerbated by the escalation of factional conflicts and tribal rivalries in the Near East in the mid 740s.[7] These contributed directly to the 'Abbasid revolt of 749, which led the following year to the overthrow of the Umayyad caliphate.[8]

In Spain close links between the first generation of Arab settlers and their counterparts in North Africa, together with a virtual break-down in communications with Egypt and Syria due to the civil wars that had broken out there, led to the establishment of a *de facto* independent government in 746. This lasted until it was overthrown ten years later by a combination of opposition groups who rallied together around the person of 'Abd al-Rahman b. Mu'awiya, a fugitive member of the former Umayyad dynasty, who had escaped the massacre of his family in Syria in 750. Although able to overthrow the last of the independent governors and establish himself as amir or king in Córdoba, it took him over twenty years to extend his authority over all of the regions of the peninsula that were still under Arab and Berber occupation.[9]

The power of the Umayyad rulers fluctuated considerably over the next two centuries. In some periods it shrank to little more than control over the Guadalquivir valley and its principal cities of Córdoba and Seville. The former remained the capital, and enjoyed the patronage of the amirs, who built numerous palaces and mosques in or close to the city. The most famous of these is the Mezquita, now the cathedral of Córdoba, whose gradual enlargement in stages extending from its foundation by 'Abd al-Rahman in 786 up to the dictatorship of the *Hajib* or Grand Vizier Al-Mansur (d. 1002) testifies to the growth of the Muslim population of the city.

The questions of how far and with what rapidity the indigenous Romano-Gothic population converted to Islam is not easy to resolve, in that there is little hard evidence available. One significant and very influential attempt to resolve these problems based itself upon a study of the changing patterns of names in the families of those Muslims of non-Arab descent who were included in the great medieval biographical encyclopaedias. In most cases the names of several generations of ancestors were included. By noting the point in such genealogies in which family names first became clearly Arabic or Muslim, it proved possible to produce graphs of the rate at which conversions took place in the major regions of the Islamic world. Not surprisingly in the light of all other available evidence, in Al-Andalus the later tenth and eleventh centuries saw the sharpest rise in the level of conversion.[10] However, this can only be used as a yardstick in measuring the rate of conversion amongst those families that did actually change their religion. It can not show what percentage of the total non-Arab population of Al-Andalus converted. Thus, even if there were a sharp rise in conversion in the tenth and eleventh centuries, there could still have been a Christian majority amongst the population as a whole.

Indeed, when the Arab traveller and geographical writer Ibn Hawqal visited Al-Andalus in 948, he reported that the population of the countryside was still predominantly Christian.[11] Although some want to deny it, there is no evidence that can be produced to contradict his claim, which is in any case perfectly credible and reasonable. The greatest pressure or incentive to convert was likely to be felt in towns, above all in Córdoba. This was particularly the case for the educated classes, who might expect to earn their living in Umayyad government service. It is clear from the accounts of the Arab historians that it was often possible for educated Christians to reach the upper levels of the bureaucracy, as well as serving in specialised but highly prestigious posts such as those of the ruler's doctor.[12]

On the other hand, there were periods when the amirs insisted that only Muslims could fill such positions. This was particularly true in the reign of Muhammad I (852–86), in the aftermath of the 'Martyr Movement'. This had been a short-lived period of confrontation in the 840s and 850s, confined almost entirely to Córdoba, in which a group of Christians had deliberately sought judicial execution by publicly reviling the prophet Muhammad and Islam. They sought to emulate the sufferings of the early Christian martyrs, and the accounts of their deaths were written up in conscious imitation of the Late Roman martyr acts. Amongst the leaders of this movement were the priest (and later titular Bishop of Toledo) Eulogius and the layman Paul Alvar. They were responsible for composing most of the descriptions of the martyrdoms, and Alvar wrote a *Life of Eulogius* after his friend's own execution in 859.[13]

The causes of this outbreak of religious conflict are varied, but may reflect conditions that were peculiar to Córdoba or were especially strongly felt in the Umayyad capital.[14] One definite element was the pressure felt within families of mixed religion. While under Islamic law it was forbidden to a Christian to marry a Muslim wife, the opposite arrangement was fully tolerated, but the children of such a union had to be brought up as Muslims. As several of the martyr acts reveal, in such cases the children of a Christian mother could, for whatever reasons, prefer her faith to that of their Muslim father, but they were forbidden from expressing it openly. Others who openly defied Islam in this period were members of the still numerous monastic communities that existed in and around Córdoba, not least in the mountainous zone immediately to the north of the city.

Such monasteries were probably also the principal preservers of Christian Latin culture in Al-Andalus. A remark in one of the works of Alvar apparently despairing at the degree to which the Christian community of Córdoba had become Arabised in language and literary taste has often been interpreted as indicating a rapid decline in the use of Latin.[15] This in turn implies an increasing loss of access to the Christian Latin literary heritage of Late Antiquity.

The Martyr Movement and a rather more peaceful if limited attempt on the part of Eulogius to foster a Latin poetic revival in Córdoba in the early 850s are taken to be reactions to this threat to the survival of Christian Latin culture under Muslim rule.[16]

Such a view underestimates the degree to which Latin continued in use in Christian circles in the south long after the period of the Martyr Movement. Beautifully inscribed and linguistically complex Latin funerary inscriptions continued to be carved in many parts of Al-Andalus even as late as the first quarter of the twelfth century. Latin manuscripts continued to be copied, and even a handful of new works were composed in the language in the same period.[17] There is increasing evidence of bilingualism, but Latin remained central to the Christian identity in the south, up to the time of the deportation of the surviving Christian communities to Morocco by the Almoravids in 1126.[18]

This should be a matter of little surprise, in that much diminished Christian communities in the area of modern Tunisia were still both existing and using Latin in their occasional contacts with the fellow believers in the West at least up to the time of Pope Gregory VII (1073–85).[19]

By this time, however, a major movement of population had already taken place in Spain. In consequence of the more restrictive and confrontational climate that developed, at least in Córdoba, in the aftermath of the Martyr Movement, and also of the period of intense local disorder and conflict that spread over virtually all of the south in the second half of the ninth century, Christians in Al-Andalus began, as individuals and groups, to migrate northwards.

It is impossible to quantify this movement, which is best documented by the spread of the distinctive style of building and of manuscript illumination, much influenced by contemporary developments in Islamic art, that the refugees took with them. This can be seen in a series of churches and chapels that they built in the tenth and eleventh centuries in an area extending from Galicia to the eastern Pyrenees, as well as in a small but significant body of manuscripts.[20]

These Christian refugees are generally known as the Mozarabs, a name taken from an Arabic word for non-Arab Muslims who had absorbed the culture of their conquerors. It is thus not technically correct to apply it to the southern Christians who had absorbed much Arab culture but had not changed their religion, but it has become accepted usage.[21]

It is by no means clear if those Mozarabs who migrated north were primarily clerics and monks, or whether the unsettled conditions in the south, which were marked by increasing inter-religious conflict and violence, also prompted significant numbers of the urban and rural Christian laity to flee northwards as well. Of those that remained, the descendants of some would pass under the rule of Christian kings as the Castillian and Aragonese kingdoms extended themselves into the middle of the peninsula from the mid-eleventh century onwards.

Those in the Guadalquivir valley and areas further south, however, would be those deported *en masse* by the Almoravids in 1126. This was an event that put an end to the continuity both of Christian traditions in southern Spain and to occupation of a wide range of settlement sites all across the region. The Mozarabs who had fled north in the earlier period had by the twelfth century begun to lose their distinctive identity and were being absorbed into the societies that had formed on the frontiers between Al-Andalus and the Christian realms.

The kingdoms of northern Spain, *c*. 718–910

It is clear from the course of events in the first half of the eighth century that the Muslims were little concerned with the north-west of the peninsula. Their initial direction of conquest was from the south-west to the north-east, along the clearly defined routes, conditioned by the mountainous geography of many parts of Spain, that had been followed by the Romans in creating their extensive system of roads. An alternative line of advance, up the Roman road that linked Seville to Mérida, Salamanca, León and the Asturias may have been used early on to impose a rapid subjection of the north-west, but this region was in geographical terms a dead-end, providing no opportunities for further expansion. Although once famed for its gold mines, it now offered relatively few economic inducements to the conquerors to make them invest their relatively limited resources of manpower in retaining control of an area of predominantly difficult mountainous terrain that seemed to promise few advantages and no serious threats.

With the advantage of hindsight it could be said that the Arabs lack of concern with the securing of this region was the one fatal mistake that nearly eight hundred years later would lead to the complete elimination of the final, much-diminished enclaves of Muslim rule in the peninsula. This is not to endorse older views of the *Reconquista* that saw it as a sustained Hispano-Christian resistance to an alien Islamic rule, that was initiated in the Asturias, developed in León and brought to triumphant conclusion by the rulers and people of Castille, who thereby earned a right to political and cultural hegemony over the whole peninsula.[22] Even so, the failure or inability of the Arab conquerors to retain their hold over the whole of the former Visigothic kingdom created centres of opposition that survived to exploit periods of weakness and division amongst the rulers of the south, with ultimately fatal consequences for the latter.

The first of these small Christian states to come into existence was a small kingdom based in the west of the Asturias, the mountainous region paralleling the centre of the northern coast of the peninsula. The history of its creation obviously became the stuff of legends in subsequent centuries, and no extant sources for these events date from before the late ninth century. These take the form of very brief chronicles composed in the 880s, but which were subject to revision and expansion in the next century.[23] The earliest of these is the *Chronicle of Albelda*, which from references in the text seems to have been compiled in or very soon after the year 883. Although this was not the place of composition of the original version, the work has received its name from the Riojan monastery in which a brief continuation of the work was composed in 976.

A second, slightly more substantial chronicle was composed in the Asturias probably not long after the compiling of the first version of the *Chronicle of Albelda* in 883. This is the work called the *Chronicle of Alfonso III*. It survives in two rather different forms, known as the *ad Sebastianum* and the Roda versions. The former was apparently given its present shape in the reign of Alfonso's son García I (910–13/14), but there is no early manuscript tradition for it. In this version the text is prefaced by a letter from Alfonso III (866–910) to a Bishop Sebastian, which if accepted as authentic establishes the king's authorship of the work. The other version, which is preserved in more numerous and earlier manuscripts than is the case with its rival, takes its name from the oldest of them, once the property of the Pyrenean see of Roda de Isábena. It may be textually the closer of the two versions to the lost original form of the work.[24]

By the time these chronicles were being composed in the Asturias in the 880s, the crucial victory that secured the kingdom's independence of Arab rule had become firmly associated with a miraculous intervention. This would receive further elaboration in twelfth century and later texts. Even the two versions of the *Chronicle of Alfonso III* contain lengthy passages of dialogue between the Christian leader and a treacherous bishop who was in collusion with the Arabs, that are quite out of keeping with the extreme brevity and un-literary character of the rest of the work.[25] It is thus not easy to recover the prosaic reality as opposed to the legend of the revolt in the Asturias.

It was led, according to tradition by a certain Pelagius, a Visigothic noble who had taken refuge in the north and who, according

to the *ad Sebastianum* version of the *Chronicle of Alfonso III*, was of
royal descent. What prompted the revolt is not clear. The Albelda
chronicler sees the objective as the restoration of liberty to the
Christians of the Asturias, and the Roda version of the Alfonso III
chronicle spins a tale involving the lecherous designs of a (Berber)
governor of Gijón called Munnuzza on Pelagius's sister.[26] Both
interpretations sound equally anachronistic, albeit in contrasting
ways. However, all of the chronicles concur in reporting Pelagius's
victory over Munnuzza, who from his name would have been a
Berber. The location of the battle at Covadonga, later the site of
a major Marian shrine, derives from the information in both
versions of the *Chronicle of Alfonso III*.

Just how seriously the Arabs took this uprising is hard to gauge,
as no mention is made of it in their accounts of this period. A
Berber garrison at Gijón on the Biscay coast was isolated and distant, and of no real military significance. It is not even easy to date
the revolt, and the traditional chronology, which would place it in
the year 718, derives entirely from deductions made from later
regnal lists. An alternative case has been made out for the year
722, but no absolute certainty can be attached to either date.[27]

Largely because no significant response was made to the revolt,
probably because the Muslims were currently concerned with their
campaigns in the Pyrenean region, Pelagius established a small
kingdom in the Asturias in the aftermath of his victory. The first
capital was at Cangas de Onis. But hardly anything else is recorded
of Pelagius's reign, until his death in 737. After his son Fafila
(737–39) was killed by a bear, Pelagius's son-in-law Alfonso I
(739–57) was chosen king by the Asturian nobles. It has to be
confessed that nothing is known about the origins, number or
social and economic standing of this aristocracy in this period.[28]

Although presented as the outcome of an unforeseen accident,
the accession of the new king probably resulted in a significant
extension of the territory of the still diminutive Asturian kingdom.
Alfonso's father, Peter, is said to have been the Duke of Cantabria,
the region to the east of the Asturias. Whether this title was a
vestige of the Visigothic administrative system or represented
some form of independent territorial authority can not be known,
but the uniting of the Asturias and Cantabria seems to have
strengthened the fledgling kingdom.

Under Alfonso I and his son Fruela I 'the Cruel' (757–68), the
frontiers of the Asturian monarchy were extended westwards into
Galicia and eastwards into the Basque regions between the Upper
Ebro and the Biscay coast. In neither case should it be assumed
that the inhabitants welcomed Asturian conquest as a liberation
by fellow Christians.[29] The Basques, other than those living in the

handful of towns of Roman origin in the western Pyrenees, seem to have remained largely free of direct Arab rule, and Berber garrisons in Galicia had already been withdrawn, probably as a result of the Berber revolts in North Africa, southern Spain and the eastern Pyrenees.

During the period of turmoil in the south in the 730s and 740s, Alfonso I of the Asturias is said to have been able to capture many of the towns of the Meseta, the high plateau that encompasses most of the inland area of the north-western quarter of the Iberian peninsula.[30] This was bounded to the south by the mountains of the Sierra de Guadarrama, beyond which lay Toledo, Talavera and Mérida, which had significant Berber garrisons. On the Meseta itself were several formerly important Roman towns, such as León and Astorga in the north and Avila, Segovia and Salamanca towards the southern edge.

According to the Asturian historiographical tradition of the late ninth century, Alfonso and Fruela after him were able to capture and depopulate virtually all of the major settlements of the Meseta. The towns themselves were left abandoned and their inhabitants were taken back into the Asturias to help populate the kingdom, leaving their old territory as a deserted *cordon sanitaire* between Christian north and Muslim south. This area would only be repopulated from the late ninth century onwards as the frontiers of the Asturian kingdom were finally pushed southwards.

The difficulty with this view of events, which has dominated the study of this period of Spanish history for a hundred years or more, is that it does not entirely make sense, and the literary evidence on which it is based gives signs of being conditioned by the particular circumstances of the later period from which it dates.

Other lines of enquiry have cast increasing doubt on the reality of the mid-eighth century depopulation of the Meseta, which can not be matched by any proof of a simultaneous major repopulating of the Asturias.[31] The impression given by the chronicles that the region had been conquered by the Asturian monarchy in the mid-eighth century particularly served the interests of Alfonso I's late ninth and early tenth century successors, at a time when they were establishing an expanding control over much of it and were redistributing it at will to favoured individuals and religious institutions. In other words, this tale of conquest and depopulation established the legal right of the later kings to impose their authority over these lands and treat it as theirs to dispose of.

It may well be that Asturian campaigns in the time of Alfonso I and Fruela I were less wide-ranging, frequent and successful than the later chroniclers claimed, particularly as far as the southern sections of the Meseta were concerned. Here the best

archaeological evidence for continuity across this supposed period of depopulation has been found in settlements such as Avila
and Segovia.[32]

The end of the reign of Alfonso I also saw major changes taking
place in *Al-Andalus*. In 756 the Umayyad refugee 'Abd al-Rahman
crossed from Africa and overthrew the regime of Yusuf al-Fikri.
However, it took him nearly twenty years to establish his control
over the centre of the peninsula and to begin extending it into
the Ebro valley. As with the earlier governors, it is notable that
this was the direction in which he clearly saw his interests as lying,
in preference to an advance into the less economically and militarily interesting north-west.

The resulting continuing lack of large-scale military response
from the south allowed the Asturian kingdom to develop territorially and institutionally in relative tranquillity for most of the
century. It did, though, encounter internal conflicts of its own,
that are all too briefly recorded in the chronicles. Fruela I earned
his nickname by murdering, for reasons that are never explained,
his brother, Vimara. This led rapidly to his own assassination in
768, and the passing over of his infant son, in favour of another
adult member of the dynasty, the late king's nephew Aurelius
(768–73). In his reign there occurred a servile revolt, of which
nothing is known other than that it was suppressed.[33]

A series of short reigns followed that of Aurelius, at the inception of each of which Fruela's son Alfonso was prevented from
succeeding, probably because of his age, and possibly because of
the feuds engendered by his father's murder. The most notable
feature of this period, extending to the end of the 780s, was the
transfer of the capital from Cangas to Santianes de Pravía in the
reign of Silo (774–83). The same king issued the first extant
Asturian royal charter, endowing a new monastery.[34] This is also
one of the earliest of any of the Spanish documentary records of
the post-Visigothic period. Such texts start to become much more
numerous in the second half of the ninth century, but many of
them present problems of authenticity. Of the eighty charters of
all kinds purporting to date from before the reign of Alfonso III
(866–910), a very high percentage are either forgeries entirely
concocted in later periods or may have been interpolated.[35]

On the death of Silo, his widow Adosinda had hoped to secure
the long-delayed succession of the young Alfonso, but was thwarted
by a noble faction that gave the throne instead to an illegitimate son
of Alfonso I called Mauregatus. On his death in 788, the same or a
similar group brought about the installation of yet another member
of the family, by the name of Vermudo, later to be known as 'the
Monk'.

The death in the same year of the Umayyad ruler 'Abd al-Rahman I would, however, lead to the securing of the Asturian throne for Alfonso. A succession crisis developed in the south, with some of 'Abd al-Rahman's brothers challenging the authority of his designated successor, his son Hisham I (788–96). When the latter had finally secured himself after two years of conflict, he launched the first of series of annual expeditions against the Christian states in the north, both the Asturian kingdom and the Frankish enclave around Gerona on the eastern fringes of the Pyrenees.[36]

These do not seem to have been intended as systematic campaigns of conquest, unlike those of the earlier eighth century. Instead they were intended to inflict damage, take captives and carry off loot from the Christian territories. One of the first of these great raids achieved all three objectives when it penetrated the Asturias in 791. Vermudo I tried to resist and was heavily defeated. In the aftermath he abdicated, or may even have been compelled so to do, and the throne was given instead to Alfonso II (791–842).

The latter's long reign is usually seen as marking a fundamental change in the nature of the Asturian kingdom, symbolised by the move to yet another new capital. Here in Oviedo Alfonso is said to have commanded that 'the whole order of the Goths, as it had been in Toledo' should be established 'as much in the church as in the palace'.[37] This statement concludes the Albelda chronicler's description of the churches of San Salvador, Santa María and San Tirso which Alfonso II built in Oviedo, and it could just be a reference to artistic style. In other words the king had his new buildings decorated in the ways that had been fashionable in Visigothic Toledo.

On the other hand, it has often been argued or assumed that the phrases referring to 'the order of the Goths' do not tell us about Alfonso's artistic taste but constitute a statement of constitutional principles.[38] In other words, what the chronicler was trying to say was that Alfonso II imposed not just the aesthetics of Visigothic Toledo on his new capital, but also its character, traditions and ethos. Thus, what may be said about the Visigothic kingdom in terms of its law, the structure of government, the organisation of palatine administration, and the nature and functioning of ecclesiastical institutions, might also be taken to be true of the Asturian kingdom from the time of Alfonso II onwards.

This would seem also to imply that such Visigothic rules and procedures had not previously existed in the Asturias in the time of his predecessors. This important change, it has been argued, must mark the influence of exiles and fugitives from the south, bringing with them the essentially alien ideas and practices of the

Visigothic past. By this line of reasoning, once firmly adhered to in mainstream Spanish historiography, the Asturians was assumed to have resisted cultural absorption in the preceding Roman and Visigothic periods and to have retained exclusive indigenous social and political traditions of their own. Thus not until the time of Alfonso II, abetted by southern incomers, was the Visigothic imprint finally imposed on these independent northerners.[39]

In fact no corroborative evidence exists to support the idea that Alfonso II's reign saw any change, let alone marked a watershed, in the political or administrative organisation of the Asturian kingdom. The greater probability must lie with the view outlined above, that what the chronicler was referring to in speaking of the *Ordo Gothorum* was metropolitan artistic taste rather than administrative and legal reform.

New cultural currents may indeed have been making themselves felt in the Asturias at this time, but they came from the north rather than from the south. In 797 Alfonso II is known to have made diplomatic contact with Charlemagne, sending the Frankish ruler some spoils from a successful raid on Lisbon.[40]

While Frankish cultural influences may have continued to be felt, the diplomatic links seem to have been short-lived. When Charles established a significant Frankish presence in the eastern Pyrenees with the conquest of Barcelona in 801, there is no reference at this time to exchanges of envoys with Oviedo or any co-ordination of military activity, as had occurred in 797. This may be due to the fact that Alfonso was briefly driven from his throne in a coup at some point that can not be precisely dated, but was certainly around 801. Alfonso himself took refuge with Basque relatives of his mother, but was soon recalled to Oviedo when an aristocratic faction loyal to him murdered the unnamed usurper and seized the palace.[41]

The latter part of the reign of Alfonso II has left little record of itself, even in the Asturian chronicles, but at this time another, much smaller Christian state came into being in the north of Spain. This was the kingdom of Pamplona, or of Navarre as it later became known. Like that of the Asturias, this kingdom came into being in consequence of a revolt. In this case, though, it was directed against the Franks rather than the Arabs.

Left defenceless by Charlemagne on his retreat from the Ebro valley in 778, Pamplona had soon reverted to Arab control, but was captured by the forces of King Louis of Aquitaine in 806. Following earlier unsuccessful risings a rebellion in 824 put an end to Frankish rule. This was confirmed by the second battle of Roncesvalles later that year, when a Frankish punitive expedition was defeated and the two counts who led it were captured. The independent kingdom of Pamplona that emerged was ruled by a local Basque dynasty, founded by Iñigo Arista, until it was replaced by another ruling family in 905.[42] Relatively little is known of the history of the kingdom in the ninth century, as it produced no chronicles or annals.

The same is equally true as far as tenth century Navarrese history is concerned, but occasional mention in Arab sources and in the records of the neighbouring Leonese kingdom, successor to that of the Asturias, provides some illumination. It is clear that in both the ninth and the tenth centuries the rulers of Pamplona were willing to enter into close relations with the Muslims, particularly the often autonomous local rulers of the upper Ebro valley.[43] Iñigo Arista entered into marriage ties with the first and most powerful of these, the Banu Qasi, and the two dynasties supported each other both against the Umayyads and against the Christian Franks and Asturians.[44] The Asturians had ambitions to expand westwards into the Basque-speaking regions of the upper Ebro, with which at least one of their kings, Alfonso II, had family ties.

Up to the present, Alfonso II of the Asturias has been known in the Spanish historiographical tradition as 'Alfonso the Chaste', because he is never recorded as either marrying or producing offspring. This is mentioned with apparent approval in the later ninth century Asturian chroniclers, but it was never turned, for ideological, political or other reasons into a means of presenting the king as a man of great piety, let alone a candidate for sanctity. It is impossible now to judge what his personal motives might have been, and to some extent they may be considered irrelevant, in that numerous medieval monarchs entered into marriages for reasons of political convenience and the production of heirs was normally taken as central to the security and stability of the realm.

It may be speculated, as it has in the case of the sons of Edward the Elder who succeeded each other on the throne of Wessex in the first half of the tenth century, that some kind of compact had been made whereby Alfonso secured the throne in 791 in return for an agreement not to produce heirs of his own.[45] It is also possible, although the sources give no hint of this, that he had been forced into clerical orders at some point during the long period in which he was prevented from succeeding his father. Vermudo I was said to have been a deacon prior to his accession in 788, and his desire to return to the clerical state was used as the justification for his abdication in 791.

It is notable that on Alfonso's death in 842, it was a son of Vermudo I by the name of Ramiro who thought that he had a prescriptive right to succeed. He was, however, absent from Oviedo at the time, undertaking a second marriage on his estates in Galicia, and the throne was taken by a nephew of Alfonso II called Nepotian.[46] He may indeed have been his uncle's preferred heir, but the greater weight of noble support lay behind Ramiro, who rapidly defeated and blinded his rival.

Already elderly, Ramiro I (842–50) enjoyed only a short reign, but his triumph ensured the possession of the throne by his branch of the royal house for nearly two centuries. He himself is recorded as constructing a palace complex on the slopes of Monte Naranco, immediately to the north of Oviedo. Elements of this can still be seen, in the form of a barrel-vaulted hall (later converted into the church of Santa María de Naranco) and the western end of the palace chapel (now known as San Miguel de Lillo).[47] He was also called a 'rod of justice' by the Albelda chronicler for the penalties he imposed on wrongdoers, including the blinding of thieves and the burning of practitioners of magic. If this implies that he produced new laws, no trace of these have otherwise survived. The Visigothic code, known as the *Forum Iudicum* continued to be enforced, and although several manuscripts of it have survived that date from the ninth and tenth centuries, none contains any new enactments by the Asturian and Leonese kings.

Ramiro had faced an attempted usurpation in the course of his reign, as well as Nepotian's bid for the throne at the commencement of it, but his son Ordoño I (850–66) succeeded without opposition. In his reign the Asturian kingdom, which had hitherto expanded almost exclusively westwards and eastwards into Galicia and the Basque regions, took its first tentative steps towards the occupation of the northern fringes of the Meseta. This meant the re-establishment of settlements, such as the old Roman legionary fortresses of León and Astorga, which were located in much more militarily exposed sites to the south of the Asturian and Cantabrian mountains. Raids were also made across the Meseta and through the passes of the Guadarrama.

Such a rapid expansion in the extent and power of the Asturian kingdom was made possible by the increasingly disturbed condition of Al-Andalus. Under Muhammad I (852–86), al-Mundhir (886–8) and 'Abdallah (888–912), the central authority of the amirs of Córdoba declined rapidly in the face of revolts, banditry, and the establishment of local potentates across most parts of the south and centre of the peninsula.[48]

One of the first and most powerful of the latter was Musa ibn Musa, a member of the Banu Qasi, a family of indigenous origin that had converted to Islam, which had long dominated the upper Ebro valley. From initial deference to the Umayyads, in whose name he had originally governed Tudela, Musa moved to outright defiance and the building up of a territorial state in virtue of which he came to be described as 'the third king of Spain'.[49]

Based on the south-eastern fringes of Ordoño's kingdom, the territory controlled by Musa constituted a nearer and more active threat to the Asturias than the weakened Amirate of Córdoba. This was marked not least by Musa's creation of a fortress at Albelda. In 859 Ordoño attacked and destroyed this, and defeated Musa. The latter's death in 862 led to a temporary weakening of his dynasty's regional power.

Surprisingly little is known about the long reign of Ordoño's son and successor Alfonso III (866–910). This is in part due to the fact that the Asturian chronicles first compiled in the 880s only take their accounts up to the death of Ordoño I, and they had no successor or continuation for nearly a century and a half. By the time that the next historical work was written in northern Spain, the reign of Alfonso III was a distant memory. Even the events with which it ended, when it seems that the elderly king was overthrown in a bloodless coup led by one or more of his own sons, are briefly and ambiguously described, and contradictory traditions exist as to his eventual fate.[50]

The kingdom of León and the county of Castille, 910–1037

For the history of the last phase of the Asturian kingdom and for its continuation after 910 in a new capital at León, the evidence of narrative sources becomes even less substantial than for the preceding period. After the composition of the various sets of Asturian chronicles in the 880s, there follows a gap of well over a century before another indigenous historian began to write a very short account of period extending from the accession of Alfonso III in 866 up to the death of Vermudo II 'the Gouty' in 999. The author Sampiro has often been identified with a bishop of Astorga of the same name, who held the see in the mid-eleventh century (*c*. 1034–*c*. 1042), and also with a royal notary responsible for the drafting of a handful of extant charters.[51] The latter extend in time over the years 977–1018, and while not totally improbable, the chances that they were all the work of a single individual who twenty years later would become a bishop is rather stretching the bounds of probability. Little if anything is thus known for certain about this author.

It must also be confessed that his work, which takes the form of short accounts of the successive kings, has not survived in its original form. It is only preserved in two later versions, which when compared may be seen to be very different in length and

in some of the information offered. Both of these versions represent twelfth century re-use of Sampiro's narrative as part of new
and more extensive histories.

The longer and apparently more informative of the two versions
is that of the history written by Bishop Pelagius (or Pelayo) of
Oviedo. He, unfortunately, enjoys a well-deserved reputation as a
forger and as a fabricator of documents. His own ideological purposes, which were essentially those of furthering the power and
wealth of his own dioceses, are not hard to uncover, and in the case
of his use of the material of Sampiro's chronicle, his additions are
easily detected when his text is compared with that of the anonymous *Historia Silense* or Silos History. This work, which was probably compiled in León rather than in the monastery of Silos, seems
to have made more scrupulous use of Sampiro, though the lack of
an independent version of his text makes even the *Historia*'s treatment of it incapable of being checked, and it may be assumed that
some degree of textual corruption or interpolation took place.[52]

If the narrative sources for the tenth century become briefer
and more problematic, then at least the documentary evidence
grows in abundance. This, however, has only limited applicability.
Apart from one or two references to contemporary events and
the chronological information to be gleaned from the regnal dates
given in most of these charters, the significance of these texts lies
more in what they can reveal of legal and economic practices and
procedures in this period.[53]

The continuing weakness of the Umayyad regime in the south,
which only began to recover its former strength in the 920s,
contributed directly to the greater security of the Asturian kingdom. The more localised threat on the eastern fringes of the
kingdom presented by the Banu Qasi in the upper Ebro valley
was also eliminated with the death of the last member of this
family in 907. By this time the Asturian kings had been occupying
and redistributing lands in the Duero valley for several decades.
New settlements, such as Zamora and Burgos (884) were founded.

With the deposition of Alfonso III in 910, a move from the traditional but distant capital of Oviedo to a new location in the northern Meseta became viable. Zamora may have served this function
in the short reign of Alfonso's eldest son García I (910–13/14).
The latter's brother and successor Ordoño II (914–24), who had
previously been sub-king in Galicia, established himself in León,
which thereafter remained the principal royal centre.[54]

Colonisation and settlement was taking place in three distinct
if contiguous areas. In the West, the extension of the Asturian
kingdom to the river Miño in Galicia took place more or less in
a single phase in the mid-eighth century, and was followed by a

more gradual extension into the area between the Miño and the Atlantic coast. With that achieved the local nobility turned their attention southwards to the area between the lower Miño and the Duero valley.[55] In the east, the area between the Cantabrian mountains and the upper Duero, which became known from its numerous small fortresses as Castille, had begun to be settled in the last quarter of the ninth century. Here a significant if unquantifiable section of the new population came from the Basque regions to the north east, as demonstrated by the presence of numerous Basque personal and place names in the extant charter collections from the region.[56]

While in Galicia (which now included the northernmost part of what would in the twelfth century become the kingdom of Portugal) a number of rival aristocratic families can be detected, building localised rather than regional centres of power, one dominant house emerged in Castille.[57] This is not to say that there was no conflict between aspiring noble factions, obscure as the evidence might be, but it seems that these resolved themselves in favour of the dynasty of Fernán González (d. 970), who held the office of Count of Castille for most of the middle years of the tenth century, and transmitted it as a hereditary possession to his descendants.[58]

Unfortunately, although his later heroic status in Castillian mythology led to extravagant claims being made for Fernán González's origins, deeds and legacy, the actual evidence relating to his career is meagre, and it is not easy to see precisely how he and his family acquired their almost unchallenged control over this large and important frontier region.

That this was achieved initially with royal support is likely, but it is notable that the kings of León found it expedient to maintain Fernán González in office even when he had proved himself personally disloyal to several of them. This can only indicate the degree to which he had made himself indispensable. This is reflected not least in the contemporary charters, which differ from those of Galicia and León not least in the way most significant legal and administrative powers appear to be exercised by the count, without reference to higher royal authority.[59] The kings are frequently not mentioned in dating clauses, which refer instead to the counts.

The central section of the frontier, between southern Galicia and Castille, was essentially that of the Leonese kingdom proper. To the north of it the former heartland of the Asturias seems to have gradually declined into political and economic obscurity, as its leading families were denied access to the opportunities offered on the frontiers. It could, however, still serve as a refuge for the kings in times of trouble.

As well as the infrequent larger-scale royal campaigns, that extended down into Arab-ruled territory as far to the south as Mérida, Lisbon and Coimbra, there was more frequent, virtually endemic smaller-scale raiding of Muslim territories being conducted by the frontier lords and their followers. Umayyad responses were as much if not more directed against the latter as the former, which is why so many expeditions from Córdoba are recorded as ravaging parts of Castille.

The threat of major Umayyad reprisals was probably lifted as a result of the battle of Simancas in 939. By the late 920s 'Abd al-Rahman III (912–61) had generally restored the fortunes of his dynasty in the south and centre of the peninsula with a series of campaigns against the various local potentates and rebels who had carved out independent territories for themselves over much of Al-Andalus.[60] Only once this had been achieved was it possible for him to resume the kind of expeditions into the north that had been commonplace in the later eighth century. That in 939 proved a disaster, in that his army was defeated as it attempted to force its way across the valley of the Duero.[61] The caliph never led an expedition in person again, and such large-scale confrontations between the Umayyad state and the Leonese kingdom were not to resume until the mid-970s. However, localised raiding across the frontier in both directions remained constant.

The great period of expansion, settlement and repopulation of the northern Meseta that began in the middle of the ninth century and lasted for a hundred years or more transformed the political and economic alignments of the original Asturian kingdom, almost out of recognition. The southern frontier became the main area of expansion, with a marcher aristocracy taking form to defend and to exploit it. The processes involved are clearest in the case of monastic houses, whose records have survived to a much greater extant than those of secular landholders. However, because of the great weight placed on written evidence and documentary proofs in the legal systems of all the Christian realms of northern Spain, their charter collections usually contain several items relating to preceding periods of secular possession of estates that subsequently were gifted or sold into monastic ownership.

The relative lack of early charters and the problems of authenticity previously mentioned particularly affect the study of the early settlement period. Another type of document that is potentially very significant in the study of these processes is the *fuero* or settlement charter, in which a founding lord concedes various rights and privileges to those whom he has persuaded to come and occupy a new settlement that he has founded or revived.[62] These tended to be added to over the course of time, as circumstances changed, more concessions were made, or greater precision became necessary in defining the inhabitants' rights. It is thus not surprising that many of the earliest sets of these privileges granted to individual settlements only survive as the opening sections of later, more complex texts. Similarly, they can in several cases be shown to have been altered or interpolated at periods later than their apparent date.[63]

Allowing for these problems, it seems that the initiative for settlement was largely taken by the frontier nobility, which occupied or conquered territories that they then needed to fill with new settlers drawn from the mountain regions to the north and/or the Basque territories to the east. Such settlers would need, with the lords's support, to establish fortified centres of population to defend their land from raids coming from the Arab frontier zones to the south as well as from more localised banditry. The *fueros* specified the duties as well as the exemptions from taxes, tolls and other burdens that a founder was prepared to offer the settlers. These latter could also include modifications to the applicability of the existing law, as contained in the still authoritative Visigothic law code.[64]

As well as those able to escape from the burden of a far more restrictive and oppressive lordship in the north, in the Asturian and Galician heartlands, the new settlers on the Meseta also included groups of refugees from the Arab lands in the south. Many of these were Christian clerics and monks, who established new monastic houses in several of the abandoned and ruined churches in this region, whose existence is abundantly testified to in the documentary records. There may well have been large numbers of Christians from the south other than clergy, but their presence in the north is not so easily detected in the texts as is the case with their clerical counterparts. Quite the opposite used to be thought to be the case, as the large number of Arab names in the northern charter collections was long assumed to indicate the presence of such refugees from the south and their descendants. However, recent study has shown that naming patterns are more complex than this view allowed for, and that such names could be used almost indiscriminately in families whose origins can be shown clearly to lie in the north.[65]

Marcher societies have always been notoriously independent. Central authority usually required the services of some of those families who had already established their own local power bases in such regions to try to control the rest. Political art consisted in building up these representatives of distant central authority, allowing them to act in ways that would not be permitted to their counterparts away from the frontiers, but at the same time not letting them become so dominant locally that they could ignore or defy their royal masters.

This was a particular danger in periods when the kings were weak, either because they were not of an age to exercise personal authority or because of factional conflicts at court. These latter could be manipulated by ambitious marcher lords in the same way that their own family rivalries could be exploited by the kings in periods in which central authority was more effective.

Thus the reign of Ramiro II of Léon (931–51), victor over the Umayyad caliph in 939, was a time in which royal power was generally in the ascendant, and the frontier zones remained quiescent as far as the stability of the kingdom was concerned.[66] However, his death ushered in a period of instability that lasted with few interruptions until the end of the century.

In part the problems were created by disputed royal successions or the ambitions of members of the dynasty towards securing at least regional power for themselves. A sub-kingdom came into being in Galicia following the deposition of Alfonso III in 910, either as an appanage for the heir apparent or as a dependency to be given to a close relative of the reigning monarch. In the reign of García I (910–13/14) his brother Ordoño held Galicia, before succeeding to the Leonese throne itself. On Ordoño's death in 924 the kingdom passed to a third of the brothers, in the person of Fruela II (924–25), despite the existence of at least three sons of Ordoño II.[67]

It was not they who seem to have presented the greatest or most immediate threat to Fruela II. This came from the sons of a brother of Alfonso III called Olmund. This implies that, as in the preceding Asturian period, almost any adult male members of the royal house, extending to at least the second generation, could be considered as potential candidates for the throne. In this case Fruela seems to have taken pre-emptive action, executing the three of them and putting an immediate end to that branch of the dynasty. This action was obviously regarded as unjust and, according to Sampiro, Fruela was struck down with leprosy from which he died in 925, in consequence of it.[68]

This precipitated a brief struggle for the throne between the sons of the former king Ordoño II, only recorded in one of the fragments of the work of the Arab historian Ibn Hayyan (d. 1076).[69] The eldest of them, Sancho, took León, but was rapidly dislodged by his brother Alfonso, who had the backing of the Navarrese King Sancho I Garcés (905–25). However, Sancho maintained himself independently in Galicia until his death in 929, when he was succeeded by the third brother, Ramiro.

In 930 or 931 Ramiro reunited Galicia with the rest of the Leonese kingdom when he succeeded Alfonso IV. The latter is said, like their ancestor Vermudo I, to have abdicated in order to enter monastic life.[70] It seems far more probable that he was the victim of a coup, backed by the military force of the Galician aristocracy, as within a few weeks of his supposedly voluntary renunciation of the crown, Alfonso had escaped from his monastery and seized the city of León, while Ramiro was absent on campaign. Alfonso's attempt to regain the throne failed as he was unable to mobilise enough support. On Ramiro II's rapid return to León, he was returned to monastic seclusion and several other members of the royal house were blinded.

It is notable that in this period of conflict between the sons of Ordoño II, two of them enjoyed strong backing in Galicia, and were able to maintain themselves in that region even when one of their rivals ruled in León, while the third and initially most successful of them had Navarrese aid. The subsequent failure of Alfonso IV to maintain himself against Ramiro II or then to recover his throne may well reflect the contemporary weakness of the kingdom of Navarre, then under the regency of Queen Toda. This theme of the rival polarities of Galicia and Navarre, exerting fluctuating degrees of influence over León, remained a constant in the politics of the kingdom for the next hundred years.

The particular involvement of the royal house with Galicia rather than with Castille, where the house of Fernán González rose in due course to unchecked pre-eminence, and the creation of its sub-kingship may result from the presence of substantial dynastic land holdings in the region. As previously mentioned, Galicia had provided the backing for Ramiro I's taking of power in 842, the year in which he had married a major Galician heiress.

While Galician aristocratic factions and the power that could be derived from the royal resources in the region played a dominant role in the politics of the Leonese court in the earlier part of the tenth century, by its middle years the leading role was being taken by the Count of Castille. Fernán González had attempted to secure a large measure of practical autonomy for himself and his territory during the latter part of the reign of Ramiro II and that of the latter's elder son and successor Ordoño III (951–6), even resorting to revolt when thwarted.[71] These had been crushed, but he and his dynasty remained indispensable to the Leonese monarchs.

The early death of Ordoño III provided new opportunities, as the regime of his half-brother, Sancho I the Fat, proved weak.

This was due not least to the new king's obesity, which was so extreme as to prevent him from mounting a horse and thus exercising the personal military leadership upon which royal credibility continued to rest. He became vulnerable to a coup which was not long in coming. This centred on one of the alternative lines of the still extensive royal family, in the person of a son of Alfonso IV, who seized the Leonese throne in 958.[72] The new King Ordoño IV (958–9) was in later tradition given the sobriquet of 'the Bad', though it has to be admitted that no deeds of particular evil can be laid at his door. For one thing, even had he been so minded, and there is no evidence that he was, his tenure of the throne was hardly long enough for the perpetration of acts of extreme wickedness.

Sancho the Fat fled eastwards to his maternal uncle, the King of Navarre, who in turn sent him south to the Umayyad court. Here he was provided with both the medical treatment necessary to slim him down and with the military assistance that enabled him to regain his throne the following year. Ordoño IV continued to hold out briefly in the Asturias, but by 960 he too had to make his way to Córdoba, to petition the Caliph for aid. In his case it was refused, and he died in exile.[73]

The role played by Fernán González of Castille is noteworthy. He seems to have been involved in the conspiracy that led to the overthrow of Sancho I in 958 and he married his daughter Urraca, already the widow of Ordoño III, to the new King Ordoño IV, indicating his strong backing for the latter's regime. However, the continuing support for the deposed Sancho manifested both by the Navarrese, who were the Castillians's eastern neighbours and by the Umayyad court seems to have effected a rapid change of allegiance on the part of Fernán González. He switched back to the cause of Sancho, and prevented his daughter from accompanying Ordoño IV on his fruitless visit to Córdoba. For all of this he was well rewarded by the restored monarch whom he had betrayed only the previous year. Following the subsequent death in exile of Ordoño the Bad, Urraca was married to her cousin Sancho II Abarca ('Slipper') of Navarre (970–94), cementing the new alliance between the counts of Castille and the Navarrese royal house.[74]

In line with a policy already adopted by the court of Navarre during the long regency of Queen Toda, the Leonese monarchy became markedly more subservient in its diplomatic dealings with the Umayyads over the next decade and a half. It also came increasingly under the influence of the kings of Navarre and their Castillian allies. Castillian and Navarrese nobles frequently attended the court of Sancho I and his son Ramiro III (966–85), and there seems to have been very close relations between León, Burgos and Pamplona at this time.[75]

In consequence Galicia, whose aristocracy had been favoured under Ramiro II and Ordoño III moved from being the main source of support for the Leonese monarchy to becoming the principal focus of rebellion. In 966 Sancho I was forced to mobilise his forces against a revolt led by the leading noble house in the area south of the Miño. Unable to resist the king militarily, Count Gonzalo Muñoz opened negotiations, in the course of which he was able to poison Sancho with a gift of apples.[76]

During the reigns of Sancho's sister, the regent Elvira Ramírez (967–75) and that of his son Ramiro III, royal authority hardly extended into Galicia. Vermudo, an illegitimate son of Ordoño III, the last monarch whom the Galician nobles had openly supported, was proclaimed king in opposition to Ramiro III in 982. The latter's regime in the period of his personal rule after 975 seems to have been riven by factional conflicts, and in 984 he was ousted from León with relative ease by Vermudo II (982–99) and his Galician forces. Ramiro retained his support in Castile, but disappears from record in 985, when he may be assumed to have died.[77]

The politics of the Leonese kingdom, which lurched from periods of Galician predominance to ones of Navarrese and Castillian ascendancy, followed the same pattern into the eleventh century. Vermudo II, his son Alfonso V (999–1027) and grandson Vermudo III (1027–37) all enjoyed significant support from many of the leading families of Galicia, while relations with Navarre deteriorated as the ambitions and power of its royal house grew.[78] Sancho III the Great of Navarre (1004–35) built up a political hegemony that embraced the Count of Barcelona in the east and the Duke of Gascony to the north, both of whom had hitherto been subject to the West Frankish kings. He also followed his predecessors in extending the territories of the Navarrese kingdom southwards further into the Ebro valley. To the south-west, the county of Castille passed into direct Navarrese control upon the murder of the last descendant of Fernán González in León in 1029. The county passed by inheritance to Sancho the Great's son Fernando.

Having thus gained control of Castille, it was but a relatively small step for Sancho to try to annexe the Leonese kingdom itself. In 1031 a Navarrese invasion of León overran the capital and the territory around it without encountering much recorded resistance. Vermudo III was, however, able to retain control of the transmontane regions of Galicia and the Asturias, the traditional strongholds of his branch of the Leonese dynasty. The death of Sancho the Great in October 1035 enabled him to regain control of León, but he faced a renewed challenge two years later from two of his old adversary's sons, Fernando, Count of Castille, and García IV of Navarre (1035–54). In a battle at Tamarón Vermudo was defeated and killed. With him died the direct line of the Asturian royal house, and his kingdom passed into the hands of the Count of Castille, who then reigned as Fernando I (1037–65) of León–Castille.

18 'The dissension of kings'

Chroniclers in an age of war

Writing late in the ninth century, the anonymous author of the *Annals of Xanten* clearly felt close to despair when compiling his entry for the year 862. He abandoned the attempt at a detailed record and contented himself with the statement that 'it is now tedious to record the dissension between our kings and the desolation caused by the pagans within our kingdoms'.[1] The modern student of the history of the Carolingian Empire in the century that followed the death of Charlemagne must feel some sympathy with the sentiments of this predecessor. From 830 onwards the sources for the narrative history of these times seem to do little more than record, in varying degrees of detail, much *dissensio regum* and perhaps even more *desolatio paganorum*. Historians attracted to this period, and there have not been very many of them, have tended to repeat what the chroniclers tell them, and to adopt many of their vantage points and the judgements that they made on their own society and its rulers.[2]

In comparison with the eighth, the ninth century in Francia has left a comparatively detailed account of itself in the form of numerous relatively large-scale chronicles and annals. The most substantial of these is the text known, rather misleadingly in that it was not composed in that monastery, as *The Annals of St Bertin*.[3] These were in fact a continuation of the annals that are generally thought to have been composed at the royal court and which are called the *Annales Regni Francorum* or *Annals of the Kingdom of the Franks*. Whereas some of the latter were probably drawn up annually by anonymous scribes, in most cases working under the supervision of the royal chaplain, after 835 the continuation became essentially a private one and represents the information available to and the views of two successive identifiable authors. The first of these was the Spaniard Galindo (probably originally from Aragón), who was also known as Prudentius, and who became Bishop of Troyes (843–61). His work was taken over after his death and carried on by Archbishop Hincmar of Reims (845–82), under whose direction the annual entries became even more substantial but also more idiosyncratic.[4] Because of the persons and interests of its compilers, this chronicle was clearly best informed about and most concerned with the events relating to the independent West Frankish kingdom that came into being in the early 840s.

The principal collection of annals relating to the history of the eastern Frankish kingdom in the ninth century is that traditionally associated with the monastery of Fulda. The compositional history of this work, known as the *Annales Fuldenses* or *Fulda Annals*, remains controversial due to the lack of a comprehensive critical edition.[5] Three different versions of the text survive; the third of which includes a continuation covering the years 882–901 that was probably written in Bavaria. The second version shows a distinctive partiality towards the ill-fated emperor Charles the Fat (d. 888), but the main compilation is likely to be associated with Archbishop Liutbert of Mainz (863–89), who twice held the office of imperial chancellor. Amongst the earlier items incorporated into the works are a version of the *Annales Regni Francorum*, and the section of the text dealing with the years 838–63 may be the work of a monk and author of saints' lives from Fulda called Rudolf (d. 865). A marginal reference to him in one of the manuscripts of the first class led to the whole compilation being linked to Fulda.

The *Annals of St Bertin* and the *Annals of Fulda* are generally the most substantial and informative of these annalistic compilations, but the information they offer can on occasion be supplemented by or compared to that provided by other shorter, chronologically or geographically more restricted texts. For example the *Annals of St Vaast* give much independent information that relates to the northern regions of the Frankish kingdoms in the years 874–900, as in their way do the *Annals of Xanten* (probably written in Ghent), despite their compiler's apparently greater interest in natural phenomena and unusual weather than in the doings of men.[6] More substantial than these, and the work of an identifiable author, is the chronicle of the monk Regino of Prüm, which covers the period from 813–906, but which is primarily valuable for its account of the period from the 860s onwards.[7]

From such chronicles and annals a consistent if depressing view of the period emerges. 'Pagans', in the form of the heathen Vikings from Scandinavia in the north and west and Muslim Arabs in the south, pillage, burn and enslave with apparent impunity, while proliferating numbers of Carolingian kings squabble over increasingly weakened and diminishing kingdoms. It is necessary, however, to note that most of the literary sources previously referred to were written or compiled during or deal primarily with the last three decades of the ninth century, when the Viking depredations were at their height, and when the Carolingian monarchs were most frequently in conflict with each other, not least due to the unusually high rate of mortality amongst them at this time. Thus, it is only fair to say that the dominant historiographical

perspective, as far as the century as a whole is concerned, is one
that is actually conditioned by the events of a much more limited
period.

Even so, it must be asked whether or not certain fundamental
flaws existed in the administrative and ideological structures
of the Carolingian Empire from the time of its founder,
Charlemagne, onwards, and if these contributed to the rapid disintegration of the political unity that had been so arduously
achieved in the late eighth century. Similarly, it is necessary to
look at the part that may have been played by the personal
capacity, or lack thereof, of the successors to the first Carolingian
emperor. The compilers of the various sets of annals tended to
have strong views about many of the rulers whose actions they
recorded. Inevitably these were coloured by their personal prejudices, the concerns of the monasteries in which they wrote and a
large measure of self-interest: few of the chronicles venture an
overt criticism of the ruler in whose territory the work was being
written. Thus for adverse comment on Charles the Bald (840–77)
as a fighter against the Vikings it is necessary to turn to annals
written in the kingdom of his half-brother, Louis the German
(817–76).[8] Was this an objective criticism, that might have been
felt by Charles's own subjects, or a convenient accusation to make
against an ambitious rival of the chronicler's own king?

Historiography was and is rarely neutral. In Francia it had
manifested a high degree of ideological content ever since the
mid-eighth century. Supporters of the rising Carolingian house
rewrote the history of the late Merovingian period in their interest. Under Charlemagne the *Annals of the Kingdom of the Franks*
had deliberately suppressed and minimised Frankish reverses,
while extolling or even exaggerating triumphs. In the troubled
reign of his successor Louis partisan historiography took on even
greater importance. This extended itself to a new, or revived,
genre, that of imperial biography. Einhard's *Life of Charles* which
was modelled on Suetonius's *Life of Augustus*, was the first such
work.[9] Although, following its literary exemplar, it provides
details of the emperor's appearance, tastes and character that
would otherwise be entirely lost, it is important to remember that
this work was a product of the later 820s and that its idealised
portrait of Charles was probably intended principally to serve as
a role model for his successor.

The latter was himself to be the beneficiary of two 'Lives' of
himself, both written by supporters.[10] One of these was Thegan,
an auxiliary bishop in the diocese of Trier. His work, which unlike
that of Einhard is a chronologically organised record of the events
of the new emperor's reign, ends abruptly in the year 836 and

omits discussion of Louis's habits and tastes. A similar structure was selected by the anonymous author of the other and longer *Vita Hludovici Imperatoris*, or *Life of the Emperor Louis*. The writer of this work is often, not very helpfully, called 'The Astronomer', because of his apparent interest in natural and above all astronomical phenomena. This was a taste that he shared with several of the annalists of the period. His book is more substantial than that of Thegan, which, however, retains its independent value, and it extends its coverage up to the emperor's death in 840. Partisan as are both *Lives*, and also the final section of the *Annals of the Kingdom of the Franks* and its continuation in the form of *The Annals of St Bertin*, it must be said that it is on their testimony that Louis the Pious is often historiographically indicted and condemned. His reign, neglected as it has been in many respects, requires more intensive scholarly investigation, not least as the *dissensio regum* that is so much a theme of the history of later ninth century Francia can be traced back into this period, and the political divisions within the previously united empire are the clear products of it.

The reign of Louis the Pious, 814–840

Since the publication in 1948 of a now famous article by the Belgian historian François-Louis Ganshof, a mild debate has continued amongst historians of the Carolingian period as to whether or not the last years of the reign of Charlemagne represent a period of decline.[11] However regarded, the events of the years 800–14 do hint at several of the major problems that would afflict the Carolingian empire throughout the rest of the ninth century. These included the questions of succession and of the division of territory between the ruler's heirs, the nature of the imperial title and the way in which it should be transmitted, and the military threats posed by Viking and Arab raids. To these could be added the inherent problems of maintaining in being an Empire whose internal governmental structures were so attenuated and whose cultural, linguistic and political cohesion was so fragile.

Charles delayed drawing up a final plan for the division of his empire amongst his three legitimate sons until the year 806.[12] By the capitulary issued at Thionville in February of that year, which is known as the *Divisio Regnorum*, all his realm was to be divided on his death into three more or less equal parts. In practice this was based upon the already existing arrangements of 781, in which Pippin had been made king of the Lombards and Louis of the Aquitanians. Their future share of the empire as envisaged in 806 added additional sections of territory to these, while allotting to Charles, the eldest brother, the Frankish heartlands of Neustria and Austrasia, together with the territories conquered or subjected east of the Rhine and north of the Danube.

The *Divisio* also laid down instructions as to how these three kingdoms were to be subdivided between the survivors in the event of any of the brothers dying before their father and not leaving an heir. No mention was made of the imperial title, and it has been suggested that Charlemagne at this time regarded it as a personal honour, not to be transmitted to the next generation.[13] On the other hand, a very persuasive interpretation of the document makes the wording imply a rather sophisticated political concept: that the proposed three kingdoms, while separate, were to be seen as also constituting a single greater *Regnum*. It is suggested that this three kingdoms/one kingdom idea was influenced by the theology of the Trinity, to which some particular attention was being given in the Carolingian Church at this very time.[14]

Whatever Charlemagne's views in 806, the events of the next few years were to lead him to a simpler solution. His son Pippin died in 810, albeit leaving a son of his own called Bernard, and in 811 Charles, the eldest of the brothers, also died, aged thirty-nine. It is possible that the emperor was not particularly fond of his only surviving son, Louis. The despatch of the young Bernard to Italy in 812 may have been a sign of this, and other members of Charles's close family, including his cousins and even the illegitimate children of his daughters might have been eligible for a share in the Frankish territories.[15] While this remained debatable, the emperor resolved the problem of the imperial title. In September 813, following the holding of a major assembly of bishops, abbots and secular magnates, he summoned Louis from Aquitaine, and in a ceremony at Aachen the latter crowned himself emperor at his father's command.[16] He was, however, then sent back to Aquitaine. On 28 January 814 Charles died at Aachen, where he was to be buried. Louis, worried that one of his relatives would attempt to stage a coup, hastened to the capital and rapidly consigned most of his family to house arrest in monasteries throughout Francia.

Louis, later known to the French as *le Débonnaire* and to the rest of the world as 'the Pious', was fortunate in his brothers' premature deaths.[17] The Empire may have been less so. Despite the oath he took to his father in 813 to follow his precedents, Louis does not seem to have learned from that shrewd and intimidating man many of the real secrets of political management. Some of the criticisms that have been made against Louis are probably unjustified, but as will be suggested, at certain crucial points in his reign his own weaknesses may have exacerbated political difficulties that could have been alleviated by a more flexible or conciliatory approach. However, it is at least possible to doubt the value of some of the older accusations levelled against him.

Two of what historians have in the past regarded as his greatest mistakes were made early in the reign, even though this was in other respects a time when he enjoyed the service of advisers of the highest calibre. The first of these may have been the decision to have himself recrowned as emperor by Pope Stephen IV (816–17). The initiative for this appears to have come from Louis himself, who took advantage of the new pope's desire to come to Francia for a personal meeting to discuss problems concerned with Rome, to include a papal anointing and re-coronation in the visit.[18] This took place at Reims in October 816. Whatever the emperor may have felt this act had done to his title and office, it meant in practice that the papacy, politically subservient to and militarily dependent on the Frankish monarchy as it had been for over half a century, had regained the crucial role in the ceremonial of emperor making. In practice, all future imperial coronations followed the precedent of the papal investiture and anointing of Charles and Louis in 800 and 816, and not the purely Frankish secular coronation of 813. After 823 no legitimate emperor was to be crowned without papal participation and this in due course could come to mean without papal approval – at least until the time of Napoleon, who reverted to Charlemagne's precedent of 813.

Louis's second supposed mistake was to be too hasty in making arrangements for the succession. Charles had ruled for nearly forty years before issuing his *Divisio Regnorum*, while Louis had been on the throne for less than four before producing his equivalent, known as the *Ordinatio Imperii*. In themselves the plans that were unveiled at an assembly in Aachen in 817 were very different from those of his father, though he like Charles had three sons to accommodate, and in many respects they were strikingly innovative. The two younger sons, Pippin and Louis, were invested with relatively small kingdoms in Aquitaine and Bavaria respectively, while the lion's share of territory was promised to their elder brother, Lothar. He was also to receive the imperial title immediately, and with it a specified future authority over his brothers, even within their own realms.[19] Louis immediately invested Lothar as co-emperor, a process confirmed when the latter received a papal re-coronation and anointing in Rome in 823 at the hands of Pope Paschal I (817–24).

Whatever his subsequent errors of judgement, criticisms levelled against Louis over these decisions are not very just. In the circumstances of 816 a papal anointing presented a confirmation of rather than a threat to his imperial authority. For later developments in papal ideology and the political circumstances of later decades, that made the imperial office something the popes could use to lure Carolingian and other rulers to the defence of Rome, Louis was not responsible. Nor was he averse to repeating the purely Frankish ceremony of 813 when he made his son Lothar co-emperor in 817. Only when the latter was sent to govern Italy in 823 were the arrangements made for the further papal anointing.

In the opening period of his reign, as during most of that of his father, the secular relationship of emperor and pope was essentially that of master and servant. Rome remained a political dependency of Francia.[20] In 823 when it was reported that Pope Paschal I (817–24) had ordered the execution of two of his own leading officials, the emperor sent two of his *missi* to investigate, and the pope found it expedient at the same time to send an embassy to Louis to present his version of these events. In 824 Lothar, on his father's orders, carried out some form of inspection and reform of the workings of the City of Rome and its territory, which according to the *Annals of the Kingdom of the Franks* had 'been ruined by the perversity of recent popes'.[21] One consequence of this was even closer supervision of papal elections. Thus in 827 Gregory IV (827–44) was unable to be ordained until an imperial *missus* had come to Rome to make sure the papal election had been properly carried out.[22]

Equally unjust is criticism of Louis for the rapidity of his decision to make arrangements for his succession. The early deaths of his own brothers and a potentially fatal accident that befell him just before Easter in 817 probably made Louis sensitive to his own mortality and the danger of dying without having made arrangements for his own succession.[23] On the other hand, the precise arrangements of the *Ordinatio Imperii* of 817 led to immediate political problems, which the emperor and his advisers proved increasingly less capable of dealing with. It is only just, though, to note that many of these difficulties were not just the products of the particular scheme devised in 817, but represent fundamental structural problems within the fabric of the Carolingian Empire and were part of the legacy of unsolved problems that Louis inherited from his father.

The ambiguity over the nature and indeed precise verbal form of the imperial title was one of these. Louis, whose long residence and upbringing in Aquitaine (781–814) may have made him less aware of, or careful of, traditional Frankish susceptibilities, used an exclusively imperial title, that of *Imperator Augustus*, which had purely Roman antecedents.[24] He did not, unlike his father, employ the subsidiary titles of *Rex Francorum* and *Rex Langobardorum*.

As evidenced not least by the *Ordinatio*, Louis and his advisers, most of whom had served him in Aquitaine, held views of the nature of the imperial office that were ideologically more sophisticated than those of their predecessors.[25]

Unfortunately, the realities of Carolingian society were rather more complex. As previously discussed, the problems of turning a set of disparate peoples with separate histories, traditions, laws and in some cases languages into a viable unitary political entity had never been solved, or even been adequately recognised, in the time of Charles. Frankish ethnic separateness had if anything been strengthened. Neither the adoption of an imperial title by the ruler nor the concept of a common Christian culture had served to provide ideological cement around which a new common identity for the inhabitants of the Empire could be formed. The administrative structures were tenuous, and even the establishment of Frankish aristocratic dynasties in the principal offices and lands of the conquered territories failed to guarantee loyalty, in that, like their predecessors under the Merovingians, such families rapidly identified themselves with regional interests.

Greater emphasis on the unity of the Empire through the use of less ambiguous imperial titles and in the scheme devised in 817 for the succession could hardly in themselves solve these fundamental problems. In fact the animosities within the imperial family that were to be raised by the *Ordinatio* gave greater scope for the development of regional conflicts and the accentuation rather than the diminution of the inherent divisiveness of the society of the empire. In this respect the weaknesses of the *Ordinatio* of 817 were twofold. Firstly the arrangements then made left no room for the possible appearance of additional heirs, however unlikely this might have seemed at the time. However, Louis's wife Ermengard died in October 818 and his remarriage four months later to Judith, daughter of the Bavarian Count Welf, was to contribute directly to his subsequent political problems.[26] Charles, known as 'the Bald', the son of this second marriage, was born in 823, and the need to revise the provisions of the *Ordinatio* to create an additional kingdom for this new heir was a constant element in the politics of the rest of the reign.

The second area of weakness in the *Ordinatio* lay in the fact that it assumed the future harmony of unequally treated beneficiaries. Thus, while it gave Lothar a power and status that he was able to use against his father, at the same time it created the grounds for future resentments on the part of the less well endowed and supposedly subservient younger brothers. These personal animosities and ambitions within the ranks of the Carolingian house were fanned by regional aristocracies whose hopes for power and status were better catered for by the promotion of rival provincial monarchies than by aspirations towards influence at a distant, centralised imperial court. Marriages by the Carolingian regional rulers to members of their leading local aristocracies only furthered these fissiparous tendencies. Such considerations may have inspired the most immediate consequence of the issue of the *Ordinatio*, which was the supposed revolt of Louis's nephew Bernard, who had been formally established as king of Italy in 813. On the other hand, the latter may have been the victim of a pre-emptive strike on the part of the emperor.

A certain amount of care is needed in assesing this episode, as even the *Annals of the Kingdom of the Franks*, then being produced under the direction of the arch-chaplain, abbot Hilduin of Saint-Denis, admit that the report that Bernard was planning to make an independent kingdom for himself in Italy was 'partly true and partly false'.[27] Bernard enjoyed the loyalty of a group of Frankish counts in his service in Italy, together with the support of three bishops. Amongst the latter, supposedly, was the veteran adviser of Charlemagne, bishop Theodulf of Orléans. No immediate connection with the Italian court can be found in his case, and it has been suggested that he was the victim of a false accusation made by his political opponents, who could have included his local rival, Count Matfrid of Orléans.[28]

It is possible, though, that this was not the only piece of cynical political manipulation to be found in this rather murky episode. Late in 817 Louis had raised a large army with which to force his way into Italy, but Bernard appears to have given up even before the emperor and his troops came within sight of the Alps. He crossed into Francia and submitted to Louis at Châlon-sur-Saone in December 817.[29] In the ensuing trial Bernard and his associates were condemned to be blinded. As in the case of Constantine VI in Byzantium, this was done in such a way that Bernard died of it early in 818. Just as with Charles's treatment of Tassilo of Bavaria, the outcome of this judicial action on the part of the supposedly threatened and betrayed Frankish ruler was politically highly expedient. With the elimination of Bernard, of whom no mention had been made in the *Ordinatio Imperii*, all of the empire was now able to be divided up between Louis's own sons, and the anomalous Italian kingdom of his nephew was from 822 put into the hands of Lothar, to be his special sphere of activity.[30] As will be seen, the devising of the *Ordinatio*, the elimination of Bernard, and the elevation of Lothar both to imperial office alongside his father and to independent authority in Italy were all the products of the policies suggested to the emperor by a powerful group of advisers.

On succeeding his father in 814, Louis had purged the court and installed a new group of advisors, drawn from the ranks of those who had previously been in his service while he was King of Aquitaine.[31] A dominant figure amongst these was the Gothic abbot and monastic founder Wittiza, better known as Benedict of Aniane, under whose direction a series of reforming ecclesiastical councils were held at Aachen in 816 and 817. Amongst other things these were intended to impose the *Rule of Benedict* as the norm for basic monastic observance throughout the Frankish empire.[32]

The death of this powerful personality in 821 appears to have coincided with changes in the court. To members of the group who had been dominant in the years 814–21, who had included the former chancellor Helisachar and his successor Hilduin of Saint-Denis, were added a small number of those who had previously been influential in the last years of Charles, such as Adalhard of Corbie and his brother Wala, cousins of the late emperor who had been relegated to monasteries by Louis in 817.[33] Louis's own half-brothers, Drogo and Hugh, illegitimate sons of Charles, were liberated in 822 from similar seclusion, and were permitted to take active roles in the Church, but were not to become active members of the court inner circle.[34] The most extraordinary feature of this series of events was the public confession made by the emperor at the assembly held at Attigny in August 822, in which Louis undertook a penance to atone for what he had done to his nephew Bernard and for his treatment of the other members of his family.[35]

Traditionally, this episode has been seen as a humiliation for the emperor, forced upon him by the newly reconstructed faction that dominated the court, but such an interpretation has been strongly challenged. The explicit comparison made in the anonymous *Life* of Louis with the penance of Theodosius I might suggest that the image intended to be conveyed by the emperor's penance was far more positive.[36] His act was also paralleled and followed by a similar confession of failings on the part of the assembled bishops. What was being symbolised was a new relationship between church and state, in which the secular ruler publicly acknowledged the special authority in all spiritual matters, even over his own person, of the episcopate. This went beyond anything that Charles had ever been willing to concede to his clergy, and may also have been matched by Louis's dividing off of all major ecclesiastical decision-making processes from the work of the annual assemblies.

While doubts have often been expressed about Louis's own political judgement, it must be conceded that for more than the first half of his reign the empire appears to have been firmly and effectively governed. The ideological programmes of the last period of Charlemagne's reign were perpetuated and extended in such documents as the capitularies issued as a result of the councils held at Aachen in 816/17. Other capitularies continued the pressure for effective administration of justice on the part of the counts, while yet others contained modifications to the Frankish law codes, both *Lex Salica* and *Lex Ribuaria*. In Italy, where members of the same group of advisers who had emerged in 821 dominated the entourage of Lothar, similar capitularies were issued for the Lombard kingdom.[37]

Militarily, the posture of the empire could be said to be defensive rather than expansive.[38] This is hardly surprising in view of the rapid growth in its territories under the rule of Charlemagne. While it would be hard to say that all the empire's frontiers were 'natural' ones, in many cases their locations made strategic sense.[39] It is notable, for example, that the collapse of the Avar hegemony out on the Danubian plains after 796 had not tempted the Franks into any form of imperial extension in that direction. In any case, in an empire with such limited administrative capacity and with such problems of communication further expansion and the successful retention of newly conquered territory became less and less of a physical possibility. On the other hand, it must be said that in the period 814–29 external threats to the existing frontiers were always dealt with vigorously and normally effectively. This included problems with the Slavs beyond the Elbe and in the north-west of the Balkans, with the Lombard duchies in the south of Italy, with the Bretons, with the Bulgars and with the Arabs on the recently created Marches south of the Pyrenees.[40]

While generally successful in retaining what had been gained in the preceding reign, such frontier warfare was inevitably less profitable than that conducted for aggressive expansionary purposes. Those who under Charlemagne had hoped for status and wealth through war may have been forced increasingly to look for similar opportunities through internal conflicts. The presence of several royal heirs with established regional interests provided the context for these, as it had in the sixth century. At the same time the grip on central authority throughout the period 814–29 of a single dominant faction and the growing frustration of others denied access to such power made a violent resolution increasingly probable, especially once the emperor allowed himself to become involved in a partisan way.

It seems likely that by the later 820s Louis was falling under the influence of another faction forming in his court. By this time the Empress Judith, whom he had married in 819, and her two brothers seem to have been looking for some way both to secure a share in the imperial inheritance for her son Charles (born in 823) and to dislodge the dominant group of advisers and office-holders around the emperor. These included Hilduin of Saint Denis, Helisachar, Wala, who had now succeeded his brother Adalhard (d. 826) as Abbot of Corbie, and such secular magnates as Counts Matfrid of Orléans and Hugh of Tours. The latter was father-in-law of the co-emperor Lothar, who had also formed close ties to Wala, his principal advisor in Italy since 822. The catalyst for the resulting factional confrontation emerged, per-haps surprisingly, not in Aachen but on the frontier between the Frankish empire and the Arab rulers of Spain.

As described in the previous chapter, 'Abd ar-Rahman I (756–88) had made himself master of much of southern Spain from 756 onwards. He had expanded his rule into the centre of the peninsula in the 760s and into the Ebro valley in the immedi-ate aftermath of Charlemagne's failed attempt to take Zaragoza and Barcelona in 778.[41] On the other hand, to the north-east of the Ebro Valley the Franks had been welcomed into Gerona by the local populace in 785, and a renewed attempt to expand this frontier march had been initiated in 801 when Louis, then King of Aquitaine and acting under his father's orders, had taken Barcelona.[42] His subsequent attempts to extend the new Frankish enclave further south to Tarragona failed, but a marcher admin-istration was created, centred on Barcelona. As representing the most substantial and much lauded achievement of a ruler who otherwise took very little personal part in the military activity of his reign, the preservation of this city was dear to Louis's heart. In 827 its safety was threatened.

A local revolt, stirred up by the descendant of one of the former rulers of the region, provided the opportunity for an intervention on the part of the Umayyad Amir of Córdoba, 'Abd ar-Rahman II (822–52). An army sent from the south menaced Barcelona, then held for Louis by its count Bernard, son of one of the original conquerors of the city and a distant relative of the emperor. Louis ordered an Aquitanian army under Counts Hugh and Matfrid to go to the assistance of Bernard, but it did not arrive before the Arabs, having ravaged the countryside around Barcelona and Gerona but otherwise having achieved little, returned to Zaragoza.[43] At an assembly held at Aachen in February 828, Hugh and Matfrid were accused of deliberately delaying the arrival of the army on the March the previous year, and were dismissed from their offices. This was an extraordinary reaction in the light of the limited nature of what had actually happened in 827 and of the close ties of at least one of the accused to the Co-emperor Lothar. From their point of view and that of their allies worse was to come in 829, when Bernard of Septimania, the Count of Barcelona, who must have been their principal accuser the previous year, was given the important court office of chamberlain or head of the imperial household.[44]

This provoked a confrontation on a scale that the evidence relating to the earlier years of the reign hardly prepares one for, but which must represent the unleashing of resentments and conflicts of which all too little can now be known. In the spring of 830, after Louis had held an assembly at Aachen to plan a campaign against the Bretons, the mobilisation of the army in Neustria was used as the cover for an armed conspiracy. In April the assembled forces, led by Louis's son Pippin, the King of Aquitaine, marched instead to seize the person of the emperor at Compiègne. His wife Judith was sent to be confined in the monastery of Sainte-Croix in Poitiers, and the hated Bernard only avoided the death that the rebels planned for him by precipitate flight to the Spanish March. His brother, though, was captured and blinded. Lothar, who did not arrive from Italy until May but may have been involved in the conspiracy from the start, had his father confined to a monastery and assumed his authority.[45] The *Ordinatio Imperii* of 817 was thus put prematurely into effect.

The consequences of that may have contributed to the equally sudden and rapid reversal of the coup of the spring of 830. The sources say little, but by October of the same year Louis had been released from custody and had regained his authority. It seems from the brief account in the *Four Books of Histories* of Nithard (d. 844) that the two younger sons, Pippin and Louis, known as 'the German', relegated to their kingdoms by their brother Lothar soon found his overlordship little to their taste, and were persuaded by supporters of their father to join in a plot to reinstate him.[46] Thus by the late autumn of 830 Lothar found himself in the humiliating position of sitting beside his father at Noyon in judgement on his own supporters in the revolt of April.[47] These included such former props of Louis's own regime as his former chancellors Hilduin of Saint-Denis and Helisachar, as well as Abbot Fridugis of St Martin's, Tours. They were all sentenced to death, but this was commuted to perpetual confinement to specified monasteries. That such men, several of whom had served him from before his imperial accession, should all have leagued against him earlier in 830 is testimony to how poorly Louis had handled the growth of factionalism amongst his office-holders and advisers in the preceding years.

Although the empress was permitted to return to court, this was delayed until the following year, and Bernard was not reinstated. A liaison between the two of them in the winter of 829/30 is claimed in hostile sources, but the truth of this can not be established.[48] Louis himself may have learnt few lessons from the events of 830, and soon alienated the two sons who, whatever they may have done in the spring of that year, had been crucial to his restoration in the autumn. In the winter of 832 Pippin of Aquitaine fled from his father's Christmas court in apparent fear for his safety, and when his kingdom was taken from him in 833 he joined forces once again with his brother Lothar, who had been relegated to Italy by Louis in 831. Their other brother, Louis the German, who had been threatened with the loss of some of his kingdom to create a realm for his half-brother Charles, was not slow to join the revolt, which also gained the backing of Pope Gregory IV (827–44).[49] In the mid-summer of 833 Louis was confronted by the forces of his three sons at a site thereafter called the 'Field of Lies' in Alsace. His own supporters melted away without striking a blow and he was taken into custody once more by Lothar, and imprisoned in the monastery of Saint-Denis.[50]

This episode is characteristic of one very marked feature of the political life of the Frankish empire in this period, the role played by consensus. The various narrative sources, notably the two *Lives* of Louis and the *Annales Regni Francorum* with their continuation in the form of the *Annals of St Bertin*, also indicate the crucial role of the assemblies, at this time held at least twice annually at dates set from one meeting to the next, in the crystalising and expression of the opinions of the lay and clerical magnates of the empire. That all-important opinion could be worked upon in the intervening periods, especially in the case of those invited to attend the court over the winter or during its spring and autumn hunting seasons. However, it was only at the assemblies that its real direction would become clear. In 830 the coup against Louis earlier in the year was undone by the swing in majority support that was only able to manifest itself clearly in the October assembly. Similarly, at the 'Field of Lies' the issue was resolved by the coming together of magnate consensus around the claims and complaints of Louis's sons, manifested physically in the haemorrhaging away of the emperor's following.

But who says that history does not repeat itself? Within a year of these events Louis was once again free, liberated by the forces of his two younger sons, who seem to have preferred his occasional malice to the more thorough-going dominance of their elder brother. Lothar's lack of political finesse, to say the least, must have been considerable to have twice alienated the crucial support for a regime whose legitimacy was far from self-evident. Magnate opinion though this time may have been more divided, in that the issue was not decided as cleanly as at the 'Field of Lies' and recourse had to be made to violence. After a brief civil war in the summer of 834 against the forces of his father and brothers, Lothar was once more relegated to Italy with his principal lay supporters.[51] Those bishops who had backed him in 833 and had provided the canonical justification for the deposition of his father, such as Ebbo of Reims and Agobard of Lyon, were deposed.

The last phase of the reign of Louis saw the emperor more firmly in control of events, though he showed no signs of trying to effect a real restoration of harmony amongst his heirs or between them and himself.[52] The death of his second son Pippin in 838 provided him with the long-sought-for opportunity of investing his youngest son Charles, who had already been given territory between the Loire and Seine, with a more substantial kingdom. This meant, however, dispossessing Pippin I's son, whose supporters in the south of Aquitaine continued vigorously to resist this process until eventually this Pippin II was captured and imprisoned as a monk in the monastery of St Médard in Soissons in 852.[53]

Louis's relations with his youngest son Louis the German were also to remain strained. The emperor, anxious to secure at least one potential ally for the young Charles, decided to make a compact with Lothar, whose prospects at this point were of inheriting nothing more than Italy, promising a new division of the empire into two equal parts, in return for a promise of support for his half-brother. This agreement was sealed at an assembly at Worms in May 839.[54] Understandably enough, Louis the German, who by this new division was to be left with no more than Bavaria, resorted once more to force, and tried to make himself master of all the lands east of the Rhine. It was thus in the midst of a new campaign against this son that the old emperor died on an island in the Rhine on 20 June 840.[55]

Those who have devoted themselves to the study of the reign of Louis the Pious have long sought to find some set of deeper underlying explanations for the apparently suicidal behaviour of the Frankish empire under his direction. Some have tried to invest the participants with more abstract and perhaps overly rarefied motives. The opposition of 830 has been seen as the work of what has been called the *Einheitspartei*, or 'Unity Party', consisting of those, such as the emperor's former advisers, for whom the ideal of defending the unity of the Empire, as envisaged in the *Ordinatio* of 817, was more important than continuing political loyalty to their master. Some such construction could be made out of the writings of Bishop Agobard of Lyon, but as a motive for the wider participation of lay and clerical magnates in the events of 830–40 this perhaps fails to convince.[56]

The problem is that there is no easy structural explanation. The various divisions, actual or theoretical, conceived of by Louis and his advisers from 817 onwards do not correspond easily with underlying ethnic divisions within the empire. The coherence of some of the smaller units, such as Bavaria, clearly had a part to play in shaping the politics of the period, while the artificial nature of some larger constructions, such as the kingdom of Aquitaine, is revealed by the fissures that emerge within them in the course of these years. The latter region split into northern and southern halves in terms of the support given to Charles and Pippin II.

As has been mentioned, the reign of Louis did correspond to a period of passivity and even defensiveness as far as expanding the frontiers of the Empire was concerned. There were no longer the kind of profits or rewards to be gained from war that had existed in the time of Charlemagne, and indeed, as the case of the condemnation of Hugh and Matfrid showed, it now became an area with a high degree of political risk attached to it. In such circumstances material and political rewards could be gained from factional conflict within the Empire and not from fighting on its borders. Families, such as that of Bernard of Septimania, who, for whatever reason, were anxious to re-establish or reassert themselves either locally or on a wider stage, could do so best by exploiting the divisions within the Carolingian dynasty.

Leaving aside the role played in these events by the vagaries of individual personality and also arguments depending upon modern ideological constructs, it has to be asked what other forces may have been exerting themselves on the explosive mixture of Carolingian society in this period. As in all Early Medieval centuries, it is not easy to find wide ranging and detailed evidence relating to the functioning of the Frankish economy. At best models have to be made on the basis of limited and sometimes ambiguous information, some of which may not appear directly relevant to the enquiry. A case in point may be the evidence concerning precarial grants, which has normally been seen as an aspect of ecclesiastical reform.

Precaria were lifetime or even heritable grants of lands owned by monasteries and churches to lay tenants in return for fixed rents, and which were quite often made in response to persuasion or pressure on the part of a secular ruler, who was thereby enabled to reward his own supporters at little or no cost to himself. From the reign of Louis the Pious onwards such grants became the target for much opposition and censure on the part of the leaders of the Frankish Church, and a veritable mythology was created in which earlier rulers, especially Charles Martel, were castigated for their tyrannical oppression of the Church through such enforced *precaria*.[57]

In fact, there is nothing intrinsically wrong with such a system, nor any reason to believe that the rents originally set were necessarily disadvantageous to the monastery or church whose land was being granted. When it did become a problem was in periods in which inflationary forces were driving up prices, and when in consequence fixed rents constituted a growing decline in annual income for the recipient. It is hardly too cynical to suggest that such economic forces, as well as increased pressure for ecclesiastical 'liberty' from secular control, motivated the church's growing distaste for precarial grants. That the economy of not only Francia but also the Anglo-Saxon kingdoms was suffering from an inflationary spiral in the central decades of the ninth century may also be suggested by the widespread evidence for the debasement of the (silver) coinage.[58] For secular landowners such economic forces could make the taking of political risks more attractive, as providing a way to recoup declining income.

Whatever the contributory causes to its problems the ultimate lesson to be learnt from the reign of Louis may have been that as a functioning political entity the Carolingian empire was in many respects an irrelevancy. It became a matter of almost total indifference to its leaders as to how it could be split up. The imperial title had failed to acquire any true significance; though it was to be much coveted by individual Carolingians, possibly primarily because it had once belonged to Charlemagne, their supreme exemplar. The failure of the ideological aspirations of the age of the first emperor to make themselves felt beyond the bounds of a narrow circle of ecclesiastics and the structural inadequacies of the central administration of the empire were thus fully highlighted in the difficult second period of the reign of his son.

Kings and emperors in the West, 840–911

Ending in the fashion that his reign did, it is no surprise that the succession arrangements envisaged by Louis had little hope of being implemented after his death. Acceptance of the scheme devised in 839 whereby the empire would be divided into equal halves between Lothar and Charles, with Louis the German retaining only Bavaria, may have been no more than a temporary expedient as far as Lothar was concerned. His ambitions always seem to have exceeded his capacity to attract loyalty. He crossed the Alps immediately upon hearing of the death of his father, proclaiming his rights as emperor and demanding that oaths of fidelity should be taken to him by all principal landholders, lay and clerical. Lacking the military strength to confront Louis the German immediately, he set about trying to dispossess the young Charles, who on the basis of the agreement of 839 might otherwise have been his natural ally, of some or all of his kingdom.[59]

The fruit of this was to be an alliance between Charles and Louis the German and in due course their victory over Lothar at the battle of Fontenoy in June 841.[60] What is so striking about this attempt at an armed resolution of the conflict between the brothers was that it marked the end of the kind of consensual politics that had typified the reign of their father. In the 830s realignments of support amongst the aristocracy had led to Louis losing power in 830 and 833 and to Lothar doing the same in 830 and 834 without a blow having to be struck. The battle of Fontenoy in 841 was the direct antithesis of the Field of Lies of 833. A similar transition, which has been commented on in earlier chapters, can be seen in the way conflicts between rival claimants to imperial office were resolved in the Roman Empire in the third and fourth centuries.

Although open war between rival Carolingians never became the norm, and after Fontenoy there was never to be a major battle in which leading members of the family actually fought out their differences face to face, it clearly marked a watershed. There could be no hope of restoring the kind of system envisaged by Louis the Pious, in which one dominant ruler held a superior authority over all of the territories of the Frankish empire, underpinned by a consensus of support amongst the magnates. Division of the empire into separate and rival states became the only practical alternative.

In itself the battle of Fontenoy was not militarily decisive, but the alliance between the two kings against the emperor was cemented by a meeting and the taking of mutual oaths at Strasbourg in February 842. The text of the oaths was recorded in Nithard's *Histories*, and is particularly important in thus preserving the first known examples of French Romance and of Old High German.[61]

By the end of 842 Lothar was forced to accept the need for compromise, and in 843 an agreement was finally reached at Verdun, whereby the territory of the Empire was divided into three roughly equal portions.[62] Pippin II of Aquitaine, who had supported Lothar, was disregarded, and continued to fight Charles until 849, when he was forced to take refuge with the Basques. Adjustments were made in the proposed frontiers that as far as possible took account of the distribution of the scattered landholdings of the principal followers of the various monarchs, but in some cases these had to be ignored, and some resentments were thereby created. It has been suggested that Charles's relative and historian Nithard, lay abbot of St Riquier, failed to regain or be compensated for the lands he owned within Lothar's territories and which the latter had redistributed to his own supporters. For this failure to look after his interests Nithard's enthusiasm for his royal master seems to have declined by the time he wrote the fourth book of his *Histories*.[63]

Lothar kept his imperial title, and his allocation of lands in 843 was so arranged as to include the former imperial capital of Aachen as well as Rome. The emperor never really accepted the division made at Verdun as final and attempted until 849 to subvert his brothers' kingdoms from within, not least by suborning their supporters. His attempts had little success and the notion that the office of emperor conveyed a superior authority to and oversight of the other kings of the Frankish-ruled territories in practice died with the treaty of Verdun. In this way both Charlemagne and Louis the Pious's conceptions of it were lost, and it became possible within another half century for the title to become little more than a superior epithet awarded to the ruler of northern and central Italy.

The division of the Empire into a series of kingdoms may in some respects have been beneficial, in the light of the diverse and geographically widespread military problems that had to be faced from the 840s onwards. A single ruler, if able to call on more numerous resources of manpower and treasure, would have needed to concentrate troops on too many widely scattered frontiers to be fully effective. As in the Roman Empire of the third century a multiplicity of monarchs was needed to provide leadership in all of the major components of Francia. As will be seen, this process was to develop further with power and authority being increasingly devolved to localised *de facto* rulers: the counts and territorial *principes* or 'princes' of the late ninth and the tenth century.

The inherent danger, as in the third century, was that the various kings would spend as much time fighting each other as combating the external threats to their territories. Indeed, such internal conflicts could involve one Carolingian king in allying with or employing the enemies of another. The history of the period c. 840–82 is so complex and detailed that it is only possible here to give some examples of this phenomenon. The conflicts in Aquitaine and their ramifications are, perhaps, particularly revealing.

Despite ignoring his interests in the treaty of Verdun, Lothar I continued to give at least moral backing to Pippin II of Aquitaine, whose resistance was centred in the south of the kingdom, especially Toulouse. Charles besieged the latter city in 844, but one of

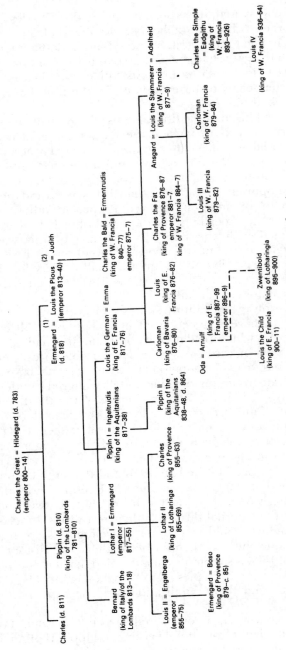

The later Carolingians (a simplified genealogy)

his armies was dramatically defeated by Pippin in the region of Angoulême. Amongst the fatalities of the battle were the historian Nithard and Charlemagne's illegitimate son Hugh.[64] It was not until 848 that Charles was able to make himself master of southern Aquitaine, assisted, albeit involuntarily, by the Viking raids on the region and their sack of Bordeaux in that year.[65] Pippin II remained in exile in the Basque duchy of Gascony south of the Garonne, until betrayed to Charles by its duke in 852. This, however, represents only the first phase and not the conclusion of the conflicts affecting the former kingdom.

In 853 an aristocratic faction in northern Aquitaine and the Loire valley, whose leader had been executed by Charles the Bald for reasons that are unknown, appealed to Louis the German, who sent his son to try and make himself king of Aquitaine. Charles may have responded by sending envoys to the Bulgars, who had replaced the Avars as the dominant confederacy in the northern Balkans and the plains north of the Danube, to persuade them to attack Louis.[66] Although Louis the German's son, the later king Louis the Younger, failed to maintain his support in Aquitaine and was expelled by Charles in 854, in the same year Pippin II escaped from monastic imprisonment and renewed his claim to his kingdom.[67] In the ensuing conflicts he was to ally with the Bretons (859) and subsequently (864) with the Vikings in the Loire, and was accused by the admittedly hostile *Annals of St Bertin* of renouncing Christianity in consequence.

In the same period the disaffected aristocracy of northern Aquitaine and the Loire valley twice more appealed to Louis the German to invade his brother Charles's territories. He rejected the request in 856, having already committed himself to a series of campaigns against the Slavs on his eastern borders, but in 858 when the Count of Anjou rebelled Louis seized his chance.[68] His invasion was militarily successful, as far as the northern parts of the West Frankish kingdom were concerned, but the refusal of the bishops, led by Hincmar of Reims, to accept the legitimacy that he claimed for his actions prevented him from establishing himself, and he was obliged to withdraw eastwards in 859.[69] In 860 a reconciliation was negotiated between the two brothers at Coblenz, largely through the intermediacy of their nephew Lothar II.[70] In the 860s the tide turned the other way, with Charles increasingly able to interfere in the politics of Louis's kingdom.

Such accounts of the rivalries and conflicts between the various Carolingian monarchs in this period could be greatly increased and expanded. It is possible to isolate a number of causes that are common to all or most of them. At the simplest level the acquisition of another kingdom or additional territory could help to solve problems of inheritance. For example, if a ruler left three legitimate heirs, his realm, like that of Lothar I in 855 and that of Louis the German in 876, might have to be broken up into yet smaller sections in order to provide separate kingdoms. Had Louis been able to install his son in Aquitaine in 853/4 part of this process would have been avoided.

A major factor in virtually all cases of conflict between the kings was aristocratic factionalism. Rival landowning families struggled to dominate the regions in which they were established, and possession of the office of count, which at this time was still theoretically in the king's gift, was the best way of gaining local supremacy and access to additional wealth through responsibility for the lands belonging to the fisc within the county.[71] Families that had once enjoyed such office but had lost it to their rivals might hope to regain it through a change of royal regime. Even those who were loyal followers of a particular king might be alienated by a change of policy that seemed to threaten their local interests. Thus, for example, Charles the Bald had sought to provide subordinate kingdoms or territories for his two sons, installing one, Charles, as King of the Aquitanians in 855 and the other, Louis the Stammerer, as Duke of Maine in 856. This also involved a settlement of the long-running conflict with the Bretons, in that the young Louis was betrothed to the daughter of their king Erispoë (851–7). In turn this threw Count Robert of Anjou (d. 866), who had previously dominated the Breton March, into opposition to the king and into adding his name to the appeals to Louis the German in 856 and 858.[72]

The continuing attraction of the imperial title, and with it the strongest claim to the inheritance of Charlemagne, was another factor that caused or exacerbated inter-Carolingian conflict, especially in the late 870s. The existence of a multiplicity of Frankish rulers made the transmission of the practically valueless but very prestigious imperial title more complex a matter than one of simple inheritance within the dynasty. After 875 the papal role in consecration enabled successive popes in practice to choose between rival claimants from amongst the rapidly proliferating royal branches of the Carolingian dynasty, but they themselves were constrained by the need to find an effective military protector as quickly as possible for a city increasingly threatened by Arab raids and the ambitions of local potentates. Therefore in practice the choice always fell on whoever seemed best able or willing to serve the material needs of Rome, above all in ensuring the protection of the city and its bishop.

The linking of the imperial title to that of 'the King of the Lombards' was made explicit by Lothar I (817–55), who entrusted northern Italy to his eldest son Louis in 844, and then had him crowned as co-emperor by Pope Leo IV in 850.[73] On Louis II's death without male heirs in 875 there followed a scramble amongst the surviving Carolingians to gain the papal gift of the title of emperor. Charles the Bald, some of whose military and other problems within his own kingdom at this time will be examined in the next chapter, launched an expedition into Italy in 875 to obtain the imperial office by making himself appear a credible protector of the papacy. In deliberate imitation of his grandfather, he was crowned emperor by Pope John VIII (872–82) on Christmas Day 875. An assembly of Italian Frankish nobles and bishops at Pavia then 'elected' him king of the Lombards in February 876.[74]

The family compact that had accepted his new status and his role in Italy was ruptured in 876, when on the death of his half-brother Louis the German, Charles tried to annex some of his kingdom, and in particular to make himself master of the imperial seat of Aachen, a necessary adjunct to his new title. However, he was resoundingly defeated by Louis's son Louis the Younger (876–82) in a battle at Andernach. Summoned to Italy in 877 by Pope John VIII, to make good the oath he had taken at his imperial coronation to defend the see of Rome, Charles found himself menaced by the forces of another nephew, Carloman King of Bavaria (876–80) and the new emperor was forced to retreat precipitately back across the Alps, only to die just north of the mountains in October 877.[75]

It was to be only a brief while before the next aspirant to the universal authority exercised by Charlemagne was to appear. This would be another Charles, one later to be known as 'the Fat'. Like his predecessor, Charles the Bald, this new Charles was not to be able to claim the imperial title on the basis of an unchallenged authority in Francia north of the Alps, but depended instead upon the prior securing of power in northern Italy and then, to a lesser extent, on papal approval. The papacy was itself subject to mounting external pressures that made the finding of a suitable candidate for the imperial office a matter of urgency. For Pope John VIII the growing designs on Rome on the part of count Lambert of Spoleto made the presence of a new imperial defender of the city ever more vital.[76] In 877 there were even more potential contenders than in 875: in the persons of three sons of Louis the German and one of Charles the Bald. However, not all of them were prepared to bid for the vacant title, being faced by military problems within their own kingdoms, and the prospect of having to take on commitments in Italy was not necessarily attractive. Nor, in practice, were all of them physically in a condition to undertake such a task.

By this time the Carolingian dynasty was suffering, through no identifiable fault of its own, something of the problem of lack of longevity that had afflicted its Merovingian predecessor. Of the four kings to whom John VIII was looking to find the new emperor in 877, only one would still be alive by the end of 882.[77] Indeed, in western Francia even the subsequent generation of Carolingians would be almost extinct by that time. Charles the Bald's son Louis the Stammerer (877–9), who was the only monarch prepared to receive John VIII in 879, died the same year, aged thirty-three. His two sons Louis III and Carloman, who succeeded him jointly as the result of a political compromise amongst the West Frankish aristocracy, followed him into the tomb from accidental deaths in 882 and 884 respectively, neither having attained the age of twenty. A posthumous son by a second wife, known as Charles the Simple, survived to reappear as king in 893.[78]

In the realm created for Lothar by the treaty of Verdun in 843, a partition between his three sons in 855 had, however, led to the extinction of the male line by 875. The emperor Louis II left only two daughters. Of his two brothers, Charles, king of Provence (855–63), left no heirs, and Lothar II (855–69) engaged in a long and ultimately fruitless struggle with the Church to obtain the annulment of his marriage, which had proved barren.[79] The immediate beneficiaries of the extinction of this particular branch of the dynasty were these monarchs' uncles Louis the German and Charles the Bald, who dismembered Lothar II's kingdom on his death.

Louis the German's own posterity, if individually longer lived than that of his younger brother Charles, proved as finite as that of his elder brother Lothar. Louis the Younger died in 882 and Carloman, who in 878 had seemed to John VIII to be the most promising candidate for the vacant imperial throne, became terminally ill in that year, finally expiring in 880. Only their younger brother Charles the Fat survived the mass extinction of the early 880s, and in consequence was able to reap, albeit temporarily, the rewards.[80]

He had inherited the small kingdom of Alamannia in southern Germany from his father in 876. The protracted illness of his brother Carloman (d. 880) led the latter to cede him his rights in northern Italy in 879, and he was formally elected as King of the Lombards at Pavia in November. His unwillingness to give the pope the guarantees he wanted in relation to the protection of Rome and the Holy See led to a delay in his selection as emperor, but by the year 881 there were no alternative candidates, and when Charles presented himself in Rome in February he was crowned.[81] The death in the next year of his only surviving brother, Louis the Younger, made him master of all of the eastern Carolingian territories, and the demise in 884 of the young west Frankish ruler Carloman left Charles the Fat as the first member of the dynasty since 817 to exercise sole rule over the whole empire created by Charlemagne. However, each of these kingdoms remained politically and administratively separate. This was not an actual re-unification of the Carolingian empire; it was instead the chance accumulation of its various contemporary components by one individual.

Charles commissioned around 884 a new work concerning his great predecessor. It is called the *Gesta Karoli* or 'Deeds of Charles', and was composed by the monk Notker the Stammerer (d. 912) of St Gall. Although very different from the biographical work of Einhard, in that it concentrates on retelling a series of anecdotes, it is testimony not only to the new emperor's interest in his ancestor, but also to the very real fear of his subjects that the dynasty was in danger of extinction. Twice in the short work Notker uses the excuse of proposing the family names Charles and Louis for future sons, thus commemorating his great ancestors, to stress that Charles the Fat still had no legitimate sons to succeed him.[82]

Whatever the appearance of the re-unification of the Carolingian empire by Charles the Fat in 884, the substance was lacking. In November 885 the Vikings besieged Paris.[83] The failure of initial efforts to lift the siege meant that the emperor had to come in person to deal with the problem in October 886. Contrary to expectations and perhaps to his self-image as the new Charlemagne, Charles the Fat bought off the Vikings without serious fighting, and made a hurried return to Alsace early the next month. By February 887 his mental health seems to have broken down.[84]

The events of this year are poorly recorded, and the contemporary sources are very partisan. Factional conflict seems to have developed within the ranks of Charles's supporters, as he was forced at an assembly held in Alamannia around June 887 to dismiss his chancellor, bishop Liutward of Vercelli, and to give the office instead to Archbishop Liutbert of Mainz.[85] The latter had previously served as chancellor to Charles's brother Louis the Younger (d. 882), and this may represent the successful political re-emergence of some of the former courtiers of that monarch. Those, such as Bishop Liutward, who had long been Charles's own personal followers, may not have forgiven him for his apparent weakness or lack of loyalty. As both Liutward and Liutbert were originally from Alamannia, this episode seems to mark a major split at the heart of the royal entourage, which also occurred at and may reflect a peculiarly sensitive time.[86]

Over the winter of 886/7 the emperor's health had shown signs of breaking down. He is reported to have suffered from a severe, if not now easily identifiable illness. Even after an initial recovery, he had to be bled to relieve the pain in his head.[87] In these circumstances, the politically charged issue of his succession took on a critical importance. At this time Charles separated from his wife, accusing her of adultery with Bishop Liutward, and it must have seemed impossible that he would produce a legitimate heir. Having previously failed to secure backing for the possible succession of his own illegitimate son, he now adopted Louis of Provence, the son of the former usurper Boso as his heir. This was most probably the direct cause of the revolt that broke out under the leadership of Arnulf, Count of Carinthia and illegitimate son of Charles's brother Carloman. Arnulf might otherwise have expected to succeed his uncle, the ailing emperor, and his position was clearly threatened by the adoption of the young and only half-Carolingian Louis.

Arnulf is recorded as winning widespread backing amongst the Saxons, the Thuringians and the Bavarians, and he was proclaimed king at an assembly near Mainz in November. By then Charles's support had melted away, even in his original kingdom of Alamannia, and he surrendered to Arnulf, who allowed him to retire to some family estates. He died in the Black Forest on 13 January 888.[88] The *Annals of St Vaast* state that he was murdered by his own men, but no other source corroborates this.[89]

Despite the apparent lack of hard achievements during his brief reign as emperor, Charles the Fat was seen by some of his contemporaries as a figure of almost saintly character. This probably testifies at least to a lack of unanimity in the matter of his deposition, heightened by doubts arising from his rapid and mysterious demise. According to the *Annals of Fulda*, when he was buried in the monastery of Reichenau 'Heaven was seen to open by many of the bystanders, thus clearly demonstrating that he who died rejected from his earthly office by men was deemed worthy by God to deserve joyfully to become a servant of the heavenly fatherland'.[90] Writing in the early tenth century, Regino of Prüm recorded of Charles that 'he was a most Christian prince, fearing God and keeping his commandments with all his heart … who, it was seen, ought to possess easily and in a brief space of time, without conflict and with none gainsaying it, all of the kingdoms of the Franks, which his predecessors had acquired not without effusion of blood and with great labour. But when near the end of his life, he was stripped of his dignities and deprived of all his goods, the suffering was, we believe, not only to be a purification but also, and which is better, a testing … which he bore most patiently, giving thanks in adversity as in prosperity, and thereby he received or doubtless has deserved to receive the crown of life that God has promised to those who delight him.'[91]

The events of this period suggest that the importance once attached to the survival of the Carolingian dynasty had greatly diminished throughout most parts of their empire. The career, described below, of Boso of Provence (879–87) had shown that it was possible for a non-Carolingian to aspire to a throne. The difficulties placed in the way of Lothar II (855–69) in the matter of his divorce and of Charles the Fat and of Arnulf in their attempts to secure the succession of illegitimate sons indicate that other principles could be given higher priority than mere Carolingian survival.[92] Admittedly, in both cases there were other members of the dynasty who had an interest in seeing that the aspirations of these two particular kings were thwarted.

While the attraction of Carolingian legitimacy continued to make itself felt well on into the tenth century, other factors could be given greater weight when a royal succession was being decided. In western Francia on the death of Charles the Fat the nobility passed over the last member of their branch of the dynasty, the nine-year-old posthumous son of Louis the Stammerer, and instead elected as king one of their own number, Count Odo of Paris. The choice was probably conditioned by the important role that he had played during the Viking siege of that city in 885–6, and the need for an active and adult king of proven military ability. But the special status of the Carolingian line continued to be recognised, in that Odo seems to have recognised the superior authority of the east Frankish Carolingian Arnulf, who provided him with regalia for his coronation at Reims.

In Italy, Duke Guido of Spoleto was elected king by the nobility of the former Carolingian kingdom in 889. His family had been trying to make themselves masters of Rome for several years, and his father Lambert had been the particular enemy of Pope John VIII (872–82). Even so, faced with the need to find a real protector for the city and see of Rome, and with the new ruler of eastern Francia clearly not willing or able to involve himself in Italy, Pope Stephen V(VI) (885–91) found it necessary to crown Guido as emperor in February 891.[93]

Guido (d. 894) had himself recrowned by the next pope, Formosus (891–6), together with his son Lambert (d. 898), but at the same time Formosus began a secret correspondence with Arnulf, to try to induce the German ruler to intervene in Italy and regain the Carolingian rights to the imperial title. This he finally did in 896 and he expelled the emperor Lambert's troops from Rome. Formosus then transferred the imperial title to

Arnulf by a coronation in February, only for the new emperor to be paralysed by a stroke and have to be carried back to Germany, where he was to die in 899.[94]

Formosus himself was probably fortunate to die in April 896, before the enraged Lambert regained Rome. His successor, Boniface VI, lasted only fifteen days before dying himself, but the next pope, Stephen VI (VII), found it expedient to be an active partisan of Lambert. Under his direction the body of Formosus was dug up, decked in pontifical robes and put on trial in what is known as 'the cadaver synod' of January 897. Found guilty of perjury and of violations of canon law, the body was then thrown into the Tiber. However, reports of miracles being performed by the washed-up corpse led to a popular revolt against Stephen, who was deposed, imprisoned and strangled in August 897. The decrees of the 'cadaver synod' were overturned and Formosus was reburied by pope Theodore II during his twenty-day pontificate in November of the same year. Picaresque as the story of the 'cadaver synod' might seem, it at least testifies to an almost obsessive concern in Rome with legal forms and procedure in such matters as the transfer of both papal and imperial authority. Behind it, however, also lies the reality that the papacy, like the imperial office, had become a prize in an increasingly localised game of central Italian politics.[95]

In Germany, as it is probably easiest now to call the eastern Frankish lands, the Carolingian dynasty was entering its terminal phase. Arnulf had managed to hold together the various regions east of the Rhine in the aftermath of the overthrow of Charles the Fat. However, his stroke in 896 weakened his personal authority, and he, like Charles before him, had faced succession problems. He could not secure acceptance of his illegitimate son Zwentibold (d. 900), whom he had created king of Lotharingia in 895, as his heir throughout the rest of his realm, and his only legitimate son was not born until 893. On Arnulf's death in 899 this infant, known as Louis the Child, succeeded, only to die still young in 911. With him the Carolingian line in the East was extinguished.[96]

In the West the dynasty was to enjoy two brief revivals, following the death of King Odo in 898. Charles the Simple (d. 929), the posthumous son of Louis the Stammerer, was put up against Odo in 893 with the backing of Archbishop Fulk of Reims (883–900) and Count Heribert of Vermandois. Sentiments of vestigial Carolingian legitimacy seems to have assisted him, and Odo lost control of most of his kingdom before his death in 898. Thereafter Charles maintained himself in office, if not always in real power, until he was deposed in 923. His attempts to maintain his control over Lotharingia at all costs had led to a revolt amongst the West Frankish nobility in 922, in the course of which they proclaimed a new king, Robert I (922–3), the brother of Odo.[97] Although Robert was killed in battle the next year, Charles was captured by his opponents and held prisoner until his death in 929.

He was replaced by another non-Carolingian, Duke Raoul of Burgundy, a son-in-law of Robert I. On Raoul's death in 936 Charles's son Louis IV was recalled from exile in Wessex by the West Frankish nobility, but he and his son Lothar (954–86) were to spend most of their reigns in conflict with different sections of it. Lothar's son Louis V (986–7) died at the age of twenty without issue, and although he had younger brothers and an uncle still living, the magnates elected Hugh Capet, a grandson of Robert I, as king. This replacement of the Carolingians, unlike that of 888, proved permanent.

Apart from the last of them, who lacked the time to demonstrate his qualities for good or for bad, none of these final West Frankish Carolingian rulers were lacking in the skill and determination needed to maintain themselves in the very difficult and changed circumstances of this period.[98] The disintegration of central authority within the already fragmented Carolingian domains can be dated to the last phase of the reign of Charles the Bald and the chaotic decade of the 880s. As will be seen in the next chapter the military problems facing the various kingdoms were acute at this time. This was also the period in which dynasties of hereditary office-holding nobles appear to have established themselves throughout the Carolingian lands.

In part this process was accelerated by such royal initiatives as the transferring of fiscal estates that had previously been administered for the crown by its local agents, the counts, into the ownership of those officials. This may not have happened all at once or in all regions, but it can certainly be documented in parts of the West Frankish kingdom in the 870s.[99] That hereditary succession to comital offices can also be shown to have begun in a number of cases in this same period is hardly coincidental.[100] In practice the central authority, the king and his immediate palatine advisers, were recognising their inability to control local society, other than in extreme cases, for which only the cumbersome mechanism of the dispatch of an army could be used. The system of *missi*, employed by Charlemagne and his successors, had in the last resort been based on the threat of force. In the circumstances of the later ninth century when, as will be seen, the military problems facing the crown were rapidly becoming insuperable, this became little more than a bluff as far as the control of local society was concerned.

Even in major cases of political disloyalty it was difficult for the monarchy to act decisively. After the death of Louis the Stammerer in 879, Boso, the count of Provence, who had been the brother of Charles the Bald's second wife, made himself king of a substantial region in the south-east of France centred on Vienne, without the West Frankish kings being able to take direct military action against him. It was only in 881, by turning his brother Richard against him, that Vienne was retaken.[101] Even afterwards Boso maintained some shadowy hold in the region until his death *c.* 887.

In practice such attempts to usurp a royal title were rare, and tended only to occur in regions that had once had their own monarchy. What was really at issue was the power that was built up from the late ninth century onwards by local dynasties of counts and dukes, who turned themselves into what have been seen as territorial 'princes'.[102] Although by the nature of their title and the origin of their offices they were formally subject to kings in western or eastern Francia, in practice they were independent masters of their own territories, taking oaths of fealty from lesser landowners, controlling the administration of justice, and taking what profits were to be gained from it and from other rights, such as tolls, that would have previously been due to the monarchy.

Political life in tenth century western and eastern Francia was largely a question of the skill or lack of it of the monarch in building and maintaining alliances amongst these firmly entrenched local 'princely' or ducal families. In eastern Francia or Germany the situation was made easier by the concentration of power into the hands of a small number of dukes, whose territories corresponded to the older ethnic divisions of Thuringia, Saxony, Bavaria, Suabia (Alamannia) and Franconia. In western Francia many more units existed, derived mainly from the long established Carolingian administrative divisions, which added to the fragmentation and to the greater political problems faced by the monarchs.

The importance of institutions of central authority, which is to say kings and their courts, became greatly reduced in many parts of Western Europe in the later ninth and tenth centuries. Their principal value was in the co-ordination of military action to be taken against such large-scale threats as the Viking raids and the incursions of the Magyars from the plains across the Danube. This was the testing ground that determined whether or not strong monarchies re-emerged in the various realms of the former Carolingian empire and adjacent areas.

In some cases, as in tenth-century England, successful military action against such a threat could lead to a rebuilding of a relatively powerful, centralised monarchy, able to impose its will

on all levels of society and to develop more complex and sophisticated forms of administration.[103] In Germany also, in the same
period, the role of the kings of the new Ottonian dynasty from
Saxony in the wars against the Magyars was crucial in the development of their power over the dukes of the component regions
of the eastern Frankish kingdom, whose equals they had originally
been. Failure, as perhaps with Charles the Fat's involvement in
the Viking siege of Paris, could, on the other hand, further
discredit a monarchy and render it less and less necessary. In this
way the 'new participants' in the history of Western Europe – the
Scandinavian Vikings, the Magyars, and even the Arabs – served
as a vital catalyst to change in the political order of the older
societies.

19 'The desolation of the pagans'

Traders and raiders

One of the first recorded Viking raids in Western Europe took place on June 8th in the year 793, when the island monastery of Lindisfarne was sacked.[1] It was to be the start of a series of such assaults on parts of Britain, Ireland, and the Channel and Atlantic coasts of France which at times would become an almost annual occurrence. Such raids in turn proved to be the forerunners of waves of migration out of Scandinavia. The destructiveness of the Viking period in the history of Western Europe, which extended from the very end of the eighth to the early eleventh centuries, has long been appreciated, despite the recent attempts made by revisionist historians to try to minimise it.[2] The resulting populist slogan that has been applied to the Vikings – 'traders not raiders' – is deceptive in implying that the same people could not be both. On the other hand, it must be admitted that, in certain of the regions that they came to settle in, the economic and cultural contributions made by the Scandinavians in the ninth to eleventh centuries represented considerable advances over what had been achieved by the indigenous culture.[3]

The Viking phenomenon is not an easy one to explain, in that the principal indigenous literary sources for their history are generally very much later in date. Serious reservations have been expressed about the worth of almost all of them, as far as the understanding of the history and society of pre-eleventh century Scandinavia is concerned.[4] Runic inscriptions constitute the only strictly contemporary source of written evidence produced by that society, and as most of these take the form of memorials to otherwise unknown individuals their evidential value is limited.[5] On the other hand, more or less contemporary ninth and tenth century West Frankish and Anglo-Saxon annals can provide an outline narrative of the impact of the Viking raids on these regions, but their authors were not interested in analysing their enemies' motives or in informing themselves about the societies that had produced them. Archaeology can help, at least in terms of the description of the material culture of the Scandinavian societies, but there are strict limits to the types of questions which it is competent to answer.

In consequence of these evidential problems there is still no consensus of opinion on such crucial questions as what factors led to the sudden development of long-distance seaborne raiding amongst the Scandinavians in the late eighth century, and which regions in particular contributed to this and to the subsequent phases of overseas settlement. The very origin of the name 'Viking' has caused some uncertainty.[6] It has proved impossible to state with confidence that the Viking raids and migrations were or were not primarily the products of such forces as overpopulation, climatic deterioration, or other ecological changes affecting Scandinavia.[7] Similarly, at a simpler and more material level it has been suggested that advances in boat-building techniques might explain the timing and character of the Viking raids, but the evidence from the excavation of a range of boats seems to indicate that Scandinavian ships had had the capability to undertake long sea voyages for some time prior to the first records of their presence in England and western Francia.[8] Some other interpretations concentrate on social change and above all on the growth of more powerful monarchies within the Scandinavian regions, that are seen as driving the recalcitrant and unruly elements in their kingdoms overseas, but there is a danger that this is possibly confusing cause with effect.[9]

Explanations that involve placing especial weight for at least some aspects of Viking activity on external causes are easier to document, but can at best be only partial, in that they have to ignore the probable role of internal changes within Scandinavian society. Although, as will be seen, it is possible to study the growth of Danish assaults on the Frankish kingdoms and southern England in the light of pressures initially exerted on their society by the expansion of Frankish power into Saxony and across the Elbe, this does not easily explain the growth of raiding by the Norwegians across the North Sea and the establishment by them of settlements in Ireland and the Northern Isles. As previously mentioned, the first Viking raids – by Norwegians on Lindisfarne and by Danes on Wessex – also precede the definite establishment of a Frankish presence on the Elbe by about ten to fifteen years.

It is probably best, though, not to look for any one explanation, nor to try to reduce the Viking period contacts between Scandinavia and Western Europe to too simple a pattern. Problems of evidence aside, what is most remarkable about the Viking phenomenon is its complexity. Simply put, different groups of Scandinavians were doing different things at different times in different places for different reasons. Thus, for example, it is likely that various families from coastal regions of south-west Norway were founding settlements in the Orkneys and the Hebrides even before the first raid on Ireland (795), and thus over half a century prior to the commencement of the largely Danish settlements in northern and eastern England.

What does seem clear is that when the Viking raids were first recorded in contemporary annals they represented, in their violence, something quite unexpected and unprecedented.[10] When Danes first appeared in Wessex, in 789, the royal official who went out to meet them (and got killed for his pains) 'did not know what they were'.[11] He probably thought they were traders. Those who were to experience the Viking attacks looked for the causes of this new and violent threat in the ills of their own society, and saw in it an element of divine retribution. Thus, Alcuin, writing to the community of Lindisfarne in the aftermath of the raid on the monastery, interpreted it as a divine chastisement: 'Truly it has not happened by chance, but is a sign that it was well merited by someone.'[12]

The unexpected nature of the initial raids did not imply, as other remarks in this letter of Alcuin's have been taken to indicate, that the raiders of Lindisfarne were members of a people unknown to all their victims. Contacts between Scandinavia and continental and insular Western Europe had been prolonged and continuous throughout the preceding centuries.[13] Economic exchange between the Roman Empire and the Baltic extended back to at least the first century AD, and appears to have intensified in the fourth.[14] In terms of material culture and also in the dynastic legends of the ruling house, evidence exists of links between the East Anglian kingdom in Britain and parts of Scandinavia in the sixth century. In particular the helmet found in the largest of the burial mounds at Sutton Hoo in East Anglia, which has been dated to the 620s, shows close parallels to a series of slightly later ones found in the cemeteries at Vendel in Sweden.[15]

The seventh and eighth centuries saw the development of extensive new trading connections along parts of the southern shores of the North Sea and the eastern end of the Channel. These involved the import, amongst other things, of goods such as furs, walrus ivory and amber from Scandinavia and the Baltic, and probably intensified existing economic links with those regions. The port of Quentovic, whose precise location near Etaples has only recently been discovered, was developed by the Franks in the vicinity of the former Roman naval base of Boulogne, and Dorestad on the junction of the river Lek with the Rhine became the principal market for this whole region by early in the eighth century.[16] To the north of the Channel two other significant *entrepôts* came into being at Hamwih (just to the east of the medieval site of Southampton) and at Ipswich in East Anglia.[17] Similarly, the emergence by the beginning of the ninth century of a number of trading settlements in Scandinavia, notably at Birka, Hedeby and Kaupang, were clearly related to these developments in the west.

It is possible that a relatively strong and unified kingship emerged in Jutland – the mainland part of Denmark – in the course of the eighth century. Furthermore, this may have been the product both of new military problems, in the form of Slavic pressure from the south-east and the growing Frankish involvement in Saxony, and of the economic opportunities created by the growth of new markets and ports in northern Francia and southern England. One of the most impressive large-scale archaeological features to be encountered in Early Medieval Denmark is a series of inter-related defensive earthworks that link the Schleifjord and the Schwansen peninsula with the valley of the river Rheide. In view of the marshy character of the land further west, this system of earthworks, known collectively as the Danevirke, controlled all land routes from the south into the Danish kingdom of Jutland.[18]

The *Annales Regni Francorum* attribute responsibility for such a work to king Godefred, dating it to 808.[19] However, archaeologists have established by dendrochronology (dating by tree rings) that the actual date of building of the Danevirke has to be placed somewhere around the year 737; at least that is the date around which the trees that were used in its construction were cut down. Like Offa's Dyke in Britain, the scale and purpose of the undertaking show that it required considerable mobilisation of labour and involved interests beyond those of a single small region. Although otherwise undocumented, the existence of these structures seems to indicate the presence of some centralised authority in Jutland at this time, able to impose an obligation to contribute to public work on at least some of its subjects.

In the course of the eighth century, paralleling the rise of the great ports in northern Francia, a number of trading settlements came into being in Scandinavia. One of the most important of these was Hedeby (Haithabu) at the southern end of the Schleifjord. This was tied into the Danevirke system of defences. It seems that by the time of Godefred (d. 810) Danish kings were taking tolls on the merchandise brought through such ports and trading stations, providing the monarchy with a regular and potentially lucrative source of revenue. The same king was reported to have destroyed a Slavic trading station at an unknown Baltic site called Reric, and to have transplanted its merchants to his own kingdom, because of the revenue this would create.[20]

Whatever the growth in political and economic complexity in Denmark in the course of the eighth century, there are strong indications that much of this was lost in the ninth. After the murder of Godefred in 810 Frankish sources record civil wars and fragmentation, and the internal disturbances and the greater turbulence throughout northern Europe must have weakened the economic benefits to be gained from peaceful trading. This would help to explain the period of predatory raiding that followed. As with African fleets under Vandal rule in the fifth century – or, for that matter, English ventures in the Caribbean in the sixteenth – possession of suitable ships enabled the same people to indulge in trade and piracy simultaneously, according to the opportunities offered and their assessments of relative profitability.

It has been doubted whether a single kingdom could have existed in Denmark at all at this time, but the Frankish chronicles do not give the impression so much of rival territorial kingdoms in Jutland and the islands as of civil wars between members of an extended royal line. Certainly the most interesting feature of the occasional references in the Frankish annals to the rulers of Denmark is the number of conflicts that were going on within what appears to be a single dynasty. Such civil wars are recorded in 812, 813, 814, 817, 819, 823, 827, 828, 850 and 854, and there were probably others besides these.[21]

From 811/12 onwards, if not earlier, it would seem fair to say on the basis of the admittedly limited information that the Frankish chroniclers had available, that kingship could be shared between all available members of a particular branch of the ruling family. Thus, for example, all of the sons of Godefred are recorded as being kings in the period *c.* 813–post-827. They did not always remain in agreement, and the heirs of other former kings from collateral branches of the dynasty frequently challenged the power of the ruling group. Thus, it is advisable to see in the Danish royal line the existence of relatively large numbers of rival leaders, whose individual political fortunes could rise and fall according to their abilities to maintain their personal followings.

Failure in the clearly bloody struggles in Denmark led the leaders of the defeated faction to go into exile, together with those who still followed them – often because they in turn had lost out in more localised struggles with rival families. Such leaders could either make a new base for themselves or, as was certainly the case by the late tenth century, gain the wealth and reputation to enable them to make another bid for power in their homeland by successful raiding in Britain, Ireland and Francia. In such circumstances it is possible that rival Danish kings and lesser war leaders found it necessary to turn to raiding to maintain themselves and their followers. Regrettably, the Frankish and Anglo-Saxon sources do not provide any information as to the origins of the principal Viking leaders overseas in the ninth century. In some cases they are clearly called *reges* or kings, but is this a reflection of their entrepreneurial leadership of the raiding armies or testimony to their inherited status within Scandinavian society?[22]

Norway, on the other hand, provides no evidence for the growth of more powerful or territorially more extensive monarchies at this time. This was to be a process that only got under way in the tenth century and is associated, at least in later tradition, particularly with the reign of a king Harald Hárfagri (d. 936?), who began to extend a kingdom centred on Vestfold into the western fjords and also northwards into the Trondelag.[23] In the eighth and ninth centuries all that can be said is that it is probable that all these regions were parcelled up between a series of petty local rulers. The same picture would seem to be equally true of Sweden.[24]

It was from parts of Norway and Sweden that the first entrepreneurial ventures overseas were undertaken, both westwards and eastwards.[25] As has been mentioned, it is suspected that the Norwegian settlements in the Orkneys and the Hebrides were already developing at the time that the first raids on Northumbria and Ireland took place in the 790s. It was probably from these northern islands rather than directly across the North Sea that the raiders came. These are areas located at best on the periphery of the zone of accelerating commercial activity in the Channel and the southern shores of the North Sea, and not generating much by way of surplus or raw materials that could be exchanged. Thus it is probable that the new settlers took to preying on their southern neighbours to provide economic resources not otherwise available to them.

Although saga material, virtually all of which was composed in the twelfth and thirteenth centuries, should generally be eschewed as a source for the narrative history of Scandinavian societies in the Viking period, it can give an imaginative impression of how raiding could fit into a pattern of life that also involved farming. Thus the Norse freemen of a settlement, for example in the Orkneys, could take to their ships with the coming of spring and after the sowing of their crops, leaving their farms to be maintained by slaves, large numbers of whom were to be found in Scandinavian society.[26] Raids either along the east coast of England or in Ireland could produce loot, that would be divided up after their return home in the autumn to take part in the harvest. Winter was passed almost hibernating (assisted by quite a lot of drink) in their farmsteads.[27] This is a pattern that is not dissimilar to the formal structure of warfare to be found in the same period in Francia. The scale is different, and there was not the central royal direction, but the integration of campaigning into a seasonal pattern that accommodated the needs of farming is identical.

The initial plundering of the island monasteries around the British, Irish and French coasts – Lindisfarne in 793, Iona, Inisbofin and Inismurray in 795, and St Philibert's monastery on Noirmoutier in 799 – was shocking to the societies that suffered the attacks because of the lack of a shared value system between raiders and victims. Other than in Ireland, where church burning was relatively common in the endemic warfare between the numerous rival kingdoms struggling for regional hegemonies, attacks on monasteries would have been inconceivable in war between Christians.[28] From the raiders' point of view such easily accessible and wealthy establishments, housing large quantities of easily portable treasure in the form of precious metal reliquaries, book covers, and liturgical ornaments, were endlessly attractive, and they returned several times to them. Iona was looted in 795, 802 and 806, and in 807 in consequence most of the community moved to Ireland to a newly established monastery in the inland site of Kells.[29]

Such practical expedients and greater wariness on the part of coastal settlements might have proved sufficient to counter the relatively small-scale, if occasionally bloody, raids of this first period. However, the relatively limited threats of the Norwegians were to be followed by much larger-scale warfare and migration on the part of the Danes, affecting regions untouched by the earlier phase of Scandinavian depredations. Whatever the causes of the Norwegian migrations across the North Sea that gave rise to the raids in Britain and Ireland, the Danish attacks on their neighbours are the products of rather different circumstances, and reflect, not least, external economic and cultural pressures on their own society.

The Vikings and Francia

The campaigns of Charlemagne against the Saxons clearly made an impact on the peoples further to the north and east, particularly on the Slavs living along the southern shores of the Baltic, and on the Danes.[30] Diplomatic contacts between the Frankish ruler and a Danish king Sigefred go back to at least 782, but Charles's tampering with the balance of power east of the Elbe in 804 may have been the cause of some of the ensuing problems. Facing continuing resistance from the Saxons living north of the Elbe, the Frankish emperor had them rounded up and transported into Francia, giving their land to the Slavic Abodrites, who had been allies of the Franks since at least 789.[31] The resulting rise in Abodrite power in this region rapidly led to a Danish attack on them in 808, and in turn the dispatch of a Frankish army to defend the Elbe. In 809 the Abodrites retaliated against other lesser Slavic tribes who had given their support to the Danes.

Conflict between the Slav allies of the Franks and of the Danes rapidly escalated into confrontation between the two kingdoms.[32] In 810 the Danish king Godefred sent a fleet to raid Frisia, which had been under the control of the Franks since the time of Charles Martel. However, in the period of internal disturbance that followed Godefred's murder in the same year, competing kings of the Danes found a new use for the Franks as potential allies in their civil wars. One of the competitors, called Harald Klak (812–13, 819–27), who had been temporarily ousted, felt it expedient to receive Christian baptism in a great ceremony at the royal palace at Ingelheim in 826, in which the Emperor Louis stood as his godfather.[33] Although he was then able to return to his kingdom with Frankish backing, in practice this did him little good in the longer term, and may have contributed directly to his renewed expulsion from Denmark the following year.

As with Rome in the fourth and fifth centuries, the growth of closer and more complex links and exchanges between a more socially and economically complex empire and its less developed neighbours led to increased predatoriness on the part of the latter when its more powerful partner showed signs of weakness. Thus, it was hardly coincidental that the first major Danish raids on imperial territory started in 834, when the civil war between Louis the Pious and his son Lothar was at its height. From 834 to 836 annual raids occurred on the trading settlement of Dorestad in Frisia.[34] Louis, who in general responded more rapidly and effectively to military than to political problems, ordered the building of a series of coastal forts in 837. Though the one on the island of Walcheren was almost immediately captured.[35]

Attacks on Francia proper commenced in 841, when the sons of Louis the Pious were engaged in civil war. In that year Rouen on the Seine was sacked, and in 842 so too was the port of Quentovic, near Boulogne.[36] In 843 a Danish fleet raided Nantes, killing the bishop, and then wintered on an island near the mouth of the Loire. In 844 this force sailed up the Garonne, and then proceeding by land, sacked Toulouse. Returning to the sea, they sailed along the north coast of Spain, and made an unsuccessful descent on Galicia, then part of the small Christian kingdom of the Asturias. From there they sailed south and looted the Arab-ruled towns of Seville and Lisbon. Spanish sources report that this fleet consisted of fifty-four ships.[37] In 845 a fleet said to consist of 120 ships sailed up the Seine to threaten Paris, but was bought off by Charles the Bald, now the undisputed master of most of western Francia, for the sum of 7000 pounds of silver.[38]

Criticism has been levelled at some of the figures given in the annals for the numbers of ships said to be involved in some of the Viking raids. Accepting that they are unlikely to be precise, it has to be asked how realistic is such a figure as that of the 120 ships given for the fleet on the Seine in 845? On the one hand, taking the reasonably conservative figure of thirty men to a ship this would indicate that the Danish fighting force numbered some 3600. This may seem at least minimal in view of the scale of the threat apparently presented and the king's unwillingness to take on the raiders in battle. On the other hand, if this figure for the manpower is approximately correct, it needs to be appreciated that the bribe they received from Charles would have netted them less than two pounds of silver per man, which is hardly impressive. The issue, like so many in Viking studies, remains inconclusive.

From the entry for this same year in the *Annals of St Bertin* it is clear that at least three separate Viking forces were operating independently at this time. There was the one in the Seine. The fleet that had devastated Toulouse and southern Aquitaine in 844 returned from its expedition to Spain, and was raiding Saintonge, and another one, reported improbably to consist of 600 ships, and which had been sent by the Danish King Horic (d. 854), sacked Hamburg and sailed up the Elbe, before being defeated by the Saxon forces of Louis the German.

This was one of the few military successes to be recorded on the part of royal armies operating against the Scandinavian raiders in this period. In 847 the Danes in Aquitaine began a blockade of Bordeaux, and Charles the Bald, then engaged in crushing the last resistance of Pippin II and his supporters, is reported to have inflicted a defeat on them in 848; but it can hardly have been of lasting consequence, in that they proceeded to take and sack Bordeaux later in the year.[39]

Overall, what is so striking about the fairly full accounts of events given in the *Annals of St Bertin* for the period 830–82 is the lack of really effective action taken by the Frankish kings to check this growing series of raids and depredations, particularly in the period from the death of Louis the Pious to the early 860s. Even the one concerted military effort made, that involved not just the army of Charles the Bald but also that of his half-brother Lothar, proved ineffectual. In 852 a Danish fleet was blockaded in the Seine by these combined Frankish armies, but in the end Charles the Bald made a treaty with its leaders, which permitted them to stay until March 853. Thus refreshed, these Vikings sailed into the Loire, where in the years to follow they were to sack Nantes, Tours, Blois, Angers, Orléans and Poitiers.[40] The causes of these failures on the part of the Carolingian rulers reflect not only the difficult nature of the military problem the Vikings posed but also the serious political difficulties they had to face within Francia, which were discussed in the previous chapter.

Large-scale as some of these Viking operations were, few if any of them seem to have been directed by Danish kings of the type represented by Godefred. The kings ruling in Denmark generally appear amenable to diplomacy, but the leaders of the great expeditions overseas, such as those in Aquitaine in the 840s, in the Loire in the 850s and in the Seine from 856 to 862 enjoyed a mobility and lack of need to defend their own land that made them very hard to contain. The Viking raiders tended to base themselves on islands, such as Thanet and Sheppey in southern England, Batavia off Frisia and a variety of isles in the rivers Seine and Loire, which gave them both secure bases that the Franks seemed little able to attack – the Anglo-Saxons were better – and places in which to store and contain their loot.[41] Although they were all too keen to get their hands on treasure and precious objects, such as books with bejewelled and ivory covers, the greater part of the proceeds of their raids was probably of the two-legged kind.

From the attack on Dorestad and Frisia in 836 onwards, the annals record the Danes 'depopulating' monasteries, towns and districts. What they were doing was carrying off slaves. In some cases their captives were of sufficient worth as to be able to command large ransoms from their families. When in April 858 Charles the Bald's cousin and chancellor, Louis, Abbot of Saint-Denis, was captured together with his brother by Vikings operating in the Seine valley, the king had to raise a ransom of 688 pounds of gold and 3250 pounds of silver to buy their release.[42] Those for whom no worthwhile ransoms could be expected were sold as slaves.

The slave trade had long existed in Western Europe, but although statistics do not exist, had probably declined considerably in importance in the period after the fall of Rome. The existence of servile status, of families tied to the land and under fixed obligations to their lords, made the need for the expensive purchasing of slaves unnecessary. When land was sold the unfree families attached to it were normally included in the price. However, from the later eighth century onwards an enormous new market for slaves brought from other parts of Europe opened up in the Islamic world. Slave armies were replacing the previous use of Arab tribal forces in Spain, North Africa and the Near East.[43] There was a considerable demand for household slaves throughout the same regions. It is also conceivable that a certain percentage of those enslaved were destined for the 'home market' back in

Scandinavia, where servile labour appears to have been used on the land.

In the same period new Scandinavian settlements were developing overseas, for which again locally captured and imported slaves would have been needed. In the 830s the Norwegian Vikings began raiding more intensively in Ireland, taking numerous captives for the slave market, as well as looting monasteries. A number of prominent ecclesiastics were also made prisoner, and like their counterparts in Francia, released in return for ransoms. Thus Forannán, Abbot of Armagh (835–48), head of the foremost monastic federation in Ireland, was held captive in 845–6.[44] In a similar paralleling of developments in Francia, the Vikings began to winter in Ireland, something that is first recorded in 840/1, when they established temporary strongholds in which to lay up their ships. At least one of these, Dublin, turned into a permanent settlement and market. Paradoxically, this made the Vikings more vulnerable, in that a fixed base of this sort needed to be defended, and its own growing wealth made it attractive to the Irish rulers. Dublin was sacked for the first time in 849 by a confederacy led by the Uí Néill King of Mide, Máel Sechnaill (843–62).[45] The Vikings also became increasingly embroiled in the inter-kingdom conflicts within Ireland, which they could sometimes exploit to their advantage, but which could also lead to military disaster.[46]

Just at the time that the Norwegians in Ireland began losing some of the advantages of mobility, so too did the Danish groups in Francia. By the late 850s the Vikings were so numerous and so well-established in the main river valleys of northern France, that it actually became easier for the western Franks to contain them. The need for the individual leaders to maintain their followings by providing them with profits meant that one group was quite willing to fight against another in the interests of the Frankish king, as long as he was able to pay them. The fact that by this time their depredations had been going on for twenty years may have also limited the degree of loot still easily accessible to them: some monasteries and larger settlements in the vulnerable areas appear to have been abandoned, and Viking slaving and ransom-seeking techniques were by now all too well known.[47] Thus, in 858 one group of Vikings established in the Seine agreed to fight for Charles the Bald, and in 862 he was able to use others then controlling the river Somme to attack the main base of those in the Seine. By such manoeuvres and also the employment of new defensive tactics, such as the establishment of fortified bridges across the vulnerable rivers, the Franks began to make the Viking operations less profitable and more risky. It is thus hardly coincidental that from 865 onwards their attacks on the Anglo-Saxon kingdoms intensified, while those on western Francia decreased. At the same time Danish groups, who had hitherto largely concerned themselves with Francia, began to operate in Ireland, and in consequence to come into conflict with the longer established Norwegians and in due course made themselves masters of Dublin.[48]

The period of relief was short-lived. In the last years of Charles the Bald Viking activity in western Francia revived. Some historians believe that it was primarily the Frankish king's defensive measures that had led the raiders to turn their attention elsewhere in the period 865–76, but when the attacks on Francia resumed the kingdom was unprepared and royal military action proved generally ineffectual. As the *Annals of St Vaast* record, in 876 an army was sent against the Vikings in the Seine but 'it did nothing useful'. In the circumstances Charles's involvements in Italy and quest for the imperial title might appear, as they did to Archbishop Hincmar of Reims, to be a dereliction of duty. From the last year of the new emperor's life (877) comes a capitulary stipulating the sums to be paid by all bishops, abbots, counts and royal vassals as a tribute to the Vikings in the Seine, 'so that they would withdraw from the kingdom'.[49]

Following the premature death of Charles's son Louis the Stammerer in 879, Viking activity in the north of Francia intensified. A dispute broke out between the principal West Frankish magnates over the succession. Some supported Louis' young sons and others wanted the East Frankish king Louis the Younger (876–82) to take over the kingdom.[50] Possibly prompted by knowledge of these divisions, a large Viking force crossed from England to sack Thérouanne and loot Brabant and the valley of the Scheldt. From 879 to 892 their depredations in northern France continued. In 881 they looted the famous monasteries of St Vaast, St Riquier (Centula) and Corbie, while in 882 they sacked Reims, and its aged Archbishop Hincmar died while a fugitive from his see.[51]

The young West Frankish King Louis III (879–82) won a victory over one Viking contingent at Saucy in 881, but as in the case of all other reported military successes in this period, this had no significant consequences.[52] In every instance the victory was not or could not be followed up, and the Vikings having withdrawn from the area they had been ravaging turned their attention to another one instead. Ultimately, their highly profitable siege of Paris in 885/6 contributed directly to the replacement of the Carolingian dynasty in western Francia.

According to the *Annals of St Vaast* the Viking army left Francia in 892 because of the famine that was then afflicting much of the land. They did not return until the winter of 896/7. From this point onwards, however, things went somewhat better for the Franks. The removal of the Vikings in 892 had been followed by, and may well have made possible, the outbreak of war between the adherents of King Odo and the supporters of the only surviving heir of the West Frankish branch of the Carolingian dynasty, Louis the Stammerer's posthumously born son Charles (later known as 'the Simple' – in the sense of 'direct and uncomplicated', not of 'simple-minded'). Despite various swings of fortune this was finally resolved, not least through the death of Odo in January 898, in favour of Charles.[53] In the latter's reign a generally more vigorous resistance was to be offered to renewed (but possibly smaller-scale) Viking threats, which was allied to a new policy of settling the invaders in vulnerable frontier regions.

The first success was secured in 897 when Vikings in the valley of the Maas retreated to their ships, fearing the size of a threatening royal army. Later in the year their leader made an agreement with Charles, accepting Christian baptism, with the king as his godfather. In 898 one of the most powerful of the territorial magnates of the West Frankish kingdom, Count Richard of Autun, defeated a Viking force raiding overland into northern Burgundy.[54] Despite these more aggressive and effective reactions, the lower valley of the Seine remained an irreducible Viking stronghold, something that came to be accepted and regularised in 911.

By this period the hitherto plentiful chronicle sources have become much rarer. The *Annals of St Bertin* terminated in 882 and those of St Vaast in 900. No major West Frankish historiography was undertaken until Flodoard, a canon of the Church of Reims, composed a set of annals covering the years 919–66. This became the main source for the monk Richer of Saint-Remi in Reims, who wrote (*c*. 996) an account of the period 888–995. He was largely content to add fictitious embroideries to his predecessor's brief accounts and his work has no independent authority for the period before the 970s.[55] This has meant that one of the most significant developments in the history of Frankish–Viking relations remains obscure. This was the agreement made in 911 between Charles the Simple and the Viking leader Rollo, who thereby appears to have become, in practice though not in title, Count of Rouen.[56]

A second settlement, based on Nantes and the frontiers of Brittany, was made in 921 after the siege and surrender of a large force of Viking marauders in the Loire valley by Duke Robert of Neustria, brother of the former King Odo.[57] This also involved the baptism of the Viking leaders at Paris. Such conversions were, as in parallel cases in England, normal after a Viking defeat and submission. In many cases it seems that such baptised Vikings reverted to paganism once they were ready to break the agreements made with their Christian conquerors. This seems like cynicism, but it is probably better to see their attitude as representing a feeling that for the time being Christ was in the ascendancy, but that in due course Odin and Thor would reassert themselves. In other words, by professing themselves as followers of Christ they were not necessarily denying the existence of their other gods.

What is significant, though, in the better documented instance of 921, is that the conversion and grant followed a military defeat and submission on the part of the Vikings. It is therefore possible that Rollo in 911 was prepared to accept baptism and responsibility for protecting western Francia from attack by other Vikings who might seek to enter via the Seine because of some prior defeat at the hands of the king. In practice Rollo remained a useful ally of Charles the Simple, and resisted the latter's two non-Carolingian successors, Robert (922–3), the brother of Odo, and his son-in-law Ralph (923–36). Admittedly, this also served his own interests best, in that his main territorial rivals, the Counts of Flanders and Vermandois, were on the opposing side. Despite occasional setbacks, Rollo and his successors were to expand their territory into what around the end of the century was to become the duchy of Normandy.[58]

Such territorial concessions were not new. As early as 827 the exiled Danish King Harald Klak had been given land around Walcheren by Louis the Pious, as part of the Franks' defensive measures against raids, and a similar agreement had been made between the Emperor Lothar and a Danish leader called Godefred, son of Heriold, which the latter broke in 852.[59] The nearest parallel to the West Frankish treaties with the Vikings was that made by the Emperor Charles the Fat with the Danish leader Godefred in 882.[60] By this the latter and his followers were settled in Frisia, and the Viking leader was adopted into the Carolingian family by marriage to Gisela, daughter of Lothar II. The intention of this treaty, like those of 911 and 921, was to fit the invaders permanently into the Frankish administrative and military structures. Thus in 911 Rollo seems to have received all royal rights over the county of Rouen, other than that of nominating its bishop.

Although, with the exception of the early tenth century settlements between the Seine and the Breton marches, Viking occupation was geographically and chronologically more limited in Francia than in England, the overall effects of their activities were equally strong. In England the elimination of the Anglo-Saxon kingdoms of Northumbria, Mercia and East Anglia in the 860s and the survival under Alfred of Wessex enabled the latter to unite all of these territories under itself in the tenth century. In Francia the nature of the threat and the limited nature of the response to it on the part of the monarchy led to the growth of greater regional independence. The dukes and counts raised their own forces and built their own fortresses to resist Viking and Arab raiding. Royal estates and regalian rights were ceded to them in the interests of maintaining such local order.

Although it might seem difficult to understand how this was rationalised at the time, the Frankish evidence relating to the Carolingian rulers' responses to Viking activities within their kingdoms gives the impression that many of them did not regard this as a problem that required their primary attention. Unlike their Anglo-Saxon counterparts, they appear to have treated the activities of the Vikings more as problems of local order than as threats to the continued existence of their kingdoms. In a sense they were right. At no point did Viking armies seem in any way poised to conquer a Frankish kingdom in the way they did in England. At their worst Viking depredations affected only certain parts of the Frankish kingdoms and did not threaten their integrity as a whole.

Even so, it is strange to see how militarily restrained Frankish reactions were, at least before the 880s. Direct confrontations between Vikings and Frankish forces, led either by kings or by their local representatives, were very rare. This changed in the 880s and 890s, but the battles of those decades fought by Louis III (879–82), Carloman (879–84) and Odo (888–98) were generally limited in their military and political effects. However, by the early tenth century the more aggressive and reactive responses on the part of the Frankish leaders when allied to a new policy of accepting Viking settlement of certain vulnerable districts and integrating them within existing administrative structures proved surprisingly successful.

It would only be fair to add that by the time of Charles the Simple it is probable that the number of Vikings active within West Francia was far less than had been the case in the 850s/860s and in the years 879–92. For one thing many of their number would have been absorbed into the substantial settlements in northern and eastern England. It was the presence of these that may also have made the Vikings in the Seine ultimately more ready to accept something similar for themselves.

The Vikings and the Anglo-Saxon kingdoms

Although the presence of Norwegian settlements in the northern islands of Britain and in Ireland had led to a series of occasional raids on vulnerable coastal sites, especially in Northumbria, large-scale attacks on the Anglo-Saxon kingdoms did not occur until the 830s. Inevitably conditions on one side of the Channel affected those on the other, and it is no surprise to find that the beginning of Danish raids on the Frankish ports in Frisia should be matched by attacks on the southern coasts of England. Thus the Isle of Sheppey was devastated in 835 and Romney Marsh, other parts of Kent and the Lincolnshire coast suffered in 841. London and Rochester were attacked in 842.[61] These latter parallel the intensified raids on northern Francia in the early 840s. Other Viking attacks occurred further to the west, and it is possible that these were actually the work of Norwegian raiders from Ireland and the northern Isles. As they were to demonstrate in Francia, the Vikings were adept at taking advantage of their enemies' weaknesses and in exploiting divisions amongst them. Thus in 838 a group of them, possibly from Ireland, allied with the Britons of Cornwall in an attack on Wessex.[62] They were, however, defeated by the West Saxon King Egbert.

In general the Anglo-Saxon rulers and their local subordinates the ealdormen, the equivalents of the Frankish counts, were active in their resistance to Viking incursions, and the shire (county) levies seem to have been quickly raised to meet such threats. Thus in 840 an ealdorman Wulfheard defeated thirty-three ships' companies of Vikings in the vicinity of Hamwih. Eanwulf, ealdorman of Somerset, won a victory at the mouth of the river Parret in 848, and his colleague Ceorl, ealdorman of Devon, was equally successful at an unidentified *Wicgeanbeorg* in 850. In the same year Athelstan the West Saxon King of Kent and his ealdorman Ealhere defeated a Viking force at Sandwich, capturing nine ships.[63]

Not all such encounters went the same way, and a number of defeats are recorded in the same period.[64] Even so, the reports of Viking attacks on towns and monasteries are far fewer than those to be found in the Frankish sources dealing with the 840s and 850s. Canterbury, for example, which should have constituted a major target, was attacked only once, in 851.[65] In part this may reflect the much more limited nature of urban settlement and the relatively small number of wealthy monasteries to be found in England, particularly in the south and west. It is not surprising in view of the limited returns and the more spirited nature of the defence put up by the West Saxons in particular that the Vikings devoted much more attention to northern Francia in these decades.

The situation changed in the mid 860s, possibly due to the more effective resistance that the Franks were then starting to offer.[66] For 865 the *Anglo-Saxon Chronicle* records the arrival in East Anglia of 'a great host of the heathens'. Although no such movement is reported in the contemporary Frankish sources, it is notable that Viking activities in West Francia ease off quite dramatically from 866 onwards, especially in the Seine valley. They were to resume again in the very late 870s, when increasing settlement and the victories of the West Saxon King Alfred brought to an end the expansion of Danish power in England.

The outline of the movements of the Viking 'Great Army' is recorded in the *Anglo-Saxon Chronicle*, although its interest in and information concerning events outside the West Saxon kingdom is very limited. The invaders descended on the kingdom of East Anglia, which made peace with them, provided maintenance for them over the winter of 865/6, and horses for their ensuing campaign. In 866 they invaded Northumbria, which was then torn by the war between the rival Kings Ælla and Osbryht, and occupied York. In consequence the two kings joined forces to try to regain the city in March 867. They were both killed in the ensuing assault, and the Viking leaders set up a new King of Northumbria of their own choosing in the person of a certain Egbert (867–72), who concluded a formal peace with them.[67]

In the very same year the Viking army moved south into Mercia, and established themselves in Nottingham over the winter. Here in the spring of 868 they were confronted by a combined Mercian and West Saxon army, but no battle ensued. Instead the Mercian King Burghred concluded a peace treaty with the Danes, who then returned to York. In 869 they crossed Mercian territory unopposed to invade East Anglia again, and to establish themselves for the winter at Thetford. Here they were attacked by the East Anglian King Edmund, who was defeated and killed.[68] In 870/1 it was to be the turn of Wessex. The Viking army came up the Thames valley, and a series of battles followed between them and the West Saxon Kings Æthelred (865–71) and Alfred (871–99) at Reading, Ashdown, Wilton and other unidentified or unnamed locations. After a series of defeats the West Saxons made peace with the invaders, as did the Mercians when they set themselves up in London for the winter of 871/2.[69] The 'peace' (*frith*) that the various Anglo-Saxon kingdoms are recorded as making with the Viking army must be assumed to have had a monetary side to it, even though the *Chronicle* makes no reference to any payments. The highly mobile invaders were hardly moving between the kingdoms just for the pleasure of the exercise. Thus, when Mercia is found 'making peace' both in 871 and 872, it is reasonable to believe that this was purchased on both occasions. In other words the Vikings were operating a highly lucrative 'protection racket' as far as the Anglo-Saxon kingdoms were concerned.

For this to be effective they had to keep in being the central authority in each monarchy, in order that treasure with which to pay them could continue to be collected. Hence their interest in setting up Egbert in Northumbria when his two predecessors perished in the battle in York. When he somehow proved unsatisfactory they replaced him with another king, called Ricsig (872–3/4). Similarly, when in 873 Burghred of Mercia was either forced or decided to relinquish his royal office and go as pilgrim to Rome the Vikings chose a new king, Ceolwulf, to replace him.[70]

By the mid 870s significant changes began to occur in Viking strategy and objectives. One of the leaders of the 'Great Army' called Halfdan split off from the rest in 874 in order to raid northwards into the kingdom of the Picts and that of the Britons of Strathclyde. In 876 he seems to have made himself King of Northumbria, and to have distributed land to his followers. In the meantime the other leaders of the host carried on as before, descending on East Anglia again in 874 and then on Wessex in 875/6.[71] Once again Alfred had to buy 'peace' (876). The *Anglo-Saxon Chronicle* perhaps exaggerates in referring to the Vikings as having to 'evade' the West Saxon armies in order to make themselves masters of Wareham. It also mentions their swearing a unique and especially sacred oath to the West Saxon King Alfred, but it seems likely that in the end Wessex, like the other kingdoms, had found it more expedient to come to terms with the raiders and to buy their withdrawal.

What may have changed the situation on this occasion was a disaster that befell the Danes at sea. Part of the fleet they had probably used to convey themselves to Wareham was destroyed by a storm off Swanage, leaving the land forces, which had moved on to Exeter, cut off in the south-west peninsula.[72] Alfred blockaded them in their fortress there, but was unable to take it. An agreement was eventually reached whereby the Vikings returned to Mercia. Here in 877, following the lead given in the north, they partitioned the kingdom with its ruler Ceolwulf and distributed land amongst themselves in the eastern part of it.[73]

At least one of their leaders appears to have determined to do something similar in Wessex, and a part of the host made a sudden attack on Alfred's winter court at Chippenham in January 878. The king, whose military following at such a time of year was minimal, managed to escape south into the Somerset marshes, and hold out in Athelney until the coming of spring made it possible for the shire levies to be concentrated. In the ensuing battle at Edington the invaders were defeated and then besieged in their fortified camp. In due course their leader Guthrum was forced to submit, and to accept Christian baptism as part of the terms of the agreement.[74] In 879 Guthrum led his followers into East Anglia and settled them on the land.

The traditional view of Alfred as saving 'England' hardly needs airing here, but it is worth considering his particular role in preserving Wessex from being overrun and perhaps turned into a kingdom ruled by a Viking dynasty. The interpretation offered here implies that when the full force of the 'Great Army' was turned against Wessex Alfred and his kingdom had to purchase peace in the way that the Northumbrian, Mercian and East Anglian rulers had. Even after the dividing of the Viking host in 874 this remained true. However, the settlements in the north in 876 and in Mercia in 877 meant that when an attempt was made to eliminate Alfred and overrun his kingdom in January 878 it was by a greatly reduced portion of the original host, under perhaps only one of its initial four leaders.

There is no question that the shire levies of the West Saxon kingdom fought hard against the invaders in 870/1 and 875/6, but despite a number of tactical successes they achieved no real victory, in the sense of securing their strategic aims of eliminating or expelling the Vikings. Nor, in the light of its limited and partisan character, should we assume that the lack of mention on the part of the *Anglo-Saxon Chronicle* of similar intensive conflicts in Northumbria and Mercia means that such resistance was an exclusively West Saxon phenomenon. Ultimately, Alfred was lucky that his kingdom was, for geographical reasons, the last on the invaders' list of targets, and even more so that he was warned in time at Chippenham in January 878.

By 879 Viking dynasties had replaced native Anglo-Saxon ones in Northumbria, East Anglia and the eastern section of Mercia. Some form of distribution of land had also taken place amongst the followers of the Danish leaders. The nature of this and the procedures employed in it are obscure, though its subsequent effects can be more easily discerned.[75] It is not at all clear how far and in what ways existing landholdings were affected. The existence of Scandinavian-influenced place names in the regions that came under Danish political control are not necessarily an accurate guide to settlement, in that they are not chronologically precise. Moreover, they are often found in economically marginal areas, that were perhaps first exploited in the period of the late ninth to eleventh centuries, and would thus have lacked earlier pre-Viking names.[76]

It is important to realise that, as in earlier periods of migration and conquest, the invaders represented at best a small minority of the total population in the territories they occupied. Thus, again like the earlier Germanic settlers within the Roman Empire, a degree of cultural assimilation between conquerors and conquered was necessary if a military occupation was to turn itself into a real settlement. This does seem to have occurred fairly rapidly in the case of the Danes in England, especially in Northumbria.

By 900 the Vikings in Northumbria were prepared to put themselves under the leadership of a fugitive West Saxon prince, Alfred's nephew Æthelwold (d. 904), and to support his unsuccessful bid to oust his cousin Edward from Wessex.[77] The rapid fusion of interests in Northumbria meant that no 'English' anti-Danish sentiment can be detected in the north in the course of the tenth century.[78] Equally instructive is the text of an agreement made c. 886 between Alfred and Guthrum, the Danish King of East Anglia. No distinction is made between Danes and Angles in referring to 'the people who are in East Anglia', and the final clause envisages – and prohibits – freemen from Wessex wishing to cross the frontier to join the Viking host.[79] If such a movement could be envisaged in Wessex, how much more likely is it to have occurred within the existing Anglo-Norse kingdoms in Northumbria, East Anglia and eastern Mercia?

Where Alfred did show his capacity as ruler and military commander to a notable extent was in preparing his kingdom against the possibility of another Viking invasion from the Continent.[80] In 879, the year Guthrum established himself in East Anglia, a large host that had been assembling in the Thames valley crossed into Francia where, as has been seen, it terrorised the northern lowland regions of the West Frankish kingdom continuously until 892. Although it has been suggested this was another body of Vikings that only crossed into England in 878 and then found that Alfred had made conditions too difficult for them to remain, this is not what the Chronicle says.[81] It is perhaps better to envisage that those of the original 'Great Army' who were unwilling or unable to take part in the land divisions and settlements carried out in 876–8 by their original leaders then gathered together in the Thames valley to put themselves under new commanders and to resume their careers as mobile raiders.

In 892 this Viking army originally formed in southern England, that had been operating in northern Francia since 879, returned from the Continent because of a widespread famine.[82] It crossed via Boulogne to southern Kent and established a fortified base at Appledore. Soon after a second Viking fleet, under a certain Haesten, sailed into the Thames. It is possible that this is the same man as the 'Hasting', who is reported in 866 and 874 as the leader of the Vikings in the Loire.[83] If so it would seem that the Loire Vikings, who had not formed part of the 'Great Army' that had invaded the Anglo-Saxon kingdoms in 865, were dislodged from Francia at this time, again possibly in consequence of the famine.

In a series of campaigns between 893 and 896 the now united Danish forces pushed through the Thames valley, up the length of western Mercia as far as the deserted Roman fortress of Chester and then into North Wales.[84] In the process they were continuously harried by the Anglo-Saxon levies of Alfred and of his son-in-law Æthelred (d. 911). The latter was in West Saxon eyes the Ealdorman of west Mercia from *c.* 883, and he may have acknowledged himself as such during Alfred's lifetime, but there are indications that he was recognised as King of Mercia, and may have been a member of the former royal dynasty.[85] The Vikings were prevented from occupying or looting any of the major settlements by continuous harrying, and by the success of Alfred's policy of fortifying such *burhs*. In the light of what must have been a disappointing series of campaigns, the Viking confederacy broke up in 896. Some of its components went off to the Danish kingdoms of Northumbria and East Anglia, and others returned to the Continent, where they were to be defeated in the Seine valley by the forces of Charles the Simple the following year. As has been seen, the reign of this West Frankish monarch saw the establishment of major Viking settlements in the region that was later to be called Normandy.

The last quarter of the ninth century and opening decades of the tenth thus saw a diminution in Viking activity, in the sense of large-scale raiding by mobile groups of Danes without fixed settlements or lands. Such bodies had existed on the basis of loose confederacies of individuals or ships' companies taking service under leaders of established reputation, whom they could leave at will. They established themselves each winter in fortified camps, normally moving on in the spring. There is evidence that in such circumstances a distribution of loot and the profits of ransoms and slave trading occurred at the beginning of each winter season. The greater the success of any given 'host', the larger it would become as others were attracted to it by the expectations of profit. These, certainly in parts of England, might well include elements of the local population.

In place of these dangerous but volatile confederacies, from 876 onwards – and earlier in Ireland – a series of more permanent settlements of population developed. As has been seen, in England these took the form of Viking domination of existing kingdoms. In Francia they were brought about by integrating Viking leaders and their followers into the local administrative structures of the Carolingian empire. In Ireland fortified coastal settlements, above all Dublin and Limerick, became the centres of territorially small but powerful local kingdoms, that drew their wealth from trade, as well as involvement in the interminable wars of the indigenous Irish realms.[86] In all cases the emergence of such Viking states was matched by growing integration with elements of the indigenous population and its culture. Not least did this involve fairly rapid conversion to Christianity.

Conversion and expansion

The origins of the evangelisation of Scandinavia are, inevitably, obscure. It is not unreasonable to suspect that increasing political and economic contact between the Frankish empire and the Baltic and Danish kingdoms was accompanied by cultural influence of the former on the latter and that this would have included growing awareness of Christianity. It is possible that some of the mid-ninth century Danish kings at least hinted at a willingness to convert, and this could well be linked to periods of co-operation between them and some of the Carolingian rulers.

The first known missionary venture intended to propagate Christianity amongst the Scandinavians was that initiated in the early ninth century by Archbishop Ebbo of Reims (817–35), with the support of Pope Paschal I.[87] This expedition has been dated to c. 823, and may have led to the conversion and baptism of the Danish King Harald Klak at Ingelheim in 826. However, after Harald's expulsion from Denmark in the following year no other Danish ruler repeated this experiment, until King Harald Bluetooth (c. 940–c. 985) was converted around the year 965. On the other hand, this did not prevent some Danish kings from on occasion allowing Christian Frankish missionaries to operate within their territories or to pass through on the way to Sweden.

The Swedish kingdom was to be an additional target for the next major Frankish evangelising ventures, those conducted by the monk Anskar who re-established the episcopal see at Hamburg, first founded in the time of Charlemagne, and worked for some years amongst the Danes. An account of his career has been preserved in a *Vita Anskari* written by his disciple Rimbert (d. 865).[88] The first mission to the Swedes is dated to 829/30 and this was followed by another in 845. The trading settlement of Birka provided the focus of and intended centre for the missions, but both proved short-lived and abortive. Both of these correspond in time with short periods of temporary stability in Frankish–Danish relations, and the Danish ruler Horic I is said to have specifically supported the re-establishment of the mission to the Swedes in 845. However, internal upheavals within Denmark and periods of Carolingian weakness undermined both ventures, and in 845 the mission centre of Hamburg was sacked. The archdiocese of Hamburg may have briefly resumed its interest in Sweden *c.* 936, but it is not before the reign of Olof Skötkonung (*c.* 995–1021/2) that a Swedish king was definitely converted.[89]

In both Norway and Sweden conversion is associated with the appearance of more powerful and geographically more extensive monarchies in the second half of the tenth century. As previously mentioned, the emergence of a dominant kingdom, absorbing other smaller ones, is dated in Norway to the time of Harald Hárfagri (d. 936?). His great grandson Olaf Tryggvason (995–1000) was the first of this line of monarchs to accept Christianity, and also to try to impose it in his kingdom. His actions may also have influenced the decision of the free Norwegian settlers of Iceland to accept the new religion in the year 1000. The process was resumed more forcefully in Norway itself by his eventual successor Olaf II (1016–30). Although Norwegian tradition emphasises the role of these two monarchs, an earlier ruler, Håkon (d. 960), son of Harald Hárfagri, who had been educated in the court of Athelstan of Wessex (925–39), is reported to have favoured Christianity, if not finally accepting baptism. Another direction from which Christian influence could make itself felt on Norway was from Denmark, after the conversion of Harald Bluetooth. In 970–5, as also from 1030 to 1035, the Norwegian kingdom became an (unwilling) dependency of the Danish realm.[90]

In turn the Danish monarchy, which had rather vanished into historiographical mist in the second half of the ninth century, had perhaps only begun to reassert itself over all of Jutland in the time of Harald Bluetooth's father Gorm the Old (d. *c.* 936). Thus in the cases of Denmark, Sweden and Norway the final acceptance of Christianity by the ruling dynasty, and within a relatively short time the imposition of it on the kingdoms, was directly related to the emergence or revival of a strong unitary kingship. Such monarchies were much more susceptible to outside political and cultural influences, such as those exerted by the Ottonian kingdom/empire in Germany, and the kingdom of Wessex, which was making itself master of most of the Scandinavian settlements in England in the period 917–54.

The conversion of their Scandinavian homeland in fact lagged considerably behind the growth of the acceptance of Christianity on the part of the Vikings settled in Western Europe. In the case of the settlements in West Francia it has been seen how such conversions were directly related to military defeats at the hands of the Frankish monarchs or their deputies, and how these were followed by the baptism of the Viking leaders. Thus, the military triumph of Christ made such an acceptance of the religion of the conquerors acceptable, though it is likely that the exclusivity of the Christian message was not immediately understood or adhered to.

In England the situation was rather different, in that, apart from the agreement between Alfred and Guthrum in 878, baptism was generally not the product of Viking military defeat. Indeed, the success of the invaders in taking over the long-established Anglo-Saxon kingdoms in the north and the east might have been expected to validate rather than challenge the hold of traditional Scandinavian paganism. Even so, both in England and in Ireland the conversion of the Vikings proceeded rapidly, and was achieved long before the same process got under way in Scandinavia. This must be seen, as in the case of the Germanic settlements inside the Roman Empire, as a manifestation of the attraction exercised on an alien minority, albeit in positions of military and political supremacy, of the more complex culture of their larger subject population.

In particular it is quite clear that the Vikings in England, as in Ireland, were rapidly involved in the dynastic politics and traditional conflicts within these societies. Thus, for example, the alliance of the Vikings of Northumbria and East Anglia against Edward the Elder of Wessex (899–925) in 903–4, involved not only the fugitive West Saxon pretender Æthelwold, but also a certain 'Beorhtsige, son of prince Beorhtnoth'. The similarity of name, together with the title, would suggest that this was a representative of the Mercian royal line of Beornwulf (823–5) and Beorhtwulf (841–52), themselves possibly related to the (?) Mercian appointee to the throne of Wessex King Beorhtric (786–802).[91] Much of the warfare in England in the first half of the tenth century makes more sense in terms of such traditional antagonisms and feuds than in terms of a conflict between Anglo-Saxons and Scandinavians or between Christians and pagans.

In the wars that led to the eventual conquest of Northumbria by Wessex in 954 religion played no part. The army of the West Saxon King Eadred (946–55) sacked and burnt the great Northumbrian monastery of Ripon, that had been founded by Wilfred, and the see of York was kept so impoverished after the conquest that it was frequently linked to that of Worcester to provide revenue for its incumbent.[92] Also this manoeuvre tied the primatial see of the north firmly to West Mercia. The north and the east remained conquered and subordinate territories, never visited by the southern kings.

The growth of the acceptance of Christianity amongst the Vikings, either by process of assimilation from the broader cultural context in which the new settlers in Western Europe had established themselves or through imposition via the new Scandinavian monarchies of the second half of the tenth century, inevitably affected other regions into which they had been moving, from the ninth century onwards. Such areas were of two kinds: north-western lands in which the Vikings found themselves effectively the first settlers, and territories to the south-east of Scandinavia on which they preyed as slave raiders or in which they came to found trading stations and other settlements. Into the first category fall the Faroe islands, Iceland (except for the possible prior establishment of a handful of Irish monks) and Greenland, and into the second come the Slav lands south of the Baltic and the overland routes via Lake Ladoga and the Volga to the Black Sea.

In the eastern expansion it was, not surprisingly, the Swedes who played the predominant part. Slave raids on the Slav territories served as an additional source for the human commodity so avidly sought by the Arab societies of the Mediterranean from the early ninth century onwards. Some of the captives were traded either by sea or overland westwards, but as the Scandinavians began exploring the routes southwards, down the great Russian river systems, so in due course they came in contact with the Muslim powers of the near East, and also with the longer established trading routes from Constantinople into the steppes of south Russia. In typical fashion such commercial possibilities could combine with the possibilities of obtaining profit by violent means. The Vikings probably first became known to the inhabitants of the truncated Eastern Roman or Byzantine Empire in the late 830s.[93] However, after they had displaced the Khazars in control of Kiev in the middle of the century the scale of their contacts with Byzantium grew, and in 860 they attempted to make a surprise raid on Constantinople.[94] Another and larger-scale attack was made in 907 by one of the first Viking 'princes' of Kiev, Oleg (*c*. 882–*c*.912/13).

This, admittedly, is to enter into very controversial waters. The brief Byzantine chronicle references to the activities of people who were known as the *Rhos* do not necessarily confirm that they were to be identified with the Vikings, who at this period seem to have been founding trading stations on the middle Volga, notably on the site of the later city of Kiev. In that the society of the south Russian steppes was still pre-literate, no indigenous literary texts exist from this period to provide fuller information on this and related questions. Not surprisingly, therefore, Russian historians have denied the association, preferring to see the *Rhos* as a predominantly or exclusively Slavic people. In as much as in England and Ireland the existence of mixed marriages and a measure of cultural assimilation between invaders and subject populations is well established, there is no reason to doubt the same processes occurred in the Viking settlements on the Volga, where a militarily dominant Scandinavian elite ruled over a more numerous Slavonic subject population. In this they were replacing the latter's previous rulers, the Khazars.[95]

The growth of such commercial contacts, supplementing the occasional military ones, together with recruitment by the Empire of mercenary soldiers from this south Russian society, inevitably opened it up to increasing Byzantine cultural influence, which had already been making itself felt there since the time of the Khazar domination and earlier.[96] Some form of Christian organisation existed in the Volga by the later 860s, and in 874 an archbishop was sent from Constantinople.[97] The first member of the ruling family of the Viking–Slavic Kievan state to be baptised was the regent Olga, who accepted Christianity, probably for political reasons, during a visit to Constantinople in 957. A definitive conversion of the dynasty, and with it the imposition of Christianity on the state, did not follow until 986 in the reign of her grandson Vladimir (*c.* 980–*c.* 1015).[98]

This was the period in which the principal ruling dynasties of Scandinavia converted, and began to force their subjects to follow suit. It is not clear how far such developments around the Baltic were known to or affected attitudes in the increasingly Slavicised principality of Kiev, though it is reported in 959 that Olga (under her baptised name of Helena) made contact with the East Frankish ruler Otto I, and requested him to send a missionary bishop and priests.[99]

Otto was at this time exerting diplomatic pressure on Denmark, whose King Harald Bluetooth converted soon after (*c.* 865), under the influence of the German priest Poppo.[100] Thus, by around the year 1000 all the major components of Scandinavian settlement, from Iceland to Kiev, had at least formally come to accept Christianity. This was a symbol of the degree to which these peoples had come to see the value of integration into a cultural tradition that extended back to the Mediterranean world of the fourth century.

20 The Ottonian Age

The problems of Italy, 875–961

Although the threat of a major Arab incursion into Western Europe never resurrected itself after the early eighth century, seaborne raids, not least linked to slave trading, presented a serious problem in the Mediterranean regions. Spanish Arab and Berber raids on the Balearic Islands in 798 led to their putting themselves under Frankish protection in 799, but by the middle of the ninth century at the latest they were under Arab rule.[1] Charlemagne is reported to have had to take precautions against Arab raids along the southern coast of France in the latter part of his reign. By the middle of the ninth century, just as Viking raids were intensifying in the north, so in the south Arab pirates were employing similar tactics. In 840, 850 and 869 they conducted large-scale raids up the Rhône, in search of slaves or those, such as the Bishop of Arles, whom they could hold to ransom.[2] Similar problems had already been encountered in Italy. In 806 raids were launched against Corsica, then part of the Italian kingdom ruled by Charles's son Pippin, and these were soon extended to Sardinia and the Italian mainland. These raids, unlike those on the Balearics, came from Africa.

After the overthrow of the Umayyad Caliphs in Syria in 750, North Africa had remained under the rule of their successors, the dynasty of the 'Abbasids, who made their capital in Baghdad in Iraq. However, the political break-up of the hitherto monolithic Arab empire had soon followed. Spain had gone its own way in 756 under a fugitive Umayyad prince, and other smaller independent amirates had come into existence in the regions now known as Morocco and western Algeria in 789 and 777 respectively. In 800 the province of *Ifriqya* (modern Tunisia) was ceded to its principal general in return for an annual tribute to the Caliph. It was under the direction of this Aghlabid dynasty in *Ifriqya* that the raids on Italy were organised, and so too from 827 was the conquest of Sicily.[3]

This island had remained the most substantial Byzantine holding in the West after the fall of the exarchate of Ravenna to the Lombards in 751. Its conquest by the Arabs took over half a century, but the maritime raids on the Italian mainland grew in frequency and seriousness throughout this period. Moreover, Arab forces also crossed to mainland Italy, took Reggio, Bari and Taranto, and by 840 were penetrating as far as the southern frontier of the papal territories. Pope Gregory IV (827–44) built a fortress called Gregoriopolis at Ostia, but its garrison fled in 846 when an Arab fleet sailed up the Tiber. The defences of Rome itself held, but the two great basilicas of St Peter's and St Paul's, which lay outside the walls, were looted. Pope Leo IV (847–55) subsequently extended the city walls to enclose St Peter's.[4]

This continuing Arab threat provided the context for papal relations with the various rival Carolingian rulers throughout the ninth century, and explains the popes' use of the imperial title as a lure to commit them to the protection of Rome. Pope John VIII (872–82) developed a small papal fleet, but in the light of the limited help that the Carolingian emperors were able to provide and the lack of support he could gain from the Lombard princes of southern Italy, he was soon reduced to buying immunity from the raiders.[5] The Emperor Louis II (850–75) had shown himself to be assiduous if not ultimately successful in trying to stem the Arab advance in the south, but his successors proved less adequate from the papal point of view. Their own internecine conflicts in the period 875–81 and the priority given by Charles the Fat to the Viking threat in the North meant that the chances of an effective Carolingian military intervention in Italy rapidly receded. That of the Emperor Arnulf (887–99) was truncated by a stroke that paralysed him in 896 and led to his early death.

By this time, however, a new actor had appeared to play a part in these complicated series of events in southern Italy – or to be more accurate it was the reappearance of one whose role had been almost entirely passive for the last century and a half. Since the time of the Emperor Leo III (717–41), the Byzantine Empire had been prevented by threats to its existence in the eastern Balkans and in Asia Minor from taking active steps to restore its former power in Italy. By the mid-ninth century the towns of Naples, Amalfi and Gaeta still belonged in name to the Empire, though largely able to conduct their own affairs under the rule of local dynasts. The other former Byzantine possessions of Bari and Otranto fell to the Arabs in the 840s. On the other hand, the rival Lombard duchies of Benevento and of Salerno belonged formally to the Frankish Empire, but would co-operate with the Byzantines if it suited them.

Under Basil I (867–86) the Empire began to take a more active interest in protecting its Italian interests. Initially he was prepared to co-operate with the western Emperor Louis II in a joint campaign against Bari in 869, but it proved impossible to co-ordinate the efforts of the two allies. At the same time, following the breakdown of negotiations for a marriage between Louis's daughter and Basil's eldest son Constantine (d. 879), the latent problem of the divisibility or otherwise of the imperial title once again reared its head. In 812 Byzantium had recognised Charlemagne as emperor of the Franks, seeing his title a strictly ethnic one that did not rival the true imperial authority of the ruler of Constantinople. In 869, however, Basil I seems to have been unwilling to call Louis II, who after all controlled no more than certain parts of northern and central Italy, anything more grandiose than King of the Franks. Particular offence had been given by the western ruler's revival of the style 'Emperor of the Romans', a title that had been abandoned by Charlemagne soon after his imperial coronation.[6]

Louis's response, the main source of our evidence for this disagreement, took the form of a lengthy letter to Basil, probably drafted for him by Anastasius, the papal librarian, who served as the western emperor's envoy to Constantinople. In this letter are to be found arguments that are identical to those contained in the forged text known as the 'Donation of Constantine'. This was produced, probably in a papal milieu in the late eighth century, in an apparent effort to find an intellectual justification for the papal choosing and investing of a western emperor. According to the 'Donation', Constantine I, when he left for the East, invested Pope Sylvester and his successors with wide-ranging rights and privileges.[7] In consequence it became possible, on the basis of this forgery, for the emperor in the East to be regarded as no more than the ruler 'of the Greeks'. This also denied the Byzantines self-identification as the *Romaioi* or Romans. It was in this way that Louis II, in the summer of 871, addressed Basil I and his subjects. In his letter to the eastern emperor he wrote that: 'It is the Greeks who, in their blindness and heretical spirit, have lost the faith, abandoned the city, and the seat of empire, the Roman nation and the very tongue of Rome, and migrated to distant parts.'[8]

In such circumstances practical co-operation between the two emperors in southern Italy was unlikely to be forthcoming. Louis, however, initially seemed to be all the papacy needed by way of an active military protector against the Arab menace. In 871 he took Bari in Apulia, which had been taken by Arab raiders in 847 and turned into a small kingdom or amirate. However, Louis's protracted stay in southern Italy, which had begun in 866, proved an increasing burden to his principal host, Adelchis (854–78), the Lombard Duke of Benevento. Probably acting with the backing of the rulers of Naples and of Salerno, Adelchis seized the poorly guarded emperor in August 872, holding him a prisoner in Benevento for a month. To gain his release, Louis took an oath to leave the duchy and never return. Later southern Italian tradition blamed the arrogance of Louis's wife, the Empress Engelberga, for alienating the Beneventan court, while Frankish sources accused the Byzantines of complicity, but the real responsibility would seem to lie with the south Italian princes. After this debacle, the 'Emperor of the Romans' and 'King of the Lombards' was forced to withdraw northwards to Ravenna.[9] He was persuaded to intervene briefly in the south once more, to protect Capua from an Arab attack, and it was there that he subsequently died in 875, leaving no male heir.

The elimination of the only Carolingian ruler with his primary, or indeed exclusive, power base being located in Italy, weakened the ties between the dynasty and the papacy that had been forged a century earlier by Charlemagne and Hadrian I. After the brief and politically weakening tenure of the imperial office by Charles the Bald (875–7), other Carolingian rulers tended to take the view that the title of emperor, despite all its reminiscences of Charlemagne, was not worth committing themselves to dangerous adventures in southern Italy for. Thus, despite the ideology of the 'Donation of Constantine' and his deep distrust of the Lombard dukes, Pope John VIII soon found himself forced to look to the papacy's former political master, the Byzantine emperor, for the help against the Arabs that the Frankish rulers after 875 were unwilling or unable to provide.[10]

Although theologically reconciled after the death of the last Iconoclast emperor, Theophilus (829–42), the churches of Rome and Constantinople had broken off relations over the deposition in 861 of the Patriarch Ignatius and the election of a layman, Photius, as his successor.[11] Pope Nicholas I (858–67) had protested that no council could be held nor could any bishop be deposed without the prior consent of the See of Peter. In a synod held in the Lateran in 863 he ordered the reinstatement of Ignatius, the relegation of Photius to his prior lay status and the excommunication of the Archbishop of Syracuse who had consecrated him. This enraged the Byzantines, who had consistently denied the validity of such papal claims to unique authority.

The murder of the Emperor Michael III (842–67) had been followed rapidly by the deposition of Patriarch Photius of Constantinople, and good relations were once again able to be restored with Rome. In return Pope Hadrian II (867–72) was even prepared to concede something that his predecessors had resisted back to the time of Leo I in the fifth century, which was the placing of Constantinople as second to Rome and ahead of Alexandria and Antioch in the table of precedence of the patriarchal sees.[12]

Unfortunately, by the time that John VIII was looking for military aid from the emperor, the situation had changed again.

After the restored Patriarch Ignatius had died in 877, Basil I re-appointed Photius. Despite the latter's condemnation by two previous popes, John VIII's secular needs were such as to make it necessary for him to co-operate with him.[13] He revoked Pope Hadrian II's excommunication of the patriarch, and sent representatives to the Eighth Ecumenical Council, which was held under Photius's presidency. The pope subsequently accepted the acts of this council, even though this seems to have involved an implicit recognition of an equality of status between the sees of Rome and of Constantinople. In return a Byzantine fleet was sent to the west coast of Italy in 879.

Basil's intervention in southern Italy proved generally successful, although nothing could be done to reverse the loss of Sicily, effectively completed by the fall of Syracuse to the Arabs in 878. On the mainland, however, maritime expeditions had already begun to achieve results that would compensate for the losses in Sicily. Otranto was regained in 873 and Bari fell to the Byzantines in 876. In 883 a major war of conquest was launched under the command of Basil's general Nicephorus Phocas, which imposed imperial rule over much of southern Italy for the first time since the seventh century. In consequence in 892 two new military themes were created in southern Italy, those of Calabria and of Langobardia.[14] The latter briefly extended itself to include Benevento (892–95), although this soon returned to Lombard princely rule. Even if truncated Lombard states survived in Salerno and Benevento, Byzantine rule was re-established over most of Apulia, Calabria and Basilicata. This fluctuated thereafter. The Lombard duchies regained some of what they had lost in a series of wars in the 920s–940s, and the Arab threat from Sicily grew in intensity in the same period. Subsequently, the revival of a somewhat stronger and more extensive western empire than had existed in the period *c.* 899–960 led to a period of competition and rivalry in southern Italy between the rulers of the old and the new Romes in the second half of the tenth century.

Germany: the kingdom and the duchies, 911–962

The extinction of the eastern branch of the Carolingian dynasty in 911, with the death of the eighteen-year-old Louis the Child, the only legitimate son of Arnulf, left a political vacuum in Germany. Unlike the 880s when Charles the Fat had effectively had the whole of the Empire fall piecemeal into his lap through the deaths of his relatives, there was in 911 no prospect that the sole surviving adult Carolingian, Charles the Simple (in the sense of straight-forward rather than simple-minded), would be able just to extend his authority to embrace the vacant eastern kingdom. He could and did, however, have hopes of acquiring Lotharingia, the region located between Eastern and Western Francia.

This kingdom, the northern part of the realm that had been conceded to Lothar I in the Treaty of Verdun in 843, had lost its last independent Carolingian ruler with the death of Arnulf's illegitimate son Zwentibold in 900, and had reverted to the nominal rule of its imperial overlord Louis the Child. On the latter's death in 911 the Lotharingian nobility preferred to put the kingdom into the hands of the Western Frankish ruler Charles the Simple rather than those of the king who had just been selected by the eastern Frankish dukes.[15] Charles, whose first wife was a member of a Lotharingian noble house, proved himself very committed to his new acquisition, so much so that this contributed to the revolt against him of a major section of the West Frankish aristocracy in 922.

In East Francia the growth of multiple military threats on the frontiers and the weakening and ultimately the extinction of the branch of the Carolingian dynasty descended from Louis the German saw the apparent re-emergence of earlier structures of political organisation. Thus in the first decade of the tenth century the title of 'duke [*dux*] of the Bavarians' appears for the first time since the deposition of Tassilo III in 788. The first holder of the revived office was probably the Duke Liutpold, who was killed in a battle against the Magyars near Bratislava in 907. He had been appointed to the lesser office of *marchio* or March Warden by the emperor Arnulf in 895 and was subsequently Count of the Palace, and it can not be said for sure that he actually assumed the title of duke. His son Arnulf, later known as 'the Bad' (d. 937), certainly did, and in a charter confirming an exchange of lands dated to 908 he can be found exercising royal authority in all but name.[16]

A similar development had already taken place in Saxony, which had also previously had a ducal dynasty up to the time of Charlemagne. Here authority in this important marcher territory confronting the northern Slavs had largely been entrusted to the family now known as the Liudolfings. Otto (d. 912) was probably the first of a new line of Saxon dukes. In Alamannia, which also came to be known as Suabia, the presence of two rival dominant families made the issue less clear cut. The holder of the office of count under Louis the Child, by the name of Burchard, had already begun to style himself 'Prince of the Alamans', but he was overthrown and executed in the course of the confused events of the year 911. His successor from the rival family took a ducal title in 915, only to be condemned for rebellion and executed in 917.

Burchard (II) emerged from the fall of his rival as the uncontested Duke of Suabia.

In the same way in the original heartlands of eastern Frankish settlement across the Rhine, the area that came to be called Franconia, feuds between the leading families made the emergence of a single dominant dynasty less easy, but the issue was finally resolved in favour of the Conradines in 906. At the beginning of the tenth century Thuringia was in the hands of another duke of the name of Burchard, up to his death in 908, but it then or soon after seems to have disappeared as a separate entity, merging with Franconia. To the west in Lotharingia the death of the Emperor Arnulf's illegitimate son Zwentibold early in 900 ended the brief period in which this region formed a separate kingdom, and power passed into the hands of a Duke Gebhard, and then after his death in battle against the Magyars in 910 to members of a quite different family.[17]

Although German scholars have labelled these revived quasi-ethnic political entities 'stem-duchies', not all of them equated to the pre-Carolingian duchies that had been used by the Frankish rulers to control the various peoples living beyond their eastern frontiers. Lotharingia in particular was an entirely artificial creation resulting from the treaty of Coulaines of 843. However, the sense of the cultural and historic distinctions between these various Germanic peoples was still clearly a major factor in the social and political articulation of the eastern Frankish realm, and claims to dynastic links with the original ducal houses was an asset to be exploited. Thus in the first *Life of Queen Matilda*, wife of the Saxon duke and then King Henry I, written for her grandson the Emperor Otto II (973–83), much attention is devoted to her descent from the Widukind who had led Saxon resistance to Charlemagne.[18] As well as looking for justification for their new status in the past, the new ducal houses made sure that they secured the ways of expressing power and the resources upon which it was to be based. They openly exercised several of the functions that would once have been royal prerogatives and in particular were able to appropriate the revenues and resources in their own regions of the former Carolingian fisc.

What they could not do, however, was stand alone against the attacks of the Magyars (on whom more will be said below), especially when other threats, notably from some of the Slav peoples on the eastern frontiers of Saxony, were also making themselves felt. Military co-operation and co-ordination required the presence of some generally recognised central authority. Nor does it ever seem to have been contemplated that the duchies should break with historical precedent and transform themselves into separate small kingdoms. Thus following the early death of Louis the Child, the dukes and other leading magnates of his realm, other than those of Lotharingia, had with considerable speed selected the Franconian Duke Conrad to be their new king.

Although it has been argued that he did, it seems unlikely that Conrad had any close family ties to the Carolingians.[19] Nor can it be assumed that his recently acquired position as Duke of Franconia, the Frankish heartland in the region east of the Rhine, gave him special claim to the vacant royal authority. He is not known to have been an outstanding military leader, but he does seem to have been the most acceptable of all the candidates to his rivals. That a matter as potentially contentious and divisive as the choice of a non-Carolingian to fill the vacant throne was settled with such apparent ease and speed was largely due to the serious military problems that the kingdom was then facing.[20]

The Avar confederacy that had long dominated the plains around the upper Danube, to the east of Bavaria, disintegrated rapidly as a result of internal conflicts and its defeats at the hands of Charlemagne's commanders in the 790s. Its place was soon largely taken by the Slav kingdom of 'Greater Moravia', the location of whose main centres has generated much scholarly controversy recently. The traditional view that associated it with the valley of the river Morava in the modern Czech Republic has been challenged by rival interpretations of the limited literary evidence that favour either an area south of the Danube around the former Roman city of Sirmium or the Hungarian Alföld.[21] This debate remains to be resolved, but wherever the location of its heartland, the Moravian kingdom, which was the most powerful eastern neighbour of the East Frankish realm, collapsed surprisingly rapidly at the very end of the ninth century under pressure from a new steppe nomad confederation, that of the Magyars, or as they were known in the East Frankish chronicles, the *Ungari* or Hungarians (probably deriving from a conflation of the name of the Magyars with that of the archaic Huns). The first appearance of the Magyars in these texts is to be found in an entry for the year 889, but from Byzantine accounts it seems clear that they had been pushed west towards the upper Danube by the growing power of the Petchenegs in the south Russian steppes.[22] By 892 they were being used as mercenaries by King Arnulf in his campaigns against the Moravian kingdom.[23] In the same decade they were also employed by the Byzantines in their wars against the Bulgars.

As with their predecessors, the Huns and the Avars, such contact with the more sophisticated and sedentary societies to the south and the west led to greater social cohesiveness amongst the nomads and in consequence a more formidable and predatory military organisation. In 899 the Magyars launched a raid across the Julian Alps into northern Italy 'killing many bishops', and this was followed by a devastating attack on Bavaria. Their raids grew in range and scale. Another attack on the Bavarians in 907 led to the death of their Duke Liutpold. In 908 the Magyars were ravaging the duchies of Thuringia and Saxony. In 909 they were in the duchy of Alamannia. In 910 they defeated a Franconian army, killing its Duke Gebhard.[24] Thus by 911 all the major duchies had suffered at the hands of the Magyars, and further raids could be expected.

The short reign of Conrad I (911–18) saw little relief. Despite a victory over them on the river Inn in 913, the Magyars are reported in 915 as devastating all of Alamannia (Suabia) and raiding through Thuringia and Saxony as far as the monastery of Fulda.[25] This monastery, founded by Boniface, was to be Conrad's burial place in 919. His death the previous December resulted from injuries received in an unsuccessful expedition against Duke Arnulf of Bavaria earlier in 918, testifying to the real problems that the kings faced in trying to impose any real authority over the duchies if the rulers of the latter were not willing to concede it. On his death bed, and seeking to avoid a contentious election, Conrad is reported to have commended Duke Henry of Saxony to the East Frankish nobles as the best choice for his successor.[26] In practice only the Franconian and Saxon magnates were present at the assembly at Fritzlar in May 919 that gave the crown to Henry, and he had to face down an immediate challenge from Arnulf of Bavaria before his new status was recognised by all of the dukes. Despite this shaky start it was to be under this new king, the founder of the Ottonian dynasty, that took its name from Henry's father Duke Otto of Saxony (d. 912), that the first effective action was to be taken against the Magyars.

Henry I (919–36), or Henry the Fowler as he was later known, was lucky that the Magyar onslaughts were suspended during the opening years of his reign, but they resumed in 924 when they 'devastated eastern Francia'.[27] Henry was forced to take refuge in the fortress of Werla. However, the fortunate capture of a Magyar leader enabled him to obtain a nine-year peace, in return for his paying them an annual tribute. Henry used this time both to develop new fortified settlements and to rebuild his army, largely through a series of campaigns against the Slavs. Thus when the truce ended and the Magyars resumed their attacks in 933, he was able to inflict a major defeat on them at the battle of Riade.[28] When they turned eastwards the following year, they were defeated again, by the forces of the Byzantine emperor Romanus I Lecapenus (920–44).[29]

This by no means put an end to the Magyar menace in the West. In 937 one of their expeditions penetrated as far as western Francia, obliging its King Louis IV (936–54) to face a siege in Laon, and it returned to the Danube by way of northern Italy, creating havoc as it went. This or another Magyar force also penetrated as far south as the duchies of Benevento and Salerno in the same year. However, the tide had certainly turned. A Magyar attack in 938, early in the reign of Henry's son Otto I (936–73), resulted in another victory over them. The Bavarians, who had suffered perhaps more than any from these raids, gained their particular revenge in 943, when Duke Arnulf the Bad's brother inflicted another major defeat on them. By 950 the eastern Franks were themselves able to take the offensive, and the king's brother Henry led a successful raid on the Magyars. The culmination of this series of victories was to be the battle won on the river Lech by Otto I in 955.[30]

The decline of the Magyar threat from the early 930s onwards released the kingdom from its most pressing problem, but also opened up new internal ones. While military activity was so constant there was less opportunity for the kings to impose themselves on the powerful dukes. As a territorial duke prior to his election in 919, Henry I was no more than one of several, and his royal title did not greatly enhance his power in practice, which tended to remain confined to his own duchy of Saxony. His authority was at least sufficient to enable him to appoint a duke of his own choosing in Suabia in 926, when that position became vacant, and he and his son Otto I gradually extended their influence through such appointments of supporters and members of their own family to the other great duchies. However, the traditions of regional independence were so strong and the lack of institutions of central government so absolute that the appointees were not necessarily thereby made dependents of the monarchy. Indeed, the greatest internal threats to the monarchy proved to be those posed by members of the Ottonian family who had been entrusted with such duchies.

Otto I faced a rebellion in 938 led by Duke Eberhard of Franconia, brother of the former King Conrad, in which both his own elder half-brother Thankmar and his full brother Henry were involved. The fighting escalated the following year, when the Duke of Lotharingia, which had reverted to eastern Frankish rule after the revolt against Charles the Simple in 922, joined the rebels and Louis IV (936–54) of western Francia invaded the kingdom.[31] However, so wracked by internal divisions was the west Frankish realm itself by this time, that many of its leading noble houses promptly gave their backing to Otto, who made an effective counter-invasion of Louis's territories, forcing him to withdraw. The deaths in this war in 939 of both the rebel Dukes of Franconia and Lotharingia then gave Otto the chance to replace them with his own appointees. He was also able to install his younger brother Henry, despite the latter's hostility to him in 938 and 941, as Duke of Bavaria, through a marriage to the daughter and heiress of Arnulf the Bad (d. 937). A similar marriage made Otto's son Liudolf Duke of Suabia.[32]

It was in the ensuing period of apparent stability both within the East Frankish kingdom and on its eastern borders that Otto was to become embroiled in the affairs of Italy. This first venture into the south on his part was to prove something of a fiasco. The non-Carolingian north Italian 'Kingdom of the Lombards', centred on Pavia, that had come into being after the deposition of the Emperor Charles the Fat in 887, had been ruled fairly effectively, if largely through forcible methods, by Hugh of Arles, formerly Count of Provence, from 926 to 947.[33] His son and successor Lothar died suddenly in 950, and the kingship was assumed by the *Marchio* or Marquis Berengar of Ivrea, who had in practice been the dominant force in the kingdom since 945.[34] However, Lothar's widow Adelheid appealed secretly to Otto I for help in overthrowing Berengar.

Otto formed his intention of intervening in Italy while celebrating Easter at Aachen in 951, and it may be that the precedent of Charlemagne influenced his decision.[35] Following the moves of his great predecessor he marched on Pavia, took it quickly and had himself crowned as King of the Lombards. Here the resemblance to Charles ended. Otto's venture into the south and his ensuing marriage to Adelheid provided so many opportunities for rebellion in the East Frankish kingdom, and aroused so much family mistrust, that a major rising against him took place in Germany, and he was forced to make a hasty retreat northwards to face a revolt, which was to embrace all of the duchies. Otto's return to Italy was to be delayed for a decade, and was then to be the product of an appeal from a pope rather than from a royal widow.[36]

The papacy at this time was in the depths of a period in its history apparently so far removed in practice from the high ideals of earlier phases of its existence that even as courtly a publication as the original *Cambridge Medieval History* felt it necessary to call it 'the Pornocracy'.[37] Exciting as are many of the tales of murder, lust and intrigue at the papal court in the tenth century, great care must be taken in assessing their veracity. The principal source for most of these stories is the truncated work by Bishop

Liutprand of Cremona, known as the *Liber de Ottone rege*, or *Book of King Otto*, written *c.* 965.[38] Liutprand (d. 972) had been a member of Otto I's court since 950, and was an extremely learned and well-read man.[39] Although his work in general has been viewed by many modern commentators as being largely idiosyncratic and scandal-mongering, this is to miss the continuity in the literary traditions of Late Antiquity that it betrays.[40]

Ever since the period of the Early Roman Empire, accusations of sexual impropriety had been used as a weapon not only in literary denigration of an opponent but also as a political tool. This tradition was subsequently to reappear in the history of the papacy. Accusations of 'adultery' were used against, for example, Pope Symmachus (498–514) by supporters of his rival Laurentius, and against Leo III (795–816) by those in Rome who sought to justify his violent overthrow in 799.[41] It is thus less surprising, and certainly not a product of the author's supposed salaciousness, to find Liutprand using the same kinds of charges to defame a recent pope and his aristocratic connections, who had opposed the author's master, Otto I.

Even if it would be unwise to place too much credence in the details of Liutprand's stories, what he describes in general does seem to indicate a strengthening of the tendency, already marked by the late eighth century, for the papal office to become the object of competition between rival aristocratic factions within the city of Rome.[42] Whereas in the previous decade an attempt had been made to preserve some semblance of legal forms in efforts made by one faction to remove a pope created by or sympathetic to another, by the early 900s resort was being made more immediately and directly to violence. Thus, Leo V was deposed after a thirty-day pontificate in September 903 by Christopher, who was in turn overthrown in January 904 by Sergius III (897 and 904–11), who had the military backing of Duke Alberic of Spoleto. Sergius III is then reported to have had both Leo V and Christopher strangled in prison. He is also accused of founding the first papal dynasty, by having a son by the fifteen-year-old daughter of the 'Consul' and commander of the Roman militia, Theophylact.[43] Again it is important to bear in mind that the source for this and many of these stories was Liutprand of Cremona, in his earlier *Antapodosis* or *Book of Revenge* of *c.* 958. His hostility to the family who came to dominate the City of Rome between 904 and 963 was a reflection both of their opposition to his master, Otto I, and of earlier Italian political conflicts in which he himself had played an, albeit minor, part.[44]

In practice, real power in the city during the pontificate of Sergius III was in the hands of the 'Consul' Theophylact (d. 920),

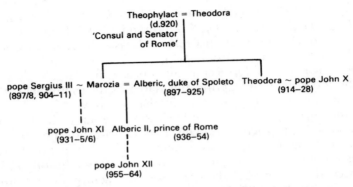

The house of Theophylact and its allies, 904–64

who was also papal treasurer, and thence it passed into those of his son-in-law Alberic I, Duke of Spoleto (d. 925). Pope John X (914–28), formerly Patriarch of Ravenna, who is accused by Liutprand of a liaison with Theophylact's other daughter Theodora, proved a more than competent pontiff in difficult circumstances, and personally took a role in raising the forces against and defeating the Arab marauders established on the mouth of the river Garigliano.[45] His legates were active in both East and West Francia, in Dalmatia, and in Constantinople. But his growing independence of the new political masters of Rome, Theophylact's daughter Marozia and her second husband Guido, the Marquis of Tuscany, may have led to his fall. He was deposed by them in 928 and murdered the following year.[46] After two short interim pontificates Marozia installed her supposed son by Sergius III as Pope John XI (931–5/6).

The power of the house of Theophylact, led by Marozia, should have further extended itself when in 932 the now once more widowed 'Senatrix' married Hugh of Arles, the King of the Lombards. However, politics within the city were intensely local-ised, and Marozia's son by her first husband, Alberic II, was able to organise a coup soon after the marriage. Hugh escaped, but Marozia and John XI became Alberic's prisoners.[47] Under the title of 'Senator' (932) and then 'Prince of the Romans' (936) he was to rule the city until his death in 954. It is important, however, to appreciate that he was only able to do this, as had his mother and grandfather before him, with the approval and support of the lead-ing figures of the long-established and deeply entrenched papal bureaucracy. Thus in 951 it was probably as much the decision of Pope Agapitus II (946–55) as of Alberic II to refuse Otto I's request that he be elevated to the vacant imperial throne.[48]

On his deathbed Alberic II is reported to have asked the leading Roman clergy and nobles to swear they would appoint his illegitimate son Octavian as the next pope. He succeeded to his father's temporal authority in 954 and was elected pope as John XII in 955, aged approximately eighteen.[49] Such a move was hardly unprecedented in Europe at this period. A number of major ecclesiastical offices were given to children, and not surprisingly this was later much criticised in the reform movement that swept through most of the western church in the eleventh century.[50] However, it needs to be appreciated that in this period the close local identification of secular and ecclesiastical power could actually benefit the church. Many of the 'princely' (that is in practice independent aristocratic comital or ducal) dynasties of Western Europe were both the military defenders of their territories against a range of external enemies and also the principal patrons of the monasteries and episcopal and other churches established within them. To continue and enhance these alliances by giving local ecclesiastical offices to junior members of such noble families made much sense in the local context. It is also unwise to assume that such dynasties would be naturally opposed to reform or to the improvement of the economic and spiritual hold of the Church in their lands. For example, the line of the Counts of Barcelona monopolised many of the abbatial and episcopal offices within the various counties under their sway in the tenth and early eleventh centuries, but were both wealthy patrons of these and other local churches, and the prime promoters of reforms in monastic life and ecclesiastical discipline.[51]

Thus, for all of his later reputation, itself a product of Liutprand's skilful pen, John XII, like some of the previous popes under his father's regime, was an active supporter of the reformed monasticism that was making itself felt in a number of houses in central Italy, western Francia and England from the mid-tenth century onwards.[52] This may represent the ability of the papal bureaucracy to maintain the ideology and the authority of the institution, irrespective of the worth of its titular head, but it must at least be allowed that John XII was willing to devote attention to the interests of the Church beyond the bounds of immediate secular political advantage. This was also part of a period in which reform of monastic life and the adoption of the *Rule of Benedict* was accepted by many of the monasteries in the city.[53] Materially, however, John XII's pontificate saw the rapid erosion of the territorial power of the papacy in central Italy, due to the aggression of the restored King of the Lombards, Berengar II (950–1, 951–63), who conquered John XII's family duchy of Spoleto in 959. Faced with this, the pope appealed to Otto I for help, with the promise of the imperial title that had been refused him in 951 as an inducement.[54] In the minds of the principal participants a reprise of the Franco-papal alliance against Lombard aggression of the times of Pippin III and Charlemagne was clearly envisaged.

Germany, Rome and Constantinople, 962–983

The rapid conquest of Berengar's kingdom by Otto was followed by his imperial coronation in Rome on 2 February 962. In return the new emperor gave the papacy the privilege known as the 'Ottonianum', confirming earlier gifts of lands made by the Carolingian rulers Pippin III, Charlemagne, and Louis.[55] These territories were considerably extended by new concessions, but the pope was obliged in return to recognise the emperor as his secular overlord in all of his lands. This was to prove a contentious legacy, especially in the period of reform and the development of new papal ideology in the eleventh and twelfth centuries. In many respects the new 'Roman Empire' that the popes had created and tried to mould for their own purposes was then to prove something of a Frankenstein's monster.

From the point of view of the new emperor, who proposed to take a more active and personal interest in Italy than had been the case with his great exemplar, Charlemagne, the papal invitation had been irresistibly attractive. For one thing, the role of the German kings was, as has been seen in the case of Otto's predecessors, a very difficult one. Their origins did not distinguish them from the other ducal houses of eastern Francia, and they lacked hereditary rights inherited from the Carolingians. Despite attempts to enhance their status by increased formality in court and liturgical ritual – far in excess of anything that had been practised by the Carolingians – their power still depended ultimately on a mixture of continuing military success and political dexterity.[56] The prospect of the imperial title, and with it both a real enhancement in status and a more clearly articulated claim to the Carolingian legacy, was thus a genuine attraction.

They would also inherit, through the simultaneous acquisition of the kingdom of the Lombards, a more complex and better governed state. In addition, the economic resources of the Italian monarchy were more immediately accessible than those of Germany, where the regional power of the duchies and the independence of the holders of those offices were so much greater. Even when members of Otto's family or other close allies could be installed as dukes, none were willing to lose the opportunities for effective autonomy that the offices provided, or to allow the kings, whose principal land holdings remained those they owned in their family duchy of Saxony, to establish a direct hold over the economic resources of these great regional principalities.

In Italy, on the other hand, the much smaller scale of the original Lombard duchies in the north and their gradual elimination under Carolingian rule, left the King of the Lombards unchallenged by such territorial 'equals' as the German dukes, and with far more by way of resources of property and patronage at his disposal. Educational traditions and the apparatus of government in Italy were also probably in advance of most of what was to be found further north. The greater sophistication of such Pavia-trained courtiers as Liutprand, who had fled to Otto in 950, must have been apparent. It is probable that Liutprand and others in Otto's entourage, such as Bishop Rather of Verona, who had experience of Italy, helped to keep the German ruler's interest in it alive in the period 951–61.

The case of Rather, however, highlights some of the dangers that Otto may not have appreciated, but of which he and his successors were to be made increasingly aware. A native of Liège in Lotharingia, Rather had been appointed to the bishopric of Verona in 931 by the King of the Lombards, Hugh of Arles, to whose court he had been attracted. However, in his diocese local xenophobia led to his twice being ejected from Verona, and to his, unwisely in the outcome, supporting the bid of Duke Arnulf the Bad of Bavaria to conquer the Lombard kingdom in 934. As an exile from 948 onwards he served as tutor to Otto's brother Bruno, later royal chancellor and Archbishop of Cologne, and was a periodic attender at the royal court. After Otto's conquest of the kingdom of the Lombards he was able to regain his see of Verona, but in general his experiences prefigured the problems that were to affect alien clergy inserted into the Italian Church. They remained acceptable locally only so long as their political masters were able to protect them with the threat of military force.[57]

This Italian lack of enthusiasm for foreign rule soon manifested itself in imperial–papal relations. By 962 John XII had begun scheming with Berengar II's son Adalbert against Otto, and is even accused by Liutprand of having entered into communication with the Magyars.[58] In consequence Otto had him deposed at a synod in Rome in 963, but once the emperor had left the city his own nominee Leo VIII (963–5) found that he lacked the local backing to stand out against John XII's supporters and was forced in turn to take to flight. Only the death of John in 964 – of a stroke while in bed with a married woman if Liutprand is to be believed – regularised the situation.[59]

Imperial nominees to the papacy, as well as to local bishoprics, were regarded with dislike by the local Italian populace, who became increasingly anti-German in attitude, and they could only maintain themselves with the emperor's armed backing. However, imperial power fluctuated. On Otto I's death in 973 his heir Otto II (973–83) had to establish himself in Germany before he could involve himself in Italy, and on his own early death the minority of his heir, Otto III (983–1002), gave rise to a long period of imperial weakness in the peninsula. In such periods imperially sponsored popes tended to come to unfortunate ends, as happened to Benedict VI (973–4) and John XIV (983–4), both of whom were deposed and murdered in the aftermath of a change of emperor.[60]

The immediate instigator of the deaths of both of these was Pope Boniface VII (974, 984–5) who, at a later date when such legal niceties mattered, was formally declared to have been an antipope. He was the candidate for the papal office of a newly dominant aristocratic faction in the city of Rome, that of the Crescentii, but in flight in 974 and in his brief restoration ten years later he was also to enjoy the backing of the Byzantine emperors, who were now anxious to do anything to discomfort the Ottonians, whom they regarded as usurpers, and to restore the authority of the rightful Roman emperor over the city from which the name derived.[61]

The Byzantine Empire had in military terms enjoyed a considerable revival in the tenth century under the direction of a succession of competent emperors, who in many cases were former generals, who made themselves co-emperors alongside the legitimate successors of Basil I. The Bulgar dominance in the eastern Balkans had fluctuated during this period, and was effectively to come to an end in the reign of the Emperor Basil II (976–1025), later and not entirely appropriately to be known as 'the Bulgar-slayer'. The eastern frontier in Asia Minor had also been successfully expanded, and the Emperor Nicephorus Phocas (963–9) regained Antioch in 969, lost by Heraclius over three centuries before. The same emperor also recovered Cyprus from the Arabs in 965.[62] In southern Italy in this period, however, the main threat in Byzantine eyes changed from that posed by the Arabs to that presented by the growing power in the region of the Ottonian empire.

In part this was a sensible perception. The Aghlabid Amirate, that had undertaken the conquest of Sicily, was overthrown in 909 by a religious rising in favour of the Fatimids, a Shi'ite Muslim dynasty, who claimed descent from the Prophet's daughter Fatima, the wife of 'Ali. Although they also took over the Aghlabid conquests in Sicily, their attention was directed primarily eastwards, and in 969 their capital was moved from Kairouan in

Ifriqya to Fustat (Cairo) in recently conquered Egypt.[63] There their interests became primarily concerned with expanding their rule into Palestine and Syria, and this in turn may have contributed to putting a term to the hitherto successful Byzantine expansion in this direction. But even with this significant shift in the power and interests of the Muslim states, Arab raids from strongholds in Calabria continued to make conditions in southern Italy unstable.

After 964, once the hold of the new emperor, Otto I, over the north and centre of the peninsula seemed secure, he was easily drawn into the complex problems of the south, not least by the need to assure his hold over Rome and central Italy. This was assisted by the more favourable situation further south. Duke Pandolf I 'Ironhead' (961–80) of Capua–Benevento looked for Ottonian help in making himself dominant in the region, both over his neighbours in Salerno and Naples and also in increasing his territory at the expense of that of the Byzantines.[64] At the same time Calabria was under increasing threat from the Fatimid rulers of Sicily and Tunisia, and an attempt to relieve this by the despatch of a Byzantine expedition to Sicily in 964 led only to military and naval disaster. In 967 Nicephorus II Phocas (963–9), ruling in tandem with two child emperors of the Macedonian dynasty, was forced to make a treaty with the Fatimids, agreeing to payment of an annual tribute. Taking advantage of these circumstances, Otto I led an army into Apulia in 968, to try to wrest Bari from the Byzantines. This failed in its objective but may have caused some damage. Otto did make rather more headway over the winter of 968/9 in further campaigning in Byzantine Calabria. He also hoped to capitalise on the military threat he was posing by sending a mission to Constantinople in 968 to secure Byzantine recognition of the new western imperial dynasty, something that he hoped would be cemented by a marriage alliance.[65]

On his return in 969 Otto's envoy to Constantinople, Bishop Liutprand of Cremona, wrote a very bitter account of his mission and of the court that he had visited. In it he likened the Emperor Nicephorus to an Ethiopian pygmy – 'one whom it would not be pleasant to meet in the middle of the night' – and claimed that he 'lives on garlic, onions and leeks, and drinks bath water'.[66] Above all, Liutprand wished to suggest that the Byzantine emperor, who was genuinely furious at the westerners' unprovoked attacks on imperial territory, was unwilling to negotiate with Otto as an equal. The Byzantine court refused to acknowledge the latter's imperial title, and insisted on referring to him as *Rex* or King.[67]

Liutprand was equally concerned to suggest that the Roman Church had been insulted by the Byzantines. This resulted from the arrival of messengers sent by Pope John XIII (965–72), who following the doctrine of the 'Donation of Constantine', referred to Nicephorus as Emperor of the Greeks and to Otto as Emperor of the Romans. The Byzantine Patrician Christophorus gave Liutprand in reply the eastern version of the supposedly crucial transfer of Constantine I from Rome to Constantinople: 'The stupid silly pope does not know that the holy Constantine transferred hither [Constantinople] the imperial sceptre, the senate and all the Roman knighthood, and left in Rome nothing but vile minions – fishers, namely, peddlers, bird catchers, bastards, plebeians, slaves.'[68]

By the time that Liutprand was writing, the situation in southern Italy had changed, which may help to explain his undiplomatic tone. Otto had been forced to return north, leaving Pandolf Ironhead to pursue the siege of Bari, but the Beneventan duke had been captured and sent a prisoner to Constantinople.[69] However, when all his hopes might have seemed to have been frustrated, Otto I was able to achieve some of his diplomatic intentions in consequence of the murder of the Emperor Nicephorus II in December 969. This was organised by one of his generals, who succeeded him as John I Tzimisces (969–76). The new emperor released Duke Pandolf, and agreed to the marriage of his niece Theophanu to Otto's son (Otto II) in 972. It is notable, though, that the chosen bride was not a member of the senior ruling house, the Macedonian dynasty, nor was she 'born in the purple', i.e. the offspring of a reigning emperor. Such imperial princesses were never to be sent to 'barbarian' husbands.[70] Theophanu's dowry was supposed to include the increasingly beleaguered Byzantine imperial possessions in Italy, but during the long period extending from 973 to 980 while Otto II was having to fight wars in Germany against his relative, the Duke of Bavaria, and against the Danish King Harald Bluetooth, and against the Slav dukes of the Poles and of the Bohemians, and against the West Frankish King Lothar (954–86), who sacked Aachen in 978, control over the south was largely lost.[71]

When Otto II finally felt able to turn his attention to Italy, he faced a complex situation in the south. His father-in-law John Tzimisces was dead and Ottonian hopes of peacefully gaining the Byzantine lands in southern Italy were at an end. War seemed the only way to make his claim a reality. Otto succeeded in expelling the Byzantine forces from Taranto, but on 13 July 982 he suffered a major defeat at the hands of the Arabs at Stilo in Calabria, and was then forced to make a hasty withdrawal to the north, where other military problems were also reasserting themselves.[72] To deal with the threat of renewed war on several fronts, Otto held a conference with the principal German dukes in Verona, where amongst other things it was agreed that his infant son and heir, also named Otto, should be formally elected and then crowned as king at Aachen later that year. This was to ensure a smooth future succession, and mirrored the early election and coronation of Otto II himself in 967. It did not indicate any expectation of the imminent end of the emperor's reign. However, while still developing his plans for future action against the Danes and the Slavs, Otto's health suddenly declined, and he died in Rome in December 983, aged only twenty-eight, and leaving his three-year-old son a host of problems.[73]

Otto III (983–1002) and the eastwards expansion of Europe

The reign of Otto III, which lasted from 983 to 1002, has long aroused scholarly interest, though more for what it appeared to promise than for what it actually achieved. The son of a Byzantine princess, he was taught and advised from 997 by Gerbert, who as Abbot of Bobbio (from 982), Archbishop of Rheims (991–97) and then pope as Sylvester II (999–1003), was undeniably the foremost scholar of the period. Others of his tutors included the pro-Byzantine John Philagathos, Abbot of Nonantula and briefly pope as John XVI (997–98). From his antecedents and training, Otto III looked as if he might have become a highly sophisticated ruler, who could have combined elements of the old and the new and from East and West into a new synthesis. It was not to be. He died aged only twenty two, and with some of what he had hoped to achieve already in ruins.

The reign of Otto III falls easily into two parts: the regencies of his mother the Byzantine Princess Theophanu (d. 991) and of his grandmother Adelheid (d. 999), and the few years in which he himself was able to direct the empire, from 994 onwards. The first and longer period is relatively little recorded, after an initial phase in which the succession was contested, as this was largely a period of governmental inactivity caused by the length of the regency and the political caution with which the two regents had to proceed. Attention has, though, been devoted recently to some of the cultural achievements of Theophanu's rule, as well as to possible Byzantine influences she mediated to the court and the art that it patronised.[74]

The standing of the imperial office remained ambiguous at this time. Although accepted as King of Germany prior to his father's

death by the magnates assembled in Verona in 983, and then confirmed as such after Duke Henry, later known as 'the Wrangler' or
'the Quarrelsome', of Bavaria (d. 994) gave up a brief bid for the
kingship in 984, Otto was not crowned as emperor and did not use
the imperial style until he received his coronation in Rome in May
996, at the hands of Gregory V (996–9), who was also his own
cousin and recent appointee to the papal office.[75] On the other
hand, his mother Theophanu had been crowned empress alongside her husband in 973, and she made use of the title up to her
death, sometimes employing her own regnal years in the dating of
charters.[76]

For evidence on his reign, beyond the testimony of a small
number of monastic annals, the formal charters of his court and
the artistic legacy of some impressive illuminated manuscripts,
there is one dominant if idiosyncratic source, the chronicle written
by Thietmar, Bishop of Merseburg (1009–1018). Thietmar was
the son of a Saxon count from Walbeck on the Aller, who began
his chronicle in 1012, intending it to be a history of his see, which
had only been founded in 968.[77] His work rapidly developed into
something much more than that. Beginning with borrowings from
the *Res Gestae Saxonicae* (Deeds of the Saxons) of the earlier Saxon
historian Widukind of Corvey, which had ended with the death
of Otto I in 973, Thietmar made his chronicle into a detailed and
very personal view of the history of the later Ottonian monarchs
and of their realm.

Although loyal to the Saxon ruling dynasty, he could be critical
of it when royal actions seemed to threaten the well-being of the
see of Merseburg. This was notably the case with Otto II, who
had secured papal support for the suppression of the diocese in
981, to provide a legal justification for its then Bishop Giseler
being transferred to the archbishopric of Magdeburg[78] (translations from one see to another were otherwise prohibited in canon
law). The diocese of Merseburg was only revived on Giseler's
death in 1004, when it was given to Wigbert, Thietmar's
predecessor.

He was still working on his chronicle at the time of his death
in 1018, and it is, not surprisingly, at its most detailed in treating
the period during which it was being composed. Even so, its
fourth book provides the fullest narrative of the reign of Otto III,
which is accompanied at the end by a series of vignettes on the
lives of some of the leading secular and ecclesiastical personages
of the period. This culminates in a remarkably candid self-portrait
of Thietmar himself: 'Know, O reader, that you would see in me
a tiny little man. My lower jaw and the side of my face are
deformed, because here there once erupted a now permanently

swollen fistula. A nose broken in childhood makes me appear ridiculous.'[79]

Thietmar's idiosyncratic but highly perceptive views on this period can usefully be complemented by the more restrained and official notices of the major annals, notably those of the convent of Quedlinburg, upon which he had himself occasionally drawn. This great monastic house to the north of Merseburg was founded in 936 as her retreat by Matilda, widow of Henry I, in the immediate aftermath of her husband's death. It was thereafter frequently visited by the royal court, notably for the celebration of Easter, and its abbesses, like those of Essen, Gernrode and one or two other such convents, were drawn from the ranks of the ladies of the royal house or those of the greater aristocracy. Its royal founder was quickly revered as a saint, and became the subject of two works of hagiography.[80] The first of these was written for her grandson Otto II, and the second was dedicated to a great-grandson, Henry II (1002–24). She was succeeded as abbess by her grand-daughter Matilda, daughter of Otto I, who held the office from 966 to 999. The abbey then passed directly to Adelheid, daughter of Otto II and sister of Otto III, who held it until her death in 1045. She also acquired the abbacies of Gernrode and Vreden in 1014 and of Gandersheim in 1039.

The Quedlinburg annals come as close as anything to presenting the Ottonian dynasty's image of itself. They also convey a very Saxon, and more specifically eastern Saxon perspective on the activities and concerns of the royal government in this period. That virtually all of the major works of Ottonian historiography were written by Saxons in Saxony, and are unmatched by comparable bodies of literary evidence from other eastern Frankish regions is bound to have a distorting effect both on the historical record and on modern interpretations of it. Relatively little sympathy is thus aroused by the activities and aspirations of the contemporary Bavarian dukes, who in later tradition came to be known by such epithets as 'the Bad' and 'the Quarrelsome', and whose actions have often in consequence been seen by modern historians as threatening and weakening the attempts of the Ottonians to create a strong, centralised monarchy. That the latter was the most desirable political development to be anticipated in medieval Germany is not necessarily as self-evident as it has often been assumed.

It was inevitable that the different components of the eastern Frankish kingdom should have varying concerns and priorities in this period. Lotharingia, for example, was bound to be more affected by developments in western Francia than was Bavaria, which on the other hand was in much closer touch with what was happening in Italy and out on the plains of the Danube. In the same way, Saxony was predominantly concerned with what was happening beyond its expanding eastern frontiers, above all the lands of the Slavs located between the Elbe and the Baltic. Numerous relatively small and often mutually antagonistic Slav tribes occupied this region, of whom the best known are the Abodrites, the Wends and the Wiltzi or Liutzi.

The western fringes of this area had once been in the hands of the Saxons, up to the time of Charlemagne, who in the final stages of his Saxon wars had deported those of them who lived to the east of the Elbe, and given their lands to his Slav allies, principally the Abodrites. The number of and rivalry between these various Slav peoples prevented a large-scale threat from building up on the eastern frontier, even during some of the most difficult times for the east Frankish Carolingians. Under Louis the German (840–76), marcher counties were established and attempts continued to be made, as they had from the time of Charlemagne, to ensure that the Slav leaders in the vicinity of the frontiers were as far as possible Frankish clients.[81] Although efforts were made, particularly by Bishop Anskar under Louis the Pious, to promote missionary ventures amongst the Danes and the Swedes, little seems to have been done to do the same for the Slavs. Though it has to be conceded that the Scandinavian missions produced few real results at this time.[82]

The emergence of the Ottonians led to more sustained efforts being made, both in terms of attempts at conversion and also in the imposition of institutionalised eastern Frankish rule or hegemony over some of the closer Slav peoples. In particular this affected those living in the region known as 'Nordalbingia', the territory lying in the angle between the river Elbe and the Baltic. In part this was probably a reflection of the previous entrepreneurial successes of various Saxon noble families on the eastern frontier in extending their personal wealth and local power at the expense of their Slav neighbours. This involved aggressive raiding and tribute taking. The greatest of such local dynasties was indeed that of the Liudolfings or Ottonians themselves. The ancestral Liudolf had been given responsibility for the control of the eastern Saxon march, with a ducal title, by his brother-in-law King Louis the Younger (876–82). That extension of their royal authority over this region and areas beyond it to the east should have been a major concern for his tenth century descendants is thus not surprising.

Henry I, when temporarily freed from the Magyar threat, conquered much of what would become Brandenburg, and established a new marcher lordship based at Meissen on the Elbe.

Otto I added two further marches to the east of the Elbe and the Saale, thus creating a layered structure of four parallel marches extending southwards from the Baltic coast to the northern edge of the lands of the Bohemians. He also instituted an aggressive programme of conversion amongst the Slavs brought under his rule. One consequence of this was that fierce Slav resistance prevented the Saxon contingents from joining the rest of the royal army for the campaign that put an end to the Magyar threat at the battle of the Lech in 955.

After the initial phases of open conflict, the political and cultural integration of these temporarily pacified Slavs into the Ottonian empire clearly required some extension of the ecclesiastical administration in northern Germany. The latter was still organised around the two great Rhineland archbishoprics of Mainz and Cologne, of which the former normally held a primacy of honour. To these had been added in 834 an archbishopric of Hamburg–Bremen, on the northern fringes of East Francia, whose main purpose was to concern itself with the Scandinavian missions.

The eastward expansion of Ottonian territory and the need for a dedicated centre for its ecclesiastical organisation and the missions to the Slavs suggested the desirability of the creation of a new archdiocese for this extensive region, which was far removed from the older centres in the Rhineland. This new metropolitan see Otto I planned to bring into being at Magdeburg, where he had founded a monastery dedicated to the soldier martyr St Maurice in 937. As previously mentioned, his mother had established her own convent of Quedlinburg only a little to the south of this in the previous year, and other important monastic centres in the region included Gernrode, founded c. 960 by Gero, who from 937 to 965 served as Warden of the East Saxon March under both Otto I and Otto II.[83]

As the presence of such religious houses indicates, an ecclesiastical administrative organisation had already had to come into existence in eastern Saxony, but this continued to depend on institutional links to the distant or otherwise involved archbishoprics of Mainz and of Hamburg–Bremen. These were not, on the other hand, easily persuaded to forgo what they saw as their rights over the new churches in the east; at least not without due compensation.

Thus, while Otto's foundation of his monastery in Magdeburg in 937 has been seen as the first step in a plan to create the new archdiocese, it would in practice prove a slow and laborious process. New bishoprics were founded in 947/8 at Aarhus, Ribe and Schleswig to serve the needs of the emerging church in southern Denmark, and these were put under the authority of the archdiocese of Hamburg–Bremen; So too was a new bishopric that was more gradually established at Oldenburg in northern Brandenburg in the course of the years 968–72. The archbishopric of Mainz, by far the largest of the German metropolitan sees, saw its authority extended through the creation of new bishoprics at Brandenburg and Havelburg. When a new bishopric was established in 973 or 976 to serve the needs of the recently converted Bohemians, it too was placed under the authority of Mainz.

Despite such concessions, there was continued opposition from vested ecclesiastical interests, not least from the Bishop of Halberstadt, whose see, located immediately to the west of Magdeburg, would have to be suppressed to endow the proposed new archbishopric. Only in 968, following the deaths of the principal ecclesiastical opponents of the scheme in Germany and when Otto I, now emperor, had also secured the support of a temporarily compliant papacy, was it possible for the new archdiocese to be established. This was accompanied by the setting up of new suffragan bishoprics at Merseburg, Meissen, and Zeitz. To the first of these was appointed the veteran missionary, Poppo, who had converted King Harald Bluetooth of Denmark earlier in the decade. At the same time the dioceses of Brandenburg and Havelburg, created in the 940s, were transferred from the authority of the Archbishop of Mainz to that of his new colleague in Magdeburg.

As with the Saxons in the time of Charlemagne, Christianisation of the northern Slavs was a dimension of a predatory lordship, which involved the establishment of small fortified centres from which the conquerors could impose their rule on and take their profits from the surrounding territory. The churches built inside these fortresses also extracted tithes from the Slav population. So, there may have been little affection felt for either Ottonian rule or the new religion to which it was allied amongst the Slavs upon whom both were being imposed. Opportunities for revolt were not overlooked, and a major Slav rising took place in 983, following closely on from Otto II's disastrous defeat at the hands of the Arabs in southern Italy the previous year. The timing can hardly have been coincidental.

The outcome was a disaster for the Saxons, from which it took them more than a generation to recover. The fortresses of Brandenburg and Havelburg, both of which were the centres of new dioceses, were destroyed by the Liutzi. At the same time Hamburg was sacked by the Abodrites. Only the intervention in August of 983 of a Saxon army led by Archbishop Giseler of

Magdeburg (981–1004) prevented further losses, but Saxon rule and with it the hold of Christianity over the area between the Elbe and the Baltic was temporarily at an end.

More constructive developments were taking place at this time amongst other Slav peoples further south and east, who were not subjected to direct Saxon rule or the immediate threat of it. While the Saxons had kept the Elbe Slavs generally disunited and divided, as well as oppressed, other larger Slavic population groupings had formed beyond this region. Some were relatively long-established. Others may have been still in the process of growth and formation.

In part this emergence of larger-scale Slav ethnic and political groups had been a response to the eastward expansion of Carolingian and then Ottonian power from the late eighth century onwards. The Bohemians, who are first recorded in Frankish annals at the very beginning of the ninth century, were probably led into uniting under a single ruler called Lecho (k. 805) in reaction to Charlemagne's conquests of Saxony and Bavaria.[84] For reasons that are not made clear in the annals, they themselves became the target of Carolingian attacks in 805/6, and seem to have lost their political unity then or soon after.

Certainly they were in no position to resist the rapid subsequent rise of the Moravian kingdom. By the mid-ninth century the Moravians, the much debated centre of whose state lay somewhere to the south-east, had made themselves into a greater threat to the Bohemians than the Franks had been. In consequence the Bohemians may have begun to contemplate entry into the Frankish cultural orbit with a greater degree of enthusiasm. Thus in 845 fourteen unnamed leaders of the Bohemians came to the eastern Frankish King Louis the German to ask for baptism, which he provided for them.[85] Despite this, the Bohemians soon seem to have fallen under Moravian domination and took an active part in raids made on east Frankish and Bavarian frontier regions. Their subjection to the Moravian ruler, Sventopulk I (*c.* 869–93) – also known by the Germanic version of his name as Zwentibald – was confirmed in a treaty made by the east Frankish King Arnulf in 890.[86]

Perhaps only with the collapse of the Moravian realm at the very end of the century did the Bohemians regain their independence under a single ruling house of their own, that of the Przemyslids. Once again this involved closer political and cultural contacts with the eastern Franks, not least as the Magyar threat grew in intensity. In 895 two leaders of the Bohemians called Spitignevo and Witizla submitted to Arnulf at Regensburg. In later tradition if not contemporary record, they are held to be brothers and to have built churches in Bohemia after their return, including the first one to be erected in Prague.

Another church was built in Prague early in the tenth century and was dedicated to St Vitus, whose cult was being actively promoted by the Saxon monastery of Corvey, on the Weser. This choice of dedication and source of relics may testify to the influence of the Saxon church on the newly developing Christianity of Bohemia at this time. The founder of this church of St Vitus was a young prince of the name of Vaclav (Wenceslas), who around 935 was murdered by his brother Boleslav. A cult of the young prince, venerated as a Christian martyr, developed rapidly, without apparently weakening the secular power wielded by his murderer. In this and other respects the cult of St Wenceslas parallels the slightly later ones of St Edward the Martyr, King of Wessex (975–8), and St Magnus, Earl of Orkney (*c.* 1105–15).[87]

A cultural dimension to this fratricidal conflict has been claimed. From around 930 Bohemia was coming increasingly under the political domination of the duchy of Bavaria under its Duke Arnulf 'the Bad', and the Bavarian church had long-established interests in extending its missionary activities in this direction. Thus it has been argued that the rivalry between Vaclav and Boleslav was a reflection of a wider struggle between two factions in the Bohemian aristocracy that supported Saxon and Bavarian political and cultural hegemony respectively. Although enticing, this argument can not be substantiated, due to the limited nature of the evidence. German chroniclers make few references to Bohemia, and an indigenous historiographical tradition would only be initiated with the writing of the *Chronica Bohemorum* of Cosmas of Prague (d. 1125).

Boleslav I (*c.* 935–67) proved a highly successful ruler, who as Duke of the Bohemians, seems to have established a relatively stable and secure state for his people within the orbit of the Ottonian empire. His successor Boleslav II (*c.* 967–1004) became a significant figure in the troubled internal politics of that empire, supporting Henry the Quarrelsome of Bavaria against Otto II in 974 and again in his short-lived bid for the crown against the infant Otto III in 984. The conversion of the Bohemians advanced steadily during the reigns of these dukes, but not in spectacular fashion. The first Bishop of Prague was only consecrated in 973 or 976, and he and his successors have been characterised as being 'little more than the chaplains of the Przemyslid dukes', who showed no interest at this time in promoting an independent Bohemian church with its own archbishopric.[88]

Bohemian influence may, however, have been in part behind the extension of Christianity into a neighbouring region at this time.

To the north east of the lands of the Bohemians and beyond 'Nordalbingia' another large Slav ethnic group seems to have been in the process of uniting under the leadership of what the Ottonians recognised as its own ducal dynasty, the Piasts. Although it has been argued that this family was of Viking origin, it ruled over the Slav population that came to be known as the Poles, of whose earlier history hardly any trace remains. It may well be that it was the military conquests of this dynasty that welded together hitherto disparate elements of population and thus forged the new Polish ethnic identity.

The Piast Duke Mieszko, the first to emerge clearly into historiographical light, married a daughter of Boleslav I of Bohemia in 964. As Thietmar reports, she quickly converted her pagan husband to Christianity. However, it is likely that Mieszko's interest in a marriage tie with the Przemyslids indicates a predisposition in favour of the wider cultural links that they represented, not least with the Ottonian empire. This was made more explicit in his second marriage in 978, this time to the daughter of Thietrich (Theoderic), warden of the Saxon North March (965–85).[89]

Mieszko was baptised in 966, and established a church dedicated to St George in his court centre at Gniezno. A bishopric (which became an archbishopric in 1000) was founded there in 968, and thence a new missionary centre and second diocese was developed at Poznan. Other sees were set up as the frontiers of Piast rule rapidly expanded in succeeding decades. To avoid the claims to authority over it of the German archbishoprics, in particular that of Magdeburg, the Polish duke placed the church in his territories under direct papal patronage in 990. This should not necessarily be seen as indicating any threat to his political loyalty to the Ottonians, but it marks a certain distancing of the duchy from too close dependence on German personnel and institutions.[90]

Mieszko (d. 992) expanded his power from this central area southwards into Silesia, which led to territorial disputes with the Bohemian dukes, and into the area around Cracow, where another bishopric was soon founded. Towards the end of his reign he also extended his conquests into Pomerania and the Baltic coast. He, like Boleslav II of Bohemia, accepted the claims made by Henry the Quarrelsome of Bavaria, and initially recognised him as king in 984. A realignment to accept the authority of Otto III did neither of the dukes any harm, especially as the ensuing regime of the two regents was largely passive as far as the eastern lands were concerned. Mieszko's son Boleslav I Chobry or 'the Mighty' (992–1025) took an even more independent line than his father in relation to the Ottonian empire, overrunning the

March of Meissen in the aftermath of the death of Otto III in 1002.

This and his attacks on the Bohemians suggest that Boleslav had little long-term interest in preserving the concord between the various Slav rulers and their imperial overlord, which Otto III seems to have hoped to foster. This had been symbolised by Otto's investing Boleslav Chobry with the title of *Frater et Cooperator Imperii* ('Brother and Partner') in the course of the emperor's ground-breaking visit to the shrine of St Adalbert at Gniezno in the year 1000.

St Adalbert, whose original name was Vojteck, was a Bohemian noble whose family, the Slavnikids, had long been hostile to the Przemyslid dukes (and were massacred by them in 995). After training at Magdeburg under its Archbishop Adalbert, whose name he subsequently took, he had been made Bishop of Prague in 983 thanks to the patronage of the Emperor Otto II. He had been forced to abandon his see in 988 after frustrated attempts at imposing reforms and quarrels with Duke Boleslav II. Following a period of exile in Rome, where he met the empress Theophanu, he was obliged to resume his episcopal duties in Prague in 992, under pressure from his ecclesiastical superior, the Archbishop of Mainz. This proved no more successful than the previous incumbency and he returned to Rome in 994, where he impressed the young Otto III when the latter came to the city for his imperial coronation. In 996 he was sent by Pope Gregory V to assist the evangelisation of the Polish frontiers. Heading into the lands of the still pagan Liutzi, he was killed by them on 23 April 997.[91] A *Life of Adalbert* was written in Rome in 999. This was followed in 1004 by a second one, written by Bruno of Querfurt, a cousin of Thietmar of Merseburg, who later became both missionary bishop and martyr in Hungary.

Otto III's visit to the tomb of Adalbert at Gniezno three years after his death has been seen both as an act of personal piety towards a man whom he knew and admired, and as a public demonstration of the new eastward extension of the remit of his imperial office. His journey, which needs to be seen as a whole, began in Rome and may be said to have ended at Aachen, where he had the grave of Charlemagne opened so that he could inspect his bones and the regalia that had been buried with him. In between these two points Otto's route had taken him to Regensburg, Meissen and Magdeburg, as well as Gniezno, where he came as the first German ruler to honour the shrine of a Slav saint in Slav lands. He approached Gniezno, the location of Adalbert's relics, 'barefoot, as a suppliant' and entering the church he appealed for the martyr's intercession. He then proclaimed the see of Gniezno to be an archbishopric. In his report of this Thietmar of Merseburg felt impelled to add the rather sardonic wish: 'legitimately, I hope'. The dioceses of Poznan, Cracow, Wroclaw and Kolberg were then made suffragans of the new metropolitan see.[92]

The emperor's actions in Gniezno, seen as part of a great journey linking the former imperial capitals of Rome and Aachen, are bound to appear highly charged with symbolism. Not the least manifestation of this was Otto's action in translating some of the relics of St Adalbert from Gniezno to Aachen, for reburial alongside Charlemagne, thus explicitly linking the new saint and the Polish duchy with the imperial founder. The young emperor was here taking new initiatives in more ways than one. As Thietmar's remark implies, the authority by which Otto intervened in the highly contentious field of ecclesiastical organisation and hierarchy to create a new archbishopric might not seem to be above challenge. Though it may be assumed that he had the full support of the new pope, Sylvester II (999–1003), his former tutor Gerbert of Aurillac. But from Thietmar's account it was clearly not papal authority but imperial decree that was employed to elevate the Polish see to archiepiscopal status. In contrast Otto I had taken perhaps as much as thirty years to bring about the comparable enhancement of Magdeburg and had secured it in the end by diplomacy, consensus and papal authorisation.

This short-lived period of very close links between pope and emperor had a further manifestation in the joint conferral of a crown and royal title on the first King of the Magyars in 1001. The Magyars had developed a geographically more stable and settled form of society in the aftermath of their final defeat by the Ottonians at the battle of the Lech in 955, and had become more receptive of the cultural influences to which they were subjected from both Byzantium and the Ottonian empire. Around 980 a Magyar ruler called Geza (d. 997) became a nominal Christian, but his son Waik seems to have been a more whole-hearted convert. He adopted the baptismal name of Stephen, by which he is better known. In his reign as first King of Hungary (1001–38) the formal conversion of the Magyars was achieved and an ecclesiastical organisation was developed for the church in the new kingdom.

The value accorded their old Magyar foes by the Ottonian rulers can be deduced from the marriage that was arranged in the mid-990s between Waik/Stephen and Gisela, the sister of Duke Henry of Bavaria. The latter, son of the infamous Henry the Quarrelsome (d. 995), would succeed his cousin Otto III as king and emperor in 1002, though this was hardly to be foreseen at the time. Even so, in comparison with the rewards offered to the Polish and Bohemian ruling houses, Stephen of Hungary's marriage into the Ottonian dynasty and his subsequent investment with a royal rather than a ducal title indicates how great a weight was placed by Otto III on securing the loyalty of the Magyar ruler.

The question remains as to whether Otto III, advised by Sylvester II, saw these concerns with the Slavs and the Magyars around the turn of the millennium primarily as a dimension of his imperial duty to promote the spread of the Christian faith or whether he was interested more in the role they could play in developing the earthly power and prestige of his office. The depiction of Otto in the illuminated Gospel book prepared for him *c.* 998–1001 shows the emperor enthroned and being approached by gift-bearing female figures representing 'Sclavinia', 'Germania', 'Gallia' and 'Roma' (in place of 'Italia' in comparable earlier versions of similar scenes).[93] The presence for the first time of the personification of the Slav lands testifies to the importance currently being accorded at the imperial court to the eastward extension of imperial hegemony.

Otto himself might not have made too much of a distinction between the extension of the bounds of his imperial authority and those of the church. Certainly the precedents from the reign of Charlemagne, with whom he was also interesting himself at this time, would have led him into looking for opportunities to further the expansion of his rule into the east as well as in Italy, and into expressing an overwhelming sense of responsibility for the spiritual well-being of his subjects. Too much of a contrast should thus not be made between the emperor's southern and eastern concerns, even though in practice the separate demands they made on him were hard to reconcile.

In Rome, where the imperial court was located for most of the relatively short time in which Otto conducted his own affairs, the missionary ventures in the east became as much a major concern as they were for the churches in Saxony and Bavaria. The monastery of San Alessio, where Adalbert stayed during his self-imposed exile from Prague, seems to have been a major centre of inspiration for such missionary ventures. Both *Lives* of Adalbert were written by monks of this community, which, as in the case of Bruno of Querfurt, was the home to several members of leading German aristocratic families.[94] Other monks from this house accompanied Adalbert on his return to Prague in 992 and were used by him to found a monastery near the Bohemian capital. The first Archbishop of Gniezno, following its elevation by Otto III in 1000 was to be Gaudentius, brother of Adalbert and another former monk of San Alessio.

Ultimately it is hard to decide exactly of what Otto III's imperial aspirations may have consisted. His actual as opposed to theoretical reign was too brief, and his views may have still been largely unformed at the time of his death. Undoubtedly, there are certain Byzantine influences to be detected on the style of his court in Rome. Here, for example, his Count of the Palace employed the Byzantine title of Protospatharios, and other officials signed imperial charters using Greek letters, albeit for clearly German names.[95] The emperor himself adopted the practice of dining publicly but alone, which was found mildly shocking by those accustomed to the more egalitarian or convivial style of other and earlier western courts.[96] While such features may be symptomatic of new ideas and experiments in protocol and imperial ideology being developed at least in Italy at this time, they proved in practice to be short-lived.

Similarly, the rhetoric of a *Renovatio Imperii Romanorum* or *Renewal of the Empire of the Romans*, which appears in a small number of works related to Otto's court, may not have been anchored on a fully developed plan of action by the time of the emperor's premature death. Its meaning, according to Thietmar, was certainly not understood or approved by all.[97] The phrase itself, which was used on Otto's imperial seal from 998 onwards, had previously been employed for the initial imperial seal of Charlemagne. It did not, therefore, for all of the classical learning of Otto's tutors and advisors, imply a revival of a Roman as opposed to a Carolingian ideology of empire. However, the first Carolingian emperor changed both his title and his seal within little more than a year of his coronation in 800, to escape from some of the implications of too close an association between his office and the city and see of Rome. This would not have been acceptable to the Franks, any more than it would have been two centuries latter to the Germans. Otto III, with a pope of his own choosing in the person of his former tutor Gerbert and perhaps bemused by the antiquarian splendours of the city, may have thought that he could avoid some of the problems that had seemed so dangerous to his great predecessor. If so, he was probably mistaken.

Like his father and grandfather before him, Otto III was caught in the dilemma of the weakness of the royal standing in Germany if the king was not present to impose his authority on the dukes and to lead his forces in person against the Slavs, Danes, Magyars or western Franks. He also needed to be equally attentive to Italian affairs if the kingship of the Lombards, and above all the imperial title, were to be maintained. As for the popes, they too were prisoners of a similar dilemma. They needed a powerful secular protector against the many external enemies and internal rivals whom they faced. Yet they did not want that protector to be too dominant or permanently present in the city of Rome, as this could inhibit their exercise of power within the territorial state that they had built up in central Italy. At the same time, the weakness of or too great an absence on the part of their imperial master could expose them to personal danger. Thus after Otto III returned to Germany in the autumn of 996 the Romans expelled his German Pope, Gregory V. Worse was to follow, in that although Otto III returned and re-established Gregory in 997, and later appointed his own former tutor Gerbert to succeed him as Sylvester II (999–1003), a revolt in Rome in 1001 forced both the emperor and his pope to flee from the city. In the aftermath of this Otto caught malaria and died in January 1002.[98]

Otto III had held high expectations of his imperial office, blending traditions deriving from his Carolingian predecessor Charlemagne with others that he may have inherited from his Byzantine mother. He had restored Aachen, looted by the western Franks in 978, and had had the body of Charlemagne dug up for his inspection and for a more grandiose reburial. Rome, even more than Aachen, became the idealised centre of his empire, and he used the title *Imperator Augustus Romanorum* with relish. In January 1001 in a charter he, rightly, dismissed the 'Donation of Constantine' as a forgery – it would take nearly 500 years before anyone else would do the same – and made it clear that papal authority was to be subordinate to imperial.[99] It is perhaps not likely that he, any more than a line of distinguished predecessors extending back to Louis the Pious, would have been able to turn these theoretical aspirations into practical reality. It was his particular misfortune that the Rome he idealised for its past had become no more than another large Italian town, prey to parochial aristocratic factionalism. Otto's imperial dreams ended with an ignominious flight into the malarial marshes.

Abbreviations

ARF	*Annales Regni Francorum* (see Bibliography); ARF Rev refers to the revised version of *c*. 814
CC	*Corpus Christianorum, series latina*
CFHB	*Corpus Fontium Historiae Byzantinae*
CHFM	*Les Classiques de l'Histoire de France au Moyen Age*
CLA	*Codices Latini Antiquiores*, ed. E. A. Lowe, 9 vols plus a Supplement (Oxford, 1934–71)
CSEL	*Corpus Scriptorum Ecclesiasticorum Latinorum*
CSHB	*Corpus Scriptorum Historiae Byzantinae*
FEHL	*Colección Fuentes y Estudios de Historia Leonesa*
Fontes	*Fontes ad Historiam Regni Francorum Aevi Karolini Illustrandam*, ed. R. Rau (3 vols, Darmstadt, 1955–60)
MGH	*Monumenta Germaniae Historica*, subdivided by series:

	AA	*Auctores Antiquissimi*
	Capit	*Capitularia*
	Epp	*Epistulae*
	LL	*Leges*
	SS	*Scriptores*
	SRG	*Scriptores Rerum Germanicarum*
	SRM	*Scriptores Rerum Merovingicarum*

MIöG	*Mitteilungen des Instituts für österreichische Geschichtsforschung*
PG	*Patrologia Graeca*, ed. J. P. Migne
PL	*Patrologia Latina*, ed. J. P. Migne
PLRE	*Prosopography of the Later Roman Empire*, ed. J. R. Martindale *et al.*, 3 vols:

vol. I: AD 260–395 (Cambridge, 1971)
vol. II: AD 395–527 (Cambridge, 1980)
vol. III: AD 527–641 (Cambridge, 1992)

RIC	*Roman Imperial Coinage*
SC	*Sources Chrétiennes*
SHF	*Société de l'Histoire de France*
SLH	*Scriptores Latini Hiberniae*

Notes

1 PROBLEM-SOLVING EMPERORS

1. Ammianus Marcellinus, *Res Gestae*, XXIII. v. 17; F. Millar, *The Roman Empire and its Neighbours* (London and New York, 1967), pp. 238–48.
2. A. A. Barrett, *Caligula: the Corruption of Power* (London, 1990), pp. xix, 1–41, 172–80.
3. Herodian, *Basileas Historias*, VI. viii. i and VII. i. 1–2.
4. *Scriptores Historiae Augustae: Maximini Duo* (ascribed to Julius Capitolinus), I. 5–7, and II. 5; see also the discussion in R. Syme, 'The Emperor Maximinus', in his *Emperors and Biography* (Oxford, 1971), pp. 179–93. For the imperial portraiture of Maximin see S. Wood, *Roman Portrait Sculpture, 217–260 A.D.* (Leiden, 1986), pp. 33–5, 66–8, 126–7.
5. Herodian, *Basileas Historias*, VIII. v. 8–9 and vi. 2.
6. F. Millar, *The Emperor in the Roman World* (London, 1977), pp. 122–31.
7. Sextus Aurelius Victor, *Liber de Caesaribus*, 28, anon. *Epitome de Caesaribus*, 28; Zosimus, *Historias Neas*, I. 18–23.
8. Sextus Aurelius Victor 29; Epitome 29; Zosimus I. 21–5. See also Wood *Roman Portrait Sculpture*, pp. 42–5, 77–9.
9. Sextus Aurelius Victor 30–2; Epitome 30–2; Zosimus I. 24–30, 36 *Scriptores Historiae Augustae: Valeriani Duo* ('Trebellius Pollio'). See Wood, *Roman Portrait Sculpture*, pp. 43–8, 109–11.
10. The capture of Valerian is graphically represented both on the Sassanian cameo of Shapur I in the Bibliothèque Nationale in Paris, and in the monumental rock carving of Naqsh-i-Rustam, see R. Ghirshman, *Iran: Parthians and Sassanians* (London, 1962), plates 195–7.
11. On the Gallic Empire see J. Drinkwater, *The Gallic Empire* (Stuttgart, 1987).
12. RIC, vol. 5(1), ed. H. Mattingly and E. A. Sydenham, pp. 248–62.
13. C. Lepelley, 'The survival and fall of the classical city in Late Roman Africa', in J. Rich (ed.), *The City in Late Antiquity* (London, 1992), pp. 50–76.
14. L. de Blois, *The Policy of the Emperor Gallienus* (Leiden, 1976), pp. 29–30.
15. R. Syme, 'The Emperor Claudius Tacitus', in his *Emperors and Biography* (Oxford, 1971), pp. 237–47 shows that Tacitus belongs to this military group, and that the presentation of him in the *SHA* as an amiable nincompoop of a senator is a deliberate distortion.
16. Sextus Aurelius Victor 38.3, Epitome 38.3.
17. Epitome 34.5 (Quintillus); Sextus Aurelius Victor 36, Zosimus I. 63–4 (Florian).
18. Sextus Aurelius Victor 37.4; Zosimus I. 71. *Scriptores Historiae Augustae: Probus*, xx (by 'Flavius Vopiscus of Syracuse') is completely unreliable.
19. Sextus Aurelius Victor 39.1–16, Zosimus I. 73.

20. Sextus Aurelius Victor 39.17–19; Eutropius, *Breviarium*, xxii; S. Williams, *Diocletian and the Roman Recovery* (London, 1985), pp. 43–8.
21. Williams, *Diocletian*, pp. 61–70; W. Seston, *Dioclétien et la Tétrarchie* (Paris, 1946), pp. 231–57. T. D. Barnes, *Constantine and Eusebius* (Cambridge, Mass., 1981), pp. 8–10.
22. P. Salway, *Roman Britain* (Oxford, 1981), pp. 288–314.
23. Seston, *Dioclétien*, pp. 137–54.
24. See RIC, vol. VI, ed. C. H. V. Sutherland and R. A. G. Carson, for the coins of the tetrarchy.
25. R. Bianchi Bandinelli, *Rome: the Late Empire* (London, 1971), plate 256; H. P. L'Orange, *Art Forms and Civic Life in the Later Roman Empire* (Princeton, 1965), pp. 37–68.
26. *XII Panegyrici Latini*, XI. xi. 4, ed. R. Mynors (Oxford, 1964), p. 265.
27. Barnes, *Constantine and Eusebius*, pp. 7–8.
28. A. H. M. Jones, *The Later Roman Empire, 284–602* (3 vols, Oxford, 1964), vol. 1, pp. 42–52.
29. Ibid., pp. 52–60; E. N. Luttwak, *The Grand Strategy of the Roman Empire* (Baltimore and London, 1976), pp. 127–90.
30. T. Frank, *Economic Survey of Ancient Rome* (Baltimore, 1940), vol. 5, pp. 310–421.
31. Jones, *Later Roman Empire*, vol. 1, pp. 68–70.
32. Suetonius, *Vita Neronis*, xvi.
33. Eusebius of Caesarea, *Ecclesiastical History*, VI. xxxix. I–VI. xlv. 5.
34. Cyprian, bishop of Carthage, *Epistolae*, lxxx.
35. Translated by H. Bettensen, *Documents of the Christian Church* (2nd edn, Oxford, 1963), III g, pp. 13–14.
36. For some arguments about the causes of the persecutions see G. E. M. de Ste Croix, 'Why were the Early Christians Persecuted?', together with a reply by A. N. Sherwin-White and de Ste Croix's riposte, all conveniently to be found in M. I. Finley (ed.), *Studies in Ancient Society* (London, 1974), pp. 210–62.
37. RIC, vol. 4 (3), ed. H. Mattingly, E. A. Sydenham and C. H. V. Sutherland, pp. 117–18 and 130–3; these coins were all struck in Milan.
38. On Christians in the Roman army see A. D. Nock, 'The Roman Army and the Roman Religious Year', *Harvard Theological Review*, 45 (1952), 186–252, especially section III. iv.
39. Eusebius of Caesarea, *Ecclesiastical History*, VI, xli. 1–xlii. 4.
40. Eusebius, *Ecclesiastical History*, VII. x. 3–9.
41. Lactantius, *De Mortibus Persecutorum*, X. 6, XI. 1–4; Barnes, *Constantine and Eusebius*, pp. 15–27.
42. Barnes, ibid., pp. 149–62.

2 THE AGE OF CONSTANTINE

1. Lactantius, *De Mortibus Persecutorum*, 19; Eutropius, *Breviarium*, IX. xxvi–xxviii.
2. Eutropius, X. i–ii. Zosimus, *Historias Neas*, II. viii.

3. Eutropius, X. ii. 2. T. D. Barnes, *Constantine and Eusebius* (Cambridge, 1981), pp. 28–9.

4. Lactantius, *De Mortibus Persecutorum*, 29.

5. Barnes, *Constantine and Eusebius*, pp. 32–3, and nn. 36 and 38, indicates that in practice neither Constantine nor Maximin used the title of *Filius Augusti* within their own territories.

6. Lactantius, *De Mortibus Persecutorum*, 35.

7. Zosimus, II. xv–xvi; Lactantius, *De Mortibus Persecutorum*, 44.

8. A. H. M. Jones, *Constantine and the Conversion of Europe* (London, 1949), pp. 94–7 for a discussion of the evidence and a possible rationalising explanation.

9. Older arguments are dealt with in N. H. Baynes, *Constantine the Great and the Christian Church* (2nd edn with preface by H. Chadwick, Oxford, 1972).

10. On the development of Constantine as both emperor and Christian see Barnes, *Constantine and Eusebius*, and Jones, *Constantine*. For Eusebius's presentation of the ideology of the Christian Empire see G. F. Chesnut, *The First Christian Histories* (Paris, 1977), pp. 61–166.

11. J. Toynbee and J. Ward Perkins, *The Shrine of St. Peter and the Vatican Excavations* (London, 1956), plate 32 and pp. 72–4.

12. P. Bruun, 'The Disappearance of Sol from the coins of Constantine', *Arctos*, ns 2 (1958), 15–37.

13. A. D. Nock, 'The Emperor's Divine *Comes*', *Journal of Roman Studies*, 37 (1947), 102–16. See also S. G. MacCormack, 'Rome, Constantinopolis, the Emperor, and His Genius', *Classical Quarterly*, 25 (1975), 131–50.

14. Toynbee and Ward Perkins, *Shrine of St. Peter*, pp. 195–239; H. P. L'Orange, *Art Forms and Civic Life in the Later Roman Empire* (Princeton, 1965), pp. 79–85; R. Krautheimer, *Early Christian and Byzantine Architecture* (Harmondsworth, 1965), pp. 17–44; idem, *Rome: Profile of a City, 312–1308* (Princeton, 1980), pp. 3–31 and 42–5. Constantine built a smaller memorial church dedicated to St Paul, which was expanded to rival that of St Peter's under Pope Damasus (366–84).

15. Krautheimer, *Rome*, pp. 7–8.

16. C.-M. Ternes, *Römisches Deutschland* (Stuttgart, 1986), p. 283.

17. S. G. MacCormack, *Art and Ceremony in Late Antiquity* (Berkeley and Los Angeles, 1981).

18. Krautheimer, *Rome*, pp. 54–8; idem, *Early Christian and Byzantine Architecture*, pp. 25–6.

19. A. Alföldi, *The Conversion of Constantine and Pagan Rome* (2nd edn, Oxford, 1969).

20. E. Kitzinger, *Byzantine Art in the Making* (London, 1977), pp. 7–9 and plates 1–4.

21. Letter of Constantine I to Anullinus, Proconsul of Africa, in Eusebius, *Ecclesiastical History*, X. v. 15–17. On Anullinus see PLRE, I, pp. 78–9 (Anullinus 2).

22. Eusebius, *Ecclesiastical History*, IX. ii. 1–iv. 4, for petitions against the Christians in Egypt, sent to Maximin II.

23. Lactantius, *De Mortibus Persecutorum*, 48; Eusebius, *Ecclesiastical History*, X. v. 1–14.

24. Eusebius, *Ecclesiastical History*, X. viii. 8–19.
25. P. Brown, *The World of Late Antiquity* (London, 1971), pp. 34–40.
26. Barnes, *Constantine and Eusebius*, pp. 62–4.
27. Ibid., pp. 64–77.
28. PLRE, vol. I, pp. 563 (Martinianus 2), and 931 (Valens 13). PLRE is wrong, however, in giving Martinianus only the title of Caesar. That he, like Valens, was an Augustus, is proved by his coinage: RIC, vol. 7, ed. P. Bruun, pp. 608 and 645.
29. Lactantius, *De Mortibus Persecutorum*, 50.
30. Barnes, *Constantine and Eusebius*, pp. 34–6 on this episode and the sources for it.
31. PLRE, vol. I, p. 233 (Crispus 4); PLRE, vol. I, pp. 325–6 (Fausta).
32. L'Orange, *Art Forms and Civic Life*, pp. 121–5.
33. G. Dagron, *Naissance d'une capitale: Constantinople et ses institutions de 330 à 451* (Paris, 1974), pp. 13–47.
34. Tacitus, *Annales*, XV. 40; *Scriptores Historiae Augustae: Commodus Antoninus*, VIII. 6–9 (attributed to Aelius Lampridius).
35. PLRE, vol. I, pp. 223 (Constantinus 3), 233 (Crispus), 509–10 (Licinius 4). The proclamation of the new Caesars occurred on 1 March 317.
36. *Codex Theodosianus*, IV. vi. 2–3 (2 laws of 336); ed. T. Mommsen (4th printing, Dublin and Zurich, 1971), vol. 1, ii, pp. 175–6. He therefore already was or was made a eunuch.
37. PLRE, vol. I, pp. 241 (Dalmatius 7), 407 (Hannibalianus 2).
38. Zosimus II, 39–40.
39. Zosimus II. 41 is confusing. See Eutropius, *Breviarium*, X. 9.
40. Julian, *Oration II: On the Heroic Deeds of Constantius*, 94, ed. W. C. Wright, *The Works of the Emperor Julian* (3 vols, Loeb Library), vol. 1, pp. 248, 250.
41. Barnes, *Constantine and Eusebius*, pp. 17–19.
42. E. Stein, *Histoire du Bas-Empire* (2 vols, Paris and Bruges, 1959), vol. 1, pp. 137–8, with references.
43. See the introduction, pp. vii–liii, of P. Dufraigne's edition of (Sextus) Aurelius Victor (Paris, 1975); also H. W. Bird, *Sextus Aurelius Victor: a Historiographical Study* (Liverpool, 1984).
44. P. Salway, *Roman Britain* (Oxford, 1981), pp. 348–53; S. Johnson, *Late Roman Fortifications* (London, 1983), pp. 204–6.
45. Zosimus II. 42. On Centcelles see R. Collins, *Oxford Archaeological Guide to Spain* (Oxford, 1998), pp. 110–13.

3 FRONTIER WARS AND CIVIL WARS, 350–395

1. On Ammianus see J. F. Matthews, *The Roman Empire of Ammianus* (London, 1989).
2. PLRE, vol. I, p. 624 (Nepotianus 5).
3. PLRE, vol. I, p. 924 (Vetranio 1).
4. Zosimus, *Historias Neas* II. 43–54 provides the most substantial account of these years. On this writer, his sources and weaknesses see W. Goffart, 'Zosimus, the First Historian of Rome's Fall', *American Historical Review*, 76 (1971), 412–41. Also A. Cameron, 'The Date of Zosimus's New History', *Philologus*, 113 (1969), 106–10.

5. Ammianus Marcellinus, *Res Gestae*, XVII. 9–10.
6. Ammianus, XVI. xii. 5.
7. Ammianus, XVI. i. 1–xi. 25.
8. Ammianus, XV. v. 1–v. 34.
9. Ammianus, XV. viii. 19, XVI. iii. 1–2.
10. Ammianus, XV. viii. 1–17.
11. Ammianus, XVI. ii. 1–13.
12. Ammianus, XVI. iii. 1–3.
13. Ammianus, XVI. iv. 1–5.
14. Ammianus, XVI. xii. 1–63.
15. Ammianus, XVII. 1. 12–13.
16. Ammianus, XVII. ii. 1–4, viii. 1–3.
17. Ammianus, XVII. ix. 1, XVIII. ii. 5–6.
18. Ammianus, XVIII. iii. 1–5.
19. Ammianus, XIX. i. 1–ix. 2.
20. Ammianus, XX. iv. 1–v. 10.
21. Ammianus, XXI. xii. 3, XXII. i. 2–ii. 1.
22. Ammianus, XIV. v. 6–9, XXII. iii. 11. For Arianism see chapter 5 below.
23. Ammianus, XXII. iv. 1–10, vii. 1–10, XXV. iv. 7–9, 19–21.
24. Ammianus, XXII. v. 1–5.
25. Ammianus, XXII. x. 7, XXV. iv. 20.
26. P. Athanassiadi, *Julian: an Intellectual Biography* (London, 1992), pp. 161–92; G. W. Bowersock, *Hellenism in Late Antiquity* (Cambridge, 1990), pp. 1–13.
27. G. W. Bowersock, *Julian the Apostate* (London, 1978), pp. 79–93. Julian's writings are edited in three volumes by W. C. Wright in the Loeb Classical Library. See vols 2 and 3 in particular.
28. Ammianus, XXII. iv. 1–2.
29. Ammianus, XXII. xiv. 1–3. The work is edited by Wright, vol. 2, pp. 420–510.
30. Eunapius, *Lives of the Philosophers*: see the accounts of Maximus of Ephesus and of Chrysanthius of Sardis; also Ammianus, XXV. iv. 17.
31. For the Persian campaign see Ammianus, XXIII. ii. 1–XXV. vii. 14. A penetrating analysis of the weaknesses of Julian's strategy can be found in A. Ferrill, *The Fall of the Roman Empire: the Military Explanation* (London, 1986), pp. 52–6.
32. Ammianus, XXV. iii. 1–24.
33. Libanius, Oration XXIV: 'On Avenging Julian', vi. In earlier works, Orations XVII and XVIII, Libanius accepts the view that a Persian had been responsible.
34. Ammianus, XXV. v. 1–x. 17.
35. Ammianus, XXVII. xii. 1–18.
36. Ammianus, XXXI. xiv. 1–8.
37. Stein, *Histoire du Bas-Empire*, vol. 1, p. 175 and references.
38. Ammianus, XXVI. v. 8–ix. 11. PLRE, vol. I, pp. 742–3 (Procopius 4).
39. Ammianus, XXVII. v. 1–10.
40. Ammianus, XXIX. i. 1–ii. 28.
41. Ammianus, XXVIII. viii. 1–57; A. Alföldi, *A Conflict of Ideas in the Late Roman Empire* (Oxford, 1952), especially pp. 48–95.

42. Ammianus, XXX. vi. 1–6.
43. Ammianus, XXX. x. 1–6.
44. J. F. Matthews, *Western Aristocracies and Imperial Court A.D. 364–425* (Oxford, 1975), pp. 51–5, 69–76.
45. Ammianus, XXXI. x. 1–22.
46. Zosimus, IV. 35.
47. PLRE, vol. I, pp. 598–9 (Merobaudes 2).
48. Matthews, *Western Aristocracies*, pp. 176–7.
49. Zosimus, IV. 42–3.
50. Zosimus, IV. 46.
51. Zosimus, IV. 53–4.
52. On this episode see H. Bloch, 'The Pagan Revival in the West at the End of the Fourth Century', in A. Momigliano (ed.), *The Conflict between Paganism and Christianity in the Fourth Century* (Oxford, 1963), pp. 193–218, and idem, 'A New Document of the Last Pagan Revival in the West', *Harvard Theological Review*, 38 (1945), 199–244.
53. For an account and analysis of the battle see Ferrill, *Fall of the Roman Empire*, pp. 71–5.
54. Zosimus, IV. 59. *Epitome de Caesaribus* xlviii. 19–20.

4   THE BATTLE OF ADRIANOPLE AND THE SACK
    OF ROME

1. J. Vogt, *Kulturwelt und Barbaren – Zum Menschheitsbild der spätantiken Gesellschaft* (Mainz, 1967).
2. Priscus of Panium, fragments, ed. and tr. R. C. Blockley, *The Fragmentary Classicising Historians of the Later Roman Empire*, vol. II (Liverpool, 1983), pp. 222–377.
3. See the arguments over the ethnic attributes of such major finds as the Pietroasa and Nagyszentmiklós Treasures; for example in G. Lázló and I. Rácz, *The Treasure of Nagyszentmiklós* (English tr., Budapest, 1984). See also the example given in note 2 of chapter 7 below, and some discussion of methodological problems in E. James, 'Burial and Status in the Early Medieval West', *Transactions of the Royal Historical Society*, 5th series, 39 (1989), 23–40, and G. Halsall, *Settlement and Social Organisation. The Merovingian Region of Metz* (Cambridge, 1995).
4. Ammianus Marcellinus, *Res Gestae*, XXXI. ii. 1–12; Jordanes, *Getica*, xlviii.
5. Ammianus, XXXI. iii. I–iv. 13.
6. C. J. Wickham, 'Pastoralism and Underdevelopment in the early Middle Ages', *Settimane di studio sull' Alto Medioevo*, 31 (1985), 401–51; see also O. Lattimore, *Inner Asian Frontiers of China* (Boston, 1951), pp. 58–80.
7. The best treatment of the Huns is to be found in the, regrettably incomplete, work of O. Maenchen-Helfen, *The World of the Huns* (Berkeley etc., 1973). See also I. Bóna, *Das Hunnenreich* (Stuttgart, 1991).
8. M. Kazanski, *Les Goths* (Paris, 1991), pp. 9–59; P. Heather, *The Goths* (Oxford, 1996), pp. 51–93.

9. On whom see A. A. Vasiliev, *The Goths in the Crimea* (Cambridge, Mass., 1936).

10. Recent work on these cultures is usefully summarised in P. Heather and J. Matthews, *The Goths in the Fourth Century* (Liverpool, 1991), pp. 51–101, and Heather, *The Goths*, pp. 11–50.

11. P. Heather, *Goths and Romans, 332–489* (Oxford, 1991), pp. 84–121.

12. As suggested by the freezing of the Sea of Azov (on which see Vasiliev, *The Goths in the Crimea* (Cambridge, Mass., 1936), pp. 31–2), and of the Rhine in 406 (see note 46 below).

13. See E. A. Thompson, *The Historical Work of Ammianus Marcellinus* (London, 1947), pp. 87–133 for discussion of the final parts of the work and for other reasons why Ammianus should have wished to terminate it in 378.

14. Ammianus, XXXI. iv. 1–8.

15. Ammianus, XXXI. v. 1–9; vi. 1–8.

16. Ammianus, XXXI. v. I–xii. 17.

17. Ammianus, XXXI. xiii. 1–19.

18. H. Wolfram, *History of the Goths* (English tr., Berkeley etc., 1988), pp. 131–9.

19. Zosimus, *Historias Neas* IV. xxiii. 4–5 (also Ammianus, XXXI. xi. 1–4) provides one example of a defeat that the Romans were able to inflict on the Goths in 378, when the latter were scattered around the countryside foraging. No great reliance should be placed on modern estimates of the size of 'barbarian' populations; not only because no real evidence of a statistical kind exists, but also because all models are conditioned by preconceived ideas of the nature of these confederacies.

20. Zosimus, IV. xxxi. 5.

21. Wolfram, *History of the Goths*, pp. 133–4, who compares and contrasts this treaty with that made in 376.

22. For criticism of Theodosius I's use of the Visigoths as allies see A. Ferrill, *The Fall of the Roman Empire: the Military Explanation* (London, 1986), pp. 75–85.

23. Wolfram, *History of the Goths*, pp. 136–7.

24. Zosimus, V. xi. 1–2; *Codex Theodosianus*, IX. xlii. 22 (22 November 408).

25. PLRE, vol. I, pp. 853–88 for the career of Stilicho.

26. For a damning critique of Stilicho see J. B. Bury, *A History of the Later Roman Empire from the death of Theodosius to the death of Justinian* (reprint, 2 vols, New York, 1958), pp. 172–3. A. Cameron, *Claudian: Poetry and Propaganda at the Court of Honorius* (Oxford, 1970), pp. 187–8 is more impressed by him.

27. Wolfram, *History of the Goths*, pp. 32–4, 143–6; P. Heather, *The Goths* (Oxford, 1996), pp. 113–17 and 166–78 is rightly sceptical of the supposed antiquity of the Amals.

28. These are (here all too briefly expressed) the arguments of W. Goffart, *Barbarians and Romans, A.D. 418–584: the Techniques of Accommodation* (Princeton, 1980). To these should now be added J. Durliat, 'Le salaire de la paix sociale dans le royaumes barbares

(Ve–VIe siècles)', in H. Wolfram and A. Schwarcz (eds), *Anerkennung und Integration* (Vienna, 1988), pp. 21–72.

29. H. Wolfram, 'Athanaric the Visigoth: Monarchy or Judgeship? A Study in Comparative History', *Journal of Medieval History*, I (1975), 259–78.
30. D. Claude, *Adel, Kirche und Königtum im Westgotenreich* (Sigmaringen, 1971), pp. 21–9.
31. E. Demougeot, *De l'unité à la division de l'empire romain* (Paris, 1951), pp. 267–81; Cameron, *Claudian*, pp. 180–7.
32. Cameron, *Claudian*, pp. 30–62.
33. Zosimus, V. xxix. 5–9; Olympiodorus fragment 5.
34. For Gainas see PLRE, vol. I, pp. 379–80. For the eastern court and politics in Constantinople at this time see A. Cameron and J. Long, *Barbarians and Politics at the Court of Arcadius* (Berkeley, 1993), pp. 199–252, and J. H. W. G. Liebeschuetz, *Barbarians and Bishops* (Oxford, 1990), pp. 89–145.
35. *Codex Theodosianus*, XIV. x. 4 (12 December 416).
36. Zosimus, V. xxxiv. 1–7.
37. Zosimus, V. xxxviii. 1–xlii. Cameron, *Claudian*, pp. 371–7 on Stilicho's use of barbarians in the Roman army – hence possibly inhibiting his use of that army against other barbarians.
38. For an analysis of Honorius's reign see B. Bleckmann, 'Honorius und das Ende der römischen Herrschaft in Westeuropa', *Historische Zeitschrift*, 265 (1997), 561–95. The most detailed presentation of the complicated pattern of events is Demougeot, *De l'unité à la division de l'empire romain*, pp. 376–494.
39. Zosimus, V. xli. 1–2; cf. Jerome *ep.* 123. xvi.
40. Zosimus, VI. vii. I–viii.; PLRE, vol. II, pp. 180–1 (Priscus Attalus 2).
41. Zosimus, VI. xii.
42. Olympiodorus fragment 3; on whom see J. F. Matthews, 'Olympiodorus of Thebes and the History of the West (A.D. 407–425)', *Journal of Roman Studies*, 60 (1970), 79–97, and E. A. Thompson, 'Olympiodorus of Thebes', *Classical Quarterly*, 38 (1944), 43–52. PLRE, vol. II, pp. 798–9 (Olympiodorus 1).
43. Olympiodorus fragment 10.
44. Zosimus, VI. ii; C. E. Stevens, 'Marcus, Gratian, Constantine', *Athenaeum*, 35 (1957), 316–47.
45. On the Alans see V. Kouznetsov and I. Lebedynsky, *Les Alains* (Paris, 1997).
46. For a discussion of the dating see Demougeot, *De l'unité à la division de l'empire romain*, pp. 381–2, note 155, which provides a full listing of the relevant sources.
47. Hydatius, *Cronica*, 42 (=AD 409).
48. PLRE, vol. II, pp. 316–17 (Constantinus 21).
49. Olympiodorus fragment 16; Zosimus, VI. v.
50. Zosimus, VI. v. For some controversial interpretations of the chroniclers' words see: E. A. Thompson, 'Britain A.D. 406–410', *Britannia*, 7 (1977), 303–18. More orthodox is P. Salway, *Roman Britain* (Oxford, 1981), pp. 426–45.

5   A DIVIDED CITY: THE CHRISTIAN CHURCH, 300–460

1. Jerome, *ep.* cxxvii. 12, citing Psalm 79. vv 1–3 and Virgil, *Aeneid* II. 361–5 and 369. On Jerome see J. N. D. Kelly, *Jerome: his Life, Writings and Controversies* (London, 1975).
2. Jerome, *ep.* cxxvii. 3.
3. Zosimus, *Historias Neas*, V. xii. 2.
4. For anti-pagan legislation of the time of Theodosius I see P.-P. Joannou, *La législation imperiale et la christianisation de l'empire romain (311–476)* (Rome, 1972), pp. 46–8, and the laws from the Theodosian Code listed on pp. 79–89; for the context see J. F. Matthews, 'A Pious Supporter of Theodosius I: Maternus Cynegius and his Family', *Journal of Theological Studies*, ns 18 (1967), 438–46, and idem, *Western Aristocracies and Imperial Court A.D. 364–425* (Oxford, 1975), pp. 101–45.
5. Edited by C. Zangemeister, *Historiarum adversum paganos libri VII*, CSEL, vol. V (reprinted Hildesheim, 1967); see also B. Lachoix, *Orose et ses idées* (Montreal, 1965).
6. E. T. Mommsen, 'Orosius and Augustine', reprinted in his *Medieval and Renaissance Studies* (New York, 1959), pp. 325–48. It is worth noting that Orosius was unwilling or unable to minimise the horrors of events occurring in his native Spain in the years 409–17.
7. See Zangemeister's edition, pp. vii–xxxv.
8. For the analysis of Augustine's views see R. A. Marcus, *Saeculum: History and Society in the Theology of St Augustine* (Cambridge, 1970), especially chs 1–4.
9. P. R. L. Brown, *Augustine of Hippo* (London, 1967), pp. 340–407.
10. See the articles of N. H. Baynes on 'The Thought-World of East Rome', 'The Byzantine State' and 'Eusebius and the Christian Empire' in his *Byzantine Studies and Other Essays* (London, 1955), pp. 24–46, 47–66 and 168–72.
11. For the history of the Arian controversy in the time of Constantine I see T. D. Barnes, *Constantine and Eusebius* (Cambridge, Mass., 1981), pp. 202–44. On fourth century Arianism see R. Williams, *Arius: A Heresy and Tradition* (London, 1987), and M. R. Barnes and D. H. Williams (eds.), *Arianism after Arius* (Edinburgh, 1993).
12. E. A. Thompson, 'The *Passio S. Sabae* and Early Visigothic society', *Historia*, 4 (1955), 331–8, and idem, *The Visigoths in the Time of Ulfila* (Oxford, 1966), pp. 64–132.
13. A. C. Vega (ed.), *Opuscula omnia Potamii Olisiponensis* (El Escorial, 1934); M. Méslin, *Les Ariens d'Occident, 335–430* (Paris, 1967).
14. For aspects of Greek Christian thought in the later fourth century see R. R. Ruether, *Gregory of Nazianzas: Rhetor and Philosopher* (Oxford, 1969).
15. Kelly, *Jerome*, pp. 141–67, 283–95, but rather brief on the exegesis.
16. Kelly, *Jerome*, pp. 227–40.
17. For Ambrose's earlier career see N. B. McLynn, *Ambrose of Milan: Church and Court in a Christian Capital* (Berkeley, 1994), pp. 1–52.
18. J. Gaudemet, *L'Eglise dans l'empire romain (IVe–Ve siècles)* (Paris, 1958), pp. 330–40.

19. Ambrose, *ep.* 20, for the fullest account.
20. McLynn, *Ambrose of Milan*, pp. 158–219; D. H. Williams, *Ambrose of Milan and the End of the Arian–Nicene Conflicts* (Oxford, 1995), pp. 185–229.
21. Ambrose, *epp.* xvii and xviii; Symmachus, *Relatio* iii, ed. R. H. Barrow, *Prefect and Emperor: the Relationes of Symmachus A.D. 384* (Oxford, 1973), pp. 32–47.
22. Ambrose, *epp.* 40 and 41.
23. Ambrose, *ep.* 51.
24. Ambrose, *ep.* 57.
25. T. D. Barnes, *Tertullian: a Historical and Literary Study* (Oxford, 1971); M. M. Sage, *Cyprian* (Cambridge, Mass., 1975).
26. On the conversion of the aristocracy of the city of Rome see P. R. L. Brown, 'Aspects of the Christianization of the Roman Aristocracy', *Journal of Roman Studies*, 51 (1961), 1–11.
27. M. Wojtowytsch, *Papsttum und Konzile von den Anfängen bis zu Leo I* (Stuttgart, 1981), pp. 205–83. E. Caspar, *Geschichte des Papsttums* (2 vols, Tübingen, 1930/1933), vol. I, pp. 196–388. For a briefer account see W. Ullmann, *A Short History of the Papacy in the Middle Ages* (corrected reprint London, 1974), pp. 10–18.
28. See O. Wermelinger, *Rom und Pelagius* (Stuttgart, 1975), pp. 88–133, 146–65.
29. C. Pietri, *Roma Christiana. Recherches sur l'Eglise de Rome, son organisation, sa politique, son idéologie de Miltiade à Sixte III 311–440* (2 vols, Paris, 1976), pp. 98–156, 461–724, 1537–96 for the administrative, liturgical and pastoral developments up to the death of Sixtus III in 440.
30. Pietri, *Roma Christiana*, pp. 431–60, 1628–51.
31. A. Dufourcq, *Etude sur les Gesta Martyrum romaine* (Paris, 1900), especially vol. I, pt iii, pp. 265–383. Pietri, *Roma Christiana*, pp. 98–156, 461–724.
32. Pope Gelasius I's attempt to suppress the Lupercalia is the best known example: *Gélase le Lettre contre les Lupercales*, ed. G. Pomarès (SC 65), with a valuable introductory study of the role of liturgy in this conflict; see also A. W. J. Holleman, *Pope Gelasius I and the Lupercalia* (Amsterdam, 1974).
33. W. Ullmann, 'Leo I and the Theme of Papal Primacy', *Journal of Theological Studies*, ns 11 (1960), 25–51, and more recently idem, *Gelasius I (492–496)* (Stuttgart, 1981), pp. 61–87. For the development of the Petrine ideology prior to the pontificate of Leo see Pietri, *Roma Christiana*, pp. 272–401, 1413–1524, 1596–1628.
34. For the conflict between the two Churches see N. H. Baynes, 'Alexandria and Constantinople: a Study in Ecclesiastical Diplomacy', in his *Byzantine Studies*, pp. 97–115.
35. On the Origenist controversy see J. Binns, *Ascetics and Ambassadors of Christ* (Oxford, 1994), pp. 201–17; also P. de Labriolle, 'Saint Jerome et l'Origenisme', in A. Fliche and V. Martin (eds), *Histoire de l'Eglise*, vol. IV (Paris, 1945), pp. 31–46, and Kelly, *Jerome*, pp. 196–209.

36. The most substantial study of Chrysostom remains that of C. Bauer, *Die heilige Johannes Chrysostomos und seine Zeit* (2 vols, Munich, 1929/1930; English tr. *John Chrysostom and his Time*, 2 vols. London, 1959), but see now also J. N. D. Kelly, *Golden Mouth: the Story of John Chrysostom, Ascetic, Preacher, Bishop* (London, 1995). For his fall see J. H. W. G. Liebeschuetz, *Barbarians and Bishops: Army, Church and State in the Age of Arcadius and Chrysostom* (Oxford, 1990), pp. 157–227.

37. E. Amann, 'L'affaire de Nestorius vue de Rome', *Revue des Sciences Réligieuses*, 23 (1949), 5–37, 207–44, and 24 (1950), 28–52, 235–65, also Pietri, *Roma Christiana*, pp. 1347–74 ('Rome, Alexandrie et Nestorius').

38. For the Council of Ephesus see Caspar, *Geschicte des Papsttums*, vol. I, pp. 389–422, and Pietri, *Roma Christiana*, pp. 1375–1405. For the Nestorian Christians beyond the Roman frontiers see J. Labourt, *Le Christianisme dans l'empire perse* (Paris, 1904) and ch. 25, 'Christians in Iran', of *Cambridge History of Iran*, ed. E. Yarshater (2 vols, Cambridge, 1983), pp. 924–48 (by J. P. Asmussen). A. C. Moule, *Christians in China before the year 1550* (London, 1930).

39. W. H. C. Frend, *The Rise of the Monophysite Movement* (Cambridge, 1972), pp. 1–49: 'The Road to Chalcedon, 428–51'. Wojtowytsch, *Papsttum und Konzile*, pp. 318–29; P. Batiffol, *Le Siège Apostolique* (2nd edn, Paris, 1924), pp. 493–527; Caspar, *Geschichte des Papsttums*, vol. I, pp. 462–503.

40. R. V. Sellers, *The Council of Chalcedon, a Historical and Doctrinal Survey* (London, 1961); Caspar, *Geschichte des Papsttums*, pp. 506–27.

41. Leo the Great, *ep.* 28, originally sent to Bishop Flavian of Constantinople, 13 June 449; Wojtowytsch, *Papsttum und Konzile*, pp. 429–50.

42. Leo the Great, *ep.* 104 to the Emperor Marcian (22 May 452); Ullmann, *Gelasius 1*, pp. 88–107; Batiffol, *Siège Apostolique*, pp. 562–89.

43. That this was already an issue by the time of the patriarchate of Acacius and the pontificate of Gelasius I was suggested by Caspar, *Geschichte des Papsttums*, vol. II, pp. 747–8.

44. Frend, *Rise of the Monophysite Movement*, pp. 143–359 for the later history of the Monophysites, up to the Arab conquests.

45. PG 26, cols 835–976. See D. Brakke, *Athanasius and the Politics of Asceticism* (Oxford, 1995), and T. D. Barnes, *Athanasius and Constantius; Theology and Politics in the Constantinian Empire* (Cambridge, Mass., 1993).

46. P. Brown, 'The Rise and Function of the Holy Man in Late Antiquity', *Journal of Roman Studies*, 61 (1971), 80–101 is fundamental to the understanding of these processes. See also P. Rousseau, *Ascetics, Authority and the Church in the Age of Jerome and Cassian* (Oxford, 1978), pp. 9–76, and D. Chitty, *The Desert a City* (Oxford, 1966), especially chs 1 and 2.

47. P. Brown, *The Making of Late Antiquity* (Cambridge, Mass., 1978), pp. 81–101; P. Rousseau, *Pachomius: the Making of a Community in Fourth Century Egypt* (Berkeley etc., 1985). For the *Lives* of Pachomius see F. Halkin (ed.), *Sancti Pachomii Vitae Graecae* (Brussels, 1932).

48. Brown, 'Rise and Function of the Holy Man', p. 83; C. C. Walters, *Monastic Archaeology in Egypt* (Warminster, 1974), pp. 7–18, with references, for evidence of the earliest communities.
49. Chitty, *The Desert a City*, pp. 2, II, 22, 41 n. 71, 44 n. 130.
50. See Binns, *Ascetics and Ambassadors of Christ*, especially pp. 80–147; also A. Vööbus, *A History of Asceticism in the Syrian Orient*, vol. II: *Early Monasticism in Mesopotamia and Syria* (Louvain, 1960).
51. For the Syrian setting see G. Tchalenko, *Villages antiques de la Syrie du nord* (3 vols, Paris, 1953); also Brown, 'Rise and Function'; for Simeon see A. J. Festugère, *Antioche païenne et chrétienne: Libanius, Chrysostome et les moines de Syrie* (Paris, 1959), pp. 347–401; H. Klengel, *Syrien zwischen Alexander und Mohammed* (Darmstadt, 1987), especially p. 54 for the reconstruction of a stylite's pillar-top living area.
52. For the text of the *Life* of Daniel see H. Delehaye, *Les Saints stylites* (Brussels, 1923), pp. 1–94; there is an English translation in E. Dawes and N. H. Baynes, *Three Byzantine Saints* (London, 1948).
53. Chitty, *The Desert a City*, pp. 82–167.
54. Rousseau, *Ascetics, Authority, and the Church*, pp. 99–139; Kelly, *Jerome*, pp. 116–40.
55. See the study of this subject by E. D. Hunt, *Holy Land Pilgrimage in the Later Roman Empire, AD 312–460* (Oxford, 1982), especially pp. 155–80.
56. Rousseau, *Ascetics, Authority and the Church*, pp. 169–234; idem, 'Cassian, Contemplation and the Coenobitic Life', *Journal of Ecclesiastical History*, 26 (1975), 113–26; O. Chadwick, *John Cassian* (2nd edn, Cambridge, 1968), especially pp. 1–81.
57. PLRE, vol. II, pp. 575–6 (Hypatia 1); Sozomen, *Ecclesiastical History*, VII. xv for the destruction of the Serapeum. On Hypatia see M. Dzielska, *Hypatia of Alexandria* (Cambridge, Mass., 1995).
58. P. R. L. Brown, 'Saint Augustine's Attitude to Religious Coercion', *Journal of Roman Studies*, 54 (1964), 107–16, and for the context Wermelinger, *Rom und Pelagius* (n. 28 above), and Pietri, *Roma Christiana*, pp. 1177–1265.
59. Brown, *Augustine of Hippo*, pp. 427–33.

6   THE DISAPPEARANCE OF AN ARMY

1. For example G. Webster, *The Roman Imperial Army* (2nd edn, London, 1979), but for this period see now P. Southern and K. R. Dixon, *The Late Roman Army* (London, 1996), and H. Elton, *Warfare in Roman Europe A.D. 350–425* (Oxford, 1996).
2. Olympiodorus fragment 12, followed by Zosimus, *Historias Neas* VI. ii.
3. Orosius, *Historiarum adversus paganos libri VII*, VII. xliii; R. Collins, *Early Medieval Spain, Unity in Diversity, 400–1000* (2nd edn, London, 1995), pp. 15–19.
4. PLRE, vol. II, pp. 237–40 (Bonifatius 3); J. M. de Lepper, *De Rebus Gestis Bonifatii* (Breda, 1941).
5. Hydatius, *Chronicon*, 69, dates this to 418; Prosper, *Epitoma Chronicon*, 1271, locates it with the events of 419. This difference has never been resolved, but it has become conventional to use the 418 date.

6. Prosper, 1298.
7. Olympiodorus fragments 17 and 19; cf. Hydatius 51 and 54, who makes no reference to the Visigoths; Prosper 1251 is very brief. PLRE, vol. II, pp. 621–2 (Jovinus 2), 983 (Sebastianus 2).
8. Prosper, 1335; for his career and death see PLRE, vol. II, pp. 684–5 (Litorius).
9. Prosper, 1322, 1324, 1326; *Chronica Gallica A CCCCLII*, 112, 117–19, 127 (use of Alans). See E. A. Thompson, *A History of Attila and the Huns* (Oxford, 1948), pp. 65–70; for the Alans see V. Kouznetsov and I. Lebedynsky, *Les Alains* (Paris, 1997), pp. 11–55.
10. *Chronica Gallica A CCCCLII*, 128.
11. For Prosper and Hydatius, and also for the brief 'Gallic Chronicle of 452', see the excellent study by S. Muhlberger, *Fifth Century Chronicles* (Liverpool, 1990).
12. I. Wood, 'The End of Roman Britain: Continental Evidence and Parallels', in M. Lapidge and D. Dumville (eds), *Gildas: New Approaches* (Woodbridge, 1984), p. 19; for the career of Aetius see PLRE, vol. II, pp. 21–9 (Aetius 7).
13. PLRE, vol. II, pp. 493–4 (Gaudentius 5).
14. For Johannes (423–25) see PLRE, vol. II, pp. 594–5 (Joannes 6); it is worth suggesting that he is identical to the Iohannes 2 of PLRE, vol. I, p. 459. Both men held office as Primicerius Notariorum, and the exercise of the office of Praetorian Prefect of Italy (412–13, 422?) by 'Johannes 2' might help explain the choice of 'Ioannes 6' to succeed the childless Honorius as emperor.
15. Prosper, 1303; for Felix see PLRE, vol. II, pp. 461–2 (Felix 14); There exists a portrait of him on his consular diptych (of 428): R. Delbrueck, *Die Consulardiptychen und verwandte Denkmäler* (Leipzig and Berlin, 1929), no. 3, pp. 93–5.
16. Prosper, 1310; *Cronica Gallica A CCCLII*, III; Hydatius 99.
17. For Sebastian see PLRE, vol. II, pp. 983–4 (Sebastianus 3).
18. Gildas, *De Excidio Britonum*, XX. 1.
19. Hydatius, 96, 98.
20. C. Courtois, *Les Vandales et l'Afrique* (Paris, 1955), pp. 155–74 for the conquest and the treaty.
21. S. I. Oost, *Galla Placidia Augusta* (Chicago, 1968), especially pp. 189–90, 228–43 for relations between the empress and Aetius.
22. B. L. Twyman, 'Aetius and the aristocracy', *Historia*, 19 (1970), 480–503 is one of the few studies touching on this area; the best narrative of Aetius's ascendancy will be found in E. Stein, *Histoire du Bas-Empire* (2 vols, Paris and Bruges, 1959), vol. 1, pp. 317–50.
23. O. Maenchen-Helfen, *The World of the Huns* (Berkeley, 1973), pp. 59–125. For a Marxist interpretation see Thompson, *History of Attila and the Huns*, pp. 41–62.
24. Thompson, *History of Attila and the Huns*, pp. 73–124; J. B. Bury, *History of the Later Roman Empire from the Death of Theodosius I to the death of Justinian* (2 vols, London, 1923), vol. I, pp. 271–88, which includes a translation of Priscus's account of his embassy to Attila; also in Blockley's edition (see Bibliography) of Priscus, pp. 246–95.

25. Hydatius, 150; Priscus, fragment 15. In fragment 16 Priscus also indicates that a cause of friction may have been a disputed succession amongst the (Ripuarian) Franks, with one contender seeking Attila's support while his brother appealed to Aetius.
26. This story comes from the *Vita Aniani Aurelianensis Episcopi*, chs vii–ix, *MGH SRM*, vol. III, pp. 104–17, and is likely to be no more than a mistaken elaboration of the account, found in Jordanes (*Getica*, 194–5), that the Alan garrison of Orléans was preparing to surrender the city to the Huns, but was frustrated by the rapid arrival of Visigothic and Roman forces.
27. Jordanes 197–215; Jordanes was writing almost exactly 100 years after the event, and it is possible to place too much reliance on the detail given in his narrative. The location of the battlefield has remained uncertain. See Bury, *Later Roman Empire*, vol. I, pp. 293, n. 1.
28. Jordanes, 215–16.
29. Prosper, 1367; Jordanes (in part following Priscus) 221–4; Hydatius 154 refers to famine and disease amongst the Huns.
30. Jordanes (following Priscus), 254–64; Prosper 1370; Hydatius 154.
31. Prosper, 1373; Hydatius 160. For this Boethius see PLRE, vol. II, p. 231 (Boethius 1).
32. Prosper, 1375; Hydatius 162.
33. *Marcellini Comitis Chronicon*, s.c. Aetii et Studii, 2, ed. Mommsen, *MGH AA*, vol. XI, p. 86. Marcellinus also refers to the deposition of Romulus in 476 (p. 91) as marking the end of the western Empire. Could he not make his mind up or is the text corrupt? For Aetius as 'the last of the Romans' see Bury, *Later Roman Empire*, vol. I, p. 300 with references.
34. PLRE, vol. I, pp. 372–3 (Flavius Fravitta), and pp. 379–80 (Gainas); Zosimus, V. xiii–xxii. See J. H. W. G. Liebeschuetz, *Barbarians and Bishops* (Oxford, 1990), pp. 89–125.
35. PLRE, vol. II, pp. 164–9 (Aspar).
36. Candidus fragment 1, preserved in the Biblioteca of Photius 79; for Candidus himself see PLRE, vol. II, p. 258 (Candidus 1).
37. PLRE, vol. II, pp. 749–51 (Maximus 22); Prosper 1375; Hydatius 162; John of Antioch fragment 201, for the brick.
38. PLRE, vol. II, pp. 196–8 (Avitus 5); as Master of the Soldiers to Petronius Maximus see Sidonius Apollinaris, Panegyric on Avitus (*Carmen* vii), lines 377–8, 392–4, 399–402, 464–8.
39. Hydatius, 173–8. Collins, *Early Medieval Spain*, pp. 19–24.
40. Hydatius, 183; *Victori Tonnennensis Episcopi Chronica*, s.c. Johannes and Varanes; and above all the continuation of Prosper's chronicle in the *Codex Havniensis*: ed. Mommsen, *MGH AA*, vol. IX, p. 304.
41. PLRE, vol. II, pp. 702–3 (Maiorianus); Stein, *Histoire du Bas-Empire*, vol. 1, pp. 371–80.
42. Hydatius, 200; for the visit to Zaragoza see the so-called *Chronicorum Caesaraugustanorum Reliquiae* (s.a. 460), ed. Mommsen, *MGH AA*, vol. XI, p. 222. On this see Collins, *Early Medieval Spain*, pp. 34–5. For *Adventus* see S. G. MacCormack, *Art and Ceremony in Late Antiquity* (Berkeley, 1981), pp. 17–89.

43. Hydatius, 209 (peace with Gaiseric), 210 (killed by Ricimer); John of Antioch fragment 203; Marcellinus s.c. Dagalaifus and Severinus 2 (ed. Mommsen, p. 88), who has him killed at Dertona.
44. Victor Tonnonnensis, s.c. Vivianus (ed. Mommsen, p. 187); PLRE, vol. II, pp. 1004–5 (Severus 18), and pp. 11–12 (Aegidius).
45. Hydatius, 228 for the death by poison or in an ambush of Aegidius, and 231 for the death of Severus. The claim that Severus was poisoned by Ricimer appears in Cassiodorus, *Chronica*, 1280. PLRE, vol. II, p. 1005 is wrong to give this reference 's.a. 464'.
46. PLRE, vol. II, pp. 96–8 (Anthemius 3).
47. Candidus fragment 2, preserved in the *Suda* or Suidas, X. 245; Procopius, *History of the Wars*, III. vi. 2–26; Courtois, *Les Vandales*, pp. 201–5.
48. Cassiodorus, 1293; Procopius, *History of the Wars*, III. vii. 1. For doubts on Anthemius being a pagan see P. Chuvin, *Chronique des derniers païens* (Paris, 1990), pp. 124–6.
49. PLRE, vol. II, pp. 796–8 (Olybrius 6).
50. *Chronica Gallica A DXI*, 651, 652, ed. Mommsen, *MGH AA*, IX, pp. 664–5.
51. PLRE, vol. II, p. 514 (Glycerius); John of Antioch fragment 209. For Gundobad and his return to Gaul see PLRE, vol. II, p. 524.
52. PLRE, vol. II, pp. 777–8 (Nepos 3).
53. PLRE, vol. II, pp. 811–12 (Orestes 2), and pp. 949–50 (Romulus 4).
54. For Glycerius's possible involvement see the résumé of the lost work of Malchus in Photius, Biblioteca, 78.
55. Malchus fragment 10.
56. *Notitia Dignitatum*, ed. O. Seeck (Berlin, 1876 – reprinted Frankfurt, 1962); see also A. H. M. Jones, *The Later Roman Empire 284–602* (3 vols, Oxford, 1964), vol. III, pp. 347–80.
57. Vegetius, *De Re Militari*, I. xx; see Ferrill, *Fall of the Roman Empire*, pp. 127–32. For a convincing redating of Vegetius to the fifth century see W. Goffart, 'The Date and Purpose of Vegetius's *De Re Militari*', *Traditio*, 33 (1977), pp. 65–100, reprinted in his *Rome's Fall and After* (London, 1989), pp. 45–80, with additional comments on p. 355.
58. E. Gibbon, *The Decline and Fall of the Roman Empire*, ed. J. B. Bury, vol. IV (London, 1901), pp. 160–3; see P. Brown, 'Gibbon's Views on Culture and Society in the Fifth and Sixth Centuries', *Daedalus*, 105 (1976), 73–88; on the development of Christian teachings on virginity see idem, *The Body and Society: Men, Women and Sexual Renunciation in Early Christianity* (New York, 1988).
59. Jones, *Later Roman Empire*, vol. II, p. 1066.
60. M. I. Rostovtzeff, *Social and Economic History of the Roman Empire* (2nd edn, Oxford, 1957).

7   THE NEW KINGDOMS

1. For reconstructions derived from archaeology see R. Christlein, *Die Alamannen: Archäologie eines lebendigen Volkes* (Stuttgart, 1978); also I. Bona, *The Dawn of the Dark Ages: the Gepids and the Lombards in the Carpathian Basin* (English tr. Budapest, 1976), pp. 35–43.

2. For example an identical type of buckle and pin can be found around the lower Loire (D. Costa, *Art mérovingien de la Musée Th. Dobrée, Nantes* (Paris, 1964), nos 268, 271, 280, 281), in the area of Paris (P. Perrin, *Collections mérovingiennes de la Musée Carnavalet* (Paris, 1985), nos 565–8, 571), but also in the centre of Spain (G. Ripoll, *La necrópolis visigoda de El Carpio de Tajo (Toledo)* (Madrid, 1985), pp. 163–73 and illustrations on pp. 213 and 219. It also turns up in southern England: for example F. R. Aldsworth, 'Droxford Anglo-Saxon Cemetery, Soberton, Hampshire', *Proceedings of the Hampshire Field Club and Archaeological Society*, 35 (1979), fig. 32, nos 9 and 10. All have been dated (independently!) to the mid-sixth century.

3. *Codex Theodosianus*, XIV. x. 2, 3 and 4.

4. *Codex Theodosianus*, XIV. x. 1.

5. For the Missorium see J. R. Melida, *El Disco de Teodosio* (Madrid, 1930); J. Beckwith, *The Art of Constantinople* (2nd edn, London, 1968), plates 14 and 22, and pp. 15–22.

6. PLRE, vol. I, pp. 163 (Bonitus 1 and 2), and pp. 840–1 (Silvanus 2); Ammianus Marcellinus, *Res Gestae*, XV. v. 16.

7. PLRE, vol. I, pp. 765–6 (Richomeres).

8. PLRE, vol. I, pp. 95–7 (Arbogastes).

9. PLRE, vol. II, pp. 128–9 (Arbogastes).

10. Sidonius Apollinaris, *epistulae*, bk IV, letter 17.

11. PLRE, vol. I, pp. 159–60 (Bauto); for his daughter the Empress Eudoxia see PLRE, vol. II, p. 410 (Eudoxia 1).

12. PLRE, vol. I, pp. 94–5 (Arbitio 2).

13. PLRE, vol. I, p. 539 (Mallobaudes).

14. Priscus fragments 7 and 8.

15. Jordanes, *Getica*, 277.

16. Gregory of Tours, *Historiarum Libri Decem*, II. 18. It would be particularly interesting to know more of the source for this brief chapter.

17. For Odovacer's career see PLRE, vol. II, pp. 791–3.

18. PLRE, vol. II, p. 806 (Onoulphus).

19. See the stimulating conference paper of W. Goffart, 'The Theme of the Barbarian Invasions in Late Antique and Modern Historiography', reprinted in his *Rome's Fall and After* (London, 1989), pp. 111–32.

20. Heruli: Procopius, *History of the Wars*, IV. iv. 30, VI. xiv. 1–xv. 4; Hydatius, *Chronica*, 171, 194. Suevi: Procopius, op. cit., V. xv. 26, xvi. 9 and 12, Isidore of Seville, *Historia Sueborum*, *passim*.

21. E. F. Gauthier, *Genseric, Roi des Vandales* (Paris, 1951) fully takes up the conspiracy theory, which makes the Vandal king the prime mover in virtually all the major events of the fifth century. See Jordanes 184 for Gaiseric inciting Attila to invade the West in 451.

22. Ammianus, XXVII. v. 6; XXXI. iii. 1. For a view that stresses continuities see H. Wolfram, *History of the Goths* (English tr. Berkeley, 1988) pp. 248–58.

23. On Jordanes see W. Goffart, 'Jordanes and his Three Histories', in his *The Narrators of Barbarian History* (Princeton, 1988), pp. 20–111; also J. J. O'Donnell, *Cassiodorus* (Berkeley, 1979), pp. 43–54.

24. Cassiodorus, *Variae*, bk IX, letter 25.
25. Jordanes, *Getica*, 79–81.
26. D. Dumville, 'Kingship, Genealogies and Regnal Lists', in P. Sawyer and I. N. Woods (eds), *Early Medieval Kingship* (Leeds, 1977), pp. 72–104 also K. Sisam, 'Anglo-Saxon Royal Genealogies', *Proceedings of the British Academy*, 39 (1953), 287–348. Although both of these deal with Anglo-Saxon and Celtic materials exclusively, their methodology and conclusions are equally significant for continental regnal lists and genealogies.
27. PLRE, vol. II, pp. 1073–7 (Theoderic 5).
28. PLRE, vol. II, pp. 151 (Arnegisclus) and 75–6 (Anagastes).
29. PLRE, vol. II, p. 936 (Recitach); John of Antioch fragment 214 (3) for the murder.
30. See A. H. M. Jones, 'The Constitutional Position of Odoacer and Theoderic', *Journal of Roman Studies*, 52 (1962), 126–30.
31. John of Antioch fragment 214a for the most vivid account.
32. For the careers of the elder Cassiodorus and Liberius see PLRE, vol. II, pp. 264–5 (Cassiodorus 3) and 677–81 (Liberius 3). Also J. Sundwall, *Abhandlungen zur Geschichte des ausgehenden Römertums* (Helsinki, 1919) pp. 106–7, 133–6.
33. PLRE, vol. II, p. 597 (Ioannes 13).
34. PLRE, vol. II, pp. 265–9 (Cassiodorus 4). See also O'Donnell, *Cassiodorus*, and R. Macpherson, *Rome in Involution: Cassiodorus' Variae in their literary and historical setting* (Poznan, 1989), especially pp. 79–118.
35. Tacitus, *Germania*, vii. 1.
36. Jordanes, 271, 281.
37. A. Chastagnol, *Le Sénat romain sous le regne d'Odoacre: Recherches sur l'épigraphie du Colisée au Ve siècle* (Bonn, 1966).
38. *Anonymi Valesiani Pars Posterior*, 70–1; see also B. Ward-Perkins, *From Classical Antiquity to the Middle Ages: Urban Public Building in Northern and Central Italy, A.D. 300–850* (Oxford, 1984), pp. 128–9, 158–66, 192–3, and M. J. Johnson, 'Toward a History of Theoderic's Building Program', *Dumbarton Oaks Papers*, 42 (1988), 73–96.
39. Anonymous Valesianus 60. J. Moorhead, *Theoderic in Italy* (Oxford, 1992), pp. 60–63.
40. Anonymous Valesianus 65. W. Ensslin, *Theoderich der Große* (Munich, 1947), pp. 111–17, and plate 5.
41. Anonymous Valesianus 48; Eugippius, *Commemoratorium Vitae Sancti Severini*, xliii. 3–5. See E. A. Thompson, 'The End of Noricum', in his *Romans and Barbarians* (Wisconsin, 1982), especially pp. 124–8.
42. Jordanes, 300–2; Moorhead, *Theoderic in Italy*, pp. 173–211; T. Burns, *A History of the Ostrogoths* (Bloomington, 1984), pp. 190–5; E. A. Thompson, *The Goths in Spain* (Oxford, 1969), pp. 7–9.
43. PLRE, vol. II, pp. 63 (Amalaberga), 63–4 (Amalafrida), 1068 (Theodegotha).
44. Gregory of Tours, *Historiae*, II. 27.
45. On the Variae of Cassiodorus see O'Donnell, *Cassiodorus*, pp. 55–102, and Macpherson, *Rome in Involution*, pp. 79–119, 151–203.

Ennodius remains neglected, but see Macpherson, ibid., pp. 123–42, and Moorhead, *Theoderic in Italy*.

46. On the arguments about two phases of composition see, decisively, W. Goffart, 'From *Historiae* to *Historia Francorum* and Back Again: Aspects of the Textual History of Gregory of Tours', in T. F. X. Noble and J. J. Contreni (eds), *Religion, Culture and Society in the Early Middle Ages* (Kalamazoo, 1987), pp. 55–76; reprinted in his Rome's *Fall and After*, pp. 255–74.

47. L. Halphen, 'Grégoire de Tours, historien de Clovis', in *Mélanges d'histoire du moyen âge offerts à M. Ferdinand Lot par ses amis et ses éleves* (Paris, 1925), pp. 235–44. Also in general J. M. Wallace-Hadrill, *The Long-Haired Kings* (London, 1962), pp. 163–85, and I. Wood, *Gregory of Tours* (Bangor, 1995).

48. A. Van der Vyver, 'La victoire contre les Alamans et la conversion de Clovis', *Revue belge de philologie et d'histoire*, 15 (1936), 859–914, and 16 (1937), 35–94; idem, 'L'unique victoire contre les Alamans et la conversion de Clovis en 506', ibid., 17 (1938), 793–813.

49. I. N. Wood, 'Gregory of Tours and Clovis', *Revue belge de philologie et d'histoire*, 63 (1985), 249–72, who does not, however, suggest that Clovis himself had been an Arian.

50. Avitus of Vienne, *ep.* 46, ed. R. Peiper, *MGH AA*, vol. VI. 2, pp. 75–6; *Epistolae Austrasicae*, nos 1 and 2; Avitus of Vienne, *ep.* 46; letter of Clovis to the bishops of Aquitaine, ed. A. Boretius, *MGH Capit.*, vol. I, pp. 1–2.

51. For Childeric's burial see P. Périn and M. Kazanski, 'Das Grab Childerichs I' in A. Wieczorek (ed.), *Die Franken. Wegbereiter Europas* (Mainz, 1996), vol. I, pp. 173–182, and vol. II, pp. 879–83 for its contents; see also R. Bruce-Mitford, 'A comparison between the Sutton Hoo burial deposit and Childeric's treasure', in *Acts du Colloque internationale d'archéologie, Rouen 3–5 Juillet 1975* (Rouen, 1978), pp. 365–71. For Alaric's burial see Jordanes 158.

52. *Epistolae Austrasicae*, no. 2.

53. PLRE, vol. II, pp. 115–18 (Apollinaris 6).

54. PLRE, vol. II, pp. 285–6 (Childericus I) E. James, *The Franks* (Oxford, 1988), pp. 64–77.

55. PLRE, vol. II, p. 945 (Riotamus); L. Fleuriot, *Les origines de la Bretagne* (Paris, 1980), pp. 163–78 wishes to make him identical to the Romano-British leader Aurelius Ambrosius!

56. V. I. Evison, *The Fifth-Century Invasions South of the Thames* (London, 1965); see also I. N. Wood, *The Merovingian North Sea* (Alingsås, 1983), pp. 12–14.

57. Gregory of Tours, *Historiae*, II. 12.

58. Gregory of Tours, *Historiae*, II. 19.

59. Gregory of Tours, *Historiae*, II. 27.

60. Gregory of Tours, *Historiae*, II. 27 and 30; see the articles by Van der Vyver cited in note 48 above.

61. James, *The Franks*, pp. 73–5, 85.

62. Gregory of Tours, *Historiae*, II. 37.

63. Gregory of Tours, *Historiae*, II. 32–3; Marius of Avenches, *Chronica*, s.a. 500 (N. B. this dating is not intrinsic to the text), ed. Mommsen, *MGH AA*, vol. XI, p. 234.
64. On the Visigothic kingdom before 507 see A. M. Jiménez Garnica, *Orígenes y desarrollo del Reino Visigodo de Tolosa* (Valladolid, 1983).
65. Gregory of Tours, *Historiae*, II. 37.
66. Gregory of Tours, *Historiae*, II. 40–2.
67. *Liber Pontificalis*, vol. I, pp. 269–74. This pontificate began in 513, but amongst the gifts recorded as having been received by the papacy at this time was *corona aurea cum gemmis pretiosis a rege Francorum Cloduveum* (ed. Mommsen, *MGH GPR*, vol. I, p. 130.)

8 THE TWILIGHT OF THE WEST, 518–68

1. Gregory of Tours, *Libri Decem Historiarum*, II. 38.
2. J. B. Bury, *History of the Later Roman Empire from the Death of Theodosius to the Death of Justinian* (2nd edn, 2 vols, London, 1923), vol. I, pp. 430–1, 436–41, with references. PLRE, vol. II, pp. 78–80 (Anastasius 4) for his career. See also P. T. R. Gray, *The Defense of Chalcedon in the East (451–553)* (Leiden, 1979), pp. 34–44.
3. The prologue to Boethius's *Liber contra Eutychen et Nestorium* reveals the theological ignorance of contemporary Rome, while the text indicates his own fuller understanding, based upon knowledge of Greek. See H. Chadwick, *Boethius: the Consolations of Music, Logic, Theology and Philosophy* (Oxford, 1981), pp. 174–222. Another, partial, exception was Bishop Avitus of Vienne, who addressed a very brief treatise *Contra Eutychianam Haeresim* to the Burgundian King Gundobad around the year 512 (ed. R. Peiper, *MGH AA*, vol. VI. 2, pp. 15–28).
4. PLRE, vol. II, pp. 1200–2 (Zenon 7).
5. A. H. M. Jones, *The Later Roman Empire, 284–602* (3 vols, Oxford, 1964), vol. I, pp. 230–1. See also PLRE, vol. II, pp. 689–90 (Longinus 6).
6. Procopius, *History of the Wars*, I. vii. 3–ix. 20; *Chronicle of Joshua the Stylite*, xlviii–lxxxi.
7. *Marcellini Comitis Chronicon*, s.c. Celer and Venantius, ed. Mommsen, *MGH AA*, vol. XI, p. 97 for the naval raid of 508.
8. For Justin I's seizure of power see A. A. Vasiliev, *Justin the First* (Cambridge Mass., 1950), pp. 68–82.
9. PLRE, vol. II, p. 438 (Eutharicus); *Cassiodori Senatoris Chronica*, 1364, ed. Mommsen, *MGH AA*, vol. XI, p. 161.
10. Vasiliev, *Justin*, pp. 160–90.
11. PLRE, vol. II, pp. 1044–6 (Symmachus 9); for possible influence of his lost work see M. A. Wes, *Das Ende des Kaisertums im Westen des römischen Reichs* ('s-Gravenhage, 1967), but also the comments of B. Croke, 'A.D. 476: the Manufacture of a Turning Point', *Chiron*, 13 (1983), 81–119.
12. PLRE, vol. II, pp. 491 (Galla 5), 907 (Probe 1); Fulgentius of Ruspe, *epp.* 2, 3, 4.

13. PLRE, vol. II, pp. 233–7.
14. For an example of possible over-interpretation of the significance of this affair see J. Matthews, 'Anicius Manlius Severinus Boethius', in M. Gibson (ed.), *Boethius: his Life, Thought and Influence* (Oxford, 1981), pp. 37–8. Wolfram, *History of the Goths* (English tr., Berkeley, 1988), pp. 331–2, is almost apocalyptic.
15. See especially Chadwick, *Boethius: the Consolations of Music, Logic, Theology, and Philosophy*.
16. Procopius, *History of the Wars*, V. i. 32–9. Gregory the Great, *Dialogorum Libri IV*, IV. 31. See in general P. Courcelle, *La consolation de philosophie dans la tradition littéraire: antecedents et posterité de Boece* (Paris, 1967) for the growth of the 'cult' of Boethius.
17. PLRE, vol. II, p. 267. For his work at this time see *Variae* bk V.
18. C. H. Coster, 'The *Iudicium Quinquevirale* in Constantinople', and 'The *Iudicium Quinquevirale* Reconsidered', in his *Late Roman Studies* (Cambridge, Mass., 1968), pp. 1–45 for the judicial process; see also P. Rousseau, 'The Death of Boethius: the Charge of Maleficium', *Studi Medievali*, 3rd ser. 20 (1979), 871–89.
19. Boethius, *De Consolatione Philosophiae*, I. iv. 13–17. See the comments of T. Burns, *A History of the Ostrogoths* (Bloomington, 1984), pp. 103–5.
20. PLRE, vol. II, pp. 215 (Basilius 9), 904 (Praetextatus 4).
21. PLRE, vol. II, p. 231 (Boethius 1).
22. Chadwick, *Boethius*, pp. 26–9, 179–81. The identification of the Deacon John with the later pope is probable, if not definite.
23. Chadwick, *Boethius*, pp. 60–4.
24. *Liber Pontificalis*, lvi: Felix IV, ed. Mommsen, p. 138: *ordinatus est ex iusso Theoderici regis*.
25. The subtitle of Vasiliev's book *Justin the First* is *An Introduction to the Epoch of Justinian the Great*, and he wrote in the preface that Justinian's 'rule, behind the throne, of course, started, in my opinion, from the moment of Justin's elevation' (p. v). See now W. Treadgold, *A History of the Byzantine State and Society* (Stanford, 1997), pp. 174–78.
26. Corippus, *In Laudem Iustini Augusti Minoris libri IV*, bk I, lines 130–45, presents the Senators as telling Justin II that the people knew that it was his advice and actions that had maintained the empire during the reign of his uncle Justinian, and that 'he achieved nothing without you'. In lines 179–80 they are made to state that Justinian himself had nominated Justin as his successor.
27. PLRE, vol. II, pp. 505–7 (Germanus 4).
28. PLRE, vol. II, pp. 645–8 (Iustinianus 7); for his appointment as Magister Militum see *Victoris Tonnennensis Episcopi Chronica*, s.c. Rusticio, 2, ed. Mommsen, *MGH AA*, vol. XI, p. 196.
29. PLRE, vol. III, pp. 750–54 (Justinus 4). He was exiled and murdered in 566. For the emperor Justin II see PLRE vol. III, pp. 754–56 (Justinus 5).
30. *Codex Theodosianus*, XV. xii. 1: gladiatorial games were abolished by Constantine I on 1 October 325, but a law of April 397 (XV. xii 3) refers to the continued existence of gladiatorial schools. Wild beast

shows were abolished by Anastasius I in 499 – with equal lack of success. See *Chronicle of Joshua the Stylite*, xxxiv.

31. J. H. W. G. Liebeschutz, *Antioch: City and Imperial Administration in the Later Roman Empire* (Oxford, 1972), pp. 208–19; for the imperial context see A. Cameron, *Circus Factions: Blues and Greens at Rome and Byzantium* (Oxford, 1976), pp. 157–92; for claques see ibid., pp. 237–49.

32. The *Relationes* are edited by R. H. Barrow in his *Prefect and Emperor* (Oxford, 1973). For riots in Rome see A. H. M. Jones, *The Later Roman Empire, 284–602* (3 vols, Oxford, 1964), vol. II, p. 693 and references.

33. Corippus, *In Laudem Iustini*, bk II, lines 278–430 provides an elaborate if formal account of the encounter of the new emperor and the populace in the Hippodrome. In general, see O. Treitinger, *Die öströmische Kaiserund Reichsidee vom öströmischen Staats- und Reichsgedanken* (2nd edn, Darmstadt, 1956).

34. Cameron, *Circus Factions*, pp. 271–96.

35. Procopius, *History of the Wars*, I. xxiv. 1–58.

36. For the change in the nature of Justinian's regime in the years 532–5 see the evocative (if evidentially impressionistic) pp. 152–4 of P. Brown, *The World of Late Antiquity* (London, 1971).

37. Procopius, *History of the Wars*, I. xxii. 16, I. xxiv. 40, III. ix. 25–6.

38. Courtois, *Les Vandales et l'Afrique* (Paris, 1955), pp. 173, 201–4 for the fifth century expeditions; also Procopius, *History of the Wars*, III. iii. 14–viii. 29. Malchus fragment 2 records Theoderic Strabo's agreement to fight for the Emperor Zeno against all enemies other than the Vandals.

39. H. Pirenne, *Mahomet et Charlemagne* (Brussels, 1937); for the emphasis on Vandal 'piracy' see N. H. Baynes, 'M. Pirenne and the Unity of the Mediterranean World', in his *Byzantine Studies and Other Essays* (London, 1955), pp. 309–16. See also the assessment of Pirenne's book by P. Brown in *Daedalus*, 102 (1973), 25–33, and Courtois, *Vandales*, pp. 205–14 for African shipping, trade and raiding.

40. J. W. Hayes, *Late Roman Pottery* (London, 1972), pp. 128–50; see also S. Tortorella, 'Produzione e circolazione della ceramica africana di Cartagine (V–VII sec.)', *Opus*, 2 (1983), 15–30.

41. Procopius, *History of the Wars*, III. x. 26–7, xi. 22–3, xxiv. 1–3, xxv. 10–26.

42. Ibid., III. xii. I–IV. viii. 1 for the narrative of the war.

43. Ibid., III. x. 1–21 for opposition to the plan, and for the Syrian Bishop. Isidore of Seville, *Historia Vandalorum*, lxxxiii states that Justinian was inspired by a vision of the martyred African Bishop Laetus.

44. A documented case is that of the family of Fulgentius of Ruspe: *Vita Fulgentii*, I; see also Courtois, *Les Vandales*, pp. 275–89.

45. Courtois, *Les Vandales*, pp. 289–310.

46. R. Collins, 'Fulgentius von Ruspe', *Theologische Realenzyklopädie*, vol. XI, 4/5, pp. 723–7.

47. C. Courtois, *Victor de Vita et son oeuvre* (Algiers, 1954).

48. *Victoris Tonnennensis Episcopi Chronica*, s.c. Maximus, 2, ed. Mommsen, *MGH AA*, vol. XI, p. 197; Courtois, *Les Vandales*, pp. 304–10.

49. Procopius, *History of the Wars*, III. vii. 29–viii. 6.

50. Ibid., III. ix. 1. PLRE, vol. II, pp. 564–5 (Hildericus).

51. Procopius, *History of the Wars*, III. ix. 3–5; Victor of Tunnunna, s.c. Maximus, 1, ed. Mommsen, pp. 196–7.

52. Cassiodorus, *Variae*, V. 16 for the creation of a fleet. Procopius, *History of the Wars*, III. ix. 6–9 for the overthrow of Hilderic. For the name Geilamir rather than Gelimer, as used by Procopius, see the king's coinage: P. Grierson and M. Blackburn, *Medieval European Coinage 1: The Early Middle Ages* (Cambridge, 1986), p. 420, and also his silver *missorium*, now in the Bibliothèque Nationale, Paris.

53. Procopius, *History of the Wars*, III. xvii. 11–12.

54. Ibid., III. ix. 10–13.

55. Ibid., III. xvii. 13; IV. ii. 8 and 32; IV. iii. 22–5.

56. Edited in C. Courtois, L. Leschi, C. Perrat and C. Saumagne, *Les Tablettes Albertini* (Paris, 1952).

57. PLRE, vol. II, pp. 748–9 (Maximus 20).

58. Procopius, *History of the Wars*, V. iv. 4–11.

59. Jordanes, *Getica*, 306; for a discussion of the context of the composition of this work see A. Momigliano, 'Cassiodorus and the Italian culture of his Time', *Proceedings of the British Academy*, 41 (1955), pp. 207–45, and for a measured view of its value see P. Heather, *Goths and Romans 332–489* (Oxford, 1991), pp. 34–67.

60. Procopius, *History of the Wars*, V. iv. 25–7.

61. Ibid., V. vi. 1–13; PLRE, vol. II, pp. 1067–8 (Theodahadus).

62. Procopius, *History of the Wars*, V. vii. 1–5.

63. Ibid., V. v. I–VIII. xxxv. 38, and Agathias, preface and bk I provide the narrative account of the war of 535–53.

64. Procopius, *History of the Wars*, V. v. 2–4.

65. Ibid., V. viii. I–x. 48 (Naples), xiv. 1–14 (Rome).

66. Ibid., V. xi. 1–9.

67. Ibid., V. v. 1–xxviii. 35.

68. Ibid., VI. xxix. 1–2.

69. Ibid., VI. xxix. 3–31.

70. Ibid., VI. xxx. 4–VII. ii. 18.

71. Ibid., II. ii. 1–12.

72. Ibid., VI. xxx. 17–VII. i. 49.

73. Ibid., VIII. xxix. 1–xxxii. 36, xxxiii. 6–xxxv. 29.

74. R. Collins, 'Theodebert I: *Rex Magnus Francorum*', in P. Wormald, D. Bullough and R. Collins (eds), *Ideal and Reality in Frankish and Anglo-Saxon Society* (Oxford, 1983), pp. 7–33.

75. For the Lombard invasion of Italy see M. Todd, *The Early Germans* (Oxford, 1992), pp. 239–52; also chapter 12, section one, below.

76. The best discussion of the Byzantine enclave in Spain will be found in E. A. Thompson, *The Goths in Spain* (Oxford, 1969), pp. 320–34; see also P. Goubert, 'Byzance et l'Espagne wisigothique', *Revue des études byzantines*, 2 (1944), 5–78.

77. Procopius, *History of the Wars*, V. xxv. 13–14.

78. Ibid., V. xxvi. 1–2.
79. Ibid., VIII. xxxiv. 6, after the battle of Busta Gallorum in 552 the Byzantine forces massacred those Goths who surrendered to them: VIII. xxxii. 20.
80. C. Wickham, 'Historical and Topographical Notes on Early Medieval South Etruria', *Papers of the British School at Rome*, 46 (1978), 132–79.

9　CONSTANTINOPLE, PERSIA AND THE ARABS

1. For a general history of the Sassanian Empire see A. Christensen, *L'Iran sous les Sassanides* (2nd edn, Copenhagen, 1944); see also individual sections of *The Cambridge History of Iran*, vol. III: *The Seleucid, Parthian and Sassanian Periods*, ed. E. Yarshater (2 vols, Cambridge, 1983); the overall political history of the Sassanian Empire is provided by R. N. Frye on pp. 116–80, and the sources are listed and discussed by G. Widengren on pp. 1269–82.
2. S. Der Nersessian, *Armenia and the Byzantine Empire* (Cambridge Mass., 1947); P. Charanis, *The Armenians in the Byzantine Empire* (Lisbon, 1964). For Byzantine–Persian relations in the fifth to seventh centuries see the chapter by N. Garsoïan in *Cambridge History of Iran*, vol. III, pp. 568–92.
3. Theophylact Simocatta, *Histories*, IV. xi. 2; Malalas 449. 19–20, and Peter the Patrician, fragment 13. Note the very different usage in Ammianus, *Res Gestae*, XVII. v. 10. See also the vivid evocation of late Sassanian Persia in P. Brown, *The World of Late Antiquity* (London, 1971), pp. 160–70
4. Menander Protector, fragment 6.2.
5. *Chronicle of Joshua the Stylite*, 10. On this chronicle see F. Hasse, 'Die Chronik des Josua Stylites', *Oriens Christianus*, ns 9 (1920), 62–73.
6. On the Hephthalites see R. Ghirshman, *Les Chionites–Hephthalites* (Cairo, 1948), especially pp. 115–34.
7. Procopius, *History of the Wars*, I. iv. 34–5, vi. 10–17; *Chronicle of Joshua the Stylite*, 19 and 24.
8. *Chronicle of Zachariah of Mitylene*, VII. iii.
9. *Chronicle of Joshua the Stylite*, 24.
10. Procopius, *History of the Wars*, I. xi. 28–9, xii. 1–19, II. xv. 1–35, II. xvii. 1–28, II. xxviii. 3–xxx. 48; Agathias, *Histories* II. xviii. 1–8 (7 reveals the strategic importance of Lazica to the Empire), II. xxi, xxvii, III, i–v, xi–xvi, xviii, xxiii, IV. i–iii, v–vii, ix–xiii, xv, xvii, xx–xxiii, xxx *passim*; Menander Protector, fragments 2, 6.1, and 9.1.
11. Procopius, *History of the Wars*, V. i. 1 is an oblique reference to Mazdakite influence on Kavad. See A. Christensen, *Le regne du roi Kawadh I et le communisme mazdakite* (Copenhagen, 1925), and ch. 27 (b) of *Cambridge History of Iran*, vol. III, pp. 991–1024 ('Mazdakism'), by E. Yarshater.
12. R. N. Frye, *The Heritage of Persia* (London, 1962), pp. 234–6; *Cambridge History of Iran*, vol. III, p. 154.
13. Ibid., p. 155; Procopius, *History of the Wars*, II. xiv. 1–4. For the possibility that Khusro I's tax reforms were based on Roman practices

see F. Altheim, *Finanzgeschichte der Spätantike* (Frankfurt, 1957), pp. 7–55; the evidence is regarded as insufficient by Garsoïan, *Cambridge History of Iran*, vol. III, pp. 587–8.

14. G. Widengren, 'Xosrau Anosurvan, les Hephthalites et les peuples turcs', *Orientalia Suecana*, I (1952), pp. 69–94.

15. Menander Protector, fragments 2, 4.2, 10.1–10.5, 19.1; see D. Obolensky, *The Byzantine Commonwealth: Eastern Europe, 500–1453* (London, 1971), pp. 164–70.

16. Procopius, *History of the Wars*, VIII. xvii. 1–8.

17. J. Ryckmans, *La Persecution des Chrétiens Himyarites au sixième siècle* (Istanbul, 1956); A. Moberg, *The Book of the Himyarites* (Lund, 1924); J. S. Trimingham, *Christianity among the Arabs in Pre-Islamic Times* (London and Beirut, 1979), pp. 287–307. See also I. Shahid, 'Byzantium in South Arabia', *Dumbarton Oaks Papers*, 33 (1979), pp. 23–94.

18. Procopius, *History of the Wars*, I. xix. I–xx. 13; A. Kammerer, *Essai sur l'histoire antique d'Abyssinie* (Paris, 1926), pp. 107–17. Trimingham, *Christianity among the Arabs*, pp. 273–6.

19. Trimingham, *Christianity among the Arabs*, pp. 154–8, 178–99; G. Rothstein, *Die dynastie der Lahmiden in al-Hira* (Berlin, 1899).

20. P. Goubert, *Byzance avant l'Islam*, vol. I: *Byzance et l'Orient* (Paris, 1951), pp. 249–72.

21. Ibid., pp. 121–90; M. Whitby, *The Emperor Maurice and his Historian* (Oxford, 1988), pp. 197–221, 292–304.

22. *The Chronicle of Theophanes* a.m. 6095–101; A. N. Stratos, *Byzantium in the Seventh Century*, vol. I: 602–34 (Amsterdam, 1968), pp. 57–65 provides a narrative of events, if rather uncritically.

23. Ibid., pp. 103–17; F. C. Conybeare, 'Antiochus Strategos' Account of the Sack of Jerusalem in A.D. 614', *English Historical Review*, 25 (1910), 502–17.

24. This is the thesis of J. Jarry, *Hérésies et factions dans l'empire byzantin du ive au vile siècle* (Cairo, 1968), especially pp. 422–529; it is disputed by A. Cameron in *Circus Factions* (Oxford, 1976), pp. 126–53. See also note 27 below.

25. *The Chronicle of Theophanes*, a.m. 6098, 6101; Jarry, *Hérésies et factions*, pp. 474–505.

26. Goubert, *Byzance avant l'Islam*, pp. 211–14 for Maurice's anti-Monophysite policy in Armenia, and W. H. C. Frend, *The Rise of the Monophysite Movement* (Cambridge, 1972), pp. 329–36.

27. A. H. M. Jones, 'Were Ancient Heresies National or Social Movements in Disguise?', *Journal of Theological Studies*, ns 10 (1959), 280–98 – with a resounding answer of 'No!'. On the Monophysites in this period see Frend, *Rise of the Monophysite Movement*, pp. 296–353.

28. Procopius, *History of the Wars*, VII. xxxviii. 1–23, xl. 1–45, VIII. xxv. 1–10; Whitby, *The Emperor Maurice*, pp. 55–91; J. J. Wilkes, *Dalamatia* (London, 1969), pp. 435–7, and in general Obolensky, *Byzantine Commonwealth*, pp. 42–68.

29. Stratos, *Byzantium in the Seventh Century*, vol. 1, pp. 173–96; F. Barisic, 'Le Siège de Constantinople par les Avares et les Slaves en 626',

Byzantion, 24 (1956), 371–95. See in general W. Pohl, 'Ergebnisse und Probleme der Awarenforschung', *MIöG*, 96 (1988), 247–74, and idem, *Die Awaren: Ein Steppenvolk im Mitteleuropa, 567–822* (Munich, 1988).

30. *Poemi*, ed. A. Pertusi (Ettal, 1960). For a useful translation of the *Paschal Chronicle* see M. and M. Whitby, *Chronicon Paschale, 284–628 A.D.* (Liverpool, 1989).

31. *Paschal Chronicle*, Olympiad 350–2, tr. Whitby, pp. 164–88; George of Pisidia, *Heracleas*; Sebeos, *History of Heraclius*, chs xxvi and xxvii; Christensen, *L'Iran sous les Sassanides*, pp. 492–4.

32. Christensen, *L'Iran sous les Sassanides*, pp. 494–509.

33. Sebeos, ch. xxix; *The Chronicle of Theophanes* a.m. 6120; N. H. Baynes, 'The Restoration of the Cross at Jerusalem', *English Historical Review*, 27 (1912), 287–99. See in general A. Frolow, *La relique de la Vrai Croix* (Paris, 1961). This event may have marked the terminal point of the now truncated *Paschal Chronicle*: see Whitby, *Chronicon Paschale*, pp. x–xii.

34. Elishe, *History of Vardan and the Armenian War*.

35. P. Peeters, 'Les ex-voto de Khosrau Aparwez à Sergiopolis', *Analecta Bollandiana*, 65 (1947), 5–56; J. Neusner, *A History of the Jews in Babylonia*, vol. V (Leiden, 1970), pp. 119–21.

36. D. M. Dunlop, *The History of the Jewish Khazars* (Princeton, 1954).

37. For the more orthodox presentation of the life of Muhammad and the origins of Islam see W. M. Watt, *Muhammad at Mecca* (Oxford, 1953), and *Muhammad at Medina* (Oxford, 1956). For a provocative alternative view see P. Crone and M. Cook, *Hagarism: the Making of the Islamic World* (Cambridge, 1977).

38. See D. M. Dunlop, *Arab Civilization to A.D. 1500* (London and Beirut, 1971), pp. 70–88, and especially 72–3.

39. *Bell's Introduction to the Qur'an*, ed. W. M. Watt (Edinburgh, 1970), especially pp. 40–56; J. Wansborough, *Quranic Studies* (Oxford, 1977), especially pp. 1–52.

40. W. M. Watt, *Companion to the Qur'an* (London, 1967), pp. 73–9.

41. Introduction to R. H. Charles's translation (see Bibliography), pp. iv–ix.

42. A useful short account of the life and work of Muhammad will be found in M. Cook, *Muhammad* (1983).

43. Cook, *Muhammad*, pp. 42–50; T. Andrae, *Mohammed: the Man and his Faith* (revised English edn, New York, 1955), pp. 53–93.

44. Watt, *Muhammad at Mecca*, pp. 1–16. See also M. J. Kister, 'Mecca and Tamim (Aspects of their Relations)', *Journal of the Economic and Social History of the Orient*, 8 (1965), 113–63.

45. Ibn Hisham's revision of Ibn Ishaq, 314–39 (pp. 212–30).

46. Ibid., 808–1013 (pp. 544–683) for the return to Mecca and the last two years.

47. Watt, *Muhammad at Medina*, pp. 121–3.

48. P. Crone, *Meccan Trade and the Rise of Islam* (Oxford, 1987).

49. S. H. M. Jafri, *The Origins and Early Development of Shi'a Islam* (London and Beirut, 1979), pp. 1–57.

50. A. N. Stratos, *Byzantium in the Seventh Century*, vol. II: *634–41* (Amsterdam, 1972), pp. 40–73.
51. This episode is interpreted as being deliberately messianic by Crone and Cook, *Hagarism*, p. 5.
52. Christensen, *L'Iran sous les Sassanides*, pp. 501–9.
53. See the monumental study of A. J. Butler, *The Arab Conquest of Egypt and the Last Thirty Years of the Roman Dominion* (2nd edn, Oxford, 1978).
54. For an account of the events see Stratos, *Byzantium*, vol. II, pp. 134–52, 175–205.
55. For the conquests see F. M. Donner, *The Early Islamic Conquests* (Princeton, 1981).
56. Ibn Abd al-Hakam, *Futah Misr wa'l-Maghrib*, bk iv.
57. Ibn Abd al-Hakam, bk v.
58. B. J. Bamberger, 'A Messianic Document of the Seventh Century', *Hebrew Union College Annual*, 15 (1940), 425–31; I. Lévi, 'L'Apocalypse de Zorobabel et le roi de Perse Siroes', *Revue des Etudes Juives*, 68 (1914), 129–60; cf. also *Doctrina Iacobi nuper baptizati*, ed. N. Bonwetsch (Göttingen, 1910).
59. Procopius, *The Buildings*, II. i. I–xi. 8; V. viii. 9 for the fort built at the foot of Mt Sinai, the only one intended for defence against Arab raids.
60. D. R. Hill, *The Termination of Hostilities in the Early Arab Conquests A.D. 634–656* (London, 1971); for some examples of this in the conquest of Spain see R. Collins, *The Arab Conquest of Spain, 710–797* (Oxford, 1989), pp. 38–44.
61. *The Chronicle of Theophanes* a.m. 6164; R. J. H. Jenkins, *Byzantium the Imperial Centuries, A.D. 610–1071* (London, 1966), pp. 43–4.

10 DECADENT AND DO-NOTHING KINGS

1. *Chronicle of 754*, 52; R. Collins, *The Arab Conquest of Spain, 710–797* (Oxford, 1989), pp. 26–30, 57–63 for discussion of this chronicle and its information concerning the overthrow of the Visigothic kingdom.
2. R. Collins, *Early Medieval Spain: Unity in Diversity, 400–1000* (2nd edn, London, 1995), pp. 88–145, and Collins, *Arab Conquest*, pp. 6–22 for the positive presentation of this society that is echoed here. For bibliography on most aspects of it consult A. Ferreiro, *The Visigoths in Gaul and Spain A.D. 418–711: a Bibliography* (Leiden, 1988).
3. *Chronicle of John of Biclar*, anno V Mauricii, 2.
4. R. Collins, 'Mérida and Toledo, 550–585', in E. James (ed.), *Visigothic Spain: New Approaches* (Oxford, 1980), pp. 189–219; L. A. García Moreno, *Historia de España visigoda* (Madrid, 1989), pp. 113–31.
5. E. A. Thompson, *The Goths in Spain* (Oxford, 1969), pp. 320–34.
6. R. Collins, *The Basques* (Oxford, 1986), pp. 82–98.
7. On the Suevic kingdom see W. Reinhart, *Historia general del reino hispánico de los Suevos* (Madrid, 1952), and the four articles of E. A. Thompson on the Sueves, reprinted in his *Romans and Barbarians* (Wisconsin, 1982), pp. 137–229.

8. For this argument see Collins, 'Mérida and Toledo', pp. 215–18, and 'King Leovigild and the Conversion of the Goths', in idem, *Law, Culture and Regionalism in Early Medieval Spain* (Aldershot, 1992), item II; for the context of the conversion see also J. Orlandis, 'El arianismo visigodo tardío', in his *Hispania y Zaragoza en la antigüedad tardía* (Zaragoza, 1984), pp. 51–64.

9. Isidore of Seville, *De Viris Illustribus*, xxviii; U. Domínguez del Val, *Leandro de Sevilla y la lucha contra el arianismo* (Madrid, 1981).

10. See J. Orlandis and D. Ramos Lissón, *Die Synoden auf der iberischen Halbisel bis zum Einbruch des Islam (711)* (Paderborn, 1981).

11. R. Collins, 'Julian of Toledo and the Education of Kings in Late Seventh-Century Spain', in idem, *Law, Culture and Regionalism*, item III, for the role of Toledo.

12. G. Martínez Díez, *La colección canónica Hispana*, vol. I (Madrid, 1966); the collection itself is to be found published in the subsequent volumes, though not yet completed.

13. P. Cazier, *Isidore de Séville et la naissance de l'Espagne catholique* (Paris, 1994), pp. 13–48; the principal study of his *Etymologiae* is that of J. Fontaine, *Isidore de Séville et la culture classique dans l'Espagne wisigothique* (3 vols, Paris, 1959–83).

14. M. Reydellet, 'Les intentions idéologiques et politiques dans la Chronique de Isidore de Séville', *Mélanges de l'Ecole française de Rome*, 82 (1970), 363–400; idem, *La royauté dans la littérature latine de Sidoine Apollinaire à Isidore de Séville* (Rome, 1981), pp. 505–97.

15. XII Toledo (681), canon vi.

16. L. A. García Moreno, *Prosopografía del reino visigodo de Toledo* (Salamanca, 1974), no. 253, p. 122.

17. P. D. King, *Law and Society in the Visigothic Kingdom* (Cambridge, 1971) for an analysis of the legal evidence.

18. S. Teillet, *Des Goths à la nation gothique* (Paris, 1984), pp. 585–636; also Collins, 'Julian of Toledo'.

19. A. Canellas López, *Diplomática hispano-visigoda* (Zaragoza, 1979), nos. 119, 178, 192, 209, 229.

20. L. Caballero Zoreda, *La iglesia y el monasterio visigodo de Santa Maria de Melque (Toledo), San Pedro de la Mata (Toledo) y Santa Comba de Bande (Orense)* (Madrid, 1980); E. Cerrillo Martín de Cáceres, *La basilica de época visigoda de Ibahernando* (Cáceres, 1983); A. González Cordero, 'Templo visigodo en el castillo de Montánchez', *Revista de Estudios Extremeños*, 40 (1984), 513–26.

21. Caballero Zoreda, *Iglesia ... de Santa Maria de Melque*, pp. 545–87; S. A. Ordax and J. A. Abasolo Alvarez, *La ermita de Santa Maria, Quintanilla de las Viñas, Burgos* (Burgos, 1982); M. A. Mateos Rodríguez, *San Pedro de la Nave* (Zamora, 1980); R. Collins, 'Doubts and Certainties on the Churches of Early Medieval Spain', in D. W. Lomax and D. Mackenzie (eds), *God and Man in Medieval Spain* (Warminster, 1989), pp. 1–18; reprinted in idem, *Law, Culture and Regionalism*, item XIV.

22. R. Collins, 'The Autobiographical Works of Valerius of Bierzo: their Structure and Purpose', in A. González Blanco (ed.),

Los Visigodos: Historia y Civilización (Murcia, 1986), pp. 425–42; reprinted in *idem, Law, Culture and Regionalism*, item IV.

23. *Vita Sancti Aemiliani* 9–34; Latxaga, *Arkaitzetako Bisigotiko Baselizak Araban/Iglesias rupestres visigóticas en Alava* (Bilbao, 1976), and L. A. Monreal Jimeno, *Eremitorios rupestres altomedievales* (*el Alto Valle del Ebro*) (Bilbao, 1989).

24. The majority of these texts were originally published in M. Gómez-Moreno, *Documentación goda en pizarra* (Madrid, 1966), but reference should be made now to the full edition in I. Velázquez Soriano, *El Latin de las pizarras visigóticas* (Murcia, 1989).

25. P. Demolon, *Le village mérovingien de Brebières* (*VIe–VIIe siècles*) (Arras, 1972).

26. C. Lorren, 'Le village de Saint-Martin de Mondeville, de l'antiquité au Haut Moyen Age', in P. Périn and L.-C. Feffer (eds), *La Neustrie. Les pays au nord de la Loire de Dagobert à Charles le Chauve* (Rouen, 1985), pp. 351–61.

27. Report in the archaeology column of *The Times*, September 1989.

28. P. de Palol i Salellas, *El Bovalar* (*Serós: Segria*): *Conjunt d'época paleocristiana i visigótica* (Lleida, 1989); idem, 'Las excavaciones del conjunto de "El Bovalar"', in *Los Visigodos*, ed. González Blanco, pp. 513–23. The full publication of the site, said to be imminent in 1991, is still awaited.

29. *Chronicle of 754*, 54–55; Collins, *Arab Conquest*, pp. 30–44.

30. Collins, *Arab Conquest*, pp. 32–6, 144–9; for views that take some of this material more seriously see M. Coll i Alentorn, *Els successors de Vititza en la zona nord-est del domini visigotic* (Barcelona, 1971).

31. See the items listed in note 29 above, and also for the coinage see G. C. Miles, *Coinage of the Visigoths of Spain, Leovigild to Achila II* (New York, 1952), pp. 442–6.

32. *Chronicle of 754*, 59–74; Collins, *Arab Conquest*, pp. 36–51.

33. W. Goffart, 'From *Historiae* to *Historia Francorum* and Back Again: Aspects of the Textual History of Gregory of Tours', in T. F. X. Noble and J. J. Contreni (eds), *Religion, Culture and Society in the Early Middle Ages* (Kalamazoo, 1987), pp. 55–76; see also J. M. Wallace-Hadrill, 'The Work of Gregory of Tours in the Light of Modern Research', in his *The Long-Haired Kings and Other Studies in Frankish History* (London, 1962), pp. 49–70.

34. These are edited by B. Krusch in *MGH SRM*, vol. I, pt ii; see P. R. L. Brown, *Relics and Social Status in the Age of Gregory of Tours* (Reading, 1977).

35. See above p. 162 and notes 47–8 of chapter 7.

36. I. N. Wood, 'Gregory of Tours and Clovis', *Revue belge de philologie et d'histoire*, 63 (1985), especially pp. 259–61.

37. For example Gregory of Tours, *Libri Decem Historiarum* III. 32. In general he has very little of any independent value to say about Italian affairs, other than for the account of the consecration of Pope Gregory I in 590 (X. 1), at which a deacon of the Church of Tours was present.

38. Ibid., V. 18, V. 44, VI. 46.

39. On the Fredegar Chronicle see R. Collins, *Fredegar* (Aldershot, 1996).

40. Ed. T. Mommsen, *MGH AA*, vol. VI, pp. 227–39.
41. For a useful survey of recent Frankish archaeology see the contributions to A. Wieczorek (ed.), *Die Franken. Wegbereiter Europas* (2 vols, Mainz, 1996).
42. Gregory of Tours, *Historiae*, V. 34; see also W. Goffart, 'Old and New in Merovingian Taxation', *Past and Present*, 96 (1982), 3–21.
43. *De Fisco Barcinonensi*; see Thompson, *Goths in Spain*, pp. 99–100.
44. Wallace-Hadrill, *The Long-Haired Kings*, pp. 231–48.
45. For an overview of this period see K. F. Werner, *Les origines*, vol. I of J. Favier (ed.), *Histoire de France* (Paris, 1984), pp. 207–497.
46. I. Wood, *The Merovingian Kingdoms, 450–751* (London, 1994), pp. 55–70 for the ideas behind, and the practice and effects of succession in the sixth century Merovingian realms.
47. E. Ewig, *Die fränkischen Teilungen und Teilreiche (511–613)* (Wiesbaden, 1953), pp. 651–67.
48. Gregory of Tours, *Historiae*, III. 11; Procopius, *History of the Wars* V. xiii. 26–8. On Gregory's account of the Burgundian war see I. N. Wood, 'Clermont and Burgundy: 511–534', in *Nottingham Medieval Studies*, 32 (1988), 119–25.
49. Gregory of Tours, *Historiae*, III. 6 and 18.
50. R. Collins, 'Theodebert I: *Rex Magnus Francorum*', in P. Wormald, D. Bullough and R. Collins (eds), *Ideal and Reality in Frankish and Anglo-Saxon Society* (Oxford, 1983), pp. 7–33.
51. *Epistulae Austrasicae*, nos 18–20; Collins, 'Theodebert', pp. 28–33.
52. M. Prou, *Catalogue des monnaies françaises de la Bibliothèque Nationale: les monnaies mérovingiennes* (Paris, 1928), pp. xxix–xxxv and 9–16. For an illustration of two unique pieces see *Ideal and Reality*, plate 1.
53. Gregory of Tours, *Historiae*, IV. 9 and 14.
54. Ibid., IV. 51.
55. Wood, *Merovingian Kingdoms*, pp. 88–101.
56. For the Fredegar Chronicle see note 39 above.
57. These will be discussed in greater detail in chapter 15 below.
58. *Vita Arnulf*, 11, 12, 17.
59. H. E. Bonnell, *Die Anfänge des karolingischen Hauses* (Munich, 1866), pp. 157–81; I. Haselbach, 'Aufstieg und Herrschaft der Karolinger in der Darstellung der sogennanten Annalen Mettenses Priores', *Historische Studien*, 406 (1970), 1–208.
60. *Annales Mettenses Priores*, pp. 1–15.
61. Photographic facsimiles of the extant original Merovingian charters will be found in H. Atsma and J. Vezin (eds), *Chartae latinae antiquiores*, vols 13–15 (Zurich, 1981–4), but for an edition of the full corpus recourse has to be made to J. M. Pardessus, *Diplomata, Chartae, Epistolae, Leges ad Res Gallo-Francicas spectantia* (2 vols, Paris, 1843).
62. *Chronicle of Fredegar*; S. McK. Crosby, *The Royal Abbey of Saint-Denis* (New Haven, 1987), pp. 29–50 for excavation of what is probably Dagobert's church.
63. For the study of charters and their particular problems see H. Bresslau, rev. H. W. Klewitz, *Handbuch der Urkundenlehre* (4th edn, Berlin, 1968/9).

64. H. Ebling, *Prosopographie der Amsträger des Merowingerreiches von Chlotar II (613) bis Karl Martel* (Munich, 1974) provides a valuable collection of the evidence relating to all known individuals of importance in this period. See also P. Geary, *Aristocracy in Provence* (Stuttgart and Philadelphia, 1985), pp. 126–52.

65. For example H. St. L. B. Moss, *The Birth of the Middle Ages* (Oxford, 1935), p. 198: 'Meroving princes are born and die, short-lived phantoms, worn out by premature debauchery, *rois fainéants*, exhibiting at best a weak piety or a pliant amiability.'

66. *Chronicle of Fredegar*, IV. 35, 56, continuations 1.

67. Wallace-Hadrill, *Long-Haired Kings*, pp. 206–48 for the kings from Chlotar II to 751.

68. *Chronicle of Fredegar*, IV. 79–80, continuations 1–2.

69. J. Nelson, 'Queens as Jezebels: the Careers of Brunhild and Baldhild in Merovingian History', in D. Baker (ed.), *Medieval Women* (Oxford, 1978), pp. 31–77; for the suggestion based on the *Vita Eligii* that Baldechildis's retirement to Chelles was forced, see pp. 51–2, but if Chlotar III had attained his majority at this very point, such a move was perhaps less surprising.

70. *Chronicle of Fredegar*, continuations 2; *Liber Historiae Francorum* 45.

71. For Ebroin see P. Fouracre, 'Merovingians, Mayors of the Palace and the Notion of a 'Low-born' Ebroin', *Bulletin of the Institute of Historical Research*, 57 (1984), 1–14, and Gerberding, *Rise of the Carolingians*, pp. 67–88.

72. *Chronicle of Fredegar*, continuations 2; *Liber Historiae Francorum* 45.

73. For example Pardessus, vol. II, nos. 400, 402, 410 (*vestra industria*) etc.

74. For towns and administration see E. James, *The Origins of France, from Clovis to the Capetians, 500–1000* (London and Basingstoke, 1982), pp. 43–63, and the various contributions in A. Wieczorek (ed.), *Die Franken*, vol. I, pp. 121–70.

75. For an example of such an assembly see the preface to the *Edictus Domni Chilperici Regis pro Tenore Pacis*, ed. K. A. Eckhardt in *MGH Leges*, vol. IV (i), p. 261, and also the records of the legal ordinances agreed on at a sequence of 'Marchfield' assemblies in the reign of Childebert II (ibid., pp. 267–9).

76. The earliest MS of Lex Salica (Wolfenbüttel, Weissenburg 97) is Eckhardt's A2, dated on the advice of B. Bischoff to *c.* 770 in R. McKitterick, *The Carolingians and the Written Word* (Cambridge, 1989), pp. 44 and 48. For the Edict of Chilperic see note 75 above.

77. Ed. Eckhardt, *MGH Leges*, vol. IV (i), pp. 269–73.

78. This first appears in the 'Epilogue' attached to some of the MSS of the 'A' class, and which cannot be dated with certainty to anything earlier than the year 715. See Eckhardt's edition, pp. 253–4.

79. For the Frankish aristocracy see F. Irsigler, *Untersuchungen zur Geschichte des frühfränkischen Adels* (2nd edn, Bonn, 1981), H. Grahn-Hoek, *Die fränkische Obersicht im 6. Jahrhundert* (Sigmaringen, 1976), and R. Sprandel, *Der merovingische Adel und die Gebiete östlich des Rheins* (Freiburg, 1957).

11 THE RE-CREATING OF BRITAIN

1. On this period see P. Salway, *Roman Britain* (Oxford, 1981).
2. D. Dumville, 'Sub-Roman Britain: History and Legend', *History*, 62 (1977), 173–92 makes an excellent introduction to the revisionist approach to post-Roman British history.
3. For 'Nennius' see the preface in J. Morris's edition of the *Historia Brittonum*, and the editor's Introduction for a somewhat optimistic view of its worth.
4. An edition of the work in which each separate manuscript will receive its own volume is currently being produced under the direction of D. Dumville: vol. 3: *The Historia Brittonum – the 'Vatican' Recension* (Cambridge, 1985). Thirteen years later this remains the only volume published.
5. Section 56 in the Harleian recension; see Morris's edition, p. 76.
6. The literature on Arthur is vast, and mostly silly. For a sensible approach see L. Alcock *Arthur's Britain* (Harmondsworth, 1971).
7. D. N. Dumville, '"Nennius" and the *Historia Brittonum*', *Studia Celtica*, 10/11 (1975/6), 78–95.
8. Section 66 in the Harleian version; see Morris's edition, p. 80.
9. A. O. H. Jarman (ed. and tr.), *Aneirin, Y Gododdin* (Llandysul, 1988); see also I. Williams, 'The Gododdin Poems', in his *The Beginnings of Welsh Poetry*, ed. R. Bromwich (2nd edn, Cardiff, 1980), pp. 50–69.
10. J. Gwenogvryn Evans (ed. and tr.), *The Book of Aneirin* (Llanbedrog, 1922).
11. See the introduction to Jarman (ed.), *Y Gododdin*, pp. xiii–lxxv.
12. See in general the studies in M. Lapidge and D. N. Dumville (eds) *Gildas: New Approaches* (Woodbridge, 1984); for a suggested locating of Gildas in the north rather than the west see E. A. Thompson, 'Gildas and the History of Britain', *Britannia*, 10 (1979), 203–26.
13. For these lives see the edition in *Cymrodorion Record Series*, vol. 3, pt II (1901), pp. 317–413.
14. Ed. L. Bieler, *Irish Penitentials*, SLH vol. V, pp. 60–5.
15. *De Excidio* 14–26. D. N. Dumville, 'The Chronology of *De Excidio Britanniae*, Book I', in Lapidge and Dumville (eds), *Gildas: New Approaches*, pp. 61–84 treats the text as being chronologically sequential.
16. The anonymous author of the *Chronica Gallica A CCCCLII*, 126, ed. T. Mommsen, *MGH AA*, vol. IX, p. 660 records for this year that Britain came under the authority of the Saxons. Such a rare continental notice of Britain and the phraseology used would make sense if some form of imperial treaty had been made, along the lines of that concluded with the Vandals in the same year.
17. Gildas, *De Excidio*, 26. 1.
18. Ibid., 28–33.
19. D. N. Dumville, 'Gildas and Maelgwn: Problems of Dating', in *Gildas: New Approaches*, pp. 51–9.
20. For these see P. C. Bartrum (ed.), *Early Welsh Genealogical Tracts* (Cardiff, 1966).

21. This is too optimistic: *The Times Atlas of Medieval Civilisations*, pt 1, 22 September 1990, p. 6, still believes that the Britons were pushed into Wales by the Anglo-Saxons! See A. S. Esmonde Cleary, *The Ending of Roman Britain* (London, 1989), especially pp. 162–205 on discontinuity in Britain after Roman rule, and K. R. Dark, *Civitas to Kingdom: British Political Continuity, 300–800* (Leicester, 1994) for an emphasis on continuities, at least in the areas under Romano-British rulers.

22. The best example of this is the 'first dynasty' of the kings of Wessex; all of this family from Cerdic to Cynewulf (d. 786) had either pure or hybrid Celtic names.

23. *Anglo-Saxon Chronicle* ('Laud' or 'E' version), s.a. 519, 560, 597.

24. *Anglo-Saxon Chronicle*, s.a. 556, 560, 568, 571, 577, 584, 593; see also J. N. L. Myres, *The English Settlements* (Oxford, 1986), pp. 162–73 for the traditional approach, including belief (unsound) in a 'Ceawlin Saga'.

25. *Anglo-Saxon Chronicle* (henceforth ASC), s.a. 495, 508.

26. He is stated to be the son of Cynric in the genealogy placed at the head of the 'A' version of ASC; on the lack of trust to be placed in such West Saxon genealogies see D. N. Dumville, 'Kingship, Genealogies and Regnal Lists' in P. H. Sawyer and I. N. Wood (eds), *Early Medieval Kingship* (Leeds, 1977), pp. 72–104.

27. ASC, s.a. 568, 571, 577; 'E' version s.a. 571; Myres, *English Settlements*, p. 169 identifies Cutha with Cuthwine.

28. J. S. Wacher, *Cirencester Roman Amphitheatre* (HMSO, 1981).

29. C. Heighway, *Anglo-Saxon Gloucestershire* (Gloucester, 1987), pp. 1–40.

30. ASC, s.a. 597, 607.

31. D. Dumville, 'The Origins of Northumbria: Some Aspects of the British Background', in S. Bassett (ed.), *The Origins of Anglo-Saxon Kingdoms* (Leicester, 1989), pp. 213–22; cf. P. Hunter Blair, *The Origins of Northumbria* (Newcastle upon Tyne, 1947).

32. See in general C. Thomas, *Christianity in Roman Britain to A.D. 500* (London, 1981).

33. Thomas, *Christianity*, pp. 275–94; Bede, *Historia Ecclesiastica* (henceforth HE) III. iv.

34. C. Thomas, *Whithorn's Christian Beginnings* (Whithorn Lecture, 1992); P. Hill, *Whithorn and St. Ninian: the Excavation of a Monastic Town 1984–91* (Stroud, 1997), pp. 1–40, 67–133.

35. On the Picts see F. T. Wainwright (ed.), *The Problem of the Picts* (London, 1955; reissued Perth, 1980), I. Henderson, *The Picts* (London, 1967), and S. M. Foster, *Picts, Gaels and Scots* (London, 1996), amongst many others.

36. Bede, HE III. iv; cf. *Vita Columbae* 102b.

37. See A. P. Smyth, *Warlords and Holy Men, Scotland A.D. 80–1000* (London, 1984), pp. 50–115.

38. Bede, HE I. xxv.

39. The point is made about Nynia in E. A. Thompson, 'The Origins of Christianity in Scotland', *Scottish Historical Review*, 37 (1958), 17–22, but applies equally to Liudhard.

40. Bede, HE I. xxvi.

41. Ibid., II. v–vi, III. viii.
42. Bede, HE II. 9 and 20; see also H. M. R. E. Mayr-Harting, 'Paulinus of York', *Studies in Church History*, 4 (1967), 15–21.
43. Bede, HE III, i, iii.
44. Ibid., I. xxix.
45. Ibid., I. xxv.
46. See index to Colgrave and Mynors's edition of Bede for references. For Wroxeter see P. A. Barker, 'The Latest Occupation of the Baths Basilica at Wroxeter', in P. J. Casey (ed.), *The End of Roman Britain* (Oxford, 1979), pp. 175–81; on Carlisle see M. R. McCarthy, *A Roman, Anglian and Medieval Site at Blackfriars Street, Carlisle; Excavations 1977–79* (Kendal, 1990), though relatively little has emerged here from the early Anglo-Saxon period.
47. B. Hope-Taylor, *Yeavering* (London, 1977).
48. On these see Bede's *Historia Abbatum*, first edited by the Irish scholar Sir James Ware in 1666; the best edition is that of C. Plummer, *Venerabilis Baedae Opera Historica* (Oxford 1896), pp. 364–87. See also E. Fletcher, *Benedict Biscop* (Jarrow Lecture 1981), and R. Cramp, 'Monkwearmouth and Jarrow: the Archaeological Evidence', in G. Bonner (ed.), *Famulus Christi* (London, 1976), pp. 5–18.
49. On the Synod of Whitby see Bede, HE III. xxv; see also H. M. R. E. Mayr-Harting, *The Coming of Christianity to Anglo-Saxon England* (London, 1972), pp. 103–13.
50. *The Earliest Life of Gregory the Great*, ed. B. Colgrave (Kansas, 1968).
51. Bede, HE IV. xviii; *Historia Abbatum*, pp. 365–7.
52. R. Bruce-Mitford, *The Art of the Codex Amiatinus* (Jarrow Lecture for 1967, publ. 1969).
53. See G. Henderson, *From Durrow to Kells: the Insular Gospel Books, 650–800* (London, 1987).
54. *The Corpus of Anglo-Saxon Stone Sculpture*, vols. I–III, ed. R. Cramp, R. Bailey and J. T. Lang (Oxford, 1984–91) for the northern counties. Vol. IV (1996) deals with the South-East.
55. Bede, HE II. 20; ASC ('Parker' or 'A' version) s.a. 626; W. Davies, 'Annals and the origin of Mercia', in A. Dornier (ed.), *Mercian Studies* (Leicester, 1977), pp. 17–29, and N. Brooks, 'The Formation of the Mercian Kingdom', in Bassett, *Origins of Anglo-Saxon Kingdoms*, pp. 159–70.
56. W. Davies and H. Vierck, 'The Context of the *Tribal Hideage*: Social Aggregates and Settlement Patterns', *Frühmittelalterliche Studien*, 8 (1974), 223–93.
57. Bede, HE I. xv, III. xxi, xxiv.
58. Ibid., II. xx.
59. Ibid., III. i.
60. Ibid., III. ii.
61. Ibid., III. xviii, xxiv; ASC s.a. 644.
62. Bede, HE III. xxiv.
63. Ibid., III. xxx, IV. iii.
64. Ibid., IV. xii cf. xxi–xxii for a Mercian defeat of Northumbria in 679.
65. Ibid., IV. 26; Smyth, *Warlords*, pp. 64–6.

66. F. M. Stenton, 'The Ascendancy of the Mercian Kings', *English Historical Review*, 33 (1918), 433–52, a classic paper in many ways, does less than justice to the late seventh century kings, largely due to the obsessive hold of Bede's list of seven kings who 'exercised a supremacy over all of the provinces which lay to the south of the Humber' (p. 433). See below and note 73 for this.
67. Bede, HE III. xxi, xxiv, IV. iii.
68. Ibid., IV. iii, vi.
69. On this see C. Stancliffe, 'Kings who Opted Out', in P. Wormald, D. Bullough and R. Collins (eds), *Ideal and Reality in Frankish and Anglo-Saxon Society* (Oxford, 1983), pp. 154–76.
70. Bede, HE V. xix; *Liber Pontificalis*, Constantine, vol. I, p. 393.
71. ASC, s.a. 688.
72. ASC, s.a. 715.
73. Bede, HE V. xxiii.
74. Ibid., II. v.
75. On this question of the 'Bretwaldaship' see P. Wormald, 'Bede, the *Bretwaldas* and the Origins of the *Gens Anglorum*' in Wormald *et al.* (eds), *Ideal and Reality*, pp. 99–129. and S. Keynes, 'Rædwald the Bretwalda' in C. B. Kendall and P. S. Wells (eds), *Voyage to the Other World: the Legacy of Sutton Hoo* (Minneapolis, 1992), pp. 103–23.
76. B. Yorke, *Kings and Kingdoms of Early Anglo-Saxon England* (London, 1990), p. 31, with references.
77. Bede, HE III. vii.
78. On Offa see J. M. Wallace-Hadrill, *Early Germanic Kingship in England and on the Continent* (Oxford, 1971), pp. 110–23.
79. See note 74 above.
80. P. H. Sawyer, *Anglo-Saxon Charters: an Annotated List* (London, 1968), nos 104–47, with comments on authenticity.
81. *Asser's Life of King Alfred*, 14, ed. W. H. Stevenson (Oxford, 1904), p. 12. The argument over the authenticity of this work has been re-opened in A. P. Smyth, *King Alfred the Great* (Oxford, 1995), pp. 149–367. Reactions have generally not been favourable to this attempt to make the *Life* a product of the late tenth century monk Byrhtferth of Ramsey.
82. For the classic boundary marker interpretation see C. Fox, *Offa's Dyke* (London, 1955); for some alternative interpretations see D. Hill, 'Offa's and Wat's Dykes: Some Aspects of Recent Work', *Transactions of the Lancashire and Cheshire Antiquarian Society*, 79 (1977), 21–33.
83. Alcuin, *Epistolae*, nos 7, 64, 100, 101, ed. E. Dümmler, *MGH Epp IV*.
84. On this episode see N. P. Brooks, *The Early History of the Church of Canterbury* (Leicester, 1984), pp. 111–27.
85. For Breedon see A. Dornier, 'The Anglo-Saxon Monastery at Breedon-on-the-Hill, Leicestershire', and R. Cramp, 'School of Mercian Sculpture', both in Dornier, *Mercian Studies*, pp. 155–68 and 191–234; for Offa's dyke see note 78 above and also D. Hill, 'The Construction of Offa's Dyke', *The Antiquaries Journal*, 65 (1985), 140–2.
86. For the reference to the (lost?) laws of Offa see the Preface to the *Code of Alfred*. The most convenient edition is that of F. Attenborough,

The Laws of the Earliest English Kings (Cambridge, 1922), p. 62. For a possible identification of the text with the acts of the legatine synod of 786 see P. Wormald, 'In search of Offa's "law-code"', in I. Wood and N. Lund (eds), *People and Places in Northern Europe 500–1600* (Woodbridge, 1991), pp. 25–45

87. On this period see Stenton, *Anglo-Saxon England*, pp. 94–5, 223–36; also N. P. Brooks, 'England in the Ninth Century: the Crucible of Defeat', *Transactions of the Royal Historical Society*, 5th ser. 29 (1979), 1–20.

88. ASC, s.a. 805, 823 (*recte* 807, 825).

89. ASC, s.a. 823, 825 (*recte* 825, 827); Florence of Worcester s.a. 825 is the source for Ludeca's death in East Anglia.

90. *Series Regum Northymbrensium*, ed. T. Arnold, Rolls Series, vol. 75, pt ii, p. 391. Also *Historia Dunelmensis Ecclesiae*, ibid., pt i, pp. 52–4.

91. ASC, s.a. 821, 823, 825, 827, 828.

92. Genealogy at the head of the 'A' version of ASC; for Eahlmund see Sawyer, *Anglo-Saxon Charters*, no. 38.

93. ASC, s.a. 784 (*recte* 786); for the Mercian line see chapter 18 below.

94. ASC, s.a. 827, 828 (*recte* 829, 830).

95. See chapter 18 below.

96. ASC, s.a. 853.

12 THE LOMBARD ACHIEVEMENT, *c*. 540–712

1. *De Origine et Situ Germanorum*, 40. 1; admittedly there could not have been many such readers, judging from the fact that, fragments of one tenth century MS apart, no pre-Renaissance copies of it are known.

2. See the map opposite p. 230 of J. G. C. Anderson's edition of the *Germania* (Oxford, 1938). For a discussion of early Lombard history see J. Jarnut, 'Zur Frühgeschichte der Langobarden', *Studi Medievali*, 24 (1983), 1–16, and N. Christie, *The Lombards* (Oxford, 1995), pp. 1–30.

3. On Paul's Beneventan interests and the probable intended dedicatee see K. H. Krüger, 'Zur "beneventanishen" Konzeption der Langobardengeschichte des Paulus Diaconus', *Frühmittelalterliche Studien*, 15 (1981), 18–35.

4. See the valuable discussion of some of these in W. Goffart, *The Narrators of Barbarian History* (Princeton, 1988), pp. 329–33.

5. Paul, *History*, I. 18; *Origo*, II; Mommsen, *MGH AA*, vol. IX, p. 499.

6. The fifth of the kings, Gudeoc, is a contemporary of Odovacer (476–93) in Paul, *History* I. 19. For a reconstruction of Lombard history in the pre-Italian phase see J. Jarnut, *Geschichte der Langobarden* (Stuttgart, 1982), pp. 17–32, and Christie, *Lombards*, pp. 31–68.

7. See the arguments of P. Amory, *People and identity in Ostrogothic Italy, 489–554* (Cambridge, 1997), pp. 13–42.

8. Procopius, *History of the Wars*, VI. xiv. I–xv. 36.

9. For Lombards and Heruls fighting in imperial armies on the Persian frontier see Agathias, *Histories*, III. xx. 10.

10. Procopius, *Histories* VII. xxxiv. 1–45; F. E. Wozniak, 'Byzantine Diplomacy and the Lombard–Gepid Wars', *Balkan Studies*, 20 (1979), 139–58.

11. Theophylact, *Chronicle*, VI. x. 9–12; Menander Protector, frs 12.1 and 2.

12. For the archaeological evidence relating to Gepid settlement north of the Danube see I. Bona, *The Dawn of the Dark Ages: the Gepids and the Lombards in the Carpathian Basin* (Budapest, 1976), pp. 14–19, 28–39, 83–7.

13. Menander Protector, fragments 12.3–8.

14. Theophylact Simocatta, *History*, I. iii. 3.

15. Bona, *Dawn of the Dark Ages*, pp. 93–105.

16. Paul the Deacon, *History of the Lombards*, II. 7.

17. Marius of Avenches, *Chronica*, s.a. (in Mommsen's ed.) 569, p. 238.

18. Isidore, *Chronica*, 402, ed. Mommsen, *MGH AA* vol. XI, p. 476; Fredegar, *Chronicle*, III. 65; Paul the Deacon, *History*, II. 5.

19. For use of Lombards in the war against Baduila see Procopius, *Histories*, VIII. xxv. 15, xxxiii. 2–3.

20. For Paul's references to Secundus see his *History*, III. 29, IV. 27, and 40. He calls him *servus Christi*, and this probably justifies our seeing him as a bishop rather than an abbot or ascetic; as does the fact that he was chosen to be godfather to King Agilulf's son Adaloald (IV. 27).

21. Paul the Deacon, *History* II. 14, 25–7.

22. G. P. Bognetti, 'Teodorico di Verona e Verona longobarda, capitale di regno', in *Scritti giuridici in onore di Mario Cavalieri* (Padua, 1959), pp. 3–39.

23. Paul the Deacon, *History*, II. 28–30; Fredegar, III. 65–6.

24. Marius of Avenches, *Chronica*, s.a. 572, ed. Mommsen, p. 238.

25. To take but one example: 'they are the anarchists of the *Völkerwanderung*, whose delight is only in destruction, and who seem incapable of culture' – T. Hodgkin, *Italy and her Invaders*, vol. V (Oxford, 1895), p. 156.

26. Fredegar, *Chronicle*, III. 65; *Epistolae Austrasicae*, 8 (letter of Bishop Nicetius of Trier to Chlotsuintha *c.* 565).

27. Paul the Deacon, *History*, III. 5–7, here largely relying on Gregory of Tours, *Histories*, V. 15.

28. G. P. Bognetti, 'La rivalitá tra Austrasia e Burgundia' in his *L'Eta longobarda*, vol. IV (Milan, 1968), pp. 559–82; C. Wickham, *Early Medieval Italy: Central Power and Local Society, 400–1000* (London, 1981), pp. 30–1 is sceptical.

29. *Epistolae Austrasicae*, 40, 41, 46; Paul the Deacon, *History*, III. 17; see W. Goffart, 'Byzantine Policy in the West under Tiberius II and Maurice', *Traditio*, 13 (1957), pp. 73–118.

30. Paul the Deacon, *History*, III. 29, 31 and 34.

31. Procopius, *Histories*, VII. xxxiv. 24.

32. Gregory I, *Libri IV Dialogorum*, III. 27–8, IV. 37; Paul the Deacon, *History*, IV. 16.

33. This is more probable than the idea that the conversion was a cynical bid initiated *c.* 565 to make the Lombards seem sympathetic to the

remnants of the Ostrogothic population in Italy: Wickham, *Early Medieval Italy*, p. 30, summarising Bognetti.

34. Bona, *Dawn of the Dark Ages*, pp. 35–43, 73–82; J. Werner, *Die Langobarden im Pannonien* (Munich, 1962).
35. Paul the Deacon, *History*, II. 32; cf. Fredegar, III. 68.
36. *Edictus Rothari*, cc. 6, and 20–5.
37. Wickham, *Early Medieval Italy*, pp. 41–2; as with all late and post-Roman administrative structures anomalies abounded.
38. G. P. Bognetti, 'Tradizione Longobarda e politica bizantina nelle origini del ducato di Spoleto', in his *L'Eta longobarda*, vol. III, pp. 441–75.
39. Paul the Deacon, *History*, III. 18–19.
40. Ibid., III. 13.
41. Ibid., III. 33 (Duke Zotto of Benevento); 32 (Authari in the South). On Zotto see S. Gasparri, *I Duchi Longobardi* (Rome, 1978), p. 86.
42. Ibid., II. 31; Marius of Avenches, s.a. 573, ed. Mommsen, p. 238.
43. Marius of Avenches, s.a. 574, ed. Mommsen, p. 238. The meaning of *puer* is unclear here, but seems to imply a youth in the royal entourage.
44. Paul the Deacon, *History*, II. 32.
45. For a discussion see Wickham, *Early Medieval Italy*, pp. 31–2; also H. Fröhlich, *Studien zur langobardischen Thronfolge von de Anfängen bis zur Eroberung des italienischen Reiches durch Karl den Grossen* (Diss. Univ. of Tübingen, 1971), vol. I, pp. 105–16.
46. G. P. Bognetti, 'L'influsso delle istituzioni militari romane sulle istituzioni longobarde del secolo VI e la nature della "fara" ', in his *L'Eta longobarda*, vol. III (Milan, 1967), pp. 3–46, especially 9–11.
47. R. Schneider, *Königswahl und Königserhebung im Frühmittelalter* (Stuttgart, 1972), p. 24 (and note 112 for other references).
48. S. Barnish, 'Taxation, Land and Barbarian Settlement in the Western Empire', *Papers of the British School at Rome*, 54 (1986), 170–95.
49. W. Goffart, *Barbarians and Romans A.D. 418–584: the Techniques of Accommodation* (Princeton, 1980), pp. 176–89.
50. Is it actually 'out of the question to suppose that Roman officials … presided over a peaceful and harmonious accommodation between barbarians and provincials', or entirely accurate to say that 'the Lombards imposed themselves by force, in considerable confusion, and with brutality'? ibid., p. 176.
51. II. 32, quoting from W. D. Foulke's translation (Philadelphia, 1907), pp. 89–91. See note 1, pp. 91–3 for older arguments concerning this passage.
52. Goffart, *Barbarians and Romans*, pp. 180–1 and note 14 discusses the historiography: his own views (pp. 181–5) are judicious.
53. J. Niermeyer, *Mediae Latinitis Lexicon Minus* (Leiden, 1976), p. 1043, following usages in Gregory of Tours, *Lex Salica* and so on.
54. See, for example, Authari's adoption of the title of Flavius; on this see H. Wolfram, *Intitulatio I. Lateinishe Königs- und Fürstentitel bis zum Ende des 8 Jh.* (Vienna, 1967), pp. 56–76.
55. III. 16: *Populi tamen adgravati per Langobardos hospites partiuntur.* W. D. Foulke, pp. 114–16, note 2 for the arguments in the older historiography.

56. See Goffart, *Barbarians and Romans*, pp. 185–9. His argument that the *populi adgravati* were the 'settled, hereditarily burdened slaves and *coloni* of the late Roman world' (p. 187) is hard to accept.
57. Niermeyer, *Lexicon*, p. 30.
58. A modification (and over-simplication) of the basic arguments of Goffart, *Barbarians and Romans*.
59. Paul, *History*, III. 16; Goffart, *Barbarians and Romans*, p. 185 for a more sensible understanding of *substantiae* than that of Bognetti, *L'Eta longobarda*, pp. 651–2, but still not going far enough. It must be admitted that C. Brühl, 'Zentral- und Finanzverwaltung im Franken- und im Langobardenreich', *Settimane di studio del Centro italiano di studi sull' alto medioevo*, 20 (1973), pp. 61–94 is far more pessimistic about the survival of land tax in Lombard Italy. See also the discussion ibid., pp. 169–85.
60. Obviously in practice the Frankish and Visigothic kings faced similar problems with locally entrenched aristocracies, but none of these commanded *de jure* anything like the resources available to the Lombard dukes.
61. John of Biclar, *Chronica*, s.a. IV Mauricii, s.a. V Mauricii; ed. Mommsen, pp. 217–18.
62. Gregory of Tours, *Histories*, VIII. 18 (585), IX. 25 (588). On the latter see also Paul the Deacon, *History*, III. 23 (585), III. 29 (588).
63. Gregory X. 3 (590); Paul III. 31 and 34.
64. J. Jarnut, *Agilolfingerstudien* (Stuttgart, 1986), pp. 44–61.
65. For discussions of Bavarian ethnogenesis see, amongst many others, H. Wolfram and A. Schwarcz (eds), *Die Bayern und ihre Nachbarn*, vol. I (Vienna, 1985) and H. Friesinger and F. Daim (eds), idem, vol. II (Vienna, 1985); also H. Dannheimer, *Auf den Spuren der Baiuwaren* (Munich, 1987) for a survey of recent archaeology.
66. Paul the Deacon, *History*, III. 35; *Origo*, 6 suggests that Agilulf carried out a *coup d'état*, then legitimised it by the marriage. See Fröhlich, *Studien*, vol. 1, pp. 124–38; Schneider, *Königswahl*, pp. 28–32.
67. Paul, *History*, IV. 3 and 13 (four dukes executed). For Agilulf's reign see Jarnut, *Geschichte der Langobarden*, pp. 43–6.
68. Paul the Deacon, *History*, IV. 12, 20 and 24.
69. Gregory I, *Epistolae*, bk II, no. 45. For Gregory and the Lombards see R. Markus, *Gregory the Great and his World* (London, 1997), pp. 99–107.
70. *gens nefandissima Langobardorum: Epistolae Austrasicae*, 40; and also Gregory I, *Epistolae*, bk VII, letter 26.
71. G. P. Bognetti, 'Santa Maria foris portas di Castelseprio e la storia religiosa dei Longobardi', in his *L'Eta longobarda*, vol. II (Milan, 1966), pp. 11–673 is the most forceful attempt to make sense of it, but is rather too prone to politicise religious affiliation.
72. Gregory I, *Epistolae* bk. 1, no. 17.
73. R. Collins, 'King Leovigild and the Conversion of the Visigoths', in idem, *Law, Culture and Regionalism in Early Medieval Spain* (Aldershot, 1992), item II.
74. Wickham, *Early Medieval Italy*, pp. 34–6 discusses Bognetti's arguments, and proposes that the issue is really one of 'the near-total

irrelevance of personal religious alignment inside a resolutely secular political system', (p. 36) – wishful thinking?

75. For example Gregory I, *Libri quattuor Dialogorum*, III. 29, referring to an Arian Lombard bishop in Spoleto (580s), and III. 30 for an Arian church in Rome (of Ostrogothic foundation or earlier?).

76. Paul the Deacon, *History*, IV. 42.

77. On the 'Three Chapters' and the Istrian Schism see L. Duchesne, *L'Eglise au VIe siècle* (Paris, 1925), pp. 156–255, and Markus, *Gregory the Great*, pp. 127–33.

78. See S. C. Fanning, 'Lombard Arianism Reconsidered', *Speculum*, 56 (1981), 241–58.

79. See the useful comments of G. Tabacco, *Egemonie sociali e strutture del potere nel medioevo italiano* (Turin, 1979), pp. 119–20, 125–9.

80. For Agilulf's crown, of which only the central pendant cross survives, see M. Brozzi *et al.*, *Longobardi* (Milan, 1980), p. 110. For Bobbio see Jonas, *Vita Columbani*, I. 30; C. Brühl, *Studien zu den langobardischen Königsurkunden* (Tübingen, 1970), pp. 19–48; idem, (ed.) *Codice diplomatico longobardo*, III, 1 (Rome, 1973), pp. 3–7. Bobbio also benefited from the Arian kings Rothari and Rodoald: ibid., pp. 18–21.

81. Paul the Deacon, *History*, IV. 41.

82. Ibid., IV. 42 and 45; for the Code see the bibliography.

83. Ibid., IV. 42; *Edictus Rothari*, 386.

84. *Codex Theodosianus: Gesta Senatus Urbis Romae*, 4; Justinian, *Institutionum libri quattuor*, Preface; *Codex Iustinianus*, *lex in conf.: Edictum Theodorici Regis*, Preface. This edict contained 154 chapters, as opposed to 388 in Rothari's.

85. *Edictus Rothari*, 243; on the Lombard charters see C. Brühl, *Studien zu den langobardischen Königsurkunden* (Tübingen, 1970).

86. *Edictus Rothari*, 386 and 367.

87. Hodgkin, *Italy and her Invaders*, vol. V. I (Oxford, 1895), p. 238.

88. *Edictus Rothari*, 376 – because Christians should not believe that a woman could eat a living man from inside him.

89. B. Ward-Perkins, *From Classical Antiquity to the Middle Ages: Urban Public Building in Northern and Central Italy AD 300–850* (Oxford, 1984), pp. 173–4; J. Jarnut, 'La funzione centrale della città nel regno longobardo', *Società e storia*, 46 (1989), 967–71. *Edictus Rothari*, 244 is also significant here.

90. Ward-Perkins, *From Classical Antiquity*, pp. 196–9, with references. For Pavia in particular in the Lombard period see D. Bullough, 'Urban Change in Early Medieval Italy: the Example of Pavia', *Papers of the British School at Rome*, 34 (1966), 82–130.

91. C. La Rocca, 'Public buildings and urban change in northern Italy in the early medieval period', in J. Rich (ed.), *The City in Late Antiquity* (London, 1992), pp. 161–80.

92. Paul the Deacon, *History*, IV. 30, V. 36; M. McCormick, *Eternal Victor: Triumphal Rulership in Late Antiquity, Byzantium and the Early Medieval West* (Cambridge, 1986), pp. 287–9, 294.

93. Paul the Deacon, *History*, V. 5–12, 19–21.

94. Wickham, *Early Medieval Italy*, pp. 37–8 argues cogently that competition for the royal office is an indicator of 'the substantial cohesion of the political system'.
95. Paul the Deacon, *History*, V. 32–3. Perctarit's inclusion in the Durham monastic 'Book of Life' (*Liber Vitae Ecclesiae Dunelmensis* (London: Surtees Society, 1841), p. 1: 'Berctred') and *Vita Wilfridi*, ch. 28 indicate continuing contacts with Northumbria.
96. Paul the Deacon, *History*, V. 36–41; on Alahis see J. Jarnut, 'Des Herzogtum Trient in langobardischer Zeit', *Atti dell'Accadania Roveretana degli Agiati*, 235 (1985), pp. 167–78.
97. Paul the Deacon, *History*, VI. 35. For the events of this period see Jarnut, *Geschichte der Langobarden*, pp. 61–6, and for the royal successions Schneider, *Königswahl*, pp. 50–4 and Fröhlich, *Studien*, pp. 166–73; on Duke Theotpert see Jarnut, *Agilolfingerstudien*, p. 8.
98. For aspects of the Lombard kingdom in the eighth century see chapters 13 and 15 below.

13   THE SUNDERING OF EAST AND WEST

1. *Sancti Fulgentii Episcopi Ruspensis Opera*, ed. J. Fraipont, CC vols XCI and XCIA; R. Collins, 'Fulgentius von Ruspe', *Theologische Realenzyklopädie*, vol. XI 4/5, pp. 723–7.
2. J. Durliat, *Les dédicaces d'ouvrages de defence dans l'Afrique byzantine* (Rome, 1981).
3. On the Three Chapters Dispute see L. Duchesne, *L'Eglise au VIe siècle* (Paris, 1925), pp. 156–217, P. T. R. Gray, *The Defense of Chalcedon in the East (451–553)* (Leiden, 1979), pp. 61–8, and most recently, for its Italian dimension, R. A. Markus, *Gregory the Great and his World* (Cambridge, 1997), pp. 125–42.
4. J. Fontaine, *Isidore de Séville et la culture classique dans l'Espagne wisigothique* (3 vols, Paris, 1959–83), vol. II, pp. 854–9.
5. The possibility that the addressee of a lost grammatical treatise of Julian of Toledo was the African Abbot Hadrian of Canterbury was raised by B. Bischoff in the discussion following the lecture by T. J. Brown, 'An Historical Introduction to the use of Classical Latin Authors in the British Isles from the Fifth to the Eleventh Centuries', *Settimane di studio del Centro italiano di studi sull' alto medioevo*, vol. XXII (1975), p. 299.
6. *Vita Fructuosi*, 17; E. A. Thompson, 'Two Notes on St. Fructuosus of Braga', *Hermathena*, 90 (1957), 54–63; the interpretation of the significance of Eugenius's work is that of R. Collins, *The Arab Conquest of Spain, 710–797* (Oxford, 1989), p. 15.
7. Adamnán, *De locis sanctis*, Preface, and the introduction to Meehan's edition (see Bibliography), pp. 6–14.
8. Monotheletism remains little studied, but more attention has been paid recently to one of its principal opponents, Maximus the Confessor: A. Nichols, *Byzantine Gospel: Maximus the Confessor in Modern Scholarship* (Edinburgh, 1993), and A. Louth, *Maximus the Confessor* (London, 1996).

9. Bede, *Historia Ecclesiastica Gentis Anglorum*, IV. 17 (by the numeration of the Colgrave and Mynors edition).
10. F. X. Murphy, 'Julian of Toledo and the Condemnation of Monotheletism in Spain', in *Mélanges J. de Ghellinck* (Gembloux, 1951), pp. 361–73.
11. Leontius of Neapolis, *Life of St. John the Almsgiver*, 10.
12. For example its continued use by the notaries of Ravenna: J.-O. Tjäder (ed.), *Die nichtliterarischen Papyri Italiens aus der Zeit 445–700* (3 vols, Lund and Stockholm, 1955–82), see also H. Pirenne, 'Le commerce de papyrus dans la Gaule mérovingienne', *Comptes rendus des séances de l'Academie des Inscriptions et Belles-Lettres* (1928), 178–91. See S. Lebecq, 'Routes of Change', in L. Webster and M. Brown (eds), *The Transformation of the Roman World AD 400–900* (London, 1997), p. 70 and fig. 28.
13. P. Courcelle, *Late Latin Writers and their Greek Sources* (Cambridge, Mass., 1969), pp. 149–223. For Isidore see Fontaine, *Isidore de Séville*, vol. II, pp. 849–54. On Gregory I see G. J. M. Bartelink, 'Pope Gregory the Great's Knowledge of Greek', in J. C. Cavadini (ed.), *Gregory the Great: a Symposium* (Notre Dame, 1995), pp. 117–36.
14. For the process of compilation see A. M. Honore, *Justinian's Digest: Work in Progress* (Oxford, 1971), and idem, *Tribonian* (London, 1978), pp. 139–222.
15. For a useful overview see W. Berschin, *Greek Letters and the Latin Middle Ages, from Jerome to Nicholas of Cusa* (rev. edn, Washington DC, 1988).
16. Y. Duval, 'La discussion entre l'apocrisiaire Grégoire et le patriarche Eutychios au sujet de la résurrection de la chair', in J. Fontaine *et al.* (eds), *Grégoire le Grand* (Paris, 1986), pp. 347–66.
17. C. Courtois, 'Grégoire VII et l'Afrique du Nord', *Revue Historique*, 195 (1945), 97–122, 193–226; C.-E. Dufourcq, 'La coexistence des chrétiens et des musulmans dans *Al-Andalus* et dans le Maghrib aux Xe siècle', in *Occident et Orient au Xe Siècle* (Paris, 1979), pp. 209–34.
18. This is an insufficiently studied phenomenon, but for useful parallels see T. Canaan, *Mohammedan Saints and Sanctuaries in Palestine* (Jerusalem, 1927).
19. For the continuing intellectual vitality and leading role of Toledo in the eighth century see Collins, *Arab Conquest of Spain*, pp. 52–80 and 217–30; for Adoptionism see above all J. C. Cavadini, *The Last Christology of the West: Adoptionism in Spain and Gaul, 785–820* (Philadelphia, 1993).
20. For the reign of Justinian II see C. F. Head, *Justinian II of Byzantium* (Maddison, 1972), and vol. V of A. N. Stratos, *Byzantium in the Seventh Century* (Antwerp, 1980). Shorter but sounder is Herrin, *Formation of Christendom*, pp. 280–90.
21. See E. W. Brooks, 'The Arabs in Asia Minor (641–750), from Arabic Sources', *Journal of Hellenic Studies*, 18 (1898), 182–208; *Chronicle of Theophanes*, a.m. 6218–a.m. 6233.
22. For example, R. J. H. Jenkins, *Byzantium: the Imperial Centuries* (London, 1966), pp. 58–89, but see now M. Whittow, *The Making of*

Orthodox Byzantium, 600–1025 (London, 1996), pp. 143–49, and W. Treadgold, *A History of the Byzantine State and Society* (Stanford, 1997), pp. 346–70.

23. *Chronicle of Theophanes*, a.m. 6211.
24. *Chronicle of Theophanes*, a.m. 6217 and 6218. See M. V. Anastos, 'Leo III's Edict Against the Images in the Year 726–27 and Italo-Byzantine Relations between 726 and 730', *Byzantinische Forschungen*, 3 (1968), 5–41.
25. *Chronicle of Theophanes*, a.m. 6218.
26. For the Iconoclast conflict see Herrin, *Formation of Christendom*, pp. 307–43, and E. Kitzinger, 'The Cult of Images in the Age before Iconoclasm', *Dumbarton Oaks Papers*, 8 (1954), 83–150; also Whittow, *Making of Orthodox Byzantium*, pp. 139–64. For detailed discussion of the evidence see A. Grabar, *L'Iconoclasme byzantin* (2nd edn, Paris, 1984), pp. 17–132.
27. *Chronicle of Theophanes*, a.m. 6215. See A. Grabar, *L'Iconoclasme*, pp. 128–9 for other evidence relating to the edict of Yazid.
28. R. Cormack, *Writing in Gold: Byzantine Society and its Icons* (London, 1985), pp. 95–140; Grabar, *L'Iconoclasme*, pp. 135–210.
29. *Chronicle of Theophanes*, a.m. 6232.
30. Herrin, *Formation of Christendom*, pp. 337–40.
31. *Chronicle of Theophanes*, a.m. 6233–a.m. 6235.
32. W. Treadgold, *Byzantium and its Army, 284–1081* (Stanford, 1995), for a substantial discussion.
33. W. Goffart, *Barbarians and Romans, A.D. 418–584: the Techniques of Accommodation* (Princeton, 1980), and the contributions, especially that of J. Durliat, to H. Wolfram and A. Schwarcz (eds), *Anerkennung und Integration* (Vienna, 1988).
34. Equally thought-provoking should be the conclusions of the study of some Late Roman administrative papyri from Egypt: J. Gascou, 'L'institution des bucellaires', *Bulletin de l'Institution française d'Archéologie orientale*, 76 (1976), 143–56.
35. Treadgold, *Byzantium and its Army*, pp. 21–27; Whittow, *Making of Orthodox Byzantium*, pp. 120–21.
36. A. N. Stratos, *Byzantium in the Seventh Century*, vol. IV: *668–85* (Amsterdam, 1978), pp. 93–113; R. Browning, *Byzantium and Bulgaria* (London, 1975), pp. 45–9.
37. *Chronicle of Theophanes*, a.m. 6257–a.m. 6259.
38. PG, 10, cols 1013–92; see on this work G. Huxley, 'On the *Vita* of Saint Stephen the Younger', *Greek, Roman and Byzantine Studies*, 18 (1977), 97–108, and the use made of it in P. Brown, 'A Dark Age Crisis: Aspects of the Iconoclastic Controversy', *English Historical Review*, 88 (1973), 1–34.
39. Herrin, *Formation of Christendom*, pp. 277–80 on the Sixth Oecumenical Council, and pp. 284–9 on the Quinisext.
40. For Martin I see *Liber Pontificalis*, vol. I, pp. 336–40; E. Caspar, *Geschichte des Papstums* (2 vols, Tübingen, 1930–3), vol. II, pp. 553–78. See also Herrin, *Formation of Christendom*, pp. 253–9 and P. Llewellyn, *Rome in the Dark Ages* (London, 1971), pp. 150–6.

41. *Liber Pontificalis*, vol. I, p. 373. See A. Guillou, *Régionalisme et inde-pendence dans l'empire byzantin au vii siècle* (Rome, 1969), pp. 209–11.
42. *Liber Pontificalis*, vol. I, pp. 385–7; P. J. Nordhagen, *The Frescoes of John VII in S. Maria Antiqua* (Rome, 1968), but cf. E. Kitzinger, *Byzantine Art in the Making* (London, 1977), pp. 113–22 and refer-ences; see also J. Breckenridge, 'Evidence for the Nature of Relations between Pope John VII and the Byzantine Emperor Justinian II', *Byzantinische Zeitschrift*, 65 (1972), 364–74.
43. Caspar, *Geschichte des Papstums*, vol. II, pp. 639–40.
44. *Chronicle of Theophanes*, a.m. 6204.
45. *Chronicle of Theophanes*, a.m. 6217; see E. Caspar, 'Papst Gregor II und der Bilderstreit', *Zeitschrift für Kirchengeschichte*, 52 (1933), 29–70.
46. *Liber Pontificalis*, vol. I, pp. 403–4 for Gregory II's involvement in the revolt over taxes, but cf. p. 408 – Gregory II's opposition to the setting up of a rebel emperor called Tiberius in south Etruria. See also Caspar, *Geschichte des Papstums*, vol. II, pp. 643–64 and Llewel-lyn, *Rome in the Dark Ages*, pp. 166–8. T. F. X. Noble, *The Republic of St. Peter: the Birth of the Papal State, 680–825* (Philadelphia, 1984), pp. 28–40 argues on the other hand that 'a papal Republic' came into existence between 729 and 733.
47. *Chronicle of Theophanes*, a.m. 6224.
48. R. A. Markus, *Gregory the Great and his World* (Cambridge, 1997), pp. 97–107.
49. J. T. Hallenbeck, *Pavia and Rome: the Lombard Monarchy and the Papacy in the Eighth Century* (Philadelphia, 1982), pp. 39–44.
50. R. Krautheimer, *Rome, Profile of a City, 312–1308* (Princeton, 1980), p. 107.
51. Caspar, *Geschichte des Papstums*, vol. II, pp. 737–7; Hallenbeck, *Pavia and Rome*, pp. 45–52.
52. Hallenbeck, *Pavia and Rome*, pp. 52–3.
53. As argued by Hallenbeck, *Pavia and Rome*, pp. 21–9 (for Liutprand) and 55–61 (for Aistulf in the years 749–52), but seeing a deliberate intent on Aistulf's part to try to take Rome in 753 (pp. 64–9).
54. *Liber Pontificalis*, vol. I, p. 441.
55. *Chronicle of Theophanes*, a.m. 6243.

14   MONKS AND MISSIONARIES

1. D. Obolensky, *The Byzantine Commonwealth* (London, 1971), especially chs 1–5.
2. R. Fletcher, *The Conversion of Europe* (London, 1997), pp. 327–68.
3. W. Ullmann, *The Growth of Papal Government* (2nd edn, London, 1962), pp. 36–7, and idem, *A Short History of the Papacy in the Middle Ages* (corrected reprint, London, 1974), pp. 51–70; his thesis that Gregory launched the mission to extend papal authority into areas beyond the emperor's control is firmly put to rest in R. Markus, 'Gregory the Great's Europe', *Transactions of the Royal Historical Society*, 5th ser. 31 (1981), 21–36.

4. R. R. Ruether, *Gregory of Nazianzus: Rhetor and Philosopher* (Oxford, 1969), pp. 18–33, 136–55.
5. *Vita Martini*, VIII. 1–3; X. 1–9. On the early medieval remains at Ligugé see J. Coquet, *L'intérêt des fouilles de Ligugé* (2nd edn, Ligugé, 1978).
6. For Honoratus see the text of and introduction to M.-D. Valentin's edition of Hilary's *Vita Honorati* (Bibliography).
7. R. Collins, 'Faustus von Reji', *Theologische Realenzyklopädie*, vol. XI, pp. 63–7.
8. For the suggestion that the Rule for Nuns is Caesarius's *only* authentic rule see R. Collins, 'Caesarius von Arles', ibid., vol. VII, pp. 531–6; in general on Caesarius see W. E. Klingshirn, *Caesarius of Arles: the Making of a Community in Late Antique Gaul* (Cambridge, 1994).
9. *Cassiodori Senatoris Instituta*, ed. R. Mynors (Oxford, 1947); J. J. O'Donnell, *Cassiodorus* (Berkeley, 1979), pp. 177–222.
10. For editions of the *Rule of the Master* and of the *Rule of Benedict* see Bibliography; on the priority of the former, against older arguments, see D. Knowles, 'The *Regula Magistri* and the *Rule* of St Benedict' in his *Great Historical Enterprises* (London, 1962), pp. 135–95, and the introduction to de Vogüé's edition, (SC 181–6) vol. 1, pp. 245–314. An attempt to reverse this verdict is made and refuted in exchanges to be found in *English Historical Review*, 105 (1990), 567–94 and 107 (1992), 95–111.
11. Book II of the *Dialogues* (Grégoire le Grand, *Dialogues*, ed. A. de Vogüé (SC vols. 251, 260, 265), bk II, vol. 2, pp. 126–249) is the main source for the life of Benedict.
12. J. M. Wallace-Hadrill, *The Barbarian West* (revised edn, Oxford, 1985), pp. 47–9.
13. *Regula Benedicti*, vii.
14. *MGH Epp.*, vols I and II; D. Norberg, *Critical and Exegetical Notes on the Letters of St. Gregory the Great* (Stockholm, 1982) and idem, 'Qui a composé les lettres de Grégoire le Grand?', *Studi Medievali*, 21 (1980), 1–17.
15. J. McClure, *Gregory the Great: Exegesis and Audience* (DPhil thesis, University of Oxford, 1979), and also C. Strav, *Gregory the Great: Perfection in Imperfection* (Berkeley, 1988).
16. R. A. Markus, *Gregory the Great and his World* (Cambridge, 1997), pp. 17–33 and 68–82.
17. L. Bieler, *Ireland: Harbinger of the Middle Ages* (London, 1963), pp. 85–93: 'The Franks were … nominal Christians … a decadent nobility, and a worldly clergy'! (p. 85); C. Dawson, *The Making of Europe, 400–1000 AD* (London, 1939), pp. 196–213.
18. For example, D. A. Binchy, 'Irish History and Irish Law', *Studia Hibernica*, 15 (1975), 7–36, and 16 (1976), pp. 7–45.
19. Ibid., and also Binchy, 'The Linguistic and Historical Value of the Irish Law Tracts', *Proceedings of the British Academy*, 29 (1943), 3–35.
20. J. F. Kenney, *The Sources for the Early History of Ireland (Ecclesiastical)*, revised by L. Bieler (Dublin, 1979) provides a comprehensive treatment of individual works; valuable generic accounts will be found in

K. Hughes, *Early Christian Ireland: Introduction to the Sources* (London, 1972).

21. See items in notes 8 and 9 above; also D. O. Corráin, L. Breatnach and A. Breen, 'The Laws of the Irish', *Peritia*, 3 (1984), 382–438 (with bibliography cited there).

22. A. P. Smyth, 'The Earliest Irish Annals: Their First Contemporary Entries and the Earliest Centres of recording', *Proceedings of the Royal Irish Academy*, 72C, no. 1 (1972), 1–48 argues that some entries from the mid-sixth century onwards are contemporary; Hughes, *Sources*, pp. 99–162 is more cautious.

23. For such largely fictional works, once much relied on, as *Cogadh Gaedhel re Gallaibh* see Hughes, *Sources*, pp. 284–301; also in this category belongs some (but not all) of *Fragmentary Annals of Ireland*, ed. J. Radnor (Dublin, 1978).

24. Hughes, *Sources*, pp. 217–47.

25. The literature on Patrick is enormous; see for some of the arguments R. P. C. Hanson, *Saint Patrick: his Origins and Career* (Oxford, 1968) (early dating), J. Carney, *The Problem of St. Patrick* (Dublin, 1973) (late dating); E. A. Thompson, *Who was St. Patrick* (Woodbridge, 1985) (either, neither or both), and, for a real counsel of despair: T. F. O'Rahilly, *The Two Patricks* (Dublin, reprinted 1981). See also D. Dumville *et al.*, *Saint Patrick, A.D. 493–1993* (Woodbridge, 1993).

26. Kenney, *The Sources*, nos 127 and 128, pp. 329–35.

27. Ibid., no. 135, pp. 342–5. See R. Sharpe, 'St. Patrick and the See of Armagh', *Cambridge Medieval Celtic Studies*, 4 (1982), 33–59 for some doubts on Armagh's claims.

28. E. A. Thompson, 'St. Patrick and Coroticus', *Journal of Theological Studies*, n.s. 31 (1980), 12–27, and idem, *Who was St. Patrick?*, pp. 125–43 offer a new approach to the identity of this man; it is certainly a corrective to the older, poorly grounded, certainties.

29. *Confessio*, 1–23.

30. Thompson, 'St. Patrick and Coroticus', pp. 12–27.

31. D. N. Dumville, 'Some British Aspects of the Earliest Irish Christianity', in P. Ní Chatháin and M. Richter (eds), *Irland und Europa* (Stuttgart, 1984), pp. 16–24 extends the logic of Thompson's argument (see note 20) to include Palladius.

32. L. Laing, 'The Romanization of Ireland in the Fifth Century', *Peritia*, 4 (1985), 261–78 for the material culture. Some discussion of possible earlier Roman influences has been generated recently by the discovery of what might be a Roman fort, or more likely a trading station, near Dublin.

33. Prosper, *Chronica*, 1307, ed. Mommsen, p. 473.

34. Muirchú, *Vita Patricii*, 8–9.

35. C. Thomas, *Christianity in Roman Britain to AD 500* (London, 1981), especially pp. 275–94 and 347–55; for his views on Patrick see pp. 307–46.

36. F. Henry, 'Early Irish Monasteries, Beehive Huts and Dry-Stone Houses in the Neighbourhood of Caherciveen and Waterville', *Proceedings of the Royal Irish Academy*, 58C (1957), 45–166; T. Fanning,

'Excavation of the Early Christian Cemetery and Settlement at Reask, County Kerry', ibid., 81C (1981), 67–172; *Royal Commission on the Ancient and Historical Monuments of Scotland: Argyll*, vol. IV: *Iona* (Edinburgh, 1982), pp. 31–48 for excavations of early Irish monastic foundations. See now A. Ritchie, *Iona* (London, 1997), pp. 31–46.

37. K. Hughes, *The Church in Early Irish Society* (London, 1966), pp. 65–78. The existence of Irish monasteries in the mid-sixth century rests largely upon the identification of a certain *Vennianus*, who was a correspondent of Gildas (*c.* 540), with the author of the *Penitentialis Vinniani*. This is at best a pious hope.

38. Much of value can still be found in the introduction and notes to W. Reeves' edition of Adamnán's *Life of Columba*, as well as in the introduction to the more recent edition by the Andersons (for these see Bibliography); see also A. D. S. Macdonald, 'Aspects of the Monastery and Monastic Life in Adamnán's Life of Columba', *Peritia*, 3 (1984), 271–302.

39. Hughes, *The Church in Early Irish Society*, pp. 79–90 for a statement of the orthodox view. See also J. Ryan, *Irish Monasticism* (Dublin, 1931), pp. 167–90.

40. R. Sharpe, 'Some Problems Concerning the Organization of the Church in Early Medieval Ireland', *Peritia*, 3 (1984), 230–70 is superbly and rightly iconoclastic.

41. For Ireland in the sixth century see D.Ó. Crónín, *Early Medieval Ireland, 400–1200* (London, 1995).

42. E. Mac Neill, *Celtic Ireland* (Dublin, 1921), pp. 96–113 and F. J. Byrne, *Irish Kings and High Kings* (London, 1973), pp. 28–47 give detailed and learned presentations of the traditional view.

43. Hughes, *Church in Early Irish Society*, pp. 65–78.

44. J. E. C. Williams, 'The Court Poet in Medieval Ireland', *Proceedings of the British Academy*, 57 (1971), 1–51; R. Flower, *The Irish Tradition* (Oxford, 1947) make useful starting points for the immense literature on the Bards.

45. J. Stevenson, 'The Beginnings of Literacy in Ireland', *Proceedings of the Royal Irish Academy*, 89C (1989), 127–65, and idem, 'Literacy in Ireland: the Evidence of the Patrick Dossier in the Book of Armagh', in R. McKitterick (ed.), *The Uses of Literacy in Early Medieval Europe* (Cambridge, 1990), pp. 11–35.

46. For aspects of the Irish role in the transmission of such learning see V. Law, *The Insular Latin Grammarians* (Woodbridge, 1982), but see also the doubts expressed in L. Holtz, 'Les grammairiens hiberno-latins étaient-ils des Anglo-Saxons?', *Peritia*, 2 (1983), 169–84.

47. T. M. Charles-Edwards, 'The Social Background to Irish *Peregrinatio*' *Celtica*, II (1976), 43–59. A real danger exists that the cart is being put before the horse: that the Irish texts relating to *Peregrinatio* are rationalising and systematising a practice recently developed within the Irish Church under external influence, rather than it being an inherent feature that caused the Irish monks to have a decisive and unique impact on the Continent.

48. Adamanán, *Vita Columbae*, I. 14, 38–40, 42, 49–50, 11. 2, 36.

49. See the *Life of Columbanus* (Bibliography), and for various studies see H. B. Clarke and M. Brennan (eds), *Columbanus and Merovingian Monasticism* (Oxford, 1981), and M. Lapidge (ed.), *Columbanus: Studies on the Latin Writings* (Woodbridge, 1997).

50. For discussion of the identity of 'Vinnian' see D. N. Dumville (ed.), 'Gildas and Uinniau', in *Gildas: New Approaches* (Woodbridge, 1984), pp. 207–14; for the penitential see L. Bieler (ed.), *The Irish Penitentials* (Dublin, 1963), pp. 74–95. See also note 27 above.

51. Columbanus, *Epistulae*, 1–3, ed. Walker, pp. 2–25.

52. *Vita Columbani*, I. 18–29; see also *Codice diplomatico del monasterio di S. Colombano di Bobbio*, ed. C. Cipolla, vol. I (Rome 1918), docs I–V.

53. This remains controversial, but the thesis of direct and unmediated links between southern Spain and Ireland is weak. See the three papers on the subject collected in J. N. Hillgarth, *Visigothic Spain, Byzantium and the Irish* (London, 1985), items VI–VIII, and E. James, 'Ireland and Western Gaul in the Merovingian Period', in D. Whitelock, R. McKitterick and D. Dumville (eds), *Ireland in Early Medieval Europe* (Cambridge, 1982) pp. 362–86.

54. Bertulf, the second abbot, was a Frankish noble and relative of bishop Arnulf of Metz, the progenitor of the Arnulfing line: *Vita Columbani*, II. 23.

55. F. Prinz, *Frühes Mönchtum im Frankenreich* (2nd edn, Darmstadt, 1988), pp. 121–51.

56. Prinz, *Frühes Mönchtum*, pp. 131–3; *Vita (prima) Sancti Wandregisili*, ed. B. Krusch, *MGH SRM*, vol. V, pp. 1–24.

57. Prinz, *Frühes Mönchtum*, map VIIA, p. 674.

58. For example M. and L. de Paor, *Early Christian Ireland* (London, 1958), pp. 48, 64–8.

59. C. Stancliffe, 'Early "Irish" Biblical Exegesis', *Studia Patristica*, XII (Berlin, 1975), 361–70; W. Stevens, 'Scientific Instruction in Early Insular Schools', in M. W. Herren (ed.), *Insular Latin Studies* (Toronto, 1981), pp. 83–111; and see also note 36 above.

60. Prinz, *Frühes Mönchtum*, pp. 263–92.

61. Bede, *Historia Ecclesiastica*, III. vii. See the Commentary by J. M. Wallace-Hadrill, p. 99.

62. See P. Rousseau, 'The Spiritual Authority of the "Monk-bishop"', *Journal of Theological Studies*, n.s. 22 (1971), 380–419.

63. H. I. Marrou, *A History of Education in Antiquity* (English tr., New York, 1956), pp. 419–51.

64. For example, IV Toledo (633), c. lii, ed. Vives, p. 209; Conc. Parisiense (614), xiv, ed. de Clercq, p. 279, etc.

65. C. Stancliffe, St. *Martin and his Biographer* (Oxford, 1983) is an excellent study of Sulpicius and his Martinian writings; see in particular pp. 328–40 for 'Martin's Campaign against Paganism'.

66. Gregory of Tours, *De Virtutibus Sancti Martini*, I. xi; idem, *Libri Decem Historiarum*, V. xxxvii.

67. Bede, *Historia Ecclesiastica*, III. iv; see also the Commentary by J. M. Wallace-Hadrill, p. 92.

68. Bede, ibid., I. xxiv; Commentary p. 32; further letters will be found in Gregory, *Epistolae*, bk XI, nos 55–62.

69. Bede, *Historia Ecclesiastica*, III. vii; IV. xii; II. xv; Commentary pp. 99, 148, 77–8.

70. The idea of such a hegemony is based primarily upon the mistranslation of one phrase in Gregory the Great's letter of 596 to the Frankish Kings Theuderic II and Theudebert II: *Epistolae*, VI. 49; see I. Wood, 'Frankish Hegemony in England', in M. Carver (ed.), *The Age of Sutton Hoo* (Woodbridge, 1992), pp. 235–41.

71. C. A. Bernoulli, *Die Heiligen der Merowinger* (Tübingen, 1900), pp. 73–149; see also F. Graus, *Volk, Herrscher und Heiliger im Reich der Merowinger. Studien zur Hagiographie der Merowingerzeit* (Prague, 1965).

72. For discussions of datings see Krusch's introductions to the items in *MGH SRM*, vols 3–7; for modern revisions see I. N. Wood, 'Forgery in Merovingian Hagiography', in *Fälschungen im Mittlealter*, vol. V (*Schriften* of the *MGH*, Hanover, 1988), pp. 369–84.

73. *Vita Amandi*, 14, and also 24.

74. See the introduction to Krusch's edition of the *Vita* for a late dating, cf. Wood 'Forgery', pp. 371–2, and R. Collins, 'The *Vaccaei*, the *Vaceti* and the Rise of *Vasconia*', in idem, *Law, Culture and Regionalism in Early Medieval Spain* (Aldershot, 1992), item XI, especially p. 212 for a mid-eighth century date. Some (for example Dierkens in note 85 below) believe it to be genuinely late seventh century.

75. *Vita Amandi*, 4; Prinz, *Frühes Mönchtum*, pp. 19–46 for the cult.

76. *Vita Amandi*, 6–7; C. Straw, *Gregory the Great*, pp. 194–212.

77. *Liber Pontificalis*, vol. I, pp. 323–7; J. N. D. Kelly, *Dictionary of Popes* (Oxford, 1986), pp. 70–1.

78. For the royal land grant see Amandus's instruction for the disposition of his body: *MGH SRM*, vol. V, pp. 483–4. Acharius had been a monk at Luxeuil, and so his role in all of this is seen (unnecessarily) as representing 'Irish influence'.

79. *Vita Amandi*, 16; the combination of Slavs and 'across the Danube' might locate this venture in Samo's kingdom (?), another area of special interest to Dagobert I: Fredegar, *Chronica*, IV. 48, 68, 75.

80. *Vita Amandi*, 17.

81. Fredegar, *Chronica*, IV. 59, 75.

82. *Vita Amandi*, 20–1; R. Collins, *The Basques* (2nd edn, Oxford, 1990), pp. 102–4.

83. M. Werner, *Der Lütticher Raum im frühkarolingischer Zeit* (Göttingen, 1980), pp. 235–56.

84. It is preserved in a text known as the *Suppletio Milonis*: edited by Krusch, *MGH SRM*, vol. V, pp. 452–6 for the letter.

85. I am convinced by the reconstruction of these events offered by A. Dierkens, 'Saint Amand et la fondation de l'abbaye de Nivelles', *Revue du Nord*, 69 (1986), 325–32.

86. A. Dierkens, *Abbayes et chapitres entre Sambre et Meuse (VII–XI siècles)* (Paris, 1985), pp. 65–76.

87. *Vita Amandi*, 23.

88. Bede, *Historia Ecclesiastica*, III. xix; Commentary pp. 114–15.

89. *Liber Historiae Francorum*, 43; for an analysis of these events see R. A. Gerberding, *The Rise of the Carolingians and the Liber Historiae Francorum* (Oxford, 1987), pp. 47–66.
90. The best study of the Frisians, although primarily concerned with them as traders and navigators, is S. Lebecq, *Marchands et navigateurs frisons du haut moyen âge* (2 vols, Lille, 1983); for their history in the seventh century see especially pp. 106–10.
91. (Eddius) Stephanus, *Vita Wilfridi*, xxvi. The identification of the author of this work, Stephanus, with the cantor Aedde derives from Bede, *Historia Ecclesiastica*, IV. ii, but is not strong.
92. *Vita Wilfridi*, xxviii and xxxiii.
93. *Vita Wilfridi*, xxiv. See also W. Goffart, 'Bede and the Ghost of Bishop Wilfrid', in his *Narrators of Barbarian History* (Princeton, 1988), pp. 235–328.
94. D. O'Cróinin, 'Rash Melsigi, Willibrord, and the Earliest Echternach Manuscripts', *Peritia*, 3 (1984), 17–42.
95. Alcuin, *Vita Willibrordi Archepiscopi Traiectensis*, 3 and 4.
96. Bede, *Historia Ecclesiastica*, V. xi; Commentary, pp. 183–5.
97. Alcuin, *Vita Willibrordi*, 6–8.
98. J. M. Wallace-Hadrill, *The Frankish Church* (Oxford, 1983), pp. 144–7; W. Levison, *England and the Continent in the Eighth Century* (Oxford, 1946), pp. 45–69.
99. Pardessus, vol. II, nos 449, 458, 459, 461, 467, 474, 476, 481, 483, 485, 490, 500, 502, 503, 519–21, 537–40.
100. No all-embracing modern study of Aldhelm exists, but see M. Winterbottom, 'Aldhelm's Prose Style and its Origins', *Anglo-Saxon England*, 6 (1977), 39–76, which stresses his continental as opposed to Irish intellectual and stylistic debts; also A. Orchard, *The Poetic Art of Aldhelm* (Cambridge, 1994).
101. For Boniface's career see Levison, *England and the Continent*, pp. 70–94, Wallace-Hadrill, *Frankish Church*, pp. 150–61, and idem, 'A Background to St. Boniface's mission', in P. Clemoes and K. Hughes (eds), *England before the Conquest* (Cambridge, 1971), pp. 35–48, reprinted in his *Early Medieval History* (Oxford, 1975), pp. 138–54, but above all T. Schieffer, *Winfrid-Bonifatius und die christliche Grundlegung Europas* (Freiburg, 1954).
102. CLA 1197; see also M. B. Parkes, 'The Handwriting of St. Boniface: a Reassessment of the Problems', in *Beiträge zur Geschichte der deutschen Sprache und Literatur*, 98 (2) (1976), 161–79.
103. On the Rhineland aristocracy see R. Sprandel, *Der merovingische Adel und die Gebiete östlich des Rheins* (Freiburg, 1957); see Wallace-Hadrill, 'Background', pp. 141–50, and also Boniface, *epp.* 50, 51, 57, 60. See also Wallace-Hadrill, *Frankish Church*, pp. 132–42 for the Church in Francia under Charles Martel.
104. Boniface, *ep.* 12. See also A. Angenendt, 'Bonifatius und die Sacramentum initiationis', *Römische Quartalschaft*, 72 (1977), 133–83.
105. H. Löwe, 'Bonifatius und die bayerisch-fränkische Spannung', *Jahrbuch für fränkische Landesforschung*, 15 (1955), 85–127.

106. For the Bavarian ducal house see J. Jarnut, *Agilolfingerstudien* (Stuttgart, 1986); see also H.-D. Kahl, 'Die Baiern und ihre Nachbarn bis zum Tode des Herzogs Theodo (717/18)', in H. Wolfram and A. Schwarcz (eds), *Die Bayern und ihre Nachbarn*, I (Vienna, 1985), pp. 160–225, and J. Jahn, *Ducatus Baiuvariorum. Das bairische Herzogtum der Agilolfinger* (Stuttgart, 1991).

107. Boniface, *ep.* 80; on *Virgil* see Schieffer, *Winfrid-Bonifatius*, pp. 246–9. See also H. Löwe, 'Salzburg als Zentrum literarischen Schaffens im 8. Jahrhundert', *Mitteilungen der Gesellschaft für Salzburger Landeskunde*, 115 (1975), 99–143.

108. Boniface, *epp.* 40, 41, 89.

109. Schieffer, *Winfrid-Bonifatius*, pp. 199–256.

110. J. Jarnut, 'Wer hat Pippin 751 zum König gesalbt?', *Frühmittelalterliche Studien*, 16 (1982), 45–57; for the origins of the ceremony see R. Schneider, *Königswahl und Königserhebung im Frühmittelalter* (Stuttgart, 1972); see also A. Angenendt, 'Rex et Sacerdos. Zur Genese der Königsalbung', in N. Kamp and J. Wollasch (eds), *Tradition als historische Kraft* (Berlin and New York, 1982), pp. 100–18.

111. Arbeo of Freising, *Vita vel Passio Sancti Haimhramni Martyris*, ed. B. Bischoff (Munich, 1953).

112. *Conversio Bagoariorum et Carantanorum*, ed. H. Wolfram (Vienna, 1979), pp. 34–8, and 60–70 for comment.

113. See for Emmeram, Rupert and Corbinian, H. Wolfram, *Die Geburt Mitteleuropas* (Berlin, 1987), pp. 109–26.

15 TOWARDS A NEW WESTERN EMPIRE, 714–800

1. *Chronicle of Fredegar*, continuations, 34.

2. *Annales Mosellani*, s.a. 708, ed. G. Pertz, *MGH SS*, vol. XVI, p. 494; *Annales Sancti Amandi*, s.a. 708, *MGH SS*, vol. I, p. 6, etc. For some discussion of these annals see R. Collins, 'The *Vaccaei*, the *Vaceti* and the Rise of *Vasconia*' in idem, *Law, Culture and Regionalism in Early Medieval Spain* (Aldershot, 1992), item XI, especially pp. 216–19.

3. R. A. Gerberding, *The Rise of the Carolingians and the 'Liber Historiae Francorum'* (Oxford, 1987), pp. 150–9.

4. *Liber Historiae Francorum*, 50; Fredegar continuations, 7.

5. Fredegar, continuations, 8–9.

6. Liber Historiae Francorum, 51; Fredegar continuations, 8.

7. *Liber Historiae Francorum*, 52; Fredegar continuations, 9.

8. *Liber Historiae Francorum*, 53; Fredegar continuations, 10. For the period 714–18 in the *LHF* see Gerberding, *Rise of the Carolingians*, pp. 116–45.

9. Fredegar continuations, 10; see, for the history of Aquitaine at this time M. Rouche, *L'Aquitaine des Wisigoths aux Arabes, 418–751: Naissance d'une région* (Paris, 1979), pp. 98–111. For the use of Basque mercenaries by the dukes of Aquitaine see R. Collins, *The Basques* (2nd edn, Oxford, 1990), pp. 106–12.

10. Fredegar continuations, 11–13 cover the years 719–33.

11. Fredegar, continuations, 5.
12. *Annales Mettenses Priores*, s.a. 687; *Gesta Abbatum Fontanellensis*, IV. 1. For Audramnus as Count of the Palace see Pardessus, vol. II no. 431.
13. Gerberding, *Rise of the Carolingians*, pp. 109–15.
14. Pardessus, vol. II, nos 440, 477–8.
15. Gerberding, *Rise of the Carolingians*, p. 104; see also in general P. Fouracre, '*Placita* and the Settlement of Disputes in Later Merovingian Francia', in W. Davies and P. Fouracre (eds), *The Settlement of Disputes in Early Medieval Europe* (Cambridge, 1986), pp. 23–43.
16. *Gesta Abbatum Fontanellensis*, IV. 1.
17. Gerberding, *Rise of the Carolingians*, pp. 138–9.
18. I am convinced by the analysis offered in ibid., pp. 116–24.
19. Ibid., p. 130; see also M. Werner, *Der Lütticher Raum im frühkarolingischer Zeit* (Göttingen, 1980), pp. 126–39.
20. *Chronicle of Fredegar*, IV. 74.
21. Fredegar continuations, 11 and 19; *Annales Sancti Amandi* s.a. 718 and 720.
22. Fredegar continuations, 12.
23. For the background to the Battle of Poitiers, and for some arguments on its dating, see R. Collins, *The Arab Conquest of Spain, 710–797* (Oxford, 1989), pp. 24–5, 89–92.
24. Fredegar continuations, 15; Rouche, *L'Aquitaine*, pp. 115–16.
25. Fredegar continuations, 14 and 18.
26. Fredegar continuations, 20. For Maurontus and his supporters see P. J. Geary, *Aristocracy in Provence: The Rhône Basin at the Dawn of the Carolingian Age* (Stuttgart, 1985), pp. 123–7, 138–43.
27. R. Collins, 'Deception and Misrepresentation in Early Eighth Century Frankish Historiography: Two Case Studies', in J. Jarnut, U. Nonn and M. Richter (eds.), *Karl Martell in seiner Zeit* (Sigmaringen, 1994), pp. 227–47.
28. Fredegar continuations, 20.
29. Fredegar continuations, 21.
30. J. M. Wallace-Hadrill, *The Frankish Church* (Oxford, 1983), pp. 123–42, 270–1 is judicious on this; see also R. Collins, 'Pippin I and the Kingdom of Aquitaine', in P. Godman and R. Collins (eds), *Charlemagne's Heir: New Perspectives on the Reign of Louis the Pious* (Oxford, 1990), especially pp. 370–2.
31. Fredegar continuations, 35 (and implied in 32); *Annales Regni Francorum* (henceforth ARF), s.a. 741, 747, 748, 753. Revised Version of ARF (henceforth ARF Rev), s.a. 747.
32. Fredegar continuations, 25 and ARF, s.a. 742.
33. Fredegar continuations, 28; on the terminology see Collins, '*Vaccaei*, the *Vaceti*, and the rise of *Vasconia*', pp. 211–23.
34. Fredegar continuations, 25, 27, 29; ARF, s.a. 742 (only). See J. Jarnut, 'Alemannien zur zeit der Doppelherrschaft der Hausmeier Karlmann und Pippin', in R. Schieffer (ed.), *Beiträge zur Geschichte des Regnum Francorum* (Sigmaringen, 1990), pp. 57–66.
35. Fredegar continuations, 25, 26, 32; ARF, s.a. 743, 748.

36. ARF, 745 and 746; ARF Rev, 746, and Fredegar continuations, 30 (the implied 747 of the Fredegar continuator is to be preferred to the 746 of ARF); on the ideological background see C. Stancliffe, 'Kings who Opted Out', in P. Wormald, D. Bullough and R. Collins (eds), *Ideal and Reality in Frankish and Anglo-Saxon Society* (Oxford, 1983), pp. 154–76, and K. H. Krüger, 'Königskonversionen im 8. Jahrhundert', *Frühmittelalterliche Studien*, 7 (1973), 169–222. For the political context see M. J. Enright, *Iona, Tara and Soissons* (Berlin and New York, 1985), pp. 110–14 with references.

37. Boniface, *ep.* 79 as evidence for the brief tenure of authority on the part of Drogo. See M. Becher, 'Drogo und die Königserhebung Pippins', *Frühmittelalterliche Studien*, 23 (1989), 131–53.

38. P. Fouracre, 'Observations on the Outgrowth of Pippinid Influence in the "Regnum Francorum" after the Battle of Tertry (687–715)', *Medieval Prosopography*, 5 (1984), 1–31. See also O. P. Clavadetscher, 'Zur Verfassungsgeschichte des merowingischen Rätien', *Frühmittelalterliche Studien*, 8 (1974), 60–70.

39. Doubts on Aquitaine: see Collins, 'The *Vaccaei*, the *Vaceti* and the Rise of *Vasconia*', and 'Pippin I and the Kingdom of Aquitaine', especially pp. 387–9; for Burgundy see I. Wood, 'Ethnicity and the Ethnogenesis of the Burgundians', in H. Wolfram and W. Pohl (eds), *Typen der Ethnogenese unter besonderer Berücksichtung der Bayern*, vol. I (Vienna, 1990), pp. 53–69.

40. Geary, *Aristocracy in Provence*, pp. 101–43.

41. Fredegar, *Chronica*, IV. 48, 68, 72, 74–5, 77, 87.

42. J. Jarnut, *Agilolfingerstudien* (Stuttgart, 1986), pp. 44–90.

43. Rouche, *L'Aquitaine*, pp. 98–109 prefers to see Aquitaine as an independent kingdom under Eudo.

44. Gregory of Tours, *Libri Historiarum*, IV. 49–50; Fredegar, *Chronica* IV. 38.

45. B. L. Bachrach, *Merovingian Military Institution, 481–751* (Minneapolis, 1972), and idem, 'Was the Marchfield part of the Frankish Constitution?', in his *Armies and Politics in the Early Medieval West* (Aldershot, 1993), item IX.

46. Childeric III receives no mention in narrative sources, but appears in a small number of charters. The problems of the dating of his reign and its end are discussed by B. Krusch in *MGH SRM*, vol. VII, pp. 508–10.

47. ARF, s.a. 749.

48. Fredegar continuations, 33.

49. See J. Nelson, 'Inauguration Rituals', in P. H. Sawyer and I. N. Wood (eds), *Early Medieval Kingship* (Leeds, 1977), pp. 50–71.

50. ARF, s.a. 754; the contemporary continuator of Fredegar makes no reference to this event whatsoever.

51. For the argument involving an Irish origin see Enright, *Iona, Tara, Soissons*, but the views of A. Angenendt, 'Rex et Sacerdos. Zur Genese der Königsalbung', in N. Kamp and E. Wollasch (eds), *Tradition als historische Kraft* (Berlin, 1982), pp. 100–18 are to be preferred.

52. J. T. Hallenbeck, *Pavia and Rome: the Lombard Monarchy and the Papacy in the Eighth Century* (Philadelphia, 1982), pp. 69–78.

53. Ibid., pp. 78–80; Fredegar continuations, 36 and 37. See D. H. Miller, 'The Motivation of Pepin's Italian Policy, 754–768', *Studies in Medieval Culture*, 4 (1973), 44–54.

54. *Liber Pontificalis*, vol. I, pp. 444–50.

55. Fredegar continuations, 38 and 39; Hallenbeck, *Pavia and Rome*, pp. 81–5.

56. ARF, s.a. 758; not mentioned by the continuator of Fredegar.

57. ARF, s.a. 760–8; Fredegar continuations, 41–52; Rouche, *L'Aquitaine*, pp. 122–32.

58. Fredegar continuations, 53 is by far the most reliable account. ARF gives no details and ARF Rev claims, tendentiously, that all of Aquitaine was allotted to Charles. For the division in Neustria see Map I (d) on p. 438 of P. Perrin and L.-C. Feffer (eds), *La Neustria: les pays au nord de la Loire de Dagobert à Charles le Chauve* (Rouen, 1985).

59. M. Lintzel, 'Karl der Grosse und Karlaman', *Historische Zeitschrift*, 140 (1929), 1–22; P. D. King, *Charlemagne* (London, 1986), pp. 6–8.

60. ARF, s.a. 771.

61. It has been suggested that the intention to convert was inherent in Charlemagne's Saxon wars from the start. This is based on the very generalised presentation in Eigil, *Vita Sancti Sturmi*, 22 (ed. G. Pertz, *MGH SS*, vol. II, pp. 375–6. The probable date of composition of this work (*c.* 814–20) gives it no independent value. It is better to see Charles's first campaigns as one of containment, like those of Charles Martel and Pippin III, and to see a change to a planned conquest and integration (via conversion) occurring in 775.

62. ARF, s.a. 772.

63. ARF, s.a. 774 and 775.

64. ARF, Rev makes significant additions for 775, including a near-disaster for the Franks.

65. ARF, s.a. 776 and 777.

66. A. Genrich, *Die Altsachsen* (Hanover, 1981); W. Winkelmann, 'Eine westfälische Siedlung des 8. Jahrhundert bei Warendorf, Kr. Warendorf' and 'Die Ausgrabung in der frühmittelalterlichen Siedlung bei Warendorf', in his *Beiträge zur Frühgeschichte Westfalens* (Münster, 1984), pp. 30–42 and 43–54, and plates 21–39.

67. *Liber Pontificalis*: Vita Hadriani, 9, vol. I, p. 488.

68. ARF and ARF Rev, s.a. 773 and 774.

69. H. Wolfram, *Intitulatio*, I (Vienna, 1967), p. 222 discusses the title only in relation to Charles's son Pippin, and (pp. 185–94) the use of it *prior* to 774.

70. See O. Bertolini, 'Carlomagno e Benevento' in W. Braunfels (ed.), *Karl der Grosse. Lebenswerk und Nachleben*, vol. I (Dusseldorf, 1967), pp. 609–71.

71. ARF, s.a. 775–6.

72. ARF and ARF Rev, s.a. 777.

73. The deliberate omissions and distortions of AF 778 are exposed by comparison with ARF Rev, 778 and Einhard, *Vita Karoli*, 9; for the actual context of this campaign – as opposed to Frankish perceptions of it – see Collins, *Arab Conquest of Spain*, pp. 168–82.

74. ARF and ARF Rev, s.a. 778–80.
75. For the royal investitures of 781 see P. Classen, 'Karl der Grosse und die Thronfolge im Frankenreich', in *Festschrift für Hermann Heimpel* (2 vols, Göttingen, 1972), vol. II, pp. 109–34.
76. ARF and ARF Rev, s.a. 782.
77. ARF, s.a. 785.
78. Bertolini, 'Carlomagno e Benevento'; ARF Rev, s.a. 786 and 787.
79. *Chronicle of Theophanes*, a.m. 6241.
80. *Chronicle of Theophanes*, a.m. 6277–80.
81. ARF, s.a. 787 and 788. Here the ARF is an almost exactly contemporary source. Cf. ARF Rev, s.a. 787 and 788.
82. *Council of Frankfurt*, canon 3, ed. A. Boretius, *MGH Capit.*, vol. I, no. 28.
83. ARF, s.a. 788.
84. ARF, s.a. 791, 795–7, 799; ARF Rev, s.a. 790–3, 795–7, 799; see W. Pohl, *Die Awarenkriege Karls des Grossen, 788–803* (Vienna, 1988); also H. Wolfram, *Die Geburt Mitteleuropas* (Berlin, 1987), pp. 251–67.
85. W. Kaemmerer, 'Die Aachener Pfalz Karls des Grossen', in Braunfels (ed.), *Karl der Grosse*, vol. I, pp. 322–48.
86. A. Freeman, 'Theodulf of Orléans and the *Libri Carolini*', *Speculum*, 32 (1957), 663–705, idem, 'Further Studies in the *Libri Carolini*', ibid., 40 (1965), 203–89, idem, 'Further Studies in the *Libri Carolini* III', ibid., 46 (1971), 597–612, and P. Meyvaert, 'The Authorship of the "Libri Carolini": Observations Prompted by a Recent Book', *Revue Bénédictine*, 89 (1979), 29–57.
87. ARF Rev, s.a. 788; cf. *Chronicle of Theophanes*, a.m. 6281.
88. *Chronicle of Theophanes*, a.m. 6282–4.
89. *Chronicle of Theophanes*, a.m. 6289.
90. *Annales Laureshamenses*, s.a. 801, ed. Pertz, *MGH SS*, vol. I, p. 38.
91. P. Llewellyn, *Rome in the Dark Ages* (London, 1971), pp. 221–51 on the city and the papacy in the reign of Charles; also T. F. X. Noble, *The Republic of St. Peter: the Birth of the Papal State, 680–825* (Philadelphia, 1984), pp. 122–255.
92. ARF and ARF Rev, s.a. 796.
93. *Liber Pontificalis*: Leo III, 11–16, vol. II, pp. 4–6; ARF and ARF Rev, s.a. 799 (with some differences in their accounts).
94. *Liber Pontificalis*: Leo III, 14–15, vol. II, p. 5; Alcuin, *epp.* 177–8.
95. That the accusations against Leo had reached the ears of some of the clergy in Francia by at least 798 is clear from Alcuin, *epp.*, 159 and 184.
96. Alcuin, *ep.* 179, drawing on doctrines developed in a set of forged documents supposedly dating to the time of Constantine, but actually produced in the course of the Laurentian schism in the papacy, around the year 500.
97. ARF and ARF Rev, s.a. 800 and 801; *Annales Laureshamenses*, s.a. 800. For a detailed reconstruction of events see R. Folz, *The Coronation of Charlemagne* (English tr., London, 1974), pp. 132–50.
98. For imperial ideas in the circle of Charlemagne's advisers in the late 790s see Folz, *Coronation of Charlemagne*, pp. 118–31, and Alcuin, *epp.*, 174, 177, and 178, all from 799.

16   THE NEW CONSTANTINE

1. Pope Hadrian I compared Charles to Constantine I, in a context redolent of the spurious doctrines of the forged *Donation of Constantine: Codex Carolinus*, 60 (May 778). See also the reconstructions of the decoration of the Lateran triclinium, in which explicit parallels were drawn between Constantine I/Pope Sylvester and Charles/Pope Leo III: R. Krautheimer, *Rome, Profile of a City, 312–1308* (Princeton, 1980), pp. 115–16 and ill. 89.
2. For the ceremonial see ARF, s.a. 800–1. For an analysis see R. Folz, *The Coronation of Charlemagne* (English tr., London, 1974), pp. 144–8 and 231–3.
3. Einhard, *Vita Karoli*, 28. An argument in favour of dating the work to *c.* 817 is advanced in M. Innes and R. McKitterick, 'The Writing of History' in R. McKitterick (ed.), *Carolingian Culture: Emulation and Innovation* (Cambridge, 1994), pp. 193–220.
4. *Annales Laureshamenses*, s.a. 800 indicate that the question was discussed at the council held in Rome early in December 800, but it is reasonable to suspect an earlier phase of discussion during Leo III's stay in Paderborn in the winter of 799. Folz, *Coronation*, pp. 139–43.
5. On the usage in Bede see J. McClure, 'Bede's Old Testament Kings', in P. Wormald, D. Bullough and R. Collins (eds), *Ideal and Reality in Frankish and Anglo-Saxon Society* (Oxford, 1983), especially pp. 96–8.
6. Folz, *Coronation*, pp. 118–31.
7. For litanies and fasts prior to the Avar campaign of 791 see Charles's letter to his wife Fastrada: *MGH Epp.*, vol. IV, p. 528–9; for the changed view on the 778 campaign see *Annales Mettenses Priores*, s.a. 778.
8. See J. Deer, 'Zum Patricius Romanorum Titel Karl des Grossen', *Archivum Historiae Pontificiae*, 3 (1965), 32–86; see also D. H. Miller, 'The Roman Revolution of the Eighth Century: a Study of the Ideological Background of the Papal Separation from Byzantium and Alliance with the Franks', *Medieval Studies*, 36 (1974), 79–133, but with reservations.
9. *Chronicle of Theophanes*, a.m. 6303–4; for a gentlemanly defence of Irene see S. Runciman, 'The Empress Irene the Athenian', in D. Baker (ed.), *Medieval Women* (Oxford, 1978), pp. 101–18; on her reign see W. Treadgold, *The Byzantine Revival 780–842* (Stanford, 1988), pp. 60–126.
10. P. Classen, 'Romanum gubernans Imperium', *Deutsches Archiv*, 9 (1951), 103–21; F. L. Ganshof, 'The Imperial Coronation of Charlemagne: Theories and Facts', in his *The Carolingians and the Frankish Monarchy* (tr. J. Sondheimer, London, 1971), pp. 41–54.
11. *Vita Karoli*, 29.
12. Procopius, *History of the Wars*, V1. vi. 17. For the power of the emperor see W. W. Buckland, *A Text Book of Roman Law from Augustus to Justinian* (3rd edn, corrected reprint, Cambridge, 1975), pp. 7–20.
13. This is the 'K' or Karolina redaction in Eckhardt's edition (see Bibliography).

14. For a brief statement of the conservative Germanic tradition on the origin and nature of the supposedly customary codes see W. Ullmann, *Law and Politics in the Middle Ages* (London, 1975), pp. 193–8; on the codes of 802/3 see R. Büchner, *Die Rechtsquellen*, a 'Beiheft' of Wattenbach-Levison, *Deutschlands Geschichtsquellen im Mittlelater* (Weimar, 1953), pp. 39–44.
15. *Leges Saxonum*, cc. xxi, xxiii, xxiv.
16. This argument is developed in R. Collins, 'The *Vaccaei*, the *Vaceti* and the Rise of *Vasconia*', in idem, *Law, Culture and Regionalism in Early Medieval Spain* (Aldershot, 1992), item XI.
17. The contrary view of an overriding and long-lasting Aquitanian identity is presented in M. Rouche, *L'Aquitaine des Wisigoths aux Arabes, 418–781* (Paris, 1979).
18. R. Collins, 'Pippin I and the Kingdom of Aquitaine', in P. Godman and R. Collins (eds), *Charlemagne's Heir: New Perspectives on the Reign of Louis the Pious* (Oxford, 1990), especially pp. 386–9.
19. I. N. Wood, 'Ethnicity and the Ethnogenesis of the Burgundians', in H. Wolfram and W. Pohl (eds), *Typen der Ethnogenese*, vol. I (Vienna, 1990), pp. 53–69.
20. See J. M. Wallace-Hadrill, 'The *Via Regia* of the Carolingian Age', reprinted in his *Early Medieval History* (Oxford, 1975), p. 195.
21. See Büchner, *Rechtsquellen*, p. 5.
22. As argued by R. Collins, *Early Medieval Spain: Unity in Diversity, 400–1000* (2nd edn, London, 1995), pp. 24–30.
23. A. N. Sherwin White, *The Roman Citizenship* (2nd edn, Oxford, 1973).
24. On Arab clientage see P. Crone, *Slaves on Horses: The Evolution of the Islamic Polity* (Cambridge, 1980), pp. 37–57.
25. It could be speculated that such feelings influenced Frankish hostility to the restoration of icon veneration in Byzantium, as evidenced by c. 2 of the Council of Frankfurt of 794.
26. F. L. Ganshof, 'L'échec de Charlemagne', *Academie des Inscriptions et Belles Lettres, comptes rendues des séances* (1947), pp. 248–54; tr. as 'Charlemagne's Failure' in idem, *Carolingians*, pp. 256–60. This is seminal.
27. For the imperial administration see John Lydus, *De Magistratibus*, ed. I Bekker, *CSHB* (Bonn, 1837), pp. 119–272 (Greek text/Latin tr.). For an overview of the government and politics of the Byzantine Empire in the time of Charlemagne see W. Treadgold, *A History of the Byzantine State and Society* (Stanford, 1997), pp. 417–29.
28. See, for example, I. Wood, 'Disputes in late fifth- and sixth-century Gaul: some problems', in W. Davies and P. Fouracre (eds), *The Settlement of Disputes in Early Medieval Europe* (Cambridge, 1986), especially pp. 12–14 on the survival of *Gesta Municipalia*; for Aquitanian towns see Rouche, *L'Aquitaine*, pp. 261–300.
29. The best introduction is the two contributions of F. L. Ganshof to Braunfels (ed.), *Karl der Grosse* on Institutions under Charlemagne and on the Administration of Justice; these are both conveniently translated by B. and M. Lyon in F. L. Ganshof, *Frankish Institutions under Charlemagne* (New York, 1968), pp. 3–55 and 71–97 (plus notes).

30. T. Reuter, 'Plunder and Tribute in the Carolingian Empire', *Transactions of the Royal Historical Society*, 5th ser. 35 (1985), 75–94.

31. T. Reuter, 'The End of Carolingian Military Expansion', in Godman and Collins, Charlemagne's Heir, pp. 391–405.

32. F. L. Ganshof, 'Charlemagne et l'usage de l'écrit en matière administrative', *Le Moyen Age*, 57 (1951), 1–25; English tr. in idem, *Carolingians and Frankish Monarchy*, pp. 125–42. R. McKitterick, *The Carolingians and the Written Word* (Cambridge, 1989), pp. 25–7 wishes to be more optimistic. See also J. L. Nelson, 'Literacy in Carolingian Government', in R. McKitterick (ed.), *The Uses of Literacy in Early Medieval Europe* (Cambridge, 1990), pp. 258–96.

33. Ganshof, 'Charlemagne et l'usage de l'écrit'; McKitterick, *Carolingians and the Written Word*, pp. 26, 28–9.

34. F. L. Ganshof, 'Charlemagne's Programme of Imperial Government' (English tr. of a conference paper published in Faenza in 1963) in his *Carolingians and the Frankish Monarchy*, pp. 55–85.

35. *Vita Karoli*, 25.

36. G. Brown, 'The Carolingian Renaissance', in R. McKitterick (ed.), *Carolingian Culture: Emulation and Innovation* (Cambridge, 1994), pp. 1–51

37. Well discussed in L. Nees, *A Tainted Mantle: Hercules and the Classical Tradition at the Carolingian Court* (Philadelphia, 1991), pp. 3–17.

38. V. Law, 'The Study of Grammar', in McKitterick (ed.), *Carolingian Culture* , pp. 88–110.

39. See D. Bullough, '*Aula Renovata*: the Carolingian Court before the Aachen Palace', *Proceedings of the British Academy*, 71 (1985), 267–301.

40. Einhard, *Vita Karoli*, 25.

41. W. Goffart, 'Paul the Deacon and Lombard History', in his *The Narrators of Barbarian History* (Princeton, 1988), pp. 329–431; also D. Bullough, 'Ethnic History and the Carolingians: an Alternative Reading of Paul the Deacon's *Historia*', in C. Holdsworth and T. P. Wiseman (eds), *The Inheritance of Historiography, 350–900* (Exeter, 1986), pp. 85–105. For the probable dedication of the *Historia* see K. H. Krüger, 'Zur beneventanischen Konzeption der Langobardengeschichte des Paulus Diaconus', *Frühmittelalterliche Studien*, 15 (1981), 18–35.

42. J. M. Wallace-Hadrill, *The Frankish Church* (Oxford, 1983), pp. 217–25. For a proposal as to Theodulf's origins see R. Collins, 'Poetry in Ninth-Century Spain', *Papers of the Liverpool Latin Seminar*, vol. 4 (Liverpool, 1983), 181–95.

43. See note 86 of chapter 15 above.

44. For a general account of Alcuin recourse has still to be made to C. J. B. Gaskoin, *Alcuin: his Life and Work* (Cambridge, 1904), but, while awaiting publication of his book *Alcuin: Achievement and Reputation*, the articles of Donald Bullough, usefully collected in his *Carolingian Renewal* (Manchester, 1991) provide masterly guidance.

45. For Alcuin and Adoptionism see the introduction to G. Blumenshine (ed.), *Liber Alcuini contra haeresem Felicis* (Vatican, 1980), pp. 9–41, and D. Bullough, 'Alcuin and the Kingdom of Heaven', in

U.-R. Blumenthl (ed.), *Carolingian Essays* (Washington, DC, 1983), pp. 1–69.

46. For example Alcuin, *epp.* 61, 64, 100, 101. See also J. M. Wallace-Hadrill, *Early Germanic Kingship in England and on the Continent* (Oxford, 1971), pp. 114–20.

47. R. Wright, *Late Latin and Early Romance in Spain and Carolingian France* (Liverpool, 1982), pp. 108–22. Even if the idea is accepted, it is hard to envisage such a project being put fully into practice.

48. For the Mass Book see H. Lietzmann (ed.), *Das Sacramentarium Gregorianum nach dem Aachener Urexemplar* (Munster, 1921). For the formal reception of the Dionyiso-Hadriana see *Annales Laureshamenses*, s.a. 802. It was, however, already the basis for most of the regulations of the *Admonitio Generalis* of 789. See also R. McKitterick, 'Knowledge of Canon law in the Frankish Kingdoms before 789: the Manuscript Evidence', *Journal of Theological Studies*, n.s. 36 (1985), 97–117.

49. P. Godman, *Poets and Emperors* (Oxford, 1987), pp. 38–92, and idem (ed.), *Poetry of the Carolingian Renaissance* (London, 1985), pp. 9–33.

50. Wallace-Hadrill, *Frankish Church*, p. 195.

51. Ibid., pp. 195–204; to these Fardulf should almost certainly be added. On him see ARF Rev, s.a. 792.

52. On the nature and purposes of capitularies recourse has to be made to F. L. Ganshof, *Recherches sur les Capitulaires* (French tr. of Flemish original, Paris, 1958). See also H. Mordek, 'Karolingische Kapitularien', in idem (ed.), *Uberlieferung und Geltung normativer Texte des frühen und hohen Mittelalters* (Sigmaringen, 1986), pp. 25–50.

53. K. F. Werner, 'Gouvener l'empire chrétien', in Godman and Collins, *Charlemagne's Heir*, especially pp. 83–8.

54. A. H. M. Jones, *The Later Roman Empire* (3 vols, Oxford, 1964), vol. I, pp. 470–9.

55. *MGH Capit.*, vol. I, ed. A. Boretius, nos 22 and 23, items 1–16.

56. Ibid., no. 22, *praef.* The translation is that of P. D. King, *Charlemagne: Translated Sources* (Kendal, 1987), p. 209.

57. ARF Rev, s.a. 792; the by this time probably contemporary ARF deliberately omit to mention this episode. W. Goffart, 'Paul the Deacon's "Gesta Episcopum Mettensium" and the Early Design of Charlemagne's Succession', *Traditio*, 42 (1986), 59–93 argues that Pippin the Hunchback had been excluded from the succession to the component parts of the Frankish empire in 781.

58. *MGH Capit.*, vol. I, nos 24 and 25. See F. L. Ganshof, 'Charlemagne et le serment', in *Mélanges Louis Halphen* (Paris, 1951), pp. 259–70, and English tr. in his *Carolingians*, pp. 111–24.

59. *Annales Laureshamenses*, s.a. 792.

60. *MGH Capit.*, vol. I, no. 21.

61. Ibid., no. 33, items 1–9.

62. Ibid., no. 44, item 9.

63. Ibid., no. 33, item 3; tr. King, p. 234.

64. Ibid., no. 33, items 4 and 8; tr. King, pp. 234–5.

65. Ibid., no. 33, item 9; tr. King, p. 235.

66. Ibid., no. 29; tr. King, pp. 232–3.

67. Council of Frankfurt, canon 1: *MGH Capit.*, vol. I, no. 28; on the Frankish response to Adoptionism see J.C. Cavadini, *The Last Christology of the West: Adoptionism in Spain and Gaul, 785–820* (Philadelphia, 1993), pp. 71–102.

17   FRONTIER SOCIETIES: CHRISTIAN SPAIN, 711–1037

1. D. Pérez Sánchez, *El ejército en la sociedad visigoda* (Salamanca, 1989), pp. 129–88.
2. R. Collins, 'Julian of Toledo and the Education of Kings in Late Seventh-Century Spain', in idem, *Law, Culture and Regionalism in Early Medieval Spain* (Aldershot, 1992), item III.
3. A. A. Duri, *The Rise of Historical Writing among the Arabs* tr. F. M. Donner, (Princeton, 1983), pp. 136–51.
4. A. Noth, *The Early Arabic Historical Tradition. A Source-Critical Study* (Darwin, 1994); R. Brunschvig, 'Ibn 'Abdalhakam et la conquête de l'Afrique du Nord par les Arabes; étude critique', *Annales de l'Institut des études orientales*, 6 (1942–7), 110–55.
5. R. Collins, *The Arab Conquest of Spain, 710–797* (Oxford, 1989), pp. 23–65.
6. Ibid., pp. 39–42; cf. D. R. Hill, *The Termination of Hostilities in the Early Arab Conquests, 634–656* (London, 1971).
7. M. Brett, 'The Arab Conquest and the Rise of Islam in North Africa', in J. D. Fage (ed.), *The Cambridge History of Africa*, vol. 2 (Cambridge, 1978), pp. 490–555.
8. M. A. Shaban, *The 'Abassid Revolt* (Cambridge, 1970); P. Crone, *Slaves on Horses: the Evolution of the Islamic Polity* (Cambridge, 1980), pp. 37–57.
9. Collins, *Arab Conquest*, pp. 168–82.
10. R. Bulliett, *Conversion to Islam in the Medieval Period* (Cambridge, Mass., 1979), pp. 114–27.
11. M. J. Romani Suay (tr.), *Ibn Hawkal, Configuración del mundo* (Valencia, 1971), p. 63.
12. J. Vernet, 'Los médicos andaluces en el "Libro de las Generaciones de Médicos" de Ibn Yulyul', *Anuario de Estudios Medievales*, 5 (1968), 445–62.
13. D. Millet-Gérard, *Chrétiens mozarabes et culture islamique* (Paris, 1984); also C. M. Sage, *Paul Albar of Cordoba: Studies on his Life and Writings* (Washington, 1943), and K. B. Wolf, *Christian Martyrs in Muslim Spain* (Cambridge, 1988), pp. 51–74.
14. J. A. Coope, *The Martyrs of Córdoba* (Lincoln, 1995); Collins, *Early Medieval Spain*, pp. 210–17.
15. Alvar, *Indiculus Luminosus*, xxxv; D. Wasserstein, 'The Language Situation in Al-Andalus', in A. Jones and R. Hitchcock (eds.), *Studies on the Muwassah and the Kharja* (Oxford, 1991), p. 5; R. Wright, 'La muerte del ladino escrito en Al-Andalus', *Euphrosyne*, 22 (1994), 255–68.
16. R. Collins, 'Poetry in Ninth Century Spain', *Papers of the Liverpool Latin Seminar*, 4, (1984), 181–95.

17. Not all of these inscriptions have been published. Those that have will be found in A. Hübner, *Inscriptiones Hispaniae Christianae* (Berlin, 1900), pp. 69–75 and 99–105.

18. M. C. Hernández, *El Islam de al-Andalus. Historia y estructura de su realidad social* (Madrid, 1992), pp. 172–3; R. Fletcher, *Moorish Spain* (London, 1992), pp. 112–13.

19. Brett, 'The Arab Conqust and the Rise of Islam in North Africa', p. 546.

20. L. A. Gomez-Moreno, *Iglesias mozarabes* (2 vols Madrid, 1919); M. Mentré, *La peinture mozarabe* (Paris, 1984).

21. R. Hitchcock, 'El supuesto mozarabismo andaluz', *Actas del I Congreso de Historia de Andalucia*, 1 (Córdoba, 1978), 149–51.

22. An underlying theme in much of the medieval Spanish historiography of the early and middle decades of the twentieth century; e.g. J. Pérez de Urbel, *Historia del condado de Castilla* (3 vols, Madrid, 1945).

23. J. I. Ruiz de la Peña, 'Estudio preliminar', in J. Gil Fernández, J. L. Moralejo and J. I. Ruiz de la Peña, *Crónicas asturianas* (Oviedo, 1985), pp. 13–42.

24. J. Gil, 'Introducción', in ibid. pp. 45–105.

25. *Chronicle of Alfonso III* (both versions) ch. 9, pp. 124–27. See J. Montenegro and A. del Castillo, 'Don Pelayo y los orígenes de la Reconquista', *Hispania*, 52 (1992), 5–32.

26. Ibid., ch. 8, pp. 122–24; *Chronicle of Albelda*, XV. 1, p. 173.

27. C. Sánchez-Albornoz, 'Data de la batalla de Covadonga', in idem, *Orígenes de la nación española*, vol. 2 (Oviedo, 1974), pp. 97–135.

28. S. Barton, *The Aristocracy in Twelfth-Century León and Castile* (Cambridge, 1997), pp. 28–9; M. Carlé, 'Gran propriedad y grandes proprietarios', *Cuadernos de Historia de España*, 57/8 (1973), 1–224.

29. C. Baliñas Pérez, *Do Mito á Realidade: a definición social e territorial de Galicia na Alta Idade Media (Séculos VIII e IX)* (Santiago de Compostela, 1992), pp. 59–86.

30. *Chronicle of Alfonso III* (both versions – with differences), ch. 14, pp. 132–33.

31. S. de Moxó, *Repoblación y sociedad en la España cristiana medieval* (Madrid, 1979); C. Sánchez-Albornoz, 'Repoblación del Reino asturleonés', in idem, *Viejos y nuevos estudios sobre las instituciones medievales españolas*, vol. 2 (Madrid, 1976), pp. 581–790; anon. (ed.), *Despoblación y colonización del valle del Duero (siglos VIII–XX)* (Avila, 1995).

32. P. Barraca de Ramos, 'La ciudad de Avila entre los siglos V al X', *IV Congreso de Arqueología Medieval Española*, vol. 2 (Alicante, 1994), pp. 39–46.

33. C. Sánchez-Albornoz, 'Los siervos en el noroeste hispano hace un milenio', in idem, *Viejos y nuevos estudios*, 3 (Madrid, 1979), 1525–1611.

34. E. Sáez (ed.), *Colección documental del Archivo de la Catedral de León (775–1230)*, vol. I, doc. 1 (León, 1987), pp. 3–5.

35. A. C. Floriano, *Diplomática española del periodo astur*, vol. 1 (Oviedo, 1949).

36. Collins, *Arab Conquest*, pp. 201–7.

37. *Chronicle of Albelda*, XV. 9, p. 174.

38. C. García de Castro Valdés, *Arqueología cristiana de la Alta Edad Media en Asturias* (Oviedo, 1995).

39. J. Pérez de Urbel and R. del Arco y Garay, *España cristiana: comienzo de la Reconquista (711–1038)*, vol. VI of R. Menéndez Pidal (ed.), *Historia de España* (Madrid, 1956), pp. 47–51; C. Sánchez-Albornoz, 'La restauración del orden gótico en el palacio y en la iglesia', in his *Orígenes de la nación española*, vol. 2 (Oviedo, 1974), pp. 623–39.

40. Einhard, *Vita Karoli*, xvi.

41. *Chronicle of Albelda*, XV. 9, p. 174; no mention is made of this in the *Chronicle of Alfonso III*.

42. R. Collins, *The Basques* (2nd edn, Oxford, 1990), pp. 134–71.

43. C. Sánchez-Albornoz, 'Problemas de la Historia Navarra del siglo IX', *Cuadernos de Historia de España*, 25/6 (1957), 5–82.

44. A. Cañada Juste, 'Los Banu Qasi (714–924)', *Príncipe de Viana*, 41 (1980), 5–95.

45. P. Stafford, *Unification and Conquest: a Political and Social History of England in the Tenth and Eleventh Centuries* (London, 1989), pp. 24–44.

46. *Chronicle of Alfonso III*, ch. 23, pp. 142–43; J. E. Casariego, 'Una revolución asturiana en el siglo IX: el interregno del conde Nepociano', *Boletín del Instituto de Estudios Asturianos*, 68 (1969), 4–29, who unlike the medieval compilers of the Asturian regnal lists does not recognise Nepotian as a legitimate if short-reigned king.

47. For recent excavations on Monte Naranco see A. Arbeiter and S. Noack-Haley, *Asturische Königsbauten des 9. Jahrhunderts* (Mainz, 1994).

48. H. Kennedy, *Muslim Spain and Portugal* (London, 1996), pp. 63–81.

49. C. Sánchez-Albornoz, 'El tercer rey de España', *Cuadernos de Historia de España*, 49/50 (1969), 5–49.

50. J. Valdeón Baruque, 'Evolución histórica del reinado de Alfonso III', in F. J. Fernández Conde (ed.), *La época de Alfonso III y San Salvador de Valdedíos* (Oviedo, 1994), pp. 19–26.

51. J. Pérez de Urbel, *Sampiro, su crónica y la monarquía leonesa en el siglo X* (Madrid, 1957), pp. 437–84 for documents relating to various bishops and notaries called Sampiro.

52. P. Linehan, *History and the Historians of Medieval Spain* (Oxford, 1993), pp. 125–31.

53. R. Collins, '*Sicut lex Gothorum continet*: Law and Charters in Ninth- and Tenth-Century León and Catalonia', *English Historical Review*, 100 (1985), 489–512.

54. On the city of León in the tenth century see C. Sánchez-Albornoz, *Una ciudad de la España cristiana hace mil años* (Madrid, 1976).

55. C. Baliñas, *Defensores e traditores: un modelo de relación entre poder monárquico e oligarquía na Galicia altomedieval (718–1037)* (Santiago de Compostela, 1988), pp. 57–84; A. Isla Frez, *La sociedad gallega en la Alta Edad Media* (Madrid, 1992), pp. 129–202.

56. A. Herrero Alonso, *Voces de origen vasco en la geografía castellana* (Bilbao, 1977).

57. A process described in detail in J. Pérez de Urbel, *Historia del Condado de Castilla* (Madrid, 1945), vol. 1, and documented in vol. 3.

58. Ibid., vol. 2.
59. See vol. 3 of the 1945 edition of Pérez de Urbel, *Condado de Castilla* (note 57 above); these texts are not included in the 1969 reprint.
60. Kennedy, *Muslim Spain*, pp. 82–97.
61. J. Rodríguez, *Ramiro II Rey de León* (Madrid, 1972), pp. 339–90.
62. G. Martínez Díez, 'Los fueros leoneses: 1017–1336', in J. M. Fernández Catón (ed.), *El Reino de León en la Alta Edad Media*, vol. 1: *Cortes, concilios y fueros* (León, 1988), pp. 285–352.
63. G. Martínez Díez, *Fueros locales en el territorio de la Provincia de Burgos* (Burgos, 1982), pp. 11–116.
64. R. Collins, 'Visigothic Law and Regional Custom in Disputes in Early Medieval Spain', in W. Davies and P. Fouracre (eds), *The Settlement of Disputes in Early Medieval Europe* (Cambridge, 1986), pp. 85–104.
65. V. Aguliar and F. R. Mediano, 'Antroponomía de origen árabe en la documentación leonesa, sigloo VIII–XIII', *El Reino de León en la alta Edad Media*, vol. 6 (1994), pp. 499–633.
66. Rodríguez, *Ramiro II*, pp. 391–507.
67. J. Rodríguez Fernández, *Reyes de León: García I, Ordoño II, Fruela II, Alfonso IV* (Burgos, 1997), pp. 137–88 for the reign of Fruela II.
68. Sampiro, *Chronica*, 20, ed. Pérez de Urbel, pp. 318–9.
69. Ibn Hayyan, *al-Muqtabis*, V. 233, tr. M. J. Viguera and F. Corriente, *Crónica del Califa 'Abdarrahman III an-Nasir entre los años 912 y 942* (Zaragoza, 1981), pp. 258–60.
70. Rodríguez, *Ramiro II*, pp. 74–76 and 105–32; idem, *Reyes de León*, pp. 210–23.
71. Rodríguez, *Ramiro II*, pp. 405–17; idem, *Ordoño III* (León, 1982), pp. 59–64.
72. J. Rodríguez Fernández, *Sancho I y Ordoño IV, Reyes de León* (León, 1987), pp. 137–57.
73. Rodríguez, *Sancho I y Ordoño IV*, pp. 170–85.
74. R. Collins 'Queens-Dowager and Queens-Regent in Tenth-Century León and Navarre', in J. C. Parsons (ed.), *Medieval Queenship* (New York, 1993), pp. 79–92.
75. Ibid. pp. 87–91.
76. Sampiro, *Chronica*, 27, ed. Pérez de Urbel, pp. 338–9.
77. Ibid. 29, pp. 342–3.
78. On the reign of Alfonso V see J. M. Fernández del Pozo, 'Alfonso V, Rey de León', in J. M. Fernández Catón (ed.), *León y su Historia*, vol. 5 (León, 1984), pp. 11–262.

18 'THE DISSENSION OF KINGS'

1. *Annales Xantenses*, s.a. 862.
2. See in general T. Reuter, *Germany in the Early Middle Ages 800–1056* (London, 1991), pp. 45–111; further bibliographical guidance can be obtained from E. Hlawitschka, *Vom Frankenreich zur Formierung der europäischen Staaten- und Völkergemeinschaft 840–1046: ein Studienbuch* (Darmstadt, 1986), pp. 239–87.

3. For the *Annales Bertiniani* (henceforth AB) see J. L. Nelson, 'The *Annals of St Bertin*', in M. T. Gibson and J. L. Nelson (eds), *Charles the Bald: Court and Kingdom* (2nd edn, Aldershot, 1990), pp. 23–40.
4. Ibid.; also J. M. Wallace-Hadrill, 'History in the Mind of Archbishop Hincmar', in R. H. C. Davis and J. M. Wallace-Hadrill (eds), *The Writing of History in the Middle Ages* (Oxford, 1981), pp. 43–70.
5. See the introduction to T. Reuter (tr.), *The Annals of Fulda* (Manchester, 1992), pp. 1–14.
6. H. Löwe, 'Studien zu den Annales Xantenses', *Deutsches Archiv*, 8 (1950), 59–99.
7. On this author, writing *c*. 908, see H. Löwe, 'Regino von Prüm und das historische Weltbild der Karolingerzeit', in W. Lammers (ed.), *Geschichtsdenken und Geschichtsbild im Mittelalter* (Darmstadt, 1961), pp. 91–134.
8. *Annales Xantenses*, s.a. 869; Louis the German is *sapientior et iustior caeteris*, whereas Charles in his dealings with the Vikings *semper* [*que*] *eis censum opponens et numquam in bello victor existens*.
9. F. L. Ganshof, 'Notes critiques sur Eginhard, biographe de Charlemagne', *Revue belge de philologie et d'histoire*, 3 (1924), 725–58, and idem, 'Eginhard, biographe de Charlemagne', *Bibliothèque d'humanisme et renaissance*, 13 (1951), 217–30, with good discussion of the previous literature. W. S. M. Nicoll, 'Some Passages in Einhard's *Vita Karoli* in Relation to Suetonius', *Medium Aevum*, 44 (1975), 117–20 suggests that Einhard was constricted by his fidelity to his literary model, but M. S. Kempshall, 'Some Ciceronian Models for Einhard's Life of Charlemagne', *Viator*, 26 (1995), 11–37 uncovers other literary debts.
10. On the two *Lives* see E. Tremp, 'Thegan und Astronomus, die beiden Geschichtsschreiber Ludwigs des Frommen', in P. Godman and R. Collins (eds), *Charlemagne's Heir: New Perspectives on the Reign of Louis the Pious* (Oxford, 1990), pp. 691–700, and idem, *Die Überlieferung der Vita Hludowici imperatoris des Astronomus* (Hanover, 1991), as well as his edition of both works in *MGH SRG*, vol. 64 (1995).
11. F. L. Ganshof, 'La fin du regne de Charlemagne. Une décomposition', *Zeitschrift für Schweizerische Geschichte*, 28 (1948), 533–52, which is challenged by the optimism of P. D. King, *Charlemagne* (London, 1986), pp. 45–7.
12. P. Classen, 'Karl der Grosse und die Thronfolge im Frankenreich', *Festschrift für Hermann Heimpel* (Göttingen, 1972), vol. 2, pp. 109–34, who sees the 781 coronations as the first step towards the *Divisio* of 806. However, the eldest son Charles received no royal title or realm at any stage prior to the *Divisio*.
13. *MGH Capit.*, vol. I, ed. A. Boretius, no. 45. L. Halphen, *Charlemagne et l'empire carolingien* (reprint, Paris, 1968), pp. 124–6.
14. R. Folz, *The Coronation of Charlemagne* (English tr., London, 1974), pp. 167–71.
15. ARF, s.a. 810, 811, 813.
16. Thegan, *Vita Hludovici imperatoris*, 6.

17. R. Schieffer, 'Ludwig "der Fromme". Zur Entstehung eines karolingischen Herrscherbeinamens', *Frühmittelalterliche Studien*, 16 (1982), 58–73.

18. ARF, s.a. 816; T. F. X. Noble, *The Republic of St. Peter: the Birth of the Papal State, 680–825* (Philadelphia, 1984), pp. 202–3, 298–308.

19. *MGH Capit.*, vol. I, no. 136; see F. L. Ganshof, 'Oservations sur l'*Ordinatio Imperii* de 817', in *Festschrift für Guido Kisch* (Stuttgart, 1955), pp. 15–31 for an alternative view.

20. J. Fridh, 'Ludwig der Fromme, das Papsttum und die fränkische Kirche', in Godman and Collins, *Charlemagne's Heir*, pp. 231–73; Noble, *Republic of St. Peter*, pp. 256–324, who prefers to see it as 'an alliance'.

21. ARF, s.a. 823 and 824; see the discussion of this episode in Noble, *Republic of St. Peter*, pp. 308–12.

22. ARF, s.a. 827.

23. ARF, s.a. 817: a covered arcade leading from the palace chapel collapsed on the emperor and his suite on Maundy Thursday.

24. See in general H. Wolfram, 'Lateinische Herrschertitel im neunten und zehnten Jahrhundert', in idem (ed.), *Intitulatio*, II (Vienna, 1973), pp. 19–178 (MIöG, vol. XXIV).

25. E. Boshof, 'Einheitsidee und Teilungsprinzip in der Regierungszeit Ludwigs des Frommen', in Godman and Collins (eds), *Charlemagne's Heir*, pp. 161–89.

26. ARF, s.a. 818 and 819. Thegan, *Vita Hludovici*, 25 and 26.

27. ARF, s.a. 817.

28. For a view of Theodulf as being driven into conspiring with Bernard by the provisions of the *Ordinatio* see T. F. X. Noble, 'The Revolt of King Bernard of Italy in 817: Its Causes and Consequences', *Studi Medievali*, 15 (1974), 315–26, but cf. the argument of P. Godman, 'Louis "the Pious" and his poets', *Frühmittelalterliche Studien*, 19 (1985), especially pp. 245–8.

29. ARF, s.a. 817. Thegan, *Vita Hludovici*, 22–3.

30. J. Jarnut, 'Ludwig der Fromme, Lothar I und das Regnum Italiae', in Godman and Collins, *Charlemagne's Heir*, pp. 349–62.

31. Halphen, *Charlemagne et l'empire carolingien*, pp. 199–201.

32. The novel or positive elements that Ganshof detected in his 'Louis the Pious reconsidered' almost all relate to the period of the ascendancy of Benedict of Aniane. See also F. L. Ganshof, 'A propos de la politique de Louis le Pieux avant la crise de 830', *Revue belge d'archéologie et d'histoire de l'art*, 37 (1968), 37–48, and J. Semmler, '*Renovatio Regni Francorum*: Die Herrschaft Ludwigs des Frommen im Frankenreich 814–829/30', in Godman and Collins, *Charlemagne's Heir*, pp. 125–46.

33. ARF, s.a. 821; L. Weinrich, *Wala, Mönch, Graf und Rebel: Die Biographie eines Karolingers* (Lübeck, 1963), pp. 33–43; on Adalhard see B. Kasten, *Adalhard von Korbie. Die Biographie eines karolingischen Politikers und Klostervorstehers* (Dusseldorf, 1985).

34. ARF, s.a. 822 and 823.

35. Anonymous, *Vita Hludovici*, 35 for the comparison with Theodosius I. See also ARF, s.a. 822.

36. See M. de Jong, 'Power and Humility in Carolingian Society: The Public Penance of Louis the Pious', *Early Medieval Europe*, 1 (1992), pp. 29–52.
37. J. Jarnut, 'Ludwig der Fromme, Lothar I. und das Regnum Italiae', in Godman and Collins, *Charlemagne's Heir*, pp. 349–62.
38. T. Reuter, 'The End of Carolingian Military Expansion', in ibid., pp. 391–405.
39. T. F. X. Noble, 'Louis the Pious and the Frontiers of the Frankish Realm', in ibid., pp. 333–48.
40. ARF, s.a. 814–29.
41. For the developments in Spain and these interpretations see R. Collins, *The Arab Conquest of Spain, 710–797* (Oxford, 1989), pp. 113–40, 168–216.
42. J. M. Salrach, *El procés de formació nacional de Catalunya (segles VIII–IX)* (2nd edn, 2 vols, Barcelona, 1981), vol. I, pp. 27–50.
43. ARF, s.a. 826 and 827; Anonymous, *Vita Hludovici*, 40–1. Salrach, *El procés*, vol. I, pp. 73–90.
44. ARF, s.a. 828 and 829. For the suggestion that the fall of Hugh and Matfried was deliberately planned see R. Collins, 'Pippin I and the Kingdom of Aquitaine', in Godman and Collins (eds), *Charlemagne's Heir*, especially pp. 377–81.
45. Anonymous, *Vita Hludovici*, 43–5; Thegan, *Vita Hludovici*, 36; *Annales Bertiniani*, s.a. 830.
46. Nithard, *Historiae*, I. 3.
47. *Annales Bertiniani*, s.a. 830; Anonymous, *Vita Hludovici*, 45.
48. Thegan, *Vita Hludovici*, 36; also Paschasius Radbertus, *Epitaphium Arsenii*; translated in A. Cabaniss, *Charlemagne's Cousins* (Syracuse, NY, 1967), pp. 83–204. See D. Ganz, 'The *Epitaphium Arsenii* and Opposition to Louis the Pious', in Godman and Collins (eds), *Charlemagne's Heir*, pp. 537–50.
49. *Annales Bertiniani*, s.a. 831–3; Anonymous, *Vita Hludovici*, 46–9; Collins, 'Pippin I and the Kingdom of Aquitaine', in Godman and Collins (eds), *Charlemagne's Heir*, especially pp. 383–6.
50. Anonymous, *Vita Hludovici*, 49–52; *Annales Bertiniani*, s.a. 833–4.
51. Anonymous, *Vita Hludovici*, 52–3.
52. An optimistic view of this period is taken by J. Nelson, 'The Last Years of Louis the Pious', in Godman and Collins (eds), *Charlemagne's Heir*, pp. 147–60.
53. Collins, 'Pippin I and the Kingdom of Aquitaine', ibid., pp. 386–9. See also J. Martindale, 'Charles the Bald and the Government of the Kingdom of Aquitaine', in Gibson and Nelson, *Charles the Bald*, pp. 115–38. See ch. 18 below for some of the later adventures of Pippin II.
54. *Annales Bertiniani*, s.a. 839; Nithard, *Historiae*, I. 7.
55. *Annales Bertiniani*, s.a. 840; Anonymous, *Vita Hludovici*, 62–4. For a more enthusiastic view of the reign than that offered here see T. Schieffer, 'Die Krise des karolingischen Imperiums', in *Aus Mittelalter und Neuzeit* (Bonn, 1957), pp. 1–15 (no notes), and by F. L. Ganshof, 'Louis the Pious Reconsidered', *History*, 42 (1957), 171–80; Ganshof

himself became less enthusiastic about Louis personally in his subsequent publications.

56. E. Boshof, 'Einheitsidee und Teilungsprinzip in der Regierungzeit Ludwigs des Frommen', in Godman and Collins (eds), *Charlemagne's Heir*, pp. 161–89; idem, *Erzbischof Agobard von Lyon: Leben uncle Werk* (Cologne, 1969).
57. J. M. Wallace-Hadrill, *The Frankish Church* (Oxford, 1983), pp. 268–74.
58. D. M. Metcalf, 'A Sketch of the Currency in the time of Charles the Bald', in Gibson and Nelson, *Charles the Bald* (2nd edn), pp. 65–97.
59. Nithard, *Historiae*, II. 1–4; *Annales Bertiniani*, s.a. 840–1.
60. Nithard, *Historiae*, II. 9–10.
61. Nithard, *Historiae*, III. 5.
62. F. L. Ganshof, 'Zur Entstehungsgeschichte und Bedeutung des Vertrages von Verdun (843)', *Deutsches Archiv*, 12 (1956), 313–30, English tr. 'The Genesis and Significance of the Treaty of Verdun', in idem, *The Carolingians and the Frankish Monarchy* (London, 1971), pp. 289–302.
63. J. L. Nelson, 'Public *Histories* and Private History in the Work of Nithard', *Speculum*, 60 (1985), 251–93.
64. For discussion of the dating see Nelson, 'Public *Histories*', app. 2.
65. Martindale, 'Charles the Bald and the Government of the Kingdom of Aquitaine', in Gibson and Nelson, *Charles the Bald*, pp. 135–8 tabulates documentary references to the presence of the Carolingian kings in Aquitaine up to 854.
66. *Annales Bertiniani*, s.a. 853; *Annales Fuldenses*, s.a. 853; for this part of his reign see J. L. Nelson, *Charles the Bald* (London, 1992), pp. 160–89.
67. *Annales Bertiniani*, s.a. 854; see chapter 18 below for Pippin's dealings with the Vikings.
68. *Annales Bertiniani* s.a. 856 and 858; *Annales Fuldenses*, s.a. 858.
69. J. Devisse, *Hincmar, Archevêque de Reims 845–882* (3 vols, Geneva, 1975) vol. I, pp. 281–366; C. Brühl, 'Hinkmariana', *Deutsches Archiv*, 20 (1964) 55–77.
70. *Annales Fuldenses*, s.a. 870.
71. K. F. Werner, '*Missus–Marchio–Comes*. Entre l'administration centrale et l'administration locale de l'empire carolingien', in W. Paravicini and K. F. Werner (eds), *Histoire comparée de l'administration* (Frankfurt, 1980) pp. 193–239.
72. *Annales Bertiniani*, s.a. 858; see Nelson, *Charles the Bald*, pp. 183–7 and 194–7.
73. *Annales Bertiniani*, s.a. 844 (a papal anointing as king) and 850.
74. *Annales Bertiniani*, s.a. 875–6.
75. *Annales Bertiniani*, s.a. 876–7; *Annales Fuldenses*, s.a. 876–7 for an eastern Frankish account of these events.
76. John VIII, *epp.* 1, 8, 22, 23, 27, 32, 56, 63.
77. Halphen, *Charlemagne et l'empire carolingien*, pp. 379–83. See John VIII, *epp.* 193, 205, 220, 221, 224, 225, 251, 257 for appeals to sundry Carolingians, and eventual concentration on Charles the Fat.

78. *Annales Vedastini*, s.a. 882, 884, 893.
79. Halphen, *Charlemagne et l'empire carolingien*, pp. 327–42; see also Devisse, *Hincmar*, vol. I, pp. 369–459.
80. *Annales Bertiniani*, s.a. 882; *Annales Vedastini*, s.a. 880 and 882, *Annales Fuldenses*, s.a. 880 and 882. On the historical writing of this period see H. Löwe, 'Geschichtschreibung der ausgehenden Karolingerzeit', *Deutsches Archiv*, 23 (1967), 1–30.
81. Regino of Prüm, *Chronica*, s.a. 881; Halphen, *Charlemagne et l'empire carolingien*, pp. 383–9.
82. Notker Balbulus, *Gesta Karoli Magni*, 11 and 14.
83. The epic poem *Bella Parisiacae urbis*, written by the monk Abbo of Saint-Germain-des Prés before 897, provides the fullest account of the Siege. (See Bibliography.) For the background see chapter 18 below.
84. *Annales Fuldenses*, s.a. 887; Halphen, *Charlemagne et l'empire carolingien*, pp. 398–400.
85. On these two see J. Fleckenstein, *Die Hofkapelle der deutschen Könige* (Stuttgart, 1959), vol. 1, pp. 185–200.
86. Reuter, *Germany in the Early Middle Ages*, pp. 119–20.
87. *Annales Fuldenses*, s.a 887.
88. *Annales Fuldenses*, s.a. 888.
89. *Annales Vedastini*, s.a. 887. cf. Regino of Prüm, *Chronica*, s.a. 887 and 888; *Annales Fuldenses*, s.a. 887. On the causes of the fall of Charles the Fat see H. Keller, 'Zum Sturz Karls III', *Deutsches Archiv*, 22 (1966), 333–84, and E. Hlawitschka, 'Die lotharische Blutslinie und der Sturz Karls III', reprinted in idem (ed.), *Königswahl und Thronfolge in fränkisch-karolingischer Zeit* (Darmstadt, 1975), pp. 495–547.
90. *Annales Fuldenses*, s.a. 887.
91. Regino of Prüm, *Chronica*, s.a. 888.
92. On Lothar's divorce see P. R. McKeon, *Hincmar of Laon and Carolingian Politics* (Urbana, 1978), pp. 39–56.
93. C. Wickham, *Early Medieval Italy: Central Power and Local Society, 400–1000* (London, 1981), pp. 169–74.
94. *Annales Fuldenses*, s.a. 893, 895, 896; Regino of Prüm, *Chronica*, s.a. 896; see G. Arnaldi, 'Papa Formoso e gli imperatori della case di Spoleto', *Annali della Facolta di Lettere di Napoli*, 1 (1951), 84–104.
95. J. Duhr, 'Le concile de Ravenne en 898: la rehabilitation du pape Formose', *Recherches de science réligieuse*, 22 (1932), 541–79.
96. E. Hlawitschka, *Vom Frankenreich zur Formierung der europäischen Staatenund Völkergemeinschaft, 840–1046* (Darmstadt, 1986), pp. 76–96.
97. For Charles the Simple see A. Eckel, *Charles le Simple* (Paris 1899), and J. Dunbabin, *France in the Making, 843–1180* (Oxford, 1985), pp. 30–36.
98. Dunbabin, *France in the Making*, pp. 27–43; R. McKitterick, *The Frankish Kingdoms under the Carolingians* (London, 1983), pp. 305–36; see also B. Schneidmuller, *Karolingische Tradition und frühes französischen Monarchie im 10. Jahrhundert* (Wiesbaden, 1979).
99. Hlawitschka, *Vom Frankenreich*, pp. 264–6 for a bibliography of works relating to this subject.

100. E. Bourgeois, *Le Capitulaire de Kiersy-sur-Oise (877)* (Paris, 1885), especially pp. 127–54, argued that this capitulary institutionalised hereditary office holding, but see Halphen, *Charlemagne et l'empire carolingien*, pp. 371–4, 411–21.

101. *Annales Bertiniani*, s.a. 879, 880, 881; for his death in 887 see *Annales Fuldenses*, s.a. 887.

102. J. Dhondt, *Etudes sur la naissance des principautés térritoriales en France (IXe–Xe siècles)* (Bruges, 1948); Dunbabin, *France in the Making*, pp. 44–100.

103. See, *inter alia*, M. Wood, 'The Making of King Æthelstan's Empire: an English Charlemagne?', in P. Wormald, D. Bullough and R. Collins (eds), *Ideal and Reality in Frankish and Anglo-Saxon Society* (Oxford, 1983), pp. 250–72.

19 'THE DESOLATION OF THE PAGANS'

1. *Anglo-Saxon Chronicle*, s.a. 793 ('E' or Laud version); *Historia Dunelmensis Ecclesiae*, v.

2. For a more balanced view of the Vikings see J. M. Wallace-Hadrill, *The Vikings in Francia* (Reading, 1974), reprinted in his *Early Medieval History* (Oxford, 1975), pp. 217–36.

3. For an overview of recent historiography and its controversies see C. P. Wormald, 'Viking Studies: Whence and Whither?', in R. T. Farrell (ed.), *The Vikings* (Chichester, 1982), pp. 128–53.

4. P. H. Sawyer, *Kings and Vikings: Scandinavia and Europe, 700–1100* (London, 1982), pp. 8–38.

5. For these see C. W. Thompson, *Studies in Upplandic Runography* (Austin, 1975), and S. B. F. Jansson, *The Runes of Sweden* (English tr., London, 1962).

6. For its primary association with the inhabitants of the region of Viken, see S. Hellberg, 'Vikingatidens *vikingar*', *Archiv fot nordisk filologi*, 95 (1980), 25–88; for the modern usage see Sawyer, *Kings and Vikings*, p. 1.

7. D. Ó Corráin, *Ireland before the Normans* (Dublin, 1972), pp. 80–1 is categoric on the role of overpopulation, but greater caution is indicated: Sawyer, *Kings and Vikings*, pp. 67–9.

8. S. Lebecq, *Marchands et navigateurs frisons du haut moyen âge* (2 vols, Lille, 1983), vol. I, pp. 165–224 for eighth century shipping and navigation.

9. For some discussion of Viking motivation see G. Jones, *A History of the Vikings* (Oxford, 1968), pp. 182–203.

10. Except in Ireland where inter-kingdom warfare, including the destruction of churches, was almost unending: Ó Corráin, *Ireland before the Normans*, pp. 85–8.

11. *Anglo-Saxon Chronicle*, s.a. 787 (*recte* 789) – only in the 'A' or Parker version.

12. Alcuin, *Epistolae*, 20. tr. H. R. Loyn and J. Percival, *The Reign of Charlemagne* (London, 1975) p. 110.

13. See J. Hines, *The Scandinavian Character of Anglian England in the pre-Viking Period* (Oxford, 1984), and idem, 'The Scandinavian Character of Anglian England: an update', in M. Carver (ed.), *The Age of Sutton Hoo* (Woodbridge, 1992), pp. 315–29.

14. M. Wheeler, *Rome beyond the Imperial Frontiers* (London, 1954), pp. 26–47, 83–117; Sawyer, *Kings and Vikings*, pp. 65–8.

15. R. Bruce-Mitford, 'The Sutton Hoo Ship-Burial: Comments on General Interpretation' (1949), reprinted in his *Aspects of Anglo-Saxon Archaeology* (London, 1974), discusses the Swedish connections on pp. 47–60. For still pertinent doubts as to the royal status of the burial see J. M. Wallace-Hadrill, 'The Graves of Kings: An Historical Note on some Archaeological Evidence', reprinted in his *Early Medieval History* (Oxford, 1975), pp. 39–59, and see J. Campbell, 'The Impact of the Sutton Hoo Discovery on the Study of Anglo-Saxon History', in C. B. Kendall and P. S. Wells (eds), *Voyage to the Other World: the Legacy of Sutton Hoo* (Minneapolis, 1992), pp. 79–101.

16. For Dorestad see W. A. Van Es and W. J. H. Verwers, *Excavations at Dorestad*, vol. I (Amersfoort, 1980), also S. Lebecq, *Marchands et navigateurs frisons du haut moyen âge* (2 vols, Lille, 1983), vol. I, pp. 139–63.

17. R. Hodges and D. Whitehouse, *Mohammed, Charlemagne and the Origins of Europe* (London, 1983), pp. 93–101; R. Hodges, *The Anglo-Saxon Achievement* (London, 1989), pp. 69–114.

18. D. M. Wilson, *Civil and Military Engineering in Viking Age Scandinavia* (Basildon, 1978), pp. 3–6.

19. ARF, s.a. 808.

20. Ibid.

21. ARF and *Annales Bertiniani* under these years.

22. Attempts have been made to locate some of these men in their Scandinavian contexts, but as this largely depends on the use of later saga or legendary-historical materials, they have rarely convinced: see A. P. Smyth, *Scandinavian Kings in the British Isles, 850–880* (Oxford, 1977), pp. 17–100.

23. Jones, *History of the Vikings*, pp. 86–9, and note 1 on p. 89.

24. Sawyer, *Kings and Vikings*, pp. 46–56.

25. For the eastward expansion of the Vikings see pp. 387–9 below.

26. Sawyer, *Kings and Vikings*, pp. 39–42 for slaves and freedmen.

27. Good examples to be found in *Orkneyinga Saga*: 105–6, tr. H. Pálsson and P. Edwards (Harmondsworth, 1981), pp. 214–15.

28. For example *Annals of Ulster*, ed. S. MacAirt and G. MacNiocaill (Dublin, 1983), s.a. 780, 783, 784, 788, 789, 790, and so on.

29. Ibid., s.a. 802, 806 (68 killed), 807; see also *Argyll: an Inventory of the Monuments*, vol. 4, *Iona* (Edinburgh, 1982), pp. 47–8.

30. R. Ernst, *Die Nordwestslaven und das frankische Reich* (Berlin, 1976), pp. 110–87.

31. ARF, s.a. 802, 804.

32. Ibid., s.a. 809, 810.

33. Ermoldus Nigellus, *In Honorem Hludovici Augusti*, II. 2167–513; on the significance of the emperor as godfather see A. Angenendt,

Kaiserherrschaft und Königstaufe. Kaiser, Könige und Papste als geistliche Patröne in der abendlandischen Missionsgeschichte (Berlin, 1984).

34. *Annales Bertiniani*, s.a. 834, 835, 836.
35. Sawyer, *Kings and Vikings*, pp. 82–3; ASB, s.a. 837.
36. *Annales Bertiniani*, s.a. 841, 842.
37. Ibid., s.a. 844–8; for the Spanish raid see W. E. D. Allen, *The Poet and the Spae-Wife* (Dublin, 1960), pp. 1–13, and E. Lévi-Provençal, *Histoire de l'Espagne musulmane* (Leiden, 1950), vol. I, pp. 218–25.
38. *Annales Bertiniani*, s.a. 845.
39. Ibid., s.a. 847, 848.
40. Ibid., s.a. 852–8.
41. For Viking use of islands see *Anglo-Saxon Chronicle*, s.a. 832, 855 (Sheppey), s.a. 853, 865 (Thanet), AB s.a. 847, 850, 859 (Batavia) cf. s.a. 859 Vikings in the Rhône: 'in insula quae Camarias dicitur sedes ponunt'.
42. *Annales Bertiniani*, s.a. 858.
43. On the slave trade in this period see C. Verlinden, *L'ésclavage dans l'Europe médiévale*, vol. I (Brugge, 1955), pp. 181–247.
44. *Annals of Ulster*, s.a. 845, for other examples of prominent captives see s.a. 831, 832, 840 and so on.
45. Ó Corráin, *Ireland before the Normans*, pp. 89–93.
46. For some of the consequences of all this see D. A. Binchy, 'The Passing of the Old Order', in B. Ó Cuív (ed.), *The Impact of the Scandinavian Invasions on the Celtic-speaking Peoples c. 800–1100 A.D.* (Dublin, 1975), pp. 119–32.
47. This is largely a question of what weight to put on negative evidence. It has been suggested that Bordeaux was abandoned by the late ninth century, but is this a fair deduction from what is no more than an absence of evidence to show that it did still function? Archaeology cannot always help: there are still no certain traces of pre-Norman Dublin, but plenty of documentary references to its existence.
48. See A. P. Smyth, *Scandinavian York and Dublin*, vol. I (Dublin, 1975).
49. *MGH Capit.*, vol. II, no. 280, p. 354.
50. *Annales Vedastini*, s.a. 879.
51. AB, s.a. 880, 881, 882; *Annales Vedastini*, s.a. 879–82.
52. For other inconsequential victories over Vikings see *Annales Vedastini*, s.a. 882, 888, 891.
53. *Annales Vedastini*, s.a. 893–8. A. Eckel, *Charles le Simple* (Paris, 1899), pp. 1–29.
54. *Annales Vedastini*, s.a. 897, 898.
55. R. H. Bautier, 'L'historiographie en France aux X et XI siècles', in *Settimane di studi sull' Alto Medioevo*, 17 (Spoleto, 1970), 793–850; see also the introduction to Latouche's edition of Richer.
56. On the agreement of 911 see A. Eckel, *Charles le Simple* (Paris, 1899), pp. 64–90. On Richer and his work see the introduction to Latouche's edition, and the bibliography there cited on pp. xvi–xvii.
57. Richer, *Historia*, I. 28–33; Flodoard, *Annales*, s.a. 921.
58. D. Bates, *Normandy before 1066* (London, 1982), pp. 2–43 for the tenth century. Rollo and his successors are attributed with a variety

of titles in the sources: normally that of count, occasionally that of *princeps* or prince, and sometimes that of duke.

59. Anonymous, *Vita Hludovici imperatoris*, 40; *Annales Bertiniani*, s.a. 852.
60. *Annales Vedastini*, s.a. 882.
61. ASC – 'A' or Parker version – s.a. 832, 839. The chronology of the ASC is normally three years out in its dating of the events of this period.
62. Ibid., s.a. 835; the chronicler calls them 'Danes', but all Vikings were Danes to the scribes of Alfred's time.
63. ASC (Parker version), s.a. 837, 845, 851 (*recte* 840, 848, 850).
64. Ibid., s.a. 833, 837, 838, 839, 840 (*recte* 836, 840, 841, 842, 843).
65. N. Brooks, *The Early History of the Church of Canterbury* (Leicester, 1984), pp. 30–1, 49, 150–2.
66. *Annales Bertiniani*, s.a. 865.
67. ASC, s.a. 867; *Historia Regum*, p. 106.
68. ASC, s.a. 868, 869, 870 (*recte* 867, 868, 869); for a controversial discussion of the killing of King (St) Edmund, see Smyth, *Scandinavian Kings*, pp. 201–13; for pertinent methodological criticisms see R. Frank, 'Viking Atrocity and Skaldic Verse: the Rite of the Blood-Eagle', *English Historical Review*, 99 (1984), 332–43.
69. ASC, s.a. 871, 872 (*recte* 870, 871). For Alfred's wars in the early 870s see A. P. Smyth, *King Alfred the Great* (Oxford, 1995), pp. 51–66
70. *Historia Dunelmensis Ecclesiae*, p. 56; ASC, s.a. 874.
71. ASC, s.a. 875, 876 (*recte* 874–6); see Smyth, *Scandinavian Kings*, pp. 255–66 (with reservations as to the use of late sources).
72. ASC, s.a. 877.
73. ASC, s.a. 877.
74. ASC, s.a. 878; D. Whitelock, *The Importance of the Battle of Edington A.D. 878* (Westbury, 1977); Smyth, *Alfred the Great*, pp. 66–98.
75. P. Stafford, *The East Midlands in the Early Middle Ages* (Leicester, 1985) provides the best discussion of Viking settlement in that region.
76. G. Fellows Jensen, *Scandinavian Settlement Names in Yorkshire* (Copenhagen, 1972), and idem, 'The Vikings in England: a Review', *Anglo-Saxon England*, 4 (1975), 181–206. See also F. M. Stenton, 'The Danes in England', *Proceedings of the British Academy*, 13 (1927), 203–46, and A. L. Binns, *The Viking Century in East Yorkshire* (Beverley, 1963), pp. 35–52.
77. ASC, MS 'D' (B. L. Cotton Tiberius B iv), s.a. 901 (*recte* 899).
78. For the Viking kingdom in the north, from 867 to 954, see Smyth, *Scandinavian York and Dublin*, vols I and II (Dublin, 1975–9).
79. F. L. Attenborough, *The Laws of the Earliest English Kings* (Cambridge, 1922), pp. 98–101; for the frontier see R. H. C. Davis, 'Alfred and Guthrum's Frontier', *English Historical Review*, 97 (1982), 803–10.
80. Usefully described in S. Keynes and M. Lapidge, *Alfred the Great* (Harmondsworth, 1983), pp. 23–41.
81. ASC, s.a. 879, 880. For the view of the army in the Thames as recently arrived see Asser, *Vita Alfredi*, 58.
82. *Annales Vedastini*, s.a. 892.

83. Regino of Prüm, *Chronica*, s.a. 867, 874; see F. Amory, 'The Viking Hastings in Franco-Scandinavian Legend', in M. H. King and W. M. Stevens (eds), *Saints, Scholars and Heroes*, vol. II (Collegeville, Minn., 1979), pp. 265–86.

84. ASC, s.a. 893–7 (*recte* 892–6); on this war see Smyth, *Alfred the Great*, pp. 117–46.

85. P. Stafford, *Unification and Conquest* (London, 1989), pp. 25–9 for a discussion of the evidence.

86. For the Vikings in Ireland in this period see Ó Corráin, *Ireland before the Normans*, pp. 80–110.

87. *MGH Epp.* VI, no. 16, p. 163.

88. For an assessment (perhaps overly critical?) of this work see I. Wood, 'Christians and Pagans in Ninth Century Scandinavia', in B. Sawyer *et al.* (eds), *The Christianization of Scandinavia* (Alingsås, 1987), pp. 36–67. This also provides a useful discussion of the relationship between mission and politics in this period.

89. P. Sawyer, 'The Process of Scandinavian Christianization in the Tenth and Eleventh Centuries', in ibid., pp. 68–87.

90. Ibid., pp. 70–3 on this and other indications of Christian influence in Norway in the mid-tenth century.

91. ASC, s.a. 905 (*recte* 904).

92. ASC, 'D' version, s.a. 948. See D. Whitelock, 'The Dealings of the Kings of England with Northumbria in the Tenth and Eleventh Centuries', in P. A. M. Clemoes (ed.), *The Anglo-Saxons* (London, 1959), pp. 70–88.

93. The Emperor Theophilus sent a group of captured *Rhos* to the Frankish ruler Louis the Pious: *Annales Bertiniani*, s.a. 839; see J. Shephard, 'The Rhos guests of Louis the Pious: whence and wherefore?', *Early Medieval Europe*, 4 (1995), 41–60.

94. Continuator of the *Chronicle of Theophanes*, 196; on the eastern movement of the Vikings and their relations with Byzantium see H. R. Ellis Davidson, *The Viking Road to Byzantium* (London, 1976).

95. On whom see D. M. Dunlop, *A History of the Jewish Khazars* (Princeton, 1954). In general for the history of early Russia see S. Franklin and J. Shephard, *The Emergence of Rus 750–1200* (London, 1996), especially ch. 1–4.

96. Franklin and Shephard, *Emergence of Rus*, pp. 112–38.

97. D. Obolensky, *The Byzantine Commonwealth* (London, 1971), pp. 183–5; see also note 98 below.

98. J. Fennell, *A History of the Russian Church to 1448* (London, 1995), pp. 20–44. The principal source, *The Russian Primary Chronicle* (tr. S. H. Cross and O. P. Sherbowitz-Wetzor, Cambridge, Mass., 1973), is both relatively late in date and prone to fictional elaboration of events. It was first compiled in the late eleventh century, and exists now in two slightly later redactions.

99. Adalbert's continuation of the *Chronicle of Regino of Prüm*, s.a. 959.

100. Widukind, *Res gestae Saxonicae*, III. 65; for Olga see Franklin and Shephard, *Emergence of Rus*, pp. 133–9 and 300–3.

20   THE OTTONIAN AGE

1. ARF, s.a. 798, 799.
2. AB, s.a. 840, 850, 869.
3. G. Marçais, 'Aghlabids', in *Encyclopaedia of Islam* (2nd edn, Leiden and London, 1960), vol. I, pp. 247–9.
4. *Liber Pontificalis*, vol. II, pp. 81–2; S. Gibson and B. Ward-Perkins, 'The Surviving Remains of the Leonine Wall', pt I: *Papers of the British School at Rome*, 47 (1979), pp. 30–57; pt II: ibid., 51 (1983), pp. 222–39.
5. F. E. Endgreen, 'Pope John VIII and the Arabs', *Speculum*, 20 (1945), 318–30.
6. R. Jenkins, *Byzantium: the Imperial Centuries AD 610 to 1071* (London, 1966), pp. 185–90.
7. *Constitutum Constantini*, 18: Constantine transferring his *imperium* and his *regni potestas* to the East; 11: *potestas, dignitas, honorificentia imperialis* given to the see of Peter, together with the gift of Constantine's own imperial diadem and robes.
8. Translated Jenkins, *Byzantium: the Imperial Centuries*, p. 190.
9. C. Wickham, *Early Medieval Italy: Central Power and Local Society, 400–1000* (London, 1981), pp. 60–3, with references.
10. John VIII, *ep.* 207.
11. On the conflict between the churches of Rome and Constantinople in this period see F. Dvornik, *The Photian Schism* (Paris, 1950); see also idem, *Byzantium and the Roman Primacy* (2nd edn, New York, 1979), pp. 101–23, which is rather too inclined to play down conflict in the interests of a modern ecumenical ideal.
12. Anastasius Bibliotecarius, *ep.* 5. Cf. the traditional Roman view of the order of precedence in *Constitutum Constantini*, 12.
13. Dvornik, *Photian Schism*, pp. 172–225.
14. A. Toynbee, *Constantine Porphyrogenitus and his World* (Oxford, 1973), pp. 267–8 and note 4 on p. 268.
15. A. Eckel, *Charles le Simple* (Paris, 1899), pp. 91–101.
16. T. Reuter, *Germany in the Early Middle Ages, 800–1056* (London, 1991), p. 130.
17. On Lotharingia see ibid., pp. 153–60.
18. *Vita antiquior Mathildis reginae*, 1, ed. B. Schütte, *MGH SRG*, vol. 66 (1994), pp. 113–4.
19. Discussed in D. C. Jackman, *The Konradiner. A Study in Genealogical Methodology* (Frankfurt am Main, 1990), pp. 78–80.
20. For bibliography on Conrad see E. Hlawitschka, *Vom Frankenreich zur Formierung der europaischen Staaten- und Völkergemeinschaft 840–1046* (Darmstadt, 1986), pp. 278–9.
21. C. R. Bowlus, *Franks, Moravians and Magyars. The Struggle for the Middle Danube, 788–907* (Philadelphia, 1995) for a Moravia centred around the lower Sava, and Martin Eggers, *Das 'Großmährische Reich'. Realität oder Fiktion?* (Stuttgart, 1995) for the Hungarian alternative.
22. Regino of Prüm, *Chronica*, s.a. 889.
23. *Annales Fuldenses*, s.a. 892.

24. *Annales Fuldenses*, s.a. 900–2; Adalbert's continuation of Regino of Prüm, s.a. 907–10 (whose dates in general are one year behind the real ones); on which see K. Hauck, 'Erzhbishof Adalbert von Magdeburg als Geschichtsschreiber', in H. Beumann (ed.), *Festshrift für Walter Schlesinger* (Cologne, 1974), vol. II, pp. 298–305; Widukind of Corvey, *Res Gestae Saxonicae*, I. xx.

25. Adalbert's continuation of Regino, s.a. 913.

26. Adalbert's continuation of Regino, s.a. 919; Thietmar of Merseburg, *Chronica*, I. 8. See in general K. J. Leyser, 'Henry I and the Beginnings of the Saxon Empire', *English Historical Review*, 83 (1968), 1–32.

27. Adalbert's continuation of Regino, s.a. 924; Widukind *Res Gestae Saxonicae*, I. xxxii. On Widukind see H. Beumann 'Historiographische Konzeption und politische Ziele Widukinds von Corvey', *Settimane di studio sull'alto medioevo*, 17 (Spoleto, 1970), pp. 857–94.

28. Widukind, I. xxxviii.

29. G. Ostrogorsky, *History of the Byzantine Empire* (English tr. of 3rd edn, Oxford, 1968), p. 282; see also M. Whittow, *The Making of Orthodox Byzantium, 600–1025* (London, 1996), pp. 235–40 for Byzantium and the Magyars in the ninth century.

30. Adalbert's continuation of Regino, s.a. 938 and 944; Widukind, *Res Gestae Saxonicae*, II xiv, III. xxx, and III. xliv. See K. J. Leyser, 'The Battle at the Lech, 955', *History*, 50 (1965), 1–25.

31. Adalbert's continuation of Regino, s.a. 938, 939; see also K. J. Leyser, 'Otto I and his Saxon Enemies', in his *Rule and Conflict in an Early Medieval Society* (London, 1979), pp. 9–42.

32. Widukind, *Res Gestae Saxonicae*, II. xxiv–xxvi and xxxvi. Adalbert's continuation of Regino, s.a. 947, 950 (for Liudolf).

33. Wickham, *Early Medieval Italy*, pp. 177–83.

34. Liutprand of Cremona, *Antapodosis*, V. xxvii–VI. ii.

35. Adalbert's continuation of Regino, s.a. (correctly) 951.

36. Ibid., s.a. 952, 953; Thietmar of Merseburg, *Chronica*, II. 6–8.

37. *Cambridge Medieval History*, vol. III (Cambridge, 1922), p. 151.

38. On Liutprand see M. Lintzel, *Studien über Liudprand von Cremona* (Berlin, 1933), especially section I for the *Historia Ottonis*.

39. For aspects of Liutprand's reading see the notes to Bauer and Rau's edition (see Bibliography), and also K. Leyser, 'Liudprand of Cremona, Preacher and Homilist', in K. Walsh and D. Wood (eds), *The Bible in the Medieval World* (Oxford, 1985), pp. 43–60; in general the bibliography concerning Lintprand is smaller than it ought to be.

40. See the introduction to J. Becker's edition of Liutprand: *MGH SRG*, pp. xii–xvi.

41. For the Laurentian Schism see J. Moorhead, *Theoderic in Italy* (Oxford, 1992), pp. 114–39; also W. T. Townsend, 'Ennodius and Pope Symmachus', in L. W. Jones (ed.), *Studies in Honor of E. K. Rand* (New York, 1938), pp. 277–91.

42. P. Llewellyn, *Rome in the Dark Ages* (London, 1971), pp. 286–315; a substantial modern study of the tenth century papacy is much to be desired.

43. Liutprand, *Antapodosis*, II. 48. L. Duchesne, 'Serge III et Jean XI', *Mélanges d'archéologie et d'histoire*, 33 (1913), 25–55.
44. See introduction to Bauer and Rau's edition, pp. 235–6.
45. Liutprand, *Antapodosis*, II. 48.
46. The fullest account of this pontificate will be found in T. Venni, 'Giovanni X', *Archivio della Deputazione Romana di Storia Patria*, 59 (1936), 1–136.
47. Liutprand, *Antapodosis*, III. 43–6.
48. P. Toubert, *Les structures du Latium médiéval* (Rome, 1973), pp. 974–98 gives an admirable assessment of Alberic's aims and the limitations on his personal power in Rome.
49. Toubert, *Structures*, pp. 997–8.
50. For the reform movement in the Church in the eleventh century and its attack on such practices see G. Tellenbach, *Church, State and Christian Society at the time of the Investiture Contest* (Oxford, 1940).
51. This still awaits a full study, but some impressions can be formed from the career of the Count-Abbot-Bishop Oliba: see R. d'Abadal i de Vinyals, *L'abat Oliba i la seva epocà* (Barcelona, 1948) and A. M. Albareda, *L'abat Oliba* (new edn, Montserrat, 1972).
52. P. Jaffe, *Regesta Pontificum Romanorum* (2 vols, Leipzig, 1885), nos 3675–6, 3678–80, 3684, 3688, 3689, 3692, 3694, 3696.
53. B. Hamilton, 'Monastic Revival in Tenth Century Rome', *Studia Monastica*, 4 (1962), pp. 35–68.
54. Liutprand, *Liber de Ottone rege*, i-iii; Adalbert s.a. 961.
55. *MGH Constitutiones*, vol. I, pp. 23–7; see also W. Ullmann, 'The Origins of the Ottonianum', *Cambridge Historical Journal*, II (1953), 114–28.
56. K. Leyser, 'Sacral Kingship', in his *Rule and Conflict*, pp. 75–107.
57. See the introduction to P. L. D. Reid's edition of Rather, CC, *cont. med.*, vol. 46, for an outline of his life and works.
58. Liutprand, *de Ottone rege*, vi.
59. Liutprand, *de Ottone rege*, xx.
60. *Liber Pontificalis*, vol. II, pp. 255–7 (Benedict VI), 259 (John XIV).
61. H. Zimmermann, *Papstabsetzungen des Mittelalters* (Graz, 1968), pp. 99–103.
62. W. Treadgold, *A History of the Byzantine State and Society* (Stanford, 1997), pp. 446–579 for an outline history of Byzantium between 842 and 1025.
63. H. Kennedy, *The Prophet and the Age of the Caliphates* (London, 1986), pp. 309–45.
64. B. M. Kreutz, *Before the Normans. Southern Italy in the Ninth and Tenth Centuries* (Philadelphia, 1991), pp. 102–6.
65. See not least K. Leyser, 'The Tenth Century in Byzantine-Western Relations', in D. Baker (ed.), *The Relations between East and West in the Middle Ages* (Edinburgh, 1973), pp. 29–63.
66. Liutprand of Cremona, *Legatio ad Imperatorem Constantinopolitanum Nicephorum Phocam*, iii, and xl; the translation is that of L. H. Nelson and M. V. Shirk, *Liutprand of Cremona, Mission to Constantinople (968 AD)* (Lawrence, 1972), pp. 3, 32.
67. Liutprand, *Legatio*, ii, tr. Nelson, p. 2.

68. Ibid., li, tr. Nelson, p. 40.
69. The principal source for these events in southern Italy is the *Chronicon Salernitanum*, ed. U. Westerbergh (Stockholm, 1956); on which see Kreutz, *Before the Normans*, pp. 94–5.
70. K. Leyser, '*Theophanu Divina Gratia Imperatrix Augusta*: Western and Eastern Emperorship in the Later Tenth Century', in idem, *Communications and Power in Medieval Europe: The Carolingian and Ottonian Centuries* (London, 1994), pp. 143–64.
71. For Otto II's reign see K. Uhlirz, *Jahrbücher des Deutschen Reiches unter Otto II und Otto III*, vol. I: Otto II. 973–83 (Berlin, 1902).
72. Thietmar of Merseburg, *Chronica*, III. 20–5.
73. For Otto III's reign see Uhlirz, *Jahrbücher*, vol. II: *Otto III. 983–1002* (Berlin 1954).
74. For example, A. von Euw and G. Sporbeck, *Abenländische Buchkunst zur Zeit der Kaiserin Theophanu* (Cologne, 1991); R. McKitterick, 'Ottonian Intellectual Culture in the Tenth Century and the Role of Theophanu', *Early Medieval Europe*, vol. 2 (1993), 53–74.
75. Thietmar, IV. 27.
76. Leyser, '*Theophanu Divina Gratia Imperatrix Augusta*', p. 164.
77. K. Leyser, 'Three Historians: c) Thietmar of Merseburg', in his *Carolingian and Ottonian Centuries*, pp. 27–28.
78. Reuter, *Germany in the Early Middle Ages*, pp. 163–5.
79. Thietmar, IV. 75.
80. Bernd Schütte (ed.), *Die Lebensbeschreibungen der Königin Mathilde, MGH SRG*, vol. 66 (1994).
81. For relations with the Slavs in the time of Louis the German see Reuter, *Germany in the Early Middle Ages*, pp. 77–84.
82. On the conversion of Scandinavia see Richard Fletcher, *The Conversion of Europe* (London, 1997), pp. 369–417.
83. L. Grote, *Die Stiftskirche in Gernrode* (Burg bei Magdeburg, 1932).
84. *Annales Regni Francorum*, s.a. 805 and 806.
85. *Annales Fuldenses*, s.a 845; tr. T. Reuter, *The Annals of Fulda* (Manchester, 1992), p. 24.
86. Regino of Prüm, s.a. 890.
87. R. Folz, *Les saints rois du Moyen Age en Occident (vie–xiiie siècles)* (Brussells, 1984), pp. 31–6.
88. Reuter, *Germany in the Early Middle Ages*, p. 262.
89. Thietmar of Merseburg, IV. 55–7.
90. On the history of Poland in this period see H. Ludat, 'The Medieval Empire and the Early Piast State', *Historical Studies*, 6 (1968), 1–21, and various sections of G. Barraclough (ed.), *Eastern and Western Europe in the Middle Ages* (London, 1970).
91. Fletcher, *Conversion of Europe*, pp. 427–9.
92. Thietmar, IV. 45.
93. On this manuscript and its art see H. Mayr-Harting, *Ottonian Book Illumination: an Historical Study*, vol. 1: *Themes* (London, 1991), pp. 157–78.
94. Bernard Hamilton, 'The monastery of San Alessio and the religious and intellectual renaissance in tenth-century Rome' in *idem, Monastic*

Reform, Catharism and the Crusades, 900–1300 (London, 1979), item III.

95. *MGH Diplomata*, vol. II, pt. 2, pp. 844–46: judgement in favour of the monastery of St. Felix, Pavia, dated 14th October 1001.
96. Thietmar, IV. 47; see Karl Leyser, 'Ritual, Ceremony and Gesture: Ottonian Germany', in his *Communications and Power in Medieval Europe: The Carolingian and Ottonian Centuries* (London, 1994), pp. 189–213, especially p. 202.
97. Thietmar, IV. 47.
98. Thietmar of Merseburg, *Chronica*, IV. 47–9.
99. *MGH Diplomata*, vol. II. ii, pp. 818–20; a deed of gift to the church of St Peter.

Bibliography

A: Primary sources

Suggested editions and, where possible, English translations are here given for many of the sources that are referred to in the notes to the chapters of this book. For texts that are used sparingly references are given in the notes.

Abbo, *Bella Parisiacae Urbis*, ed. H. Waquet, CHFM, 1964.

Adalbert of Trier, continuation of the *Chronicle* of Regino of Prüm, ed. A. Bauer and R. Rau (2nd edn, Darmstadt, 1977), pp. 190–231.

Adamnán, *De Locis Sanctis*, ed. D. Meehan, SLH, vol. III (1958); see also *Vita Columbae*.

Agathias, *Histories*, ed. R. Keydell, tr. J. D. Frendo, CFHB, vols II and IIA.

Alcuin, *Epistolae*, ed. E. Dümmler, *MGH Epp.* vol. IV.

Alvar of Córdoba, *Indiculus Luminosus*, ed. J. Gil, *Corpus Scriptorum Muzarabicorum* (2 vols, Madrid, 1973), vol. 1, pp. 270–315.

Ambrose, *Epistolae*, in PL, vol. XVI, *cc.* 913–1342; tr. M. M. Beyenka, FC vol. 26 (rev. edn 1967).

Ammianus Marcellinus, *Res Gestae*, ed. and tr. J. C. Rolfe (Loeb Library, 3 vols) or ed. A. Loren (3 vols, Paris, 1960); abridged tr. W. Hamilton (Penguin Classics, 1986).

Anglo-Saxon Chronicle, ed. C. Plummer, *Two Saxon Chronicles in Parallel* (2 vols, Oxford, 1892); tr. G. N. Garmonsway (rev. edn, London, 1960).

Annales Bertiniani, ed. F. Grat, J. Vielliard, S. Clémencet, SHF, 1964; also ed. R. Rau, *Fontes*, vol. II, pp. 12–287; tr. J. L. Nelson, *The Annals of St-Bertin* (Manchester, 1991).

Annales Fuldenses, ed. R. Rau, *Fontes*, vol. II, pp. 20–177; tr. T. Reuter, *The Annals of Fulda* (Manchester, 1992).

Annales Laureshamenses, ed. G. Pertz, *MGH SS*, vol. I, pp. 22–39; partial tr. P. D. King, *Charlemagne: Translated Sources* (Lancaster, 1987), pp. 137–45.

Annales Mettenses Priores, ed. B. de Simson, *MGH SRG*; partial tr. P. Fouracre and R. A. Gerberding, *Late Merovingian France. History and Hagiography 640–720* (Manchester, 1996), pp. 330–70.

Annales Mosellani, ed. G. Pertz, *MGH SS*, vol. XVI, p. 494–9.

Annales Regni Francorum, ed. F. Kurze, *MGH SRG*

ARF Revised Version – same edition on opposite pages. The sections of both versions relating to Charlemagne's reign, tr. P. D. King, *Charlemagne: Translated Sources* (Lancaster, 1987), pp. 74–131.

Annales Sancti Amandi, ed. G. Pertz, *MGH SS*, vol. I, pp. 6–14.

Annals of Ulster, ed. and tr. S. Mac Airt and G. MacNiocaill (Dublin, 1983).

Annales Vedastini, ed. R. Rau, *Fontes*, vol. II, pp. 291–337.

Annales Xantenses, ed. R. Rau, *Fontes*, vol. II, pp. 340–71.

501

Anonymus Valesianus (part II), ed. J. Moreau, *Excerpta Valesiana* (Leipzig, 1968); tr. in vol. 3 of Rolfe's edn of Ammianus Marcellinus – see above.

Bede, *Historia Ecclesiastica Gentis Anglorum*, ed. B. Colgrave and R. A. B. Mynors (Oxford, 1969). Commentary: the companion volume of commentary by J. M. Wallace-Hadrill (Oxford, 1988), updated by the notes in J. McClure and R. Collins, *Bede: Ecclesiastical History of the English People* (Oxford, 1994), which also tr. Bede's *Greater Chronicle*.

Boethius, *De Consolatione Philosophiae*, ed. L. Bieler, CC vol. XCIV; also ed. and tr. H. F. Stewart, E. K. Rand and S. J. Tester (Loeb Library, rev. edn, 1973).

Boniface, *Epistolae*, ed. M. Tangl, *MGH Epistolae Selectae*, vol. I; tr. E. Emerton, *The Letters of Saint Boniface* (New York, 1940).

Candidus, fragments, ed. and tr. R. Blockley, *Fragmentary Classicising Historians*, vol. II (Liverpool, 1983).

Cassiodorus, *Chronica*, ed. T. Mommsen, *MGH AA*, vol. XI, pp. 111–61; Variae, ed. T. Mommsen, *MGH AA*, vol. XII.

Chronica Gallica A CCCCLII, ed. T. Mommsen, *MGH AA*, vol. IX, pp. 615–62.

Chronicle of Albelda, ed. J. Gil Fernández, J. L. Moralejo and J. I. Ruiz de la Peña, *Crónicas asturianas* (Oviedo, 1985), pp. 153–88.

Chronicle of Alfonso III (both versions): ibid., pp. 114–49; Roda version translated in K. B. Wolf, *Conquerors and Chroniclers of Early Medieval Spain* (Liverpool, 1990), pp. 159–77.

Chronicle of John of Nikiu, ed. and tr. R. H. Charles (London, 1916).

Chronicle of Joshua the Stylite, ed. and tr. W. Wright (Cambridge, 1882).

Chronicle of Zachariah of Mitylene, tr. F. J. Hamilton and E. W. Brooks (London, 1899).

Chronicle of 754 or *Mozarabic Chronicle*, ed. J. E. López Pereira, *Crónica mozárabe de 754* (Zaragoza, 1980); tr. K. B. Wolf, *Conquerors and Chroniclers of Early Medieval Spain* (Liverpool, 1990), pp. 111–58.

Codex Carolinus, ed. W. Gundlach, *MGH Epp*, vol. III, pp. 476–653; partial tr. P. D. King, *Charlemagne: Translated Sources* (Lancaster, 1987), pp. 269–307.

Codex Iustinianus, ed. P. Krueger, vol. II of *Corpus Iuris civilis* (Berlin, 1900).

Codex Theodosianus, ed. T. Mommsen (3 vols, 4th edn, Dublin and Zurich, 1971); tr. C. Pharr, *Theodosian Code* (repr. New York, 1969).

Columbanus, *Epistolae*, ed. and tr. G. S. M. Walker, SLH vol. II; *Penitential*, ed. and tr. L. Bieler, SLH vol. V, pp. 96–107.

Corippus, *In laudem Iustini Augusti Minoris*, ed. and tr. A. Cameron (London, 1976).

Councils of Toledo: ed. J. Vives, *Concilios visigóticos e hispano-romanos* (Barcelona and Madrid, 1963).

Edictus Rothari, ed. F. Bluhme, *MGH Fontes Iuris Germanici Antiqui*; tr. K. F. Drew, *The Lombard Laws* (Philadelphia, 1973).

Einhard, *Vita Karoli Magni*, ed. O. Holder-Egger, *MGH SRM*; tr. P. E. Dutton, *Carolingian Civilization: A Reader* (Peterborough, Ontario, 1993), pp. 24–42.

Elishé, *History of Vardan and the Armenian War*, tr. R. W. Thomson (Cambridge, Mass., 1982).

Epistolae Austrasicae, ed. W. Gundlach, *MGH Epp.*, vol. III, pp. 110–53.

Epitome de Caesaribus, ed. F. Pichlmayr (Leipzig, 1970).

Ermoldus Nigellus, ed. E. Faral, CHFM (1964).

Eugippius, *Vita Severini*, ed. R. Noll (Berlin, 1963; Passau, 1981); tr. L. Bieler, FC vol. 55 (1965).

Eunapius, *Lives of the Philosophers*, ed. and tr. W. C. Wright (Loeb Library).

Eusebius of Caesarea, *Historia Ecclesiastica*, ed. and tr. H. J. Lawlor and J. E. L. Oulton (2 vols, London, 1954).

Eutropius, *Breviarium*, ed. F. Ruehl (Leipzig, 1909); tr. H. W. Bird (Liverpool, 1993).

Fragmentary Annals of Ireland, tr. J. Radnor (Dublin, 1978).

Fredegar, Chronicle of – book IV and the Continuations – ed. and tr. J. M. Wallace-Hadrill (London, 1960).

Gesta Abbatum Fontanellensis, ed. F. Lohier and J. Laporte (Rouen, 1936).

Gildas, *De Excidio Britonum*, ed. and tr. M. Winterbottom (London, 1978).

Gregory the Great, Pope, *Dialogorum Libri IV*, ed. with French tr. A. de Vogüé, SC, vols 254, 260, 265.

Gregory of Tours, *Libri Decem Historiarum*, ed. B. Krusch and W. Levison, *MGH SRM*, vol. I (rev. edn, 1951); tr. O. M. Dalton, *The History of the Franks by Gregory of Tours* (2 vols, Oxford, 1927).

Herodian, ed. and tr. C. R. Whittaker (2 vols, Loeb Library).

Historia Dunelmensis Ecclesiae, ed. T. Arnold, Rolls Series, vol. 75. 1.

Hydatius, *Chronica*, ed. and tr. R. W. Burges, *The Chronicle of Hydatius and the Consularia Constantinopolitana* (Oxford, 1993), pp. 69–123.

Ibn Abd al-Hakam, *Futah Misr*, tr. J. H. Jones (Göttingen, 1858).

Ibn Ishaq, *Sirat Rasul Allah*, tr. A. Guillaume, *The Life of Muhammad* (Lahore, 1955).

Isidore of Seville, *Historia Gothorum, Vandalorum et Sueborum*, ed. C. Rodríguez Alonso, FEHL, vol. 13 (León, 1975); tr. K. B. Wolf, *Conquerors and Chroniclers of Early Medieval Spain* (Liverpool, 1990), pp. 81–110.

Isidore, *De Viris Illustribus*, ed. C. Codoñer Merino (Salamanca, 1964).

Jerome, *Epistolae*, ed. Hilberg, CSEL, vols LIV, LV and LVI.

John of Antioch, fragments, ed. and tr. R. Blockley – *see under* Candidus.

John of Biclar, *Chronica*, ed. J. Campos, *Juan de Bíclaro* (Madrid, 1960); tr. K. B. Wolf, *Conquerors and Chroniclers of Early Medieval Spain* (Liverpool, 1990), pp. 61–80.

John VIII, Pope, *Epistolae*, ed. E. Caspar, *MGH Epp*, vol. VII, pp. 1–333.

Jordanes, *Getica*, ed. T. Mommsen, *MGH AA*, vol. V; tr. C. C. Mierow, *The Gothic History of Jordanes* (Princeton, 1915).

Julian, the Emperor, *Works*, ed. and tr. W. C. Wright (3 vols, Loeb Library).

Lactantius, *De Mortibus Persecutorum*, ed. J. Creed (rev. reprint, Oxford, 1989).

Leo the Great, Pope, *Epistolae*, ed. C. Silva-Tarouca (3 vols, Rome, 1932–5); tr. E. Hunt, FC, vol. 34 (1957).

Lex Salica, ed. A. Eckhardt, *MGH LL*, vol. IV. 1; tr. T. J. Rivers, *Laws of the Salian and Ripuarian Franks* (New York, 1986), pp. 39–152.

Lex Saxonum, ed. C. von Schwerin, MGH *Fontes Iuris Germanici Antiqui*.

Lex Visigothorum (or *Forum Iudicum*), ed. K. Zeumer, *MGH LL*, vol. I.

Libanius, *Orations*, selection ed. and tr. A. F. Norman (2 vols, Loeb Library).

Liber Historiae Francorum, ed. B. Krusch, *MGH SRM*, vol. II, pp. 215–328.

Liber Pontificalis, ed. L. Duchesne (3 vols, reprinted Paris, 1955–7); tr. R. Davis (3 vols. Liverpool, 1989, 1992, 1995).

Life of St. John the Almsgiver, of Leontius, tr. E. Dawes and N. H. Baynes, *Three Byzantine Saints* (London, 1948), pp. 199–262.

Liutprand of Cremona, *Antapodosis, De Ottone Rege, Legatio*, ed. J. Becker, *MGH SRG*; tr. F. A. Wright, *Liudprand of Cremona: the Embassy to Constantinople and other Writings* (London, 1930; reprinted 1993), pp. 1–156.

Marcellinus Comes, *Chronica*, ed. T. Mommsen, *MGH AA*, vol. XI, pp. 60–108; tr. B. Croke, *The Chronicle of Marcellinus* (Sydney, 1995).

Marius of Avenches, *Chronica*, ed. T. Mommsen, *MGH AA*, vol. XI, pp. 232–9.

Menander Protector, fragments, ed. and tr. R. Blockley, *The History of Menander the Guardsman* (Liverpool, 1985).

Muirchú, *Vita Patricii*, ed. and tr. Hood – *see under* Patrick.

'Nennius' or the *Historia Brittonum*, ed. and tr. J. Morris (London, 1978); a 'volume per manuscript' edition is currently being published under the editorship of D. Dumville (Cambridge, 1985-?).

Nithard, *Historiae*, ed. with French tr. P. Lauer, CHM (1964).

Notker Balbulus, *Gesta Karoli Magni*, ed. R. Rau, *Fontes*, vol. III, pp. 320–427.

Olympiodorus of Thebes, fragments of, ed. and tr. R. Blockley – *see under* Candidus.

Paschal Chronicle, tr. M. and M. Whitby (Liverpool, 1989).

Patrick, *Epistolae*, ed. and tr. A. B. E. Hood (London, 1978).

Paul The Deacon, *Historia Gentis Langobardorum*, ed. G. Waitz, *MGH SRG*; tr. W. D. Foulke, *History of the Lombards* (Philadelphia, 1907; reprinted 1974).

Photius, *Biblioteca*, ed. and French tr. R. Henry (8 vols, Paris, 1959–77).

Priscus of Panium, fragments of, ed. and tr. R. Blockley – *see under* Candidus.

Procopius, *History of the Wars*, and *The Buildings*, ed. and tr. H. B. Dewing (6 vols, Loeb Library).

Prosper, *Chronica*, ed. T. Mommsen, *MGH AA*, vol. IX, pp. 342–499.

Regino of Prüm, *Chronica*, ed. R. Rau, *Fontes*, vol. III, pp. 180–319.

Regula Magistri, ed. and French tr. A. de Vogüé, SC, 105–7.

Regula Sancti Benedicti, ed. and French tr. A. de Vogüé, SC, vols 181–6.

Richer, *Historia*, ed. and French tr. R. Latouche, CHFM (2 vols, 1967).

Sampiro, *Chronica*, ed. J. Pérez de Urbel, *Sampiro, su crónica y la monarquía leonesa en el siglo X* (Madrid, 1952).

Scriptores Historiae Augustae, ed. and tr. D. Magie (3 vols, Loeb Library).

Sebeos, *History of Heraclius*, French tr. F. Macler (Paris, 1904).

Sextus Aurelius Victor, *De Caesaribus*, ed. P. Dufraigne (Paris, 1975); English tr. H. W. Bird (Liverpool, 1994).

Sidonius Apollinaris, *Epistolae*, ed. and tr. W. B. Anderson (2 vols, Loeb Library).

Simeon of Durham, *Historia Regum*, ed. T. Arnold, Rolls Series, vol. 75. ii.
Suetonius, *De Caesaribus*, ed. and tr. J. C. Rolfe (2 vols, Loeb Library).
Tacitus, *Germania*, ed. J. G. C. Anderson (Oxford, 1938); tr. H. Mattingly (rev. edn, Penguin Classics, 1970).
Thegan, *Vita Hludovici Imperatoris*, ed. R. Rau, *Fontes*, vol. I, pp. 216–53; tr. P. E. Dutton, *Carolingian Civilization: a Reader* (Peterborough, Ontario, 1993), pp. 141–55.
Theophanes, *Chronicle*, ed. C. de Boor (2 vols, Leipzig, 1883–5); tr. H. Turtledove (Philadelphia, 1982), and C. Mango (Oxford, 1997).
Theophylact Simocatta, *Histories*, tr. M. and M. Whitby (Oxford, 1986).
Thietmar of Merseburg, *Chronica*, ed. R. Holtzman and W. Trillmich (Darmstadt, 1957).
Vegetius, *De Re Militari*, ed. C. Lang (Stuttgart, 1967); tr. N. P. Milner, *Vegetius: Epitome of Military Science* (Liverpool, 1993).
Victor Tonnennensis, *Chronica*, ed. T. Mommsen, *MGH AA*, vol. XI, pp. 164–206.
Vita Aemiliani, of Braulio, ed. L. Vázquez de Parga (Madrid, 1943); tr. A. T. Fear, *Lives of the Visigothic Fathers* (Liverpool, 1997), pp. 15–43.
Vita Amandi, anon., ed. B. Krusch, *MGH SRM*, vol. V, pp. 395–485; tr. J. N. Hillgarth, *Christianity and Paganism, 350–750* (Philadelphia, 1986), pp. 139–49.
Vita Arnulfi., anon., ed. B. Krusch, *MGH SRM*, vol. II, pp. 426–46.
Vita Columbae, of Adamnán, ed. W. Reeves (Dublin, 1857), and ed. and tr. A. O. and M. O. Anderson (London, 1961).
Vita Columbani, of Jonas, ed. B. Krusch, *MGH SRM*, vol. IV, pp. 1–61.
Vita Fructuosi, anon., ed. M. C. Díaz y Díaz (Braga, 1974); tr. A. T. Fear, *Lives of the Visigothic Fathers* (Liverpool, 1997), pp. 123–44.
Vita Fulgentii, of Ferrandus, ed. G.-G. Lapèyre (Paris, 1929).
Vita Hludovici Imperatoris, of 'the Astronomer'/anon., ed. R. Rau, *Fontes*, vol. I, pp. 258–381; tr. A. Cabaniss, *Son of Charlemagne: a Contemporary Life of Louis the Pious* (Syracuse, New York, 1961).
Vita Honorati, of Hilary, ed. and French tr. M.-D. Valentin, SC, vol. 235.
Vita Martini, of Sulpicius Severus, ed. and French tr. J. Fontaine, SC, vol. 133.
Vita Wilfridi, of Stephanus, ed. and tr. B. Colgrave (Cambridge, 1927).
Vita Wilibrordi, of Alcuin, ed. H.-J. Reischmann, *Willibrord. Apostel der Friesen* (Darmstadt, 1989), pp. 44–89.
Widukind of Corvey, *Res Gestae Saxonicae*, ed. A. Bauer and R. Rau (Darmstadt, 1977).
Zosimus, *Historias Neas*, ed. F. Paschoud (3 vols in 5, Paris, 1971–86); tr. J. J. Buchanan and H. T. Davis, *Zosimus: Historia Nova* (San Antonio, 1967).

B: Selected secondary reading

Only a limited number of the most pertinent books and articles are listed here. More detailed suggestions can be gained from the references in the notes to each chapter.

1   PROBLEM-SOLVING EMPERORS

T. D. Barnes, *The New Empire of Diocletian and Constantine* (Cambridge, Mass., 1982).
P. Brown, *The World of Late Antiquity* (London, 1971).
E. R. Dodds, *Pagan and Christian in an Age of Anxiety* (Cambridge, 1965).
W. H. C. Frend, *Martyrdom and Persecution in the Early Church* (Oxford, 1965).
H. P. L'Orange, *Art Forms and Civic Life in the Late Roman Empire* (Princeton, 1965).
E. N. Luttwak, *The Grand Strategy of the Roman Empire* (Baltimore, 1976).
F. Millar, *The Roman Empire and its Neighbours* (London, 1967).
F. Millar, *The Emperor in the Roman World (31 BC–337 AD)* (London, 1977).
W. Seston, *Dioclétien et la tétrarchie* (Paris, 1946).
S. Williams, *Diocletian and the Roman Recovery* (London, 1985).
S. Wood, *Roman Portrait Sculpture 217–260 AD* (Leiden, 1986).

2   THE AGE OF CONSTANTINE

A. Alföldi, *The Conversion of Constantine and Pagan Rome* (2nd edn, Oxford, 1969).
T. D. Barnes, *Constantine and Eusebius* (Cambridge, Mass., 1981).
N. H. Baynes, *Constantine the Great and the Christian Church* (2nd edn, Oxford, 1972).
G. Dagron, *Naissance d'une capitale: Constantinople et ses institutions de 330 à 451* (Paris, 1974).
A. H. M. Jones, *Constantine and the Conversion of Europe* (London, 1949).
R. MacMullen, *Christianizing the Roman Empire A.D. 100–400* (New Haven, 1984).
A. Momigliano (ed.), *The Conflict between Paganism and Christianity in the Fourth Century* (Oxford, 1963).
J. Straub, *Regeneratio Imperii* (Darmstadt, 1972) – selected studies.

3   FRONTIERS WARS AND CIVIL WARS, 350–395

A. Alföldi, *A Conflict of Ideas in the Late Roman Empire* (Oxford, 1952).
P. Athanassiadi, *Julian: an Intellectual Biography* (London, 1992).
G. W. Bowersock, *Julian the Apostate* (London, 1978).
G. W. Bowersock, *Hellenism in Late Antiquity* (Cambridge, 1990).
P. Chuvin, *Chronique des derniers païens* (Paris, 1990).
A. Ferrill, *The Fall of the Roman Empire: the Military Explanation* (London, 1986), chs 1–4.
A. Lippold, *Theodosius der grosse und seine Zeit* (Stuttgart, 1968).
J. Matthews, *Western Aristocracies and Imperial Court A.D. 364–425* (Oxford, 1975).
J. Matthews, *The Roman Empire of Ammianus Marcellinus* (London, 1989).
S. Williams and G. Friell, *Theodosius: the Empire at Bay* (London, 1994).

4 THE BATTLE OF ADRIANOPLE AND THE SACK OF ROME

A. Cameron, *Claudian: Poetry and Propaganda at the Court of Honorius* (Oxford, 1970).

P. Courcelle, *Histoire littéraire des grands invasions germaniques* (3rd edn, Paris, 1964), pp. 31–77.

E. Demougeot, *De l'unité à la division de l'empire romain 395–410* (Paris, 1951).

H. Elton, *Warfare in Roman Europe AD 350–425* (Oxford, 1996).

A. Ferrill, *The Fall of the Roman Empire: the Military Explanation* (London, 1986), ch. 5.

O. Maenchen-Helfen, *The World of the Huns* (Berkeley etc., 1973).

E. A. Thompson, *A History of Attila and the Huns* (Oxford, 1948).

E. A. Thompson, *The Visigoths in the Time of Ulfila* (Oxford, 1966).

M. Todd, *The Barbarians: Goths, Franks and Vandals* (London, 1972).

H. Wolfram, *History of the Goths* (English edn, Berkeley etc., 1988), pp. 1–171.

5 A DIVIDED CITY: THE CHRISTIAN CHURCH, 300–460

J. Binns, *Ascetics and Ambassadors of Christ* (Oxford, 1994)

D. Brakke, *Athanasius and the Politics of Asceticism* (Oxford, 1995)

P. Brown, *Augustine of Hippo* (London, 1967).

P. Brown, *The Making of Late Antiquity* (Cambridge, Mass., 1978).

P. Brown, *Society and the Holy in Late Antiquity* (London, 1982) – selected studies.

P. Brown, *The Body and Society* (London, 1989), especially pts 2 and 3.

S. Elm, *Virgins of God: The Making of Asceticism in Late Antiquity* (Oxford, 1994).

A. J. Festugière, *Antioch païenne et chrétienne* (Paris, 1959).

E. D. Hunt, *Holy Land Pilgrimage in the Later Roman Empire AD 312–400* (Oxford, 1982).

N. B. McLynn, *Ambrose of Milan: Church and Court in a Christian Capital* (Berkeley, 1994).

J. N. D. Kelly, *Jerome* (London, 1975).

P. Rousseau, *Basil of Caesarea* (Berkeley, 1994).

C. Stancliffe, *St. Martin and his Hagiographer* (Oxford, 1983).

D. H. Williams, *Ambrose of Milan and the End of the Arian–Nicene Conflicts* (Oxford, 1995).

6 THE DISAPPEARANCE OF AN ARMY

A. Cameron and J. Long, *Barbarians and Politics at the Court of Arcadius* (Berkeley, 1993).

P. Courcelle, *Histoire littéraire des grandes invasions germaniques* (3rd edn, Paris, 1964).

E. Demougeot, *L'Empire romain et les barbares d'occident (IVe–VIIe siècles – scripta varia)* (Paris, 1988).

S. Johnson, *Late Roman Fortifications* (London, 1983).

W. E. Kaegi, Jnr, *Byzantium and the Decline of Rome* (Princeton, 1968).
J. H. W. G. Liebescuetz, *Barbarians and Bishops* (Oxford, 1990).
P. Southern and K. R. Dixon, *The Late Roman Army* (London, 1996).
E. A. Thompson, *Romans and Barbarians: the Decline of the Western Empire* (Madison, 1982) – selected studies.
R. Van Dam, *Leadership and Community in Late Antique Gaul* (Berkeley, 1985).

7   THE NEW KINGDOMS

P. Amory, *People and Identity in Ostrogothic Italy, 489–554* (Cambridge, 1997).
Anon. (ed.), *Die Alamannen* (Stuttgart, 1997).
P. S. Barnwell, *Emperor, Prefects and Kings: the Roman West, 395–565* (London, 1992).
T. S. Burns, *The Ostrogoths: Kingship and Society* (Wiesbaden, 1980).
T. S. Burns, *A History of the Ostrogoths* (Bloomington, 1984).
R. Christlein, *Die Alamannen: Archäologie eines lebendigen Volkes* (Stuttgart, 1978).
J. Harries, *Sidonius Apollinaris and the Fall of Rome* (Oxford, 1995).
P. Heather, *The Goths* (Oxford, 1996).
E. James, *The Franks* (Oxford, 1988).
J. Moorhead, *Theoderic in Italy* (Oxford, 1992).
J. J. O'Donnell, *Cassiodorus* (Berkeley, 1979).
J. M. Wallace-Hadrill, *The Barbarian West 400–1000* (rev. edn, Oxford, 1985).
H. Wolfram, *History of the Goths* (tr. T. Dunlap, Berkeley, 1988).
H. Wolfram, *The Roman Empire and Its Germanic Peoples* (tr. T. Dunlap, Berkeley, 1997).

8   THE TWILIGHT OF THE WEST, 518–568

A. Cameron, *Agathias* (Oxford, 1970).
A. Cameron, *Procopius* (London, 1985).
A. Cameron, *Continuity and Change in Sixth-Century Byzantium* (London, 1981) – selected studies.
C. Courtois, *Les Vandales et l'Afrique* (Paris, 1955).
A. Honore, *Tribonian* (London, 1978).
M. Maas, *John Lydus and the Roman Past* (London, 1992).
J. Moorhead, *Justinian* (London, 1994).
A. A. Vasiliev, *Justin I* (Cambridge, Mass., 1950).
O. G. von Simson, *Sacred Fortress* (Chicago, 1948).

9   CONSTANTINOPLE, PERSIA AND THE ARABS

A. J. Butler, *The Arab Conquest of Egypt* (2nd edn, Oxford, 1978).
A. Cameron, *Circus Factions* (Oxford, 1976).
P. Crone, *Meccan Trade and the Rise of Islam* (Oxford, 1987).

P. Goubert, *Byzance avant l'Islam*, vol. I (Paris, 1951).
J. Jarry, *Hérésies et factions dans l'empire byzantin du IVe au VII siècles* (Cairo, 1968).
H. Kennedy, *The Prophet and the Age of the Caliphates* (London, 1986).
D. W. Phillipson, *Ancient Ethiopia* (London, 1998)
M. Rodinson, *Mohammed* (English tr., Harmondsworth, 1971).
I. Shahid, *Byzantium and the Arabs in the Sixth Century* (2 vols, Washington, 1995).
W. M. Watt, *Muhammad at Mecca* (Oxford, 1953).
W. M. Watt, *Muhammad at Medina* (Oxford, 1956).
M. Whitby, *The Emperor Maurice and his Historian* (Oxford, 1988).

10   DECADENT AND DO-NOTHING KINGS

Spain (*507–711*)

R. Collins, *Early Medieval Spain: Unity in Diversity, 400–1000* (2nd edn. London, 1995).
J. Fontaine, *Isidore de Seville et la culture classique dans l'Espagne wisigothique* (3 vols, Paris, 1959–83).
L. A. García Moreno, *Historia de España visigoda* (Madrid, 1989).
J. N. Hillgarth, *Visigothic Spain, Byzantium and the Irish* (collected studies, London, 1985).
P. D. King, *Law and Society in the Visigothic Kingdom* (Cambridge, 1972).
J. Orlandis, *Historia del reino español visigodo* (Madrid, 1988).
E. A. Thompson, *The Goths in Spain* (Oxford, 1969).

Francia (*511–687*)

E. Ewig, *Die Merowinger und das Frankenreich* (2nd edn, Stuttgart, 1993).
L. C. Feffer and P. Perrin, *Les Francs*, vol. 2 (Paris, 1987).
F. Irsigler, *Untersuchungen zur Geschichte des frühfränkischen Adels* (Bonn, 1981).
E. James, *The Franks* (Oxford, 1988).
O. Pontal, *Histoire des conciles mérovingiens* (Paris, 1989).
G. Tessier, *Le baptême de Clovis* (Paris, 1964).
J. M. Wallace-Hadrill, *The Long Haired Kings* (London, 1961).
J. M. Wallace-Hadrill, *The Frankish Church* (Oxford, 1983).
A. Wieczorek (ed.), *Die Franken. Wegbereiter Europas* (2 vols, Mainz, 1996).
I. Wood, *The Merovingian Kingdoms, 450–751* (London, 1994).

11   THE RE-CREATING OF BRITAIN

S. Bassett (ed.), *The Origins of Anglo-Saxon Kingdoms* (Leicester, 1989).
J. Campbell (ed.), *The Anglo-Saxons* (Oxford, 1982).
J. Campbell, *Essays in Anglo-Saxon History* (London and Ronceverte, 1986).
C. Cubitt, *Anglo-Saxon Church Councils c. 650–c. 850* (Leicester, 1995)
A. S. Esmonde Cleary, *The Ending of Roman Britain* (London, 1989).
D. Hill, *An Atlas of Anglo-Saxon England* (Oxford, 1981).

E. John, *Reassessing Anglo-Saxon England* (Manchester, 1996).
M. E. Jones, *The End of Roman Britain* (Ithaca, 1996).
D. P. Kirby, *The Earliest English Kings* (London, 1991).
H. M. R. E. Mayr-Harting, *The Coming of Christianity to Anglo-Saxon England* (2nd edn, London, 1972; rev. edn, 1991).
P. Salway, *Roman Britain* (Oxford, 1981).
P. H. Sawyer, *From Roman Britain to Norman England* (London, 1978).
A. P. Smyth, *Warlords and Holy Men* (London, 1984) – for Scotland.
B. Yorke, *Kings and Kingdoms of Early Anglo-Saxon England* (London, 1990).

12   THE LOMBARD ACHIEVEMENT, *c.* 540–712

G. P. Bognetti, *L'Eta longobarda* (4 vols of collected studies, Milan, 1966–8).
T. S. Brown, *Gentlemen and Officers: Imperial Administration and Aristocratic Power in Byzantine Italy A.D. 554–800* (Rome, 1984).
C. Brühl, *Studien zu den langobardischen Königsurkunden* (Tübingen, 1970).
N. Christie, *The Lombards* (Oxford, 1995).
S. Gasparri, *I Duchi Longobardi* (Rome, 1978).
J. Jarnut, *Geschichte der Langobarden* (Stuttgart, 1982).
W. Menghin, *Die Langobarden* (Stuttgart, 1985).
G. Tabacco, *The Struggle for Power in Medieval Italy* (English tr., Cambridge, 1989).
J. Werner, *Die Langobarden in Pannonien* (Munich, 1962).

13   THE SUNDERING OF EAST AND WEST

N. H. Baynes, *Byzantine Studies and Other Essays* (London, 1960).
R. Cormack, *Writing in Gold* (London, 1985), chs 1–3.
P. Courcelle, *Late Latin Writers and their Greek Sources* (English tr., Cambridge, Mass., 1969).
A. Grabar, *L'Iconoclasme byzantin* (2nd edn, Paris, 1984).
J. T. Hallenbeck, *Pavia and Rome: the Lombard Monarchy and the Papacy in the Eighth Century* (Philadelphia, 1982).
J. Herrin, *The Formation of Christendom* (Oxford, 1987).
P. Llewellyn, *Rome in the Dark Ages* (London, 1971).
R. Macmullen, *Christianity and Paganism in the Fourth to Eighth Centuries* (New Haven, 1997).
T. F. X. Noble, *The Republic of St. Peter: the Birth of the Papal State 680–825* (Philadelphia, 1984).
J. Richards, *The Popes and the Papacy in the Early Middle Ages 476–752* (London, 1979).

14   MONKS AND MISSIONARIES

F. J. Byrne, *Irish Kings and High Kings* (London, 1973).
F. Homes-Dudden, *Gregory the Great* (2 vols, London, 1905).
K. Hughes, *The Church in Early Irish Society* (London, 1966).

K. Hughes, *Early Christian Ireland: an Introduction to the Sources* (London, 1972).

R. A. Markus, *Gregory the Great and his World* (Cambridge, 1997).

D. ó Cróinín, *Early Medieval Ireland, 400–1200* (London, 1995).

T. Schieffer, *Winfrid-Bonifatius und die christliche Grundlegung Europas* (Freiburg, 1954).

H. Wolfram, *Die Geburt Mitteleuropas* (Berlin, 1987).

J. M. Wallace-Hadrill, 'A background to St. Boniface's mission', in his *Early Medieval History* (Oxford, 1975), pp. 138–54.

15   TOWARDS A NEW WESTERN EMPIRE, 714–800

R. Collins, *The Arab Conquest of Spain, 710–797* (Oxford, 1989).

R. Collins, *Fredegar* (Aldershot, 1996).

P. J. Geary, *Aristocracy in Provence. The Rhône Basin at the Dawn of the Carolingian Age* (Stuttgart, 1985).

R. A. Gerberding, *The Rise of the Carolingians and the 'Liber Historiae Francorum'* (Oxford, 1987).

C. Landes (ed.), *Les derniers romaine en Septimanie, IV–VIII siècles* (Lattes, 1988).

R. McKitterick (ed.), *New Cambridge Medieval History*, vol. II: *c. 700– c. 900* (Cambridge, 1995).

M. Rouche, *L'Aquitaine des Wisigoths aux Arabes, 418–781* (Paris, 1979).

J. M. Wallace-Hadrill, *The Frankish Church* (Oxford, 1983).

16   THE NEW CONSTANTINE

B. Bischoff (tr. M. M. Gorman), *Manuscripts and Libraries in the Age of Charlemagne* (Cambridge, 1994).

R. Collins, *Charlemagne* (London, 1998).

H. Fichtenau, *The Carolingian Empire* (English tr., Oxford, 1968).

R. Folz, *The Coronation of Charlemagne* (English tr., London, 1974).

F. L. Ganshof, *Recherches sur les capitulaires* (Paris, 1958).

F. L. Ganshof, *Frankish Institutions under Charlemagne* (New York, 1968).

F. L. Ganshof, *The Carolingians and the Frankish Monarchy* – English tr. of selected studies (London, 1971).

J. L. Nelson, *The Frankish World, 750–900* (London, 1996) – selected studies.

W. Ullmann, *The Carolingian Renaissance and the Idea of Kingship* (Cambridge, 1969).

L. Wallach, *Alcuin and Charlemagne* (Ithaca, 1959).

17   FRONTIER SOCIETY: CHRISTIAN SPAIN, 711–1037

R. Collins, *The Arab Conquest of Spain, 710–797* (Oxford, 1989).

R. Collins, 'Spain: The Northern Kingdoms and the Basques, 711–910', in R. McKitterick (ed.), *New Cambridge Medieval History*, vol. II: *c. 700– c. 900* (Cambridge, 1995), pp. 272–89.

J. Coope, *The Martyrs of Córdoba* (Lincoln, Nebraska, 1995).
P. García Toraño, *Historia de el Reino de Asturias* (Oviedo, 1986).
T. F. Glick, *Islamic and Christian Spain in the Early Middle Ages* (Princeton, 1979).
H. Kennedy, *Muslim Spain and Portugal* (London, 1996).
P. Linehan, *History and the Historians of Medieval Spain* (Oxford, 1993).
J. Pérez de Urbel, *Historia del Condado de Castilla* (3 vols, Madrid, 1945).
J. Rodríguez, *Ramiro II, Rey de León* (Madrid, 1972).
C. Sánchez-Albornoz, *Orígenes de la Reconquista: el Reino de Asturias* (3 vols, Oviedo, 1972–75).
K. B. Wolf, *Christian Martyrs in Muslim Spain* (Cambridge, 1988).

18   'THE DISSENSION OF KINGS'

J. Devisse, *Hincmar, Archevêque de Reims* (3 vols, Geneva, 1975).
F. L. Ganshof, 'L'Historiographie dans la monarchic franque sous les Mérovingiens et les Carolingiens', *Settimane di studio del Centro italiano di studi sull' alto medioevo*, 17 (1970), 631–750.
M. T. Gibson and J. Nelson (eds), *Charles the Bald: Court and Kingdom* (2nd edn, Aldershot, 1990).
P. Godman and R. Collins (eds), *Charlemagne's Heir: New Aspects of the Reign of Louis the Pious* (Oxford, 1990).
P. Godman, *Poets and Emperors: Frankish Politics and Carolingian Poetry* (Oxford, 1987).
R. McKitterick, *The Carolingians and the Written Word* (Cambridge, 1989).
R. McKitterick (ed.), *Carolingian Culture: Emulation and Innovation* (Cambridge, 1994).
J. L. Nelson, *Charles the Bald* (London, 1992).
J. M. Wallace-Hadrill, *Early Germanic Kingship in England and on the Continent* (Oxford, 1971).
J. M. Wallace-Hadrill, 'A Carolingian Renaissance Prince', *Proceedings of the British Academy*, 64 (1978), 155–84.
J. M. Wallace-Hadrill, 'History in the Mind of Archbishop Hincmar', in R. H. C. Davis and J. M. Wallace-Hadrill (eds), *The Writing of History in the Middle Ages* (Oxford, 1981), pp. 43–70.

19   'THE DESOLATION OF THE PAGANS'

H. R. Ellis, *The Road to Hell* (Cambridge, 1943).
H. R. Ellis Davidson, *The Viking Road to Byzantium* (London, 1976).
G. Jones, *A History of the Vikings* (Oxford, 1968).
P. H. Sawyer, *The Age of the Vikings* (London, 1962).
P. H. Sawyer, *Kings and Vikings* (London, 1982).
P. H. Sawyer (ed.), *The Oxford History of the Vikings* (Oxford, 1997).
A. P. Smyth, *Alfred the Great* (Oxford, 1997).

20   THE OTTONIAN AGE

Arabs, Lombards and Byzantines in the western Mediterranean

A. Ahmad, *A History of Islamic Sicily* (Edinburgh, 1975), chs 1–3.

N. Cilento, *Italia meridionale longobarda* (2nd edn, Milan, 1971).

A. Guillou, *Studies on Byzantine Italy* (London, 1970).

B. M. Kreutz, *Before the Normans: Southern Italy in the Ninth and Tenth Centuries* (Philadelphia, 1991).

W. Treadgold, *The Byzantine Revival, 780–842* (Stanford, 1988)

W. Treadgold, *A History of the Byzantine State and Society* (Stanford, 1997), part IV.

C. Wickham, *Early Medieval Italy: Central Power and Local Society, 400–1000* (London, 1981).

The Ottonians

G. Althoff, *Otto III* (Darmstadt, 1996).

E. Hlawitschka, *Vom Frankenreich zur Formierung der europaischen Staaten- und Volkergemeinschaff 840–1046* (Darmstadt, 1986).

K. J. Leyser, *Rule and Conflict in an Early Medieval Society* (London, 1979).

K. J. Leyser, *Medieval Germany and her Neighbours, 900–1250* (London, 1982) – selected studies.

K. J. Leyser, *Communications and Power in Medieval Europe: the Carolingian and Ottonian Centuries* (London, 1994) – selected studies

T. Reuter, *Germany in the Early Middle Ages, 800–1056* (London, 1991).

H. Zimmermann (ed.), *Otto der Grosse* (Darmstadt, 1976) – a collection of articles.

Index